MATHEMATICAL METHODS AND MODELS
IN ECONOMIC DYNAMICS

Mathematical Methods and Models in Economic Dynamics.

Giancarlo GANDOLFO

Università di Siena, Istituto di Economia, Italy

1971

NORTH-HOLLAND PUBLISHING COMPANY — AMSTERDAM · LONDON

© NORTH-HOLLAND PUBLISHING COMPANY, 1971

Library of Congress Catalog Card Number 71-157033
North-Holland ISBN 0 7204 3053 4
American Elsevier ISBN 0 444 10106 3

Publishers:

NORTH-HOLLAND PUBLISHING COMPANY – AMSTERDAM
NORTH-HOLLAND PUBLISHING COMPANY, LTD – LONDON

Sole distributors for the U.S.A. and Canada:

AMERICAN ELSEVIER PUBLISHING COMPANY, INC.
52 VANDERBILT AVENUE, NEW YORK, N.Y. 10017

PRINTED IN THE NETHERLANDS

PREFACE

This book has evolved from undergraduate and graduate courses given by the author at the Universities of Rome and of Siena in the last five years. Criticism and comments by the students on a provisional Italian edition helped in the preparation of the English edition.

The book aims at giving a simple but comprehensive treatment of some mathematical methods commonly used in economic dynamics and at showing how they are utilised to build and to analyse dynamic models. Accordingly, the book focuses on methods, and every new mathematical technique introduced is followed by its application to selected models. The unifying principle in the exposition of the different economic models is then seen to be the common mathematical technique. The process should ultimately enable the student to build and to analyse his own models.

The material is arranged in two Parts and four Appendixes. The latter contain relatively more advanced material (from the mathematical point of view) and also the treatment is relatively less simple. The two Parts, as far as the mathematics is concerned, follow the same scheme. Although a unified treatment of both difference and differential equations (linear and with constant coefficients) would have been more elegant, the author has preferred to keep them apart, at the cost of some repetition, in order to avoid confusion to the beginner and to make it possible to teach and to study them separately. In the appropriate places the formal similarities (and dissimilarities) between the two kinds of equations are pointed out. The Appendixes are also independent of one another (though each requires the knowledge of some of the material contained in the text) so that the teacher (and the student) has freedom of choice.

The various economic models can usually be read independently; where necessary or useful, the connections with other models (whether or not included in the book) are indicated. The models included in the book were selected to serve the purpose stated at the beginning of this preface; other models might often have served equally well. The author thinks, however, that the selection — which includes both old and new contributions — offers a general idea of the scope of modern economic dynamics.

The exercises are problems involving the solution of economic models with numerically given values of the parameters. Some of them are fully worked out in order to serve both as numerical examples of what has been explained and as a guide for the solution of the proposed exercises.

The reader of this book is assumed to have an elementary knowledge of the basic principles of economic theory (such as that provided by any good *general* introductory textbook). As far as the mathematics is concerned, no previous familiarity with the topics treated is assumed, so that everything is worked out in great detail and no essential steps in the argument are omitted. The required background for the text consists of elementary algebra and (for Part II) of the rudiments of calculus. Knowledge of some advanced matrix algebra is needed to understand a few proofs in Part I, ch. 8, and Part II, chs. 8 and 9, such proofs, however, are given in footnotes (and can be omitted without loss to the main argument, which is developed in non-matricial terms). Some more mathematical background is needed for the Appendixes (e.g., the implicit function theorem and the first- and second-order conditions for a free or constrained extremum in n variables are used in Appendix I) where the treatment may also, in some places, be a bit harder than in the text.

University of Siena, 1970

CONTENTS

INTRODUCTION

"A system is dynamical if its behavior over time is determined by functional equations in which variables at different points of time are involved in an essential way" (Frisch's and Samuelson's definition). ★

Before commenting on this definition, it may be recalled that, according to another definition, economic dynamics is identified with those parts of economic theory where every quantity must be dated, whereas in economic statics we need not trouble about dating. But in this way we would include in dynamics many non-dynamic phenomena. As an example, think of a case where all quantities have the same date. This may mean that a certain phenomenon has taken place at a certain point of time (and this may be important, but it is not dynamics), or that a variable at time t depends on another variable at the same time t (and this too may be important — e.g., consumption is assumed to depend on current income and not on lagged income — but, again, it is not dynamics). The definition based on 'dating', then, is too vague and cannot be accepted.

Let us now turn back to the initial definition and explain what a *functional equation* is. The general theory of functional equations is outside the scope of this book, and we shall give only some basic notions, which are sufficient for our purposes.

The basic concept is the following: *a functional equation is an equation where the unknown is a function.* Everybody knows that to solve an equation means to find that value (or those values) of the unknown which satisfy the equation. Now, to solve a functional equation means to find an unknown

---

★ This definition is based on the *formal* characteristics common to all problems studied by economic dynamics. Other definitions, based on the economic substance of those problems, are possible (e.g., economic dynamics is concerned with growth, or stability, etc.: see the interesting survey by Machlup). But these definitions are inevitably partial (a complete definition of this type would reduce to a cumbersome list of problems, with the danger of omitting some of them). The formal definition, on the contrary, is precise and general.

function ★ which satisfies the functional equation *identically*. It is important to understand that *'to satisfy identically'* means that the function we have to find must satisfy the functional equation for *any* admissible value of the independent variable appearing in the function. The following simple example may clarify this point.

Let us consider the functional equation $y'(x) - y(x) = 0$. We must find a specific function (in one independent variable) which satisfies identically the stated equation, i.e. a function such that, for any value of its argument, the value of the function and the value of its first derivative are equal. It is easy to check that this function is $y(x) = Ae^x$, since, from elementary calculus, $y'(x) = Ae^x = y(x)$ for any x. Now consider the function $y = ax + b$, which gives $y' = a$; if we put $x = (a - b)/a$, we have also $y = a$, i.e. $y' = y$. However, for any other value of x the value of the function will be different from a; therefore, the function $y = ax + b$ does *not* satisfy identically our functional equation. As a matter of terminology, from now on we shall usually omit the adjective 'identically', it being understood that 'to satisfy' a functional equation means to satisfy it identically.

Now, if we suppose that the symbol x stands for time★★, we are ready to understand the second part of the definition of economic dynamics. In fact, $y'(x) = y(x)$ can be considered as a relation which involves the value of y at any point of time and the value it has at an arbitrarily close point, determined by y'. The 'different points of time' clause is necessary to exclude the case, already mentioned above, of quantities dated at the same point of time. Time must enter in an 'essential' way: for example, if it enters only as a unit of measurement (i.e. because we are dealing with quantities which are flows per unit of time) the system is not dynamic.

The types of functional equations most widely used in economic dynamics are linear, constant-coefficient difference and differential equations (the meaning of these words will be clarified in the following treatment), and to

---

★ It must be stressed that by 'function' we mean the *form* of the function, apart from arbitrary constants (e.g., $y = Ae^x$, where A is an arbitrary constant). As we shall see when expounding the various functional equations appearing in this book, the solution of a functional equation determines the form of the unknown function, and the determination of the arbitrary constant(s) requires additional conditions.

★★ Of course, the symbol x can stand for any variable. This obvious remark is useful to avoid the mistake of believing that in economics functional equations are used only in dynamic problems (as an example of a case outside economic dynamics, the classic. problem of obtaining a utility function knowing the marginal rate(s) of substitution may be recalled). Since this is a book on economic dynamics only, from now on we shall use t instead of x, as this convention is commonly adopted.

them the text is devoted; Appendixes III and IV are aimed at those wanting
to know some more types.

References *

Baumol, W.J., 1970, *Economic Dynamics*, ch. 1 and appendix to ch. 8.
Frisch, R., 1936, On the Notion of Equilibrium and Disequilibrium.
Hicks, J.R., 1939, 1946, *Value and Capital*, ch. IX, § 1.
Hicks, J.R., 1965, *Capital and Growth*, ch. I.
Machlup, F., 1959, Statics and Dynamics: Kaleidoscopic Words.
Samuelson, P.A., 1947, *Foundations of Economic Analysis*, ch. XI, pp. 311–17.
Samuelson, P.A., 1949, Dynamic Process Analysis, §§I, II.
Volterra, V., 1959, *Theory of Functionals and of Integral and Integro-Differential Equations*, ch. I, pp. 1–7.

* References will be indicated only by name(s), date, title. Complete information as
to publisher, place of publication, etc., is contained in the Bibliography at the end of the
volume.

PART I

DIFFERENCE EQUATIONS (LINEAR AND WITH CONSTANT COEFFICIENTS)

1

General Principles

Given a function $y = f(t)$, its first difference is defined as the difference between the value of the function when the argument assumes the value $t + h$ and the value of the function corresponding to the value t of the argument. In symbols, $\Delta y = f(t+h) - f(t)$. Without loss of generality we can assume unit increments of the independent variable, i.e. $\Delta y = f(t+1) - f(t)$.

If we consider successive equally-spaced values of the independent variable $(t+1, t+2, t+3,$ etc.) [*], we can obtain successive first differences:

$$\Delta y_t \quad = f(t+1) - f(t) = y_{t+1} - y_t \, ,$$

$$\Delta y_{t+1} = f(t+2) - f(t+1) = y_{t+2} - y_{t+1} \, ,$$

$$\Delta y_{t+2} = f(t+3) - f(t+2) = y_{t+3} - y_{t+2} \, ,$$

and so on. We can now compute the *second differences*, i.e. the sequence of differences between two successive first differences:

---

[*] It makes no difference whether the values run forwards or backwards ($t - 1; t - 2, t - 3,$ etc.).

7

$$\Delta^2 y_t = \Delta y_{t+1} - \Delta y_t = (y_{t+2} - y_{t+1}) - (y_{t+1} - y_t)$$

$$= y_{t+2} - 2y_{t+1} + y_t \, ,$$

$$\Delta^2 y_{t+1} = \Delta y_{t+2} - \Delta y_{t+1} = y_{t+3} - 2y_{t+2} + y_{t+1} \, ,$$

$$\Delta^2 y_{t+2} = \Delta y_{t+3} - \Delta y_{t+2} = y_{t+4} - 2y_{t+3} + y_{t+2} \, ,$$

and so on. Note that the superscript 2 means that the operation of computing the difference has been repeated twice, i.e. that the operator Δ has been applied twice.

Proceeding similarly, we can compute the differences between two successive second differences and obtain the *third differences* of the function:

$$\Delta^3 y_t = \Delta^2 y_{t+1} - \Delta^2 y_t = (\Delta y_{t+2} - \Delta y_{t+1}) - (\Delta y_{t+1} - \Delta y_t)$$

$$= \Delta y_{t+2} - 2\Delta y_{t+1} + \Delta y_t$$

$$= (y_{t+3} - y_{t+2}) - 2(y_{t+2} - y_{t+1}) + (y_{t+1} - y_t)$$

$$= y_{t+3} - 3y_{t+2} + 3y_{t+1} - y_t \, ,$$

$$\Delta^3 y_{t+1} = \Delta^2 y_{t+2} - \Delta^2 y_{t+1} = y_{t+4} - 3y_{t+3} + 3y_{t+2} - y_{t+1} \, ,$$

and so on. Higher-order differences can be computed by the reader as an exercise.

We can now define an *ordinary difference equation* as a functional equation involving one or more of the differences Δy, $\Delta^2 y$, etc., of an unknown function of time. Since the argument t varies in a discontinuous way, taking on equally spaced values, it follows that our unknown function will be defined only corresponding to these values of t (i.e. the graph of the function will be a succession of separated points, as we shall see in detail in ch. 2).

We have called this equation *ordinary* because the unknown function is a function of only one argument. When the partial differences of a function having more than one argument are involved, the equation becomes a partial difference equation, a type of functional equation that will not be treated in this book.

The *order* of a difference equation is that of the highest difference appearing in the equation. If, for example, the highest difference contained is the third difference, the equation is of the third order; note that the equation is of the third order independently of the fact that lower-order differences are or are not contained in the equation.

Since the differences of any order can be expressed, as we have seen above, in terms of various values of the function, a difference equation may also be defined as a functional equation involving two or more of the values y_t, y_{t+1}, etc., of an unknown function of time. As an example, the difference equation $a\Delta y_t + by_t = 0$ transforms, if we substitute $\Delta y_t = y_{t+1} - y_t$, into $ay_{t+1} + (b-a)y_t = 0$. In this form, the order of the equation is given by the highest difference between time subscripts: if the equation, for example, contains y_{t+3}, y_{t+1} and y_t, it is of the third order. We shall consider difference equations expressed in this second form, as it is the form they commonly take in economic models.

Let us note again that it makes no difference whether the equally spaced values of t are computed forwards or backwards, so long as the structure of time lags remains unaltered. The equation $ay_{t+1} + (b-a)y_t = 0$, for example, is identical with the equation $ay_t + (b-a)y_{t-1} = 0$. The reason is that to solve a difference equation means, as we know from the Introduction, to find a function (or functions) which satisfies (satisfy) the equation for any admissible value of t. This allows us to shift all the time subscripts as we like, provided that they are all shifted by the same amount (neglecting this proviso would alter the structure of the equation).

Consider now the equation $\Delta y_t = a$, i.e. $y_{t+1} - y_t = a$. In words, the problem is: find a function such that its first difference equals the given constant a for any value of t. It can be checked that the linear function $y = at + b$ satisfies the equation, since

$$y_{t+1} - y_t = [a(t+1) + b] - (at+b) = a \ . \ ^\star$$

Note that in the solution function an arbitrary constant (b) appears. This is not surprising, since the constancy of first differences is not affected by a parallel shift of the straight line. More generally, in the operation of differencing, the presence of an arbitrary constant, that is eliminated in the course of the operation, does not alter the result. Therefore, an arbitrary constant always appears in the solution of a first-order difference equation, and no more than one can appear.

---

* Actually, this function is also the only one that satisfies the equation. This is shown by the 'existence and uniqueness' theorem, which we shall not treat. All types of equations considered in this book are 'well-behaved', i.e. their solution exists and is unique.

Proceeding further, consider the equation $\Delta^2 y_t = 0$ (find a function such that its second difference equals zero for any value of t). The solution is always the linear function $y = at + b$, but now both a and b are arbitrary constants; in fact, *any* straight line has a zero second difference. In general, the computation of second differences eliminates in succession *two* (and only two) arbitrary constants.

We shall see in the following chapters how the arbitrary constant(s) can be determined through additional conditions; what interests us here is to note that we can induce, from the reasoning given above, the important principle that *the general solution of a difference equation of order n is a function of t involving exactly n arbitrary constants.*

We can now summarize precisely the scope of our treatment. In Part I we shall be concerned with linear, constant-coefficient difference equations. The general n-th order form of such equations is

$$c_n y_{t+n} + c_{n-1} y_{t+n-1} + \ldots + c_1 y_{t+1} + c_0 y_t = g(t) , \qquad (1.1)$$

where the c's are given constants and $g(t)$ is a known function. Some c's may be zero, but of course *both c_n and c_0* must be different from zero if the equation is of order n.

In order to avoid cumbersome sentences, from now on we shall use the expression 'difference equations' (or even, when there is no danger of misunderstanding, simply 'equations') in the sense of 'ordinary difference equations, linear and with constant coefficients'.

We must now distinguish between homogeneous and non-homogeneous equations. Eq. (1.1) is non-homogeneous; the n-th order homogeneous equation is

$$c_n y_{t+n} + c_{n-1} y_{t+n-1} + \ldots + c_1 y_{t+1} + c_0 y_t = 0 . \qquad (1.2)$$

The following theorems are fundamental in the theory of difference equations:

(1) *If $y_1(t)$ is a solution of the homogeneous equation, then $Ay_1(t)$, where A is an arbitrary constant, is also a solution.*

The proof is simple. Assume that $y_1(t)$ satisfies eq. (1.2). Substitute $Ay_1(t)$ in the same equation, obtaining

$$c_n Ay_1(t+n) + c_{n-1} Ay_1(t+n-1) + \ldots + c_1 Ay_1(t+1) + c_0 Ay_1(t) = 0 ;$$

therefore

$$A[c_n y_1(t+n) + c_{n-1} y_1(t+n-1) + ... + c_1 y_1(t+1) + c_0 y_1(t)] = 0 .$$

If $Ay_1(t)$ has to be a solution, the last relationship must be satisfied. Since $y_1(t)$ is a solution of eq. (1.2), the expression in square brackets vanishes, and so the relationship

$$A[c_n y_1(t+n) + c_{n-1} y_1(t+n-1) + ... + c_1 y_1(t+1) + c_0 y_1(t)] = 0$$

is satisfied. This proves the theorem.

(2) *If $y_1(t)$, $y_2(t)$ are two distinct* ★ *solutions of the homogeneous equation* ($n > 1$), *then $A_1 y_1(t) + A_2 y_2(t)$ is also a solution for any two constants A_1, A_2.*

The proof is similar to that of theorem (1) and is left as an exercise. Theorem (2) — called the 'superposition theorem' — can easily be extended to any number $k \leqslant n$ of distinct solutions of eq. (1.2). ★★

To obtain the general solution of eq. (1.2), find n distinct solutions $y_1(t)$, $y_2(t)$, ..., $y_n(t)$ and combine them (theorem (2)) into the function

$$f(t; A_1, A_2, ..., A_n) = A_1 y_1(t) + A_2 y_2(t) + ... + A_n y_n(t) , \qquad (1.3)$$

where $A_1, A_2, ..., A_n$ are arbitrary constants. Since this function contains exactly n arbitrary constants, we can conclude — from the general principle expounded before — that it is the general solution of eq. (1.2). The practical problem of how to find the n functions $y_1(t), y_2(t), ..., y_n(t)$ will be tackled in the following chapters.

(3) *If $\bar{y}(t)$ is any particular solution of the non-homogeneous equation, the general solution of this same equation is obtained adding $\bar{y}(t)$ to the general solution* † *of the corresponding homogeneous equation*, i.e.

★ By 'distinct solutions' we mean *linearly independent* solutions.

★★ Given a homogeneous equation of order n, a set of n linearly independent solutions is called a *fundamental set*.

† The general solution of the homogeneous equation is then only a part of the general solution of the non-homogeneous equation, and so it is not 'general' with respect to the latter. This means that the expression 'general solution' must always be qualified. As a matter of terminology, note the following: (1) some authors use the word 'integral' (particular or general) instead of 'solution' but with the same meaning; (2) the expres-

$$\bar{y}(t) + f(t; A_1, A_2, ..., A_n) \tag{1.4}$$

is the general solution of the non-homogeneous equation.

The proof of this theorem can be given substituting (1.4) into (1.1) and checking that the latter is satisfied. Since the function (1.4) contains exactly n arbitrary constants, it is the general solution of eq. (1.1).

Theorem (3) contains the method to solve the non-homogeneous equation:

(a) find a particular solution $\bar{y}(t)$ of the non-homogeneous equation;

(b) put $g(t) \equiv 0$ and solve the resulting homogeneous equation (often called the 'reduced' equation);

(c) add the two results.

Steps (a) and (b) can be taken in any order; step (c) gives the general solution of the non-homogeneous equation.

The particular solution of the non-homogeneous equation will depend, *ceteris paribus*, on the form of the known function $g(t)$. This suggests the following general approach: *to find a particular solution of the non-homogeneous equation, try a function having the same form of $g(t)$ but with undetermined coefficient(s) (e.g., if $g(t)$ is a constant, try an undetermined constant; if it is an exponential function, try the same exponential function with an undetermined multiplicative constant, and so on). Substitute this function in the non-homogeneous equation and determine the coefficient(s) so that the equation is satisfied.* This method will be expounded in more detail in the following chapter.

We now have enough general principles to pass on to a detailed treatment of the difference equations of the various orders.

References

Allen, R.G.D., 1959, *Mathematical Economics*, ch. 6, §§6.1, 6.2.

sion 'particular solution' is also used (a) in the sense of a solution obtained from the general solution by giving specific values to the arbitrary constants, and (b) in the sense of any single non-general solution of the homogeneous equation (i.e., to indicate any one of $y_1(t)$, $y_2(t)$, etc.); (3) the expression 'complementary function' is used to indicate the general solution of the homogeneous equation when considered as a part of the general solution of the non-homogeneous equation, and the expression 'reduced equation' is used to indicate the homogeneous part of a non-homogeneous equation, i.e. the corresponding homogeneous equation obtained putting $g(t) \equiv 0$ in the course of the procedure to solve a non-homogeneous equation. To avoid confusion, we shall not adopt these uses.

Boole, G., 1960, *A Treatise on the Calculus of Finite Differences*, ch. IX, pp. 157–61.
Goldberg, S., 1958, *Introduction to Difference Equations*, ch. 1, §§ 1.1, 1.2, 1.3; ch. 2, §§ 2.1, 2.2, 2.3; ch. 3, § 3.1.
Huang, D.S., 1964, *Introduction to the Use of Mathematics in Economic Analysis*, ch. 7, § 7.2.
Papandreou, A.G., 1965, *Introduction to Macroeconomic Models*, ch. 5, §§ 5.0, 5.1, 5.3.

2

First-order Equations

The general form of these equations is

$$c_1 y_t + c_0 y_{t-1} = g(t),$$ (2.1)

where c_0, c_1 are given constants and $g(t)$ is a known function. The constants c_0, c_1 must be both different from zero, since if even only one of them is zero the equation is no longer a difference equation.

Let us begin with the study of the homogeneous equation, whose form is

$$c_1 y_t + c_0 y_{t-1} = 0,$$ (2.2)

or

$$y_t + b y_{t-1} = 0,$$ (2.3)

where $b \equiv c_0/c_1$. Suppose that in the initial period (i.e. for $t = 0$) the function y takes on an arbitrary value A; from eq. (2.3) we can then compute the following sequence:

$$y_1 = -b y_0 = -bA,$$

$$y_2 = -by_1 = -b(-bA) = b^2A \ ,$$

$$y_3 = -by_2 = -b(b^2A) = -b^3A \ ,$$

$$y_4 = -by_3 = -b(-b^3A) = b^4A \ ,$$

. . . .

and so the solution appears to be

$$y_t = A(-b)^t \ . \tag{2.4}$$

As a check, substitute this function in eq. (2.3):

$$A(-b)^t + bA(-b)^{t-1} = 0 \ . \tag{2.5}$$

If our function is a solution, eq. (2.5) must hold identically. Now, since

$$bA(-b)^{t-1} = -(-b)A(-b)^{t-1} = -A(-b)^t \ ,$$

eq. (2.5) can be written as

$$A(-b)^t - A(-b)^t = 0 \ , \tag{2.6}$$

and is indeed satisfied for any value of t.

Since the function we have found satisfies the difference equation and contains one arbitrary constant, we may conclude from general principles that it is the general solution.

The problem remains of how to determine the arbitrary constant. To do this we need an additional condition. This need derives from the fact that relation (2.4) gives only the *form* of the function y_t but not its position in the Cartesian plane (t, y_t). As soon as the function is constrained to pass through a given point, say (t^*, y^*), its position, which depends on one arbitrary constant only, is determined and the arbitrariness of the constant disappears. More formally, the additional condition says that $y_t = y^*$ for $t = t^*$, where t^* and y^* are known values. Substituting these values in (2.4) we get $y^* = A(-b)^{t^*}$ and so

$$A = y^*/(-b)^{t^*} \ . \tag{2.7}$$

In economic problems the value of y in the initial period is usually assumed as known, at least in principle, i.e. $y_t = y_0$ for $t = 0$, which gives $A = y_0$.

The behaviour over time of the function $y_t = A(-b)^t$ depends on the sign and on the absolute value of the parameter b.

As for the sign, if b is negative then $-b$ is positive and the movement is monotonic. On the other hand, if b is positive then $-b$ is negative and the values of the function will alternate in sign, since the power of a negative number is positive (negative) if the exponent is even (odd). This case is usually described as an 'oscillatory' movement. However, to distinguish terminologically this kind of movement from the trigonometric (sine or cosine) oscillations (which, as we shall see, can arise only in second- or higher-order equations), we suggest the expression 'improper oscillations' or 'alternations'. 'Proper oscillations' or simply 'oscillations' would then specifically indicate trigonometric oscillations.

As for the absolute value, if b is in absolute value less (greater) than unity, the movement will be convergent (divergent). This conclusion is a consequence of the properties of powers: the absolute value of a power, as the exponent increases, tends to zero (to infinity) if the absolute value of the base is less (greater) than one. In the particular case of $|b| = 1$, the function shows improper oscillations of constant amplitude (when $b = 1$) or takes on the constant value A (when $b = -1$).

In fig. 2.1 all kinds of movements are shown (A is assumed to be positive; if it were negative, the qualitative behaviour of the solution would not change). Note that the diagrams show only a succession of points. This is because, as we know, t varies over a set of equally spaced values (0, 1, 2, 3, etc.), and so the solution function is defined only corresponding to equally spaced values of t. The graphical counterpart of this is a succession of points.

Of course, in reality time is a continuous variable. When we formalize an economic problem in difference equations terms, we (implicitly or explicitly) assume that, to all relevant purposes, only what happens at the end of each time interval does matter, so that the variables we are analysing may be thought of as varying by discrete 'jumps'. What happens during the period is not considered, in the sense that all relevant economic activity of each period is assumed to be concentrated in a single point of time (the end of the period, which is the same as the beginning of the following period). These assumptions may or may not be justified according to the nature of the problem we are examining; for some further comments on this point, as well as on the related point of the use of discrete or of continuous time tools in economics, see Part II, ch. 1 (at the end), Part II, ch. 3, §2 (at the end) and Appendix IV, §3 (at the beginning).

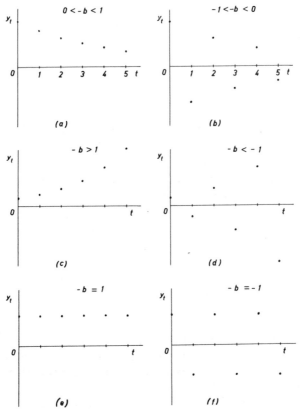

Fig. 2.1. (a) Monotonic and convergent; (b) Oscillatory and convergent; (c) Monotonic and divergent; (d) Oscillatory and divergent; (e) Constant; (f) Oscillatory with constant amplitude.

Going back to the diagrams, the points are usually joined with segments. Fig. 2.2 shows two alternative ways of doing this (diagram (b) of fig. 2.1 is exemplified). It must be emphasized that *the joining of the successive points is performed only to help the eye to follow the movement of the solution over time*. It would be a gross mistake to interpret the segments as describing the movement of y_t in each instant of the period: it is *not* possible to say, for example, that for $t = \overline{OB}$ the value of y is $\overline{OC}$. Such an inference would be wrong, since y_t is defined only for $t = 0, 1, 2, 3, \ldots$, as represented in fig. 2.1. If that is understood, graphical representations of the kind depicted in fig. 2.2 may be adopted safely as a visual aid.

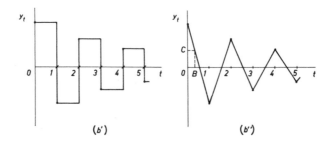

Fig. 2.2.

To complete the study of first-order equations we must now explain how to find a particular solution of the non-homogeneous equation. The application of the general method expounded in Part I, ch. 1, will be explained in relation to the commoner functions.

Case (1): g(t) is a constant.

In this case, equation (2.1) becomes

$$c_1 y_t + c_0 y_{t-1} = a , \tag{2.8}$$

where a is a given constant. As a particular solution, try an undetermined constant, and call it μ. Substitution into eq. (2.8) yields $(c_1 + c_0)\mu = a$, from which

$$\mu = a/(c_1 + c_0) , \tag{2.9}$$

and so $\bar{y}_t = a/(c_1 + c_0)$ is a particular solution.

The method obviously breaks down if $c_1 + c_0 = 0$. In this case, equation

(2.8) may be written as

$$y_t - y_{t-1} = a/c , \tag{2.10}$$

where $c = c_1 = -c_0$.

As a particular solution, try now μt. Substituting in (2.10) we have

$$\mu t - \mu(t-1) = a/c ,$$

whence

$$\mu = a/c . \tag{2.11}$$

A particular solution is then $\bar{y}_t = (a/c)t$.

It is important to note that the above treatment illustrates the following general prescription (which is a necessary complement of the general principle expounded in Part I, ch. 1): *if the function you try as a particular solution does not work, try next the same function multiplied by t.* ★

Since the general solution of the homogeneous equation $y_t - y_{t-1} = 0$ is $y_t = A$, where A is an arbitrary constant, the general solution of eq. (2.10) is $y_t = A + (a/c)t$. The same result could be obtained directly, seeing that the function whose first difference is constant is a linear function (see Part I, ch. 1, for a similar case), but it is important to understand how the same result is reached by applying general principles.

Case (2): g(t) is an exponential function.

When $g(t) = Bd^t$, where B and d are given constants, ★★ as a particular solution try Cd^t, C being an undetermined constant. Substituting in (2.1) we have

$$c_1 Cd^t + c_0 Cd^{t-1} = Bd^t .$$

Therefore

$$d^{t-1}(c_1 Cd + c_0 C - Bd) = 0 .$$

The last equation is satisfied for any t if, and only if,

★ In second- or higher-order equations it may be necessary, as we shall see, to multiply by t^2, t^3, etc.

★★ If $g(t) = B\alpha^{\lambda t}$, where B, α, λ are given constants, put $\alpha^\lambda = d$ and proceed as before.

$$c_1 Cd + c_0 C - Bd = 0 ,$$

whence

$$C = \frac{Bd}{c_1 d + c_0} .$$

A particular solution is then

$$\bar{y}_t = \frac{Bd}{c_1 d + c_0} d^t .$$

The method fails if $c_1 d + c_0 = 0$; note that this implies that the general solution of the corresponding homogeneous equation is Ad^t. As a particular solution, try then tCd^t. Substitute in (2.1) and obtain

$$c_1 tCd^t + c_0 (t-1)Cd^{t-1} = Bd^t ;$$

thus

$$d^{t-1}[(dc_1 + c_0)tC - c_0 C - Bd] = 0 .$$

Since $c_1 d + c_0 = 0$ by assumption, it follows that

$$d^{t-1}(-c_0 C - Bd) = 0 ,$$

which is satisfied for any t if, and only if,

$$-c_0 C - Bd = 0 ,$$

so that

$$C = -Bd/c_0 .$$

A particular solution is then

$$\bar{y}_t = \frac{-Bd}{c_0} td^t .$$

Case (3): $g(t)$ is a polynomial function of degree m.

As an example, consider $g(t) = a_0 + a_1 t$, where a_0 and a_1 are given constants. Try $\bar{y}_t = \alpha + \beta t$ as a particular solution, α and β being undetermined constants. Substituting in (2.1) we have

$$c_1(\alpha + \beta t) + c_0[\alpha + \beta(t-1)] = a_0 + a_1 t \ ;$$

therefore

$$(c_1\beta + c_0\beta - a_1)t = a_0 - (c_0 + c_1)\alpha + c_0\beta \ .$$

The only way to satisfy the last equation for any t is to let both $c_1\beta + c_0\beta - a_1$ and $a_0 - (c_0 + c_1)\alpha + c_0\beta$ be equal to zero, and so we have the following linear system:

$$(c_0 + c_1)\beta = a_1 \ ,$$

$$(c_0 + c_1)\alpha - c_0\beta = a_0 \ ,$$

whose solution determines the values of α and β.

The student should be able by now to examine by himself the case where the method fails (i.e. when $c_1 + c_0 = 0$).

Case (4): $g(t)$ is a trigonometric function of the sine–cosine type.

In this case, $g(t) = B_1 \cos \omega t + B_2 \sin \omega t$, where B_1, B_2, ω are known constants. As a particular solution, try the function $\alpha \cos \omega t + \beta \sin \omega t$, where α and β are undetermined constants. Substitution in (2.1) gives

$$c_1\alpha \cos \omega t + c_1\beta \sin \omega t + c_0\alpha \cos (\omega t - \omega) + c_0\beta \sin (\omega t - \omega)$$

$$= B_1 \cos \omega t + B_2 \sin \omega t \ .$$

Simple manipulations ★ yield

$$[(c_1 + c_0 \cos \omega)\alpha - c_0\beta \sin \omega - B_1] \cos \omega t$$

$$+ [\alpha c_0 \sin \omega + (c_1 + c_0 \cos \omega)\beta - B_2] \sin \omega t = 0 \ .$$

★ Recall from trigonometry that

$$\cos (\omega t \pm \omega) = \cos \omega t \cos \omega \mp \sin \omega t \sin \omega \ ,$$

$$\sin (\omega t \pm \omega) = \sin \omega t \cos \omega \pm \sin \omega \cos \omega t \ .$$

This equation is satisfied for any t if, and only if,

$$(c_1 + c_0 \cos \omega)\alpha - (c_0 \sin \omega)\beta - B_1 = 0 ,$$

$$(c_0 \sin \omega)\alpha + (c_1 + c_0 \cos \omega)\beta - B_2 = 0 ,$$

which is a linear system whose solution determines the values of α and β. The student may examine, as an exercise, the case in which the method fails.

The four cases treated ★ cover all the cases we are likely to meet in economic applications. Actually, only case (1) — which is the most usual — and case (2) will be met in the following chapters on economic applications.

Having found a particular solution of the non-homogeneous equation, its general solution will be

$$y_t = A(-b)^t + \bar{y}_t .
\tag{2.12}$$

We must now determine the arbitrary constant A. It is important to keep in mind that this constant must be determined, given an additional condition, in relation to the general solution of the equation concerned. This means that, if the equation is non homogeneous, we cannot use formula (2.7) but must find a new one. The method, however, is the same: given $y_t = y^*$ for $t = t^*$, substitute in the general solution (2.12). This yields

$$A = \frac{y^* - \bar{y}_{t^*}}{(-b)^{t^*}} .$$

In economics, as we have already said, the initial value of y is usually assumed known, at least in principle, so that $A = y_0 - \bar{y}_0$.

It is interesting to note, from the economic point of view, that in the general solution of the non-homogeneous equation the particular solution $\bar{y}_t$ may usually be interpreted as the *equilibrium value* of the variable y (a stationary equilibrium or a moving equilibrium according to whether $\bar{y}_t$ is a constant or a function of t). The component $A(-b)^t$ in (2.12) may then be interpreted as giving the *deviations* from equilibrium, since $y_t - \bar{y}_t = A(-b)^t$.

These considerations can be extended to any difference equation: if $y_t = \bar{y}_t + f(t; A_1, A_2, ..., A_n)$ is the general solution of a n-th order non-homoge-

---

★ If $g(t)$ is a combination of the functions seen above in the various cases, as a particular solution we may try the same combination with undetermined coefficients, etc.

neous equation, and if the particular solution $\bar{y}_t$ may be interpreted as the equilibrium value of y, then $f(t; A_1, A_2, ..., A_n)$ expresses the deviations from equilibrium. Of course, from the mathematical point of view it is always true that $y_t - \bar{y}_t = f(t; A_1, A_2, ..., A_n)$, independently of the possibility of giving an economic interpretation to the particular solution $\bar{y}_t$.

References

Allen, R.G.D., 1959, *Mathematical Economics*, ch. 6, §6.3.

Baumol, W.J., 1970, *Economic Dynamics*, ch. 9.

Goldberg, S., 1958, *Introduction to Difference Equations*, ch. 2, §2.4.

Papandreou, A.G., 1965, *Introduction to Macroeconomic Models*, ch. 5, §5.3, 5.4.

Tintner, G., and Millham, C.B., 1970, *Mathematics and Statistics for Economists*, ch. 9, §§41, 42.

3

Some Economic Applications
of First-order Equations

§1. The cobweb theorem

This is a dynamic model derived from the static supply and demand model. Assume that supply reacts to price with a lag of one period, while demand depends on current price and that both functions are linear. In symbols

$$D_t = a + bp_t,$$

$$S_t = a_1 + b_1 p_{t-1}.$$

Why should supply behave in that way? First of all, the model relates to goods whose production is not instantaneous nor continuous, but requires a fixed period of time (which we take as the unit of measurement of time); at the end of each period the output 'started' at the beginning of the period appears and the market determines its price (e.g., agricultural production). Producers think – and this is a crucial assumption – that this price will hold also in the next period and so start the new production according to current price. When output materializes (one period later), the price by which it has been determined is obviously the price of the period before.

A last assumption is that in each period the market determines the price in such a way that demand absorbs exactly the quantity supplied, i.e. no producer is left with unsold output and no consumer with unsatisfied demand. This means that

$$D_t = S_t ,$$

whence

$$bp_t - b_1 p_{t-1} = a_1 - a . \tag{3.1}$$

The general solution of the corresponding homogenous equation is $A(b_1/b)^t$ and a particular solution of eq. (3.1) is $p_e = (a_1 - a)/(b - b_1)$. On the assumption that p_0, the initial value of price, is known, the arbitrary constant is determined as $A = p_0 - p_e$. The general solution of eq. (3.1) is then

$$p_t = (p_0 - p_e) \left(\frac{b_1}{b}\right)^t + p_e . \tag{3.2}$$

Can we give an economic interpretation to the particular solution p_e? The answer is yes: it is the static equilibrium value of price (the subscript e stands for 'equilibrium'). We can see from (3.2) that, if the initial price happens to be p_e, then $p_t = p_e$, i.e. price stays fixed at p_e (of course, if no exogenous disturbances occur) and that is what we mean by '(static) equilibrium'. Another way to arrive at the same interpretation is to check that the value of p_e given above is the same as that obtained by the solution of the static supply and demand model:

$$D = a + bp ,$$

$$S = a_1 + b_1 p ,$$

$$D = S .$$

Let us now analyse the behaviour over time of price, as given by eq. (3.2). Usually demand has a negative slope ($b < 0$) and supply a positive one ($b_1 > 0$). Then $b_1/b < 0$, and so price will have an oscillatory movement around its equilibrium value. These improper oscillations will be explosive, of constant amplitude, or damped according as $|b_1| \gtreqless |b|$, i.e. according as supply has a slope greater than, equal to or smaller than the absolute value of the slope of demand.

In fig. 3.1 the three cases are shown. The cobweblike aspect of the diagrams on the left justifies the name given (by Kaldor) to the model. Take, for

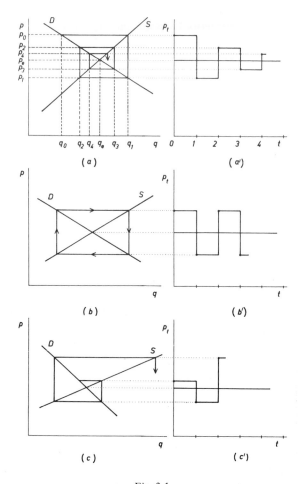

Fig. 3.1.

example, diagram (a). Let us suppose that in the initial period the system is
not in equilibrium because of an exogenous disturbance (e.g., a drought),
and let q_0 be the initial quantity; the corresponding initial price is p_0. The
price p_0 induces entrepreneurs to produce the quantity q_1, which, as we
know, materializes in period 1. This quantity will be exactly absorbed by
demand at price p_1, which in turn induces output q_2, and so on. The succession of prices over time is shown in diagram (a'). The movement converges
toward equilibrium, i.e. we are in a case where the slope of supply is smaller

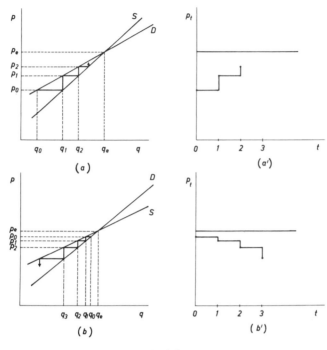

Fig. 3.2.

in absolute value than the slope of demand (in checking this, it must be re-membered that demand and supply functions have been written with price as the independent variable; slopes must then be computed with reference to the p axis).

We have so far considered only 'normal' cases, i.e. those in which demand has a negative slope and supply has a positive slope. Two among the conceiv-able 'abnormal' cases are shown in fig. 3.2. Here the movement is monotonic. The conditions on slopes hold here too. As we can see from the general solu-tion (3.2), the stability condition, i.e. the condition that the price converges – no matter how – towards its equilibrium value, is in any case $|b/b_1| < 1$, i.e. $|b| < |b_1|$.

This completes the examination of the traditional cobweb theorem. This model can be considered as a particular case of the more general model

$$D_t = a + bp_t,$$
$$S_t = a_1 + b_1\hat{p}_t,$$
$$D_t = S_t,$$

(3.3)

where $\hat{p}_t$ indicates the expected price, i.e. the price that producers, at the moment of 'starting' the production, think will hold when output materializes. In the original cobweb theorem the (implicit or explicit) assumption is, as we have seen above, that $\hat{p}_t = p_{t-1}$. Now it seems very implausible to assume that producers continue to expect that price will remain constant to its previous level when, on the contrary, it goes on varying period after period. Even animals learn from experience. The formation of expectations inherent in the traditional cobweb theorem cannot be accepted as a plausible description of reality. A more realistic way of treating expectations in this model will be shown later on, since it involves a second-order equation (see Part I, ch. 5, §4). Here we have tried to substitute a more plausible assumption on the formation of expectations, while remaining in the field of first-order equations. The result is the following.

First of all, define the 'normal price' as that price which producers think will sooner or later obtain in the market. Then if the current price is different from the normal price, they think that the former will modify, moving towards the latter. The simplest way of formalizing this is to put

$$\hat{p}_t = p_{t-1} + c(p_N - p_{t-1}), \qquad 0 < c < 1.$$

(3.4)

If, for example, the current price is lower than the normal price, an increase in price is expected for the next period. The fact that the positive constant c is assumed to be less than unity is equivalent to the assumption that producers do not think that price will immediately become the normal price (this would be the case if $c = 1$, whence $\hat{p}_t = p_N$), but think that the process will require a certain amount of time (measured by the reciprocal of c). Let us note, incidentally, that when $c = 0$ we are back to the original cobweb theorem.

What we have said above would be little more than a tautology if we did not specify how to determine the normal price. A simple way of doing this is to assume that p_N is a constant and equals p_e, the static equilibrium price. This admittedly simplifying assumption ★ may be perfectly valid and realistic

---

★ Yet it is difficult to improve on it while (1) keeping expectations endogenous to the model (in the contrary case we could assume that p_N is a given function of time, but this seems rather arbitrary) and (2) respecting the constraint of not using equations of order higher than the first.

when, for example, the system has been in equilibrium for some time before the exogenous disturbance, so that producers have formed the belief that the price to which they have become accustomed is the norm.

Now let us turn to mathematics. Substituting (3.4), where $p_N = p_e$, in (3.3), we obtain

$$b_1(1-c)p_{t-1} - bp_t = a - a_1 - b_1 c p_e ,\qquad(3.5)$$

whose solution is

$$p_t = A\left[\frac{b_1(1-c)}{b}\right]^t + p_e .\qquad(3.6)$$

The stability condition is

$$|b_1(1-c)| < |b| .\qquad(3.7)$$

The quantity $1 - c$ is positive and less than unity, since $0 < c < 1$. Then the absolute value of $b_1(1-c)$ is smaller than the absolute value of b_1. If we compare our new model with the original cobweb theorem we obtain the following results (the first term in the comparisons refers to the original cobweb theorem):

(1) A convergent movement remains convergent and the convergence is faster. In fact, since

$$\left|\frac{b_1(1-c)}{b}\right| < \left|\frac{b_1}{b}\right| < 1 ,$$

the absolute value of $[b_1(1-c)/b]^t$ tends to zero more rapidly than the absolute value of $(b_1/b)^t$.

(2) An improper oscillation of constant amplitude becomes damped. This is so because, if $|b_1| = |b|$, then $|b_1(1-c)| < |b|$.

(3) A divergent movement may become convergent (or of constant amplitude) if the parameter c is sufficiently close to unity and, when it remains divergent, the divergence is slower. This is so because the greater is c the smaller is $(1-c)$ — remember that in any case $0 < c < 1$ — and so the more likely it is that $|b_1(1-c)| \leqslant |b|$ even if $|b_1| > |b|$. In any case

$$\left|\frac{b_1(1-c)}{b}\right| < \left|\frac{b_1}{b}\right| ,$$

and so, if the movement remains divergent, the absolute value of $[b_1(1-c)/b]^t$ increases at a slower rate than the absolute value of $(b_1/b)^t$. Note that a greater value of c means that producers expect a faster approach of current price towards its equilibrium value.

Our conclusions show that in any case the introduction of expectations based on a normal price (assumed to be equal to the equilibrium price) makes the model more stable, and this is a sensible result.

Exercises

1. Given the following functions

$$D_t = 100 - 2p_t ,$$

$$S_t = -20 + 3p_{t-1} ,$$

find the equilibrium value of price and check if it is stable or unstable. Assume that the initial value of price is $p_0 = 24$ and compute the numerical values of p_t up to $t = 4$.
25

Calculation. Putting $D_t = S_t$ we have

$$100 - 2p_t = -20 + 3p_{t-1} ,$$

and dividing through by 2 and rearranging terms we obtain

$$p_t + 1.5p_{t-1} = 60 . \tag{3.8}$$

The equilibrium value of price is obtained setting $p_t = p_{t-1} = p_e$ (an undetermined constant) in (3.8), whence

$$p_e + 1.5p_e = 60 ,$$

therefore

$$p_e = 24 , \tag{3.9}$$

which is also a particular solution of (3.8). The corresponding homogeneous equation is

$$p_t + 1.5p_{t-1} = 0 , \tag{3.10}$$

whose general solution is

$$p_t = A(-1.5)^t , \tag{3.11}$$

where A is an arbitrary constant. Adding (3.9) and (3.11) we obtain the general solution of (3.8):

$$p_t = A(-1.5)^t + 24 . \tag{3.12}$$

Since -1.5 is negative and in absolute value greater than unity (improper oscillations of ever increasing amplitude), the equilibrium is unstable. Given $p_0 = 25$, we can determine the value of the arbitrary constant A. From (3.12)

$$p_0 = A(-1.5)^0 + 24 ,$$

and so (remember that any number to the zeroth power gives as a result one)

$$25 = A + 24$$
$$A = 1 .$$

We have then

$$p_t = (-1.5)^t + 24 . \tag{3.13}$$

To compute the numerical values of p_t we may either make use of eq. (3.8) recursively or utilise eq. (3.13). The following table shows the computations.

t	$p_t = -1.5p_{t-1} + 60$	$p_t = (-1.5)^t + 24$
0	$p_0 = 25$	$p_0 = 25$
1	$p_1 = -1.5 \times 25 + 60 = 22.5$	$p_1 = (-1.5)^1 + 24 = -1.5 + 24 = 22.5$
2	$p_2 = -1.5 \times 22.5 + 60 = 26.25$	$p_2 = (-1.5)^2 + 24 = 2.25 + 24 = 26.25$
3	$p_3 = -1.5 \times 26.25 + 60 = 20.625$	$p_3 = (-1.5)^3 + 24 = -3.375 + 24 = 20.625$
4	$p_4 = -1.5 \times 20.625 + 60 = 29.0625$	$p_4 = (-1.5)^4 + 24 = 5.0625 + 24 = 29.0625$

From the computational point of view the first method of finding the successive values of p_t is more efficient, since in general it involves a smaller number of operations. The second method, however, is preferable when we have to compute the value of p_t for a single given value of t, since we do not have to compute all the preceding values of p.

2. Same problem as in exercise 1, but with the following data:

$$D_t = 5 + 3p_t , \qquad S_t = 35 + 1.5p_{t-1} , \qquad p_0 = 10 .$$

Calculation. From the condition $D_t = S_t$, dividing through by 3 and rearranging terms, we have

$$p_t - 0.5p_{t-1} = 10 . \tag{3.14}$$

The equilibrium value p_e (particular solution of (3.14)) is found to be

$$p_e = 20 . \tag{3.15}$$

The non-homogeneous equation corresponding to (3.14) is

$$p_t - 0.5p_{t-1} = 0 , \tag{3.16}$$

and its general solution is

$$p_t = A(0.5)^t , \tag{3.17}$$

where A is an arbitrary constant. The general solution of (3.14) is then

$$p_t = A(0.5)^t + 20 . \tag{3.18}$$

Since 0.5 is a positive number smaller than unity, the movement is monotonic and converges towards equilibrium. Given $p_0 = 10$, from (3.18) we have

$$10 = A(0.5)^0 + 20 ,$$

therefore

$$A = -10 ,$$

and so

$$p_t = -10(0.5)^t + 20 . \tag{3.19}$$

The numerical succession of p_t, computed with any of the two methods expounded in exercise 1, is shown in the following table.

t	0	1	2	3	4
p_t	10	15	17.5	18.750	19.375

3. Same problem as in exercise 1, but with the following data:

(a) $D_t = 80 - 4p_t$, $S_t = -10 + 2p_{t-1}$, $p_0 = 18$;

(b) $D_t = 80 - p_t$, $S_t = -10 + p_{t-1}$, $p_0 = 50$;

(c) $D_t = 20 + p_t$, $S_t = -10 + 2p_{t-1}$, $p_0 = 31$.

4. Consider the model

$$D_t = 100 - 2p_t ,$$

$$S_t = -20 + 3\hat{p}_t ,$$

where $\hat{p}_t$ is determined according to the normal price hypothesis. Assume that $p_N = 24$ and $c = 1/3$. What is the behaviour of price over time?

Calculation. First of all, substitute $\hat{p}_t = p_{t-1} + \frac{1}{3}(24 - p_{t-1})$ in S_t, obtaining $S_t = 4 + 2p_{t-1}$. Then go on with the usual procedure ($D_t = S_t$, etc.). The resulting equation is

$$p_t + p_{t-1} = 48 ,$$

and its general solution is

$$p_t = A(-1)^t + 24 .$$

The improper oscillation, which would have been of increasing amplitude in the original cobweb theorem (see exercise 1) is now of constant amplitude.

5. With the same demand and supply functions as in exercise 4, examine the following cases:

   (a) $c = \frac{1}{2}$;

   (b) $c = \frac{1}{5}$.

§2. The dynamics of multipliers

We know from elementary Keynesian macroeconomics that in a model without government or foreign sector, an increase ΔI in autonomous investment (or, more generally, in autonomous expenditure) brings about an increase in national income according to the multiplier equation

$$\Delta Y = \frac{1}{1-b} \Delta I ,$$

where b is the marginal propensity to consume. This is a result of the *comparative statics* kind, i.e., given an equilibrium position (where income is, say, Y_0) and given an autonomous shift of investment from I to $I + \Delta I$, the *new* equilibrium value of income is

$$Y_0 + \frac{1}{1-b} \Delta I .^{\star}$$

This result, however, does not say anything about the *movement* from the old to the new equilibrium — we do not even know if income will move towards (or away from) its new equilibrium value. Only a dynamical model can elucidate these points. The usual dynamical assumption is that consumption depends on income with a one-period lag, i.e.

$$C_t = a + bY_{t-1} , \qquad a \geq 0 , \qquad 0 < b < 1 . \tag{3.20}$$

Investment, for the moment, is assumed to be wholly autonomous, and in the initial period shifts from I_0 to $I_0 + \Delta I$ (remaining at this level in all subsequent

---

   $\star$ The student wanting to know more about comparative statics is referred to Appendix I.

periods):

$$I_t = I_0 + \Delta I .$$ (3.21)

The equation

$$Y_t = C_t + I_t$$ (3.22)

closes the model. This equation may be interpreted both as a definitional equation and as an equilibrium condition.

In the first sense, starting from the definitional equation

$$Y_t \equiv C_t + S_t ,$$

and using the *ex post* identity between S_t and I_t,

$$S_t \equiv I_t ,$$

which, as we know from elementary macroeconomics, is an accounting identity, we obtain

$$Y_t \equiv C_t + I_t ,$$

which is a definitional relation.

In the second sense, starting from the definitional equation

$$S_t \equiv Y_t - C_t ,$$

and using the *ex ante* equality between S_t and I_t,

$$S_t = I_t ,$$

which, as we know, is an *equilibrium condition*, we obtain

$$Y_t - C_t = I_t ;$$

therefore

$$Y_t = C_t + I_t ,$$

which is an equilibrium condition.

Both interpretations are formally possible, but the second is preferable from the economic point of view, at least in the present writer's opinion, for the first interpretation is compatible with an *ex ante* inequality between saving and investment. This inequality may, and usually will, bring about some economic reactions which are *not* contemplated in the model. No such problem arises with the second interpretation. Since equation (3.22) appears in many of the models examined in this book, the reader is recommended to keep in mind that the interpretation of that equation will always be the one given here, unless otherwise explicitly stated. ★

Substituting from (3.20) and (3.21) in (3.22) we obtain

$$Y_t - bY_{t-1} = a + I_0 + \Delta I, \tag{3.23}$$

whose solution is

$$Y_t = A(b)^t + \frac{a + I_0 + \Delta I}{1 - b}. \tag{3.24}$$

The new equilibrium value $(a + I_0 + \Delta I)/(1 - b)$ and the initial equilibrium value $(a + I_0)/(1 - b)$ of income differ by the quantity $(\Delta I)/(1 - b)$, which is the result stated at the beginning. But eq. (3.24) says something more. Since $0 < b < 1$, the term $A(b)^t$ tends to zero as time goes on and this means that income actually moves (with a monotonic movement) towards its new equilibrium value. In fig. 3.3 a graphical representation of this approach is given. The 'static' part of the diagram is the well-known 'Keynesian cross'. The initial level of investment is $\overline{OR}$ (this means that we have assumed here $a = 0$) and $\overline{OR'}$ is its new level (the shift has been exaggerated for graphical convenience). The corresponding equilibria are Y_0 and Y_E respectively. Let us now examine the dynamic process. In period 1, consumption – which depends on income in period zero – is $\overline{A_1 P_1}$. Adding it to the (new) investment $\overline{OR'} = \overline{A_1 Y_0}$ we obtain income in period 1, which is then $\overline{Y_0 P_1}$. By means of the 45° line we transfer this segment to the Y axis, obtaining point Y_1. In period 2, consumption is $\overline{A_2 P_2}$ and income is $\overline{Y_1 P_2} = \overline{A_2 P_2} + \overline{A_2 Y_1}$; by means of the 45° line we obtain point Y_2 on the abscissae, and so on. As we see, the system tends monotonically towards point P_E, i.e. towards Y_E.

★ It must be noted that in any case, when from the other equations of a model we substitute in equation $Y_t = C_t + I_t$ an investment *function* (that is, *ex ante* investment) and a consumption function (that is, *ex ante* consumption), then the only correct interpretation is the equilibrium condition one. This can also be seen by remarking that in such a case the equation $C_t + I_t = Y_t$ is nothing else but the equilibrium between *ex ante* aggregate demand $(C_t + I_t)$ and aggregate supply (Y_t).

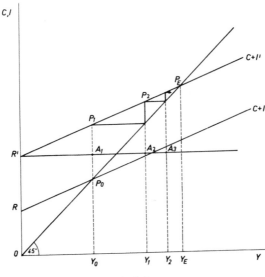

Fig. 3.3.

We have so far examined the case in which investment is entirely autonomous. Let us now assume that it is partly autonomous and partly depending
on income, i.e. $I_t = hY_{t-1} + I_0$ * where h is the marginal propensity to invest,
and $0 < h < 1$. Eq. (3.21) above becomes

$$I_t = hY_{t-1} + I_0 + \Delta I , \qquad\qquad (3.21')$$

and eq. (3.23) becomes

$$Y_t - (b+h)Y_{t-1} = a + I_0 + \Delta I , \qquad\qquad (3.23')$$

whose solution is

$$Y_t = A(b+h)^t + \frac{a + I_0 + \Delta I}{1 - b - h} . \qquad\qquad (3.24')$$

Since b and h are both positive magnitudes, the movement is monotonic.

---

* The student may check as an exercise that, if we put $I_t = hY_t + I_0$, the multiplier
and the stability condition below are not altered.

Stability requires that $b + h < 1$, i.e.

$$h < 1 - b .\tag{3.25}$$

Since $1 - b$ is the marginal propensity to save, condition (3.25) says that the marginal propensity to invest must be smaller than the marginal propensity to save if equilibrium is to be stable. Let us note, incidentally, that from (3.25) it follows that $0 < 1 - b - h$, and this ensures that the multiplier $1/(1 - b - h)$ is positive. ★

As a last example of multiplier analysis, we shall now examine a foreign trade multiplier. Imports are a function of income and exports are assumed to be wholly exogenous (for a more general model see Part I, ch. 9, §1). In an open economy, aggregate supply is the sum of national product and imports; aggregate demand is national consumption plus national investment plus exports. The equilibrium condition is then no more $Y = C + I$, but $Y + M = C + I + X$ or $Y = C + I + X - M$. The formal model is then the following:

$$C_t = a + bY_{t-1} ,$$

$$I_t = hY_{t-1} + I_0 + \Delta I ,$$

$$X_t = X_0 + \Delta X ,$$

$$M_t = mY_{t-1} + M_0 , \qquad 0 < m < 1 ,$$

$$Y_t = C_t + I_t + X_t - M_t .$$

Substituting from the first four equations of the above system into the fifth, we obtain

$$Y_t - (b + h - m)Y_{t-1} = a + I_0 + X_0 - M_0 + \Delta I + \Delta X ,\tag{3.26}$$

whose solution is

$$Y_t = A(b + h - m)^t + \frac{a + I_0 + X_0 - M_0 + \Delta I + \Delta X}{1 - b - h + m} .\tag{3.27}$$

Note that the multiplier is now $1/(1 - b - h + m)$. The 'leakage' due to im-

---

★ This is an application of the 'correspondence principle'. See Appendix I.

ports is represented by m, the marginal propensity to import.

The sum $b + h$ is surely greater than m. This apparently unwarranted statement can be justified on the following economic grounds. Take a unit increment in income, which causes an increment in both consumption and investment; this increment is measured by $b + h$ and contains both national and foreign goods. The part pertaining to the latter is measured by m, which is then only a part of the total increment $b + h$. It follows that $b + h - m$, which measures the marginal propensity to spend on domestic goods, is a positive quantity. Hence the movement given by (3.27) is monotonic.

The stability condition is that $b + h - m < 1$. This inequality is equivalent to the inequality $1 - b - h + m > 0$ and so the stability condition ensures that the multiplier $1/(1 - b - h + m)$ is positive. The condition may also be written in the form

$$h < 1 - b + m , \tag{3.28}$$

i.e. the marginal propensity to invest must be smaller than the sum of the marginal propensity to save and of the marginal propensity to import.

A related and interesting question is whether the foreign trade multiplier brings about a complete adjustment in the balance of trade. Assume that trade is initially balanced (i.e., $X = M$) and that exports autonomously increase. Income increases according to the foreign trade multiplier and also imports increase, since they are an increasing function of income. Will the (induced) increase in imports exactly offset the (exogenous) increase in exports? Formally, we have

$$\Delta Y = \frac{1}{1 - b - h + m} \Delta X$$

and

$$\Delta M = m\Delta Y = \frac{m}{1 - b - h + m} \Delta X .$$

It follows that $\Delta M = \Delta X$ if, and only if, $m/(1 - b - h + m) = 1$, so that $h = 1 - b$. It must be emphasized that the last equality cannot be ruled out by stability considerations. It is true that in a closed economy h must be smaller than $1 - b$ (see condition (3.25) above), but here we are in an open economy and the stability condition (3.28) is compatible with h being equal to $1 - b$. In general, $\Delta M \lessgtr \Delta X$ according as $h \lessgtr 1 - b$, any of the three cases being in principle possible.

Exercises

1. In a certain period income is in equilibrium at the level $Y_0 = 100$; C_0 is 60 and I_0 is 40. The consumption function is $C_t = 0.60\, Y_{t-1}$ and investment is entirely autonomous. Assume that investment shifts from 40 to 50 and compute the final increment in income. Is the new equilibrium a stable position?

Calculation. The increment in income is obtained applying the static multiplier $1/(1 - 0.6)$ to the increment in autonomous investment; the result is 25. The new equilibrium value of income is then 125. Substituting the given functions in the equation $Y_t = C_t + I_t$, we obtain

$$Y_t = 0.60\, Y_{t-1} + 50 , \qquad (3.29)$$

whose solution is

$$Y_t = A(0.60)^t + 125 ,$$

where

$$A = Y_0 - 125 = 100 - 125 = -25 ,$$

and so

$$Y_t = -25(0.60)^t + 125 . \qquad (3.30)$$

Since $(0.60)^t$ tends monotonically to zero as t increases, Y_t tends to 125, and so the equilibrium is stable.

As a further exercise, the following table can be computed

Period	Investment	Consumption	Income
0	40	60	100
1	50	60	110
2	50	66	116
3	50	69.6	119.6
4	50	71.76	121.76
5	50	73.056	123.056
6	50	73.8336	123.8336
...	...	...	...
$t \to \infty$	50	$C_t \to 75.00$	$Y_t \to 125$

2. Same initial data as in exercise 1, but now the investment function is
$I_t = 0.20\,Y_{t-1} + 20$ (the consumption function is the same); the autonomous
component in the investment function shifts from 20 to 30. Compute the
new equilibrium level of income and check its stability.

Calculation. The multiplier $1/(1 - 0.6 - 0.2)$ applied to the increment in
autonomous investment gives an increment in income of 50. The new equilibrium value of income is then 150. Substituting the given functions in the
equation $Y_t = C_t + I_t$, we obtain

$$Y_t = 0.60\,Y_{t-1} + 0.20\,Y_{t-1} + 30 \ ;$$

therefore

$$Y_t - 0.80\,Y_{t-1} = 30 \ ,$$

whose solution is

$$Y_t = A(0.80)^t + 150 \ ,$$

where

$$A = Y_0 - 150 = 100 - 150 = -50 \ ,$$

and so

$$Y_t = -50(0.80)^t + 150 \ .$$

Since $(0.80)^t$ tends to zero monotonically as t increases, Y_t tends to 150:
equilibrium is stable.

3. Examine the following cases:
    (a) $Y_0 = 100, C_0 = 80, I_0 = 20, C_t = 0.8\,Y_{t-1}.\,I_t$ is entirely exogenous
and shifts from 20 to 25.
    (b) $Y_0 = 100, C_0 = 64, I_0 = 36, C_t = 0.64\,Y_{t-1}, I_t = 0.20\,Y_{t-1} + 16$. The
autonomous component in I_t shifts from 16 to 24.
    (c) $Y_0 = 100, C_0 = 60, I_0 = 40, X_0 = 30, M_0 = 30, C_t = 0.60\,Y_{t-1}$,
$I_t = 0.20\,Y_{t-1} + 20, M_t = 0.3\,Y_{t-1}$. Exports shift exogenously from 30 to 40.

§3. A formalization of Harrod's model

The correct formalization of this model, which was set forth in non-formal terms by its author, has occasioned much discussion in the literature. *

The formalization we give here, adopted by some authors, is probably not the best one. It has, however, the advantage of simplicity and may be considered as a step towards more complicated formulations.

Assume that *ex ante* saving is given by the function

$$S_t = sY_{t-1} \, ,$$

and *ex ante* investment by the function

$$I_t = k(Y_t - Y_{t-1}) \, .$$

The marginal (and average) propensity to save, s, and the acceleration coefficient k, are given constants; the symbol Y denotes national income. In equilibrium, *ex ante* saving and *ex ante* investment must be equal and so

$$sY_{t-1} = k(Y_t - Y_{t-1}) \, , \tag{3.31}$$

whence

$$kY_t - (k+s)Y_{t-1} = 0 \, ;$$

therefore

$$Y_t - \frac{k+s}{k} Y_{t-1} = 0 \, .$$

The solution of this homogeneous equation is

$$Y_t = A \left(\frac{k+s}{k} \right)^t = A \left(1 + \frac{s}{k} \right)^t , \tag{3.32}$$

where the arbitrary constant A equals the initial value of income, say Y_0. Eq. (3.32) tells us that income increases over time at the constant rate of growth s/k. This rate is called by Harrod the 'warranted' rate of growth. It is a rate such that, when income grows according to it, there is a continuous equality over time between *ex ante* saving and *ex ante* investment, i.e. a dynamic equilibrium obtains. This can be checked easily. We have

---

* For a survey of the various formalizations of Harrod's model, see Miconi's article. He also puts forward his own interpretation.

$$S_t = sY_{t-1} = sA \left(\frac{k+s}{k} \right)^{t-1},$$

$$I_t = k(Y_t - Y_{t-1}) = k \left[A \left(\frac{k+s}{k} \right)^t - A \left(\frac{k+s}{k} \right)^{t-1} \right].$$

The investment equation can be manipulated as follows:

$$I_t = kA \left(\frac{k+s}{k} \right)^{t-1} \left(\frac{k+s}{k} - 1 \right) = kA \left(\frac{k+s}{k} \right)^{t-1} \frac{s}{k},$$

and so

$$I_t = sA \left(\frac{k+s}{k} \right)^{t-1},$$

which equals the expression for S_t. This is as it ought to be, since we have obtained Y_t as a function of time, imposing the condition that $S_t = I_t$.

The warranted rate of growth has the peculiarity of being unstable. This means that, if for any reason income deviates from its equilibrium path given by (3.32), it will go on deviating further and further from that path. An intuitive proof is the following. Suppose that in period t income is not $A[(k+s)/k]^t$ but is, say, $A[(k+s)/k]^t + B$, where B is the effect of an exogenous disturbance. Assume, for example, that $B > 0$. Then, as can easily be checked, $I_t > S_t$, and this will give an additional impulse to income (we know that when $I_t > S_t$, aggregate demand is greater than aggregate supply and this exerts an upward pressure on national income) which will then start growing faster than it previously had.

Exercises

1. Assume that the (marginal and average) propensity to save is 0.20 and that the acceleration coefficient is 2. Determine the warranted rate of growth and, given the initial value of income $Y_0 = 100$, compute the values of income, of consumption and of investment up to $t = 4$.

Calculation. With the given numerical values of s and of k we have

$$S_t = 0.20\, Y_{t-1},$$

$$I_t = 2(Y_t - Y_{t-1}),$$

$$S_t = I_t,$$

whence

$$Y_t - 1.10\,Y_{t-1} = 0 . \tag{3.33}$$

The solution of eq. (3.33) is

$$Y_t = Y_0(1.10)^t . \tag{3.34}$$

The warranted rate of growth is 0.10.
    Since $C_t = Y_t - S_t$, we have

$$C_t = Y_t - 0.20\,Y_{t-1} = Y_0(1.10)^t - 0.20\,Y_0(1.10)^{t-1}$$

$$= Y_0(1.10)^{t-1}(1.10 - 0.20)$$

and so

$$C_t = 0.90\,Y_0(1.10)^{t-1} . \tag{3.35}$$

For the investment function, we have

$$I_t = 2(Y_t - Y_{t-1}) = 2[Y_0(1.10)^t - Y_0(1.10)^{t-1}]$$

$$= 2Y_0(1.10)^{t-1}(1.10 - 1) ,$$

and so

$$I_t = 0.20\,Y_0(1.10)^{t-1} . \tag{3.36}$$

Since $S_t = 0.20\,Y_{t-1}$, we have $S_t = 0.20\,Y_0(1.10)^{t-1}$, which equals I_t as given by (3.36). To compute the required succession of Y_t, C_t and I_t, we may either proceed recursively or utilize eqs. (3.34), (3.35) and (3.36). The result is shown in the following table

t	$Y_t = C_t + I_t = 1.10\,Y_{t-1}$ $= 100(1.10)^t$	$C_t = Y_t - 0.20\,Y_{t-1}$ $= 90(1.10)^{t-1}$	$I_t = 2(Y_t - Y_{t-1})$ $= 20(1.10)^{t-1}$
0	100	90/1.10	20/1.10
1	110	90	20
2	121	99	22
3	133.1	108.9	24.2
4	146.41	119.79	26.62

2. Examine the following cases:
   (a) $s = 0.15, k = 3$;
   (b) $s = 0.30, k = 5$.

§4. A simple dynamic model of income inflation

By 'income inflation' we mean the kind of inflationary process resulting
from the attempts of different income groups to raise their relative real incomes by raising their monetary incomes. Define money national income as

$$Y_t = P_t y_t ,$$
(3.37)

where P_t is the level of prices and y_t is real national income. Assume that the
relevant distributive classes are only two, wage-earners (workers) and profit-
earners (entrepreneurs); the substantial conclusions of the model would not
change if we considered a greater number of distributive classes. We then have

$$Y_t = W_t + E_t ,$$
(3.38)

where W_t is aggregate money wages and E_t aggregate money profits. Suppose
now that entrepreneurs want to obtain a given *share* of real profits in real
income, say a. Then $e_t = a y_t$, where e_t is the (desired) level of profits. We
now make the assumption that entrepreneurs have the power to modify
prices in order to pursue their aim. In money terms we have

$$E_t = e_t P_t = a y_t P_t .$$
(3.39)

Since, from eq. (3.37), $E_t = Y_t - W_t$, substituting into (3.39) we obtain

$$a y_t P_t = Y_t - W_t ,$$
(3.40)

and substituting $Y_t = P_t y_t$ we have

$$P_t = \frac{1}{(1-a)y_t} W_t .$$
(3.41)

Eq. (3.41) indicates the price that entrepreneurs have to fix if they want to
obtain a given share a of real national income.

Suppose now that workers as a group also want to obtain a given share, say b, of real national income and that they act to obtain the corresponding money wage. Wage bargains and the like, however, take some time and so it is plausible to think that wages react to prices with a lag. Assuming that the length of the lag is constant, we have

$$W_t = b y_{t-1} P_{t-1} .$$ (3.42)

Substituting from (3.42) into (3.41) we obtain

$$P_t = \frac{b y_{t-1}}{(1-a) y_t} P_{t-1} .$$ (3.43)

The ratio y_{t-1}/y_t must be known if we want to solve eq. (3.43). Two cases will be considered:

(1) income is constant at some level (e.g. at full employment);
(2) income is growing at a constant rate of growth, say r.

In case (1), $y_t = y_{t-1}$ and so

$$P_t = \frac{b}{1-a} P_{t-1} ,$$ (3.43')

whose solution is

$$P_t = P_0 \left(\frac{b}{1-a} \right)^t ,$$ (3.44)

where P_0 is the initial price level. Since $1 - a > 0$, the movement is monotonic. The price level will increase when $b/(1-a) > 1$, i.e. when

$$a + b > 1 .$$ (3.45)

The interpretation of condition (3.45) is straightforward: when the shares of national income that entrepreneurs and workers want to appropriate are as a whole excessive, inflation results, given of course the behaviour assumptions that we have made. Note that a and b are *desired* values; if we indicate by a_1 and b_1 the actual shares, then $a_1 + b_1 = 1$ by definition. It should be clear from the model that $a_1 = a$ while, owing to the lag, $b_1 < b$ if inflation is going on ($b_1 = W_t/Y_t = (W_t/P_t)(Y_t/P_t)^{-1} = (b y_{t-1} P_{t-1}/P_t)(1/y_t) = b(P_{t-1}/P_t)$. If inflation is going on, $P_{t-1}/P_t < 1$ and so $b_1 < b$).

In case (2), $y_t = y_0(1+r)^t$, whence $y_{t-1}/y_t = 1/(1+r)$, and so

$$P_t = \frac{b}{(1-a)(1+r)} P_{t-1} , \tag{3.43''}$$

whose solution is

$$P_t = P_0 \left[\frac{b}{(1-a)(1+r)} \right]^t . \tag{3.46}$$

The movement is monotonic and inflation results when $b/(1-a)(1+r) > 1$, i.e. when

$$a + b > 1 + r - ar . \tag{3.47}$$

The interpretation of this condition is the same as the one given for condition (3.45); we only note that the critical value of $a+b$ is now greater, owing to the fact that income increases and so can accomodate greater claims. However, in this case too b_1 is smaller than b (check as an exercise).

Some more general results can be given, independently of any assumption about the behaviour of y_t. Write the ratio y_t/y_{t-1} as $1 + r_t$ (where r_t is defined as $(y_t - y_{t-1})/y_{t-1}$). Inflation results if $P_t > P_{t-1}$, i.e., from eq. (3.43), if

$$\frac{by_{t-1}}{(1-a)y_t} \equiv \frac{b}{(1-a)(1+r_t)} > 1 ,$$

whence

$$a + b > 1 + r_t - ar_t . \tag{3.48}$$

The interpretation of this condition — of which particular cases are conditions (3.45) and (3.47) — is the same as before.

It must be stressed that the model does *not* allow us to tell which of the two desired shares is excessive when inflation is going on: it simply says that their *sum* is excessive. In order to tell which share is excessive, some additional considerations must be made; these considerations are not contained in the model and are, at least in part, of a non-economic nature. Assume, as an example, that in a certain moment the sum $a + b$ does not exceed its critical value, so that prices are constant; suppose now that the value of b increases. The value of a must be adjusted accordingly; if this does not happen inflation results. Now, if we think that it is socially just to increase workers' share, then the excessive share is a; if, on the contrary, we think that the increase in b is unjustified, b is the excessive share.

Exercises

1. Assume that real income is given at the full employment level and that workers' share and entrepreneurs' share are respectively 0.52 and 0.48. Workers then claim a greater share, say 0.60, and obtain wage increases, but entrepreneurs want to preserve their own share and modify prices. Compute the rate of inflation.

Calculation. In this case we obtain the equation

$$P_t = \frac{0.60}{0.52} P_{t-1} \, ,$$

whose solution is

$$P_t = P_0 \left(\frac{0.60}{0.52}\right)^t ,$$

i.e.

$$P_t = P_0 (1.1538)^t .$$

Prices increase at a rate of 15.38% per period.

2. Same initial data as in exercise 1, but now entrepreneurs are willing to accept a reduction in their share from 48% to 45%.

References

Ackley, G., 1961, *Macro-economic Theory*, ch. XIII; ch. XVIII, pp. 518–29.
Allen, R.G.D., 1959, *Mathematical Economics*, ch. I, §§ 1.1, 1.2, 1.4; ch. 2, §§ 2.1, 2.5, 2.6, 2.7, 2.8.
Allen, R.G.D., 1967, *Macro-Economic Theory: A Mathematical Treatment,* ch. 5, § 5.2; ch. 9, §§ 9.1, 9.2, 9.3; ch. 11. §§ 11.1, 11.4.
Baumol, W.J., 1970, *Economic Dynamics*, ch. 4.
Bronfenbrenner, M. and Holzman, F.D., 1963, Survey of Inflation Theory, § III.F.
Buchanan, N.S., 1939, A Reconsideration of the Cobweb Theorem.
Dernburg, T.F. and Dernburg, J.D., 1969, *Macroeconomic Analysis: An Introduction to Comparative Statics and Dynamics*, ch. 6.
Ezekiel, M., 1938, The Cobweb Theorem.
Harrod, R.F., 1939, An Essay in Dynamic Theory.
Harrod, R.F., 1948, *Towards a Dynamic Economics*, pp. 63–100.

Henderson, J.M. and Quandt, R.E., 1958, *Microeconomic Theory: A Mathematical Approach*, ch. 4, §4.8.
Kaldor, N., 1960, Determinateness of Static Equilibrium, pp. 4, 30–3.
Kindleberger, C.P., 1968, *International Economics*, ch. 16.
Kogiku, K.C., 1968, *An Introduction to Macroeconomic Models*, chs. 1; 2; 3, §§3.1–3.5; ch. 7, §§7.1, 7.2.
Miconi, B., 1967, On Harrod's Model and Instability.

4

Second-order Equations

The general form of these equations is

$$c_2 y_t + c_1 y_{t-1} + c_0 y_{t-2} = g(t),$$ (4.1)

where c_0, c_1, c_2 are given constants and $g(t)$ is a known function. The coefficients c_2 and c_0 must be *both* different from zero, since if either one is zero the equation becomes of the first order.

Consider now the homogeneous equation

$$c_2 y_t + c_1 y_{t-1} + c_0 y_{t-2} = 0,$$ (4.2)

which can be written in the form

$$y_t + a_1 y_{t-1} + a_2 y_{t-2} = 0,$$ (4.3)

where

$$a_1 \equiv c_1/c_2, \qquad a_2 \equiv c_0/c_2.$$

We have seen in Part I, ch. 2, that the general solution of the first-order equation involves a function of the type λ^t, where λ is a constant determined by

50

means of the coefficients of the equation. Analogy leads us to think that the solution function of eq. (4.3) might be of the same type. Let us then substitute $y_t = \lambda^t$ in eq. (4.3), the constant λ being for the moment undetermined. We obtain

$$\lambda^t + a_1\lambda^{t-1} + a_2\lambda^{t-2} = 0 , \qquad (4.4)$$

whence

$$\lambda^{t-2}(\lambda^2 + a_1\lambda + a_2) = 0 . \qquad (4.4')$$

If λ^t has to be a solution, eq. (4.4') must be satisfied for any value of t, and this is true — apart from the trivial case $\lambda = 0$ — if, and only if, the expression in parentheses, which does not involve t, is zero, i.e.

$$\lambda^2 + a_1\lambda + a_2 = 0 . \qquad (4.5)$$

Eq. (4.5) is called the *characteristic* (or *auxiliary*) *equation* of the difference equation (4.3). It is remarkable that in this way we have reduced the solution of a functional equation to the solution of an algebraic equation. The two roots of eq. (4.5) are given by the well-known formula

$$\lambda_1, \lambda_2 = \frac{-a_1 \pm (a_1^2 - 4a_2)^{1/2}}{2} .$$

We must now examine in some detail the nature of these roots — and hence of the solution of eq. (4.3) — according to the sign of the discriminant $\Delta \equiv a_1^2 - 4a_2$. Three cases are possible.

Case (1)

$$\Delta > 0 .$$

The roots λ_1, λ_2 are real and distinct. Then both λ_1^t and λ_2^t satisfy eq. (4.3) and, according to general principles, we can combine them linearly and obtain the general solution

$$y_t = A_1\lambda_1^t + A_2\lambda_2^t , \qquad (4.6)$$

where A_1, A_2 are two arbitrary constants.

The kind of movement (monotonic or oscillatory or combination of the two) depends on the *sign* of λ_1, λ_2. We know that the t-th power of a positive number is always positive (monotonic movement), whereas the power of a negative number is positive or negative according as to whether the exponent is even or odd (improper oscillations, as we have defined them in Part I, ch. 2). Since, in principle, each root may have any sign (no root, however, can be zero, since $a_2 \neq 0$) ★ a great variety of movements is possible. In any case the movement will be *convergent* if, and only if, *both* roots are in absolute value less than unity, since in that case both terms on the right-hand side of (4.6) tend to zero in absolute value. As t increases, the movement of y_t will be dominated by the root numerically greater, which is called the dominant root.

Case (2)

$$\Delta = 0 .$$

Eq. (4.5) has two real and equal roots: $\lambda_1 = \lambda_2 = -\frac{1}{2} a_1$; call it λ^*. We must find another solution of eq. (4.3), since we have only one solution, λ^{*t}. Let us try $t\lambda^{*t}$. Substituting in (4.3) we have

$$t\lambda^{*t} + a_1(t-1)\lambda^{*t-1} + a_2(t-2)\lambda^{*t-2} = 0 ; \tag{4.7}$$

therefore

$$\lambda^{*t-2}[t\lambda^{*2} + a_1(t-1)\lambda^* + a_2(t-2)] = 0 ,$$

from which

$$(-\tfrac{1}{2}a_1)^{t-2}(\tfrac{1}{4}a_1^2 t - \tfrac{1}{2}a_1^2 t + \tfrac{1}{2}a_1^2 + a_2t - 2a_2)$$

$$= (-\tfrac{1}{2}a_1)^{t-2}(-\tfrac{1}{4}a_1^2 t + a_2t + \tfrac{1}{2}a_1^2 - 2a_2) = 0 . \tag{4.8}$$

★ The signs of the roots can be ascertained by Descartes' theorem ("In any algebraic equation, complete or incomplete, the number of positive roots cannot exceed the number of changes of signs of the coefficients, and in any complete equation the number of negative roots cannot exceed the number of continuations in the signs of the coefficients.") In our case – given of course that $\Delta > 0$ – there are the following possibilities:
+ + +   two negative roots,
+ + −   one negative and one positive root (the negative root being greater in absolute value),
+ − +   two positive roots,
+ − −   one negative and one positive root (the positive root being greater in absolute value),
+ 0 −   one negative and one positive root (both having the same absolute value).

If $t\lambda^{*t}$ has to be a solution, eq. (4.8) must be satisfied for any t. Since $a_1^2 - 4a_2 = 0$ by assumption, then $a_2 = \frac{1}{4}a_1^2$. Substituting in the expression in the second set of parentheses, this expression vanishes, and this proves that

$$t\lambda^{*t} \tag{4.9}$$

in a solution of eq. (4.3) in the case under consideration. The general solution is then

$$y_t = A_1\lambda^{*t} + A_2 t\lambda^{*t} = (A_1 + A_2 t)\lambda^{*t} . \tag{4.10}$$

Let us note that, when $|\lambda^*| < 1$, the solution will be damped, since, in the term $t\lambda^{*t}$, the damping due to λ^{*t} dominates the explosive tendency of the multiplicative t. ★

Case (3)

$$\Delta < 0 .$$

In this case the roots are two complex conjugate numbers, i.e. numbers having the form $\alpha \pm i\theta$, where $i = +\sqrt{-1}$ is the imaginary unit and α, θ are real numbers. α is called the real part of the complex number and $i\theta$ the imaginary part. Here $\alpha = -\frac{1}{2}a_1$, $\theta = \frac{1}{2}(4a_2 - a_1^2)^{\frac{1}{2}}$. The solution is then

$$y_t = A'(\alpha + i\theta)^t + A''(\alpha - i\theta)^t ,$$

where A' and A'' are two arbitrary constants which we may take as arbitrary complex conjugate numbers. After some manipulation ★★ the solution can be

---

★ The student may check as an exercise that, when $|\lambda^*| < 1$, the inequality $(t+1)|\lambda^*|^{t+1} < t|\lambda^*|^t$ is satisfied for any value of t greater than $|\lambda^*|/(1 - |\lambda^*|)$.

★★ The following elementary results in complex number theory will now be used in the text:

(1) Polar form of complex numbers. Any complex number $\alpha \pm i\theta$ can be written in the equivalent trigonometric form $r(\cos \omega \pm i \sin \omega)$ by a transformation from Cartesian to polar coordinates, i.e.

$$r \cos \omega = \alpha , \qquad r \sin \omega = \theta , \qquad r^2 = \alpha^2 + \theta^2 .$$

The positive number $r = +(\alpha^2 + \theta^2)^{\frac{1}{2}}$ is called the *modulus* or *absolute value* of the complex number.

(2) De Moivre's theorem. The relation

written in a more suitable form. First, change $\alpha \pm i\theta$ into $r(\cos \omega \pm i \sin \omega)$ and obtain

$$y_t = A'[r(\cos \omega + i \sin \omega)]^t + A''[r(\cos \omega - i \sin \omega)]^t$$

$$= A'r^t(\cos \omega + i \sin \omega)^t + A''r^t(\cos \omega - i \sin \omega)^t$$

$$= r^t[A'(\cos \omega + i \sin \omega)^t + A''(\cos \omega - i \sin \omega)^t] .$$

Then apply De Moivre's theorem and obtain

$$y_t = r^t[A'(\cos \omega t + i \sin \omega t) + A''(\cos \omega t - i \sin \omega t)]$$

$$= r^t[(A'+A'') \cos \omega t + (A'-A'') i \sin \omega t] .$$

Now, A' and A'' are arbitrary complex conjugate numbers, say $a \pm ib$, where a and b are arbitrary real numbers. Then $A' + A'' = 2a$, which is a real number (call it A_1), and $(A'-A'')i = (2ib)i = 2i^2 b = -2b$, which is a real number too (call it A_2). The final formula is then

$$y_t = r^t(A_1 \cos \omega t + A_2 \sin \omega t) , \tag{4.11}$$

where r and ω are determined by the relations

$$r \cos \omega = -\tfrac{1}{2}a_1 , \qquad r \sin \omega = \tfrac{1}{2}(4a_2 - a_1^2)^{1/2} . \tag{4.12}$$

$$(\cos \omega \pm i \sin \omega)^n = \cos n\omega \pm i \sin n\omega$$

holds for any positive integer n.

The proof is by induction. Consider first $n = 1$: the relation obviously holds. Next we show that if it holds for $n - 1$, then it holds also for n, and this completes the proof. Assume then that $(\cos \omega \pm i \sin \omega)^{n-1} = \cos (n-1)\omega \pm i \sin (n-1)\omega$ is true. We must prove that $(\cos \omega \pm i \sin \omega)^n = \cos n\omega \pm i \sin n\omega$ is also true. Now

$$(\cos \omega \pm i \sin \omega)^n = (\cos \omega \pm i \sin \omega)(\cos \omega \pm i \sin \omega)^{n-1}$$

$$= (\cos \omega \pm i \sin \omega)[\cos (n-1)\omega \pm i \sin (n-1)\omega] .$$

Performing the multiplications (the order of the signs is of course plus with plus and minus with minus) and rearranging terms (remember that $i^2 = -1$), we have

$$[\cos \omega \cos (n-1)\omega - \sin \omega \sin (n-1)\omega] \pm i[\cos \omega \sin (n-1)\omega + \cos (n-1)\omega \sin \omega].$$

Now, from elementary trigonometry, the first expression in square brackets is $\cos n\omega$ (write $\cos n\omega$ as $\cos [\omega + (n-1)\omega]$ and apply the addition formulae) and that in the second brackets is $\sin n\omega$, so that we have obtained the expression $\cos n\omega \pm i \sin n\omega$. Q.E.D.

An alternative form of the solution is

$$y_t = A r^t \cos(\omega t - \epsilon), \tag{4.13}$$

where r and ω are the same as before and the arbitrary constants A and ϵ are connected to the arbitrary constants A_1 and A_2 by the transformation

$$A_1 = A \cos \epsilon,$$
$$A_2 = A \sin \epsilon. \tag{4.14}$$

In fact, if we substitute (4.14) into (4.11), we have

$$y_t = r^t(A \cos \epsilon \cos \omega t + A \sin \epsilon \sin \omega t),$$

i.e.

$$y_t = A r^t(\cos \epsilon \cos \omega t + \sin \epsilon \sin \omega t). \tag{4.15}$$

Now, from elementary trigonometry,

$$\cos \epsilon \cos \omega t + \sin \epsilon \sin \omega t = \cos(\omega t - \epsilon), \tag{4.16}$$

and so, substituting into (4.15), we obtain (4.13). This second form is perhaps easier to interpret, since it involves only one trigonometric function instead of two. The first form, however, is more suitable for the determination of the values of the arbitrary constants. In any case the resulting movement is the same: a trigonometric oscillation whose period $\star$ is $2\pi/\omega$ and whose amplitude will be increasing, constant or decreasing if, respectively, r is greater than, equal to or smaller than unity.

Of course, we must remember that t is a discontinuous variable which may take on only the values 0, 1, 2, 3, etc., and so y_t can be represented graphically by a succession of discrete points. These points may be connected, *as a mere visual aid* (see remarks in Part I, ch. 2), with a continuous line, which in our case is a sinusoidal function (for some more remarks on this point, see exercise 2 in Part I, ch. 5, §1).

We have seen above that the amplitude of the oscillation is governed by the

---

$\star$ The *period* of an oscillation is the interval of time in which a complete oscillation takes place. The *frequency* is the number of oscillations per unit of time, and is the reciprocal of the period.

magnitude of r. A simple formula connecting r to the coefficients of the characteristic equation can be obtained. Return to (4.12), square both members of each equation and add the corresponding members, obtaining $r^2(\cos^2 \omega + \sin^2 \omega) = a_2$. Since $\cos^2 \omega + \sin^2 \omega = 1$ for any ω, we have $r^2 = a_2$, and so

$$r = \sqrt{a_2}, \tag{4.17}$$

where the square root is to be taken with the positive sign (this is because r, the modulus or absolute value of the complex number $\alpha \pm i\theta$ — see footnote ** on page 53 — has a positive value). Now, since $\sqrt{a_2} \gtreqless 1$ as $a_2 \gtreqless 1$, it follows that the oscillation will have an increasing, constant or decreasing amplitude according to whether $a_2 \gtreqless 1$. The stability condition, i.e. the necessary and sufficient condition that the oscillation be damped, is then

$$a_2 < 1. \tag{4.18}$$

At this point we may wonder whether also in the cases of real roots conditions exist by means of which we can check *on the coefficients of the characteristic equation* whether the roots are in absolute value less than unity. Such conditions exist, and it can be proved that the following inequalities:

$$1 + a_1 + a_2 > 0,$$
$$1 - a_2 > 0, \tag{4.19}$$
$$1 - a_1 + a_2 > 0,$$

constitute a set of necessary and sufficient conditions in order that the roots — *be they real or complex* — of the characteristic equation (4.5) be less than unity in absolute value. A heuristic proof is the following.

First, note that the second inequality in (4.19) is identical with inequality (4.18). The complex roots case is then included in (4.19) *. For the real roots, consider the graph of the parabola $f(\lambda) = \lambda^2 + a_1\lambda + a_2$. The real roots of $\lambda^2 + a_1\lambda + a_2 = 0$ are the points of intersection of $f(\lambda)$ with the λ axis. Now,

---

* Note that, when the roots are complex, the first and third inequalities in (4.19) are automatically satisfied, so that they do not impose any additional restraint. In fact, when the roots are complex, the parabola $f(\lambda) = \lambda^2 + a_1\lambda + a_2$ lies wholly in the positive half plane above the λ axis. This means that $f(-1)$, which is $1 - a_1 + a_2$, and $f(1)$, which is $1 + a_1 + a_2$, are both positive quantities.

we have

$$f(1) = 1 + a_1 + a_2 , \qquad f(-1) = 1 - a_1 + a_2 .$$

The first and third inequalities in (4.19) then mean that both $f(1)$ and $f(-1)$ are positive. This is necessary and sufficient to *exclude* the following cases:

(1) + 1 and/or −1 is a root of the equation (since in this case it would be $f(1) = 0$ and/or $f(-1) = 0$);

(2) one root is less than −1, the other greater than +1 (in this case it would be $f(-1) < 0, f(1) < 0$, see e.g. fig. 4.1 below);

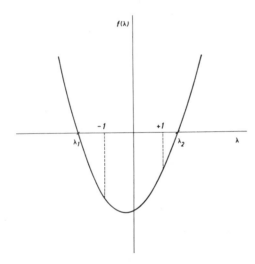

Fig. 4.1.

(3) one root is less than −1, the other lying between −1 and +1 (in this case it would be $f(-1) < 0, f(1) > 0$, as the student may check graphically);

(4) one root lying between −1 and +1 and the other greater than +1 (check graphically that in this case it would be $f(-1) > 0, f(1) < 0$).

Only three cases then remain, all compatible with $f(-1)$ and $f(1)$ both positive (check graphically):

(a) both roots negative and less than −1;

(b) both roots positive and greater than 1;

(c) both roots lying between −1 and +1.

Now, in cases (a) and (b) the *product* of the roots is positive and greater than unity. Since the product of the roots is a_2 (as the student may check by straightforward multiplication of the explicit expressions for λ_1, λ_2), the second inequality in (4.19) is necessary and sufficient to exclude cases (a) and (b). Only case (c) is then possible, and this completes the proof.

We should like to stress the importance of stability conditions (4.19), since they are of great help in the analysis of the qualitative behaviour of second-order economic models (see Part I, ch. 5, for some examples).

We have now completed the study of the homogeneous equation and may turn to the non-homogeneous equation. All that we need is a particular solution of the latter. We shall exemplify the general method of undetermined coefficients (see Part I, ch. 1) in the case in which $g(t) = G$, a constant. In other cases the student may proceed along the same lines as in the examples we worked out dealing with first-order equations (see Part I, ch. 2).

Assume then that

$$c_2 y_t + c_1 y_{t-1} + c_0 y_{t-2} = G . \tag{4.20}$$

As a particular solution try $\bar{y}_t = B$, where B is an undetermined constant. Direct substitution in (4.20) gives $c_2 B + c_1 B + c_0 B = G$, from which

$$B = \frac{G}{c_0 + c_1 + c_2} .$$

If $c_0 + c_1 + c_2 = 0$, try Bt. Substitution in (4.20) gives

$$c_2 Bt + c_1 B(t - 1) + c_0 B(t - 2) = G ;$$

therefore

$$(c_2 + c_1 + c_0)Bt - B(c_1 + 2c_0) = G ,$$

which gives

$$B = \frac{-G}{c_1 + 2c_0} .$$

If also $c_1 + 2c_0 = 0$, try Bt^2. Substitution in (4.20) yields, after some manipulation,

$$B = \frac{G}{2c_0} .$$

Since c_0 must be different from zero if the equation is of the second order, no more complications may arise.

The particular solution of the non-homogeneous equation may usually be interpreted, as we shall see in the economic applications, as the (stationary or moving) equilibrium of the variable y_t.

In the general solution, as we have seen above, two arbitrary constants appear. In order to determine them, we need two additional conditions. These conditions will take the form

$$y_t = y^* \qquad \text{for} \qquad t = t^*,$$

$$y_t = y^{**} \qquad \text{for} \qquad t = t^{**},$$

where t^*, t^{**}, y^*, y^{**} are all known values. Substituting these values in the general solution, we obtain a set of two linear equations in the two unknown values of A_1, A_2. The solution of this system yields the values of the two arbitrary constants which satisfy the additional conditions given above. Let us note that the determination of the arbitrary constants is to be made according to the general solution of the equation under consideration (i.e., if the equation is non-homogeneous, its own general solution, and not the general solution of the corresponding homogeneous equation, must be used).

In principle, the values t^* and t^{**} may be any two different values of t. In economic models, however, the additional conditions are usually given for $t = 0$ and $t = 1$ and this is why they are called 'initial' conditions.

Let us end the study of second-order equations with a final warning. When the numerical values of the coefficients c_0, c_1, c_2, of the parameters appearing in $g(t)$ and of the initial conditions are known, the successive values of y_t may be computed recursively, without any apparent need to find the general solution of the equation. The warning is that, having computed the succession of y_t up to some t, it may be dangerous to extrapolate the behaviour we have observed, so that in order to avoid mistakes it is better to find the solution of the equation also in this case. As an example, consider the equation

$$y_t + 1.8\,y_{t-1} + 0.8\,y_{t-2} = 0, \qquad y_0 = 0, \qquad y_1 = -2.$$

To compute the successive values of y_t recursively, write the equation in the form

$$y_t = -1.8\,y_{t-1} - 0.8\,y_{t-2}.$$

Then

$$y_2 = -1.8\,y_1 - 0.8\,y_0 = -1.8 \times (-2) - 0.8 \times 0 = 3.6\,,$$

$$y_3 = -1.8 \times 3.6 - 0.8 \times (-2) = -4.88\,,$$

$$y_4 = -1.8 \times (-4.88) - 0.8 \times 3.6 = 5.904\,,$$

$$y_5 = -1.8 \times 5.904 - 0.8(-4.88) = -6.7232\,.$$

The values alternate in sign and are increasing in absolute value. We might then be tempted to say that the movement is an improper oscillation of increasing amplitude, i.e. a divergent movement. Let us now check by solving the equation. Its characteristic equation is

$$\lambda^2 + 1.8\,\lambda + 0.8 = 0\,,$$

whose roots are $-1, -0.8$. The general solution of the difference equation under consideration is then

$$y_t = A_1(-1)^t + A_2(-0.8)^t\,.$$

The arbitrary constants are now determined according to the initial conditions. We have

$$y_0 = A_1(-1)^0 + A_2(-0.8)^0 = A_1 + A_2 = 0\,,$$

$$y_1 = A_1(-1)^1 + A_2(-0.8)^1 = -A_1 - 0.8\,A_2 = -2\,.$$

The solution of the system

$$A_1 + A_2 = 0\,,$$

$$-A_1 - 0.8\,A_2 = -2\,,$$

yields $A_1 = 10, A_2 = -10$, and so

$$y_t = 10(-1)^t - 10(-0.8)^t\,.$$

From this equation we can see that, as t increases, y_t tends to an improper oscillation of constant amplitude, given by the term $10(-1)^t$, since the term $-10(-0.8)^t$ tends to zero. The overall fluctuation is actually of increasing amplitude, but it does not diverge, since it tends to a limit cycle of constant amplitude. (Fig. 4.2 below shows the actual fluctuation and its limits (broken lines)). The inference we were tempted to make on the basis of the succession of values computed recursively is clearly wrong.

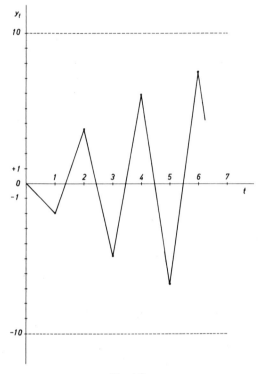

Fig. 4.2.

Other examples could be shown, e.g. the case of a trigonometric oscillation whose period is relatively great, so that it may happen that the value of t at which we stop our recursive computations is situated before that value of t where the first turning point in y_t occurs, so that the data lead us to think that the movement is monotonic. But we think that the warning is now sufficiently clear.

References

Allen, R.G.D., 1959, *Mathematical Economics*, ch. 4, § § 4.1–4.5; ch. 6, § 6.4.

Baumol, W.J., 1970, *Economic Dynamics*, chs. 10, 11.

Baumol, W.J., 1958, Topology of Second Order Difference Equations with Constant Coefficients.

Goldberg, S., 1958, *Introduction to Difference Equations*, ch. 3, § § 3.3, 3.4, 3.5; ch. 4, § 4.1.

Papandreou, A.G., 1965, *Introduction to Macroeconomic Models*, ch. 5, § § 5.3, 5.4.

Tintner, G., and Millham, C.B., 1970, *Mathematics and Statistics for Economists*, ch. 9, § § 43, 44.

5

Some Economic Applications
of Second-order Equations

§1. Samuelson's multiplier—accelerator model

This model, which was built by Samuelson following a suggestion by Hansen, may justly be considered as the pioneer of all the multiplier—accelerator models of income determination and of the business cycle. The 'ingredients' of such models are a consumption function, an investment function (in which both induced and autonomous investment appear) and the relation which defines the equilibrium value of income. In the model under consideration we have the following equations:

$$C_t = bY_{t-1}, \qquad 0 < b < 1. \tag{5.1}$$

Consumption depends on national income with a one-period lag. The constant b is the (marginal and average) propensity to consume. As far as investment is concerned, we distinguish between induced investment I_t' and autonomous investment I_t''. Then

$$I_t = I_t' + I_t'', \tag{5.2}$$

where I_t is total investment.

Autonomous investment (essentially public expenditure) is assumed constant:

$$I_t'' = G ,\tag{5.3}$$

where G is a positive constant.

Induced investment depends on the variation in the demand for consumption goods, according to the acceleration principle:

$$I_t' = k(C_t - C_{t-1}) ,\tag{5.4}$$

where k is the acceleration coefficient (the 'relation' in Hansen's terminology).

The equilibrium condition (see Part I, ch. 3, §2)

$$Y_t = C_t + I_t\tag{5.5}$$

closes the model.

Simple substitutions yield the following second-order equation:

$$Y_t - b(1+k)Y_{t-1} + bkY_{t-2} = G .\tag{5.6}$$

The solution of this functional equation gives the behaviour over time of national income; substitution in eqs. (5.1) and (5.4) will then give the behaviour over time of consumption and of induced investment.

A particular solution of eq. (5.6) is easily found by trying $\bar{Y}_t$ = constant, from which

$$\bar{Y}_t = \frac{G}{1-b} .\tag{5.7}$$

This is the value we obtain applying the multiplier $1/(1-b)$ to autonomous expenditure G. The particular solution determines the (stationary) equilibrium value of national income.

The deviations from this value will be given by the general solution of the homogeneous equation corresponding to eq. (5.6), i.e. of

$$Y_t - b(1+k)Y_{t-1} + bkY_{t-2} = 0 .$$

The characteristic equation is

$$\lambda^2 - b(1+k)\lambda + bk = 0 .\tag{5.8}$$

A qualitative analysis of eq. (5.8) will now be made. As a first step, we apply the stability conditions (see (4.19) in Part I, ch. 4). We obtain

$$1 - b(1+k) + bk = 1 - b > 0 ,$$

$$1 - bk > 0 , \qquad\qquad (5.9)$$

$$1 + b(1+k) + bk > 0 .$$

The first inequality is satisfied since we have assumed that the marginal propensity to consume is less than unity (and this is an empirically plausible assumption); the third inequality is satisfied too, the left-hand side being a sum of quantities which are all positive. The crucial inequality is then the second one. Therefore we may say that the stability condition is

$$bk < 1$$

or

$$b < 1/k . \qquad\qquad (5.10)$$

In order to ascertain the type of the movement (monotonic, oscillatory, etc.) let us begin to note that the succession of the signs of the coefficients of eq. (5.8) is $+ - +$. This means (Descartes' rule of signs) that no negative root may occur. We can then exclude movements involving 'improper' oscillations. The next step is to compute the discriminant of eq. (5.8). It is

$$\Delta = b^2(1+k)^2 - 4bk , \qquad\qquad (5.11)$$

and so $\Delta \gtreqless 0$ if $b^2(1+k)^2 \gtreqless 4bk$, whence

$$\Delta \gtreqless 0 \quad \text{as} \quad b \gtreqless \frac{4k}{(1+k)^2} . \qquad\qquad (5.12)$$

Putting together (5.10) and (5.12) we have all the possible cases, which can be conveniently plotted on the following diagram (fig. 5.1), due to Samuelson. In the diagram are plotted the function $b = 4k/(1+k)^2$ (the curve OPS) and the function $b = 1/k$ (the curve PQ). Since $b < 1$, we are interested only in that part of the positive quadrant which is below the broken line (this is why we have not drawn the upper part of the rectangular hyperbola $b = 1/k$). Four regions are then individuated (remember that real roots are positive).

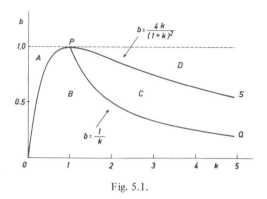

Fig. 5.1.

Region A. Any point in this region lies *below* the function $b = 1/k$ and *above* the function $b = 4k/(1+k)^2$. This is the graphical counterpart of the inequalities $b < 1/k$, $b > 4k/(1+k)^2$. Therefore, by (5.10) and (5.12), the stability condition is satisfied and the roots are real. The system will show a monotonic movement converging towards the equilibrium value $G/(1-b)$.

Region B. Any point in this region satisfies the inequalities $b < 1/k$, $b < 4k/(1+k)^2$. The stability condition is satisfied and the roots are complex. The result is a damped oscillation around the equilibrium value.

Region C. Here we have $b > 1/k$, $b < 4k/(1+k)^2$. The stability condition is not satisfied and the roots are complex. The result is an explosive oscillation around the equilibrium value.

Region D. In this region we have $b > 1/k$, $b > 4k/(1+k)^2$. The stability condition is not satisfied and the roots are real. The movement is monotonically explosive.

   In order to complete our analysis we have to examine the points which happen to lie on the boundary lines demarcating the four regions. Since b and k are both positive in this model, and $b < 1$, we must exclude from consideration the points on the b axis, the points on the k axis, the origin and point P. We may then have the following particular cases:
   (1) Points on the demarcation line between region A and region B. Here we have $b = 4k/(1+k)^2$, i.e. a real root of multiplicity two. Since the stability condition $b < 1/k$ is satisfied, this root is smaller than unity. Therefore the

function $(A_1 + A_2t)\lambda^{*t}$ will be dominated, as $t \to \infty$, by the component λ^{*t} and the movement will eventually converge monotonically towards equilibrium.

(2) Points falling on the demarcation line between region B and region C. We have $b < 4k/(1+k)^2$ and $bk = 1$, i.e. complex roots with unit modulus, which imply a constant amplitude oscillation, that is to say a movement separating stability from instability.

(3) Points falling on the line demarcating region C and region D. Here we have $b = 4k/(1+k)^2$, $b > 1/k$, i.e. a root with multiplicity two and greater than unity. The result is a movement which will be eventually dominated by the monotonically divergent term λ^{*t}.

Exercises

1. In a certain period the economic system is in equilibrium. Take the initial equilibrium levels of the various variables as their origin of measurement (i.e. $Y_0 = 0$, $C_0 = 0$, $I_0 = 0$) and assume that in period 1 autonomous investment increases by 100, afterwards remaining at the new level. Examine the behaviour over time of Y_t (both recursively and by solving the difference equation) given that the propensity to consume is 0.8 and that the acceleration coefficient is 3.

Calculation. To compute recursively the successive values of Y_t we prefer to use the equation

$$Y_t = 0.8\ Y_{t-1} + 3(C_t - C_{t-1}) + 100$$

instead of the final equation

$$Y_t = 3.2\ Y_{t-1} - 2.4\ Y_{t-2} + 100 .$$

The reason is that the first form allows a better economic understanding of the recursive procedure. The table on page 68 shows the computations.

In period 0 the system is in its initial equilibrium, which gives the row of zeros, according to our convention. In period 1 autonomous investment increases, consumption does not change since it depends on previous period income, and so there is no induced investment. In period 2 consumption increases by 80 and this induces an investment of 240. Proceeding in like manner we see that the values of Y_t increase monotonically.

With the given values of the marginal propensity to consume and of the

t	G	$C_t = 0.8\,Y_{t-1}$	$C_t - C_{t-1}$	$I'_t = 3(C_t - C_{t-1})$	$Y_t = G + C_t + I'_t$
0	0	0	0	0	0
1	100	0	0	0	100
2	100	80	80	240	420
3	100	336	256	768	1204
4	100	963.2	627.2	1881.6	2944.8
5	100	2355.84	1392.64	4177.92	6633.76
"	"	"	"	"	"

acceleration coefficient we are in region D in Samuelson's diagram, and this tells us that the tendency shown by the first five values of Y_t will actually be maintained.

Let us now solve the difference equation

$$Y_t = 3.2\,Y_{t-1} - 2.4\,Y_{t-2} + 100 .$$

A particular solution is $100/(1 - 3.2 + 2.4) = 100/(1 - 0.8) = 500$. The characteristic equation of the homogeneous equation $Y_t - 3.2\,Y_{t-1} + 2.4\,Y_{t-2} = 0$ is

$$\lambda^2 - 3.2\,\lambda + 2.4 = 0 ,$$

whose roots are 1.2 and 2. The general solution of the non-homogeneous equation is then

$$Y_t = A_1(1.2)^t + A_2(2)^t + 500 ,$$

where A_1 and A_2 are two arbitrary constants. Given the initial conditions $Y_0 = 0$, $Y_1 = 100$, we have

$$Y_0 = A_1(1.2)^0 + A_2(2)^0 + 500 = A_1 + A_2 + 500 = 0 ,$$

$$Y_1 = A_1(1.2)^1 + A_2(2)^1 + 500 = 1.2\,A_1 + 2\,A_2 + 500 = 100 .$$

Solving the system

$$A_1 + A_2 = -500 ,$$
$$1.2\,A_1 + 2\,A_2 = -400 ,$$

we obtain $A_1 = -750, A_2 = 250$, and so

$$Y_t = -750(1.2)^t + 250(2)^t + 500 .$$

This solution confirms again that the movement will keep on being monotonically explosive.

The solution allows us to compute the value of Y_t for any t without having to compute all the preceding values. For $t = 5$, for example, we have

$$Y_5 = -750(1.2)^5 + 250(2)^5 + 500 = -750(2.48832) + 250(32) = 6633.76 .$$

This result is the same — as it must be if we have made no mistakes — as that obtained in the table above.

2. Same problem as in exercise 1, but now the marginal (and average) propensity to consume is $(\sqrt{3}-1) \simeq 0.73205$ and the acceleration coefficient is $1/(\sqrt{3}-1) \simeq 1.36602$.

Calculation. The product of the two parameters is 1, so that we know that the movement will be a constant amplitude oscillation. Before continuing with the computations we may wonder why the author of this book has not chosen simpler values (as, e.g., 0.5 and 2 or 0.8 and 1.25) to illustrate the case of a constant amplitude oscillation. The reason is that, with values such as 0.5 and 2, 0.8 and 1.25, 0.4 and 2.5, etc., the recursive computation of Y_t will not show (as the student may check as an exercise) an oscillation whose amplitude is exactly constant. This is rather intriguing, since the product of the values listed above is, in any case, 1 and we know from theory that the oscillation should then be of constant amplitude. The explanation is that the oscillation would be of constant amplitude if time were considered as a continuous variable in the sinusoidal function $A_1 \cos \omega t + A_2 \sin \omega t$. But since t can take on only the discrete values 0, 1, 2, 3, etc., only the corresponding points of the underlying continuous sinusoidal function can be considered. Now, there is no reason why the turning points of the recursive sequence should always coincide with the peaks and troughs of the sinusoidal function. The following diagram (fig. 5.2) may serve as an illustration.

The statement usually made (i.e. that when the roots are complex and $r = 1$ a constant amplitude fluctuation follows) must then be qualified: what is true is that the points of the succession of the values of Y_t will lie on a sinusoidal function whose amplitude is constant. Therefore the actual oscillation as t increases can be neither explosive nor convergent, although it may

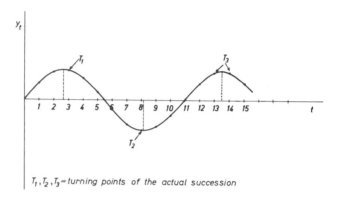

$T_1, T_2, T_3 =$ turning points of the actual succession

Fig. 5.2.

not show an exactly constant amplitude. As a matter of terminology, we shall continue to use the expression 'constant amplitude oscillations', according to the meaning clarified here. A similar problem arises, of course, when $r \gtreqless 1$ (explosive or damped oscillations), but in such cases it is not apparent, since the fact that the turning points of the succession may not coincide with those of the sinusoidal function is of no consequence as to the increasing or decreasing amplitude of the oscillation shown by the succession.

Let us now turn back to our example. With the values of the propensity to consume and of the acceleration coefficient given at the beginning, the succession actually shows a strictly constant amplitude oscillation. The reason why in the turning points two successive equal values occur is that we have constructed the example in such a way that the peaks and troughs of the sinusoidal function occur exactly half-way between two successive integer values of t (i.e. all the turning points of the succession are as T_3 in fig. 5.2.

Let us now solve the difference equation

$$Y_t - \sqrt{3} Y_{t-1} + Y_{t-2} = 100 . \tag{5.13}$$

Note that we have used the exact values of the two parameters and not their approximated values, in order to avoid the cumulation of approximations. A particular solution of eq. (5.13) is

$$\bar{Y}_t = \frac{100}{2 - \sqrt{3}} . \tag{5.14}$$

t	G	C_t	$C_t - C_{t-1}$	I'_t	Y_t
0	0	0	0	0	0
1	100	0	0	0	100
2	100	73.205	73.205	100	273.205
3	100	200	126.795	173.205	473.205
4	100	346.410	146.410	200	646.410
5	100	473.205	126.795	173.205	746.410
6	100	546.410	73.205	100	746.410
7	100	546.410	0	0	646.410
8	100	473.205	− 73.205	−100	473.205
9	100	346.410	−126.795	−173.205	273.205
10	100	200	−146.410	−200	100
11	100	73.205	−126.795	−173.205	0
12	100	0	− 73.205	−100	0
13	100	0	0	0	100
14	100	73.205	73.205	100	273.205
"	"	"	"	"	"
"	"	"	"	"	"

The homogeneous equation corresponding to the non-homogeneous equation
(5.13) has the characteristic equation

$$\lambda^2 - \sqrt{3}\lambda + 1 = 0, \tag{5.15}$$

whose roots are

$$\lambda_1, \lambda_2 = \tfrac{1}{2}(\sqrt{3} \pm \sqrt{-1}) = \tfrac{1}{2}\sqrt{3} \pm \tfrac{1}{2}i.$$

Since $r = \sqrt{1} = 1$, the general solution of the homogeneous equation is

$$Y_t = A_1 \cos \omega t + A_2 \sin \omega t, \tag{5.16}$$

where

$$\cos \omega = \tfrac{1}{2}\sqrt{3},$$

$$\sin \omega = \tfrac{1}{2}.$$

From the trigonometric tables we find that the angle whose sine is $\frac{1}{2}$ and
whose cosine is $\frac{1}{2}\sqrt{3}$, is $30°$. Then eq. (5.16) becomes

$$Y_t = A_1 \cos 30°t + A_2 \sin 30°t,$$

and the general solution of eq. (5.13) is

$$Y_t = A_1 \cos 30°t + A_2 \sin 30°t + \frac{100}{2 - \sqrt{3}}. \tag{5.17}$$

Given the initial conditions $Y_0 = 0$, $Y_1 = 100$ we have, substituting in (5.17),

$$0 = A_1 \cos 0 + A_2 \sin 0 + \frac{100}{2 - \sqrt{3}},$$

$$100 = A_1 \cos 30° + A_2 \sin 30° + \frac{100}{2 - \sqrt{3}}.$$

Since $\cos 0 = 1$, $\sin 0 = 1$, from the first equation we obtain immediately $A_1 = -100/(2 - \sqrt{3})$. Substituting into the second equation this value and also the values of $\cos 30°$ and of $\sin 30°$, we have

$$\frac{-100\sqrt{3}}{(2 - \sqrt{3})2} + \tfrac{1}{2}A_2 + \frac{100}{2 - \sqrt{3}} = 100,$$

which gives, after some simple manipulation, $A_2 = 100$. Eq. (5.17) then becomes

$$Y_t = \frac{-100}{2 - \sqrt{3}} \cos 30°t + 100 \sin 30°t + \frac{100}{2 - \sqrt{3}}. \tag{5.18}$$

If we want to put the solution into the alternative form mentioned in Part I, ch. 4, we use the transformation

$$\frac{-100}{2 - \sqrt{3}} = A \cos \epsilon,$$

$$100 = A \sin \epsilon,$$

so that $A = +(A_1^2 + A_2^2)^{\frac{1}{2}}$ and $\tan \epsilon = -(2 - \sqrt{3})$. The result is $A = 200/(2 - \sqrt{3})^{\frac{1}{2}}$ and $\epsilon = 165°$. The alternative form of the solution is then

$$Y_t = \frac{200}{(2 - \sqrt{3})^{\frac{1}{2}}} \cos(30°t - 165°) + \frac{100}{2 - \sqrt{3}}. \tag{5.18'}$$

As a check we may compute some value of Y_t, e.g. Y_3. Using eq. (5.18) we have (remember that $\sin 90° = 1$ and $\cos 90° = 0$)

$$Y_3 = 100 + \frac{100}{2 - \sqrt{3}} \simeq 100 + 373.205 = 473.205 \ .$$

Using eq. (5.18′) we have

$$Y_3 = \frac{200}{(2 - \sqrt{3})^{1/2}} \cos(-75°) + \frac{100}{2 - \sqrt{3}} \ .$$

Now, $\cos(-75°) = \cos 75° = \frac{1}{4}\sqrt{2}(\sqrt{3} - 1)$. Substituting in the last equation and using the fact that $(\sqrt{3} - 1)\sqrt{2} = 2(2 - \sqrt{3})^{1/2}$ (the student may check by squaring both members), we have

$$Y_3 = 100 + \frac{100}{2 - \sqrt{3}} \simeq 473.205 \ , \qquad \text{as before .}$$

3. Same problem as in exercise 1, but with the following values of the two parameters (the first number in the parentheses is the propensity to consume, and the second is the acceleration coefficient): $(0.5 , 1)$; $(0.9 , 0.5)$; $(0.6 , 3)$.

§2. Hicks' trade cycle model

This is a model of the accelerator—multiplier kind, which has some interesting characteristics that distinguish it from Samuelson's model and that we shall clarify during our exposition. Here we shall expound the 'simple' version of Hicks' model, since the general version gives rise to a higher-order equation (see Part 1, ch. 7, §1).

The basic equations of the model are the following:

$$Y_t = C_t + I_t \ , \tag{5.19}$$

$$C_t = bY_{t-1} \ , \tag{5.20}$$

$$I_t = I_t' + I_t'' \ , \tag{5.21}$$

$$I_t'' = A_0(1+g)^t \ , \tag{5.22}$$

$$I_t' = k(Y_{t-1} - Y_{t-2}) \ . \tag{5.23}$$

Firstly, note that autonomous investment is assumed to increase over time at the constant rate of growth g. Secondly, note that induced investment does not depend solely on the variations in consumption demand, but it depends on the variations in total demand. Thirdly, note that the variations which induce investment are lagged one period, i.e. $Y_{t-1} - Y_{t-2}$ and not $Y_t - Y_{t-1}$ is the argument of the investment function; this means that some time must elapse in order that the new capital goods required to accomodate the increased demand can be produced.

After the standard substitutions we obtain the second-order difference equation

$$Y_t - (b+k)Y_{t-1} + kY_{t-2} = A_0(1+g)^t .$$ (5.24)

The known function of time is an exponential function, so that as a particular solution we may try (see Part I, ch. 1)

$$\overline{Y}_t = Y_0(1+g)^t ,$$ (5.25)

where Y_0 is an undetermined constant. Substituting in (5.24) we have

$$Y_0(1+g)^t - (b+k)Y_0(1+g)^{t-1} + kY_0(1+g)^{t-2} = A_0(1+g)^t ;$$

therefore

$$(1+g)^{t-2}[Y_0(1+g)^2 - (b+k)Y_0(1+g) + kY_0 - A_0(1+g)^2] = 0 .$$

The last equation is satisfied for any t if, and only if, the expression in square brackets is zero:

$$Y_0(1+g)^2 - (b+k)Y_0(1+g) + kY_0 - A_0(1+g)^2 = 0 ,$$

which gives

$$Y_0 = \frac{A_0(1+g)^2}{(1+g)^2 - (b+k)(1+g) + k} .$$ (5.26)

In order that our particular solution be economically meaningful, Y_0 must be positive, i.e. the denominator in (5.26) must be positive, the numerator being positive. Let us assume, as Hicks does, that Y_0 is positive ★. The particular solution can then be interpreted as the equilibrium trend of national income,

★ See footnote on following page

viz. a moving equilibrium implying the growth of income at the constant rate
of growth g.

The homogeneous equation corresponding to (5.24) has the characteristic
equation

$$\lambda^2 - (b+k)\lambda + k = 0 . \tag{5.27}$$

The stability conditions are (see (4.19) in Part I, ch. 4)

$$1 - (b+k) + k = 1 - b > 0 ,$$

$$1 - k > 0 , \tag{5.28}$$

$$1 + (b+k) + k > 0 .$$

The first inequality is satisfied since we assume a propensity to consume
smaller than unity; the third is satisfied since the left-hand side is a sum of
positive magnitudes. The crucial inequality is then the second one, and so the
stability condition in this model is

$$k < 1 . \tag{5.29}$$

In Samuelson's model the stability condition is, as we know, $bk < 1$. Now,
since $b < 1$, stability condition (5.29) is more stringent. Hicks' model is then
intrinsically less stable than Samuelson's model. This is not surprising, since
in the former induced investment depends on the variations in total demand,
whereas in the latter it depends on the variations in consumption demand,
which are evidently smaller.

In order to ascertain the type of movement (monotonic, oscillatory, etc.)
let us begin by noting that the succession of the signs of the coefficients in
eq. (5.27) is $+ - +$, and this excludes negative real roots (no 'improper' oscillation may occur).

The discriminant of eq. (5.27) is

---

* Actually, it can be proved that, if the roots of eq. (5.27) below are complex, then
the denominator in (5.26) is positive; if, on the contrary, such roots are real, then the
denominator in (5.26) is positive for those values of g such that $(1+g) < \lambda_1$ or $(1+g)$
$> \lambda_2$, where $\lambda_1 \leqslant \lambda_2$ are the roots of eq. (5.27). The proof can be given by examining
the inequality $(1+g)^2 - (b+k)(1+g) + k > 0$ in relation to the characteristic equation
$\lambda^2 - (b+k)\lambda + k = 0$.

$$\Delta = (b+k)^2 - 4k = k^2 - (4-2b)k + b^2 .$$

We must investigate the conditions under which $\Delta \gtreqless 0$. The inequality

$$k^2 - (4-2b)k + b^2 \gtreqless 0$$

is a second-degree inequality. Consider the parabola $f(k) = k^2 - (4-2b)k + b^2$ and call k_1, k_2 its intersections (if any) with the k-axis. It is apparent from the diagram that $f(k) > 0$ for $k < k_1$ and for $k > k_1$; $f(k) = 0$ for $k = k_1$ and for $k = k_2$; $f(k) < 0$ for $k_1 < k < k_2$; whereas, if k_1 and k_2 coincide, then $f(k)$ is always positive, except for $k = k_1 = k_2$, where it is zero. Finally, if $f(k)$ does not intersect the k-axis (which means that the roots of eq. (5.30) below are complex), then it is always positive ★.

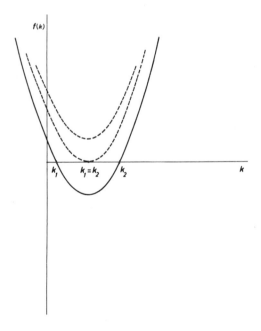

Fig. 5.3.

Now, k_1, k_2 are the roots of the equation

★ This is a general method for examining second-degree inequalities, and it will be used also in the study of other models.

$$k^2 - (4 - 2b)k + b^2 = 0 ,\tag{5.30}$$

which are

$$k_1, k_2 = \tfrac{1}{2}\{4 - 2b \pm [(4 - 2b)^2 - 4b^2]^{\frac{1}{2}}\} .$$

Simple manipulation yields

$$k_1, k_2 = 1 + s \pm 2\sqrt{s} = (1 \pm \sqrt{s})^2 ,$$

where $s = 1 - b$ is the (marginal and average) propensity to save. Therefore we have the following cases (remember that the roots of eq. (5.27), if real, must be positive)

If	Then	Roots of eq. (5.27)
$k < (1 - \sqrt{s})^2$	$\Delta > 0$	Real and distinct
$k = (1 - \sqrt{s})^2$	$\Delta = 0$	Real and equal
$(1 - \sqrt{s})^2 < k < (1 + \sqrt{s})^2$	$\Delta < 0$	Complex conjugate
$k = (1 + \sqrt{s})^2$	$\Delta = 0$	Real and equal
$k > (1 + \sqrt{s})^2$	$\Delta > 0$	Real and distinct

We can now combine these results with the stability condition (5.29). In order to do that, note that, since $s < 1$, $\sqrt{s}$ is smaller than unity and so $0 < 1 - \sqrt{s} < 1$, so that $(1 - \sqrt{s})^2 < 1$. The following table shows the complete results.

If	Roots of eq. (5.27)	Behaviour of the deviations from the trend, as $t \to \infty$
$k < (1 - \sqrt{s})^2$	R, D, $\mu < 1$	Monotonic and convergent
$k = (1 - \sqrt{s})^2$	R, E, $\mu < 1$	Monotonic and convergent
$(1 - \sqrt{s})^2 < k < 1$	C, $\mu < 1$	Oscillatory and damped
$k = 1$	C, $\mu = 1$	Oscillatory, with const. ampl.
$1 < k < (1 + \sqrt{s})^2$	C, $\mu > 1$	Oscillatory and divergent
$k = (1 + \sqrt{s})^2$	R, E, $\mu > 1$	Monotonic and divergent
$k > (1 + \sqrt{s})^2$	R, D, $\mu > 1$	Monotonic and divergent

Key: R = real (and positive); D = distinct; E = equal; C = complex conjugate; μ = modulus

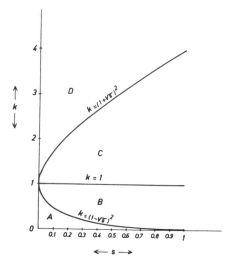

Fig. 5.4.

In fig. 5.4 we have plotted the three functions $k = (1 - \sqrt{s})^2$, $k = 1$, $k = (1 + \sqrt{s})^2$. In region A, we have $k < (1 - \sqrt{s})^2 < 1$, and so the movement is monotonic and convergent. The reader may ascertain as an exercise the remaining correspondences between the inequalities listed in the last table above and the regions shown in the diagram.

Now, according to Hicks, the acceleration coefficient is always greater than unity (even a simple glance at real-life data will show this to be true), and this puts the model in the unstable regions ★. The explosiveness of the model, however, is checked by some non-linearities built in the model in an ingenious way. These non-linearities are an *upper limit* and a *lower limit* to

---

★ It must be noted that Hicks assumes that not only the *absolute* deviations from the trend (given, as we know, by the general solution of the homogeneous equation) are explosive, but that also the *relative* deviations are explosive. The relative deviations are the ratio between the absolute deviations and the trend, and can be measured graphically as the vertical difference between the actual values of income and the corresponding values of the trend in a semi-logarithmic diagram (log Y_t in the vertical scale and natural values of t in the horizontal scale; remember that the difference of two logarithms is the logarithm of the ratio of the two natural values). Mathematically, the condition for the relative deviations to be explosive is $k > (1+g)^2$. To prove this condition, divide the equation $Y_t - (b + k)Y_{t-1} + kY_{t-2} = 0$, which gives the absolute deviations, by the trend as given by eq. (5.25). We have

income, which check its otherwise explosive behaviour and give rise to cycles of constant amplitude *. It is interesting to note that the presence of the limits reduces to a matter of secondary importance the problem whether the 'free' movement (i.e. the movement that would occur in absence of the limits) is monotonic or oscillatory, since the 'rebound' (speaking loosely) against the limits gives rise in any case to a fluctuating movement. If we are interested only in the general features of the model, the study of the discriminant of eq. (5.27) may then be omitted, since the instability of the free movement is the relevant thing, and it can be checked immediately, by applying the stability conditions.

The upper limit (or 'ceiling', as Hicks calls it) is full employment income, beyond which output cannot expand by definition. The ceiling is growing over time (essentially because of population and productivity growth), and the assumption is that it grows at the same rate as autonomous investment does, i.e.

$$B_t = B_0(1+g)^t, \tag{5.31}$$

where B_t is the value of the ceiling and the positive constant B_0 is assumed to be greater than Y_0, since it is plausible to assume that the ceiling lies above the trend.

Let us now study the ascending phase of the cycle, postponing the determination of the lower limit (the 'floor') for our study of the descending phase.

The system is in equilibrium on the trend when an exogenous disturbance

$$\frac{1}{Y_0(1+g)^t}\,[Y_t - (b+k)Y_{t-1} + kY_{t-2}] = 0 \ ;$$

therefore

$$\frac{Y_t}{Y_0(1+g)^t} - \frac{b+k}{(1+g)}\,\frac{Y_{t-1}}{Y_0(1+g)^{t-1}} + \frac{k}{(1+g)^2}\,\frac{Y_{t-2}}{Y_0(1+g)^{t-2}} = 0 \ ,$$

and

$$D_t - \frac{b+k}{(1+g)}\,D_{t-1} + \frac{k}{(1+g)^2}\,D_{t-2} = 0 \ ,$$

where $D_t \equiv Y_t/Y_0(1+g)^t$ represents relative deviations. Applying the stability conditions to the last equation, we find that the crucial condition is $k/(1+g)^2 < 1$. It follows that in the opposite case, i.e. when $k/(1+g)^2 > 1$, D_t will be divergent anyhow. Note that with empirically plausible values of k and g the instability condition is certainly satisfied, and so Hicks' assumption is not unwarranted.

* In relative terms. See further on, in the text.

occurs, which gives an upward shock to income. An explosive movement then starts, which brings income towards the ceiling. What happens when income 'hits' the ceiling? ★ We have said above that a 'rebound' occurs, but we must now explain why, since someone might wonder whether income might not keep on 'crawling' along the ceiling. Let us begin to recall that the ceiling grows by assumption at the same constant rate g as the equilibrium trend. Now income can grow at the constant rate g *only on the trend*, since the latter has been found as the (only) exponential function of the type $Y_0(1+g)^t$ compatible with the non-homogeneous difference equation defining the movement of income over time. Therefore income must turn down towards the trend, since the constant rate of growth g is sustainable only there. It can be proved that, if the trend lies below the ceiling, then income cannot stay along the ceiling for more than two periods ★★.

Once the descending phase has begun, the explosiveness of the movement causes income to overtake the trend and to go further down. We must now turn to the explanation of the 'floor'. The first thing to expound is a non-linearity in the acceleration mechanism. When income decreases, net investment must be negative, according to the acceleration principle. But the absolute value of negative net investment (i.e. of disinvestment) obviously cannot exceed the absolute value of the (physical) depreciation of the capital stock. To disinvest means to reduce the capital stock, and the maximum rate at which the capital stock can be reduced is obtained when capital goods are not replaced. If, for example, the acceleration coefficient is 2 and the decrease in income is 150, net investment should be -300; now, if the current replace-

---

★ We neglect possible special cases in which income is stopped, before it hits the ceiling, by bottlenecks of various types, since those cases are outside the main body of the argument.

★★ The proof is the following. Assume that Y_{t-1} and Y_{t-2} have been equal to the corresponding values of the ceiling, i.e. $Y_{t-1} = B_0(1+g)^{t-1}$, $Y_{t-2} = B_0(1+g)^{t-2}$. Substituting in (5.24) we have

$$Y_t = (b+k)B_0(1+g)^{t-1} - kB_0(1+g)^{t-2} + A_0(1+g)^t .$$

The proposition to prove is that such a value of Y_t is smaller than the value of the ceiling in time t, i.e. we have to show that the inequality

$$(b+k)B_0(1+g)^{t-1} - kB_0(1+g)^{t-2} + A_0(1+g)^t < B_0(1+g)^t \qquad (*)$$

is true. Simple manipulations show that inequality $(*)$ is actually satisfied if, and only if, $Y_0 < B_0$. If, on the contrary, $Y_0 > B_0$ (i.e. the trend lies *above* the ceiling), then Y_t would be greater than B_t and so income will continue indefinitely along the ceiling.

ments of capital goods ought to amount to, say, 200 (i.e., depreciation = 200), then net investment cannot be -300 but will be only -200. Formally, all this means that in the descending phase eq. (5.23) holds only as long as induced investment is not greater than depreciation in absolute value; in the opposite case eq. (5.23) must be replaced ★ by the equation

$$I'_t = -a_t ,\qquad\qquad (5.23')$$

where $a_t > 0$ is the absolute value of depreciation. Now, a_t must be known in order that we may solve the equation

$$Y_t - bY_{t-1} = -a_t + A_0(1+g)^t ,\qquad\qquad (5.24')$$

which is the basic equation of the model when eq. (5.23′) is substituted for eq. (5.23). The simplifying assumption made by Hicks is that $a_t = a$, where a is a constant (e.g., the depreciation corresponding to the capital stock in existence when the descending phase begins).

As a particular solution of eq. (5.24′), when $a_t = a$, try the function

$$H_1(1+g)^t + H_2 ,$$

where H_1 and H_2 are undetermined constants. Substituting into (5.24′) and manipulating in the usual way, we obtain

$$H_1 = \frac{A_0}{1 - b(1+g)^{-1}} , \qquad H_2 = -\frac{a}{1-b} ,$$

and so

★ This 'switch' is a non-linear feature of the model, which can be more formally expressed as

$$I'_t = \begin{cases} k(Y_{t-1} - Y_{t-2}) & \text{if } k(Y_{t-1} - Y_{t-2}) \geqslant -a_t , \\ -a_t & \text{if } k(Y_{t-1} - Y_{t-2}) < -a_t . \end{cases}$$

In a similar way we can express the other non-linearity of the model seen above in the ascending phase:

$$Y_t = \begin{cases} (b+k)Y_{t-1} - kY_{t-2} + A_0(1+g)^t & \text{if } (b+k)Y_{t-1} - kY_{t-2} + A_0(1+g)^t \leqslant B_0(1+g)^t , \\ B_0(1+g)^t & \text{if } (b+k)Y_{t-1} - kY_{t-2} + A_0(1+g)^t > B_0(1+g)^t . \end{cases}$$

$$\overline{Y}_t = \frac{A_0(1+g)^t}{1 - b(1+g)^{-1}} - \frac{a}{1-b} \tag{5.32}$$

is a particular solution of eq. (5.24'). The corresponding homogeneous equation $Y_t - bY_{t-1} = 0$ has the general solution $A_1(b)^t$, and so the general solution of eq. (5.24') is

$$Y_t = A_1(b)^t + \frac{A_0(1+g)^t}{1 - b(1+g)^{-1}} - \frac{a}{1-b}. \tag{5.33}$$

Considering as the initial period that in which we substitute eq. (5.23') in the place of eq. (5.23), the arbitrary constant A_1 is determined as the difference existing in that period between the value of income and the value of $\overline{Y}_t$ for $t = 0$.

The behaviour of Y_t, as given by eq. (5.33), is a monotonic approach to the *lower limit* (or '*floor*') given by the particular solution (5.32). The floor, then, is seen to be equal to the output corresponding to the multiplier $1/[1 - b(1+g)^{-1}]$ applied to autonomous investment *less* the output corresponding to the multiplier $1/(1 - b)$ applied to (the absolute value of) depreciation. This has an economic meaning. In the descending phase, total investment equals autonomous investment less induced disinvestment, the latter being at worst equal to the amount of depreciation; therefore, income cannot fall below the minimum level obtained applying the multiplier to that difference. To be exact, the multiplier to be applied to autonomous investment and that to be applied to depreciation are slightly different, owing to the lag in the consumption function ★, but this does not significantly alter the general economic idea.

Let us note that the floor as given by (5.32) increases at a (proportional)

★ If such a lag did not exist, eq. (5.24') would become

$$Y_t - bY_t = -a + A_0(1+g)^t,$$

and the floor would be

$$Y_t = \frac{A_0(1+g)^t - a}{1-b},$$

which is the result obtained applying the multiplier $1/(1-b)$ to the difference between autonomous investment and depreciation. Of course, if we assume that no lag exists in the consumption function, we must also alter the initial equations and we obtain another model.

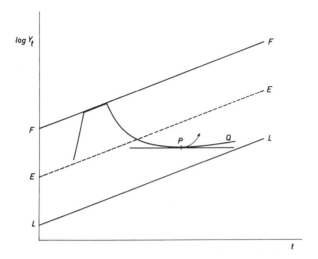

Fig. 5.5.

rate approximately equal to g. The 'approximately' is due to the fact that, owing to the presence of the term $-a/(1-b)$, the actual rate of growth is slightly different from g.

We must now explain the lower turning point. This is rather simple. In the descending phase, income moves asymptotically towards the floor. But since the floor is increasing, in the course of the approach to it income must sooner or later begin to *increase*. At this point the accelerator comes back into gear and brings about a positive induced investment. Income starts increasing explosively towards the ceiling and then the story repeats itself. In fig. 5.5 a graphical illustration is given. To interpret the diagram, remember that in a semi-log scale exponential functions become straight lines, equal slopes imply equal rates of growth and vertical differences represent ratios [*]. Now, the straight lines FF, EE, LL represent respectively the ceiling, the trend and the floor. They are all parallel since ceiling, trend and floor grow at the same rate

---

[*] Any function $Y_t = A(1+g)^t$ becomes, when the logarithms of both sides are taken, $\log Y_t = \log A + t \log(1+g)$. In semi-log paper this is a straight line with slope $\log(1+g)$. Equal slopes must then correspond to the same rate of growth g, although the slope itself is *not* the rate of growth. As for ratios, $\log(a/b) = \log a - \log b$. Constant vertical differences in semi-log diagrams then mean *constant ratios*, and this implies, if the values are increasing, *increasing differences* in natural values.

(the difference in the rate of growth of the floor is here neglected). As we can see, when income approaches the floor, it starts increasing from point P, and so it cannot go on following the path PQ but 'explodes' towards the ceiling, as indicated by the arrow.

The fluctuations in income are then contained between the two limits and so are of approximately constant amplitude in *relative terms*, i.e. when measured as relative deviations from the trend. In absolute value they are actually of increasing amplitude.

Exercises

1. The following data are known:

marginal and average propensity to consume = 0.5;

acceleration coefficient = 2;

rate of growth of autonomous investment and of the ceiling = 0.1 (initial values: 100 for autonomous investment and 500 for the ceiling);

maximum rate of disinvestment possible = 200 per period (in absolute value).

Compute recursively a table showing the behaviour of Y_t over time.

Calculation. The table that we have computed is the following:

t	$I_t''=100(1.1)^t$	$C_t=0.5Y_{t-1}$	$Y_{t-1}-Y_{t-2}$	$I_t'=2(Y_{t-1}-Y_{t-2})$	$Y_t=C_t+I_t'+I_t''$	$500(1.1)^t$
0	100	100	0	0	200	500
1	110	100	0	0	210	550
2	121	105	10	20	246	605
3	133	123	36	72	328	665
4	146	164	82	164	474	730
5	161	237	146	292	690	805
6	177	345	216	432	(954) →	885
7	195	442.5	195	390	(1027.5) →	975
8	214	487.5	90	180	881.5	1070
9	236	440.75	− 93.5	−187	489.75	1180
10	259	244.88	−391.75	(−783.5) − 200	303.88	1295
11	285	151.94	−185.87	(−371.74) − 200	236.94	1425
12	314	118.47	− 66.94	−133.88	298.59	1570
13	345	149.30	+ 61.65	+123.3	617.60	1725
14	380	308.80	319.01	638.02	1326.82	1900
15	418	663.41	709.22	1418.44	(2499.85) →	2090
"	"	"	"	"	"	"

The headings of the columns are self-explanatory. Note that, giving to consumption the initial value 100 and to the variation in income the initial value zero, we have implicitly assumed that income was 200 in each of the two periods immediately preceding period zero. These are the two initial conditions which, as we know, are required to 'start' the model. Given their arbitrariness in numerical examples, we have chosen them so as to simplify computations.

We see from the table that income moves explosively towards the ceiling: in period 6 the 'collision' occurs. This means that we must substitute the value of the ceiling to the value that income would have assumed in the case of a 'free' movement; this operation is indicated by the arrow. It is obvious that the value 885, and not the value 954, must be used to compute consumption in period 7 and the variation in income on which induced investment in period 7 depends. In period 7 income is still on the ceiling. In period 8 the descending phase begins. Note that income has 'crawled' along the ceiling for only two periods. In period 9 induced investment becomes negative. Since its absolute value is smaller than the maximum rate admissible, the value -187 is used in the computations. In period 10, negative induced investment should be -783.5, but this exceeds the maximum rate admissible and so for -783.5 we must substitute -200. A similar thing happens in period 11. In period 12 the value -133.88 is admissible and is a symptom of recovery: in fact, in period 12 income begins to increase. A new 'explosion' towards the ceiling occurs, etc. etc. We hope that this numerical example will help the student to obtain a clearer understanding of the working of Hicks' model, which in formal terms may seem rather complicated.

2. Check that, in the absence of the limits, in exercise 1 the deviations of income from the trend would have been an oscillation of increasing amplitude (both in absolute and in relative terms).

3. Find the explicit expression of the floor (same data as in exercise 1).

§3. Metzler's inventory cycle model

Metzler was the first to investigate formally the consequences of an effort by sellers to maintain a desired level of inventories, through appropriate variations in production. Here we shall expound the basic characteristics of the models he built to that purpose, and then we shall examine one of his second-order models.

Total current output is the sum of the output of consumption goods and of the output of investment goods, the latter being assumed an exogenous constant. The former is made up of two components:

(1) output to be currently sold, according to producer's *expectations* on sales;

(2) output to bring inventories to their *desired* level.

Component (2) may, of course, be negative, which means simply that sellers will produce *less* than expected sales, the difference being provided for, in their plans, by the desired decrease in inventories.

Of course, expectations may not be exact, i.e. actual sales may be different from expected sales, the difference implying an *unintended* variation in inventories. Note that actual sales coincide with current *consumption demand*; the latter must not be confused with the output of consumption goods, since in Metzler's models the output of (as specified above), and the demand for, consumption goods, are allowed to be different.

A lot of specific models can be obtained from these general characteristics, according to the specific assumptions made on the formation of expectations and on how the desired level of inventories is determined.

Let us now assume that expectations are of the 'naive' type, i.e. current expected sales U_t are equal to the sales realized in the previous period; then

$$U_t = C_{t-1} , \tag{5.34}$$

where U_t is also component (1) above and C_{t-1} is the demand of consumption goods in the previous period. No lag is assumed to exist in the consumption function, i.e.

$$C_t = bY_t , \qquad 0 < b < 1 , \tag{5.35}$$

and so

$$U_t = bY_{t-1} . \tag{5.36}$$

To specify component (2), let us assume that producers want to maintain a constant *ratio* between inventories and sales: call it k (the inventory 'accelerator'). Since actual sales will be known only *ex post facto*, producers apply such a ratio to *expected* sales in order to compute the desired level of inventories, $\hat{Q}_t$, to which actual current inventories must be brought:

$$\hat{Q}_t = kU_t , \qquad k > 0 . \tag{5.37}$$

Component (2) – investment in inventories – is then given by

$$\hat{Q}_t - Q_{t-1} = kU_t - Q_{t-1} = kbY_{t-1} - Q_{t-1} , \qquad (5.38)$$

where Q_{t-1} is the existing level of inventories at the moment when producers make their plans (the beginning of period t, i.e. the end of period $t-1$). Now, Q_{t-1} is the level of inventories that producers had planned for period $t-1$, i.e. $kU_{t-1} = kbY_{t-2}$, *minus* the unintended variation in inventories (if any) which occurred in period $t-1$ because of the difference (if any) in that period between realized sales, $C_{t-1} = bY_{t-1}$, and expected sales, $U_{t-1} = bY_{t-2}$. Thus we have

$$Q_{t-1} = kbY_{t-2} - b(Y_{t-1} - Y_{t-2}) , \qquad (5.39)$$

and so (5.38) becomes

$$\hat{Q}_t - Q_{t-1} = (1+k)bY_{t-1} - (1+k)bY_{t-2} . \qquad (5.40)$$

As we said at the beginning, national product (income) is given by

$$Y_t = U_t + (\hat{Q}_t - Q_{t-1}) + I_0 , \qquad (5.41)$$

where I_0 is autonomous investment.

After simple substitutions we obtain the second-order non-homogeneous equation

$$Y_t - (2+k)bY_{t-1} + (1+k)bY_{t-2} = I_0 . \qquad (5.42)$$

A particular solution is obtained trying $\overline{Y}_t$ = constant, which gives

$$\overline{Y}_t = \frac{1}{1-b} I_0 , \qquad (5.43)$$

i.e. the stationary equilibrium given as usual by the multiplier applied to the constant exogenous expenditure.

The corresponding homogeneous equation has the characteristic equation

$$\lambda^2 - (2+k)b\lambda + (1+k)b = 0 . \qquad (5.44)$$

Applying the stability conditions (inequalities (4.19) of Part I, ch. 4) we have that, since the propensity to consume is smaller than unity, the crucial condition is

$$b < \frac{1}{1+k}. \tag{5.45}$$

The succession of the signs of the coefficients in eq. (5.44) is $+ - +$ and so no real negative root may occur. The discriminant of eq. (5.44) is

$$\Delta = (2+k)^2 b^2 - 4(1+k)b ,$$

so that

$$\Delta \gtreqless 0 \qquad \text{if} \qquad b \gtreqless \frac{4(1+k)}{(2+k)^2}. \tag{5.46}$$

Since the inequality

$$\frac{4(1+k)}{(2+k)^2} > \frac{1}{1+k} \tag{5.47}$$

is true for any $k > 0$, we have the following movements (referred to the stationary equilibrium position):

$$0 < b < \frac{1}{1+k} , \qquad \text{oscillatory and convergent;}$$

$$b = \frac{1}{1+k} , \qquad \text{oscillatory and with constant amplitude;}$$

$$\frac{1}{1+k} < b < \frac{4(1+k)}{(2+k)^2} , \qquad \text{oscillatory and divergent;}$$

$$b \geqslant \frac{4(1+k)}{(2+k)^2} , \qquad \text{monotonic and divergent.}$$

It is interesting to note that no stable monotonic movement can occur: stability can take on only the form of damped oscillations. Note also that, *ceteris paribus*, the *smaller* the ratio that producers want to keep between inventories and sales, the more probable it is that a stable movement will occur. The following diagram (fig. 5.6) shows as usual the various regions, which the student may interpret as an exercise.

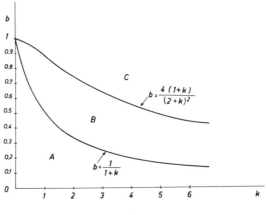

Fig. 5.6.

Exercises

1. In the initial period income is in equilibrium at 2000; the output (and sales) of consumption goods is 1000; inventories are at their desired level and autonomous investment is 1000. In period 1 autonomous investment shifts to 1100 and maintains this level in subsequent periods. Given that the propensity to consume is 0.5 and that the desired inventories/sales ratio is 0.2, compute the values of Y_t for a certain number of periods, and check mathematically the type of movement.

Calculation. The recursive computation is laid down in the table on p. 90. The headings of the columns are self-explanatory. The value in the columns marked with an asterisk (∗) add up to Y_t; the other columns are there to keep track of the computations.

In period 0 the system is in equilibrium. In period 1 autonomous investment shifts to 1100; output of consumption goods remains fixed at 1000; income is 2100 and consumption is 1050, greater than expected consumption (output of consumption goods for sale, U_t): the difference causes a decrease in inventories. In period 2 the output of consumption goods is 1050 for expected consumption plus 60 to bring the inventories to their desired level. Income turns out to be 2210 and so consumption is 1105, again greater than its expected level, the difference coming out of inventories, etc., etc. The values of Y_t have been computed up to $t = 17$ by a direct application of the equation

$$Y_t = 1.1\,Y_{t-1} - 0.6\,Y_{t-2} + 1100\,.$$

t	$I_0^{(*)}$	$U_t^{(*)}$	$\hat{Q}_t$	$\hat{Q}_t - Q_{t-1}^{(*)}$	Y_t	C_t	$C_t - U_t$	Q_t
0	1000	1000	200	0	2000	1000	0	200
1	1100	1000	200	0	2100	1050	50	150
2	1100	1050	210	60	2210	1105	55	155
3	1100	1105	221	66	2271	1135.5	30.5	190.5
4					2272.1			
5					2236.71			
6					2197.12			
7					2174.81			
8					2174.02			
9					2186.54			
10					2200.78			
11					2208.93			
12					2209.36			
13					2204.94			
14					2199.82			
15					2196.84			
16					2196.63			
17					2198.19			

The student should complete the other columns of the table as an exercise.

Let us now comment on the movement. It is clearly a damped oscillation, around the equilibrium value $\overline{Y}_t = [1/(1-0.5)] \times 1100 = 2200$. As a check, it can be easily seen that the roots of the characteristic equation

$$\lambda^2 - 1.1\,\lambda + 0.6 = 0$$

are complex conjugate with modulus smaller than unity $(r = \sqrt{0.6})$, and this confirms the nature of the movement.

2. Given that $Y_0 = 2000$, $Y_1 = 2100$, examine the following cases:

b	0.8	0.9	0.9
k	0.25	0.2	1

§4. Expectations and cobweb theorem (Goodwin)

We saw in Part I, ch. 3, §1 that the expectations which underlie the original formulation of the cobweb theorem are rather unrealistic; a more realistic assumption on expectations was examined in that section (the 'normal price' hypothesis). Here we shall analyse the case in which expectations are assumed to be formed according to the relation

$$\hat{p}_t = p_{t-1} + \rho(p_{t-1} - p_{t-2}), \tag{5.48}$$

where $\hat{p}_t$ is expected price and ρ is a coefficient of expectations (see Goodwin). The case $\rho = 0$ corresponds to the original cobweb theorem; when the parameter ρ is positive (negative), price is expected to continue moving in the same direction (to reverse its movement).

The model is then made up of the following equations:

$$D_t = a + bp_t,$$

$$S_t = a_1 + b_1 \hat{p}_t = a_1 + b_1[p_{t-1} + \rho(p_{t-1} - p_{t-2})],$$

$$D_t = S_t.$$

After simple substitutions we obtain the second-order difference equation

$$bp_t - b_1(1+\rho)p_{t-1} + b_1\rho p_{t-2} = a_1 - a. \tag{5.49}$$

As a particular solution, let us try an undetermined constant p_e. Substituting in (5.49) and solving, we have

$$p_e = \frac{a_1 - a}{b - b_1}, \tag{5.50}$$

which is the equilibrium value of price. The characteristic equation of the corresponding homogeneous equation is

$$\lambda^2 - \frac{b_1(1+\rho)}{b}\lambda + \frac{b_1\rho}{b} = 0. \tag{5.51}$$

Applying the stability conditions — see (4.19) of Part I, ch. 4 — we have

$$1 - \frac{b_1(1+\rho)}{b} + \frac{b_1\rho}{b} = 1 - \frac{b_1}{b} > 0 ,$$

$$1 - \frac{b_1\rho}{b} > 0 , \tag{5.52}$$

$$1 + \frac{b_1(1+\rho)}{b} + \frac{b_1\rho}{b} = 1 + \frac{b_1(1+2\rho)}{b} > 0 .$$

To analyse those inequalities, it is convenient to distinguish two cases: $\rho > 0$ and $\rho < 0$. In what follows it is assumed that the demand and supply functions are 'normal', i.e. $b < 0$, $b_1 > 0$.

Case (1): $\rho > 0$
The first and second inequalities in (5.52) are always satisfied and so the crucial inequality is the third, which may be written as

$$\frac{1}{(1+2\rho)} > \frac{b_1}{-b} ,$$

i.e.

$$\frac{b_1}{-b} < \frac{1}{1+2\rho} . \tag{5.53}$$

Let us now compare inequality (5.53) with the stability condition holding in the original cobweb theorem, which is, in the case of normal demand and supply functions,

$$b_1/-b < 1 . \tag{5.54}$$

Since $1/(1+2\rho)$ is smaller than 1, stability condition (5.53) is more restrictive than (5.54). Expectations such that price is expected to continue moving in the same direction ('extrapolative' expectations) are an element of instability, and so the region of stability is smaller. The discriminant of eq. (5.51) is

$$\Delta = \frac{b_1^2(1+\rho)^2}{b^2} - 4\frac{b_1\rho}{b} .$$

Since $\rho > 0$, $b_1 > 0$, $b < 0$, Δ is always positive. The roots are real and distinct.

Since the succession of the signs of the coefficients in (5.51) is $+\ +\ -$, one root is negative and the other is positive, and this means the superposition of an improper oscillation on a monotonic movement.

Case (2): $\rho < 0$
The first inequality in (5.52) is always satisfied, and so the remaining two are the relevant ones. The second may be written as

$$\frac{b_1}{-b} < \frac{1}{-\rho}. \tag{5.55}$$

As for the third, two sub-cases must be distinguished. If $\rho \leqslant -\frac{1}{2}$, then such inequality is always satisfied, and so the only relevant inequality is (5.55). If $\rho > -\frac{1}{2}$, then $1 + 2\rho > 0$, and the inequality under consideration may be written as

$$\frac{b_1}{-b} < \frac{1}{1+2\rho}. \tag{5.56}$$

Now, we must check which inequality is more stringent, and this is equivalent to checking whether

$$\frac{1}{-\rho} \lessgtr \frac{1}{1+2\rho} \tag{5.57}$$

in the range $-\frac{1}{2} < \rho < 0$. From (5.57) we have

$$1 + 2\rho \lessgtr -\rho \ ;$$

therefore

$$3\rho \lessgtr -1 \ ,$$

and

$$\rho \lessgtr -\tfrac{1}{3} \ ,$$

and so

$$\frac{1}{-\rho} \lessgtr \frac{1}{1+2\rho} \qquad \text{for} \quad \rho \lessgtr -\tfrac{1}{3} \ . \tag{5.58}$$

The results for $\rho < 0$ may then be laid down in the following table (eq. 5.59), where the crucial inequality is written below the different ranges of ρ:

$$
\begin{array}{|c|c|}
\hline
\rho \leqslant -\frac{1}{3} & -\frac{1}{3} \leqslant \rho < 0 \\
\hline
\dfrac{b_1}{-b} < \dfrac{1}{-\rho} \quad (5.55) & \dfrac{b_1}{-b} < \dfrac{1}{1+2\rho} \quad (5.56) \\
\hline
\end{array}
\qquad (5.59)
$$

Let us now compare, as before, such stability conditions with that holding in the original cobweb theorem. The result is that, if $-1 < \rho < 0$, then the stability condition is *less* restrictive than (5.54); if $\rho = -1$, they are the same; if $\rho < -1$, then the stability condition is *more* restrictive than (5.54). In fact, for $-\frac{1}{3} < \rho < 0$, the stability condition is (5.56), which is less restrictive than (5.54) since $1/(1+2\rho) > 1$. For $-1 < \rho \leqslant -\frac{1}{3}$ the stability condition is (5.55) and, since $1/-\rho > 1$, it is less restrictive than (5.54). For $\rho \leqslant -1$ the stability condition is again (5.55) and, if $\rho = -1$, then $1/-\rho = 1$ and so (5.55) and (5.54) coincide; if $\rho < -1$, then $1/-\rho < 1$ and so (5.55) is more restrictive than (5.54). The economic meaning of such results is the following. The fact that producers expect price to reverse its movement is an element of stability, *provided that the expected inversion is not too great*, since in the opposite case it would have the contrary effect, with the result that the stability conditions would have to be more stringent than in the original cobweb theorem (which is the case when $\rho < -1$).

The discriminant of the characteristic equation may now have any sign, and precisely

$$
\Delta \gtreqqless 0 \qquad \text{if} \qquad \frac{b_1}{-b} \gtreqqless \frac{-4\rho}{(1+\rho)^2} . \qquad (5.60)
$$

Note that, when the roots are real, they are both negative if $\rho > -1$ (the succession of the signs of the coefficients of the characteristic equations is $+\;+\;+$) and both positive if $\rho < -1$ (the signs are $+\;-\;+$); for $\rho = -1$ only complex roots may occur.

The results obtained from the qualitative analysis of Goodwin's model may be represented in a familiar way in fig. 5.7.

Only the parts of the various curves lying in the positive half plane have been drawn, since $b_1/-b > 0$ by assumption. The curves drawn more heavily separate the stable regions (points *below* the curves) from the unstable ones (points *above* the curves). Two curves are needed for such separation since, as we have seen above, for $\rho \leqslant -\frac{1}{3}$ the relevant stability condition is

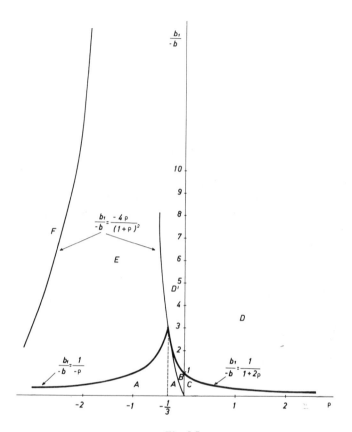

Fig. 5.7.

$b_1/{-b} < 1/{-\rho}$ (ineq. (5.55)), whereas for $\rho \geqslant -\frac{1}{3}$ the relevant stability condition is $b_1/{-b} < 1/(1+2\rho)$ (inequalities (5.56) and (5.53)). The other curves
separate in a similar way the real roots regions from the complex roots regions
(the curve $b_1/{-b} = -4\rho/(1+\rho)^2$ has two branches, one to the left and one to
the right of the vertical asymptote (not shown in the diagram) $\rho = -1$). The
letters demarcate the various regions, whose nature the student can ascertain
as an exercise ★. The diagram helps us to see that, when ρ is negative, complex

★ The letter A has been repeated to avoid confusion, since the broken line serves only
to distinguish the point $(-\frac{1}{3}, 3)$ where the three curves meet but does *not* serve to separate two regions. On the contrary, region D is different from region D′; in both regions
the roots are real and unstable, but in D one root is negative and the other is positive,
whereas in D′ both roots are negative.

roots are more likely to occur than real roots, except when ρ is very small or very great in absolute value and the slope of the supply function is much greater than the slope of the demand function (in absolute value, of course). For example, if $\rho = -\frac{1}{2}$, $\Delta > 0$ for $b_1/-b > 8$, i.e. b_1 must exceed 8 times the absolute value of b.

Exercises

1. The demand function is $D_t = 80 - 4p_t$, the supply function is $S_t = -10 + \hat{p}_t$, where $\hat{p}_t = p_{t-1} + \rho(p_{t-1} - p_{t-2})$. Assume that $\rho = -1$ and check whether price converges or not, and how, towards its equilibrium value.

Calculation. The point $(-1, \frac{1}{4})$ falls in region A of fig. 5.7 and so the movement will be a damped oscillation around the equilibrium price.

Equating demand and supply we have

$$80 - 4p_t = -10 + [p_{t-1} - (p_{t-1} - p_{t-2})] \; ;$$

therefore

$$p_t + \tfrac{1}{4} p_{t-2} = 22.5 \; . \tag{5.61}$$

A particular solution can be found, as usual, trying $p_t = p_{t-2} = p_e$ (undetermined constant), so that

$$p_e = 18 \; ,$$

which is the static equilibrium price, which can also be checked by solving the static system

$$D = 80 - 4p \; , \quad S = -10 + p \; , \quad D = S \; .$$

The characteristic equation of $p_t + \tfrac{1}{4} p_{t-2} = 0$ is

$$\lambda^2 + \tfrac{1}{4} = 0 \; ,$$

whence

$$\lambda_1, \lambda_2 = \pm \tfrac{1}{2} i \; .$$

The roots are 'pure imaginary', i.e. complex roots lacking the real part. From the relations

$$r \cos \omega = 0 \,,$$

$$r \sin \omega = \tfrac{1}{2} \,,$$

we have $\omega = 90°$, $r = \tfrac{1}{2}$. Let us note, incidentally, that when the roots are pure imaginary the arc ω is always $90°$. The general solution of eq. (5.61) is then

$$p_t = (\tfrac{1}{2})^t (A_1 \cos 90° t + A_2 \sin 90° t) + 18 \,.$$

2. In period 0 price is in equilibrium and in period 1 an initial disturbance shifts it to 20. Compute the values of the arbitrary constants in the solution of exercise 1.

3. Same data as in exercise 1, but for $\rho = 3$.

§5. Monetary factors and multiplier–accelerator interaction (Smyth)

The business cycle models * that we have previosuly examined in this chapter (Samuelson's, Hicks', Metzler's; see also Pasinetti's model) are models which explain the cyclical phenomenon on the basis of real factors, without introducing monetary factors **. On the contrary, monetary factors had a place in the older theories of the business cycle, and this place was sometimes pre-eminent (purely monetary theories of the business cycle). We think that the emphasis given since to real factors has been determined, at least in part, by the attractive possibility of 'explaining' theoretically, and in a formally elegant way, the cyclical phenomenon by a combination of the multiplier and of the accelerator (in its various forms), without any need of monetary factors.

Since the 'real' wave, however, model builders have included monetary factors, partly because the observation of reality suggests that such factors have often played an important role in the business cycles that have occurred

---

* The expression 'business cycle models' is here used broadly, since the quoted models, as we have seen, can give rise not only to oscillatory movements, but also to monotonic movements.

** To be exact, in Hicks' book (chs. IX and X) monetary factors are treated too. However, he does not introduce them formally into his model and, moreover, allots to them only the task of attenuating or strengthening the effects of real factors. Thus we are not far from the truth when we say that Hicks' model is essentially a real model.

in the Western world since the end of the Second World War. This does not mean that theory has shifted to the opposite extreme (purely monetary models), but that it has tried to formulate models in which real and monetary factors are blended. Among such models we have chosen Smyth's, since it illustrates rather simply the mechanism of the interaction between monetary factors and real factors (of the multiplier—accelerator kind). The equations of the model are the following:

$$C_t = bY_{t-1} , \qquad 0 < b < 1 , \qquad\qquad (5.62)$$

which is a consumption function of the usual type, and

$$I_t = k(Y_{t-1} - Y_{t-2}) + aR_{t-1} , \qquad k > 0 , \quad a < 0 . \qquad (5.63)$$

Eq. (5.63) is the investment function where, in addition to the acceleration principle, the influence of the rate of interest (lagged one period) is present. Of course, according to traditional theory, $a < 0$, since an increase (decrease) in the rate of interest has a negative (positive) effect on investment; or

$$Y_t = C_t + I_t + A_t . \qquad\qquad (5.64)$$

In eq. (5.64), A_t is autonomous expenditure, and no trend term is assumed in it. From (5.62), (5.63) and (5.64) we have

$$Y_t = (b+k)Y_{t-1} - kY_{t-2} + aR_{t-1} + A_t . \qquad\qquad (5.65)$$

For the monetary aspects of the model, let us begin with the demand for money. It depends, as we know, positively on income and negatively on the rate of interest. Assuming that the influence of the two variables can be separated into transactions demand depending only on income, and speculative demand depending only on the rate of interest, and that the functions are linear, we have

$$L_t = dY_t + (n + jR_t) , \qquad\qquad (5.66)$$

where $d > 0, n > 0, j < 0$. Note that in the model price changes are assumed away, as in the 'real' models. The money supply is determined by the monetary authorities, who follow a stabilization policy, i.e. they increase (decrease) the money supply in proportion to the decrease (increase) in income:

$$L_{S_t} - L_{S_{t-1}} = w(Y_{t-1} - Y_{t-2}), \qquad w < 0. \tag{5.67}$$

Eq. (5.67) may also be written as

$$\Delta L_{S_t} = w \Delta Y_{t-1},$$

so that

$$L_{S_t} = wY_{t-1} + c,$$

where c is an arbitrary constant. Assuming that L_{S_1}, the money supply in period 1, and Y_0, the national income in period 0, are known, from $L_{S_1} = wY_0 + c$ we have $c = L_{S_1} - wY_0$, and so

$$L_{S_t} = wY_{t-1} + (L_{S_1} - wY_0) = wY_{t-1} + e, \tag{5.68}$$

where $e \equiv L_{S_1} - wY_0$.

Monetary equilibrium requires that the demand for and the supply of money are equal, that is

$$L_t = L_{S_t}. \tag{5.69}$$

Substituting in (5.69) from (5.66) and (5.68) we have

$$dY_t + n + jR_t = wY_{t-1} + e; \tag{5.70}$$

therefore

$$R_t = \frac{1}{j}(-dY_t + wY_{t-1} + e - n),$$

and thus we have, shifting all time subscripts backwards by one period,

$$R_{t-1} = \frac{1}{j}(-dY_{t-1} + wY_{t-2} + e - n). \tag{5.71}$$

Substituting (5.71) in (5.65) and collecting terms, we have

$$Y_t - \left(b + k - \frac{ad}{j}\right)Y_{t-1} + \left(k - \frac{aw}{j}\right)Y_{t-2} = \frac{a}{j}(e - n) + A_t. \tag{5.72}$$

If A_t is assumed constant, a particular solution is

$$\overline{Y}_t = \frac{a(e-n)+jA}{(1-b)j+a(d-w)}.$$ (5.73)

The interesting thing, however, is to examine the deviations of income from its equilibrium level and to compare them with those occurring in purely 'real' models; as a standard for comparison Hicks' model is used, since Smyth's model is actually Hicks' model with monetary factors added. Let us recall that in Hicks' model the characteristic equation is

$$\lambda^2 - (b+k)\lambda + k = 0,$$ (5.74)

and that the stability condition is

$$k < 1.$$ (5.75)

In Smyth's model, the characteristic equation is

$$\lambda^2 - \left(b + k - \frac{ad}{j}\right)\lambda + \left(k - \frac{aw}{j}\right) = 0.$$ (5.76)

Let us now apply the stability conditions — see (4.19) of Part I, ch. 4 — to eq. (5.76). We have

$$1 - b - k + \frac{ad}{j} + k - \frac{aw}{j} = 1 - b + \frac{ad}{j} - \frac{aw}{j} > 0,$$

$$1 - k + \frac{aw}{j} > 0,$$

$$1 + b + k - \frac{ad}{j} + k - \frac{aw}{j} > 0.$$

The first inequality is certainly satisfied, since, given the assumptions on the various parameters, $1 - b > 0$, $ad/j > 0$, $-aw/j > 0$.

From the second inequality we have

$$k < 1 + \frac{aw}{j},$$ (5.77)

and from the third

$$b > \frac{a}{j}(w+d) - 2k - 1 . \tag{5.78}$$

Comparing inequality (5.77) with (5.75), it can be easily seen that (5.77) is more stringent than (5.75), since aw/j is a negative magnitude. The conclusion is that the introduction of monetary factors makes the model more likely to be unstable $\star$. Another interesting conclusion is that the possibility of oscillations is greater. First of all, 'improper' oscillations may occur (they cannot occur in Hicks' model): if $b + k - ad/j < 0$, the succession of the signs of the coefficients in (5.76) is $+ + +$ and so the roots, if real, are both negative. Secondly, if $2(b+k) > ad/j$, then 'proper' oscillations are more likely to occur than in Hicks' model. In fact, the conditions that such oscillations occur are

$$\left(b + k - \frac{ad}{j} \right)^2 - 4\left(k - \frac{aw}{j} \right) < 0 , \tag{5.79}$$

$$(b+k)^2 - 4k < 0 , \tag{5.80}$$

respectively, for Smyth's model and for Hicks' model. Now, if $2(b+k) > ad/j$, then

$$\left(b + k - \frac{ad}{j} \right)^2 < (b+k)^2 . \tag{5.81}$$

Since $aw/j < 0$, it is always true that $4(k - aw/j) > 4k$; from this and from (5.81) it follows that

---

$\star$ Smyth points out that this conclusion depends in an essential way on the fact that the rate of interest appears with a lag in the investment function. If one puts R_t instead of R_{t-1} in (5.63), then the characteristic equation of the homogeneous part of the model becomes:

$$\lambda^2 - \frac{b + k + aw/j}{1 + ad/j} \lambda + \frac{k}{1 + ad/j} = 0 ,$$

and, applying the usual stability conditions, the critical value of k turns out to be $1 + ad/j$. Since $ad/j > 0$, such a critical value is greater than in Hicks' model, and so the model is now more likely to be stable, an opposite conclusion to that reached before. All this offers the opportunity to remark that, in building difference-equation models, lags cannot be freely poured over the model, but their presence (or absence) must be justified according to sound economic reasoning.

$$\left(b + k - \frac{ad}{j}\right)^2 - 4\left(k - \frac{aw}{j}\right) < (b+k)^2 - 4k , \qquad (5.82)$$

which proves that (5.79) is more likely to be satisfied than (5.80).

Exercises

1. Complete the qualitative discussion of the model finding the regions where $\Delta \gtreqless 0$ and combining the results with the stability conditions.

2. The following data are given: $b = 0.8$, $k = 4$, $a = -100$, $d = 0.5$, $n = 2500$, $j = -250$, $w = -4$. Examine the behaviour of the deviations of national income from its equilibrium value.

Calculation. With the given data, the homogeneous part of the basic equation of the model becomes

$$Y_t - 4.6 Y_{t-1} + 5.6 Y_{t-2} = 0 ,$$

whose characteristic equation is

$$\lambda^2 - 4.6\lambda + 5.6 = 0 .$$

The roots are

$$\lambda_1, \lambda_2 \simeq 2.3 \pm 0.55677\, i .$$

From the relations

$$r \cos \omega = 2.3 ,$$

$$r \sin \omega = 0.55677 ,$$

$$r \qquad = + \sqrt{5.6} ,$$

we obtain

$$r \simeq 2.36643 ,$$

$$\omega \simeq 13° 36' ,$$

and so the solution of the above homogeneous difference equation is

$$Y_t = (2.36643)^t (A_1 \cos 13° 36't + A_2 \sin 13° 36't) \, .$$

The movement is an explosive oscillation. Let us note that, given $b = 0.8$, $k = 4$, in Hicks' model the movement would also be explosive, but monotonic, since the roots of the equation

$$\lambda^2 - 4.8 \lambda + 4 = 0$$

are real, positive and both greater than unity.

3. Same problems as in exercise 2, but with the following data: $b = 0.7$, $k = 2, a = -100, d = 0.5, n = 2500, j = -250, w = -1$.

References

Dernburg, T.F. and Dernburg, J.D., 1969, *Macroeconomic Analysis: An Introduction to Comparative Statics and Dynamics*, ch. 8.

Duesenberry, J.S., 1958, *Business Cycles and Economic Growth*, chs. 9, 10.

Goodwin, R.M., 1947, Dynamical Coupling with Especial Reference to Markets Having Production Lags, §IV.

Hicks, J.R., 1949, Mr. Harrod's Dynamic Theory.

Hicks, J.R., 1950, *A Contribution to the Theory of Trade Cycle*, chs. I–VIII and mathematical appendixes.

Kuh, E., 1963, *Capital Stock Growth: A Micro-Econometric Approach*, ch. 9.

Metzler, L.A., 1941, The Nature and Stability of Inventory Cycles.

Minsky, H.P., 1959, A Linear Model of Cyclical Growth.

Pasinetti, L.L., 1960, Cyclical Fluctuations and Growth.

Samuelson, P.A., 1939, Interactions between the Multiplier Analysis and the Principle of Acceleration.

Smyth, D.J., 1963, Monetary Factors and Multiplier–Accelerator Interaction.

6

Higher-order Equations

As we know, the general form of an n-th order difference equation is

$$c_0 y_t + c_1 y_{t-1} + \dots + c_n y_{t-n} = g(t) , \quad c_0 \neq 0 , \quad c_n \neq 0 . \quad (6.1)$$

To obtain the solution of the corresponding homogeneous equation, let us try, as for second-order equations, the function λ^t, where λ is a constant to be determined. Substituting in the equation we have

$$c_0 \lambda^t + c_1 \lambda^{t-1} + \dots + c_n \lambda^{t-n} = 0 ;$$

therefore

$$\lambda^{t-n}(c_0 \lambda^n + c_1 \lambda^{n-1} + \dots + c_n) = 0 . \quad (6.2)$$

If λ^t is a solution, eq. (6.2) must be satisfied for any t, and this — excluding the trivial case $\lambda = 0$ — is possible if, and only if,

$$c_0 \lambda^n + c_1 \lambda^{n-1} + \dots + c_n = 0 , \quad (6.3)$$

which is the characteristic equation of the homogeneous difference equation. Eq. (6.3) may also be written as

$$\lambda^n + a_1\lambda^{n-1} + ... + a_n = 0,$$ (6.4)

where $a_i \equiv c_i/c_0, i = 1, 2, ..., n$.

The solution of eq. (6.4) yields exactly n roots, which may be real or complex, simple or repeated. In the case of distinct real roots, we have n functions λ_i^t, each being a solution of the homogeneous equation. According to general principles, we can combine them with n arbitrary constants, and obtain the general solution

$$y_t = A_1\lambda_1^t + A_2\lambda_2^t + ... + A_n\lambda_n^t .$$ (6.5)

If λ^* is a repeated root of multiplicity $m \leq n$, then also $t\lambda^{*t}, t^2\lambda^{*t}, ...$ ..., $t^{m-1}\lambda^{*t}$ are solutions of the homogeneous equation. In general, the solution of the homogeneous equation in the case of repeated real roots is

$$y_t = \sum_{j=1}^k P_j(t)\lambda_j^{*t},$$ (6.6)

where λ_j^* are the roots of eq. (6.4), each with its multiplicity, and $P_j(t)$ are polynomials of the type

$$P_j(t) = A_{1_j} + A_{2_j}t + ... + A_{m_j}t^{m_j-1},$$

where the A's are arbitrary constants and m_j is the multiplicity of the j-th root. In the case of complex roots (that occur always in conjugate pairs), each pair will give rise to a trigonometric component of the kind

$$r^t(A_1 \cos \omega t + A_2 \sin \omega t),$$

in exactly the same way as in second-order equations. If some pairs of complex roots are repeated, then we shall have terms of the kind

$$r_j^t[(A_{11_j} + A_{12_j}t + ... + A_{1m_j}t^{m_j-1}) \cos \omega t$$
$$+ (A_{21_j} + A_{22_j}t + ... + A_{2m_j}t^{m_j-1}) \sin \omega t],$$ (6.7)

where m_j is the number of times that the j-th pair of complex roots is repeated and the A's are $2m_j$ arbitrary constants. Of course, in the same equation complex (simple or repeated) roots may occur together with real (simple or repeated) roots, and so a great variety of movements is possible.

A particular solution of the non-homogeneous equation can usually be found by applying the general method of undetermined coefficients (see Part I, ch. 1) [*].

In order to determine the n arbitrary constants, n additional conditions are needed, which usually take the form of $y_0, y_1, ..., y_{n-1}$ being known values. Substituting such values in the general solution, we obtain a system of n linear equations in the n unknowns $A_1, A_2, ..., A_n$ [**].

As we see, there are no *conceptual* difficulties greater than those met in relation to second-order equations [†]. The greater difficulty of higher-order equations lies in the practical problem of how to find the roots of the characteristic equation. This problem in numerical analysis is outside the scope of this book and, anyway, it is *not* of great importance for the economic theorist, who works with *qualitative* information only. In this connection it would be highly desirable to have stability conditions (of the kind of (4.19) in Part I, ch. 4) to check whether the roots of the characteristic equation are all in modulus less than unity [‡] by means of inequalities involving the coefficients of the characteristic equation itself. Such conditions exist, and can be given in two forms.

---

[*] We shall exemplify in the case in which $g(t) = G$, a constant. As a particular solution try $\bar{y}_t = B$, an undetermined constant. Substitution in (6.1) yields $B = G/(c_0 + c_1 + ... + c_n)$. If $c_0 + c_1 + ... + c_n = 0$, try $\bar{y}_t = Bt$. Substituting in (6.1) and collecting terms we have $(c_0 + c_1 + ... + c_n)Bt - B(c_1 + 2c_2 + ... + nc_n) = G$ and so $B = -G/(c_1 + 2c_2 + ... + nc_n)$. If also $c_1 + 2c_2 + ... + nc_n = 0$, try $\bar{y}_t = Bt^2$, and so on.

[**] Consider the case in which the characteristic roots are all distinct. Then the equations for the determination of the arbitrary constants are

$$\sum_{j=1}^{n} \lambda_j^i A_j = y_i - \bar{y}_i, \qquad i = 0, 1, ..., n-1, \qquad (*)$$

where $\bar{y}_i \equiv 0$ if the system is homogeneous. Since the roots are all distinct, the matrix $[\lambda_j^i]$ is non-singular and so system $(*)$ can be solved. Some complications may arise when there are multiple roots, but we need not treat them here.

[†] The 'jump' in conceptual difficulty occurs when we pass from first- to second-order equations (complex roots, etc.). From the second-order on we do not think that the conceptual difficulties are greater.

[‡] Another way of saying the same thing is that the roots all lie within the unit circle in the complex plane, that is, they are 'stable' roots. The reason why also the roots with unit modulus are to be excluded is that we want *asymptotic* stability, that is $\lim_{t \to +\infty} y(t) = 0$, where $y(t)$ is the general solution of the homogeneous equation. Now, a root with unit modulus gives rise, in the solution, either to a constant term (root = +1) or to a constant amplitude alternation (root = −1) or to a constant amplitude oscillation (pair of complex conjugate roots with unit modulus). In each of these cases the time path, while not being divergent, is not stable in the sense defined above.

(1) *Necessary and sufficient stability conditions (Samuelson's form)*
Given equation (6.4), form the following sums ($a_0 = 1$):

$$\bar{a}_0 = \sum_{i=0}^{n} a_i \,,$$

$$\bar{a}_1 = \sum_{i=0}^{n} a_i(n-2i) \,,$$

$$\cdots\cdots\cdots\cdots\cdots$$

$$\bar{a}_r = \sum_{i=0}^{n} a_i \sum_{k=0}^{n} \binom{n-i}{r-k}(-1)^k \binom{i}{k} \,,$$

$$\cdots\cdots\cdots\cdots\cdots\cdots\cdots\cdots$$

$$\bar{a}_n = 1 - a_1 + a_2 - \dots + (-1)^{n-1}a_{n-1} + (-1)^n a_n \,.$$

Then the stability conditions are

$$\bar{a}_0 > 0 \,,$$

$$\Delta_1 > 0 \,,$$

$$\Delta_2 > 0 \,,$$

$$\cdots\cdots$$

$$\Delta_n > 0 \,,$$

where the Δ's are the leading principal minors of the matrix (of which only the first n rows and columns must be considered)

$$\begin{bmatrix} \bar{a}_1 & \bar{a}_3 & \bar{a}_5 & \cdots \\ \bar{a}_0 & \bar{a}_2 & \bar{a}_4 & \cdots \\ 0 & \bar{a}_1 & \bar{a}_3 & \cdots \\ 0 & \bar{a}_0 & \bar{a}_2 & \cdots \\ \cdots & \cdots & \cdots & \cdots \\ \cdots & \cdots & \cdots & \cdots \end{bmatrix} \,.$$

(2) *Necessary and sufficient stability conditions (Schur's form: see Chipman)*
The following n determinants (the broken lines are inserted only to bring out their symmetry):

$$
\begin{vmatrix} a_0 & a_n \\ a_n & a_0 \end{vmatrix} , \quad
\begin{vmatrix} a_0 & 0 & a_n & a_{n-1} \\ a_1 & a_0 & 0 & a_n \\ a_n & 0 & a_0 & a_1 \\ a_{n-1} & a_n & 0 & a_0 \end{vmatrix} , \quad \dots
$$

$$
\dots , \quad
\begin{vmatrix}
a_0 & 0 & \cdots & 0 & a_n & a_{n-1} & \cdots & a_{n-r+1} \\
a_1 & a_0 & \cdots & 0 & 0 & a_n & \cdots & a_{n-r+2} \\
\cdot & \cdot & & \cdot & \cdot & & & \cdot \\
a_{r-1} & a_{r-2} & \cdots & a_0 & 0 & 0 & \cdots & a_n \\
a_n & 0 & \cdots & 0 & a_0 & a_1 & \cdots & a_{r-1} \\
a_{n-1} & a_n & \cdots & 0 & 0 & a_0 & \cdots & a_{r-2} \\
\cdot & \cdot & & \cdot & \cdot & & & \cdot \\
a_{n-r+1} & a_{n-r+2} & \cdots & a_n & 0 & 0 & & a_0
\end{vmatrix} , \quad \dots
$$

$$
\dots , \quad
\begin{vmatrix}
a_0 & 0 & \cdots & 0 & a_n & a_{n-1} & \cdots & a_1 \\
a_1 & a_0 & \cdots & 0 & 0 & a_n & \cdots & a_2 \\
\cdot & \cdot & & \cdot & \cdot & & & \cdot \\
a_{n-1} & a_{n-2} & \cdots & a_0 & 0 & 0 & \cdots & a_n \\
a_n & 0 & \cdots & 0 & a_0 & a_1 & \cdots & a_{n-1} \\
a_{n-1} & a_n & \cdots & 0 & 0 & a_0 & \cdots & a_{n-2} \\
\cdot & \cdot & & \cdot & \cdot & & & \cdot \\
a_1 & a_2 & \cdots & a_n & 0 & 0 & \cdots & a_0
\end{vmatrix} .
$$

must be all positive (in eq. (6.4), $a_0 = 1$).

The Schur conditions may seem easier to apply, since no previous transformations on the coefficients of the equation are required, and in fact some authors prefer them to the Samuelson conditions. However, the latter conditions, once the transformations are made, imply the expansion of smaller-order determinants (the maximum order of the determinants to expand is n with (1) and $2n$ with (2), and this is a rather important thing in the economy of the computations). So Schur's form may not be more convenient than Samuelson's form, and this is why we have given both. In the following chapters we shall use the Samuelson conditions, but this is a choice that perhaps reflects personal tastes.

In either form the stability conditions become increasingly complicated as the order of the equation increases and, correspondingly, their economic interpretation becomes more and more intricate. Indeed, there is little hope of extricating a clear economic meaning from the stability conditions when the equation is of order higher than the third.

For a third-order equation, the explicit form of the stability conditions is

$$1 + a_1 + a_2 + a_3 > 0,$$

$$3 - a_1 - a_2 + 3a_3 > 0,$$

$$1 - a_1 + a_2 - a_3 > 0,$$

$$3 + a_1 - a_2 - 3a_3 > 0,$$

$$(3 + a_1 - a_2 - 3a_3)(3 - a_1 - a_2 + 3a_3)$$

$$- (1 + a_1 + a_2 + a_3)(1 - a_1 + a_2 - a_3) \equiv -a_3^2 + a_1 a_3 - a_2 + 1 > 0.$$

(6.8)

It can easily be seen that either the second or the fourth inequality can be eliminated, since one of them is clearly redundant *. However, we have given them both, since in the economic applications that we shall see it will be convenient sometimes to drop the second (see Part I, ch. 7, §2) and sometimes to drop the fourth (see Part I, ch. 9, §2).

Finally, let us note that when all the coefficients of eq. (6.4) are positive, then a *sufficient* stability condition is that

---

* Call d_1, d_2, d_3, d_4, d_5 the five inequalities in (6.8). Inequality d_5 is not implied by the others and so is independent. Now, d_5, d_1, d_2, d_3 together imply d_4, and d_5, d_1, d_3, d_4 together imply d_2. On the contrary, d_5, d_1, d_2, d_4 together do *not* imply d_3 and d_5, d_2, d_3, d_4 together do *not* imply d_1. This proves that the redundant inequality is either d_4 or d_2.

$$1 > a_1 > a_2 > ... > a_n \ . \tag{6.9}$$

For further details on this and similar cases, see Sato (1970). Another *sufficient* stability condition (which does not require the coefficients to be positive) is that

$$\sum_{i=1}^{n} |a_i| < 1 \ , \tag{6.10}$$

whereas a *necessary* stability condition is that

$$- \sum_{i=1}^{n} a_i < 1 \ . \tag{6.11}$$

For these conditions, see Smithies (1942).

References

Allen, R.G.D., 1959, *Mathematical Economics*, ch. 6, § 6.5.
Baumol, W.J., 1970, *Economic Dynamics*, ch. 10, § 5; ch. 12.
Chipman, J.S., 1950, The Multi-Sector Multiplier, § VI.
Goldberg, S., 1958, *Introduction to Difference Equations*, ch. 3, § 3.7.
Papandreou, A.G., 1965, *Introduction to Macroeconomic Models*, ch. 5, § 5.5
Samuelson, P.A., 1941, Conditions that the Roots of a Polynomial be less than Unity in Absolute Value.
Samuelson, P.A., 1947, *Foundations of Economic Analysis*, Appendix B, § 37.
Sato, R., 1970, A Further Note on a Difference Equation Recurring in Growth Theory.
Smithies, A., 1942, The Stability of Competitive Equilibrium, p. 269.
Yamane, T., 1968, *Mathematics for Economists: An Elementary Survey*, ch. 12, § 12.5.

7

Some Economic Applications

of Higher-order Equations

§1. Distributed lags and multiplier–accelerator interaction (Hicks)

In Part I, ch. 5, §2, we have examined Hicks' trade cycle model in its 'simple' form. Its general form will be examined here. The basic idea is that, in any period, investment and consumption depend on the values of national income in the n preceding periods.

For the investment function, the assumption is that the investment induced by a variation in income is not entirely carried out in a single period, but is spread over n successive periods. Thus, if ΔY is the variation in income and $k\Delta Y$ is the induced investment, given the acceleration coefficient k, a fraction $e_1(k\Delta Y)$ will be invested in the next period, another fraction $e_2(k\Delta Y)$ two periods after, and so on up to $e_n(k\Delta Y)$. Of course, $e_1 + e_2 + \ldots$ $\ldots + e_n = 1$. Call $e_i k \equiv k_i$; thus $\sum_{i=1}^{n} k_i = k$. From all this it follows that total induced investment actually carried out in any period t consists of a part depending on ΔY_{t-1}, of another part depending on ΔY_{t-2}, and so on up to the part depending on ΔY_{t-n}. Calling I_t' total induced investment carried out in period t, we have

$$I_t' = k_1(Y_{t-1} - Y_{t-2}) + k_2(Y_{t-2} - Y_{t-3}) + \ldots + k_n(Y_{t-n} - Y_{t-n-1}). \quad (7.1)$$

For the consumption function, the assumption is that consumption depends on the values of national income in the last n periods, i.e.

$$C_t = b_1 Y_{t-1} + b_2 Y_{t-2} + \dots + b_n Y_{t-n} \, , \tag{7.2}$$

where

$$b_1 + b_2 + \dots + b_n = b \, .$$

Eq. (7.2) is based on the assumption that the variation in consumption depending on a variation in income is spread over n successive periods, as for induced investment.

With equations (7.1) and (7.2), the model gives rise to a difference equation of order $n + 1$. Here we shall analyse the case in which investment is distributed over two successive periods and so is consumption, so that a third-order equation results. The equations of the model are then

$$Y_t = C_t + I_t \, , \tag{7.3}$$

$$C_t = b_1 Y_{t-1} + b_2 Y_{t-2} \, , \qquad\qquad b_1 + b_2 = b \, , \tag{7.4}$$

$$I_t = I_t' + I_t'' \, , \tag{7.5}$$

$$I_t' = k_1 (Y_{t-1} - Y_{t-2}) + k_2 (Y_{t-2} - Y_{t-3}) \, , \qquad k_1 + k_2 = k \, , \tag{7.6}$$

$$I_t'' = A_0 (1+g)^t \, . \tag{7.7}$$

After the usual substitutions we obtain the third-order equation

$$Y_t - (b_1 + k_1) Y_{t-1} - (k_2 + b_2 - k_1) Y_{t-2} + k_2 Y_{t-3} = A_0 (1+g)^t \, . \tag{7.8}$$

As a particular solution, let us try $\overline{Y}_t = Y_0 (1+g)^t$, where Y_0 is an undetermined constant. Substituting in (7.8) and performing the usual manipulations — the details are left as an exercise — we obtain

$$\overline{Y}_t = \frac{A_0 (1+g)^3}{(1+g)^3 - (b_1 + k_1)(1+g)^2 - (k_2 + b_2 - k_1)(1+g) + k_2} (1+g)^t \, . \tag{7.9}$$

We assume that the denominator in (7.9) is positive, so that the particular solution is economically meaningful and can be interpreted, as usual, as the equilibrium trend of national income. The characteristic equation of the homogeneous part of (7.8) is

$$\lambda^3 - (b_1 + k_1)\lambda^2 - (k_2 + b_2 - k_1)\lambda + k_2 = 0 . \qquad (7.10)$$

Before examining this equation, let us show that k_2 is presumably greater than 1. First of all, as Hicks points out, it is very likely that the greatest part of induced investment is concentrated not in the period immediately following the variation in income, but in the farthest periods. In our case the implication is that k_2 is greater than k_1. Now, empirical data allow us to assume that the value of the overall acceleration coefficient k is not smaller than 2. From $k_1 + k_2 = k \geqslant 2$ and from $k_2 > k_1$ it follows that $k_2 > 1$.

Now, if $k_2 > 1$, the deviations of national income from the trend, whatever their nature, are certainly unstable. To show this there is no need to apply the stability conditions to eq. (7.10), since we can use the well-known fact that in any n-th-degree algebraic equation (written in such a way that the coefficient of the term of highest power is unity) *the product of the roots equals* $(-1)^n$ *times the constant term.* In our case we have

$$\lambda_1 \lambda_2 \lambda_3 = -k_2 , \qquad \text{in the case of three real roots;}$$

$$\lambda_1 r^2 = -k_2 , \qquad \text{in the case of one real root and a pair of complex conjugate roots with modulus } r \;\text{*}.$$

If we consider only absolute values, it is obvious that at least one root must be in absolute value greater than 1 since $k_2 > 1$. In other words, $k_2 > 1$ is a sufficient (although *not* a necessary) *in*stability condition.

Once we have proved that the movement is unstable, the nature of the movement (monotonic, oscillatory, etc.) is of secondary importance, since the presence of the limits will give rise in any case to a constant-amplitude oscillation (in relative terms), as we have seen in the second-order model. However, we can say that two cases are possible:

(1) Three real roots. Since the succession of the coefficients in eq. (7.10) is + − − +, two roots will be positive and one negative (monotonic movement plus an improper oscillation).

(2) One real root and two complex conjugate roots. Since the product of

---

 * If $\alpha \pm i\theta$ is a pair of complex conjugate numbers, then $(\alpha + i\theta)(\alpha - i\theta) = \alpha^2 + \theta^2$ as $i^2 = -1$. Since the modulus or absolute value of a complex number $\alpha + i\theta$ or $\alpha - i\theta$ is defined as $r = +(\alpha^2 + \theta^2)^{1/2}$, the statement in the text follows.

the roots is $-k_2 < 0$, and since $r^2 > 0$, it follows that the real root must be negative (an improper oscillation plus a proper oscillation).

Exercises

1. Check the instability of the model (given that $k \geqslant 2$), applying conditions (6.8) of Part I, ch. 6. (*Hint*: drop the second inequality; the fourth inequality is certainly not satisfied if $k \geqslant 2$.)

2. Examine the deviations of national income from the trend given the following data: $k_1 = 0.8$, $k_2 = 4$, $b_1 = 0.3$, $b_2 = 0.6$.

Calculation. Such deviations are given by the solution of the homogeneous equation

$$Y_t - 1.1 Y_{t-1} - 3.8 Y_{t-2} + 4 Y_{t-3} = 0 ,$$

whose characteristic equation is

$$\lambda^3 - 1.1 \lambda^2 - 3.8 \lambda + 4 . \tag{7.11}$$

A root is 2, as the student may check by straightforward substitution in (7.11). As we know from elementary algebra, eq. (7.11) may be divided by $\lambda - 2$, with remainder zero. We obtain

$$\lambda^3 - 1.1 \lambda^2 - 3.8 \lambda + 4 = (\lambda - 2)(\lambda^2 + 0.9 \lambda - 2) = 0 ,$$

and so the remaining two roots of (7.11) are given by the solution of

$$\lambda^2 - 0.9 \lambda - 2 = 0 ,$$

whose roots are

$$\frac{-0.9 \pm \sqrt{8.81}}{2} \simeq \begin{cases} 1.034 , \\ -1.934 . \end{cases}$$

The general solution for the deviations is then

$$Y_t = A_1 2^t + A_2 (1.034)^t + A_3 (-1.934)^t , \tag{7.12}$$

where A_1, A_2, A_3 are arbitrary constants. The movement is divergent, with an explosive monotonic component (first two terms in the right-hand side of (7.12)) on which an improper oscillation of increasing amplitude is superimposed.

3. Same problem as in exercise 2, but with the following data: $k_1 = 1.2$, $k_2 = 1.8$, $b_1 = 0.2$, $b_2 = 0$. (*Hint*: a root of the characteristic equation is -1.)

§2. Expectations and inventory cycles (Metzler)

In the inventory cycle model that we examined in Part I, ch. 5, §3, expectations were of the 'naïve' kind, i.e. expected sales for period t were equal to realized sales in period $(t-1)$. A more realistic assumption is that expected sales are related to realized sales according to the equation

$$U_t = C_{t-1} + \rho(C_{t-1} - C_{t-2}) = bY_{t-1} + \rho(bY_{t-1} - bY_{t-2}), \quad (7.13)$$

where U_t indicates expected sales for period t, C_{t-1} and C_{t-2} are consumption demand (i.e. realized sales) in periods $t-1$ and $t-2$, and ρ is an expectation coefficient. If $\rho > 0$, sales are expected to continue moving in the same direction as before ('extrapolative' expectations), whereas if $\rho < 0$ they are expected to reverse their movement [*]. We assume that $\rho > 0$.

The other characteristics of the model are the same as before (see Part I, ch. 5, §3). Thus the desired level of inventories is

$$\hat{Q}_t = kU_t = kbY_{t-1} + k\rho(bY_{t-1} - bY_{t-2}) = kb(1+\rho)Y_{t-1} - bk\rho Y_{t-2},$$

and so investment in inventories is

$$\hat{Q}_t - Q_{t-1} = kb(1+\rho)Y_{t-1} - bk\rho Y_{t-2} - Q_{t-1}, \quad (7.14)$$

where Q_{t-1} is the existing level of inventories; it is equal to the level of inventories planned for period $t-1$ minus the unintentional variation due to the difference in period $t-1$, if any, between realized sales and expected sales:

---

[*] We have already met this type of expectations in the model of Part I, ch. 5, §4. Chronologically, Metzler's paper comes first.

$$Q_{t-1} = [kb(1+\rho)Y_{t-2} - bk\rho Y_{t-3}] - \{bY_{t-1} - [b(1+\rho)Y_{t-2} - b\rho Y_{t-3}]\}$$

$$= -bY_{t-1} + b(1+k)(1+\rho)Y_{t-2} - (1+k)b\rho Y_{t-3} . \tag{7.15}$$

Substitution in (7.14) yields

$$\hat{Q}_t - Q_{t-1} = b[k(1+\rho)+1]Y_{t-1} - b[k\rho + (1+k)(1+\rho)]Y_{t-2} + (1+k)b\rho Y_{t-3} . \tag{7.16}$$

National income (product) is

$$Y_t = U_t + (\hat{Q}_t - Q_{t-1}) + I_0 , \tag{7.17}$$

where I_0 is autonomous expenditure.

Substituting (7.13) and (7.16) in (7.17) we obtain

$$Y_t - b[(1+k)(1+\rho)+1]Y_{t-1} + b(1+k)(1+2\rho)Y_{t-2} - (1+k)b\rho Y_{t-3} = I_0 . \tag{7.18}$$

A particular solution is obtained trying $\overline{Y}_t$ = constant, which gives

$$\overline{Y}_t = \frac{I_0}{1-b} , \tag{7.19}$$

which is the stationary equilibrium, given by the multiplier applied to the constant exogenous expenditure.

The homogeneous equation corresponding to the non-homogeneous equation (7.18) has the characteristic equation

$$\lambda^3 - b[(1+k)(1+\rho)+1]\lambda^2 + b(1+k)(1+2\rho)\lambda - (1+k)b\rho = 0 . \tag{7.20}$$

Let us apply the stability conditions (6.8) of Part I, ch. 6, dropping the second inequality. We have

$$1 - b[(1+k)(1+\rho)+1] + b(1+k)(1+2\rho) - (1+k)b\rho \qquad > 0 ,$$

$$1 + b[(1+k)(1+\rho)+1] + b(1+k)(1+2\rho) + (1+k)\rho \qquad > 0 ,$$

$$3 - b[(1+k)(1+\rho)+1] - b(1+k)(1+2\rho) + 3(1+k)b\rho \qquad > 0 ,$$

$$-(1+k)^2 b^2 \rho^2 + b^2(1+k)\rho[(1+k)(1+\rho)+1] - b(1+k)(1+2\rho) + 1 > 0 .$$

The first and second inequalities are always satisfied, since the propensity to consume is smaller than unity and the expectation coefficient is positive. The relevant inequalities are then the third and the fourth, which, after simple manipulation, may be written as

$$3 - b(2k+3) > 0 ,$$

$$(1+k)(2+k)\rho b^2 - (1+k)(1+2\rho)b + 1 > 0 . \tag{7.21}$$

From inequalities (7.21) we can see that, if $\rho = 0$, the stability condition becomes $b < 1/(1+k)$ ★, the same as the condition holding in the simplified model expounded in Part I, ch. 5, § 3. If, instead, $\rho = 1$, the condition becomes more restrictive, as we can see from fig. 7.1 ★★. Given ρ, the stable (unstable) regions are those below (above) the appropriate curve. When $\rho = 1$ the stable region is much smaller, and such that the economic system is not likely to be stable. In fact, even in the extreme case in which $k = 0$ (no inventory accelerator), the propensity to consume must be smaller than 0.5 in order

---

★ From the first inequality in (7.21) we have $b < 3/(2k + 3)$, which gives $b < 1/(1 + \frac{2}{3}k)$. From the second we have, for $\rho = 0$, $b < 1/(1 + k)$. Now,

$$\frac{1}{1 + k} < \frac{1}{1 + \frac{2}{3}k}$$

for any positive k, and so the crucial inequality is $b < 1/(1 + k)$.

★★ Formally the stable region is determined by $b < b_1$, where b_1 is the smaller root of the equation $(1+k)(2+k)b^2 - 3(1+k)b + 1 = 0$.

Proof. For $\rho = 1$, inequalities (7.21) become

$$3 - b(2k+3) > 0 ,$$

$$(1+k)(2+k)b^2 - 3(1+k)b + 1 > 0 . \tag{7.22}$$

The first inequality is satisfied for $b < 3/(2k+3)$. The second one is satisfied for $b < b_1$ and for $b > b_2$, where b_1, b_2 are the roots of the equation

$$(1+k)(2+k)b^2 - 3(1+k)b + 1 = 0 .$$

(It can easily be checked that such roots are real, distinct and both positive.) Inequalities (7.22) are then satisfied in the following intervals

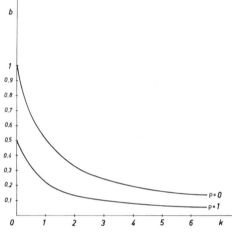

Fig. 7.1.

that the system be stable. We may then conclude, with Metzler, that either (1) in real life the expectation coefficient is much smaller than unity, or (2) the economic system is inherently unstable but is kept from exploding by the action of various stabilizers (such as the full employment limit, credit restrictions, etc.).

$$b < \frac{3}{2k+3},$$

$$b < b_1,$$

$$b > b_2.$$

(7.23)

Consider now the parabola $f(b) = (1+k)(2+k)b^2 - 3(1+k)b + 1$. From what we have said above it follows that $f(b) > 0$ for $b < b_1$ and for $b > b_2$ and $f(b) < 0$ for $b_1 < b < b_2$. Substituting in $f(b)$ the value $b^* = 3/(2k+3)$, we see that $f(b^*)$ takes on a negative value, and so b^* lies between b_1 and b_2. The interval $b > b_2$ must then be discarded, and, since the inequality $b < 3/(2k+3)$ is absorbed by the more stringent inequality $b < b_1$, the latter is the crucial stability condition. Substituting $b = 1/(1+k)$ in $f(b)$, we see that $f(b) < 0$, and so $b_1 < 1/(1+k) < b_2$. This proves that the inequality $b < b_1$ is more stringent than the inequality $b < 1/(1+k)$.

Exercises

1. The following data are given: $b = 0.8$, $k = 1$, $\rho = 1$, $I_0 = 100$, $Y_0 = 400$, $Y_1 = 420$, $Y_2 = 450$. Determine the behaviour of income over time.

Calculation. With the given data, eq. (7.18) of the text becomes

$$Y_t - 4Y_{t-1} + 4.8\,Y_{t-2} - 1.6\,Y_{t-3} = 100 . \qquad (7.24)$$

A particular solution is obtained trying $\overline{Y}_t =$ constant, which gives

$$\overline{Y}_t = 500 .$$

The characteristic equation of the reduced equation is

$$\lambda^3 - 4\lambda^2 + 4.8\lambda - 1.6 = 0 . \qquad (7.25)$$

A root is 2, as can be checked by straightforward substitution. Equation (7.25) may then be divided by $\lambda - 2$, and so

$$\lambda^3 - 4\lambda^2 + 4.8\lambda - 1.6 = (\lambda - 2)(\lambda^2 - 2\lambda + 0.8) = 0 .$$

Thus the remaining two roots are given by the solution of the equation

$$\lambda^2 - 2\lambda + 0.8 = 0 ,$$

which yields the values 1.447 and 0.553. The general solution of eq. (7.24) is then

$$Y_t = A_1 2^t + A_2 (1.447)^t + A_3 (0.553)^t + 500 . \qquad (7.26)$$

The result is an explosive monotonic movement.

From (7.26) we have

$$Y_0 = A_1 2^0 + A_2 (1.447)^0 + A_3 (0.553)^0 + 500 ,$$

$$Y_1 = A_1 2^1 + A_2 (1.447)^1 + A_3 (0.553)^1 + 500 ,$$

$$Y_2 = A_1 2^2 + A_2 (1.447)^2 + A_3 (0.553)^2 + 500 ,$$

from which, given the initial conditions, we obtain the system

$$A_1 + A_2 + A_3 = -100,$$

$$2A_1 + 1.447A_2 + 0.553A_3 = -80,$$

$$4A_1 + 2.093809A_2 + 0.305809A_3 = -50,$$

whose solution (which is left as an exercise) determines the values of the arbitrary constants A_1, A_2, A_3.

2. Same problem as in exercise 1, but with the following data: $b = 0.9$, $k = 0.5$, $\rho = 1$, $I_0 = 100$, $Y_0 = 900$, $Y_1 = 910$, $Y_2 = 920$. (*Hint*: a root of the characteristic equation is 1.5.)

References

Allen, R.G.D., 1959, *Mathematical Economics*, ch. 7, §§7.7, 7.9.
Coppock, D.J., 1965, The Post-War Short Cycle in the U.S.A.
Hicks, J.R., 1950, *A Contribution to the Theory of the Trade Cycle*.
Metzler, L.A., 1941, The Nature and Stability of Inventory Cycles, pp. 126–9.

8

Simultaneous Systems

Two (or more) difference equations in which two (or more) unknown functions are involved, form a simultaneous system. For the system to be solvable, the number of equations must be equal to the number of unknowns, provided that the equations are independent and consistent.

The simplest type of system is the following first-order system in 'normal' form *

$$y_{t+1} = a_{11}y_t + a_{12}z_t + g_1(t),$$

$$z_{t+1} = a_{21}y_t + a_{22}z_t + g_2(t),$$

(8.1)

where the coefficients a_{ij} are given constants and $g_1(t), g_2(t)$ are known functions. System (8.1) is a non-homogeneous system; the corresponding homogeneous system is

---

* The system is first-order because only two adjacent points of time appear ($t + 1$ and t; or t and $t - 1$) and is called 'normal' because in each equation only one unknown function in turn appears evaluated at time $t + 1$. It must be noted that the *order* of a system is equal to the *degree* of its characteristic equation (see below). Therefore, the expression 'first-order system' must be understood only in the sense defined above, and not as indicating the order of the system (actually the order of system (8.1) is 2).

$$y_{t+1} = a_{11}y_t + a_{12}z_t \, ,$$

$$z_{t+1} = a_{21}y_t + a_{22}z_t \, . \tag{8.2}$$

Let us begin with (8.2) since, as in single equations, the general solution of (8.1) is obtained adding a particular solution of (8.1) to the general solution of (8.2) (the proof can be given by straightforward substitution, and is left as an exercise).

A method of solving (8.2) consists of reducing it to a single equation in which only one unknown function appears; this reduction is always possible by suitable transformations. From the first equation of system (8.2) we obtain, provided that $a_{12} \neq 0$ *,

$$z_t = \frac{1}{a_{12}} y_{t+1} - \frac{a_{11}}{a_{12}} y_t \, , \tag{8.3}$$

whence

$$z_{t+1} = \frac{1}{a_{12}} y_{t+2} - \frac{a_{11}}{a_{12}} y_{t+1} \, . \tag{8.4}$$

Substituting (8.3) and (8.4) in the second equation of system (8.2), we have

$$\frac{1}{a_{12}} y_{t+2} - \frac{a_{11}}{a_{12}} y_{t+1} = a_{21}y_t + \frac{a_{22}}{a_{12}} y_{t+1} - \frac{a_{11}a_{22}}{a_{12}} y_t \, .$$

Multiplying both members by a_{12} and rearranging terms, we have

$$y_{t+2} - (a_{11} + a_{22})y_{t+1} - (a_{12}a_{21} - a_{11}a_{22})y_t = 0 \, , \tag{8.5}$$

i.e.

$$y_t - (a_{11} + a_{22})y_{t-1} - (a_{12}a_{21} - a_{11}a_{22})y_{t-2} = 0 \, . \tag{8.6}$$

Thus we have a second-order difference equation in which only one unknown function, y_t, appears. We solve it in the usual way, and to obtain z_t we have only to substitute in (8.3). Suppose, for example, that the roots of the

---

* If $a_{12} = 0$, then we use the second equation to isolate y_t etc. (the steps are the same as those expounded in the text for z_t; note that, when $a_{12} = 0$, a_{21} must be different from zero, since, if also $a_{21} = 0$, we would no more have a simultaneous system, but two separate equations with no interdependency). Another method, when either a_{12} or a_{21} is zero, is to solve separately the equation where only one unknown function appears and to substitute the result in the other equation.

characteristic equation of (8.6) are real and distinct. Then the general solution of (8.6) is, as we know,

$$y_t = A_1\lambda_1^t + A_2\lambda_2^t,$$ (8.7)

where A_1, A_2 are arbitrary constants. Substituting from (8.7) in (8.3) we have

$$z_t = \frac{A_1\lambda_1^{t+1} + A_2\lambda_2^{t+1}}{a_{12}} - \frac{a_{11}(A_1\lambda_1^t + A_2\lambda_2^t)}{a_{12}}.$$

Since $\lambda_1^{t+1} = \lambda_1\lambda_1^t, \lambda_2^{t+1} = \lambda_2\lambda_2^t$, we can collect terms and obtain

$$z_t = \frac{\lambda_1 - a_{11}}{a_{12}} A_1\lambda_1^t + \frac{\lambda_2 - a_{11}}{a_{12}} A_2\lambda_2^t.$$ (8.8)

Eqs. (8.7) and (8.8) are the general solution of system (8.2); of course, if the roots of the characteristic equation of (8.6) are real and equal or are complex, we shall proceed as expounded in Part I, ch. 4 to obtain y_t, and then substitute in (8.3) to obtain z_t. If such roots are real and equal, the solution for y_t is, as we know,

$$y_t = (A_1 + A_2 t)\lambda^{*t}.$$ (8.9)

Substituting in (8.3) we have

$$z_t = \frac{1}{a_{12}} [A_1 + A_2(t+1)]\lambda^{*t+1} - \frac{a_{11}}{a_{12}}(A_1 + A_2 t)\lambda^{*t}$$

$$= \lambda^{*t} \left[\frac{\lambda^*}{a_{12}}(A_1 + A_2 + A_2 t) - \frac{a_{11}}{a_{12}}(A_1 + A_2 t) \right];$$

therefore

$$z_t = \left[\frac{(\lambda^* - a_{11})A_1 + \lambda^* A_2}{a_{12}} + \frac{\lambda^* - a_{11}}{a_{12}} A_2 t \right] \lambda^{*t}.$$ (8.10)

Making use of the fact that $\lambda^* = \frac{1}{2}(a_{11} + a_{22})$, eq. (8.10) may also be written as

$$z_t = \left[\frac{(a_{22} - a_{11})A_1 + (a_{11} + a_{22})A_2}{2a_{12}} + \frac{a_{22} - a_{11}}{2a_{12}} A_2 t \right] \lambda^{*t} . \qquad (8.10')$$

If, finally, the roots of the characteristic equation of (8.6) are complex, then, as we know,

$$y_t = r^t(A_1 \cos \omega t + A_2 \sin \omega t) . \qquad (8.11)$$

Substituting in (8.3) we have

$$z_t = \frac{r^{t+1}[A_1 \cos(\omega t + \omega) + A_2 \sin(\omega t + \omega)] - a_{11} r^t(A_1 \cos \omega t + A_2 \sin \omega t)}{a_{12}}$$

$$= r^t \left\{ \frac{r[A_1(\cos \omega t \cos \omega - \sin \omega t \sin \omega) + A_2(\sin \omega t \cos \omega + \cos \omega t \sin \omega)]}{a_{12}} \right.$$

$$\left. - \frac{a_{11}(A_1 \cos \omega t + A_2 \sin \omega t)}{a_{12}} \right\} ,$$

which gives

$$z_t = r^t \left(\frac{A_1 r \cos \omega + A_2 r \sin \omega - a_{11} A_1}{a_{12}} \cos \omega t \right.$$

$$\left. + \frac{A_2 r \cos \omega - A_1 r \sin \omega - a_{11} A_2}{a_{12}} \sin \omega t \right) . \qquad (8.12)$$

The method that we have expounded is undoubtedly rather simple and yields the required solution. There is, however, another method, which, although it may seem more complicated, has the advantage of being more *direct*, in the sense that it gives simultaneously the unknown functions y_t and z_t, without any need to reduce the system to a single equation in one unknown function. Such a method, moreover, can easily be generalized. It consists in trying directly as a solution — by analogy with single equations — the functions $y_t = \alpha_1 \lambda^t$, $z_t = \alpha_2 \lambda^t$, where α_1, α_2 are constants not both zero. Substituting in (8.2) we have

$$\alpha_1 \lambda^{t+1} = a_{11} \alpha_1 \lambda^t + a_{12} \alpha_2 \lambda^t ,$$

$$\alpha_2 \lambda^{t+1} = a_{21} \alpha_1 \lambda^t + a_{22} \alpha_2 \lambda^t ,$$

from which

$$\lambda^t [(a_{11} - \lambda)\alpha_1 + a_{12}\alpha_2] = 0 ,$$

$$\lambda^t [a_{21}\alpha_1 + (a_{22} - \lambda)\alpha_2] = 0 .$$

(8.13)

The functions that we have tried will be a solution of system (8.2) if, and only if, system (8.13) is satisfied for any t, i.e. (apart from the trivial case $\lambda = 0$) if, and only if,

$$(a_{11} - \lambda)\alpha_1 + a_{12}\alpha_2 = 0 ,$$

$$a_{21}\alpha_1 + (a_{22} - \lambda)\alpha_2 = 0 .$$

(8.14)

System (8.14) has the trivial solution $\alpha_1 = \alpha_2 = 0$, but we have excluded it from the beginning for obvious reasons. From elementary algebra we know that the necessary and sufficient condition for a linear and homogeneous system to have non-trivial solutions, in addition to the trivial one, is that the determinant of the system be zero. In our case, then, it must be ★

$$\begin{vmatrix} a_{11} - \lambda & a_{12} \\ a_{21} & a_{22} - \lambda \end{vmatrix} = 0 .$$

(8.15)

Expanding the determinant we have

$$(a_{11} - \lambda)(a_{22} - \lambda) - a_{12}a_{21} = \lambda^2 - (a_{11} + a_{22})\lambda + (a_{11}a_{22} - a_{12}a_{21}) = 0 .$$

(8.15′)

The determinantal equation (8.15) and its expanded form (8.15′) are called the characteristic equation of the system of difference equations (8.2). Let us

★ The student knowing some matrix algebra will recognize in (8.15) − as in (8.32) and in (8.33) below − the characteristic equation, $|A - \lambda I| = 0$, of the matrix $A \equiv [a_{ij}]$ whose elements are the coefficients of the difference system, and in $[\alpha_1^{(i)}, \alpha_2^{(i)}, ..., \alpha_n^{(i)}]$ below the characteristic vector associated with the characteristic root λ_i. The student not knowing sufficient matrix algebra can ignore this footnote and go on with the text. Actually, the use of matrix algebra would have allowed a more compact treatment, but without its use nothing is lost as far as the understanding of the 'direct' method of solution of systems of difference equations is concerned.

note that such an equation is the same as the characteristic equation of (8.6) above, and this is correct, since the λ values must obviously be the same whichever method is followed to solve the system of difference equations.

From the solution of (8.15') we obtain two values of λ; let us assume for the moment that they are real and distinct. Thus the determinant of system (8.14) equals zero for $\lambda = \lambda_1$ and for $\lambda = \lambda_2$; correspondingly, we shall have two solutions of that system. Let us call $[\alpha_1^{(1)}, \alpha_2^{(1)}]$ the solution that we obtain putting $\lambda = \lambda_1$ in (8.14) and $[\alpha_1^{(2)}, \alpha_2^{(2)}]$ the solution that we obtain putting $\lambda = \lambda_2$. For $\lambda = \lambda_1$ we have

$$(a_{11} - \lambda_1)\alpha_1^{(1)} + a_{12}\alpha_2^{(1)} = 0 ,$$

$$a_{21}\alpha_1^{(1)} + (a_{22} - \lambda_1)\alpha_2^{(1)} = 0 . \tag{8.14'}$$

From elementary algebra we know that, since the determinant of the system is zero, we can fix arbitrarily [*] the value of one of the unknowns and then determine the value of the other (in other words, only the ratio between the two unknowns is determined). We choose to fix $\alpha_1^{(1)} = 1$ whence, from the first equation of (8.14'),

$$\alpha_2^{(1)} = \frac{\lambda_1 - a_{11}}{a_{12}} .$$

Note that, from the second equation, $\alpha_2^{(1)} = a_{21}/(\lambda_1 - a_{22})$. The two values, however, are equal since λ_1 is a root of the characteristic equation, i.e.

$$(a_{11} - \lambda_1)(a_{22} - \lambda_1) - a_{12}a_{21} = 0 ,$$

so that

$$\frac{\lambda_1 - a_{11}}{a_{12}} = \frac{a_{21}}{\lambda_1 - a_{22}} .$$

In a similar way for $\lambda = \lambda_2$ we fix $\alpha_1^{(2)} = 1$ and obtain

---

[*] Such arbitrariness does not give any trouble in the solution of system (8.2), since it combines in a multiplicative way with the arbitrary constants A_1, A_2 which appear in the general solution. Thus we have chosen $\alpha_1^{(1)} = 1$ (and similarly we shall choose $\alpha_1^{(2)} = 1$) in order that the solution of system (8.2) that we shall obtain be immediately comparable, without any need of further manipulations, with (8.7) and (8.8) above.

$$\alpha_2^{(2)} = \frac{\lambda_2 - a_{11}}{a_{12}} = \frac{a_{21}}{\lambda_2 - a_{22}} .$$

Thus we have reached the result that $y_{1t} = \alpha_1^{(1)}\lambda_1^t$, $z_{1t} = \alpha_2^{(1)}\lambda_1^t$ is a solution of system (8.2) and $y_{2t} = \alpha_1^{(2)}\lambda_2^t$, $z_{2t} = \alpha_2^{(2)}\lambda_2^t$ is another solution. We can then combine them linearly with two arbitrary constants A_1, A_2 and obtain the general solution of system (8.2) *:

$$y_t = A_1\alpha_1^{(1)}\lambda_1^t + A_2\alpha_1^{(2)}\lambda_2^t , \tag{8.16}$$

$$z_t = A_1\alpha_2^{(1)}\lambda_1^t + A_2\alpha_2^{(2)}\lambda_2^t , \tag{8.17}$$

i.e., with the values of $\alpha_i^{(j)}$, $i, j, = 1, 2$, found above,

$$y_t = A_1\lambda_1^t + A_2\lambda_2^t , \tag{8.18}$$

$$z_t = A_1 \frac{\lambda_1 - a_{11}}{a_{12}} \lambda_1^t + A_2 \frac{\lambda_2 - a_{11}}{a_{12}} \lambda_2^t , \tag{8.19}$$

which are the same as (8.7) and (8.8) above.

The solution of the system may also be written in the equivalent form, which sometimes appears in the literature,

$$y_t = A_1\lambda_1^t + A_2\lambda_2^t ,$$
$$z_t = A_1'\lambda_1^t + A_2'\lambda_2^t , \tag{8.20}$$

where the arbitrary constants A_1, A_2, A_1', A_2' are connected by the relations

$$\frac{A_1'}{A_1} = \frac{\lambda_1 - a_{11}}{a_{12}} = \frac{a_{21}}{\lambda_1 - a_{22}} , \qquad \frac{A_2'}{A_2} = \frac{\lambda_2 - a_{11}}{a_{12}} = \frac{a_{21}}{\lambda_2 - a_{22}} . \tag{8.21}$$

Since the ratios A_1'/A_1, A_2'/A_2 are uniquely determined in terms of the λ's and of the coefficients of the system, the independent arbitrary constants are actually only two.

---

* The student may check by direct substitution that (8.18) and (8.19) indeed satisfy system (8.2). The number of arbitrary constants appearing in the general solution of this system is two, since the system is reducible to a second-order equation, as we have seen above.

If the characteristic equation has two real and equal roots, $\lambda_1 = \lambda_2 = \lambda^*$, let us try

$$y_t = (A_1 + A_2 t)\lambda^{*t} ,$$
$$z_t = (A_1' + A_2' t)\lambda^{*t} ,$$

(8.22)

where the arbitrary constants A_1, A_2, A_1', A_2' are related in some way. Substituting in system (8.2) we have

$$[A_1 + A_2(t+1)]\lambda^{*t+1} = a_{11}(A_1 + A_2 t)\lambda^{*t} + a_{12}(A_1' + A_2' t)\lambda^{*t} ,$$
$$[A_1' + A_2'(t+1)]\lambda^{*t+1} = a_{21}(A_1 + A_2 t)\lambda^{*t} + a_{22}(A_1' + A_2' t)\lambda^{*t} .$$

(8.23)

Dividing through by $\lambda^{*t} \neq 0$ and rearranging terms we obtain

$$[A_2(\lambda^* - a_{11}) - a_{12}A_2']t + [(\lambda^* - a_{11})A_1 + A_2\lambda^* - a_{12}A_1'] = 0 ,$$
$$[(\lambda^* - a_{22})A_2' - a_{21}A_2]t + [(\lambda^* - a_{22})A_1' - a_{21}A_1 + A_2'\lambda^*] = 0 .$$

(8.24)

Eqs. (8.24) are identically satisfied if, and only if, the expressions in square brackets are all zero, i.e.

$$A_2(\lambda^* - a_{11}) - a_{12}A_2' \qquad = 0 ,$$

(8.25)

$$(\lambda^* - a_{11})A_1 + A_2\lambda^* - a_{12}A_1' = 0 ,$$

(8.26)

$$(\lambda^* - a_{22})A_2' - a_{21}A_2 \qquad = 0 ,$$

(8.27)

$$(\lambda^* - a_{22})A_1' - a_{21}A_1 + A_2'\lambda^* = 0 ,$$

(8.28)

whence

$$A_2' = \frac{\lambda^* - a_{11}}{a_{12}} A_2 ,$$

(8.25a)

$$A_1' = \frac{(\lambda^* - a_{11})A_1 + \lambda^* A_2}{a_{12}} ,$$

(8.26a)

$$A_2' = \frac{a_{21}}{\lambda^* - a_{22}} A_2 ,$$

(8.27a)

$$A_1' = \frac{a_{21}}{\lambda^* - a_{22}} A_1 - \frac{\lambda^*}{\lambda^* - a_{22}} A_2' .$$ (8.28a)

Since λ^* is a root of the characteristic equation, $(\lambda^* - a_{11})/a_{12} = a_{21}/(\lambda^* - a_{22})$ and so (8.25a) and (8.27a) coincide. Using (8.25a) and the fact that $(\lambda^* - a_{11})/a_{12} = a_{21}/(\lambda^* - a_{22})$, (8.28a) can be written as

$$A_1' = \frac{\lambda^* - a_{11}}{a_{12}} A_1 - \frac{\lambda^*(\lambda^* - a_{11})}{a_{12}(\lambda^* - a_{22})} A_2 ,$$ (8.28b)

which coincides with (8.26a) if, and only if, $-(\lambda^* - a_{11}) = \lambda^* - a_{22}$, i.e. if, and only if, $\lambda^* = \frac{1}{2}(a_{11} + a_{22})$, which is indeed true if, and only if, λ^* is a double root of the characteristic eq. (8.15'). Thus (8.22) is indeed the (general) solution of the system; using (8.26a) and (8.25a) to express A_1', A_2' in terms of A_1, A_2, it can be seen that eqs. (8.22) coincide with (8.9) and (8.10) above.

If the roots of the characteristic equation are complex, $\lambda_1, \lambda_2 = \alpha \pm i\theta$, then the solution can at first be written (the procedure is the same as for the case of distinct real roots) as

$$y_t = B_1(\alpha + i\theta)^t + B_2(\alpha - i\theta)^t ,$$

$$z_t = \frac{(\alpha + i\theta) - a_{11}}{a_{12}} B_1(\alpha + i\theta)^t + \frac{(\alpha - i\theta) - a_{11}}{a_{12}} B_2(\alpha - i\theta)^t$$ (8.29)

$$= \frac{B_1(\alpha + i\theta)^{t+1} + B_2(\alpha - i\theta)^{t+1}}{a_{12}} - \frac{a_{11}[B_1(\alpha + i\theta)^t + B_2(\alpha - i\theta)^t]}{a_{12}} ,$$

where B_1, B_2 are arbitrary complex conjugate constants. Using the transformations on complex numbers expounded in Part I, ch. 4, we obtain

$$B_1(\alpha + i\theta)^t + B_2(\alpha - i\theta)^t = r^t(A_1 \cos \omega t + A_2 \sin \omega t) ,$$

$$B_1(\alpha + i\theta)^{t+1} + B_2(\alpha - i\theta)^{t+1} = r^{t+1}[A_1 \cos(\omega t + \omega) + A_2 \sin(\omega t + \omega)]$$ (8.30)

$$= r^{t+1}[(A_1 \cos \omega + A_2 \sin \omega) \cos \omega t$$

$$+ (A_2 \cos \omega - A_1 \sin \omega) \sin \omega t] ,$$

where $A_1 \equiv (B_1 + B_2), A_2 \equiv (B_1 - B_2)i$ are arbitrary real constants and r, ω are related to α, θ in the usual way. Substituting (8.30) in eqs. (8.29) and collecting terms where necessary, we obtain

$$y_t = r^t(A_1 \cos \omega t + A_2 \sin \omega t),$$

$$z_t = r^t \left(\frac{A_1 r \cos \omega + A_2 r \sin \omega - a_{11}A_1}{a_{12}} \cos \omega t \right. \tag{8.31}$$

$$\left. + \frac{A_2 r \cos \omega - A_1 r \sin \omega - a_{11}A_2}{a_{12}} \sin \omega t \right),$$

which coincide with (8.11) and (8.12) above.

This completes the exposition of the 'direct' method of solution. As we said above, this method can easily be generalized to first-order systems of type (8.2) having any number of equations. Considering, for example, the system

$$y_{t+1} = a_{11}y_t + a_{12}z_t + a_{13}w_t,$$

$$z_{t+1} = a_{21}y_t + a_{22}z_t + a_{23}w_t,$$

$$w_{t+1} = a_{31}y_t + a_{32}z_t + a_{33}w_t,$$

we can write immediately its characteristic equation

$$D(\lambda) = \begin{vmatrix} a_{11}-\lambda & a_{12} & a_{13} \\ a_{21} & a_{22}-\lambda & a_{23} \\ a_{31} & a_{32} & a_{33}-\lambda \end{vmatrix} = 0. \tag{8.32}$$

Expanding the determinant we have a third-degree algebraic equation in the unknown λ, whose solution will give three values $\lambda_1, \lambda_2, \lambda_3$. Since the stable or unstable behaviour over time of the solution depends exclusively on the roots $\lambda_1, \lambda_2, \lambda_3$, to analyse the stability of the system we can examine only the nature of such roots, without any need to compute the coefficients $\alpha_i^{(j)}$. For this purpose we can apply to the characteristic equation the stability conditions stated in Part I, ch. 6, which allow us to check whether the roots of a polynomial are in absolute value less than unity without finding them explicitly.

In general, the characteristic equation of a first-order system of type (8.2) with n equations [*] is

$$D(\lambda) = \begin{vmatrix} a_{11}-\lambda & a_{12} & \cdots & a_{1n} \\ a_{21} & a_{22}-\lambda & \cdots & a_{2n} \\ \cdots\cdots\cdots\cdots\cdots\cdots\cdots \\ a_{n1} & a_{n2} & \cdots & a_{nn}-\lambda \end{vmatrix} = 0 . \tag{8.33}$$

The application of the stability conditions recalled above requires that the determinant be expanded in order to obtain the explicit polynomial. Such expansion is rather laborious if n is great, so that it would be highly desirable to have stability conditions which can be applied directly to the coefficients a_{ij} of the system, *without having to expand the determinant*. Such conditions exist, and the most important are expounded below; let us note that in our list all conditions but the first are either sufficient (but not necessary) or necessary (but not sufficient), and this must be kept in mind when applying them to economic models.

In what follows, by 'stability conditions' we mean, as usual, 'conditions that the roots of the characteristic equation (8.33), be they real and/or complex, are less than unity in absolute value, or, which is the same thing, that these roots all lie within the unit circle in the complex plane [**].

---

[*] Of course, this system can also be reduced, by a procedure similar to that used in relation to the 2 × 2 system, to a single n-th order equation in one unknown function. Let us note that the converse is also true, i.e. a n-th order equation can always be transformed into a first-order system in normal form having n equations in n unknown functions. To do this, new variables $y_{1t}, y_{2t}, ..., y_{n-1,t}$ are defined such that $y_{t+1} = y_{1t}$, $y_{1t+1} = y_{2t}, ..., y_{n-2,t+1} = y_{n-1,t}$. Substituting in the given n-th order equation in y, a first-order equation in $y_{n-1,t+1}, y_{n-1,t}, ..., y_{1t}, y_t$ is obtained, which, together with the equations defining the new variables, forms a first-order system in normal form.

[**] Conditions I through III', although they might be (and actually have been by some authors) proved independently, are essentially applications of some corollaries of the theorems of Perron (cond. II), of Frobenius (cond. III') and of the extension of the latter to arbitrary non-negative matrices (conds. I and III); for proofs of such theorems and corollaries, see e.g. Gantmacher (1959). This is the line that we shall follow in the proofs below. Here is a sketch of proofs of the various conditions (for other proofs of some of them, see e.g. Baumol (1970), Fisher (1962), Solow (1952)). In what follows λ_M denotes the dominant root of eq. (8.33), i.e. the root whose absolute value is not smaller than the absolute value of any other root.

Conditions I follow from the theorem according to which a necessary and sufficient condition that the real number ρ be greater than the dominant root of a non-negative

I. Let $a_{ij} \geqslant 0$. Then necessary and sufficient stability conditions are that the following n inequalities

$$
1 - a_{11} > 0, \qquad
\begin{vmatrix}
1 - a_{11} & -a_{12} \\
-a_{21} & 1 - a_{22}
\end{vmatrix} > 0,
$$

$$
\begin{vmatrix}
1 - a_{11} & -a_{12} & -a_{13} \\
-a_{21} & 1 - a_{22} & -a_{23} \\
-a_{31} & -a_{32} & 1 - a_{33}
\end{vmatrix} > 0, ...,
\begin{vmatrix}
1 - a_{11} & -a_{12} & \cdots & -a_{1n} \\
-a_{21} & 1 - a_{22} & \cdots & -a_{2n} \\
\multicolumn{4}{c}{\dotfill} \\
-a_{n1} & -a_{n2} & \cdots & 1 - a_{nn}
\end{vmatrix} > 0
$$

matrix A is that all the leading principal minors of the matrix $[\rho I - A]$ be positive (Gantmacher (1959) pp. 85 and 88). Now, if we put $\rho = 1$, conditions I follow immediately.

Conditions III' and II follow from the fact that for indecomposable non-negative matrices (and so a fortiori for positive matrices), min $S_j \leqslant \lambda_M \leqslant$ max S_j, where the sign of equality to the left or right of λ_M holds only when min $S_j =$ max S_j (Gantmacher (1959) p. 76; he uses row sums, but the same property holds for column sums, since a matrix and its transpose have the same characteristic roots). It follows that max $S_j = 1$ is a sufficient condition that $\lambda_M < 1$, provided that min $S_j < 1$.

Conditions III follow from the fact that for arbitrary non-negative decomposable matrices, min $S_j \leqslant \lambda_M \leqslant$ max S_j, where the sign of equality to the left or right of λ_M may hold also if min $S_j \neq$ max S_j (Gantmacher (1959) p. 82), so that max $S_j = 1$ must be excluded in order to have a sufficient condition that $\lambda_M < 1$.

Note that from the above bounds for λ_M, it follows that a sufficient instability condition is that min $S_j > 1$, and this is condition IV.

Conditions V follow from the theorem (see e.g. McKenzie (1960)), according to which, if λ is any characteristic root of an arbitrary matrix $A \equiv [a_{ij}]$, then $|\lambda| \leqslant$ max$_j$ $\Sigma_{i=1}^n |a_{ij}|$.

To prove conditions VI and VII, it must be recalled that in the expansion of (8.33) the coefficient of λ^{n-1} is equal to $-\Sigma_{i=1}^n a_{ii}$ and the constant term is equal to $(-1)^n (\det A)$. Now, from elementary algebra, the coefficient of λ^{n-1} is equal to the sum of the roots multiplied by -1 and the constant term is equal to the product of the roots multiplied by $(-1)^n$. Thus we have $\Sigma a_{ii} = \Sigma \lambda_i$ and, taking absolute values, $|\Sigma a_{ii}| = |\Sigma \lambda_i|$. Now, $|\Sigma \lambda_i| \leqslant \Sigma |\lambda_i|$, and, if $|\lambda_i| < 1$, then $\Sigma |\lambda_i| < n$, so that $|\lambda_i| < 1$ implies (although it is not implied by) $|\Sigma a_{ii}| < n$, which is then a necessary (although not a sufficient) stability condition. We have also $\det A = \Pi_i \lambda_i$, and, taking absolute values, $|\det A| = |\Pi \lambda_i|$. Now, $|\Pi \lambda_i| = \Pi |\lambda_i|$ and, if $|\lambda_i| < 1$, then $\Pi |\lambda_i| < 1$, so that $|\lambda_i| < 1$ implies (although it is not implied by) $|\det A| < 1$, which is then a necessary (although not a sufficient) stability condition.

be all satisfied. In other words, the leading principal minors of the matrix $[I - A]$, where $A \equiv [a_{ij}]$ is the matrix of the coefficients of the difference system, must be all positive.

II. Let $a_{ij} > 0$ (the coefficients must be all positive). Form the n sums $S_j = \sum_{i=1}^{n} a_{ij}$, $j = 1, 2, ..., n$. Then a set of sufficient stability conditions is that no S_j is greater than 1 and at least one of them is smaller than 1.

III. Let $a_{ij} \geqslant 0$. Then a set of sufficient stability conditions is that all S_j (as defined in II) are smaller than 1.

III′. Let $a_{ij} \geqslant 0$ as in III, but in addition let the matrix of the coefficients of the difference system, $A \equiv [a_{ij}]$, be indecomposable ★. Then a set of sufficient stability conditions is the same as in II above. Actually condition III′ absorbs condition II, since a positive matrix is *a fortiori* indecomposable, but we have stated them separately for greater clarity.

IV. Let $a_{ij} \geqslant 0$. Then a set of sufficient *in*stability conditions is that all S_j (as defined in II) are greater than 1.

V. Let a_{ij} be arbitrary. Form the n sums $|S_j| = \sum_{i=1}^{n} |a_{ij}|$, $j = 1, 2, ..., n$. Then a set of sufficient stability conditions is that all $|S_j|$ are smaller than 1. Note that this condition absorbs condition III (when $a_{ij} \geqslant 0$, then $\sum |a_{ij}| = \sum a_{ij}$), but we have stated them separately for didactic purposes.

VI. A necessary stability condition is that $|\sum_{i=1}^{n} a_{ii}| < n$.

VII. A necessary stability condition is that the determinant of the matrix of the coefficients of the difference system, $\det A$, be less than 1 in absolute value.

★ Let us recall that a matrix $A \equiv [a_{ij}]$ is indecomposable (or irreducible) if there is *no* permutation of the indices (i.e., interchange of rows followed by the same interchange of columns, or vice versa) which reduces it to the form

$$A = \begin{bmatrix} B & C \\ 0 & D \end{bmatrix},$$

where B and D are square matrices (not necessarily of the same order). If such reduction is possible, the matrix is decomposable or reducible.

Note, finally, that conditions II, III, III′, IV and V may be phrased in terms of the sums $S_i = \sum_{j=1}^{n} a_{ij}$, $i = 1, 2, ..., n$, and be equally true *.

We can now turn to the problem of finding a particular solution of system (8.1). The general method of undetermined coefficients (see Part I, ch. 1) can be applied here too, and we shall illustrate it in the case in which $g_1(t), g_2(t)$ are two given constants, say b_1, b_2. Thus we have

$$y_{t+1} = a_{11}y_t + a_{12}z_t + b_1 ,$$

$$z_{t+1} = a_{21}y_t + a_{22}z_t + b_2 . \qquad (8.1')$$

As a particular solution let us try $\bar{y}_t = \mu_1$, $\bar{z}_t = \mu_2$, where μ_1, μ_2 are undetermined constants. Substituting in (8.1′) and rearranging terms, we have

$$(a_{11} - 1)\mu_1 + a_{12}\mu_2 = -b_1 ,$$

$$a_{21}\mu_1 + (a_{22} - 1)\mu_2 = -b_2 , \qquad (8.34)$$

whence **

$$\mu_1 = \frac{-b_1(a_{22}-1) + b_2 a_{12}}{(a_{11}-1)(a_{22}-1) - a_{12}a_{21}} , \qquad \mu_2 = \frac{-b_2(a_{11}-1) + b_1 a_{21}}{(a_{11}-1)(a_{22}-1) - a_{12}a_{21}} .$$

The determination of the arbitrary constants which appear in the general solution can be made as usual by a number of additional conditions equal to the number of the arbitrary constants. These conditions give the information that, for a given value of t (usually for $t = 0$), the values of the various functions are known values (e.g., in the case of systems (8.1) or (8.2), that y_0 and

---

* This follows from the fact that a matrix and its transpose have the same characteristic roots.

** The method is successful only if the determinant of system (8.34) is different from zero, i.e.

$$\begin{vmatrix} a_{11} - 1 & a_{12} \\ a_{21} & a_{22} - 1 \end{vmatrix} \neq 0 .$$

Note that this condition means that + 1 is *not* a root of the characteristic equation of the homogeneous difference system (8.2). When this occurs, the method fails; a way out is to reduce the non-homogeneous system to a single equation (the procedure is the same as for the homogeneous system) and then apply to the latter the methods that we have illustrated for single equations (see, e.g., Part I, ch. 4).

z_0 are known). Substituting in the general solution of the system under consideration, we obtain a system of linear equations which can be solved for the unknowns $A_1, A_2, ..., A_n$ [*].

The systems that we have so far examined have the peculiarity that in each equation only one unknown function in turn appears at two different points of time, which moreover are adjacent (t and $t+1$, or t and $t-1$) [**]. But, in general, in each equation *each* unknown function might appear at different points of time, not necessarily adjacent. As an illustration, consider the system

$$a_3 y_{t+3} + a_2 y_{t+2} + b_1 z_{t+1} + b_0 z_t = g_1(t),$$

$$c_1 y_{t+1} + c_0 y_t + d_2 z_{t+2} = g_2(t),$$

(8.35)

and its homogeneous counterpart

---

[*] Consider, for example, the case in which the characteristic roots are all distinct. Then the equations for the determination of the arbitrary constants turn out to be

$$\sum_{j=1}^{n} A_j \alpha_i^{(j)} + \bar{y}_i(0) = y_i(0), \qquad i = 1, 2, ..., n,$$

(*)

where $\bar{y}_i(0) \equiv 0$ if the system is homogeneous. It is a well-known theorem in matrix algebra that characteristic vectors associated with distinct characteristic roots are linearly independent; therefore the matrix $[\alpha_i^{(j)}]$ is non-singular and system (*) can be solved. Some complications may arise when there are multiple roots, but we need not treat them here.

[**] This is why the system is called first-order and normal, as defined above. Note that a system might be first-order but not in normal form, and this occurs when the different points of time involved are still two and adjacent, but in each equation two (or more) functions appear evaluated at time $t + 1$. A first-order system not in normal form can always be put in such form by means of suitable manipulations. In matrix terms, the general first-order homogeneous system can be written as $A y_{t+1} + B y_t = 0$. If A is non-singular, we obtain immediately the normal form $y_{t+1} = C y_t$, where $C = -A^{-1}B$. If A is singular, we must first reduce the number of equations and of unknowns to the rank of A by means of suitable substitutions, and then express the remaining $y_{it+1}, i = 1, 2, ..., r$; $r < n$, in terms of the y_{it} as before, obtaining the normal form. Note that when A is singular, the degree of the characteristic equation is no more n, but r, the rank of A.

Of course a first-order system not in normal form can also be solved directly as expounded below in the text in relation to an arbitrary system (i.e., substitute $y_{it} = \alpha_i \lambda^t$ etc.) without any need to reduce it first to the normal form. The reason why such reduction might be preferable is that we can apply to it the stability conditions expounded above in the text in relation to first-order normal systems.

$$a_3 y_{t+3} + a_2 y_{t+2} + b_1 z_{t+1} + b_0 z_t = 0 ,$$

$$c_1 y_{t+1} + c_0 y_t + d_2 z_{t+2} \qquad = 0 . \tag{8.36}$$

To solve system (8.36) we can follow the same direct method expounded above, trying as a solution $y_t = \alpha_1 \lambda^t$, $z_t = \alpha_2 \lambda^t$, where α_1, α_2 are not both zero *. Substituting in system (8.36) we have

$$a_3 \alpha_1 \lambda^{t+3} + a_2 \alpha_1 \lambda^{t+2} + b_1 \alpha_2 \lambda^{t+1} + b_0 \alpha_2 \lambda^t = 0 ,$$

$$c_1 \alpha_1 \lambda^{t+1} + c_0 \alpha_1 \lambda^t + d_2 \alpha_2 \lambda^{t+2} \qquad = 0 ,$$

from which

$$\lambda^t [(a_3 \lambda^3 + a_2 \lambda^2)\alpha_1 + (b_1 \lambda + b_0)\alpha_2] = 0 ,$$

$$\lambda^t [(c_1 \lambda + c_0)\alpha_1 + d_2 \lambda^2 \alpha_2] \qquad = 0 . \tag{8.37}$$

If $\alpha_1 \lambda^t$, $\alpha_2 \lambda^t$ are a solution, system (8.37) must be satisfied for any t and this is possible — apart from the trivial case $\lambda = 0$ — if, and only if,

---

* Alternatively, we could reduce the system to a single difference equation (but the manipulations would be more complicated than for normal first-order systems), or transform the system into an equivalent normal first-order system. Such a transformation can always be performed by an appropriate introduction of new variables. In relation to system (8.36), define $y_{t+1} = w_t$, $w_{t+1} = e_t$, $z_{t+1} = j_t$ (whence, e.g., $y_{t+3} = e_{t+1}$, etc.) and substitute suitably in system (8.36). The result, together with the equations which define the new variables, is the following first-order system (which is already in 'normal' form; when, after the definition of the new variables, the resulting system is first-order but not in normal form, we can use the procedure expounded in the previous footnote):

$$y_{t+1} = w_t , \qquad w_{t+1} = e_t , \qquad z_{t+1} = j_t ,$$

$$e_{t+1} = -\frac{b_0}{a_3} z_t - \frac{a_2}{a_3} e_t - \frac{b_1}{a_3} j_t ,$$

$$j_{t+1} = -\frac{c_0}{d_2} y_t - \frac{c_1}{d_2} w_t .$$

The reader may check as an exercise that the expanded form of the characteristic equation of such a system is the same as that obtained from (8.39). Of course the procedure explained in the text is more rapid, but there might be a reason to perform the transformation of a general system into a first-order normal system: see the next footnote.

$$(a_3\lambda^3 + a_2\lambda^2)\alpha_1 + (b_1\lambda + b_0)\alpha_2 = 0 \,,$$

$$(c_1\lambda + c_0)\alpha_1 + d_2\lambda^2\alpha_2 \qquad\qquad = 0 \,,$$

(8.38)

and system (8.38) will yield a non-trivial solution for α_1, α_2 if, and only if, its determinant is zero, i.e.

$$\begin{vmatrix} a_3\lambda^3 + a_2\lambda^2 & b_1\lambda + b_0 \\ c_1\lambda + c_0 & d_2\lambda^2 \end{vmatrix} = 0 \,.$$

(8.39)

The determinantal equation (8.39) and its expanded form are called the characteristic equation of system (8.38). Expanding the determinant, we obtain a fifth-degree equation in the unknown λ. From this point on, the procedure is the same as that expounded above for first-order systems. If, for example, the characteristic equation yields five real and distinct roots (to each of them we can associate a couple of values $\alpha_1^{(j)}$, $\alpha_2^{(j)}$), then the solution will have the form

$$y_t = A_1\alpha_1^{(1)}\lambda_1^t + A_2\alpha_1^{(2)}\lambda_2^t + A_3\alpha_1^{(3)}\lambda_3^t + A_4\alpha_1^{(4)}\lambda_4^t + A_5\alpha_1^{(5)}\lambda_5^t \,,$$

$$z_t = A_1\alpha_2^{(1)}\lambda_1^t + A_2\alpha_2^{(2)}\lambda_2^t + A_3\alpha_2^{(3)}\lambda_3^t + A_4\alpha_2^{(4)}\lambda_4^t + A_5\alpha_2^{(5)}\lambda_5^t \,,$$

(8.40)

where A_1, A_2, A_3, A_4, A_5 are arbitrary constants.

In any case, the stability of the system can be examined by applying the stability conditions (see Part I, ch. 6) to the explicit form of the characteristic equation. Let us note that for the system under consideration (as, in general, for systems which are not of type (8.2)) there are no stability conditions directly applicable to the coefficients of the system, so that the explicit polynomial form of the characteristic equation must be obtained in order that the stability conditions can be applied [*].

In the case of a non-homogeneous system, a particular solution can be found by the method of undetermined coefficients. The arbitrary constants, finally, can be determined given a sufficient number of additional conditions. In the case of systems (8.35) or (8.36), such additional conditions could be, for example, that y_0, y_1, y_2, z_0 and z_1 are all known values.

---

[*] Of course we can always transform the system into an equivalent normal first-order system, and then apply the stability conditions expounded above.

References

Baumol, W.J., 1970, *Economic Dynamics*, chs. 15, 16.

Boole, G., 1960, *A Treatise on the Calculus of Finite Differences*, ch. XII, pp. 231–2.

Fisher, F.M., 1962, An Alternate Proof and Extension of Solow's Theorem on Nonnegative Square Matrices.

Fisher, F.M., 1965, Choice of Units, Column Sums, and Stability in Linear Dynamic Systems with Nonnegative Square Matrices.

Gantmacher, F.R., 1959, *Applications of the Theory of Matrices*, ch. III, §§ 1, 2, 3.

Hadar, J., 1965, A Note on Dominant Diagonals in Stability Analysis.

McKenzie, L., 1960, Matrices with Dominant Diagonals and Economic Theory, p. 49.

Samuelson, P.A., 1947, *Foundations of Economic Analysis*, Appendix B, §§ 30–35.

Solow, R.M., 1952, On the Structure of Linear Models.

Yamane, T., 1968, *Mathematics for Economists: An Elementary Survey*, ch. 12, §§ 12.6–12.9.

9

Some Economic Applications

of Simultaneous Systems

Actually all economic models, even the simplest ones, are simultaneous systems. The fact that a lot of them are usually examined as giving rise to a single equation is because the reduction of the system to a single equation suggests itself quite naturally (i.e. only direct substitutions are required, without any previous manipulations) and is actually easier than simultaneous methods. For example, the homogeneous part of the multiplier model

$$C_t - bY_{t-1} = 0$$

$$I_t = I_0$$

$$C_t + I_t - Y_t = 0$$

has the characteristic equation

$$\begin{vmatrix} \lambda & 0 & -b \\ 0 & 1 & 0 \\ 1 & 1 & -1 \end{vmatrix} = -\lambda + b = 0,$$

whence $\lambda = b$, etc. However, direct substitution from the first two equations into the third immediately suggests itself and is actually simpler. The same considerations apply to the models expounded in the previous chapters. On the other hand, there are some economic models in which, when all direct substitutions have been performed, two (or more) simultaneous equations still remain, to which simultaneous methods can be profitably applied.

§1. Multiplier effects in an open economy

In Part I, ch. 3, §2, we examined, among others, the dynamics of the foreign trade multiplier in the case in which exports are assumed to be exogenous. Actually exports may depend indirectly on national income. Suppose, for example, that in a country (call it country 1) a variation in income occurs. Then also imports, which depend on income, change and this change means a change in the exports of the rest of the world (that, for simplicity's sake, we consider as a single country — call it country 2) to country 1. The change in exports in country 2 causes a change in income in that country and consequently country 2 imports from country 1 change. This means a change in country 1 exports and consequently in country 1 income and so on.

This chain of events is known under the name of 'foreign repercussions', and the multiplier which takes account of them is called multiplier with foreign repercussions; for terminological convenience we shall call 'foreign trade multiplier without repercussions' the foreign trade multiplier treated in Part I, ch. 3, §2.

Let us begin with the static model, which is made up of the following equations:

Country 1	Country 2
$C_1 = b_1 Y_1$,	$C_2 = b_2 Y_2$,
$I_1 = I_{01} + h_1 Y_1$,	$I_2 = I_{02} + h_2 Y_2$,
$M_1 = M_{01} + m_1 Y_1$,	$M_2 = M_{02} + m_2 Y_2$,
$X_1 = M_2$,	$X_2 = M_1$,
$Y_1 = C_1 + I_1 + X_1 - M_1$.	$Y_2 = C_2 + I_2 + X_2 - M_2$.

The equations express, in this order, the consumption function, the invest-ment function, the import function, the fact that the exports of one country are the same as the imports of the other country and the determination of national income in an open economy. I_0 and M_0 are autonomous compo-nents. Subscripts 1 and 2 indicate, respectively, country 1 and country 2 [*].

Substituting, for both countries, from the first four equations into the fifth and rearranging terms, we have

$$(1-b_1-h_1+m_1)Y_1 - m_2Y_2 = I_{01} + M_{02} - M_{01} \, ,$$

$$- m_1Y_1 + (1-b_2-h_2+m_2)Y_2 = I_{02} + M_{01} - M_{02} \, ,$$

(9.1)

from which

$$Y_1 = \frac{(1-b_2-h_2)(I_{01}+M_{02}-M_{01}) + m_2(I_{01}+I_{02})}{(1-b_1-h_1+m_1)(1-b_2-h_2+m_2) - m_1m_2} \, ,$$

$$Y_2 = \frac{(1-b_1-h_1)(I_{02}+M_{01}-M_{02}) + m_1(I_{01}+I_{02})}{(1-b_1-h_1+m_1)(1-b_2-h_2+m_2) - m_1m_2} \, ,$$

(9.2)

and, considering the variations,

$$\Delta Y_1 = \frac{(1-b_2-h_2)(\Delta I_{01}+\Delta M_{02}-\Delta M_{01}) + m_2(\Delta I_{01}+\Delta I_{02})}{(1-b_1-h_1+m_1)(1-b_2-h_2+m_2) - m_1m_2} \, ,$$

$$\Delta Y_2 = \frac{(1-b_1-h_1)(\Delta I_{02}+\Delta M_{01}-\Delta M_{02}) + m_1(\Delta I_{01}+\Delta I_{02})}{(1-b_1-h_1+m_1)(1-b_2-h_2+m_2) - m_1m_2} \, .$$

(9.3)

Now the dynamics. The assumptions are the same as in Part I, ch. 3, §2, i.e. that in both countries C_t, I_t and M_t depend on Y_{t-1}. After the usual substi-tutions we have the difference system

$$Y_{1_t} = (b_1+h_1-m_1)Y_{1_{t-1}} + m_2Y_{2_{t-1}} + (I_{01}+M_{02}-M_{01}) \, ,$$

$$Y_{2_t} = m_1Y_{1_{t-1}} + (b_2+h_2-m_2)Y_{2_{t-1}} + (I_{02}+M_{01}-M_{02}) \, .$$

(9.4)

A particular solution of system (9.4) is obtained trying $Y_{1_t} = Y_{1_{t-1}} = \overline{Y}_1$, $Y_{2_t} = Y_{2_{t-1}} = \overline{Y}_2$, where $\overline{Y}_1, \overline{Y}_2$ are constants; the values that we obtain are the same as the static equilibrium values (9.2).

[*] When we use b, h, m without subscripts, it will be because we refer generically to both countries.

The characteristic equation of the homogeneous form of system (9.4) is

$$\begin{vmatrix} (b_1+h_1-m_1) - \lambda & m_2 \\ m_1 & (b_2+h_2-m_2) - \lambda \end{vmatrix} = 0 . \tag{9.5}$$

Now, since $b + h > m$ (see Part I, ch. 3, §2, for the explanation), the coefficients are positive, so that we can apply the stability conditions expounded in Part I, ch. 8. From conditions I we obtain the following necessary and sufficient stability conditions:

$$1 - b_1 - h_1 + m_1 > 0 ,$$
$$(1-b_1-h_1+m_1)(1-b_2-h_2+m_2) - m_1 m_2 > 0 . \tag{9.6}$$

If we want only sufficient conditions, we can apply conditions III and obtain

$$b_1 + h_1 < 1 ,$$
$$b_2 + h_2 < 1 . \tag{9.7}$$

From (9.6) and (9.7) we deduce the following conclusions:
    (1) a necessary (but not sufficient) stability condition is that $1 - b_1 - h_1 + m_1$ and $1 - b_2 - h_2 + m_2$ are both positive;
    (2) a sufficient (but not necessary) stability condition is that $b_1 + h_1$ and $b_2 + h_2$ are both less than 1;
    (3) if $b_1 + h_1 > 1$ and also $b_2 + h_2 > 1$, the model is unstable (this follows from cond. IV);
    (4) if one of the quantities $b_1 + h_1, b_2 + h_2$ is smaller than unity and the other is greater than unity, the model may be stable or unstable according to the magnitude of m_1, m_2.
    To appreciate the economic meaning of these conclusions, let us recall from Part I, ch. 3, §2, that $b + h - m < 1$ is the stability condition for the foreign trade multiplier without repercussions and that $b + h < 1$ is the stability condition for the closed economy multiplier. Thus we can say:
    (1) a necessary (but not sufficient) stability condition for the multiplier with foreign repercussions is that in both countries the foreign trade multiplier without repercussions is stable;
    (2) a sufficient (but not necessary) stability condition for the multiplier

with foreign repercussions is that in both countries in isolation the closed economy multiplier is stable;

(3) if in both countries in isolation the closed economy multiplier is unstable, the foreign trade multiplier with repercussions is unstable;

(4) if, when each country is considered in isolation, in one of them the closed economy multiplier is unstable whereas in the other it is stable, then the foreign trade multiplier with foreign repercussions may be stable or unstable.

The multiplier model with foreign repercussions can be easily extended to any number of countries. Call m_{ji}, $i \neq j$, the (partial) propensity of country i to import from country j,

$$m_i = \sum_{\substack{j=1 \\ j \neq i}}^{n} m_{ji}$$

being the (total) propensity to import of country i. Similarly,

$$M_{0i} = \sum_{\substack{j=1 \\ j \neq i}}^{n} M_{0ji},$$

where M_{0ji} is autonomous imports of country i from country j. Then for any country $i = 1, 2, ..., n$, we have

$$Y_{i_t} = C_{i_t} + I_{i_t} + X_{i_t} - M_{i_t}$$

$$= (b_i + h_i - m_i)Y_{i_{t-1}} + \sum_{\substack{k=1 \\ k \neq i}}^{n} m_{ik} Y_{k_{t-1}} + I_{0i} + \sum_{\substack{k=1 \\ k \neq i}}^{n} M_{0ik} - M_{0i}. \qquad (9.8)$$

The characteristic equation of the homogeneous part of system (9.8) is

$$\begin{vmatrix} (b_1+h_1-m_1)-\lambda & m_{12} & \cdots & m_{1n} \\ m_{21} & (b_2+h_2-m_2)-\lambda & \cdots & m_{2n} \\ \cdots & \cdots & \cdots & \cdots \\ m_{n1} & m_{n2} & \cdots & (b_n+h_n-m_n)-\lambda \end{vmatrix} = 0.$$

Applying the stability conditions, we can deduce conclusions similar to those found for the two-country case. In particular, it is interesting to note that the necessary and sufficient stability conditions also guarantee that a static equilibrium solution for the non-homogeneous system exists and is economically meaningful * and that $b_i + h_i < 1$, all i, is a sufficient stability condition, whereas if $b_i + h_i > 1$, all i, then the model is unstable.

Exercises

1. The following data are given: $b_1 = 0.60$, $h_1 = 0.20$, $m_1 = 0.10$, $b_2 = 0.80$, $h_2 = 0.25$, $m_2 = 0.30$. In country 1 autonomous investment increases by 9. Compute the new equilibrium level of the incomes in the two countries, given that the previous equilibrium level was 100 in both countries. Examine the dynamic stability of the model.

Calculation. Applying eqs. (9.3) of the text, given that $\Delta I_{01} = 9$, $\Delta I_{02} = \Delta M_{01} = \Delta M_{02} = 0$, and given the values of the various propensities, we obtain $\Delta Y_1 = 50$, $\Delta Y_2 = 20$, so that the new equilibrium values are $\overline{Y}_1 = 150$, $\overline{Y}_2 = 120$. The characteristic equation of the homogeneous part of the dynamic system is

$$\begin{vmatrix} 0.70 - \lambda & 0.30 \\ 0.10 & 0.75 - \lambda \end{vmatrix} = \lambda^2 - 1.45\,\lambda + 0.495 = 0 \,,$$

whose roots are 0.90, 0.55. Thus the general solution of the homogeneous system is (see (8.18) and (8.19) of Part I, ch. 8)

$$Y_{1_t} = A_1(0.90)^t + A_2(0.55)^t \,,$$

$$Y_{2_t} = A_1 \tfrac{2}{3}(0.90)^t - A_2 0.5(0.55)^t \,,$$

and the general solution of the non-homogeneous system is

$$Y_{1_t} = A_1(0.90)^t + A_2(0.55)^t + 150 \,,$$

$$Y_{2_t} = A_1 \tfrac{2}{3}(0.90)^t - A_2 0.5(0.55)^t + 120 \,,$$

---

* A particular solution of system (9.8) is $\overline{Y} = [I-A]^{-1} v$, where v is the column vector of the autonomous terms and A is the matrix (obviously non-negative) of the coefficients of the difference system. It is well known (see, e.g., Solow (1952)) that the positivity of the leading principal minors of $[I-A]$ guarantees that $[I-A]^{-1}$ is non-negative.

from which we see that the equilibrium solution is stable.

The initial conditions appear to be $Y_{01} = 109$, $Y_{02} = 100$. In fact, in country 1 income in period 0 goes from 100 to 109 because of the increment in autonomous investment, while in country 2 it still remains at the previous equilibrium level. Thus we have

$$Y_{01} = 109 = A_1(0.90)^0 + A_2(0.55)^0 + 150 ,$$

$$Y_{02} = 100 = A_1 \tfrac{2}{3}(0.90)^0 - A_2 0.5(0.55)^0 + 120 ;$$

therefore

$$A_1 + A_2 = -41 ,$$

$$\tfrac{2}{3}A_1 - 0.5 A_2 = -20 ,$$

which give $A_1 = -34.7143$, $A_2 = -6.2857$.

2. Apply the stability conditions to exercise 1.

§2. Capital stock adjustment and extrapolative expectations

The capital stock adjustment principle is considered a generalization of the acceleration principle; here we shall expound it and build a model based on it.

According to that principle, net induced investment depends on the existence of a gap between the desired capital stock and the existing capital stock. This gap induces entrepreneurs to invest (positively or negatively) in order to eliminate it. In symbols

$$I_{N_t} = \beta(K_t^* - K_{t-1}) ,$$

where I_{N_t} is the net investment, K_t^* the desired capital stock, K_{t-1} the existing capital stock and β is a reaction coefficient, of course positive, which indicates how rapidly entrepreneurs intend to make up the gap. It is plausible to think that the gap is not made up completely in one period, so that probably β is smaller than unity.

So expressed, the capital stock adjustment principle is little more than a truism, and to give it operational content it is necessary to specify how the desired capital stock is determined. It seems obvious that the desired capital stock is that which will be needed to produce the *expected* output. Now, if we assume a constant desired capital/output ratio, it follows that

$$K_t^* = k\hat{Y}_t \, ,$$

where $\hat{Y}_t$ is expected output. Thus

$$I_{N_t} = \beta(k\hat{Y}_t - K_{t-1}) \, .$$

Expressed in this way, the investment function is rather general and includes the acceleration principle as a particular case. To show this, assume that the adjustment is complete, i.e. $\beta = 1$. Thus we have $I_{N_t} = k\hat{Y}_t - K_{t-1}$. If, in addition, we assume that expectations are verified (i.e. perfect forecast), then $\hat{Y}_t = Y_t$ and $I_{N_t} = kY_t - K_{t-1}$; and, since the adjustment is complete, $K_{t-1} = kY_{t-1}$, so that $I_{N_t} = k(Y_t - Y_{t-1})$, which is the accelerator equation (unlagged form). If, instead, we assume that expectations are of the naïve kind, i.e. $\hat{Y}_t = Y_{t-1}$, then $I_{N_t} = kY_{t-1} - K_{t-1}$; and, since the adjustment is complete but with a lag (i.e. in period t the capital stock is brought to the level kY_{t-1}, and similarly $K_{t-1} = kY_{t-2}$), we have $I_{N_t} = k(Y_{t-1} - Y_{t-2})$, which is the lagged form of the accelerator equation. Let us note that, if we do not assume that the adjustment is complete, and assume that $\hat{Y}_t = Y_{t-1}$, then we obtain as a particular case the investment equation $I_{N_t} = \alpha Y_{t-1} - \beta K_{t-1}$ (where $\alpha = \beta k$), which is also referred to in the literature as a capital stock adjustment equation.

We should like to note that the assumptions by which we have obtained the accelerator equation are rather unrealistic, and this is a reason why the acceleration principle has never given good empirical results; on the contrary, capital stock adjustment equations have given better empirical results (Smyth, 1964).

Once we have linked the desired capital stock with expected output, we can take the last step, which is to specify how expectations are formed. In our model we use expectations of the kind

$$\hat{Y}_t = Y_{t-1} + \rho(Y_{t-1} - Y_{t-2}) \, , \qquad \rho > 0 \, ,$$

that we have already met in other models (see Part I, ch. 5, §4, and Part I, ch. 7, §2). Thus we have

$$I_{N_t} = \beta k[Y_{t-1} + \rho(Y_{t-1} - Y_{t-2})] - \beta K_{t-1}$$

$$= \beta k(1+\rho)Y_{t-1} - \beta k\rho Y_{t-2} - \beta K_{t-1} \ .$$

We may now write down the complete model.

$$Y_{L_t} = C_t + I_{L_t} + A \ , \tag{9.9}$$

where Y_{L_t} is gross national income (output), C_t is consumption, I_{L_t} is gross investment and A is autonomous expenditure (assumed constant).

$$Y_{N_t} = Y_{L_t} - \gamma K_{t-1} \ , \qquad 0 < \gamma < 1 \ , \tag{9.10}$$

where Y_{N_t} is net national income (output) and γK_{t-1} represents depreciation, assumed to be a constant fraction of the existing capital stock (so-called 'radioactive' depreciation or depreciation 'by evaporation').

$$C_t = b Y_{N_t} \ , \tag{9.11}$$

i.e. consumption depends linearly on net national income; no lag is assumed.

$$I_{L_t} = \beta k(1+\rho)Y_{L_{t-1}} - \beta k\rho Y_{L_{t-2}} + (\gamma - \beta)K_{t-1} \ , \tag{9.12}$$

i.e. gross investment is obtained adding depreciation to net investment.

$$K_t = K_{t-1} + I_{L_t} - \gamma K_{t-1} \tag{9.13}$$

is a definitional equation.

Now let us substitute from (9.10) in (9.11) and then in (9.9), and from (9.12) in (9.9) and in (9.13). We obtain

$$Y_{L_t} = b(Y_{L_t} - \gamma K_{t-1}) + A + \beta k(1+\rho)Y_{L_{t-1}} - \beta k\rho Y_{L_{t-2}} + (\gamma - \beta)K_{t-1}, \tag{9.14}$$

$$K_t = \beta k(1+\rho)Y_{L_{t-1}} - \beta k\rho Y_{L_{t-2}} + (1-\beta)K_{t-1} \ ,$$

from which, rearranging terms and shifting time subscripts, we have

$$(1-b)Y_{L_{t+2}} - (\beta k + \beta k\rho)Y_{L_{t+1}} + \beta k\rho Y_{L_t} + (\beta + b\gamma - \gamma)K_{t+1} = A \ , \tag{9.15}$$

$$-(\beta k + \beta k\rho)Y_{L_{t+1}} + \beta k\rho Y_{L_t} + K_{t+2} + (\beta - 1)K_{t+1} = 0 . \tag{9.15}$$

A particular solution is easily found trying $\overline{Y}_{L_t} = Y_{L_e}$, $\overline{K}_t = K_e$, where Y_{L_e} and K_e are constants to be determined. Substituting in (9.15) and solving, we obtain

$$Y_{L_e} = \frac{A}{(1-b)(1-k\gamma)} , \qquad K_e = kY_{L_e} . \tag{9.16}$$

The characteristic equation of the homogeneous part of system (9.15) is

$$\begin{vmatrix} (1-b)\lambda^2 - (\beta k + \beta k\rho)\lambda + \beta k\rho & (\beta + b\gamma - \gamma)\lambda \\ -(\beta k + \beta k\rho)\lambda + \beta k\rho & \lambda^2 + (\beta - 1)\lambda \end{vmatrix} = 0 . \tag{9.17}$$

Expanding the determinant and discarding the trivial root $\lambda = 0$, we have

$$(1-b)\lambda^3 + (b + \beta - 1 - \beta k - \beta k\rho - b\beta)\lambda^2$$

$$+ (\beta k + 2\beta k\rho + b\beta k\gamma + b\beta k\rho\gamma - bk\gamma - \beta k\rho\gamma)\lambda$$

$$+ (\beta k\rho\gamma - \beta k\rho - b\beta k\rho\gamma) = 0 , \tag{9.17a}$$

which can be written as

$$\lambda^3 + \frac{b + \beta - 1 - \beta k - \beta k\rho - b\beta}{1-b} \lambda^2$$

$$\tag{9.17b}$$

$$+ \frac{\beta k + 2\beta k\rho + b\beta k\gamma + b\beta k\rho\gamma - bk\gamma - \beta k\rho\gamma}{1-b} \lambda + \frac{\beta k\rho\gamma - \beta k\rho - b\beta k\rho\gamma}{1-b} = 0 .$$

Let us now apply to eq. (9.17b) the stability conditions relevant for a third-degree polynomial ★. We obtain

$$\beta(1-b)(1-k\gamma) > 0 \tag{9.18}$$

$$4(1-b) + \beta[(1-b)(k\gamma - 1) + 4k\rho(\gamma - b\gamma - 1)] > 0$$

★ See Part I, ch. 6, inequalities (6.8), of which we have chosen to drop the fourth.

$$1 - \frac{b+\beta-1-\beta k-\beta k\rho-b\beta}{1-b} + \frac{\beta k+2\beta k\rho+b\beta k\gamma+b\beta k\rho\gamma-bk\gamma-\beta k\rho\gamma}{1-b}$$

$$-\frac{\beta k\rho\gamma-\beta k\rho-b\beta k\rho\gamma}{1-b} > 0 , \qquad (9.18)$$

$$(k\rho+bk\rho\gamma-k\rho\gamma)(k\rho\gamma-bk\rho\gamma-1+k+b)\beta^2$$

$$+ (1-b)(k\gamma-k-k\rho-bk\gamma)\beta + (1-b)^2 > 0 .$$

The first inequality is satisfied, since $\beta > 0$, $0 < b < 1$ and $1 - k\gamma > 0$ [*]. The third inequality is also satisfied, given the assumptions on the various parameters [**]. The relevant inequalities are then the second and the fourth. Taking account of the fact that the expression in square brackets in the second inequality is negative, such inequality yields

$$\beta < \frac{4(1-b)}{(1-b)(1-k\gamma) + 4k\rho(1+b\gamma-\gamma)} . \qquad (9.19)$$

The fourth inequality will be satisfied for $\beta < \beta_1$ and for $\beta > \beta_2$, where β_1, β_2 are the roots of the equation

$$(k\rho+bk\rho\gamma-k\rho\gamma)(k\rho\gamma-bk\rho\gamma-1+k+b)\beta^2$$

$$+ (1-b)(k\gamma-k-k\rho-bk\gamma)\beta + (1-b)^2 = 0 . \qquad (9.20)$$

Such roots are real and both positive, and it can be proved that β_2 is greater than the fraction on the right-hand side of (9.19) [‡]. Thus the interval $\beta > \beta_2$

[*] Let us note that the assumption $1 - k\gamma > 0$ is necessary in order that the system be viable. In fact, since to produce one unit of output k units of capital are required, of which $k\gamma$ need be replaced, it follows that if $1 - k\gamma < 0$, then even employing the entire capital stock in the production of capital it would not be possible to prevent the capital stock from dwindling to zero; and, if $1 - k\gamma = 0$, then the entire capital stock would be necessary just to produce replacements (so that consumption goods could be produced only at the expense of a continuous reduction in the capital stock).

[**] In addition to the assumptions already mentioned, $\beta > 0$, $0 < b < 1$, $1 - k\gamma > 0$, the other assumptions are $0 < \gamma < 1$, $\rho > 0$ and $k > 1$ (the capital/output ratio can be assumed to be greater than unity on empirical grounds).

[‡] The succession of the signs of the coefficients of eq. (9.20) is $+ - +$, so that the roots, if real, are both positive. Consider now the parabola $g(\beta)$ associated with (9.20). We have $g(0) = (1-b)^2 > 0$, $g(+\infty) = +\infty$ and $g(\beta) < 0$ for $\beta = (1-b)/(k\rho+bk\rho\gamma-k\rho\gamma)$ as

must be discarded. From the various results so far obtained it follows that the stability conditions will be all satisfied for $\beta < \bar{\beta}$, where

$$\bar{\beta} = \min \left[\frac{4(1-b)}{(1-b)(1-k\gamma)+4k\rho(1+b\gamma-\gamma)} , \beta_1 \right]. \qquad (9.21)$$

All this proves the following theorem:

There always exists a positive value $\bar{\beta}$ – given by (9.21) – such that the model is stable for $\beta < \bar{\beta}$ and unstable for $\beta > \bar{\beta}$. (9.22)

The economic interpretation of (9.22) is simple: if the reaction to the gap between the desired and the existing capital stock is not too strong, then the model will be stable, and it will be unstable in the opposite case; eq. (9.21) gives the critical value of the reaction coefficient as a function of all the other parameters of the model.

Exercises

1. Given $b = 0.7$, $\rho = 0.9$, $k = 2$, $\gamma = 0.10$, compute the critical value of the reaction coefficient.

Calculation. With the given values, the right-hand side of (9.19) becomes $1.2/7.224 \simeq 0.1661$. Eq. (9.20) becomes

$$3.062484\,\beta^2 - 1.122\,\beta + 0.09 = 0 ,$$

whose roots are 0.2477 and 0.1186.

The smaller value between (0.1661; 0.1186) is 0.1186, which is the critical value of the reaction coefficient. Let us note, incidentally, that in empirical studies (Kuh, 1963) the value of the reaction coefficient has been found to be normally about 0.10.

2. Same problem as in exercise 1, but for $b = 0.6$.

can be checked by substitution in (9.20). This proves that $g(\beta)$ must intersect twice the positive β semiaxis and that the value

$$\beta = \frac{1-b}{k\rho+bk\rho\gamma-k\rho\gamma}$$

lies between the two roots. But that value is greater, clearly, than the fraction on the right-hand side of (9.19), and so the latter is smaller than β_2.

§3. Smithies' model

This model tries to combine cycles and growth, and has several interesting features. Let us begin by analysing the investment function, in which three arguments appear:

(1) Profits, which have a positive influence on investment for two reasons. The expectation of making profits is one of the principal incentives to invest (of course, in a non-collectivistic economy) and, moreover, profits are a source of finance for investment. Regarding the second reason, it is true that investment can also be financed by borrowing, but it is a well-known fact that entrepreneurs prefer internal (profits) to external (credit) financing.

(2) A component similar to the capital stock adjustment principle, with the difference that, instead of the capital stock, full capacity output and normal output are considered. By 'full capacity output' we mean the output obtainable utilising fully, but under normal working conditions, the existing capital stock. Thus if the output deemed normal exceeds full-capacity output, there is an incentive to increase the capital stock.

(3) A trend element, which represents exogenous factors.

The investment function may then be written as

$$I_t = h_1 Y_{t-1} + h_2 \overline{Y} - h_3(Y_{F_{t-1}} - \overline{Y}) + d^t \tag{9.23}$$

where h_1, h_2, h_3 are positive constants and the other symbols have the following meaning:

I = gross investment,

Y = gross national income (product),

$\overline{Y}$ = highest level of Y so far,

Y_F = full capacity output,

d^t = trend element $(d > 1)$.

The first two terms on the right-hand side of (9.23) represent the influence of profits, given the assumption that profits are an approximately constant fraction of Y (i.e. no appreciable shifts in distribution occur). Now, if we assume that profit expectations are based on realized profits (which also influence investment for the second reason mentioned above) and on the highest level of profits so far obtained, and that there is a lag between the decision to invest and the carrying out of investment, we have the first two terms on the right-hand side of (9.23).

The term $-h_3(Y_{F_{t-1}} - \overline{Y})$ represents the influence of the second element mentioned above, given the assumptions that the output considered normal is related to $\overline{Y}$ and that there is as before a lag.

The term d^t represents, as we said above, the trend element.

Let us now examine the consumption function. In addition to current income, it has as argument $\overline{Y}$; the inclusion of the highest income so far obtained represents a 'ratchet effect', of the kind introduced into aggregate consumption theory by Modigliani (1949) and Duesenberry (1949). Thus we have

$$C_t = b_1 Y_t + b_2 \overline{Y}, \tag{9.24}$$

where b_1, b_2 are positive constants and smaller than unity, and $b_1 + b_2 < 1$. Let us note that the long-run propensity to consume (i.e. when $\overline{Y} = Y_t$) is $b_1 + b_2$; the corresponding long-run propensity to save is $1 - (b_1 + b_2)$.

We have now the equilibrium relation

$$Y_t = C_t + I_t \tag{9.25}$$

or

$$S_t = I_t . \tag{9.25'}$$

To complete the model we have to examine the relationship between investment and full capacity output. Smithies assumes, following Domar (for Domar's model, see Part II, ch. 3, §3) that each unit of investment increases capacity output by a factor σ, so that $Y_{F_t} - Y_{F_{t-1}} = \sigma I_{t-1}$. But, in addition, he takes into account the influence of depreciation, of obsolescence and of technical progress. Depreciation is assumed to be proportional to the capital stock, i.e. to full capacity output. Obsolescence is divided into two categories: 'normal' and 'extraordinary' obsolescence. Normal obsolescence is assumed to be proportional to gross investment and its influence is included in the coefficient σ. Extraordinary obsolescence is assumed to be proportional to the difference between full capacity output and current output (with a lag); the reason is that when current demand is low relative to capacity output, abnormal scrapping can be expected, whereas when demand is relatively high it may happen that capital goods which would normally be scrapped are retained in operation, so that extraordinary obsolescence is negative. Technical progress, finally, is represented as a trend element. Thus we have

$$Y_{F_t} - Y_{F_{t-1}} = \sigma I_{t-1} - D_1 - D_2 + l^t , \tag{9.26}$$

where D_1 is depreciation and D_2 is extraordinary obsolescence, and

$$D_1 = \gamma_1 Y_{F_{t-1}}, \qquad 0 < \gamma_1 < 1, \qquad (9.27)$$

$$D_2 = \gamma_2(Y_{F_{t-1}} - Y_{t-1}), \qquad 0 < \gamma_2 < 1. \qquad (9.28)$$

The term l^t represents technical progress ($l > 1$).

In the solution of the model, two situations are considered. The first
— called 'state 1' — is when the ratchet is not operating, so that $\overline{Y} = Y_{t-1}$ in
(9.23) and $\overline{Y} = Y_t$ in (9.24). The second — called 'state 2' — is when those
equalities do not hold. In the first case, after standard substitutions (in (9.26),
use $I_{t-1} = Y_{t-1} - C_{t-1}$ etc.), we obtain the system

$$Y_t = a_{11} Y_{t-1} + a_{12} Y_{F_{t-1}} + gd^t, \qquad (9.29)$$

$$Y_{F_t} = a_{21} Y_{t-1} + a_{22} Y_{F_{t-1}} + l^t,$$

where

$$a_{11} = \frac{h_1 + h_2 + h_3}{1 - (b_1 + b_2)}, \qquad (9.30)$$

$$a_{12} = \frac{-h_3}{1 - (b_1 + b_2)},$$

$$a_{21} = \sigma[1 - (b_1 + b_2)] + \gamma_2,$$

$$a_{22} = 1 - \gamma_1 - \gamma_2,$$

$$g = \frac{1}{1 - (b_1 + b_2)}.$$

In the second case we obtain

$$Y_t = a'_{11} Y_{t-1} + a'_{12} Y_{F_{t-1}} + r\overline{Y} + g'd^t, \qquad (9.31)$$

$$Y_{F_t} = a'_{21} Y_{t-1} + a'_{22} Y_{F_{t-1}} + e\overline{Y} + l^t, \qquad (9.32)$$

where

$$a'_{11} = \frac{h_1}{1 - b_1},$$

$$a'_{12} = \frac{-h_3}{1 - b_1} ,$$

$$a'_{21} = \sigma(1 - b_1) + \gamma_2 ,$$

$$a'_{22} = 1 - \gamma_1 - \gamma_2 ,$$

$$g' = \frac{1}{1 - b_1} ,$$

$$r = \frac{b_2 + h_2 + h_3}{1 - b_1} ,$$

$$e = -\sigma b_2 .$$

Let us begin with 'state 1'. The characteristic equation of the homogeneous part of system (9.29)–(9.30) is

$$\begin{vmatrix} a_{11} - \lambda & a_{12} \\ a_{21} & a_{22} - \lambda \end{vmatrix} = \lambda^2 - (a_{11} + a_{22})\lambda + (a_{11}a_{22} - a_{12}a_{21}) = 0 ,$$

which gives

$$\lambda_1, \lambda_2 = \tfrac{1}{2} \{(a_{11} + a_{22}) \pm [(a_{11} + a_{22})^2 - 4(a_{11}a_{22} - a_{12}a_{21})]^{\frac{1}{2}} \} .$$

The solution of the homogeneous part of the system is then

$$Y_t = A_1 \lambda_1^t + A_2 \lambda_2^t$$

$$Y_{F_t} = A'_1 \lambda_1^t + A'_2 \lambda_2^t$$

where (see (8.20) and (8.21) of Part I, ch. 8)

$$\frac{A'_1}{A_1} = \frac{\lambda_1 - a_{11}}{a_{12}} = \frac{a_{21}}{\lambda_1 - a_{22}} , \qquad \frac{A'_2}{A_2} = \frac{\lambda_2 - a_{11}}{a_{12}} = \frac{a_{21}}{\lambda_2 - a_{22}} .$$

For the particular solution, in order to simplify things, Smithies assumes that only one of the two trend elements is operating, e.g. d^t. As a particular solution let us try $Y_t = \mu_1 d^t$, $Y_{F_t} = \mu_2 d^t$, where μ_1, μ_2 are undetermined coefficients. Substituting in (9.29) and (9.30) we have

$$\mu_1 d^t = a_{11}\mu_1 d^{t-1} + a_{12}\mu_2 d^{t-1} + g d^t ,$$

$$\mu_2 d^t = a_{21}\mu_1 d^{t-1} + a_{22}\mu_2 d^{t-1} ,$$

and dividing through by d^{t-1} we have

$$(a_{11}-d)\mu_1 + a_{12}\mu_2 = -gd$$

$$a_{21}\mu_1 + (a_{22}-d)\mu_2 = 0 ,$$

so that

$$\mu_1 = \frac{gd(d-a_{22})}{(a_{11}-d)(a_{22}-d) - a_{12}a_{21}} ,$$

$$\mu_2 = \frac{a_{21}gd}{(a_{11}-d)(a_{22}-d) - a_{12}a_{21}} .$$

Now,

$$(a_{11}-d)(a_{22}-d) - a_{12}a_{21} = d^2 - (a_{11}+a_{22})d + (a_{11}a_{22}-a_{12}a_{21}) ,$$

and the last expression can be written, as we know from elementary algebra, as $(d-d_1)(d-d_2)$ where d_1, d_2 are the roots of

$$d^2 - (a_{11}+a_{22})d + (a_{11}a_{22}-a_{12}a_{21}) = 0 .$$

But this equation is the same as the characteristic equation of the homogeneous part of the system under examination, so that $d_1 = \lambda_1, d_2 = \lambda_2$. It follows that

$$\mu_1 = \frac{gd(d-a_{22})}{(d-\lambda_1)(d-\lambda_2)} ,$$

$$\mu_2 = \frac{a_{21}gd}{(d-\lambda_1)(d-\lambda_2)} ,$$

so that

$$\frac{\mu_2}{\mu_1} = \frac{a_{21}}{d-a_{22}} .$$

The general solution for 'state 1' is then

$$Y_t = A_1\lambda_1^t + A_2\lambda_2^t + \mu_1 d^t ,$$

$$Y_{F_t} = A_1'\lambda_1^t + A_2'\lambda_2^t + \mu_2 d^t .$$

Given the initial conditions $Y_t = Y_0$, $Y_{F_t} = Y_{F_0}$ for $t = 0$, we substitute in the general solution and obtain, after simple manipulations,

$$A_1 = \frac{Y_0(a_{11}-\lambda_2) + a_{12}Y_{F_0} - \mu_1[a_{21}a_{12}/(d-a_{22})+a_{11}-\lambda_2]}{\lambda_1 - \lambda_2} ,$$

$$A_2 = \frac{Y_0(a_{11}-\lambda_1) + a_{12}Y_{F_0} - \mu_1[a_{21}a_{12}/(d-a_{22})+a_{11}-\lambda_1]}{\lambda_2 - \lambda_1} .$$

We now want to find the conditions under which the solution for 'state 1' gives rise to an equilibrium growth; the possibility of oscillations will be examined later on. For that purpose it is expedient to write the general solution in the form

$$Y_t = B_1\lambda_1^t + B_2\lambda_2^t$$

$$+ \mu_1 \left[-\frac{a_{21}a_{12}/(d-a_{22})+a_{11}-\lambda_2}{\lambda_1 - \lambda_2} \lambda_1^t - \frac{a_{21}a_{12}/(d-a_{22})+a_{11}-\lambda_1}{\lambda_2 - \lambda_1} \lambda_2^t + d^t \right],$$

$$Y_{F_t} = B_1'\lambda_1^t + B_2'\lambda_2^t$$

$$+ \mu_2 \left[-\frac{a_{21}a_{12}/(d-a_{22})+a_{11}-\lambda_2}{\lambda_1 - \lambda_2} \cdot \frac{d-a_{22}}{\lambda_1-a_{22}} \lambda_1^t \right.$$

$$\left. - \frac{a_{21}a_{12}/(d-a_{22})+a_{11}-\lambda_1}{\lambda_2 - \lambda_1} \cdot \frac{d-a_{22}}{\lambda_2-a_{22}} \lambda_2^t + d^t \right],$$

where

$$B_1 = \frac{Y_0(a_{11}-\lambda_2) + a_{12}Y_{F_0}}{\lambda_1 - \lambda_2} ,$$

$$B_2 = \frac{Y_0(a_{11}-\lambda_1) + a_{12}Y_{F_0}}{\lambda_2 - \lambda_1} ,$$

and B_1', B_2' are related to B_1, B_2 in the same way as A_1', A_2' are related to A_1, A_2 (see above).

In considering constant equilibrium growth, let us examine first a situation in which the trend elements are absent; they will be taken into consideration later on. Thus we have the relations

$$Y_t = B_1 \lambda_1^t + B_2 \lambda_2^t, \tag{9.33}$$

$$Y_{F_t} = B_1' \lambda_1^t + B_2' \lambda_2^t. \tag{9.34}$$

In order that constant equilibrium growth occurs, it is necessary that $Y_t = Y_{F_t}$ and that both grow at a constant rate, i.e.

$$Y_t = Y_{F_t} = A z^t, \tag{9.35}$$

where $z - 1$ is the rate of growth. In order that (9.33) and (9.34) reduce to (9.35), the roots λ_1, λ_2 must be real and positive; only one of the two terms λ_1^t, λ_2^t must remain in (9.33) and in (9.34), and the coefficients of this term must be equal in both equations. We may assume without loss of generality that such a term is λ_1^t. Since

$$B_1' = B_1 \frac{a_{21}}{\lambda_1 - a_{22}} = B_1 \frac{\lambda_1 - a_{11}}{a_{12}},$$

putting $B_1 = B_1'$ we have

$$\lambda_1 = a_{21} + a_{22} = a_{11} + a_{12},$$

and so $\star$

$$\lambda_2 = a_{11} - a_{21} = a_{22} - a_{12}.$$

In terms of the original coefficients (σ, b, etc.) we have

$$\lambda_1 = \sigma[1 - (b_1 + b_2)] + 1 - \gamma_1,$$

$$\lambda_2 = 1 - \gamma_1 - \gamma_2 + \frac{h_3}{1 - (b_1 + b_2)}.$$

$\star$ Consider the equation $\lambda^2 - (a_{11} + a_{22})\lambda + (a_{11}a_{22} - a_{12}a_{21}) = 0$. It is a well-known fact in elementary algebra that $\lambda_1 + \lambda_2 = a_{11} + a_{22}$. Substituting the expression for λ_1 we obtain λ_2.

Substituting the values of λ_1, λ_2 into the formulae for B_1, B_2, we obtain

$$Y_t = \frac{a_{21}Y_0 + a_{12}Y_{F_0}}{a_{21} + a_{12}} \lambda_1^t + \frac{a_{12}(Y_0 - Y_{F_0})}{a_{21} + a_{12}} \lambda_2^t ,$$

$$Y_{F_t} = \frac{a_{21}Y_0 + a_{12}Y_{F_0}}{a_{21} + a_{12}} \lambda_1^t - \frac{a_{21}(Y_0 - Y_{F_0})}{a_{21} + a_{12}} \lambda_2^t ,$$

from which we can see that the term containing λ_2^t disappears if, and only if, $Y_0 = Y_{F_0}$. In other words, constant equilibrium growth requires that capacity is fully utilized in the initial period. Assuming that $Y_0 = Y_{F_0}$, we have

$$Y_t = Y_{F_t} = Y_0 \lambda_1^t = Y_{F_0} \lambda_1^t ,$$

and the rate of growth is $\lambda_1 - 1$, i.e. $\sigma[1 - (b_1 + b_2)] - \gamma_1$. This rate is the same as the 'warranted' rate of growth in Harrod's model, with the difference that it is expressed in terms of *gross* product instead of net product. In fact, σ is the reciprocal of the capital/output ratio and $1 - (b_1 + b_2)$ is the (long-run) propensity to save, so that $\sigma[1 - (b_1 + b_2)] = s/k$, the warranted rate of growth; subtracting from this rate the rate of depreciation γ_1, we have the *net* rate of growth (in Harrod's model all quantities are net, so that there is no need to subtract the rate of depreciation).

When $Y_0 \neq Y_{F_0}$, it is still possible to achieve equilibrium growth in the limit provided that $|\lambda_2| < 1$: in that case, in fact, the dominant term in the solution is λ_1^t and the term containing λ_2^t tends to zero as t increases.

When the trend element is considered, equilibrium growth will not be possible except in very special circumstances (and even then only in the limit), i.e. when, in addition to the conditions stated above for the case of no trend, the condition $d = \lambda_1$ holds. When $d = \lambda_1$, a particular solution of the non-homogeneous system is $Y_t = \delta_1 t \lambda_1^t$, $Y_{F_t} = \delta_2 t \lambda_1^t$, ($\delta_1, \delta_2$ are constants that can be determined in terms of coefficients of the system). Now, if $\lambda_1 = a_{11} + a_{12} = a_{21} + a_{22}$, $Y_0 = Y_{F_0}$ and $|\lambda_2| < 1$, the general solution of the system can be seen to approach, as t increases, a limit of the kind $Y_t = Y_{F_t} = (Y_0 + \delta_3 t)\lambda_1^t$, ($\delta_3$ = constant), which, for t sufficiently large, tends to be dominated by λ_1^t.

Let us now consider oscillations. When they occur, two cases are possible:

(a) the oscillations are mild, so that in the general solution the influence of the trend elements (particular solution of the non-homogeneous system) dominates in the sense that no decrease in income occurs (the sum of an oscillation and of an exponentially increasing function may still be a monotonic increasing function);

(b) the oscillations are such that in the downward phase a decrease in income occurs.

In case (a), the system remains in 'state 1' and a situation of cyclical growth occurs. In case (b) the system cannot remain in 'state 1', since the permanence of that state requires that income always increases, and it switches to 'state 2'. The general solution for the system obtaining in 'state 2' is (the trend elements are ignored for simplicity)

$$Y_t = H_1 \lambda_1'^t + H_2 \lambda_2'^t + F\overline{Y},$$

$$Y_{F_t} = H_1' \lambda_1'^t + H_2' \lambda_2'^t + F'\overline{Y},$$

where

$$F = \frac{r(1 - a_{22}') + a_{12}'e}{1 - (a_{11}' + a_{22}') + a_{11}' a_{22}' - a_{21}' a_{12}'},$$

$$F' = \frac{ra_{21}' + e(1 - a_{11}')}{1 - (a_{11}' + a_{22}') + a_{11}' a_{22}' - a_{21}' a_{12}'},$$

and λ_1', λ_2' are the roots of the characteristic equation

$$\begin{vmatrix} a_{11}' - \lambda' & a_{12}' \\ a_{21}' & a_{22}' - \lambda' \end{vmatrix} = 0.$$

When the system has switched to 'state 2', it may remain there or it may also happen that it goes back to 'state 1' and then again to 'state 2', and so on. In conclusion, the model admits of a great variety of movements, combining cycles and growth.

Exercises
1. The following data are given: $h_1 = 0.15, h_2 = 0.05, h_3 = 0.10, b_1 = 0.60,$ $b_2 = 0.20, \sigma = 0.30, \gamma_1 = 0.10, \gamma_2 = 0.05$. Assuming that the trend elements are absent, check that the system remains in 'state 1', but that equilibrium growth cannot occur.

Calculation. With the given data, the characteristic equation of the homogeneous part of the system is

$$\begin{vmatrix} 1.5 - \lambda & -0.5 \\ 0.11 & 0.85 - \lambda \end{vmatrix} = \lambda^2 - 2.35\lambda + 1.33 = 0 \,,$$

whose roots are $\lambda_1 = 1.40$, $\lambda_2 = 0.95$.

Since the roots are both positive and one of them is greater than unity, the system grows without oscillations, and this guarantees that it remains in 'state 1'. Since $\lambda_1 \neq a_{21} + a_{22}$, $(1.40 \neq 0.96)$, the coefficients B_2, B_2' in (9.33) and (9.34) do not disappear, and $B_1 \neq B_1'$, so that equilibrium growth cannot occur.

2. Examine the behaviour of the system given the following data (the trend elements are absent): $h_1 = 0.10$, $h_2 = 0.05$, $h_3 = 0.5$, $b_1 = 0.60$, $b_2 = 0.15$, $\gamma_1 = 0.15$, $\gamma_2 = 0.05$, $\sigma = 0.30$.

References

Duesenberry, J.S., 1949, *Income, Saving and the Theory of Consumer Behavior,* chs. III, V.

Hicks, J.R., 1965, *Capital and Growth*, ch. IX.

Kuh, E., 1963, *Capital Stock Growth: A Micro-Econometric Approach,* ch. 9.

Machlup, F., 1943, *International Trade and the National Income Multiplier.*

Metzler, L.A., 1942, Underemployment Equilibrium in International Trade.

Metzler, L.A., 1950, A Multiple Region Theory of Income and Trade.

Modigliani, F., 1949, Fluctuations in the Saving–Income Ratio: A Problem in Economic Forecasting, §§ 1–4.

Smithies, A., 1957, Economic Fluctuations and Growth.

Smyth, D., 1964, Empirical Evidence on the Acceleration Principle.

Vanek, J., 1962, *International Trade: Theory and Economic Policy*, ch. 7; ch. 9, § 9.3.

PART II

DIFFERENTIAL EQUATIONS (LINEAR AND WITH CONSTANT COEFFICIENTS)

1

General Principles

An ordinary differential equation is a functional equation involving one or more of the derivatives y', y'', y''', etc., of an unknown function of time $y = f(t)$, which obviously is differentiable. We have called the equation an *ordinary* differential equation since the unknown function is a function of only one argument; if the independent variables were more than one, partial derivatives would appear in the differential equation, which would be a partial differential equation (we shall not treat this type of functional equation).

The *order* of a differential equation is given by the highest derivative appearing in the equation.

After what we said in the Introduction, it will be clear that to solve (or to 'integrate') a differential equation means to find the unknown function that satisfies the relationship expressed by the equation.

Let us begin, as usual, by a simple example. Consider the differential equation $y' = a$, where a is a constant. From elementary integral calculus it follows that $y = at + b$; let us remember, incidentally, that integration — the 'inverse' operation of differentiation — represents the solution of a differential equation. We note that in the solution an arbitrary constant b appears (the other constant a is known, since it appears in the differential equation). This is not surprising, since we know that differentiation eliminates such a constant, so that from $y = at + b$ we obtain, in fact, $y' = a$. Let us now con-

163

sider the second-order differential equation $y'' = a$. Performing two successive integrations we obtain $y = \frac{1}{2} at^2 + bt + c$; now, two arbitrary constants, b and c, appear in the solution. It is easy to check that, if we differentiate the function y twice, such arbitrary constants disappear one after the other, so that from $y = \frac{1}{2} at^2 + bt + c$ we obtain, in fact, $y'' = a$, that is the differential equation from which we started.

From the above considerations we can deduce the general principle that *the general solution of a differential equation of order n is a function of t which involves exactly n arbitrary constants* [*]. We shall see in the following chapters how the arbitrary constants can be determined by means of additional conditions.

As we said in the Introduction, the differential equations most widely used in economic dynamics are linear and with constant coefficients, which are also the easiest to handle from the mathematical point of view. In this second part (Part II) of the book we shall use the expression 'differential equations' (or even, when the meaning is clear from the context, simply 'equations') in the sense of 'ordinary differential equations' linear and with constant coefficients'.

The general form of an n-th order differential equation is

$$a_0 y^{(n)} + a_1 y^{(n-1)} + \dots + a_{n-1} y' + a_n y = g(t) \,, \qquad (1.1)$$

where $y^{(n)}$, $y^{(n-1)}$, etc., indicate the derivatives of order n, $n - 1$, etc.; the a's are given constants and $g(t)$ is a known function. Some a's may be zero, but of course a_0 must be different from zero if the equation is of order n.

Eq. (1.1) is called a *non-homogeneous* equation; the corresponding *homogeneous* form is

$$a_0 y^{(n)} + a_1 y^{(n-1)} + \dots + a_{n-1} y' + a_n y = 0 \,. \qquad (1.2)$$

The following general theorems will be applied to solve (1.1) and (1.2):

---

[*] We have implicitly assumed that this function exists and is unique (apart from the arbitrary constants). Actually this assumption could be proved by means of an existence and uniqueness theorem, but we shall not treat such theorems. All types of equations considered in this book are well-behaved, in the sense that their solution exists and is unique. In general, it may be observed that the properties that the 'well behaved' functions used in economic theory are assumed to have, are usually more than enough to satisfy the requirements of any existence and uniqueness theorem.

(1) *If $y_1(t)$ is a solution of* (1.2), *then $Ay_1(t)$ – where A is an arbitrary constant – is also a solution.*

(2) *Superposition Theorem. If $y_1(t), y_2(t)$ are two distinct (i.e., linearly independent) solutions of* (1.2), *then $A_1y_1(t) + A_2y_2(t)$ is also a solution for any two arbitrary constants A_1, A_2.* The same property holds for any number $k \leqslant n$ of distinct solutions [*].

(3) *If $f(t; A_1, A_2, ..., A_n)$ is the general solution of* (1.2) – *where $A_1, A_2, ...$ ..., A_n are arbitrary constants – and $\bar{y}(t)$ is any particular solution [**] of* (1.1), *i.e. any function that satisfies* (1.1), *then $\bar{y}(t) + f(t; A_1, A_2, ..., A_n)$ is the general solution of* (1.1).

These theorems can be proved, as we did in Part I, ch. 1, for difference equations, by direct substitution in the eqs. (1.1) and (1.2).

According to (2), to find the general solution of the homogeneous equation we can find n distinct solutions $y_1(t), y_2(t), ..., y_n(t)$ and combine them linearly in the function

$$f(t; A_1, A_2, ..., A_n) = A_1y_1(t) + A_2y_2(t) + ... + A_ny_n(t) .$$

Since this function involves n arbitrary constants, it is the general solution of (1.2). According to (3), to find the general solution of the non-homogeneous equation it is enough to find a particular solution of this equation and then to add to it the general solution of the homogeneous equation obtained putting $g(t) \equiv 0$.

For the particular solution $\bar{y}(t)$, it will depend, *ceteris paribus*, on the form of the known function $g(t)$. This suggests the following general approach (the so-called *'method of undetermined coefficients'*): to find a particular solution of the non-homogeneous equation, try a function having the same form of $g(t)$ but with undetermined coefficient(s) (e.g., if $g(t)$ is a constant, try an undetermined constant; if it is an exponential function, try the same exponential function but with an undetermined multiplicative constant, and so on). Substitute this function in the non-homogeneous equation and determine the coefficient(s) in such a way that the equation is satisfied.

---

[*] Given a homogeneous equation of order n, a set of n linearly independent solutions is called a *fundamental set.*

[**] See Part I, ch. 1, footnote † to pp. 11–12: the remarks on terminology hold here too.

The practical problem of how to find the n functions $y_1(t), y_2(t), ..., y_n(t)$ and – if the equation is non-homogeneous – the function $\bar{y}(t)$, will be tackled in the following chapters.

We must note at this point the great similarity that exists between differential and difference equations, so much that the general theorems are the same. However, some dissimilarities also exist, which give rise to differences in the economic interpretation. The principal formal dissimilarity is that in differential equations t varies continuously and also the function $y = f(t)$ is continuous (that it must be so is obvious, since it is differentiable), whereas in difference equations t varies discontinuously over a set of equi-spaced values, and so the solution $y = f(t)$ is a function which is defined only corresponding to these values of t. This implies that it is *not* immaterial whether we use differential or difference equations in the formalization of an economic problem. If we think that a certain dynamic economic phenomenon takes place in a continuous way and without discontinuous lags, then the appropriate mathematical tool to use is differential equations, whereas if we think that it takes place in a discontinuous way, then the appropriate tool is difference equations. Unfortunately this sharp distinction is not often possible ★, so that if we want to avoid more complicated mathematical tools, we must give a judgement, from the economic point of view, as to which aspects are prevalent: if we think that the economic phenomenon under consideration is mainly continuous and without discontinuous lags, then we shall use differential equations; if we think that in such phenomenon discontinuous lags, etc., are the main characteristic, then we shall use difference equations. It is important that this judgement be given from the beginning and clearly, since, as we shall see (e.g., in Part II, ch. 3, §2), the use of one rather than the other tool in formalizing an economic problem may give different economic results.

References

Allen, R.G.D., 1938, *Mathematical Analysis for Economists*, ch. 16, §16.1.
Allen, R.G.D., 1959, *Mathematical Economics*, ch. 5, §§5.1, 5.2.
Baumol, W.J., 1970, *Economic Dynamics*, ch. 14, §1.
Ince, E.L., 1956, *Ordinary Differential Equations*, ch. I, §§1.1, 1.2; ch. V, §5.1.
Ince, E.L., 1959, *Integration of Ordinary Differential Equations*, ch. I, §§1, 2; ch. II, §37.

★ And when it is not possible (or if we do not want to make it), then we must use more complex mathematical tools, e.g. mixed difference–differential equations (see Appendix IV, §3).

2

First-order Equations

The general form of such equations is

$$a_0 y' + a_1 y = g(t), \qquad a_0 \neq 0, \tag{2.1}$$

where a_0, a_1 are given constants and $g(t)$ is a known function. The constant a_0 must be different from zero, since if it were equal to zero the equation would not be a differential equation; on the contrary, a_1 may be zero, in which case we have

$$y' = \frac{1}{a_0} g(t). \tag{2.2}$$

To solve eq. (2.2) means to find a function such that its derivative equals the right-hand side of (2.2). This is rather easy: integrating both sides we have

$$y(t) = \frac{1}{a_0} \int g(t)\, dt + C,$$

where C is an arbitrary constant. Thus the solution of (2.2) can be found by the usual formulae and rules of integration. Indeed, as we have already noted in Part II, ch. 1, the operation of integration (the 'inverse' operation of differentiation) represents the solution of the simplest type of first-order differential equation, expressed by (2.2).

Let us go back to (2.1), assuming now that both a_0 and a_1 are different from zero. We begin by studying the corresponding homogeneous equation:

$$a_0 y' + a_1 y = 0 , \tag{2.3}$$

which we can write as

$$y' + by = 0 , \qquad \text{where } b \equiv a_1/a_0 . \tag{2.4}$$

From (2.4) we have $y' = -by$. Thus we must find a function such that its derivative is equal to the function itself, multiplied by the constant $-b$. To solve this problem we proceed by degrees. Let us first consider the particular case in which $b = -1$, so that

$$y' = y . \tag{2.5}$$

From elementary differential calculus we know that the only function which is equal to its derivative for any value of the argument is e^t. This suggests the idea of trying, as a solution of (2.4), a function of the type $e^{\lambda t}$, where λ is a constant to be determined. Substituting in (2.4) (remember that $de^{\lambda t}/dt = \lambda e^{\lambda t}$) we have

$$\lambda e^{\lambda t} + be^{\lambda t} = 0 ,$$

i.e.

$$e^{\lambda t}(\lambda + b) = 0 . \tag{2.6}$$

If the function $e^{\lambda t}$ is a solution of (2.4), eq. (2.6) must be satisfied for any t, and this is possible if, and only if,

$$\lambda + b = 0 , \tag{2.7}$$

which is called the *characteristic equation* or the *auxiliary equation* of the differential equation (2.4).

From (2.7) we obtain $\lambda = -b$ and so, according to the general principles expounded in Part II, ch. 1, the general solution of (2.4) is

$$y(t) = Ae^{-bt},\tag{2.8}$$

where A is an arbitrary constant. The reader may check as an exercise that (2.8) indeed satisfies (2.4) for any t.

Another way to obtain the same result is the following. Write (2.4) in the form

$$y'/y = -b,\tag{2.4a}$$

and observe that $y'/y = \mathrm{d}\log_e y/\mathrm{d}t$, so that integrating both sides of (2.4a) we have

$$\log_e y = -bt + C,\tag{2.4b}$$

where C is an arbitrary constant. From (2.4b) it follows that

$$y(t) = e^{-bt+C} = e^C e^{-bt}\tag{2.4c}$$

and putting $e^C = A$ we obtain (2.8).

In order to determine the arbitrary constant we need an additional condition. In fact, the solution of a differential equation gives only the *form* of the unknown function but not its position in the (t, y) Cartesian plane. As soon as the function is constrained to pass through a given point, say (t^*, y^*), its position, which here depends on one arbitrary constant only, is determined and the arbitrariness of the constant disappears. More formally, let it be known that $y(t) = y^*$ for $t = t^*$, where t^* and y^* are given values. Substituting these values in (2.8) we have

$$y^* = Ae^{-bt^*}\tag{2.9}$$

and so

$$A = y^*/e^{-bt^*}.\tag{2.10}$$

In economic problems the value of y in the initial period is usually assumed to be known, at least in principle, i.e. $y(t) = y_0$ for $t = 0$; it follows from (2.10) that $A = y_0$.

The behaviour over time of the function Ae^{-bt} depends on the *sign* of the parameter b. When b is negative, then $-b$ is positive and e^{-bt} increases monotonically as t increases, so that Ae^{-bt} tends to $\pm\infty$ if $A \gtrless 0$. When b is positive, then $-b$ is negative and Ae^{-bt} decreases monotonically towards zero as t increases. Fig. 2.1 illustrates the various cases.

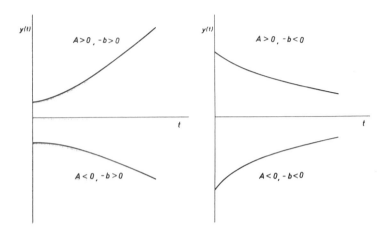

Fig. 2.1.

If we compare the solution of the homogeneous first-order differential equation with that of the homogeneous difference equation of the same order, we see that the former admits of a smaller variety of time paths than the latter. In particular, alternating movements (i.e. 'improper oscillations', as we termed them in Part I, ch. 2) cannot occur with a first-order differential equation, and this is true for differential equations of any order. Another consideration, also true generally, is that in differential equations the qualitative behaviour of the solution depends only on the *sign* of a certain parameter, whereas in difference equations such behaviour depends both on the *sign* and on the *absolute value* of a parameter.

These disparities depend formally on the different behaviour of the functions $e^{\lambda t}$ and λ^t.

The problem of finding a particular solution of the non-homogeneous equation will now be tackled, applying to the commoner functions the general method stated in Part II, ch. 1.

Case (1): $g(t)$ is a constant.

In this case, equation (2.1) becomes

$$a_0 y' + a_1 y = a , \tag{2.11}$$

where a is a given constant. As a particular solution, try $\bar{y}(t) = \mu$, where μ is an undetermined constant. Substituting in (2.11) we have $0 + a_1\mu = a$, from which

$$\mu = a/a_1 \ . \tag{2.12}$$

The method obviously fails if $a_1 = 0$; in this case let us try $\bar{y}(t) = \mu t$. Substituting in (2.11) we have $a_0\mu = a$, so that

$$\mu = a/a_0 \ . \tag{2.13}$$

It must be stressed that the above treatment illustrates the following general prescription, which is a necessary complement to the general principle expounded in Part II, ch. 1: *if the function that we try as a particular solution does not work, let us try next the same function multiplied by t* [*].

Let us note that, when $a_1 = 0$, the general solution of the homogeneous part of (2.11) is $y(t) = A$, since the characteristic equation yields $\lambda = 0$. Thus the general solution of our non-homogeneous equation is $y(t) = (a/a_0)t + A$. We could obtain the same result directly by integrating the equation $a_0 y' = a$ (see the beginning of this chapter). It is, however, important to understand how the solution is obtained even in this particular case by applying general principles.

Case (2): $g(t)$ is an exponential function.
When $g(t) = Be^{dt}$, where B and d are given constants [**], as a particular solution try Ce^{dt}, where C is an undetermined constant. Substitution in (2.1) yields

$$a_0 d C e^{dt} + a_1 C e^{dt} = B e^{dt} \ ,$$

from which

$$[(a_0 d + a_1)C - B] e^{dt} = 0 \ . \tag{2.14}$$

Eq. (2.14) will be satisfied for any t if, and only if,

$$(a_0 d + a_1)C - B = 0 \ ,$$

which gives

----

[*] In second- or higher-order equations it may be necessary, as we shall see, to multiply by t^2, t^3, etc.
[**] If $g(t) = \alpha^{\beta t}$, $\alpha > 0$, put $\beta \log_e \alpha = d$, and proceed as before.

$$C = \frac{B}{a_0 d + a_1} . \tag{2.15}$$

If $a_0 d + a_1 = 0$ (incidentally, this means that the root of the characteristic equation of the homogeneous part of the equation equals d) the method fails. Let us then try tCe^{dt}. Substituting in (2.1) we have

$$a_0(Ce^{dt} + tdCe^{dt}) + a_1 tCe^{dt} = Be^{dt} ,$$

from which

$$(a_0 d + a_1)tCe^{dt} + (a_0 C - B)e^{dt} = 0 ,$$

i.e., since $a_0 d + a_1 = 0$,

$$(a_0 C - B)e^{dt} = 0 , \tag{2.16}$$

which yields

$$C = B/a_0 . \tag{2.17}$$

Case (3): $g(t)$ is a polynomial function of degree m.

As an example, consider $g(t) = c_0 + c_1 t$, where c_0 and c_1 are given constants. Try $\overline{y}(t) = \alpha + \beta t$ as a particular solution, α and β being undetermined constants. Substitution in (2.1) yields

$$a_0 \beta + a_1(\alpha + \beta t) = c_0 + c_1 t ,$$

which gives

$$(a_1 \beta - c_1)t + (a_0 \beta + a_1 \alpha - c_0) = 0 . \tag{2.18}$$

Eq. (2.18) will be satisfied for any t if, and only if,

$$a_1 \beta - c_1 \quad\quad = 0 ,$$
$$a_0 \beta + a_1 \alpha - c_0 = 0 . \tag{2.19}$$

The solution of system (2.19) yields

$$\alpha = (a_1 c_0 - a_0 c_1)/a_1^2 , \quad\quad \beta = c_1/a_1 . \tag{2.20}$$

When $a_1 = 0$, we try $\bar{y}(t) = \alpha t + \beta t^2$. Substituting in (2.1) we obtain (the details are left as an exercise)

$$\alpha = c_0/a_0 ,$$
$$\beta = c_1/2a_0 .$$
(2.21)

Case (4): $g(t)$ is a trigonometric function of the sine–cosine type.

In this case, $g(t) = B_1 \cos \omega t + B_2 \sin \omega t$, where B_1, B_2, ω are given constants. As a particular solution, try the function $\alpha \cos \omega t + \beta \sin \omega t$, where α and β are undetermined constants. Substitution in (2.1) yields

$$a_0(-\alpha\omega \sin \omega t + \beta\omega \cos \omega t) + a_1(\alpha \cos \omega t + \beta \sin \omega t) = B_1 \cos \omega t + B_2 \sin \omega t ,$$

from which

$$(a_0\omega\beta + a_1\alpha - B_1) \cos \omega t + (a_1\beta - a_0\omega\alpha - B_2) \sin \omega t = 0 .$$
(2.22)

Eq. (2.22) will be satisfied for any t if, and only if,

$$a_0\omega\beta + a_1\alpha - B_1 = 0 ,$$
$$a_1\beta - a_0\omega\alpha - B_2 = 0 .$$
(2.23)

Eqs. (2.23) are a system of two linear equations, whose solution will give the values of α and β. By now the student should be able to examine the case in which the method fails.

If $g(t)$ is a combination of the functions seen above in the various cases, as a particular solution we may try the same combination with undetermined coefficients, etc. The four cases treated cover all the cases that we are likely to meet in economic applications; actually only cases (1), (2), and (4) will be met in the following chapters on economic applications.

Having found a particular solution of the non-homogeneous equation, we find that its general solution will be

$$y(t) = Ae^{-bt} + \bar{y}(t) .$$
(2.24)

Let us now determine the arbitrary constant A. It is important to note that this constant must be determined, given an additional condition, on the basis of the general solution of the equation concerned. This means that, if the equation is non-homogeneous, formula (2.10) does not hold any more and we must find a new one. The method is the same: given that $y(t) = y^*$ for $t = t^*$, we substitute in (2.24) and obtain

$$y^* = Ae^{-bt^*} + \bar{y}(t^*) ,$$

which gives

$$A = e^{bt^*}[y^* - \bar{y}(t^*)] .$$

As we have already said above, in economics the initial value of y is usually assumed known, at least in principle, so that $A = y_0 - \bar{y}_0$, the initial deviation between $y(t)$ and $\bar{y}(t)$.

Let us note, finally, that in economic applications the particular solution $\bar{y}(t)$ can usually be interpreted as the *equilibrium value* (a stationary equilibrium or a moving equilibrium according to whether $\bar{y}(t)$ is a constant or a function of t) of the variable y. Given this interpretation, the general solution of the homogeneous part of the equation can be interpreted as giving the time path of the *deviations* from equilibrium, since $y(t) - \bar{y}(t) = Ae^{-bt}$.

These considerations can be extended to differential equations of any order: if

$$y(t) = f(t; A_1, A_2, ..., A_n) + \bar{y}(t)$$

is the general solution of an n-th order differential equation and if $\bar{y}(t)$ can be interpreted as the equilibrium value of y, then $f(t; A_1, A_2, ..., A_n)$ expresses the deviations from equilibrium. Of course, from the mathematical point of view it is always true that

$$y(t) - \bar{y}(t) = f(t; A_1, A_2, ..., A_n) ,$$

independently of the possibility of giving an economic interpretation to the particular solution $\bar{y}(t)$.

References

Allen, R.G.D., 1959, *Mathematical Economics*, ch. 5, § 5.3.
Baumol, W.J., 1970, *Economic Dynamics*, ch. 14, § 2.

3

Some Economic Applications
of First-order Equations

§1. Stability of supply and demand equilibrium

We know from microeconomics that in a perfectly competitive market equilibrium is determined by the point at which the supply function and the demand function are equal. Here we limit ourselves to the simple case in which demand and supply of a commodity are assumed to depend only on the price of that commodity, *ceteris paribus* (i.e., we are making a partial equilibrium analysis). A general equilibrium analysis requires more complex mathematical tools and will be examined further on (see Part II, ch. 9, §1, and Appendix II, §4.1).

Let us now ask what happens when the system is not in equilibrium ★, that is, when price and quantity do not coincide with the respective equilibrium values. Will the system tend to move towards its equilibrium or not? The problem that we have posed is the problem of the *stability of equilibrium*. It is important to distinguish two concept of stability: *static stability*

★ Either because the system, previously in equilibrium, has been displaced from it by accidental causes, or because the system has never been in equilibrium. It is obvious that these are two aspects of the same problem.

and *dynamic stability* ★. Static stability only tells us whether the economic forces that act on the system tend to make it move towards the equilibrium point, but does not tell us anything about the actual time path of the system nor, therefore, whether the system converges over time to the equilibrium point. It is true that the economic forces tend to 'push' the system towards its equilibrium, but this does not exclude, for example, the case in which the equilibrium point is 'overtaken' again and again in opposite directions, giving rise to oscillations which might in principle be undamped. Therefore, the study of static stability is not sufficient, and it is necessary to study dynamic stability: the latter, being based on functional equations, is able to solve the problems left unsolved by the former. Therefore, the 'true' concept of stability is the dynamic one, which is the one that we have implicitly adopted in the preceding chapters when we have examined the stability of equilibrium in the various models.

In order to study the stability of equilibrium — be it static or dynamic — it is necessary to make *assumptions about the behaviour* of the relevant variables out of equilibrium. Since, in principle, it is usually possible to make several, and equally plausible, such assumptions, there follows the *relativity of stability conditions*, since in some cases a given equilibrium point may be stable or unstable according to the different assumptions made.

Let us now examine the problem from which we started, i.e. the stability of supply and demand equilibrium. The main behaviour assumptions are the Walrasian assumption and the Marshallian assumption. According to the *Walrasian* assumption, price tends to increase (decrease) if excess demand is positive (negative). According to the *Marshallian* assumption, quantity tends to increase (decrease) if excess demand price is positive (negative). The following diagram may be useful to clarify the distinction between 'excess demand' and 'excess demand price'. Excess demand is the difference between the quantity that buyers are willing to buy at any given price and the quantity that sellers are willing to supply at the same price. In fig. 3.1(a) at price p' excess demand is positive and is measured by the segment $\overline{A'B'}$ ($= \overline{a'b'}$); at price p'' excess demand is negative and is measured (in absolute value) by the segment $\overline{A''B''}$ ($= \overline{a''b''}$). Excess demand price is the difference between the price that buyers are willing to pay for any given quantity and the price that is required to call forth the supply of the same quantity. In fig. 3.1(b) at quantity q' excess demand price is positive and is measured by the segment

---

★ Many other distinctions are made with regard to the concept of stability (perfect and imperfect, asymptotic, local and global, etc.). Some of them will be treated later on, in this section and in Part II, ch. 9, § 1 and Appendix II, § 1.

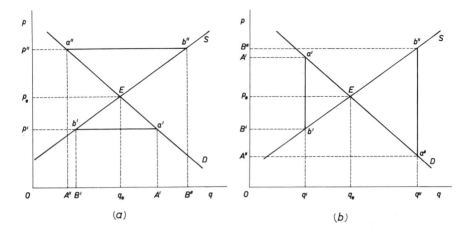

Fig. 3.1.

$\overline{A'B'}$ (= $\overline{a'b'}$); at quantity q'' excess demand price is negative and is measured (in absolute value) by the segment $\overline{A''B''}$ (= $\overline{a''b''}$).

The idea underlying the Walrasian assumption is that, when there is a positive (negative) excess demand, unsatisfied buyers (sellers) bid the price up (down). The idea underlying the Marshallian assumption is that, when there is a positive (negative) excess demand price, producers realize that they can profitably increase (decrease) the quantity supplied.

Let us now examine the stability conditions from the *static stability* point of view. If we adopt the Walrasian assumption, equilibrium is stable if a price increase (decrease) — caused by positive (negative) excess demand — diminishes (increases) excess demand, i.e. if

$$\frac{\mathrm{d}E(p)}{\mathrm{d}p} = \frac{\mathrm{d}[D(p) - S(p)]}{\mathrm{d}p} < 0 , \tag{3.1}$$

that is

$$\frac{\mathrm{d}D}{\mathrm{d}p} - \frac{\mathrm{d}S}{\mathrm{d}p} < 0 . \tag{3.2}$$

If we adopt the Marshallian assumption, equilibrium is stable if an increase (decrease) in quantity — caused by a positive (negative) excess demand price — reduces (increases) the excess demand price, i.e. if

$$\frac{dE^{-1}}{dq} = \frac{d[p_d(q) - p_s(q)]}{dq} < 0 , \tag{3.3}$$

that is

$$\frac{dp_d}{dq} - \frac{dp_s}{dq} < 0 . \tag{3.4}$$

Since $p_d = p_d(q)$ is the *inverse* of the function $D = D(p)$, and $p_s = p_s(q)$ is the inverse of the function $S = S(p)$, it follows, by a well-known theorem in elementary calculus, that

$$\frac{dp_d}{dq} = \left(\frac{dD}{dp}\right)^{-1} ,$$

and that

$$\frac{dp_s}{dq} = \left(\frac{dS}{dp}\right)^{-1} .$$

Therefore, eq. (3.4) may be written as

$$\left(\frac{dD}{dp}\right)^{-1} - \left(\frac{dS}{dp}\right)^{-1} < 0 . \tag{3.4'}$$

Before passing to compare conditions (3.2) and (3.4'), let us examine the *dynamic stability* conditions. The method used to study the dynamic stability is the following: the behaviour assumption is formalized as a functional equation, which is then solved to determine the time path of the relevant variables.

The dynamic formalization of the Walrasian assumption is the following:

$$p' = f[D(p) - S(p)] ,$$

where

$$\text{sgn} \, f[\ldots] = \text{sgn} \, [\ldots], \quad f[0] = 0, \quad f'[0] > 0 . \tag{3.5}$$

The notation $\text{sgn} \, f[\ldots] = \text{sgn} \, [\ldots]$ means that f is a *sign-preserving* function, i.e. that the dependent variable has the same sign as the independent variable (which in this case is excess demand): therefore, if excess demand is positive (negative), the time derivative of p is positive (negative), i.e. p is increasing (decreasing), and this is what the Walrasian assumption says. The condition $f[0] = 0$ means that the time derivative of p is zero when excess demand is zero, and this is obvious since zero excess demand means that the system is in equilibrium, i.e. price does not vary. The condition $f'[0] > 0$ means that the function is increasing at the point where it passes from negative to positive values.

Eq. (3.5) is a first-order differential equation and to solve it we need to know the form of the functions f, D, S. There are two methods. Either we give such functions an arbitrary form (usually linear, for simplicity's sake) or we expand them in Taylor's series at the equilibrium point and neglect all terms of order higher than the first (i.e. we make a linear approximation of the functions; thus, the results that we obtain are valid only in a neighbourhood of the equilibrium point and, consequently, the stability conditions are *local*). In both cases we obtain a first-order linear differential equation with constant coefficients, which is *****:

$$p' = c(b - b_1)(p - p_e), \tag{3.6}$$

i.e.

$$p' - c(b - b_1)p = -c(b - b_1)p_e, \tag{3.6'}$$

where $b \equiv dD/dp$, $b_1 \equiv dS/dp$, p_e is the equilibrium price and c is a positive constant.

Applying the methods expounded in Part II, ch. 2, the solution of $(3.6')$ is found to be

---

* In the first case, we have

$$p' = c[a + bp - (a_1 + b_1 p)] = c(b - b_1)p + c(a - a_1).$$

Since $p_e = (a - a_1)/(b_1 - b)$, it follows that $c(a - a_1) = -c(b - b_1)p_e$ and so $p' = c(b - b_1)(p - p_e)$. In the second case, we must linearize f, D and S. Linearizing f at the point where $D = S$, we have $p' = c[D(p) - S(p)]$, where $c \equiv f'[0]$. Linearizing D and S at the point where $p = p_e$, we obtain

$$p' = c[b(p - p_e) + D_e - b_1(p - p_e) - S_e],$$

where $b \equiv (dD/dp)^e$, $b_1 \equiv (dS/dp)^e$ (the symbol $(\ )^e$ means that the derivative is taken where $p = p_e$). Since $D_e = S_e$, it follows that

$$p' = c(b - b_1)(p - p_e).$$

$$p(t) = A \exp\left[c(b - b_1)t\right] + p_e , \tag{3.7}$$

where A is an arbitrary constant, equal to the initial deviation $p(0) - p_e$. Equilibrium is stable if $p(t)$ tends to p_e as t increases, i.e. if the term $A \exp\left[c(b - b_1)t\right]$ tends to zero. This in turn is equivalent to the quantity $c(b - b_1)$ being negative, and since $c > 0$, we arrive at the following stability condition:

$$b - b_1 < 0 . \tag{3.8}$$

Note that inequality (3.8) is the same as inequality (3.2), so that, in this case, the static and the dynamic stability conditions are the same. Let us anticipate that a similar conclusion holds in the case of the Marshallian assumption. Now, we must emphasize the fact that the coincidence between the static and dynamic stability conditions deduced from a given behaviour assumption is *not* a general rule (see Part II, ch. 9, §1). Given the greater importance of dynamic stability conditions over static stability conditions, whenever a 'disagreement' occurs between them the former must be preferred. More drastically, the study of static stability may be neglected and attention concentrated on dynamic stability only. However, both concepts are given here to demonstrate the conclusion just stated (which will be strengthened by the material contained in Part II, ch. 9, §1).

The dynamic formalization of the Marshallian assumption is the following:

$$q' = g[p_d(q) - p_s(q)] , \tag{3.9}$$

where

$$\text{sgn } g[...] = \text{sgn } [...] , \quad g[0] = 0 , \quad g'[0] > 0 .$$

The interpretation of eq. (3.9) is similar to that of eq. (3.5): it is enough to substitute 'quantity' in the place of 'price' and 'excess demand price' in the place of 'excess demand'.

From eq. (3.9) we obtain — with a similar procedure as before (i.e. either assuming linear functions or making a linear approximation at the equilibrium point) — the following differential equation:

$$q' = k\left(\frac{1}{b} - \frac{1}{b_1}\right)(q - q_e) , \tag{3.10}$$

where b and b_1 have the same meaning as before, k is a positive constant and

q_e is the equilibrium quantity. The solution of eq. (3.10) is

$$q(t) = A \exp\left[k\left(\frac{1}{b} - \frac{1}{b_1} \right) t \right] + q_e , \qquad (3.11)$$

and so the stability condition is

$$\frac{1}{b} - \frac{1}{b_1} < 0 \qquad (3.12)$$

which coincides with (3.4').

We may now compare (3.12) with (3.8). They give the same result both in the 'normal' case and in the 'extreme abnormal' case, whereas they give opposite results in the 'simple abnormal' cases. By 'normal' case we mean the case in which the demand function is a decreasing function and the supply function is an increasing function (i.e., $b < 0$ and so $1/b < 0$; and $b_1 > 0$ and so $1/b_1 > 0$). It is easy to see that in this case both (3.8) and (3.12) are satisfied, so that equilibrium is stable according to both the Walrasian and the Marshallian behaviour assumption.

By 'extreme abnormal' case we mean the case in which demand is an increasing function and supply is a decreasing function: neither (3.8) nor (3.12) are now satisfied, so that equilibrium is unstable according to both behaviour assumptions.

By 'simple abnormal' cases we mean the cases in which one of the two functions is abnormal whereas the other is normal. Let us rewrite (3.12) as

$$\frac{b_1 - b}{bb_1} < 0 . \qquad (3.13)$$

Now, in the cases under consideration the product bb_1 is a positive magnitude (since we have either $b > 0$, $b_1 > 0$, or $b < 0$, $b_1 < 0$), so that (3.13) is equivalent to

$$b_1 - b < 0 , \qquad (3.14)$$

and it is obvious that, if (3.14) holds, then (3.8) cannot hold, and vice versa. Therefore, in the 'simple abnormal' cases, if equilibrium is stable according to one behaviour assumption, then it is unstable according to the other, and vice versa. This illustrates the already mentioned principle of *relativity of stability conditions*. We may now wonder whether there is any point at all in studying stability, since the results that we obtain may no longer be valid if a different behaviour assumption is adopted. The answer is that, firstly, in the normal cases different behaviour assumptions usually give the same results. Secondly, although the possible behaviour assumptions are in principle many, those that may be deemed *plausible* in the study of the stability of a given equilibrium point are usually a very small number (two or three) and, moreover, the simple observation of facts often enables us to see that only one is the most *realistic* (i.e. best suited to describe the behaviour of the economic agents in the case under examination). Let us note, finally, that *relativity of results is a principle valid in all economic theory*, in which results depend on assumptions, so that different assumptions may (though not necessarily must) give rise to different results.

Exercises

1. Let $D = 80 - 4p$ be the demand function and $S = -10 + 2p$ the supply function. Determine the equilibrium point and study its stability (as initial point take $p_0 = 18, q_0 = 8$).

Calculation. The equilibrium point is determined equating demand and supply, and so

$$80 - 4p = -10 + 2p ,$$

so that $p_e = 15$, to which corresponds $q_e = 20$.

Let us now examine stability, beginning with the Walrasian assumption. Excess demand is

$$E(p) = 80 - 4p - (-10 + 2p) = 90 - 6p ,$$

and since $dE/dp = -6 < 0$, the static stability condition is satisfied. Dynamically we have the differential equation

$$p' = c(90 - 6p) = -6cp + 90c ,$$

whose solution is

$$p(t) = Ae^{-6ct} + 15 ,$$

where, given $p_0 = 18$, we have $A = 3$. Since c is a positive constant, the term Ae^{-6ct} tends to zero, so that equilibrium is dynamically stable.

To examine stability according to the Marshallian assumption, we must first express demand and supply price as functions of quantity. The inverse demand and supply functions are

$$p_d = 20 - \tfrac{1}{4} q \ ,$$

$$p_s = 5 + \tfrac{1}{2} q \ ,$$

which give $E^{-1}(q) = 20 - \tfrac{1}{4} q - (5 + \tfrac{1}{2} q) = 15 - \tfrac{3}{4} q$.

Since $dE^{-1}/dq = -\tfrac{3}{4} < 0$, the static stability condition is satisfied. Dynamically we have the differential equation

$$q' = k(15 - \tfrac{3}{4} q) = -\tfrac{3}{4} kq + 15 k \ ,$$

whose solution is

$$q(t) = Ae^{-\tfrac{3}{4} kt} + 20 \ ,$$

where, given $q_0 = 8$, we have $A = -12$. Since k is a positive constant, the term $Ae^{-\tfrac{3}{4} kt}$ tends to zero as t increases, so that equilibrium is dynamically stable.

2. Examine the following cases:
   (a) $D = 20 + p$, $S = -10 + 2p$; $p_0 = 31$, $q_0 = 51$,
   (b) $D = 70 - p$, $S = -10 - 3p$; $p_0 = 30$, $q_0 = 40$.

§2. A re-formulation of the cobweb theorem

In Part I, ch. 3, §1 we expounded the 'cobweb theorem' in terms of difference equations. Let us recall that the simplest formulation of that model may be considered as a particular case of the more general model

$$D_t = a + bp_t \ ,$$

$$S_t = a_1 + b_1 \hat{p}_t \ ,$$

$$D_t = S_t \ ,$$

where $\hat{p}_t$ is expected price.

Let us now assume that: (a) production (supply) is a continuous flow; (b) expectations are formed according to the equation $\hat{p}(t) = p(t) + cp'$, where c is a given constant. The sign of c is very important: if $c > 0$, expectations are of the extrapolative kind. In fact, if price is increasing, producers expect a further increase ($\hat{p}(t) = p(t) + cp' > p(t)$, since $c > 0$ and $p' > 0$); if price is decreasing producers expect a further decrease ($\hat{p}(t) = p(t) + cp' < p(t)$). On the contrary, if $c < 0$, producers expect an inversion of the current trend of price: if price is increasing, they expect a decrease ($\hat{p}(t) = p(t) + cp' < p(t)$) and vice versa [*].

Formally, we have

$$D(t) = a + bp(t) ,$$

$$S(t) = a_1 + b_1 [p(t) + cp'] ,$$

$$D(t) = S(t) ,$$

from which

$$b_1 cp' + (b_1 - b) p(t) = a - a_1 , \tag{3.15}$$

whose solution is

$$p(t) = A \exp \left(\frac{b - b_1}{c} t \right) + p_e , \tag{3.16}$$

where $p_e = (a - a_1)/(b_1 - b)$ is a particular solution of (3.15) and equals the equilibrium price, and $A = p_0 - p_e$ is the initial deviation.

In the normal case, the demand function is negatively sloped and the supply function is positively sloped, so that $b - b_1 < 0$. Then, if $c > 0$, it will be $(b - b_1)/c < 0$, so that equilibrium is stable, since $A \exp \{ [(b - b_1)/c]t \}$ tends to zero as t increases and consequently $p(t)$ tends to p_e. If $c < 0$ we reach the opposite conclusion. Note that in some abnormal cases (e.g., $b > 0$, $b_1 > 0$ and such that $b - b_1 > 0$) the results are opposite since if $c < 0$ we have stability, if $c > 0$ instability.

We should note, since it gives us the occasion for some general remarks, that in the original treatment with difference equations the 'cobweb theorem' could give rise to both monotonic and alternating movements, whereas in the present treatment only monotonic movements can take place.

---

[*] Such expectations are the continuous counterpart of those described, in the context of a 'period' analysis, in Part I, ch. 5, §4.

From the merely formal point of view the reason is that a first-order difference equation admits of both types of movement, whereas a first-order differential equation admits only of monotonic movements. But this gives rise to a difficulty: if the results that we obtain in the study of a given problem are different if we use different mathematical tools, how can we know which are the 'correct' results and how can we establish which is the 'correct' tool to use? The fact is that, as we treat the problem with one or another tool, we more or less consciously adopt *different* assumptions, so that the problem only *appears* to be the same, but is actually different. It is important that this should always be kept in mind in order to avoid doubts and confusion. To return to our example, if we use difference equations we assume that output is discrete, that expectations are of a certain type, etc.; if we use differential equations we assume that output is a continuous flow, that expectations are of a certain other type, etc. No wonder that with different assumptions we obtain different results; it is a well-known fact that, if assumptions are different, the results may (although they need not) be different. In economics, it may often seem that it makes no difference whether a given problem is formalized with difference or differential equations. But if we are careful to examine thoroughly the economic assumptions that we are making, our uncertainly usually disappears. So it is the exact setting of the problem in economic terms that suggests the choice of the appropriate mathematical tool.

Exercises
1. The following functions are given:

$$D = 80 - 4p$$

$$S = -10 + 2\hat{p} ,$$

where $\hat{p}$ is expected price, given by the equation $\hat{p} = p + cp'$. Determine the static equilibrium price and, given that $c = 1$, check whether it is stable. Assuming that $p_0 = 18$, compute the value of $p(t)$ for $t = 1.5$.

Calculation. Substituting $\hat{p} = p + cp'$ in the supply function and equating supply and demand, we obtain, after simple manipulation, the equation

$$cp' + 3p = 45 . \tag{3.17}$$

When price is in equilibrium, $p' = 0$, so that from (3.17) we obtain

$$3p_e = 45 ; \qquad \text{therefore } p_e = 15 .$$

This value is, from the mathematical point of view, a particular solution of eq. (3.17). For the homogeneous equation $cp' + 3p = 0$, let us try $p(t) = e^{\lambda t}$. We obtain

$$c\lambda e^{\lambda t} + 3e^{\lambda t} = 0 ,$$

$$e^{\lambda t}(c\lambda + 3) = 0 . \tag{3.18}$$

If $e^{\lambda t}$ is a solution, eq. (3.18) must be identically satisfied, and this is possible if, and only if,

$$c\lambda + 3 = 0 , \tag{3.19}$$

which is the characteristic equation of the homogeneous part of (3.17). From (3.19) we have $\lambda = -3/c$, so that the general solution of (3.17) is

$$p(t) = A \exp\left(-\frac{3}{c}t\right) + 15 , \tag{3.20}$$

where A is an arbitrary constant. With $c = 1$, (3.20) becomes

$$p(t) = Ae^{-3t} + 15 , \tag{3.20'}$$

so that $p(t)$ tends to 15 as t increases: the equilibrium price is stable. Given $p_0 = 18$, we substitute it in (3.20'), obtaining

$$18 = p_0 = Ae^0 + 15 ;$$

therefore

$$18 = A + 15 ,$$

$$A = 3 .$$

Thus, the value of A is the initial deviation $p_0 - p_e$. We finally have

$$p(t) = 3e^{-3t} + 15 . \tag{3.21}$$

To compute the value of $p(t)$ for $t = 1.5$, we must compute the value of $e^{-4.5}$ (if we do not have the tables of $e^{\pm x}$, we can use logarithms). It turns out that $e^{-4.5} \simeq 0.011109$, so that $p(1.5) \simeq 15.033327$.

2. Examine the following cases:
(a) $D = 80 - 4p,\qquad S = -10 + 2\hat{p},\qquad c = -1,\qquad p_0 = 18;$
(b) same data as in (a), but for $c = 2$;
(c) $D = 20 + p,\qquad S = -10 + 2\hat{p},\qquad c = 2,\qquad p_0 = 31;$
(d) same data as in (c), but for $c = -1$.

§3. Domar's model

This model and Harrod's model — formulated independently by the two authors — are often put together and called the 'Harrod–Domar model'. Others — and we among them — think that the two models must be kept distinct, although the final equation that gives the time path of income is actually the same, apart from notation. The fact is that, from an economic point of view, the two models are substantially different. In Harrod's model there is a precise behaviour assumption as to entrepreneur's investment decisions, which gives rise to an investment function. In Domar's model there is no investment function (in the behavioural sense), since his problem is different: he wants to determine the rate at which investment must grow for there to be no idle capacity, and does not introduce any investment function to explain how investment might actually grow at that rate [*].

The general idea of Domar's model is the following: investment increases productive capacity and, in order that such capacity be always fully utilized, the increment in (potential) output made possible by the increment in productive capacity must be entirely absorbed by an increment in aggregate demand. Aggregate demand is consumption plus investment. Now assume that output, and so income, increases by the full amount which utilizes all the increment in productive capacity. Since the marginal propensity to consume is less than unity, the increase in consumption absorbs only a part of the increase in output, so that an increase in investment is needed to absorb the remaining part. But the increase in investment further increases productive capacity, and so on. Thus it is necessary, in order to avoid the appearance of non-utilized productive capacity (which would eventually stop investment and so economic growth), that investment goes on increasing. It turns out (see below) that it must increase at a constant (proportional) rate, to which corresponds a constant rate of growth of income (the two rates are actually the same).

[*] From another point of view, if we accept the distinction between positive and normative economics, Harrod's model might be considered as a positive model and Domar's as a normative model.

It is important to note, before turning to the mathematics, that in this model both roles of investment (it is a component of aggregate demand, and it increases productive capacity) are taken into account. In analysing short-run problems we may, as Keynes did, consider only the first role, but in discussing long-run problems (and especially the problem of economic growth) we must consider both roles.

In what follows, $P(t)$ is potential output, Y is actual output (income), σ is the 'potential social average productivity of investment', i.e. a coefficient which indicates by how much a unit of investment increases productive capacity (productive capacity is measured directly in terms of potential output); the other symbols have the usual meanings. In continuous terms, we have

$$P' = \sigma I . \tag{3.22}$$

Let us note that the coefficient σ can be interpreted as the reciprocal of the capital/output ratio. In fact, a given investment I coincides by definition with the increment in the capital stock (we do not consider the problem of depreciation). Given a marginal (and average) capital/output ratio k, the increment in the capital stock makes possible a (potential) increase in output equal to $1/k$ times the increment in the capital stock, so that, putting $1/k = \sigma$, eq. (3.22) follows.

$$Y' = C' + I' . \tag{3.23}$$

Eq. (3.23) says that, in equilibrium, the increment in output equals the increment in aggregate demand. Assuming a consumption function with a constant average propensity, we have

$$Y' = (1 - s)Y' + I' , \tag{3.23'}$$

which gives

$$Y' = \frac{1}{s} I' . \tag{3.24}$$

We could also obtain eq. (3.24) directly, remembering that the increase in income equals the multiplier $1/s$ times the increase in investment. Assuming that in the initial period productive capacity is fully utilized, for this situation to be continued over time the increase in potential output must equal the increase in actual output, i.e.

$$Y' = P' . \qquad\qquad (3.25)$$

From (3.22), (3.24) and (3.25) we have

$$I' = \sigma s I . \qquad\qquad (3.26)$$

Eq. (3.26) expresses the relation that must be satisfied by investment in order that productive capacity be fully utilized over time. The solution of (3.26) is

$$I(t) = I_0 e^{s\sigma t} , \qquad\qquad (3.27)$$

where I_0 is the initial level of investment. Investment must grow at the constant (proportional) rate $s\sigma$. It is easy to see that, if investment grows at that rate, output (income) will grow at the same rate. Integrating with respect to time both sides of (3.24), we have $sY = I + A$, where A is an arbitrary constant, and given (3.27) we have

$$sY = I_0 e^{s\sigma t} + A ,$$

i.e.

$$Y = \frac{1}{s} I_0 e^{s\sigma t} + \frac{A}{s} .$$

Assuming that we start from an equilibrium situation, we must have $sY_0 = I_0$, so that $Y_0 = (1/s) I_0$ and, consequently, A must be zero. Thus we have

$$Y(t) = Y_0 e^{s\sigma t} , \qquad\qquad (3.28)$$

and so also Y grows at the rate $s\sigma$. Therefore, income grows at a rate which is the same as the one which obtains in Harrod's model ($s\sigma = s/k$). But the similarity between the two models, as we said at the beginning, does not go much beyond this formal fact.

Exercises

1. Given $s = 0.20$, $\sigma = 0.5$, determine the time path of income according to Domar's model and compute the value of $Y(t)$ for $t = 3$ ($I_0 = 20$, $Y_0 = 100$).

Calculation. The equation for the increment in productive capacity is

$$P' = \tfrac{1}{2} I(t) ,$$

and the equation for the increment in aggregate demand is

$$Y' = \frac{1}{0.2} I' .$$

Equating P' and Y', we have

$$\tfrac{1}{2} I(t) = \frac{1}{0.2} I' ;$$

therefore

$$I' - 0.10 I(t) = 0 ,$$

whose solution is

$$I(t) = I_0 e^{0.10t} ,$$

and so

$$I(t) = 20 e^{0.10t} .$$

Since $0.2Y' = I'$, we have $0.2 Y = I + A$, whence

$$Y(t) = 100 e^{0.10t} + 5 A .$$

For $t = 0$, $Y_0 = 100 + A$ and, since $Y_0 = 100$, it follows that $A = 0$. Therefore,

$$Y(t) = 100 e^{0.10t} .$$

For $t = 3$ we have

$$Y_3 = 100 e^{0.30} .$$

From the tables of e^x (or, lacking them, using logarithms) we obtain

$$e^{0.30} \simeq 1.3499 ,$$

and so

$$Y_3 = 134.99 .$$

2. Examine the following cases ($\sigma = 1/k$):

$$s = 0.24 \,, \quad k = 3 \,, \quad I_0 = 24 \,, \quad Y_0 = 100 \,;$$
$$s = 0.30 \,, \quad k = 2 \,, \quad I_0 = 30 \,, \quad Y_0 = 100 \,;$$
$$s = 0.15 \,, \quad k = 5 \,, \quad I_0 = 15 \,, \quad Y_0 = 100 \,.$$

§4. The neoclassical aggregate growth model (Solow)

The problem under consideration is whether a situation of growth in income with continuous full employment of labour is possible and, if so, whether such a situation is stable.

With regard to the first question (existence), it is obvious that − on the assumption of no technical progress − income and the labour force must increase at the same (proportionate) rate of growth. As a point of departure, take the fundamental relation

$$\frac{\Delta Y}{Y} = \frac{s}{k} \,, \tag{3.29}$$

where $\Delta Y/Y$ (i.e. Y'/Y in continuous terms) is the rate of growth of income and s, k have the usual meaning of average (and marginal) propensity to save and of average (and marginal) capital/output ratio. The relation is easily proved:

$$\frac{s}{k} = \frac{S}{Y} \left(\frac{\Delta K}{\Delta Y} \right)^{-1} = \frac{S}{Y} \frac{\Delta Y}{\Delta K} \,,$$

and, since $\Delta K = I$ (ignoring depreciation or working with net magnitudes) and in equilibrium $I = S$, it follows that S and $\Delta K = I$ cancel out, so that $s/k = \Delta Y/Y$. In continuous terms, $\Delta Y/Y = Y'/Y$, as said above, and $\Delta K = K'$.

On the assumption that population grows at a constant (proportionate) rate, say n, and that the labour force is a constant fraction of population so that it also grows at the same rate n, the condition for the existence of full employment growth is

$$s/k = n \,. \tag{3.30}$$

In general, if s, k and n are given and independent constants, the above equality would be purely accidental, and we would not expect it to occur. This, in fact, is the conclusion to be drawn from Harrod's model. Instead, if k is assumed to be variable, in principle it is possible to satisfy the equality, provided that k can take on the value s/n.

The neoclassical aggregate model in its simplest version assumes that the production function is homogeneous of degree one (with the usual properties) and that this function admits of an *unlimited* ★ substitutability between capital and labour. In this way it is always possible to equate k to s/n. From the static point of view, the problem is to find the capital/labour ratio which gives rise to an output/labour ratio such that the capital/output ratio is the desired one. Formally, given the production function

$$Y = f(K, L),$$ (3.31)

write it in the 'intensive' form

$$Y/L = f(r, 1)$$ (3.32)

where $r \equiv K/L$. Now,

$$k = \frac{K}{Y} = \frac{K}{Lf(r, 1)} = \frac{r}{f(r, 1)},$$ (3.33)

so that the required amount of capital per unit of labour is obtained solving the equation

$$\frac{s}{n} = \frac{r}{f(r, 1)},$$

which can be written as

$$\frac{s}{n} f(r, 1) = r,$$ (3.34)

★ By 'unlimited' substitutability we mean that, to produce any given output, any amount – from zero (excluded or included) to infinity – of capital can be (efficiently) used, obviously using with it the appropriate amount of labour. This assumption is necessary to guarantee that the capital/output ratio can take on any (positive) value; if it were not so, it might happen that the ratio which is needed to equate s/k to n cannot be attained given the state of technology expressed by the production function.

or as

$$sf(r, 1) = nr .$$ (3.35)

A simple graphical interpretation of eq. (3.34) is given by fig. 3.2.

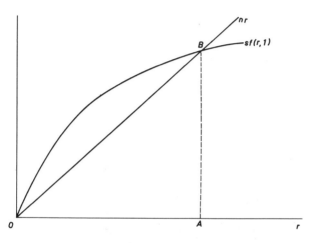

Fig. 3.2.

If the production function is 'well-behaved', an intersection, and only one, always exists. Point A gives the required amount of capital per unit of labour. It is easy to see that this amount is indeed the one which gives rise to a capital/output ratio equal to s/n. By definition,

$$\overline{OA}/\overline{AB} = \frac{K}{L} \left(s \frac{Y}{L} \right)^{-1} = \frac{K}{sY}.$$

Geometrically,

$$\overline{OA}/\overline{AB} = 1/n$$

and, equating the two results, it follows that $K/Y = s/n$.

We can now pass to the second question (stability). The basic equations of the model, already introduced, though not in this order, are

$$
\begin{aligned}
Y &= f(K, L) \\
  &= Lf(r, 1) ,
\end{aligned}
$$ (3.36)

$$S = sY , \tag{3.37}$$

$$K' = I , \tag{3.38}$$

$$K' = sY , \tag{3.39}$$

$$L = L_0 e^{nt} . \tag{3.40}$$

Eq. (3.39) implies that $I = S$ (*ex ante*) and eq. (3.40) implies that the labour force is fully employed. Consider now the definition of r,

$$r = K/L ,$$

which gives

$$K = rL_0 e^{nt} . \tag{3.41}$$

Differentiating both members with respect to time we have ★

$$K' = r'L_0 e^{nt} + nrL_0 e^{nt}$$

and, given (3.39), (3.36) and (3.40),

$$sL_0 e^{nt} f(r, 1) = r'L_0 e^{nt} + nrL_0 e^{nt} .$$

The term $L_0 e^{nt}$ cancels out, so that we have

$$r' = sf(r, 1) - nr , \tag{3.42}$$

which is the fundamental dynamic equation of the model. It can be easily seen that, if the production function is 'well-behaved', the point of equilibrium is stable. First of all, note that if we impose the condition that r be in equilibrium, i.e. that $r' = 0$, then from eq. (3.42) we obtain eq. (3.35) already discussed above. Consider now fig. 3.2: to the left (right) of point A, the function $sf(r, 1)$ lies above (below) the function nr, i.e., respectively, $sf(r, 1) - nr \gtrless 0$. Given this, from eq. (3.42) it follows that to the left (right) of point A, r is positive (negative), i.e. that r increases (decreases) according to whether it is smaller (greater) than its equilibrium value. This proves stabil-

---

★ Eq. (3.42) follows from the fact that eq. (3.41) is an *identity*, so that the derivatives of both members are equal (with equations this would *not* in general be true)..

ity *. To examine specific cases, we have only to substitute a specific function for the generic function $f(r, 1)$. For example, given the well-known Cobb–Douglas production function, $Y = K^{\alpha}L^{1-\alpha}$, we have $f(r, 1) = r^{\alpha}$, so that eq. (3.42) becomes

$$r' = sr^{\alpha} - nr .$$ (3.43)

Eq. (3.43), although being of the first order, is not linear, since r appears also to the α-th power. However, it can be brought to a linear equation by means of a simple transformation **. Define a new variable, z, connected to r by the relation

$$z = r^{1-\alpha} ,$$ (3.44)

whence, differentiating with respect to time, we have

$$z' = (1 - \alpha)r^{-\alpha}r' ,$$

i.e.

$$\frac{1}{1-\alpha}z' = r^{-\alpha}r' .$$ (3.45)

Now, multiply both members of (3.43) by $r^{-\alpha}$:

$$r^{-\alpha}r' = s - nr^{1-\alpha} ,$$

and, making use of (3.44) and (3.45),

$$\frac{1}{1-\alpha}z' = s - nz ,$$

i.e.

$$z' + n(1-\alpha)z = s(1-\alpha) ,$$ (3.46)

which is linear in z (and with constant coefficients).

---

* Similar reasoning would prove the instability of equilibrium in the case in which the function $sf(r, 1)$ were such as to cut the function nr from below.
** This transformation of variables is a general method for solving equations of type (3.43) – they are called Bernoulli equations – and will be expounded in greater detail in appendix III, §4.

The general solution of the homogeneous part of (3.46) is

$$A \exp\left[-n(1-\alpha)t\right],$$

and a particular solution of (3.46), obtained putting $z' = 0$, is

$$\bar{z}(t) = s/n,$$

so that the general solution of (3.46) is

$$z(t) = A \exp\left[-n(1-\alpha)t\right] + s/n. \tag{3.47}$$

From (3.44) we have the inverse transformation

$$r = z^{1/(1-\alpha)} \tag{3.44'}$$

so that from (3.47) we have

$$r(t) = \{A \exp\left[-n(1-\alpha)t\right] + s/n\}^{1/(1-\alpha)}. \tag{3.48}$$

Assuming that r has a known value, say r_0, for $t = 0$, from (3.48) we obtain

$$r_0 = (A + s/n)^{1/(1-\alpha)};$$

therefore

$$r_0^{1-\alpha} = A + s/n,$$

$$A = r_0^{1-\alpha} - s/n,$$

and so

$$r(t) = \{(r_0^{1-\alpha} - s/n) \exp\left[-n(1-\alpha)t\right] + s/n\}^{1/(1-\alpha)}. \tag{3.48'}$$

Since n and $(1-\alpha)$ are positive magnitudes, the term $(r_0^{1-\alpha} - s/n)\exp[-n(1-\alpha)t]$ tends to zero as t increases, so that $r(t)$ tends to its equilibrium value, $(s/n)^{1/(1-\alpha)}$.

The introduction of technical progress in this model can be made in a very simple manner if we assume that technical progress is 'labour augmenting', that is it increases the productivity of labour, so that in any time t the same physical unit of labour produces more than in time $t - dt$. In this case we have only to measure labour in 'efficiency units', instead of in natural units. Now, if technical progress occurs at a constant proportionate rate, we can reinterpret n as the rate of growth of the labour force *plus* the rate of labour augmenting technical progress (so that $L = L_0 e^{nt}$ is labour measured in efficiency units), and then proceed as before in the analysis of the model. More general types of technical progress will be examined in Appendix III, §7.2.

An interesting conclusion that has been drawn from the neoclassical model is the so-called '*golden rule*' of capital accumulation, which is the answer to the following question: given that the system is on its equilibrium path and assuming that the only goal of society is to maximize consumption per unit of labour, how is this goal to be reached? The analysis is very simple. On the equilibrium path, all variables grow at the same proportionate rate n, so that

$$K' = nK .$$

Consumption equals output minus investment, that is

$$C = f(K, L) - nK ,$$

and, given that f is homogeneous of degree one,

$$C/L = f(r, 1) - nr .$$

Now, C/L is at a maximum when

$$\frac{\mathrm{d}[f(r, 1) - nr]}{\mathrm{d}r} = f'(r, 1) - n = 0 . \tag{3.49}$$

The second derivative, $f''(r, 1)$, is negative since f is assumed to be a well-behaved function, so that the stationary point given by (3.49) is indeed a maximum. Since $f'(r, 1)$ is the marginal productivity of capital [*], the 'golden rule' states that in order to maximize consumption per unit of labour the marginal productivity of capital must be equal to the exogenously given growth rate of the labour force. For further treatment of golden rules, see Phelps (1966).

---

[*] Since $f(K, L) = Lf(r, 1)$, we have

$$\frac{\partial f}{\partial K} = Lf'(r, 1) \frac{1}{L} = f'(r, 1) .$$

Exercises

1. Assume that the aggregate production function is $Y = K^{2/3}L^{1/3}$, that the rate of growth of the labour force is 0.05 and that the average propensity to save is 0.20. Compute:

(a) the value that the capital/output ratio must have in order that full employment growth obtains;

(b) the corresponding value of the capital/labour ratio.

Solve the basic differential equation and show that equilibrium is stable. Given that the initial value of the capital/labour ratio is $r_0 = 80$, compute:

(c) the time required for the absolute deviation of $r(t)$ from its equilibrium value to be reduced to 10% of the initial deviation;

(d) the time required for the proportional deviation of $r(t)$ from its equilibrium value to be reduced to 10%.

Calculation. The answer to question (a) is obtained solving the equation

$$0.20/k = 0.05 ,$$

which gives $k = 4$.

Given the production function $Y = K^{2/3}L^{1/3}$, we have

$$\frac{K}{Y} = \frac{K}{K^{2/3}L^{1/3}} = \left(\frac{K}{L}\right)^{1/3} ,$$

so that

$$\frac{K}{L} = \left(\frac{K}{Y}\right)^{3} .$$

For $K/Y = 4$, we have $K/L = 64$, and this is the answer to question (b).

With the given values of s, n and α, the basic differential equation becomes

$$r' = 0.20\, r^{2/3} - 0.05\, r .$$

The substitution $z = r^{1/3}$ transforms the above equation into

$$z' + \frac{0.05}{3}\, z = \frac{0.20}{3} ,$$

whose solution is

$$z(t) = A \exp\left(-\frac{0.05}{3} t\right) + 4 .$$

The inverse transformation $r = z^3$ gives

$$r(t) = \left[A \exp\left(-\frac{0.05}{3} t\right) + 4 \right]^3 .$$

As $t \to \infty$, the term $A \exp [(-0.05/3)t]$ tends to zero, so that $r(t)$ tends to $4^3 = 64$, which is its equilibrium value.

Given $r_0 = 80$, the solution becomes

$$r(t) = \left[(80^{1/3} - 4) \exp\left(-\frac{0.05}{3} t\right) + 4 \right]^3 \simeq \left[0.308869 \exp\left(-\frac{0.05}{3} t\right) + 4 \right]^3 .$$

The initial deviation is 16, so that to answer question (c) we must find the value of t such that

$$r(t) - 64 = 1.6 ,$$

or

$$\left[0.308869 \exp\left(-\frac{0.05}{3} t\right) + 4 \right]^3 = 65.6 ,$$

i.e., taking the cube root of both sides,

$$0.308869 \exp\left(-\frac{0.05}{3} t\right) + 4 \simeq 4.033059 ,$$

so that

$$\exp\left(-\frac{0.05}{3} t\right) \simeq 0.1070324 .$$

Using Naperian logarithms,

$$t = -\frac{3}{0.05} \log_e 0.1070324 \simeq 134.07882 .$$

The proportional deviation is

$$\frac{r(t) - 64}{64},$$

so that to answer question (d) we must find the value of t such that

$$\left[0.308869 \exp\left(-\frac{0.05}{3} t \right) + 4 \right]^3 = 70.4,$$

whence, taking the cube root of both sides and using Naperian logarithms,

$$t \simeq -\frac{3}{0.05} \log_e \frac{0.129120}{0.308869} \simeq 52.33638.$$

For some general remarks on the speed of adjustment in the neoclassical model, see Sato (1963) and Okuguchi (1968) and the references quoted by the latter.

2. Same problems as in exercise 1, but with the following data:
$Y = K^{1/2}L^{1/2}, n = 0.01, s = 0.25, r_0 = 600.$

§5. Money and growth in the neoclassical aggregate model (Stein)

In the recent literature on growth models, increasing attention has been devoted to the introduction of money in such models. Research has been carried on along two lines: the neoclassical and the 'Keynes–Wicksell' line (Stein's terminology). The main difference between monetary growth models of the neoclassical and of the Keynes–Wicksell type is that in the former there is not an independent investment function (i.e. all saving is automatically invested), which is present in the latter. In other words, in neoclassical models the $S = I$ equilibrium always exists by assumption, whereas in the Keynes–Wicksell models S and I may be unequal (in the 'ex ante' sense) and, when they are, a disequilibrium situation occurs and adjustments take place in the price level.

As a natural extension of the previous section we shall examine a neoclassical monetary growth model; the reader interested in a Keynes–Wicksell model, as well as in a comparison of the results obtained in the two types of models, may consult Stein's (1969) paper, on which our treatment is based ★.

★ In any case, Stein's Keynes–Wicksell model could not be expounded here, since it involves a system of two simultaneous differential equations. Thus the interested reader

The production function, assumed to have the usual properties (positive and decreasing marginal products and constant returns to scale), is

$$Y = f(K, L) , \tag{3.50}$$

which can be written as

$$y = y(x) , \qquad y'(x) > 0 , \qquad y''(x) < 0 , \tag{3.50'}$$

where $y \equiv Y/K$ is output per unit of capital and $x \equiv L/K$ is labour per unit of capital. The labour force grows at the constant proportionate rate n and is always fully employed, i.e.

$$L(t) = L_0 e^{nt} . \tag{3.51}$$

Real saving is assumed to depend on output and on real net claims of the private sector on the public sector, all variables being expressed per unit of capital [*]:

$$\frac{S}{K} = S^*(y, \theta v) , \qquad \frac{\partial S^*}{\partial y} > 0 , \qquad \frac{\partial S^*}{\partial \theta v} < 0 , \tag{3.52}$$

where $v \equiv (M/p)/K$ is real balances per unit of capital (M is the stock of money and p the price level) and $\theta \equiv c/M$ is net monetary claims of the private sector upon the public sector (c) per unit of money, so that $\theta v = (c/p)/K =$ real net claims of the private sector on the public sector per unit of capital. The signs of the partial derivatives reflect the usual properties of a saving function in which a 'real balance effect' is included. Substituting $(3.50')$ into (3.52) we have

$$\frac{S}{K} = S(x, v) , \qquad \frac{\partial S}{\partial x} > 0 , \qquad \frac{\partial S}{\partial v} \leqslant 0 ; \tag{3.52'}$$

when $\theta > 0$, then $\partial S/\partial v < 0$; the case $\partial S/\partial v = 0$ corresponds to $\theta = 0$ [**].

is warned that he must study Part II, ch. 7, before tackling that part of Stein's paper. See also Stein (1970).

[*] For reasons that will become clear later, in this model all variables are expressed as ratios per unit of capital.

[**] c (and consequently θ) would be zero if there were no outside money and if government bonds were not considered by their private owners as part of their net

$\partial S/\partial x$ is positive since

$$\frac{\partial S}{\partial x} = \frac{\partial S^*}{\partial y} \, y'(x) \ .$$

Real balances are demanded for transactions purposes and as a store of value; for simplicity's sake we assume that there are only two stores of value: real capital and real balances. Thus the demand for real balances per unit of capital is positively related to real output per unit of capital and negatively related to the expected yield on real capital. This yield is the marginal product of capital, $g(x)$ ★, plus the expected proportionate rate of change of the price level, π^*. On the assumption that real balances are complementary to real net claims of the private sector on the public sector, θv is included as an argument to which the demand for real balances is positively related:

$$M_d = M_d \left[y(x), g(x) + \pi^*, \theta v \right] \ , \tag{3.53}$$

$$\frac{\partial M_d}{\partial y} > 0 \ , \qquad \frac{\partial M_d}{\partial [g(x) + \pi^*]} < 0 \ , \qquad 1 > \theta \, \frac{\partial M_d}{\partial \theta v} > 0 \ \text{★★} \ .$$

A simplifying assumption about π^* is that $\pi^* = \pi^e$, where π^e is the equilibrium rate of price change; π^e is assumed to be equal to the rate of change of the

wealth (i.e. because they take account of the taxes that will be levied in the future by the government in relation to the necessities of the public debt). On the contrary, $\theta = 1$ if all money were outside money and there were no government bonds.

★ The marginal product of capital is $\partial Y/\partial K = f_K(K, L)$. Since f is homogeneous of degree one, f_K is homogeneous of degree zero by a well-known theorem on homogeneous functions, and so

$$\frac{\partial Y}{\partial K} = f_K \left(1, \frac{L}{K} \right) = g(x) \ .$$

Obviously $g'(x) > 0$, since $g'(x) = K f_{KL}$ and $f_{KL} > 0$ because the production function is homogeneous of degree one with f_{KK} and f_{LL} both negative (remember that $f_{KL} = -(K/L) f_{KK} = -(L/K) f_{LL}$).

★★ The fact that $\partial M_d/\partial \theta v > 0$ derives from the assumption made. A further assumption is necessary to justify that $\partial M_d/\partial v = \theta(\partial M_d/\partial \theta v) < 1$. Such an assumption is that 'a unit rise in real balances and an equiproportionate rise in net real claims of the private sector upon the public sector is associated with an excess supply of real balances' (Stein (1969), p. 159). It must be stressed that the assumption that $\theta(\partial M_d/\partial \theta v) < 1$ is very important, since the basic result in the comparative dynamics of the model depends on it in an essential way. See footnote ★★ to p. 205.

money supply per worker, $\mu - n$, where $\mu \equiv M'/M$. Thus we have

$$M_d = M_d \left[y(x), g(x) + \mu - n, \theta v \right] . \tag{3.53'}$$

Monetary equilibrium is assumed to hold in every moment, so that the supply and demand for real balances per unit of capital are always equal, i.e.

$$v = M_d \left[y(x), g(x) + \mu - n, \theta v \right] . \tag{3.54}$$

Eq. (3.54) can, at least in principle, be solved for v, so that we obtain

$$v = M_d^* (x, \mu - n, \theta) . \tag{3.54'}$$

Given the assumption that $I = S$ and since $I = K'$, from (3.52') it follows that

$$K'/K = S(x, v) \tag{3.55}$$

whence, using (3.54'),

$$K'/K = S[x, M_d^* (x, \mu - n, \theta)] . \tag{3.55'}$$

Differentiating with respect to time the identity $x \equiv L/K$, we have

$$\frac{x'}{x} = \frac{L'}{L} - \frac{K'}{K} , \tag{3.56}$$

so that, since $L'/L = n$ and using (3.55') $\star$,

$$x'/x = n - S[x, M_d^* (x, \mu - n, \theta)] , \tag{3.56'}$$

which is the basic differential equation of the model. The equilibrium point is

---

$\star$ The usefulness of having expressed all variables as ratios per unit of capital manifests itself in the derivation of eq. (3.56'). It can be noted that this amounts to assuming that all functions (and not only the production function) are homogeneous of degree one if expressed in absolute values: for example,

$$S = S \left(Y, \frac{M}{p} \right) = KS \left(\frac{Y}{K}, \frac{M}{pK} \right),$$

whence $S/K = S(x, v)$, and so on.

obtained putting $x'/x = 0$ in (3.56'), from which

$$n - S[x, M_d^*(x, \mu - n, \theta)] = 0 . \tag{3.57}$$

We assume that (3.57) has one, and only one, positive solution x^e. To study the stability of the equilibrium point x^e we use a linear approximation of (3.56') at x^e. First write (3.56') as

$$x' = nx - S[x, M_d^*(x, \mu - n, \theta)]x , \tag{3.58}$$

which gives, when we expand the right-hand side in Taylor's series and neglect all terms of order higher than the first,

$$\bar{x}' = n\bar{x} - \left\{ \left(\frac{\partial S}{\partial x} + \frac{\partial S}{\partial M_d^*} \frac{\partial M_d^*}{\partial x} \right) x^e + S[x_e, M_d^*(x^e, \mu - n, \theta)] \right\} \bar{x} , \tag{3.59}$$

where $\bar{x} = x(t) - x^e$ and all derivatives are computed for $x = x^e$. Since $n - S[x^e, M_d^*(x^e, \mu - n, \theta)] = 0$ by definition of x^e, it follows that

$$\bar{x}' = - x^e \left(\frac{\partial S}{\partial x} + \frac{\partial S}{\partial M_d^*} \frac{\partial M_d^*}{\partial x} \right) \bar{x} . \tag{3.60}$$

This is a first-order equation, linear and with constant coefficients, whose solution is

$$x(t) = \bar{x}(0) \exp\left[- x^e \left(\frac{\partial S}{\partial x} + \frac{\partial S}{\partial M_d^*} \frac{\partial M_d^*}{\partial x} \right) t \right] . \tag{3.61}$$

The result is that the equilibrium point is stable (i.e. $\bar{x}(t) \to 0$ as $t \to +\infty$) if, and only if,

$$\frac{\partial S}{\partial x} + \frac{\partial S}{\partial M_d^*} \frac{\partial M_d^*}{\partial x} > 0 . \tag{3.62} \star$$

★ This inequality is not necessarily satisfied. In fact, $\partial S/\partial x > 0$, $\partial S/\partial M_d^* \leq 0$ (if the = sign holds, then (3.62) is surely satisfied) and the sign of $\partial M_d^*/\partial x$ is uncertain, since x has two effects of opposite sign on the demand for real balances. A variation in x causes a variation in the same direction in $y(x)$ and in $g(x)$ (for the sign of $g'(x)$ see footnote ★ to p. 202), but the variations in the demand for real balances determined by a given variation in $y(x)$ and in $g(x)$ are of opposite sign, given the assumptions made in relation to eq. (3.53). Strictly speaking, what we have said refers to $\partial M_d/\partial x$ and not to $\partial M_d^*/\partial x$.

One of the most interesting things to study in a monetary growth model is the effect of a change in the rate of growth of the money supply on the steady-state values of the real variables. To do so [*], first note that the solution of (3.57) depends, given the forms of the functions S and M_d^*, on the values of the parameters μ, n, θ, so that $x^e = x^e(\mu, n, \theta)$. Differentiating (3.57) with respect to μ, we have

$$-\frac{\partial S}{\partial x}\frac{\partial x^e}{\partial \mu} - \frac{\partial S}{\partial M_d^*}\left(\frac{\partial M_d^*}{\partial x}\frac{\partial x^e}{\partial \mu} + \frac{\partial M_d^*}{\partial \mu}\right) = 0 , \qquad (3.63)$$

where all derivatives are computed for $x = x^e$. Solving (3.63) for $\partial x^e/\partial \mu$, we obtain

$$\frac{\partial x^e}{\partial \mu} = -\frac{(\partial S/\partial M_d^*)(\partial M_d^*/\partial \mu)}{\partial S/\partial x + (\partial S/\partial M_d^*)(\partial M_d^*/\partial x)} . \qquad (3.64)$$

The stability condition (3.62) ensures that the denominator of the fraction on the right-hand side of (3.64) is positive. The numerator is positive if there is outside money [**], so that $\partial x^e/\partial \mu < 0$. An increase in the rate of monetary

However, it can be shown that the two derivatives have the same sign through the assumption about $\theta(\partial M_d/\partial \theta v)$. From (3.53) we have

$$\frac{\partial M_d}{\partial x} = \frac{\partial M_d}{\partial y}y'(x) + \frac{\partial M_d}{\partial [g(x)+\mu-n]}\, g'(x) ,$$

whose sign is uncertain, as we have noted above. Now, from (3.54),

$$v - M_d[y(x), g(x) + \mu - n, \theta v] = 0 .$$

Consider this as a $\phi(x, \mu - n, \theta, v) = 0$ and use the theorem on the differentiation of implicit functions:

$$\frac{\partial v}{\partial x} = \frac{\partial M_d^*}{\partial x} = -\frac{\phi_x}{\phi_v} = \frac{(\partial M_d/\partial y)y'(x) + \{\partial M_d/\partial [g(x)+\mu-n]\}g'(x)}{1 - \theta(\partial M_d/\partial \theta v)} .$$

The numerator of the last fraction is $\partial M_d/\partial x$, and the denominator is positive since it has been assumed that $1 > \theta(\partial M_d/\partial \theta v)$.

   [*] What we are doing is an exercise in comparative dynamics. For some general remarks on comparative dynamics, see Appendix I, §6.
   [**] We have seen above that $\partial S/\partial v = \partial S/\partial M_d^* < 0$ if there is outside money. For $\partial M_d^*/\partial \mu$, by the same procedure used in footnote [*] to p. 204,

$$\frac{\partial v}{\partial \mu} = \frac{\partial M_d^*}{\partial \mu} = -\frac{\phi_{\mu-n}}{\phi_v} = \frac{\partial M_d/\partial [g(x)+\mu-n]}{1 - \theta(\partial M_d/\partial \theta v)}$$

expansion causes an increase in the equilibrium capital per worker $(1/x^e)$, and consequently an increase in the equilibrium output per worker **★**. If the money supply is not considered by the public as part of its wealth, then $\partial S/\partial v = \partial S/\partial M_d^* = 0$ and a change in μ has no effect on x^e.

Exercises

1. The production function is $Y = K^{1/3}L^{2/3}$; the saving function and the demand for real balances function are

$$S/K = 0.20y - 0.01\,\theta v\,,$$

$$M_d = \frac{16}{30}y - 100[g(x)+\mu - n] + \frac{2}{3}\,\theta v\,.$$

It is also given that the rate of population growth is 0.01, that $\theta = 0.3$ and that the money supply grows at the same rate as population. Find the equilibrium point and check its stability.

Calculation. The production function can be written as

$$y = Y/K = K^{-2/3}L^{2/3} = x^{2/3}\,.$$

The marginal product of capital is

$$\frac{\partial Y}{\partial K} = \frac{1}{3}K^{-2/3}L^{2/3} = \frac{1}{3}x^{2/3} = g(x)\,.$$

Substituting $y = x^{2/3}$, $g(x) = \frac{1}{3}x^{2/3}$, $\theta = 0.3$ and $\mu - n = 0$ in S/K and in M_d, we have

$$S/K = 0.20\,x^{2/3} - 0.003\,v\,,$$

Now, given the assumptions made in relation to eq. (3.53) in the text, the numerator is negative and the denominator is positive, so that $\partial M_d^*/\partial \mu < 0$. As we said above (see footnote ★★ to p. 202), the fact that the positive quantity $\theta(\partial M_d/\partial \theta v)$ is assumed to be smaller than 1 is essential for the validity of the result stated by Stein.

★ This result cannot so far (1970) be considered as generally accepted. Other authors (e.g. Levhari and Patinkin, 1968) have found that the effect of a change in the rate of monetary expansion in a neoclassical model is indeterminate. Note that such effect would also be indeterminate in Stein's model if we dropped the assumption that $\theta(\partial M/\partial \theta v) < 1$.

$$M_d = \frac{16}{30} x^{2/3} - \frac{100}{3} x^{2/3} + 0.2\,v = -32.8\, x^{2/3} + 0.2\,v \ .$$

Equating M_d to v we have

$$v = -32.8\, x^{2/3} + 0.2\,v \ ,$$

which, solving for v, gives

$$v = -\frac{32.8}{0.8} x^{2/3} = -41\, x^{2/3} \ .$$

Substituting in S/K we obtain

$$S/K = 0.20\, x^{2/3} + 0.123\, x^{2/3} = 0.323\, x^{2/3} \ .$$

The basic differential equation

$$x'/x = n - S/K$$

becomes

$$x'/x = 0.01 - 0.323\, x^{2/3} \ . \tag{3.65}$$

The equilibrium point is obtained by solving the equation

$$0.01 - 0.323\, x^{2/3} = 0 \ ;$$

therefore

$$x = \left(\frac{10}{323}\right)^{3/2} ,$$

which gives

$$x^e \simeq \frac{1}{183.571} \ .$$

The equilibrium capital per worker is about 183.571.

Let us now examine the differential eq. (3.65). It could be linearized, but its form is such that it can be solved by a simple transformation of variables (the trick is the same as that used in Part II, ch. 3, §4). Let us make the substitution $z = x^{-2/3}$, so that $z' = -\frac{2}{3} x^{-5/3} x'$. Multiplying (3.65) by $-\frac{2}{3} x^{-2/3}$

we have

$$-\frac{2}{3}x^{-5/3}x' = -\frac{0.02}{3}x^{-2/3} + \frac{0.646}{3},$$

i.e.

$$z' + \frac{0.02}{3}z = \frac{0.646}{3},$$

whose solution is

$$z(t) = A \exp\left(-\frac{0.02}{3}t\right) + 32.3,$$

where A is an arbitrary constant. From $z = x^{-2/3}$ we have $x = z^{-3/2}$, so that

$$x(t) = \left[A \exp\left(-\frac{0.02}{3}t\right) + 32.3\right]^{-3/2}. \tag{3.66}$$

From eq. (3.66) it follows that $x(t)$ tends to its equilibrium value $(32.3)^{-3/2}$.

2. Same data as in exercise 1, but for the production function, $Y = K^{1/2}L^{1/2}$.

References

Ackley, G., 1961, *Macroeconomic Theory*, pp. 513–17.

Allen, R.G.D., 1959, *Mathematical Economics*, ch. 1, §§1.3, 1.8.

Archibald, G.C. and Lipsey, R.G., 1967, *An Introduction to a Mathematical Treatment of Economics*, ch. 13, §§13.2, 13.6, 13.8; ch. 15, §15.1.

Baumol, W.J., 1970, *Economic Dynamics*, ch. 17, §§1–5.

Beach, E.F., 1957, *Economic Models*, pp. 76–9.

Beckmann, M.J. and Wallace, J.P., 1967, Marshallian versus Walrasian Stability.

Bushaw, D.W. and Clower, R.W., *Introduction to Mathematical Economics*, ch. 1.

Deardoff, A.V., 1970, Growth Paths in the Solow Neoclassical Growth Model.

Dernburg, T.F. and Dernburg, J.D., 1969, *Macroeconomic Analysis: An Introduction to Comparative Statics and Dynamics*, ch. 10; ch. 11, §§11.1, 11.2.

Domar, E.D., 1957, *Essays in the Theory of Economic Growth*, essays III, IV.

Hahn, F.H. and Matthews, R.C.O., 1964, The Theory of Economic Growth: A Survey, §I.4.

Henderson, J.M. and Quandt, R.E., 1958, *Microeconomic Theory: A Mathematical Approach*, ch. 4, §4.7.

Levhari, D. and Patinkin, D., 1968, The Role of Money in a Simple Growth Model.

Marshall, A., 1920, *Principles of Economics*, Book V, ch. III, §6.

Okuguchi, K., 1968, The Labour Participation Ratio and the Speed of Adjustment.

Phelps, E., 1966, *Golden Rules of Economic Growth*.

Samuelson, P.A., 1947, *Foundations of Economic Analysis*, ch. IX, pp. 260—4.

Sato, R., 1963, Fiscal Policy in a Neo-Classical Growth Model: An Analysis of Time Required for Equilibrating Adjustment.

Solow, R.M., 1956, A Contribution to the Theory of Economic Growth.

Stein, J.L., 1969, "Neoclassical" and "Keynes—Wicksell" Monetary Growth Models.

Stein, J.L., 1970, Monetary Growth Theory in Perspective.

Swan, T., 1956, Economic Growth and Capital Accumulation.

Walras, L., 1954, *Elements of Pure Economics*, lesson 6, §§60, 61; lesson 7, §§66, 67.

4

Second-order Equations

The general form of second-order differential equations is

$$a_0 y'' + a_1 y' + a_2 y = g(t) , \tag{4.1}$$

where a_0, a_1, a_2 are given constants and $g(t)$ is a known function. Of course, the coefficient a_0 must be different from zero since the equation is of the second order; a_1 or a_2 or both may be zero.

Let us begin by studying the homogeneous equation

$$a_0 y'' + a_1 y' + a_2 y = 0 .$$

Since $a_0 \neq 0$, we can divide through by a_0 and write the equation as

$$y'' + b_1 y' + b_2 y = 0 , \tag{4.2}$$

where

$$b_1 \equiv a_1/a_0 , \qquad b_2 \equiv a_2/a_0 .$$

What might be the form of the unknown function $y(t)$ that satisfies the equation is not so clear as in first-order equations, at least at first sight. However, analogy suggests that this form might be similar to that found in first-order equations. Let us then try a function of the type $e^{\lambda t}$, where λ is a constant to be determined in terms of the coefficients of the equation. Substituting in (4.2) we have

$$\lambda^2 e^{\lambda t} + b_1 \lambda e^{\lambda t} + b_2 e^{\lambda t} = e^{\lambda t}(\lambda^2 + b_1\lambda + b_2) = 0 \ . \tag{4.3}$$

If $e^{\lambda t}$ has to be a solution, eq. (4.3) must be satisfied for any value of t, and this is possible if, and only if,

$$\lambda^2 + b_1\lambda + b_2 = 0 \ . \tag{4.4}$$

Eq. (4.4) is called the *characteristic* (or *auxiliary*) equation of (4.2). Note that here too we have reduced the solution of a functional equation to the solution of an algebraic equation.

The two roots of eq. (4.4) are given by the well-known formula

$$\lambda_1, \lambda_2 = \tfrac{1}{2}[-b_1 \pm (b_1^2 - 4b_2)^{1/2}] \ . \tag{4.5}$$

The nature of the solution of eq. (4.2) depends on the nature of such roots, which we are going to examine in some detail, according to the sign of the discriminant $\Delta \equiv b_1^2 - 4b_2$. Three cases are possible.

Case (1): $\Delta > 0$

The roots λ_1, λ_2 are real and distinct. Then both $\exp(\lambda_1 t)$ and $\exp(\lambda_2 t)$ satisfy eq. (4.2) so that, according to general principles, their linear combination with two arbitrary constants

$$y(t) = A_1 \exp(\lambda_1 t) + A_2 \exp(\lambda_2 t) \ , \tag{4.6}$$

is the general solution of eq. (4.2). The time path of $y(t)$ for $t \to +\infty$ is monotonic. The stability of such movement depends on the *signs* of the roots [*]. Descartes' theorem [**] enables us to reach the following general propositions, given that $\Delta > 0$:

---

[*] Note again that, contrary to the result holding for difference equations, here the absolute value of the roots is immaterial as far as stability is concerned. This is a general property, already mentioned in Part II, ch. 2, and depends on the fact that in the solution the λ's appear in one case in the form λ^t, and in the other in the form $e^{\lambda t}$.

[**] See note [*] to p. 52 (Part I, ch. 4).

(1) If b_1 and b_2 are both positive, the roots are both negative, since we have two continuations in the signs of the coefficients of eq. (4.4). From (4.6) it follows that $y(t)$ tends to zero as t increases, i.e. the movement is convergent.

(2) If b_1 and b_2 are both negative or if $b_1 > 0, b_2 < 0$, the signs of the coefficients show one variation and one continuation, so that one root is positive and the other is negative. In (4.6), the term containing the negative root converges to, and the term containing the positive root diverges from, zero as t increases. The overall movement is obviously divergent.

(3) If $b_1 < 0, b_2 > 0$ the signs of the coefficients show two variations, so that both roots are positive. The movement is clearly divergent, towards $\pm \infty$ according to whether the sign of the arbitrary constant (to be determined by means of appropriate conditions, see below) multiplying the term containing the greater root is positive or negative.

Two particular cases may arise, when either b_1 or b_2 are zero (both cannot be zero here, since $\Delta > 0$). When $b_1 = 0, b_2$ must be negative since $\Delta > 0$, and from (4.6) it is easy to see that the two roots are equal in absolute value and opposite in sign, so that a similar conclusion as in (2) holds. When $b_1 \neq 0$, $b_2 = 0$, from (4.6) it is easy to see that one root is zero and the other is equal to $- b_1$. The solution is

$$y(t) = A_1 + A_2 \exp(-b_1 t) \, ,$$

and so the movement will diverge if $b_1 < 0$ and converge if $b_1 > 0$: note, however, that in the second case it will not converge to zero but to the constant A_1.

Case (2): $\Delta = 0$

The roots λ_1, λ_2 are real and equal: $\lambda_1 = \lambda_2 = -\frac{1}{2}b_1$ — call it λ^*. Now $\exp(\lambda^* t)$ is a solution of eq. (4.2), and we must find a second one to be able to write down the general solution, according to general principles. Let us prove that $t \exp(\lambda^* t)$ is another function which satisfies eq. (4.2). Substituting in (4.2) we have

$$[2\lambda^* \exp(\lambda^* t) + t\lambda^{*2} \exp(\lambda^* t)]$$

$$+ b_1 [\exp(\lambda^* t) + t\lambda^* \exp(\lambda^* t)] + b_2 t \exp(\lambda^* t) = 0 \, ,$$

from which

$$(2\lambda^* + b_1)\exp(\lambda^* t) + (\lambda^{*2} + b_1\lambda^* + b_2)t\exp(\lambda^* t) = 0 \ . \qquad (4.7)$$

If $t\exp(\lambda^* t)$ is a solution, then eq. (4.7) must be satisfied for any t, so that, since $\exp(\lambda^* t) \neq 0$, the quantities $2\lambda^* + b_1$ and $\lambda^{*2} + b_1\lambda^* + b_2$ must both be zero. The former is zero because $\lambda^* = -\frac{1}{2}b_1$, and the latter is zero because λ^* is a root of the characteristic equation. Thus $t\exp(\lambda^* t)$ is a solution of eq. (4.2), and the general solution is

$$y(t) = A_1\exp(\lambda^* t) + A_2 t\exp(\lambda^* t) = (A_1 + A_2 t)\exp(\lambda^* t) \ , \quad (4.8)$$

where A_1 and A_2 are arbitrary constants. Note that (4.8) also holds in the particular case $\lambda^* = 0$, which gives $y(t) = A_1 + A_2 t$. Since $\lambda^* = 0$ implies $b_1 = b_2 = 0$, the differential equation is $y'' = 0$, from which, integrating twice, we actually obtain $y(t) = A_1 + A_2 t$ without any need to apply the method so far expounded. However, the fact that we can obtain the solution also from (4.8), shows that the method also works in particular cases.

The function $A_1 + A_2 t$ obviously diverges, so that the overall movement will be divergent if $\exp(\lambda^* t)$ also diverges ($\lambda^* > 0$, i.e. $b_1 < 0$). What happens when $\lambda^* < 0$? In this case $\exp(\lambda^* t)$ tends to zero, and, since it tends to zero more rapidly than $A_1 + A_2 t$ tends to infinity, the overall movement will be convergent [*].

Case (3): $\Delta < 0$

The roots are two complex conjugate numbers, say $\alpha \pm i\theta$, where $i = +\sqrt{-1}$ is the imaginary unit and

$$\alpha = -\tfrac{1}{2}b_1 \ , \qquad \theta = \tfrac{1}{2}(|b_1^2 - 4b_2|)^{1/2} \ . \qquad (4.9)$$

The solution is then

---

[*] More formally,

$$\lim_{t\to+\infty} [A_1\exp(\lambda^* t) + A_2 t\exp(\lambda^* t)] = A_1 \lim_{t\to+\infty} \exp(\lambda^* t) + A_2 \lim_{t\to+\infty} t\exp(\lambda^* t)$$

$$= 0 + A_2 \lim_{t\to+\infty} t\exp(\lambda^* t) = A_2 \lim_{t\to+\infty} \frac{t}{\exp(-\lambda^* t)} \ .$$

Applying L'Hôpital's theorem,

$$\lim_{t\to+\infty} \frac{t}{\exp(-\lambda^* t)} = \lim_{t\to+\infty} [-\lambda^*\exp(-\lambda^* t)]^{-1} = 0 \ .$$

$$y(t) = A' \exp\left[(\alpha+i\theta)t\right] + A'' \exp\left[(\alpha-i\theta)t\right]$$

$$= A' \exp\left(\alpha t + i\theta t\right) + A'' \exp\left(\alpha t - i\theta t\right), \tag{4.10}$$

where A' and A'' are two arbitrary constants that we may take as two arbitrary complex conjugate numbers. Using some elementary results in the theory of functions of a complex variable ★, the solution can be written in a more suitable form. First, write (4.10) as (4.10'):

$$y(t) = e^{\alpha t}(A' e^{i\theta t} + A'' e^{-i\theta t}), \tag{4.10'}$$

and then use the transformation

★ In the real domain, the exponential function e^x (x a real number) can be defined as the sum of the power series

$$1 + x + \frac{x^2}{2!} + \frac{x^3}{3!} + \dots .$$

In the same way we can define e^z (z a complex number) as the sum of the series of complex terms:

$$1 + z + \frac{z^2}{2!} + \frac{z^3}{3!} + \dots . \tag{1}$$

Since the series converges for all values of z, it defines a function analytic (i.e. one valued and differentiable) in the whole z-plane. It can also be proved, by multiplication of series, that the real number e with a complex exponent obeys the formal law of indices of elementary algebra (so that, for example, $e^{\alpha\pm i\theta} = e^{\alpha} e^{\pm i\theta}$). When z is pure imaginary, say $z = \pm ix$, applying (1) we have

$$e^{\pm ix} = 1 + (\pm ix) + \frac{(\pm ix)^2}{2!} + \dots . \tag{2}$$

If we recall that $i^2 = -1$, whence $i^3 = -i$, $i^4 = 1$, $i^5 = i$, etc., from (2) we have, on separating the real and the imaginary terms of the series,

$$e^{\pm ix} = \left(1 - \frac{x^2}{2!} + \frac{x^4}{4!} - \frac{x^6}{6!} + - \dots\right) \pm i\left(x - \frac{x^3}{3!} + \frac{x^5}{5!} - \frac{x^7}{7!} + - \dots\right), \tag{3}$$

so that

$$e^{\pm ix} = \cos x \pm i \sin x , \tag{4}$$

since the two power series on the right-hand side of (3) define, respectively, the cosine and the sine of the real variable x. Putting $x = \theta t$ we have (4.11) in the text.

$$e^{\pm i\theta t} = \cos\theta t \pm i \sin\theta t \tag{4.11}$$

to obtain

$$y(t) = e^{\alpha t}[A'(\cos\theta t + i\sin\theta t) + A''(\cos\theta t - i\sin\theta t)]$$

$$= e^{\alpha t}[(A' + A'')\cos\theta t + (A' - A'')i\sin\theta t] . \tag{4.12}$$

Now, since A' and A'' are complex conjugate numbers, say $a \pm ib$ (where a and b are arbitrary real numbers), it follows that $A' + A'' = 2a$, a real number (call it A_1) and that $(A' - A'')i = (2ib)i = -2b$, a real number too (call it A_2). Thus the solution becomes

$$y(t) = e^{\alpha t}[A_1\cos\theta t + A_2\sin\theta t] . \tag{4.13}$$

An alternative way of writing the solution is

$$y(t) = Ae^{\alpha t}\cos(\theta t - \epsilon) , \tag{4.13'}$$

where the new arbitrary constants A, ϵ are expressed in terms of A_1, A_2 by the transformation

$$A\cos\epsilon = A_1 ,$$
$$\tag{4.14}$$
$$A\sin\epsilon = A_2 .$$

Substituting (4.14) into (4.13) and using the fact that

$$\cos\epsilon\cos\theta t + \sin\epsilon\sin\theta t = \cos(\theta t - \epsilon) ,$$

we obtain (4.13'). This second form is perhaps easier to interpret, since it involves only one trigonometric function instead of two; the form (4.13), however, is more suitable for the determination of the values of the two arbitrary constants. In any case the resulting movement is a trigonometric oscillation, whose period [*] is $2\pi/\omega$ and whose amplitude is increasing, constant or decreasing, if, respectively, $\alpha \gtrless 0$, i.e. if the real part of the complex roots is positive, zero or negative. Thus, since $\alpha = -\frac{1}{2}b_1$, the stability condition (damped oscillations) is that $b_1 > 0$.

We have now completed the study of all cases that may arise in a homo-

---

[*] See Part I, ch. 4, footnote [*] p. 55.

geneous equation of the second order. From the point of view of stability (i.e. of the convergence towards zero of the general solution) the general condition is that the real roots are negative and that the complex roots have a negative real part ★. If we want to check the stability without solving the characteristic equation, it follows from the results obtained in the various cases that we have only to check that both b_1 and b_2 are positive. In other words, the necessary and sufficient conditions for the roots of (4.4) to be negative if real, and have negative real parts if complex, are

$$b_1 > 0 \,,$$

$$b_2 > 0 \,.$$

(4.15)

The following table provides a classification of all possible cases and sub-cases.

b_1	b_2	Δ	Kind of movement for $t \to +\infty$
			$+$ Monotonic, convergent to zero
$+$	$+$	$+$	0 Monotonic, convergent to zero
			$-$ Oscillating, damped
			$+$ Monotonic, divergent
$+$	$-$	$+$	0 Monotonic, divergent
			$-$ Oscillating, explosive
$+$	$+$	$-$	$+$ Monotonic, divergent
$+$	$-$	$-$	$+$ Monotonic, divergent
$+$	0	$+$	$-$ Oscillating, constant amplitude
$+$	0	$-$	$+$ Monotonic, divergent
$+$	$+$	0	$+$ Monotonic, convergent to an arbitrary constant
$+$	$--$	0	$+$ Monotonic, divergent
$+$	0	0	0 Monotonic (linear and not exponential as in all previous cases), divergent

Let us now examine the non-homogeneous equation. According to general principles, we have only to find a particular solution of this equation and add it to the general solution of the corresponding homogeneous equation. We shall exemplify the general method of undetermined coefficients (see Part II, ch. 1) in the case in which $g(t)$ is a constant, say F. In other cases the student

---

★ Since we are interested in the convergence towards zero, we must exclude also the case of a zero real root (convergence to a constant, see at the end of case (1)).

may proceed along the same lines as in the examples expounded with reference to first-order equations (Part II, ch. 2).

As a particular solution, try $\bar{y}(t) = B$, where B is an undetermined constant. Substituting in (4.1) we have $a_2 B = F$, so that

$$\bar{y}(t) = F/a_2 \tag{4.16}$$

is a particular solution. If $a_2 = 0$, try $\bar{y}(t) = Bt$. Substituting in (4.1) we have $a_1 B = F$, so that

$$\bar{y}(t) = \frac{F}{a_1} t \tag{4.17}$$

is a particular solution. If also $a_1 = 0$, try $\bar{y}(t) = Bt^2$ and substitute in (4.1), obtaining $2a_0 B = F$, so that

$$\bar{y}(t) = \frac{F}{2a_0} t^2 \tag{4.18}$$

is a particular solution (remember that $a_0 \neq 0$).

The particular solution of the non-homogeneous equation may usually be interpreted, as we shall see in the economic applications, as the (stationary or moving) equilibrium of the variable $y(t)$.

We must, finally, treat the determination of the arbitrary constants. Of course, two additional conditions are needed. They usually take the form that for a known value of t, say t^*, the value of $y(t)$, say y^*, and of its first derivative, say y'^*, are known (in economics t^* is generally taken to be zero). Substituting t^* and y^* in the general solution and substituting t^* and y'^* in its first derivative, we obtain two linear equations in the two unknowns A_1, A_2. The solution of this system yields the values of the two arbitrary constants that satisfy the two additional conditions. Of course, the determination of the arbitrary constants is to be made according to the general solution of the equation under consideration (for example, if the equation is non-homogeneous, its own general solution, and not the general solution of the corresponding homogeneous equation, must be used).

References

Allen, R.G.D., 1959, *Mathematical Economics*, ch. 4, §§4.1–4.5; ch. 5, §5.4.

Baumol, W.J., 1970, *Economic Dynamics*, ch. 14, §§3,4,5,6,8.

Chiang, A.C., 1967, *Fundamental Methods of Mathematical Economics*, ch. 15, §§ 15.1, 15.3, 15.4, 15.6.

Courant, R., 1937, *Differential and Integral Calculus*, Vol. I, ch. VIII, §7; ch. XI, §§2,3.

5

Some Economic Applications
of Second-order Equations

§ 1. Phillips' stabilization model for a closed economy

The level of national output (income) is determined, as we know from elementary macroeconomics, by the level of aggregate demand. The latter is made up of a part originating from private economic agents and of a part originating from the government. The government manoeuvres its expenditure in order that aggregate demand is such that national income attains a given desired level. Thus we can talk of stabilization of aggregate demand. Phillips analyses this economic policy problem from a dynamic point of view.

Let us assume that national income is initially at the desired level and that an exogenous decrease in aggregate demand occurs. The variables are measured as deviations from their desired levels, so that a negative value simply means that the actual value is smaller than the desired value. Before introducing the stabilization policy we must know, to have a standard of comparison, the 'spontaneous' behaviour of the economic system, i.e. its behaviour when there is no government expenditure. The basic dynamic mechanism is the multiplier, considered however as working in continuous and not in discrete time ★.

★ Phillips considers also the case in which the basic dynamic mechanism is of the multiplier—accelerator type. However, the simpler 'multiplier only' mechanism is sufficient to understand the basic ideas underlying his analysis.

219

The fundamental assumption is that producers react to excess demand by making adjustments in output: if aggregate demand exceeds (falls short of) current output, the latter will be increased (decreased). Obviously this mechanism operates independently of the origin of excess demand, and so it is the same both without and with government expenditure. In formal terms,

$$Y' = \alpha(D - Y), \qquad \alpha > 0, \tag{5.1}$$

where Y is national output, D is aggregate demand and α is a reaction coefficient, representing the velocity of adjustment to a discrepancy between aggregate demand and current output.

Aggregate private demand is a function of national income:

$$D = (1 - l)Y, \tag{5.2}$$

where $1 - l$ is the marginal propensity to spend (i.e. the marginal propensity to consume plus the marginal propensity to invest). This propensity is assumed smaller than unity, whence $0 < l < 1$. Introducing the exogenous disturbance u we have

$$D = (1 - l)Y - u. \tag{5.2'}$$

Substituting (5.2') into (5.1) and giving to u a unit value, we have

$$Y' + \alpha l Y = -\alpha. \tag{5.3}$$

This is a first-order equation, whose solution is

$$Y(t) = A e^{-\alpha l t} - \frac{1}{l}. \tag{5.4}$$

We assumed that in the initial period national income was at the desired level, so that $Y(0) = 0$ and so $A = 1/l$, whence

$$Y(t) = -\frac{1}{l}(1 - e^{-\alpha l t}). \tag{5.4'}$$

Since $\alpha l > 0$, $Y(t)$ tends monotonically to $-1/l$, i.e. to the value obtained applying the multiplier $1/l$ to the exogenous decrease in expenditure (-1).

We may now go on to examine the effects of a stabilization policy.

Phillips enumerates three types of stabilization policy. They are the following:

Proportional stabilization policy: government expenditure is proportional and of opposite sign to the deviation between the actual and the desired value of output, i.e. $G^* = -f_\mathrm{p}Y$, where $f_\mathrm{p} > 0$ is the coefficient of proportionality.

Derivative stabilization policy: government expenditure is proportional and of opposite sign to the variation in (that is, to the derivative of) current output, i.e. $G^* = -f_\mathrm{d}Y'$, where $f_\mathrm{d} > 0$ is the coefficient of proportionality.

Integral stabilization policy: government expenditure is proportional and of opposite sign to the sum (in continuous terms, to the integral) of all the differences that have occurred, from time zero to the current moment, between the actual and the desired values of output, i.e.

$$G^* = -f_\mathrm{i} \int_0^t Y \, dt \, ,$$

where $f_\mathrm{i} > 0$ is the coefficient of proportionality.

The reader will have noted that we have marked with an asterisk the government demand. The reason is that the various values of such demand indicated in the enumeration of the various policies are the *theoretical* or *potential* values, i.e. the values that define in theory the different policies. Now, in Phillips' words (Phillips, 1954, p. 294), "the actual policy demand will usually be different from the potential policy demand, owing to the time required for observing changes in the error, adjusting the correcting action accordingly and for changes in the correcting action to produce their full effects. ... whenever such a difference exists the actual policy demand will be changing in a direction which tends to eliminate the difference and at a rate proportional to the difference". Thus, using the symbol G to indicate *actual* government demand, we have

$$G' = \beta(G^* - G) \, , \qquad \beta > 0 \, , \tag{5.5}$$

where β is a reaction coefficient, indicating the speed of response to a discrepancy between potential and actual public expenditure.

Now, when government demand is present, equation $(5.2')$ becomes

$$D = (1 - l)Y + G - u \, . \tag{5.2''}$$

The stabilization model is made of equations (5.1), $(5.2'')$, (5.5) and of one or more of the relations defining G^*. We now manipulate the model to reduce it to a single equation. From (5.5) we have

$$G' + \beta G = \beta G^* .$$ (5.5′)

Differentiating (5.2″) we obtain

$$D' = (1 - l)Y' + G' .$$ (5.2‴)

Multiplying both members of (5.2″) by β and adding the result to eq. (5.2‴) we have

$$D' + \beta D = (1 - l)Y' + \beta(1 - l)Y + G' + \beta G - \beta u ,$$ (5.6)

whence, using (5.5′),

$$D' + \beta D = (1 - l)Y' + \beta(1 - l)Y + \beta G^* - \beta u .$$ (5.6′)

From (5.1) we obtain

$$D = \frac{Y' + \alpha Y}{\alpha} ,$$ (5.1′)

whence, differentiating both members,

$$D' = \frac{Y'' + \alpha Y'}{\alpha} .$$ (5.1″)

Now multiply both members of (5.1′) by β and add the result to (5.1″), obtaining

$$D' + \beta D = \frac{Y'' + (\alpha + \beta)Y' + \alpha\beta Y}{\alpha} .$$ (5.7)

Equating the right-hand members of (5.7) and of (5.6′) we obtain

$$\frac{Y'' + (\alpha + \beta)Y' + \alpha\beta Y}{\alpha} = (1 - l)Y' + \beta(1 - l)Y + \beta G^* - \beta u ,$$ (5.8)

so that, multiplying through by α and rearranging terms, we have, considering a unit decrease in aggregate demand,

$$Y'' + (\alpha l + \beta)Y' + \alpha \beta l Y - \alpha \beta G^* = -\alpha \beta . \tag{5.9}$$

Eq. (5.9) is the basic differential equation of the model. Inserting the various relations defining G^* we can determine the time path of output and so study the effects of the single stabilization policies or of combinations of them when two or more are used simultaneously. As examples we shall study the 'pure proportional' case and the 'mixed proportional-derivative' case. The introduction of the integral stabilization policy, alone or in conjunction with others, will have to wait until Part II, ch. 7, since it gives rise to a third-order equation.

(1) *Proportional stabilization policy*

Inserting $G^* = -f_p Y$ in (5.9) and collecting terms we have

$$Y'' + (\alpha l + \beta)Y' + \alpha \beta (l + f_p)Y = -\alpha \beta . \tag{5.9'}$$

A particular solution is

$$\bar{Y} = -\frac{1}{l + f_p} . \tag{5.10}$$

The characteristic equation of the homogeneous part of $(5.9')$ is

$$\lambda^2 + (\alpha l + \beta)\lambda + \alpha \beta (l + f_p) = 0 . \tag{5.11}$$

The succession of the signs of the coefficients is $+\ +\ +$, so that stability is ensured. To determine whether the movement will be monotonic or oscillatory we must examine the discriminant

$$\Delta = (\alpha l + \beta)^2 - 4\alpha \beta (l + f_p) , \tag{5.12}$$

and it is easy to see that the greater f_p is the more likely it is that $\Delta < 0$. More precisely,

$$\Delta \gtreqless 0 \qquad \text{according to} \qquad f_p \lesseqgtr \frac{(\alpha l - \beta)^2}{4\alpha \beta} . \tag{5.13}$$

Let us recall that the limit value of output in the absence of any stabilization policy is $-1/l$; since $f_p > 0$, the new limit value $-1/(l + f_p)$ is smaller in absolute value. This means that the decrease in income determined by an exogenous decrease in aggregate demand is smaller than the decrease occurring

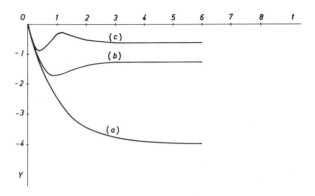

Fig. 5.1.

without the stabilization policy. The policy under consideration, however, cannot completely eliminate this decrease (an infinite value of f_p is not possible). Let us note also that the greater f_p is, the more effective is the stabilization policy (i.e. the smaller is the absolute value of $-1/(l+f_p)$). In fig. 5.1 — taken from Phillips — curve (a) is the time path of income in the absence of stabilization, curve (b) holds for $f_p = 0.5$ and curve (c) for $f_p = 2$. In all cases $\alpha = 4, l = 0.25$; the value of β is 2 and the initial conditions are $Y(0) = 0$ for curve (a) and $Y(0) = 0, Y'(0) = -4$ for curves (b) and (c). See the exercises for the solution of the various equations.

In conclusion, the drawbacks of the purely proportional stabilization policy are two:

(a) it fails to eliminate completely the reduction in income;

(b) it tends to provoke oscillations, though damped, when f_p is too great, and this contrasts with the desirability of having as great an f_p as possible, in order to minimize the reduction in income.

(2) *Mixed proportional-derivative stabilization policy*

In this case the two policies are used simultaneously, so that in eq. (5.9) we must substitute $G^* = -f_p Y - f_d Y'$, obtaining

$$Y'' + (\alpha l + \beta + \alpha\beta f_d)Y' + \alpha\beta(l+f_p)Y = -\alpha\beta .\qquad (5.9'')$$

A particular solution is

$$\bar{Y} = -\frac{1}{l+f_p} .\qquad (5.14)$$

The characteristic equation of the homogeneous part of (5.9″) is

$$\lambda^2 + (\alpha l + \beta + \alpha\beta f_d)\lambda + \alpha\beta(l+f_p) = 0 . \tag{5.15}$$

Here too the succession of the signs of the coefficients is + + +, so that as t increases $Y(t)$ will converge to the particular solution (5.14). The oscillatory or monotonic behaviour of the time path depends on the sign of

$$\Delta = (\alpha l + \beta + \alpha\beta f_d)^2 - 4\alpha\beta(l+f_p) . \tag{5.16}$$

We now have all the elements to compare the mixed policy with the pure proportional policy. The first thing to note is that (5.14) is the same as (5.10): the addition of the derivative policy has no effect as far as the reduction in income is concerned. The effect of this addition can be seen by examining Δ: the greater f_d, the greater the positive term in Δ and the less likely it is that $\Delta < 0$. Thus f_d offsets the bias towards oscillations of f_p. Moreover, even if oscillations should occur, they would be more heavily damped than in the case of a purely proportional policy. As we know, it is the real part of the complex roots that gives the damping, and, the greater the absolute value of this real part, the heavier is the damping. Now, the real part of the complex roots, when they occur, is $-\frac{1}{2}(\alpha l + \beta)$ in the case of the purely proportional policy and $-\frac{1}{2}(\alpha l + \beta + \alpha\beta f_d)$ in the case of the mixed proportional-derivative policy. The latter expression is obviously greater in absolute value than the former. We shall see later – in Part II, ch. 7, § 1 – that the general property of the derivative stabilization policy is to offset the oscillatory bias of other policies.

Exercises
1. Given $\alpha = 4$ and $l = 0.25$, determine the consequences of a unit decrease in aggregate demand. Analyse the consequences of a proportional stabilization policy when $f_p = 0.5$ and $\beta = 2$. The initial conditions are $Y(0) = 0$ and $Y'(0) = -4$.

Calculation. With the given data, eq. (5.3) in the text becomes

$$Y' + Y = -4 ,$$

whose solution is

$$Y(t) = Ae^{-t} - 4 .$$

Since $Y(0) = 0$, we have $0 = A - 4$ and so $A = 4$.

In the case of a purely proportional stabilization policy we have — see eq. (5.9') in the text — the equation

$$Y'' + 3Y' + 6Y = -8 . \qquad (5.17)$$

A particular solution is

$$\bar{Y} = -\tfrac{4}{3} \simeq -1.33 .$$

The final decrease in income is now 1.33 instead of 4. Two-thirds of the (final) influence of the exogenous disturbance have been eliminated. The characteristic equation of the homogeneous part of (5.17) is

$$\lambda^2 + 3\lambda + 6 = 0 ,$$

whose roots are

$$\lambda_1, \lambda_2 \simeq -1.5 \pm 1.936\, i .$$

Thus the general solution of (5.17) is

$$Y(t) = e^{-1.5t}(A_1 \cos 1.936\, t + A_2 \sin 1.936\, t) - \tfrac{4}{3} .$$

The use of the proportional stabilization policy has the effect of introducing an oscillation in the hitherto monotonic movement of the system. Using the initial conditions we can determine the value of the two arbitrary constants. We have

$$Y(0) = 0 = e^0(A_1 \cos 0 + A_2 \sin 0) - \tfrac{4}{3} ;$$

therefore

$$0 = A_1 - \tfrac{4}{3} ,$$

and so

$$A_1 = \tfrac{4}{3} .$$

Moreover,

$$Y' = -1.5A_1 e^{-1.5t} \cos 1.936\,t - 1.936\,A_1 e^{-1.5t} \sin 1.936\,t$$

$$-1.5A_2 e^{-1.5t} \sin 1.936\,t + 1.936\,A_2 e^{-1.5t} \cos 1.936\,t\,,$$

and so, for $t = 0$,

$$Y'(0) = -4 = -1.5A_1 + 1.936A_2\,.$$

Since $A_1 = \frac{4}{3}$, we obtain

$$A_2 = -2/1.936 \simeq -1.033\,.$$

2. Same data as in the previous exercise, but for $f_p = 2$. Check that (1) the final decrease in income is smaller; (2) the speed of damping is the same; (3) the oscillations have a greater frequency.

3. Same data as in exercise 1, but for $\beta = 8$. Check that the oscillation is more heavily damped. Can you say anything in general as to the influence of β?

§2. A model of foreign exchange speculation under floating exchange rates

From the elementary theory of maximizing behaviour it follows that, in general, a speculator will be in equilibrium when the marginal revenue from his operations — represented by the difference between the expected and the current value of the variable (in our case, of the spot exchange rate) — equals the marginal cost. The latter, whose main 'objective' elements are the costs of the operation and interest forgone at home net of interest earned abroad (or vice versa) for the period of the operation, is defined as including a risk coefficient. It can be safely assumed that this coefficient is an increasing function of the scale of operations, so that the overall marginal cost is an increasing function even if its 'objective' components are constant. Thus if marginal revenue increases, the scale of operations will be increased (up to the point where marginal cost has increased to match marginal revenue), and so the amount of funds employed by speculators is an increasing function of the difference between expected and actual exchange rate. For simplicity we assume a relation of proportionality, i.e.

$$E_s(t) = m\,[ER(t) - SR(t)]\,, \qquad m > 0\,, \qquad\qquad (5.18)$$

where $E_s(t)$ is the speculative excess demand of foreign exchange at time t, $ER(t)$ the expected rate of exchange at time t [*] and $SR(t)$ the current spot rate of exchange at time t (we consider only speculation in the spot market).

Note that we adopt the convention of defining the rate of exchange — both current and expected — as the price in terms of local currency of one unit of foreign currency. Eq. (5.18) says that, if the expected rate of exchange is greater (smaller) than the current rate — that is if the exchange rate is expected to depreciate (appreciate) — speculators' excess demand is positive (negative), and the greater in absolute value the greater the difference between ER and SR.

Non-speculators are also operating in the foreign exchange market, e.g. traders engaged in commercial operations with foreign countries [**]. Their excess demand $E_n(t)$ depends only on the current rate of exchange:

$$E_n(t) = a_0 + a_1 SR(t) + B \cos \omega t , \qquad a_0 > 0, \ a_1 < 0, \ B > 0 , \qquad (5.19)$$

where $B \cos \omega t$ represents external factors, such as seasonal influences, arising both on the demand and on the supply side.

When speculators are absent, the equilibrium rate of exchange is determined putting $E_n(t) = 0$, so that

$$SR(t) = B_1 \cos \omega t + B_2 , \qquad B_1 \equiv B/-a_1, \quad B_2 \equiv a_0/-a_1 . \qquad (5.20)$$

The values of the parameters must obviously be such that non-positive values of the exchange rate cannot occur. Since the interval of variation of $\cos \omega t$ is ± 1, non-positive values of $SR(t)$ are excluded if $B_1 < B_2$, i.e. if $B < a_0$.

When speculators are operating, the equilibrium rate of exchange is determined by the relation

---

[*] Expectations formed at time t obviously refer to a value that is expected to materialize at some given date in the future.

[**] In practice it is difficult to distinguish between speculators and non-speculators. Even if they are not professionally engaged in speculation, traders too can, and do, speculate, e.g. anticipating payments for imports and delaying encashments from exports or vice versa (the 'leads and lags' of trade). Thus the two categories are only *functionally* distinguishable (the same person may be a speculator or a non-speculator at different times, or both at the same time). From the functional point of view, a sale (or purchase) of foreign exchange is speculative if it is undertaken with the expectation of a variation in the exchange rate as the primary consideration (or at least as one of the primary considerations). See also Glahe (1966).

$$E_n(t) + E_s(t) = 0 ,$$ (5.21)

i.e.

$$mER(t) + (a_1 - m)SR(t) + a_0 + B \cos \omega t = 0 .$$ (5.21')

In order to solve (5.21') it is necessary to know how expectations are formed. We assume that speculators base their expectations on the current rate of exchange and on its first and second derivatives (i.e. they take account not only of whether the rate of exchange is increasing or decreasing, but also of the acceleration of its movement) according to a linear combination:

$$ER(t) = b_0 SR(t) + b_1 SR' + b_2 SR'' ,$$ (5.22)

where b_0, b_1, b_2 are given constants, whose signs reflect the attitudes of speculators. To leave the analysis as general as possible we do not fix such signs. Substituting in (5.21') and rearranging terms we have

$$m b_2 SR'' + m b_1 SR' + [a_1 - m(1-b_0)] SR = -a_0 - B \cos \omega t .$$ (5.23)

The characteristic equation of the homogeneous part of (5.22) is

$$\lambda^2 + \frac{b_1}{b_2} \lambda + \frac{a_1 - m(1-b_0)}{m b_2} = 0 .$$ (5.24)

So that the exchange rate does not behave explosively the following stability conditions must be satisfied:

$$b_1/b_2 > 0 ,$$

$$\frac{a_1 - m(1-b_0)}{m b_2} > 0 .$$ (5.25)

Inequalities (5.25) may be satisfied in two ways:

case (1)

$$b_1 > 0 ,$$

$$b_2 > 0 ,$$ (5.25a)

$$a_1 - m(1-b_0) > 0 , \text{ i.e. } b_0 > 1 - a_1/m ;$$

or

case (2)

$$b_1 < 0 \,,$$
$$b_2 < 0 \,, \tag{5.25b}$$
$$a_1 - m(1-b_0) < 0 \,, \text{ i.e. } b_0 < 1 - a_1/m \,.$$

Note that in case (1) the coefficient b_0 must be greater than 1, so that in-stability is certain if the current rate of exchange is given the weight 1 in the formation of expectations. In case (2) this is no longer true. Thus, if we think that a plausible specification of (5.22) is

$$ER(t) = SR + b_1 SR' + b_2 SR'' \,, \tag{5.22'}$$

i.e. that expectations are formed 'correcting' the current exchange rate by means of the expression $b_1 SR' + b_2 SR''$, then from (5.25b) the stability conditions are that both b_1 and b_2 be negative.

Let us now find a particular solution of (5.23), trying

$$\overline{SR}(t) = C_1 \cos \omega t + C_2 \sin \omega t + C_3 \,,$$

where C_1, C_2, C_3 are undetermined coefficients. We have

$$\overline{SR}' = -\omega C_1 \sin \omega t + \omega C_2 \cos \omega t \,,$$

$$\overline{SR}'' = -\omega^2 C_1 \cos \omega t - \omega^2 C_2 \sin \omega t \,.$$

Substituting in (5.23) and collecting terms we have

$$\{ [a_1 - m(1-b_0+b_2\omega^2)] C_1 + mb_1 \omega C_2 + B \} \cos \omega t$$

$$+ \{ -mb_1 \omega C_1 + [a_1 - m(1-b_0+b_2\omega^2)] C_2 \} \sin \omega t$$

$$+ \{ [a_1 - m(1-b_0)] C_3 + a_0 \} = 0 \,. \tag{5.26}$$

Eq. (5.26) is identically satisfied if, and only if, the three expressions in curly brackets are all zero, i.e.

$$[a_1 - m(1 - b_0 + b_2\omega^2)]C_1 + mb_1\omega C_2 + B = 0 ,$$

$$-mb_1\omega C_1 + [a_1 - m(1 - b_0 + b_2\omega^2)]C_2 = 0 , \qquad (5.27)$$

$$[a_1 - m(1 - b_0)]C_3 + a_0 = 0 .$$

This is a system in the three unknowns C_1, C_2, C_3. From the first two equations we obtain

$$C_1 = \frac{-B[a_1 - m(1 - b_0 + b_2\omega^2)]}{[a_1 - m(1 - b_0 + b_2\omega^2)]^2 + m^2 b_1^2 \omega^2} ,$$

$$C_2 = \frac{Bmb_1\omega}{[a_1 - m(1 - b_0 + b_2\omega^2)]^2 + m^2 b_1^2 \omega^2} , \qquad (5.28)$$

and from the third

$$C_3 = \frac{-a_0}{a_1 - m(1 - b_0)} . \qquad (5.29)$$

We now want to write the particular solution in a form more easily comparable with (5.20). Let us make the substitutions

$$C_1 = C \cos\gamma ,$$

$$C_2 = -C \sin\gamma . \qquad (5.30)$$

Since, from (5.30)

$$C = +(C_1^2 + C_2^2)^{1/2} ,$$

it follows, using (5.28), that

$$C = \frac{B}{+\{[a_1 - m(1 - b_0 + b_2\omega^2)]^2 + m^2 b_1^2 \omega^2\}^{1/2}} . \qquad (5.31)$$

Using (5.30) and the addition formulae for the cosine, we have

$$C_1 \cos\omega t + C_2 \sin\omega t = C \cos(\omega t + \gamma) , \qquad (5.32)$$

and so the particular solution can be rewritten as

$$\overline{SR}(t) = C \cos(\omega t + \gamma) + C_3 \ . \tag{5.33}$$

This can be interpreted as the (moving) equilibrium solution, and in order that this time path be economically meaningful, non-positive values must be excluded, so that the following inequalities must hold:

$$C_3 > 0 \ ,$$

$$C < C_3 \ , \tag{5.34}$$

i.e., since $a_0 > 0$,

$$a_1 - m(1 - b_0) < 0$$

$$\frac{B}{+ \{[a_1 - m(1 - b_0 + b_2 \omega^2)]^2 + m^2 b_1^2 \omega^2\}^{1/2}} < \frac{-a_0}{a_1 - m(1 - b_0)} \ . \tag{5.34'}$$

It is important to note that the first inequality in (5.34') implies that only case (2) — see conditions (5.25b) above — can be considered in the analysis of stability. In other words, if we want the time path of the exchange rate not to behave explosively *and* the limiting movement to be economically meaningful (the first requirement leads obviously to the second one), then we must exclude case (1) above.

We can now compare (5.33) with (5.20). Both express a constant amplitude oscillation, having the same frequency $\omega/2\pi$ [*], around a constant value. The latter is, in general, different in the two cases, except when specification (5.22') of the expectations equation is used: in fact, when $b_0 = 1$ then $C_3 = B_2$.

All this offers the opportunity for some considerations on a very important problem, that is whether speculation is stabilizing or destabilizing. Many discussions have been made in the literature on this problem [**] and the concept itself of 'stabilizing' or 'destabilizing' speculation is not so easily defined. However, in our model a very simple answer can be given. Taking as a standard of comparison the basic movement of the exchange rate in the absence of

---

[*] The parameter γ just shifts the whole function along the t-axis, leaving unaltered its intrinsic properties (amplitude and frequency).

[**] See Friedman (1953), Baumol (1957), Telser (1959), Cutilli (1963), Kemp (1963), Glahe (1966), Obst (1967) and the references quoted by the last author.

speculative activity, i.e. the time path given by (5.20), we can say that speculative activity will be stabilizing, at least in the limit, if the time path of the exchange rate converges to a constant amplitude fluctuation (around a stationary trend) whose amplitude is *smaller* than the one given by (5.20). It must be stressed that we can concentrate on amplitude only because the two oscillations (the basic one given by (5.20) and the one given by the particular solution (5.33)) have the same frequency and both have a stationary trend. When two constant amplitude oscillations taking place around a stationary trend have the same frequency, the more 'stable' undoubtedly is the one which has the smaller amplitude, whereas when the frequencies are different it is not so easy to say which one is more 'stable' *. Let us then *assume* that the echange rate converges to the particular solution (5.33). Can it be proved that $C < B_1$? The answer is definitely *no*: on *a priori* grounds, the inequality $C \lessgtr B_1$ can be satisfied with any sign **. Thus we have reached the conclusion that speculation, even when it does not give rise to an explosive path (in which case it would surely be considered as destabilizing), cannot be proved to be 'stabilizing' in the sense explained above ‡.

---

* Telser has given a measure of stability based on variance, but such a measure has been shown unsatisfactory by Obst, who has proposed an alternative measure based on squared deviations from the trend. But Obst's criterion also is not above criticism. For example, consider two identical oscillations (same amplitude and frequency) around two different trends, a stationary trend and an increasing trend. According to Obst's criterion they would be indistinguishable, whereas common sense suggests that the first time path (oscillations around the stationary trend) is the more 'stable'.

** C and B_1 have the same numerator, but we cannot say anything about denominators. Squaring both denominators, we have

$$[a_1 - m(1 - b_0 + b_2\omega^2)]^2 + m^2 b_1^2 \omega^2 \gtreqless a_1^2 ,$$

from which

$$m^2(1 - b_0 + b_2\omega^2)^2 - 2a_1 m(1 - b_0 + b_2\omega^2) + m^2 b_1^2 \omega^2 \gtreqless 0 . \qquad (*)$$

Since we have assumed the convergence, we must be in case (2), as we said above, and so $b_2 < 0$. The sign of the expression $1 - b_0 + b_2\omega^2$ cannot be determined *a priori*, so that (*) is indeterminate. Note that, if we assumed $b_0 = 1$ (a plausible *a priori* specification of (5.22), then this sign would be negative, and (*) would remain indeterminate.

‡ A related and much discussed problem is whether *profitable* speculation is necessarily stabilizing. If it were so, then speculation would be beneficial (and would not endanger a floating exchange rate system) at least in the long run, since destabilizing speculators would make losses and so be compelled to leave the market. Friedman and Telser have tried to prove that profitable speculation must be stabilizing; Baumol, Cutilli and Kemp have produced counterexamples. See also Obst and the references quoted by him.

Exercises

1. The following data are given: $a_0 = 200$, $a_1 = -10$, $B = 10$, $\omega = 4\pi$, $m = 1$, $b_1 = -0.4$, $b_2 = -0.2$, $b_0 = 1$.
What is the influence of speculation on the time path of the exchange rate?

Calculation. With the given numerical values of the parameters, non-speculators' excess demand is

$$E_n(t) = 200 - 10\,SR(t) + 10\cos 4\pi t \ ,$$

and so the time path of the exchange rate, obtained by putting $E_n(t) = 0$, is

$$SR(t) = 20 + \cos 4\pi t \ .$$

Speculators' excess demand is

$$E_s(t) = ER(t) - SR(t) \ ,$$

where

$$ER(t) = SR - 0.4\,SR' - 0.2\,SR'' \ ,$$

and so

$$E_s(t) = -0.4\,SR' - 0.2\,SR'' \ .$$

The time path of the exchange rate is obtained putting $E_n(t) + E_s(t) = 0$, which gives

$$-0.2\,SR'' - 0.4\,SR' - 10\,SR = -200 - 10\cos 4\pi t \ .$$

The characteristic equation of the homogeneous part is

$$\lambda^2 + 2\lambda + 50 = 0 \ ,$$

so that

$$\lambda_1, \lambda_2 = \tfrac{1}{2}(-2 \pm \sqrt{-196}) = -1 \pm 7\,\mathrm{i} \ .$$

Using the general formulae found in the text, a particular solution turns out to be

$$\overline{SR}(t) = 20 + 0.4512\cos(4\pi t + \gamma) \ ,$$

and so the general solution is

$$SR(t) = e^{-t}(A_1 \cos 7t + A_2 \sin 7t) + 20 + 0.4512 \cos(4\pi t + \gamma).$$

We can conclude that, in the limit, speculation will have a stabilizing influence, since the exchange rate converges to an oscillation whose amplitude is smaller than the one obtaining without speculative activity.

2. Determine the value of γ in the previous exercise.

3. Same data as in exercise 1, but for $m = 0.3$. Can you say something general on the influence of m on the limiting solution?

References

Allen, R.G.D., 1959, *Mathematical Economics*, ch. 8, §§8.8, 8.9.
Allen, R.G.D., 1967, *Macro-Economic Theory: A Mathematical Treatment,* ch. 18, §§18.3, 18.4.
Baumol, W.J., 1957, Speculation, Profitability and Stability.
Cutilli, B., 1963, The Role of Commercial Banks in Foreign Exchange Speculation.
Friedman, M., 1953, The Case for Flexible Exchange Rates, pp. 174–7.
Glahe, F.R., 1966, Professional and Nonprofessional Speculation, Profitability, and Stability.
Kemp, M.C., 1963, Speculation, Profitability, and Price Stability.
Obst, N.P., 1967, A Connection Between Speculation and Stability in the Foreign Exchange Market.
Phillips, A.W., 1954, Stabilisation Policy in a Closed Economy.
Telser, L.G., 1959, A Theory of Speculation Relating Profitability and Stability.

6

Higher-order Equations

In this chapter we shall examine the general n-th order differential equation

$$a_0 y^{(n)} + a_1 y^{(n-1)} + \dots + a_{n-1} y' + a_n y = g(t) \,, \quad a_0 \neq 0 \,. \quad (6.1)$$

To solve the corresponding homogeneous equation

$$a_0 y^{(n)} + a_1 y^{(n-1)} + \dots + a_{n-1} y' + a_n y = 0 \,, \quad (6.2)$$

we can follow the same method which has worked successfully in first- and second-order equations, so that we substitute $y = e^{\lambda t}$ in (6.2), obtaining

$$a_0 \lambda^n e^{\lambda t} + a_1 \lambda^{n-1} e^{\lambda t} + \dots + a_{n-1} \lambda e^{\lambda t} + a_n e^{\lambda t} = 0 \,, \quad (6.3)$$

i.e.

$$e^{\lambda t}(a_0 \lambda^n + a_1 \lambda^{n-1} + \dots + a_{n-1} \lambda + a_n) = 0 \,. \quad (6.3')$$

Now, if $e^{\lambda t}$ is a solution of (6.2), eq. (6.3') must be identically satisfied. Since $e^{\lambda t} \neq 0$, the necessary and sufficient condition that (6.3') be identically satisfied is

$$a_0 \lambda^n + a_1 \lambda^{n-1} + \ldots + a_{n-1}\lambda + a_n = 0 \ . \tag{6.4}$$

Eq. (6.4) is called the *characteristic* (or auxiliary) *equation* of the differential equation (6.2). Thus we have reduced the solution of a differential equation to the solution of an algebraic equation. The solution of eq. (6.4) yields exactly n roots, which may be real or complex, simple of repeated. In the case of distinct real roots, we have n functions $\exp(\lambda_i t)$, each being a solution of the homogeneous equation (6.2). According to general principles, the general solution of (6.2) is then

$$y(t) = A_1 \exp(\lambda_1 t) + A_2 \exp(\lambda_2 t) + \ldots + A_n \exp(\lambda_n t) \ , \tag{6.5}$$

where $A_1, A_2, \ldots, A_n$ are arbitrary constants.

If λ^* is a repeated real root of multiplicity $m \leqslant n$, then also $t \exp(\lambda^* t)$, $t^2 \exp(\lambda^* t), \ldots, t^{m-1} \exp(\lambda^* t)$ are solutions of the homogeneous equation. In general, the solution of the homogeneous equation in the case of repeated real roots is

$$y(t) = \sum_{j=1}^{k} P_j(t) \exp(\lambda_j^* t) \ , \tag{6.6}$$

where λ_j^* are the roots of eq. (6.4), each with its multiplicity, and $P_j(t)$ are polynomials of the type

$$P_j(t) = A_{1_j} + A_{2_j}t + \ldots + A_{m_j}t^{m_j - 1} \ ,$$

where the A's are arbitrary constants and m_j is the multiplicity of the j-th root.

In the case of complex roots (that always occur in conjugate pairs), each pair will give rise to a trigonometric oscillation of the kind

$$e^{\alpha t}(A_1 \cos\theta t + A_2 \sin\theta t)$$

in exactly the same way as in second-order equations. A further complication (which we did not meet in second-order equations, where it could not arise) is that one pair (or more) of complex roots may be repeated. Then in the solution we shall have terms of the kind

$$e^{\alpha t}[(A_{11_j} + A_{12_j}t + ... + A_{1m_j}t^{m_j-1})\cos\theta t$$

$$+ (A_{21_j} + A_{22_j}t + ... + A_{2m_j}t^{m_j-1})\sin\theta t] ,$$ (6.7)

where m_j is the number of times that the j-th pair of complex roots is repeated and the A's are $2m_j$ arbitrary constants.

Of course, in the same equation, complex (simple or repeated) roots may occur together with real (simple or repeated) roots, so that a great variety of movements is possible.

For a particular solution of the non-homogeneous equation, it can usually be found by applying the general method of undetermined coefficients (see Part II, ch. 1). We shall exemplify in the case in which $g(t) = G$, a constant. As a particular solution, try $\bar{y} = B$, an undetermined constant. Substitution in (6.1) yields $a_n B = G$ and so $B = G/a_n$. If $a_n = 0$, try $\bar{y} = Bt$. Substituting in (6.1) and solving for B we obtain $B = G/a_{a-1}$. If also $a_{n-1} = 0$, try $\bar{y} = Bt^2$, and so on. In the extreme case in which all coefficients but a_0 are zero, a particular solution will be $\bar{y} = Bt^n$, where $B = G/a_0 n!$. [*]

In order to determine the n arbitrary constants appearing in the solution, n additional conditions are needed; they usually take the form of $y(0), y'(0),...$ $..., y^{(n-1)}(0)$ being known values. Substituting such values in the general solution, we obtain a system of n linear equations in the n unknowns A_1, $A_2, ..., A_n$ [**].

---

[*] The characteristic equation of the homogeneous equation $a_0 y^{(n)} = 0$ is $a_0 \lambda^n = 0$, which has a root $\lambda^* = 0$ repeated n times. Applying (6.6) and since $e^0 = 1$, the general solution of the homogeneous equation is $A_1 + A_2 t + ... + A_n t^{n-1}$, and so the general solution of the non-homogeneous equation $a_0 y^{(n)} = G$ is $y(t) = A_1 + A_2 t + ... + A_n t^{n-1} + Bt^n$. We could obtain the same result directly by integrating the differential equation n times.

[**] Consider the case in which all roots are distinct. The equations for the determination of the arbitrary constants are

$$\sum_{j=1}^{n} A_j \lambda_j^i = y^{(i)}(0) - \bar{y}^{(i)}(0) , \qquad i = 0, 1, ..., n-1 ,$$ (*)

and

$$\bar{y}^{(i)}(0) \equiv 0 ,$$

if the system is homogeneous, where i is the order of the derivative ($i=0$ means no differentiation) and the $y^{(i)}(0)$ are the given initial values. It can be checked that the determinant of system (*) (the 'Wronksian' determinant of the functions $\exp(\lambda_j t)$ for $t=0$) is different from zero since the roots are all distinct. Thus we can solve (*) for the A's. Some complications may arise when there are repeated roots, but we need not treat them here.

As we said in the discussion of difference equations (p. 106), the n-th order equation does not confront us with greater conceptual difficulties than the second-order equation. The practical problem of how to find the roots of the characteristic equation is a problem in numerical analysis and will not be treated in this book; anyway, it is relatively unimportant for the economic theorist, who works with *qualitative* information only. From this point of view the true problem is whether it is possible to check the stability of the roots * by means of inequalities involving only the coefficients of the characteristic equation itself. The condition that all the non-zero coefficients in (6.4) have the same sign excludes, by Descartes' theorem, positive real roots, and the condition $a_n \neq 0$ excludes zero real roots, but all this is not sufficient to exclude complex roots with non-negative real part. However, general conditions exist which are necessary and sufficient for all the roots to be stable. We shall first state the classical Routh–Hurwitz theorem and then the Liénard–Chipart stability criteria (usually overlooked in the mathematical economics literature) which allow a great simplification in the conditions.

Let there be given the polynomial equation with real coefficients

$$a_0\lambda^n + a_1\lambda^{n-1} + \dots + a_{n-1}\lambda + a_n = 0 , \qquad (a_0 > 0) , \qquad (6.4)$$

where without loss of generality a_0 can be taken as positive. Then we may state the following theorems.

(1) *Necessary and sufficient stability conditions (Routh–Hurwitz)*
Form the array of coefficients

$$\begin{bmatrix} a_1 & a_3 & a_5 & a_7 & \cdots & 0 \\ a_0 & a_2 & a_4 & a_6 & \cdots & 0 \\ 0 & a_1 & a_3 & a_5 & \cdots & 0 \\ 0 & a_0 & a_2 & a_4 & \cdots & 0 \\ 0 & 0 & a_1 & a_3 & \cdots & 0 \\ \cdots & \cdots & \cdots & \cdots & \cdots & \cdots \\ \cdots & \cdots & \cdots & \cdots & \cdots & a_n \end{bmatrix} . \qquad (6.8)$$

---

* By a 'stable' root we mean a root having negative real part — that is, strictly lying in the left half of the complex plane — (this includes both complex and real roots). Roots with zero real part are excluded from the definition of 'stable' roots, because we want

It must be noted that all the a's with a subscript greater than n or with a negative subscript, must be treated as zero. Only the first n rows and columns of (6.8) have to be considered. The Routh–Hurwitz theorem states that necessary and sufficient conditions for all roots of (6.4) to have negative real parts are given by the following inequalities (which must hold simultaneously):

$$\Delta_1 > 0, \Delta_2 > 0, ..., \Delta_n > 0 , \tag{6.9}$$

where $\Delta_1, \Delta_2, ..., \Delta_n$ are the leading principal minors of (6.8), i.e.

$$\Delta_1 = a_1, \Delta_2 = \begin{vmatrix} a_1 & a_3 \\ a_0 & a_2 \end{vmatrix} ,$$

$$\Delta_3 = \begin{vmatrix} a_1 & a_3 & a_5 \\ a_0 & a_2 & a_4 \\ 0 & a_1 & a_3 \end{vmatrix} , ..., \Delta_n = \begin{vmatrix} a_1 & a_3 & a_5 & a_7 & \cdots & 0 \\ a_0 & a_2 & a_4 & a_6 & \cdots & 0 \\ 0 & a_1 & a_3 & a_5 & \cdots & 0 \\ 0 & a_0 & a_2 & a_4 & \cdots & 0 \\ 0 & 0 & a_1 & a_3 & \cdots & 0 \\ \cdots & \cdots & \cdots & \cdots & \cdots & \\ \cdots & \cdots & \cdots & \cdots & & a_n \end{vmatrix} . \tag{6.10}$$

For example, in the case of a third-order equation, the basic array is

$$\begin{bmatrix} a_1 & a_3 & 0 \\ a_0 & a_2 & 0 \\ 0 & a_1 & a_3 \end{bmatrix} ,$$

and only $\Delta_1, \Delta_2, \Delta_3$ have to be considered, so that the stability conditions are

$$a_1 > 0 , \tag{6.11}$$

asymptotic stability, that is $\lim_{t \to +\infty} y(t) = 0$, where $y(t)$ is the general solution of the homogeneous equation. Now, a zero real root gives rise to an additive arbitrary constant, and a complex root with zero real part to a constant amplitude oscillation, in the general solution, so that in both cases the stability is not asymptotic.

$$a_1 a_2 - a_0 a_3 > 0 \,,$$

$$a_3(a_1 a_2 - a_0 a_3) > 0 \,. \tag{6.11}$$

The third inequality, given the second, is equivalent to $a_3 > 0$, so that we may rewrite the conditions as

$$a_1 > 0 \,,$$

$$a_3 > 0 \,, \tag{6.11$'$}$$

$$a_1 a_2 - a_0 a_3 > 0 \,.$$

Note also that, since $a_0 > 0$, the three inequalities together imply that $a_2 > 0$ ($a_0 a_3$ is positive, so that the third inequality implies that $a_1 a_2$ is positive, i.e., since $a_1 > 0$, that $a_2 > 0$). If we prefer, $a_2 > 0$ can be substituted for the first inequality in (6.11$'$), since the inequalities

$$a_2 > 0 \,,$$

$$a_3 > 0 \,, \tag{6.12}$$

$$a_1 a_2 - a_0 a_3 > 0 \,,$$

imply that $a_1 > 0$. Another way of noting the same thing is to state the stability conditions ★ as

$$a_1 > 0 \,,$$

$$a_2 > 0 \,,$$

$$a_3 > 0 \,, \tag{6.13}$$

$$a_1 a_2 - a_0 a_3 > 0 \,,$$

and to note that one of the first two inequalities can be eliminated since it is implied by the remaining three.

★ Such conditions can be proved independently and in a rather simple way. The positivity of all the coefficients ensures that no non-negative real roots may occur. We shall

(2) *Necessary and sufficient stability conditions (Liénard–Chipart)*
Necessary and sufficient conditions for eq. (6.4) to have only roots with negative real parts may be expressed in any one of the four following alternative forms:

(a) $a_n > 0, a_{n-2} > 0, ...; \Delta_1 > 0, \Delta_3 > 0, ...$,   (6.14a)

(b) $a_n > 0, a_{n-2} > 0, ...; \Delta_2 > 0, \Delta_4 > 0, ...$,   (6.14b)

(c) $a_n > 0, a_{n-1} > 0, a_{n-3} > 0, ...; \Delta_1 > 0, \Delta_3 > 0, ...$,   (6.14c)

(d) $a_n > 0, a_{n-1} > 0, a_{n-3} > 0, ...; \Delta_2 > 0, \Delta_4 > 0, ...$,   (6.14d)

where $\Delta_1, \Delta_2, ..., \Delta_n$ are as defined in (6.10).

The advantage of the Liénard–Chipart conditions over the Routh–Hurwitz conditions is that the former involve about half as many determinantal inequalities as the latter, and this is an important simplification, especially when the degree of the characteristic equation is high (and so the determinants Δ_i arrive at a high order). In either form, however, the conditions become increasingly complicated as the order of the equation increases and, correspondingly, their economic interpretation becomes more and more difficult. Indeed, there is not much hope of extricating a clear economic meaning from the stability conditions (except in particular cases) when the order of the equation is even moderately high (say four or more).

now use the well-known relations between the coefficients and the roots of an algebraic equation (see e.g. Turnbull, 1957, p. 66), that are – assuming that $a_0 = 1$ –

$$a_1 = -(\lambda_1 + \lambda_2 + \lambda_3) ,$$

$$a_2 = \lambda_1\lambda_2 + \lambda_1\lambda_3 + \lambda_2\lambda_3 ,$$

$$a_3 = -\lambda_1\lambda_2\lambda_3 .$$

Now, suppose that $\lambda_2, \lambda_3 = \alpha \pm i\theta$. The positivity of all the coefficients ensures that $\lambda_1 < 0$. Furthermore, we have

$$-(\lambda_1 + 2\alpha) = a_1 > 0 ,$$

$$2\alpha\lambda_1 + \alpha^2 + \theta^2 = a_2 > 0 ,$$

$$-\lambda_1(\alpha^2 + \theta^2) = a_3 > 0 ,$$

$$a_1 a_2 - a_3 = 2[-(\lambda_1 + 2\alpha)\lambda_1 - (\alpha^2 + \theta^2)]\alpha > 0 .$$

Since $-(\lambda_1 + 2\alpha) > 0$ by the first inequality, and $\alpha^2 + \theta^2 > 0$, it follows that $a_1 a_2 - a_3 > 0$ implies $\alpha < 0$ and vice versa.

References

Allen, R.G.D., 1959, *Mathematical Economics*, ch. 5, § 5.5.

Baumol, W.J., 1970, *Economic Dynamics*, ch. 14, § 7.

Bushaw, D.W. and Clower, R.W., 1957, *Introduction to Mathematical Economics*,
    Part II, ch. 12, § 9.

Gantmacher, F.R., 1959, *Applications of the Theory of Matrices*, ch. V, §§ 6, 13.

Ince, E.L., 1956, *Ordinary Differential Equations*, ch. VI, pp. 133–41.

Kooros, A., 1965, *Elements of Mathematical Economics*, ch. 9, § 9.3.

Samuelson, P.A., 1947, *Foundations of Economic Analysis*, Appendix B, § 36.

Turnbull, H.W., 1957, *Theory of Equations*, pp. 66, 68, 102.

Yamane, T., 1968, *Mathematics for Economists· An Elementary Survey*, ch. 12, § 12.10.

7

Some Economic Applications
of Higher-order Equations

While higher-order difference equations are quite frequently met in economics, examples of the use of 'direct' * higher-order differential equations are not numerous. The reason is that in the context of a period analysis lags can usually be freely and plausibly poured over the model (e.g., in any macroeconomic model built in discrete time, investment and consumption functions with distributed lags could be inserted), whereas in the context of a continuous analysis it is more difficult to give an economic meaning to derivatives of the third or higher orders. Here we shall examine Phillips' stabilization model in the case of an integral policy, and an inventory adjustment model.

---

* We must explain what we mean by 'direct'. As we shall see in the next chapter, a simultaneous system of differential equations can be transformed into a single differential equation of a certain order. Thus a higher-order differential equation can result from the transformation of a system. The adjective 'direct' means that we are referring to differential equations that arise directly, and not as a transformation of a system, in economic dynamics. See, however, what we shall say at the beginning of Part II, ch. 9.

§ 1. Phillips' integral stabilization policy

For the basic aspects of this model the reader is referred back to Part II, ch. 5, § 1. Now inserting $G^* = -f_i \int_0^t Y \, dt$ in eq. (5.9) of that section, we obtain

$$Y'' + (\alpha l + \beta)Y' + \alpha\beta lY + \alpha\beta f_i \int_0^t Y \, dt = -\alpha\beta . \tag{7.1}$$

The integral can be eliminated differentiating with respect to time, which gives

$$Y''' + (\alpha l + \beta)Y'' + \alpha\beta lY' + \alpha\beta f_i Y = 0 . \tag{7.2}$$

The first thing to note is that (7.2) is a homogeneous equation, so that the movement of Y is referred to zero. Therefore, if we find that such a movement is convergent, it follows that the integral stabilization policy succeeds where the other policies have failed, i.e. in eliminating completely the decrease in income due to an exogenous decrease in aggregate demand.

The characteristic equation of (7.2) is

$$\lambda^3 + (\alpha l + \beta)\lambda^2 + \alpha\beta l\lambda + \alpha\beta f_i = 0 . \tag{7.3}$$

All the coefficients of eq. (7.3) are positive, so that it does not have any positive roots. Thus the instability, if any, can only be oscillatory. Applying stability conditions (6.13) of Part II, ch. 6, we find that, since all the coefficients are positive, the crucial condition is

$$(\alpha l + \beta)\alpha\beta l - \alpha\beta f_i > 0 , \tag{7.4}$$

from which

$$f_i < (\alpha l + \beta)l . \tag{7.4'}$$

It follows that the integral stabilization policy is successful provided that the intervention coefficient f_i is *smaller* than a certain critical value (the right-hand side of (7.4')). In the contrary case, such policy causes income to diverge from (with explosive oscillations around) the desired value. Thus the integral policy has, if successful, the advantage of being able to completely eliminate the effects of the exogeneous disturbance, but there is also the risk that an unstable movement may take place (this could not occur with the other policies). These are rather interesting conclusions, and it should be noted that we could not have reached them in all generality without the use of the stability conditions, which gave us the inequality (7.4').

Let us now see what happens when the integral policy is used together with one or more of the other policies. When the integral and the proportional stabilization policies are used together, we have

$$G^* = -f_i \int_0^t Y \, dt - f_p Y ,$$

and so eq. (5.9) of Part II, ch. 5, §1, becomes

$$Y'' + (\alpha l + \beta)Y' + \alpha\beta(l + f_p)Y + \alpha\beta f_i \int_0^t Y \, dt = -\alpha\beta . \tag{7.5}$$

Differentiating with respect to time we obtain

$$Y''' + (\alpha l + \beta)Y'' + \alpha\beta(l + f_p)Y' + \alpha\beta f_i Y = 0 . \tag{7.6}$$

This too is a homogeneous equation, whose characteristic equation is

$$\lambda^3 + (\alpha l + \beta)\lambda^2 + \alpha\beta(l + f_p)\lambda + \alpha\beta f_i = 0 . \tag{7.7}$$

All the coefficients are positive, and so no positive roots may occur. The crucial stability condition is

$$(\alpha l + \beta)\alpha\beta(l + f_p) - \alpha\beta f_i > 0 , \tag{7.8}$$

from which

$$f_i < (\alpha l + \beta)(l + f_p) . \tag{7.8'}$$

The critical value of f_i is now *greater* than in the case of a pure integral policy. The conclusion is that the addition of the proportional policy reduces the danger of explosive oscillations.

The student may check as an exercise that in the case of a mixed integral–derivative policy the crucial stability condition is

$$f_i < (\alpha l + \beta + \alpha\beta f_d)l , \tag{7.9}$$

and that in the case in which all three policies are simultaneously adopted the
crucial stability condition is

$$f_i < (\alpha l + \beta + \alpha \beta f_d)(l + f_p) .$$ (7.10)

(In both cases no positive roots may occur, so that here too instability, if any,
is oscillatory.)

Comparing the various conditions, it follows that the technically preferable
choice is to use the three policies simultaneously, since the critical value of
f_i is greater than when the integral policy is used in conjunction with only one
of the other two policies.

Assuming (as a didactic exercise) that Phillips' model could be applied
bodily to the real world, some general conclusions can be drawn. If the government knows with certainty the values of α and of l and can determine exactly
the values of the parameters that it controls (f_d, f_p, f_i and β), it should undoubtedly use the integral policy since it allows the complete elimination, at
least in the limit, of the effects of an exogenous disturbance, and since f_i
could be kept below its critical value, known exactly. But, if the above conditions do not hold (as perhaps is true in real world policy problems), there
is a certain degree of risk in the use of the integral policy, which can be reduced, but not removed, by using this policy in conjunction with the other
two. Thus a 'risk averting' government may prefer to leave aside the integral
policy and use only the mixed proportional–derivative policy (which does
not completely eliminate the effects of an exogenous disturbance but is 'safe'
since it cannot give rise to a divergent movement).

Exercises
1. Given $\alpha = 4$, $l = 0.25$, $f_i = 0.504$, $\beta = 2$, determine the time path of income
after a unit disturbance.

Calculation. With the given numerical values, eq. (7.2) in the text becomes

$$Y''' + 3Y'' + 2Y' + 4.032 Y = 0 ,$$ (7.11)

and its characteristic equation is

$$\lambda^3 + 3\lambda^2 + 2\lambda + 4.032 = 0 .$$

The crucial stability condition is satisfied, since

$$3 \times 2 - 4.032 > 0 \ .$$

This is enough to say that income will converge somehow to the desired value. If we want to know its precise time path we must solve the characteristic equation. The exercise has been built in such a way that $\lambda_1 = -2.8$ is a root of the characteristic equation, as the student may check by direct substitution. From elementary algebra we know that a polynomial is exactly divisible by $\lambda - \lambda_i$, where λ_i is any one of its roots. Performing the division by $\lambda + 2.8$ we obtain $\lambda^2 + 0.2\lambda + 1.44$, so that

$$\lambda^3 + 3\lambda^2 + 2\lambda + 4.032 = (\lambda + 2.8)(\lambda^2 + 0.2\lambda + 1.44) = 0 \ ,$$

and thus the other two roots are given by the solution of

$$\lambda^2 + 0.2\lambda + 1.44 = 0 \ ,$$

which gives

$$\lambda_2, \lambda_3 \simeq -0.10 \pm 1.195826 \ \mathrm{i} \ .$$

The general solution of (7.11), which gives the time path of income, is

$$Y(t) = A_1 e^{-2.80t} + e^{-0.10t}(A_2 \cos 1.195826 \ t + A_3 \sin 1.195826 \ t) \ ,$$

where A_1, A_2, A_3 are arbitrary constants.

2. Given the initial conditions $Y(0) = 0$, $Y'(0) = 4$, $Y''(0) = 4$, determine the values of the arbitrary constants in the previous exercise and compute the time approximately required for the deviation of income from its desired level to be reduced below 10% (in absolute value). (*Hint*: after having found the values of the arbitrary constants, write $A_2 \cos 1.195826 \ t + A_3 \sin 1.195826 \ t$ in the form $A \cos (1.195826 \ t - \epsilon)$ and use the fact that the range of variation of $\cos x$ is ± 1.)

3. Same data as in exercise 1, but for $f_i = 2$. Use the stability conditions and check that the movement is divergent.

4. The following data are given: $\alpha = 4, l = 0.25, \beta = 2, f_i = 0.5, f_p = 0.5$. Check that the movement converges and has an oscillatory component whose damping is more rapid than in exercise 1.

Calculation. With the given numerical values, eq. (7.6) in the text becomes

$$Y''' + 3Y'' + 6Y' + 4Y = 0 \tag{7.12}$$

and its characteristic equation is

$$\lambda^3 + 3\lambda^2 + 6\lambda + 4 = 0 \ .$$

The student may check by direct substitution that $\lambda_1 = -1$ is a root. Dividing by $\lambda + 1$ we have

$$\lambda^3 + 3\lambda^2 + 6\lambda + 4 = (\lambda + 1)(\lambda^2 + 2\lambda + 4) = 0 \ ,$$

and so λ_2, λ_3 are given by the solution of

$$\lambda^2 + 2\lambda + 4 = 0 \ ,$$

which gives

$$\lambda_2, \lambda_3 = -1 \pm i\sqrt{3} \simeq -1 \pm 1.732051 \, i \ .$$

Thus the general solution of (7.12) is

$$Y(t) = A_1 e^{-t} + e^{-t}(A_2 \cos 1.732051 \, t + A_3 \sin 1.732051 \, t) \ ,$$

where A_1, A_2, A_3 are arbitrary constants. The damping factor in the oscillatory component of the solution is e^{-t}, whereas in exercise 1 this factor was $e^{-0.10t}$. Since e^{-t} tends to zero more rapidly than $e^{-0.10t}$, the oscillation is now more heavily damped (the contrary is true for the monotonic component).

5. Same data as in exercise 4, but for $f_i = 2, f_p = 2$.

6. The following data are given: $\alpha = 4, l = 0.25, \beta = 2, f_i = 8, f_p = 8, f_d = 1$. Check that the movement is convergent applying the stability conditions and compare the result with the one obtaining if $f_p = f_d = 0$.

§2. Expectations and inventory adjustment

The basic assumption in this model is that producers vary their output in relation to the difference between the desired and the actual level of their inventories (of finished goods): if the desired level is greater (smaller) than the actual level, they increase (decrease) output to bring inventories to the desired level. Thus we can write

$$Y' = \beta [\hat{Q}(t) - Q(t)] ,$$ (7.13)

where $Y(t)$ is national product (income), $\hat{Q}(t)$ is the desired level of inventories and $Q(t)$ the actual level; β is a reaction coefficient: if $\beta = 1$, the variation in output is equal to the difference between desired and actual inventories, i.e. producers want to eliminate immediately and fully such a difference. However, it seems more plausible to assume that $\beta < 1$.

We know from elementary macroeconomics that a difference between 'ex ante' saving and 'ex ante' investment gives rise to an equivalent variation in inventories. In this model we admit that such a difference may exist (instead of postulating a continuous ex ante equality between saving and investment), so that

$$Q' = S(t) - I(t) .$$ (7.14)

Saving is assumed to be a function of national income and investment is assumed to be entirely exogenous, so that

$$S(t) = -a + sY(t) , \qquad a > 0 , \qquad 0 < s < 1 ,$$ (7.15)

and

$$I(t) = I_0 , \qquad I_0 > 0 .$$ (7.16)

To use the model some assumptions have to be made about the desired level of inventories. We assume that this desired level is proportional to expected output $\hat{Y}$. Regarding the latter, we assume that expectations are formed by extrapolating the rate of change of current output and by considering also whether this rate is increasing or decreasing, i.e.

$$\hat{Y} = Y + a_1 Y' + a_2 Y'' , \qquad a_1 > 0 , \qquad a_2 > 0 .$$ (7.17)

Thus, for example, if current output is increasing at an increasing rate ($Y' > 0$, $Y'' > 0$), a further increase is expected, whereas if it is increasing at a decreasing rate ($Y' > 0$, $Y'' < 0$), an increase or a decrease may be expected, according to the magnitudes of Y', Y'' and of the expectations coefficients a_1, a_2. In other words, extrapolative expectations are modified using the second derivative. This sounds more plausible than pure extrapolative expectations, since when, for instance, output is increasing at a decreasing rate, it seems reasonable to think that producers may expect a decrease as well as an increase in output.

Differentiating both members of the equation $Y' = \beta(\hat{Q} - Q)$, we have

$$Y'' = \beta \hat{Q}' - \beta Q' . \tag{7.18}$$

Since $\hat{Q}' = k \hat{Y}'$, where $k > 0$ is the proportionality coefficient, and $Q' = S - I_0 = sY - (a + I_0)$, we obtain

$$Y'' = \beta k Y' + \beta k a_1 Y'' + \beta k a_2 Y''' - \beta s Y + \beta(a + I_0) , \tag{7.19}$$

from which

$$\beta k a_2 Y''' + (\beta k a_1 - 1)Y'' + \beta k Y' - \beta s Y = -\beta(a + I_0) . \tag{7.20}$$

A particular solution of (7.20) is obtained trying $\overline{Y}$ = constant, whence, substituting in (7.20) and solving for $\overline{Y}$, we obtain

$$\overline{Y} = \frac{a + I_0}{s} , \tag{7.21}$$

which is the equilibrium level of output.

The characteristic equation of the homogeneous part of (7.20) is

$$\beta k a_2 \lambda^3 + (\beta k a_1 - 1)\lambda^2 + \beta k \lambda - \beta s = 0 . \tag{7.22}$$

It can immediately be seen that the stability conditions are not satisfied, since $-\beta s < 0$, so that the model is unstable ★. The interesting thing to note is that there is no way of making the model stable by changing the coefficients of expectation: as the student may check as an exercise, there is no combination of the signs and absolute values of a_1, a_2, that makes it possible to satisfy all the inequalities required by the stability conditions.

★ It can also be proved that at least one root is real and positive (unstable monotonic component in the solution). Consider the cubic function

$$h(\lambda) = \beta k a_2 \lambda^3 + (\beta k a_1 - 1)\lambda^2 + \beta k \lambda - \beta s .$$

The real roots of (7.22) are the points of intersection of $h(\lambda)$ with the λ-axis. Now, $h(0) = -\beta s < 0$ and $h(\lambda) \to +\infty$ as $\lambda \to +\infty$, since the term $\beta k a_2 \lambda^3$ predominates for sufficiently high values of λ, and $\beta k a_2 > 0$. Since $h(\lambda)$ is a continuous function, it follows that it must cross at least once the positive part of the λ-axis.

Exercises

1. The following data are given: $\beta = 0.80, k = 0.50, s = 0.25, a_1 = 0.50,$
$a_2 = 1.50, a = 10, I_0 = 50$. Determine the time path of income.

Calculation. With the given numerical data, eq. (7.20) in the text becomes

$$0.6\,Y''' - 0.8\,Y'' + 0.4\,Y' - 0.2\,Y = -48 \ .$$

A particular solution is obtained trying $\bar{Y}$ = constant, whence $\bar{Y}$ = 240 (the same value is obtained applying the multiplier $1/s = 4$ to exogenous expenditure $a + I_0 = 60$).

The characteristic equation

$$0.6\,\lambda^3 - 0.8\,\lambda^2 + 0.4\,\lambda - 0.2 = 0$$

has a root equal to 1, as can be checked by direct substitution. The characteristic equation can then be divided by $\lambda - 1$, which gives

$$0.6\,\lambda^3 - 0.8\,\lambda^2 + 0.4\,\lambda - 0.2 = (\lambda - 1)(0.6\,\lambda^2 - 0.2\,\lambda + 0.2) = 0 \ ,$$

so that the remaining two roots are given by the solution of

$$0.6\,\lambda^2 - 0.2\,\lambda + 0.2 = 0 \ ,$$

which gives

$$\lambda_1, \lambda_2 = 0.1\bar{6} \pm i\,\frac{1}{1.2}\sqrt{0.44} \simeq 0.1\bar{6} \pm 0.5527\,i \ .$$

The general solution is then

$$Y(t) = A_1 e^t + e^{0.1\bar{6}t}(A_1 \cos 0.5527\,t + A_2 \sin 0.5527\,t) \ ,$$

where A_1, A_2, A_3 are arbitrary constants.

2. Same data as in the previous exercise, but for $\beta = 1, a_1 = 1, a_2 = 0.5$.
(*Hint*: $\lambda = 1$ is a root of the characteristic equation.)

References

Allen, R.G.D., 1959, *Mathematical Economics*, ch. 8, § 8.9.

Allen, R.G.D., 1967, *Macro-Economic Theory: A Mathematical Treatment,* ch. 18, §§ 18.3, 18.4, 18.5.

Phillips, A.W., 1954, Stabilisation Policy in a Closed Economy.

Phillips, A.W., 1957, Stabilisation Policy and the Time-Form of Lagged Responses.

8

Simultaneous Systems

A simultaneous system is made up of two (or more) differential equations in which two (or more) unknown functions are involved. In order that the system be solvable, it must have as many equations as unknowns, provided that the equations are independent and consistent.

The simplest system is a first-order system in 'normal' form [*]; in the 2×2 case it has the form

$$y'(t) = a_{11}y(t) + a_{12}z(t) + g_1(t),$$

$$z'(t) = a_{21}y(t) + a_{22}z(t) + g_2(t),$$
(8.1)

where the coefficients a_{ij} are given constants and $g_1(t), g_2(t)$ are known functions. System (8.1) is a non-homogeneous system; the corresponding homogeneous system is

---

[*] The system is called first-order because in it second- (or higher-) order derivatives of the unknown functions do not appear; and it is called 'normal' because each equation involves the derivative of only one function in turn. It must be noted that the *order* of a system is equal to the *degree* of its characteristic equation (see below). Therefore, the expression 'first-order system' must be understood only in the sense defined above, and not as indicating the order of the system (actually, the order of system (8.1) is 2).

$$y'(t) = a_{11}y(t) + a_{12}z(t) ,$$
$$z'(t) = a_{21}y(t) + a_{22}z(t) .$$

(8.2)

It can be proved by direct substitutions (which are left as an exercise) that, as in single equations, the general solution of (8.1) is obtained by adding a particular solution of (8.1) to the general solution of (8.2). So let us begin with the homogeneous system.

A method of solving (8.2) consists in reducing it to a single equation in which only one unknown function appears; this reduction is always possible by means of suitable transformations. From the first equation of system (8.2) we obtain, provided that $a_{12} \neq 0$ *,

$$z = \frac{1}{a_{12}} y' - \frac{a_{11}}{a_{12}} y ,$$

(8.3)

so that, differentiating with respect to time,

$$z' = \frac{1}{a_{12}} y'' - \frac{a_{11}}{a_{12}} y' .$$

(8.4)

Substituting (8.3) and (8.4) in the second equation of system (8.2) we have

$$\frac{1}{a_{12}} y'' - \frac{a_{11}}{a_{12}} y' = a_{21}y + \frac{a_{22}}{a_{12}} y' - \frac{a_{11}a_{22}}{a_{12}} y .$$

(8.5)

Multiplying through by a_{12} and rearranging terms we obtain

$$y'' - (a_{11} + a_{22})y' + (a_{11}a_{22} - a_{12}a_{21})y = 0 .$$

(8.6)

Eq. (8.6) is a second-order equation in the unknown function $y(t)$. We solve it in the usual way (see Part II, ch. 4) and to obtain $z(t)$ we have only to substitute the solution of (8.6) into (8.3). Suppose that the characteristic equation of (8.6) has two real and distinct roots. Then the general solution of (8.6) is, as we know,

---

* If $a_{12} = 0$, we can use the second equation to isolate $y(t)$, etc. (the steps are the same as those expounded in the text for $z(t)$; note that when $a_{12} = 0$, then a_{21} must be different from zero, because if a_{21} were also zero, we would no more have a simultaneous system, but two separate equations without any interdependency). Another method, when either a_{12} or a_{21} is zero, is to solve separately the equation in which only one unknown function appears and to substitute the result in the other equation.

$$y(t) = A_1 \exp(\lambda_1 t) + A_2 \exp(\lambda_2 t), \tag{8.7}$$

where A_1, A_2 are arbitrary constants. Substituting from (8.7) in (8.3) we have

$$z(t) = \frac{\lambda_1 A_1}{a_{12}} \exp(\lambda_1 t) + \frac{\lambda_2 A_2}{a_{12}} \exp(\lambda_2 t) - \frac{a_{11} A_1}{a_{12}} \exp(\lambda_1 t) - \frac{a_{11} A_2}{a_{12}} \exp(\lambda_2 t),$$

so that

$$z(t) = \frac{\lambda_1 - a_{11}}{a_{12}} A_1 \exp(\lambda_1 t) + \frac{\lambda_2 - a_{11}}{a_{12}} A_2 \exp(\lambda_2 t). \tag{8.8}$$

Equations (8.7) and (8.8) are the general solution of system (8.2) in the case of real and distinct roots of the characteristic equation of (8.6). Suppose now that such roots are real and equal; then — see Part II, ch. 4, eq. (4.8) — the solution of (8.6) is

$$y(t) = A_1 \exp(\lambda^* t) + A_2 t \exp(\lambda^* t). \tag{8.9}$$

From (8.9) we have

$$y'(t) = \lambda^* A_1 \exp(\lambda^* t) + A_2 \exp(\lambda^* t) + \lambda^* A_2 t \exp(\lambda^* t), \tag{8.9'}$$

and substituting (8.9) and (8.9') in (8.3) we have

$$z(t) = \frac{\lambda^* A_1}{a_{12}} \exp(\lambda^* t) + \frac{A_2}{a_{12}} \exp(\lambda^* t) + \frac{\lambda^* A_2 t}{a_{12}} \exp(\lambda^* t)$$

$$- \frac{a_{11} A_1}{a_{12}} \exp(\lambda^* t) - \frac{a_{11} A_2 t}{a_{12}} \exp(\lambda^* t),$$

so that, rearranging terms, we have

$$z(t) = \left[\frac{(\lambda^* - a_{11})A_1 + A_2}{a_{12}} + \frac{\lambda^* - a_{11}}{a_{12}} A_2 t \right] \exp(\lambda^* t). \tag{8.10}$$

Using the fact that $\lambda^* = \frac{1}{2}(a_{11} + a_{22})$, eq. (8.10) may also be written as

$$z(t) = \left[\frac{(a_{22} - a_{11})A_1 + 2A_2}{2a_{12}} + \frac{a_{22} - a_{11}}{2a_{12}} A_2 t \right] \exp(\lambda^* t). \tag{8.10'}$$

Consider finally the case in which the roots of the characteristic equation of (8.6) are complex. The solution of (8.6) is − see Part II, ch. 4, eq. (4.13) −

$$y(t) = e^{\alpha t}(A_1 \cos \theta t + A_2 \sin \theta t) \,. \tag{8.11}$$

From (8.11) we have

$$y'(t) = \alpha e^{\alpha t}(A_1 \cos \theta t + A_2 \sin \theta t) + e^{\alpha t}(-\theta A_1 \sin \theta t + \theta A_2 \cos \theta t)$$

$$= e^{\alpha t}[(\alpha A_1 + \theta A_2) \cos \theta t + (\alpha A_2 - \theta A_1) \sin \theta t] \,. \tag{8.11'}$$

Substituting (8.11) and (8.11') in (8.3) we have

$$z(t) = \frac{e^{\alpha t}[(\alpha A_1 + \theta A_2) \cos \theta t + (\alpha A_2 - \theta A_1) \sin \theta t)]}{a_{12}}$$

$$- \frac{a_{11} e^{\alpha t}(A_1 \cos \theta t + A_2 \sin \theta t)}{a_{12}} \,,$$

whence, rearranging terms,

$$z(t) = e^{\alpha t} \left[\frac{(\alpha - a_{11})A_1 + \theta A_2}{a_{12}} \cos \theta t + \frac{(\alpha - a_{11})A_2 - \theta A_1}{a_{12}} \sin \theta t \right]. \tag{8.12}$$

The method that we have expounded is conceptually rather simple and yields the required solution. We shall now explain another method, which at first sight might look more complicated, but has two advantages: (1) it is more *direct*, in the sense that it gives simultaneously both unknown functions, and (2) it is easily generalizable to the point that the characteristic equation of an *n*-equation system can be obtained in a simple manner. This method consists in trying directly as a solution − by analogy with single equations − the functions $y(t) = \alpha_1 e^{\lambda t}$, $z(t) = \alpha_2 e^{\lambda t}$, where α_1, α_2 are constants not both zero. Substituting in (8.2) we have

$$\lambda \alpha_1 e^{\lambda t} = a_{11} \alpha_1 e^{\lambda t} + a_{12} \alpha_2 e^{\lambda t} \,,$$

$$\lambda \alpha_2 e^{\lambda t} = a_{21} \alpha_1 e^{\lambda t} + a_{22} \alpha_2 e^{\lambda t} \,,$$

from which

$$e^{\lambda t}[(a_{11} - \lambda)\alpha_1 + a_{12}\alpha_2] = 0 \ ,$$

$$e^{\lambda t}[a_{21}\alpha_1 + (a_{22} - \lambda)\alpha_2] = 0 \ . \tag{8.13}$$

The functions that we have tried will be a solution of system (8.2) if, and only if, they satisfy it identically, i.e. if, and only if, equations (8.13) are satisfied for any t, i.e. if, and only if,

$$(a_{11} - \lambda)\alpha_1 + a_{12}\alpha_2 = 0 \ ,$$

$$a_{21}\alpha_1 + (a_{22} - \lambda)\alpha_2 = 0 \ . \tag{8.14}$$

System (8.14) has the trivial solution $\alpha_1 = \alpha_2 = 0$, but we have excluded it from the beginning for obvious reasons. It is a well-known theorem in elementary algebra that a linear homogeneous system has non-trivial solutions (in addition to the trivial one) if, and only if, its determinant is zero. In our case, then, it must be *

$$\begin{vmatrix} a_{11} - \lambda & a_{12} \\ a_{21} & a_{22} - \lambda \end{vmatrix} = 0 \ . \tag{8.15}$$

Expanding the determinant we have

$$(a_{11} - \lambda)(a_{22} - \lambda) - a_{12}a_{21}$$

$$= \lambda^2 - (a_{11} + a_{22})\lambda + (a_{11}a_{22} - a_{12}a_{21}) = 0 \ . \tag{8.15'}$$

The determinantal equation (8.15) and its expanded form (8.15') are called the *characteristic* equation of the differential system (8.2). Note that this equation is the same as the characteristic equation of (8.6) above, and this is as it

---

* The student knowing some matrix algebra will recognize in (8.15) — as well as in (8.32) and in (8.34) below — the characteristic equation $|A - \lambda I| = 0$, of the matrix $A \equiv [a_{ij}]$ whose elements are the coefficients of the differential system, and in $[\alpha_1^{(i)}, \alpha_2^{(i)}, ..., \alpha_n^{(i)}]$ below the characteristic vector associated with the characteristic root λ_j. The student not knowing sufficient matrix algebra can ignore this footnote and go on with the text. Actually, the use of matrix algebra would have allowed a more compact treatment, but without it nothing is lost as to the understanding of the 'direct' method of solution of systems of differential equations.

must be, since the solution of the differential system must be independent of the method followed to obtain it.

From the solution of (8.15′) two values of λ are obtained. The usual three cases may occur. Consider first the case of two real and distinct roots. The determinant of system (8.14) equals zero for $\lambda = \lambda_1$ and for $\lambda = \lambda_2$; correspondingly, we shall have two solutions of that system. Let $[\alpha_1^{(1)}, \alpha_2^{(1)}]$ be the solution that we obtain putting $\lambda = \lambda_1$ in (8.14) and $[\alpha_1^{(2)}, \alpha_2^{(2)}]$ the solution that we obtain putting $\lambda = \lambda_2$. For $\lambda = \lambda_1$ we have

$$(a_{11} - \lambda_1)\alpha_1^{(1)} + a_{12}\alpha_2^{(1)} = 0 ,$$

$$a_{21}\alpha_1^{(1)} + (a_{22} - \lambda_1)\alpha_2^{(1)} = 0 . \tag{8.14′}$$

From elementary algebra we know that, since the determinant of the system is zero, we can fix arbitrarily * the value of one of the unknowns and then determine the value of the other (in other words, only the ratio between the two unknowns is determined). We choose to fix $\alpha_1^{(1)} = 1$ **, so that, from the first equation in (8.14′), $\alpha_2^{(1)} = (\lambda_1 - a_{11})/a_{12}$. Using the second equation, we have also $\alpha_2^{(1)} = a_{21}/(\lambda_1 - a_{22})$. The two values are equal, since for $\lambda = \lambda_1$ the determinant of the system is zero, i.e. $(a_{11} - \lambda_1)(a_{22} - \lambda_1) - a_{12}a_{21} = 0$, and so $(\lambda_1 - a_{11})/a_{12} = a_{21}/(\lambda_1 - a_{22})$.

In a similar way for $\lambda = \lambda_2$ we fix $\alpha_1^{(2)} = 1$ and obtain $\alpha_2^{(2)} = (\lambda_2 - a_{11})/a_{12}$ $= a_{21}/(\lambda_2 - a_{22})$.

Recapitulating the results so far obtained, we have found that $y(t) = \alpha_1^{(1)} \exp(\lambda_1 t)$, $z(t) = \alpha_2^{(1)} \exp(\lambda_1 t)$ is a solution of system (8.2) and that $y(t) = \alpha_1^{(2)} \exp(\lambda_2 t)$, $z(t) = \alpha_2^{(2)} \exp(\lambda_2 t)$ is another solution. We can then combine them with two arbitrary constants A_1, A_2 and obtain the general solution of system (8.2) ‡:

$$y(t) = A_1\alpha_1^{(1)} \exp(\lambda_1 t) + A_2\alpha_1^{(2)} \exp(\lambda_2 t) , \tag{8.16}$$

---

* Such arbitrariness does not give any trouble, since it combines in a multiplicative way with the arbitrary constants A_1, A_2 appearing in the general solution of system (8.2). Thus we have chosen $\alpha_1^{(1)} = 1$ (and similarly we shall choose $\alpha_1^{(1)} = 1$) in order that the solution that we shall obtain be immediately comparable, without further manipulations, with (8.7) and (8.8) above.

** See the previous footnote.

‡ The student may check by direct substitution that (8.18) and (8.19) do satisfy (8.2). The number of arbitrary constants appearing in the general solution is two, since the system is reducible to a second-order equation, as we have seen above. In general, the number of arbitrary constants is equal to the *order* of the system, that is to the *degree* of its characteristic equation.

$$z(t) = A_1 \alpha_2^{(1)} \exp(\lambda_1 t) + A_2 \alpha_2^{(2)} \exp(\lambda_2 t), \tag{8.17}$$

i.e., with the values of $\alpha_i^{(j)}$ found above,

$$y(t) = A_1 \exp(\lambda_1 t) + A_2 \exp(\lambda_2 t), \tag{8.18}$$

$$z(t) = A_1 \frac{\lambda_1 - a_{11}}{a_{12}} \exp(\lambda_1 t) + A_2 \frac{\lambda_2 - a_{11}}{a_{12}} \exp(\lambda_2 t), \tag{8.19}$$

which are the same as (8.7) and (8.8) above.

The solution may also be written in the alternative form, which sometimes appears in the literature,

$$y(t) = A_1 \exp(\lambda_1 t) + A_2 \exp(\lambda_2 t),$$
$$z(t) = A_1' \exp(\lambda_1 t) + A_2' \exp(\lambda_2 t), \tag{8.20}$$

where the arbitrary constants A_1, A_2, A_1', A_2' are connected by the relations

$$\frac{A_1'}{A_1} = \frac{\lambda_1 - a_{11}}{a_{12}} = \frac{a_{21}}{\lambda_1 - a_{22}}, \qquad \frac{A_2'}{A_2} = \frac{\lambda_2 - a_{11}}{a_{12}} = \frac{a_{21}}{\lambda_2 - a_{22}}. \tag{8.21}$$

Since the ratios $A_1'/A_1, A_2'/A_2$ are uniquely determined in terms of the coefficients of the system, the independent arbitrary constants are actually only two★.

If the characteristic equation has two real and equal roots, $\lambda_1 = \lambda_2 = \lambda^*$, let us try

$$y(t) = (A_1 + A_2 t) \exp(\lambda^* t),$$
$$z(t) = (A_1' + A_2' t) \exp(\lambda^* t), \tag{8.22}$$

where the arbitrary constants A_1, A_2, A_1', A_2' are related in some way. From (8.22) we have

$$y'(t) = (\lambda^* A_1 + A_2 + \lambda^* A_2 t) \exp(\lambda^* t), \tag{8.22'}$$

★ Comparing eqs. (8.20) with eqs. (8.16) and (8.17), it follows that A_1'/A_1 must be equal to $A_1 \alpha_1^{(1)}/A_1 \alpha_2^{(1)}$, etc. This is indeed true, since $\alpha_1^{(1)}/\alpha_2^{(1)} = (\lambda_1 - a_{11})/a_{12} = a_{21}/(\lambda_1 - a_{22})$, etc.

$$z'(t) = (\lambda^* A_1' + A_2' + \lambda^* A_2' t) \exp(\lambda^* t). \tag{8.22'}$$

Substituting (8.22) and (8.22') in system (8.2) we have

$$(\lambda^* A_1 + A_2 + \lambda^* A_2 t) \exp(\lambda^* t)$$

$$= a_{11}(A_1 + A_2 t) \exp(\lambda^* t) + a_{12}(A_1' + A_2' t) \exp(\lambda^* t),$$

$$(\lambda^* A_1' + A_2' + \lambda^* A_2' t) \exp(\lambda^* t) \tag{8.23}$$

$$= a_{21}(A_1 + A_2 t) \exp(\lambda^* t) + a_{22}(A_1' + A_2' t) \exp(\lambda^* t).$$

Dividing through by $\exp(\lambda^* t) \neq 0$ and rearranging terms we obtain

$$[(\lambda^* - a_{11})A_2 - a_{12}A_2'] t + [(\lambda^* - a_{11})A_1 + A_2 - a_{12}A_1'] = 0,$$

$$[(\lambda^* - a_{22})A_2' - a_{21}A_2] t + [(\lambda^* - a_{22})A_1' + A_2' - a_{21}A_1] = 0. \tag{8.24}$$

Eqs. (8.24) are identically satisfied if, and only if, each one of the four expressions in square brackets is zero, i.e.

$$(\lambda^* - a_{11})A_2 - a_{12}A_2' \quad\quad = 0, \tag{8.25}$$

$$(\lambda^* - a_{11})A_1 + A_2 - a_{12}A_1' = 0, \tag{8.26}$$

$$(\lambda^* - a_{22})A_2' - a_{21}A_2 \quad\quad = 0, \tag{8.27}$$

$$(\lambda^* - a_{22})A_1' + A_2' - a_{21}A_1 = 0, \tag{8.28}$$

which give

$$A_2' = \frac{\lambda^* - a_{11}}{a_{12}} A_2, \tag{8.25a}$$

$$A_1' = \frac{\lambda^* - a_{11}}{a_{12}} A_1 + \frac{1}{a_{12}} A_2, \tag{8.26a}$$

$$A_2' = \frac{a_{21}}{\lambda^* - a_{22}} A_2, \tag{8.27a}$$

$$A_1' = \frac{a_{21}}{\lambda^* - a_{22}} A_1 - \frac{1}{\lambda^* - a_{22}} A_2' . \tag{8.28a}$$

Since λ^* satisfies by definition the characteristic equation, $(\lambda^* - a_{11})/a_{12} = a_{21}/(\lambda^* - a_{22})$ and so (8.25a) and (8.27a) coincide. Using (8.25a) and the relation just recalled, (8.28a) can be written as

$$A_1' = \frac{\lambda^* - a_{11}}{a_{12}} A_1 - \frac{\lambda^* - a_{11}}{a_{12}(\lambda^* - a_{22})} A_2 , \tag{8.28b}$$

which coincides with (8.26a) if, and only if, $-(\lambda^* - a_{11})/(\lambda^* - a_{22}) = 1$, i.e. $\lambda^* = \frac{1}{2}(a_{11} + a_{22})$, which is indeed true if, and only if, λ^* is a double root of the characteristic equation (8.15′). Thus (8.22) is indeed the (general) solution of the system; using (8.26a) and (8.25a) to express A_1', A_2' in terms of A_1, A_2, it follows immediately that eqs. (8.22) coincide with eqs. (8.9) and (8.10) above.

Consider, finally, the case in which the roots of the characteristic equation are complex numbers, say $\alpha \pm i\theta$. Then the solution can at first be written as (the procedure is the same as in the case of distinct real roots):

$$y(t) = B_1 \exp[(\alpha + i\theta)t] + B_2 \exp[(\alpha - i\theta)t]$$

$$z(t) = \frac{(\alpha + i\theta) - a_{11}}{a_{12}} B_1 \exp[(\alpha + i\theta)t] + \frac{(\alpha - i\theta) - a_{11}}{a_{12}} B_2 \exp[(\alpha - i\theta)t] , \tag{8.29}$$

where B_1, B_2 are arbitrary complex conjugate numbers. Using the transformation on complex numbers expounded in Part II, ch. 4, we obtain

$$y(t) = e^{\alpha t}(A_1 \cos \theta t + A_2 \sin \theta t) ,$$

as explained there, where $A_1 \equiv B_1 + B_2$, $A_2 \equiv (B_1 - B_2)i$ are arbitrary real constants. For $z(t)$, we have

$$z(t) = e^{\alpha t}\left[\frac{(\alpha - a_{11}) + i\theta}{a_{12}} (B_1 \cos \theta t + B_1 i \sin \theta t) \right.$$

$$\left. + \frac{(\alpha - a_{11}) - i\theta}{a_{12}} (B_2 \cos \theta t - B_2 i \sin \theta t) \right]$$

$$= e^{\alpha t} \left[\frac{(\alpha - a_{11})(B_1 + B_2) + i\theta(B_1 - B_2)}{a_{12}} \cos \theta t \right.$$

$$\left. + \frac{(\alpha - a_{11})(B_1 - B_2) + i\theta(B_1 + B_2)}{a_{12}} i \sin \theta t \right]$$

$$= e^{\alpha t} \left[\frac{(\alpha - a_{11})(B_1 + B_2) + \theta(B_1 - B_2)i}{a_{12}} \cos \theta t \right.$$

$$\left. + \frac{(\alpha - a_{11})(B_1 - B_2)i + i^2\theta(B_1 + B_2)}{a_{12}} \sin \theta t \right] . \tag{8.30}$$

Now, $B_1 + B_2 = A_1$, $(B_1 - B_2)i = A_2$, $i^2 = -1$ and so the general solution of the differential system is obtained:

$$y(t) = e^{\alpha t}(A_1 \cos \theta t + A_2 \sin \theta t) ,$$
$$\tag{8.31}$$
$$z(t) = e^{\alpha t} \left[\frac{(\alpha - a_{11})A_1 + \theta A_2}{a_{12}} \cos \theta t + \frac{(\alpha - a_{11})A_2 - \theta A_1}{a_{12}} \sin \theta t \right] ,$$

which coincide with (8.11) and (8.12) above.

This completes the exposition of the 'direct' method of solution in the case of a 2×2 system. As we said above, this method is easily generalizable to first-order systems in 'normal' form having any number of equations. Considering, for example, the system

$$y' = a_{11}y + a_{12}z + a_{13}w ,$$

$$z' = a_{21}y + a_{22}z + a_{23}w ,$$

$$w' = a_{31}y + a_{32}z + a_{33}w ,$$

we can write immediately its characteristic equation

$$D(\lambda) = \begin{vmatrix} a_{11} - \lambda & a_{12} & a_{13} \\ a_{21} & a_{22} - \lambda & a_{23} \\ a_{31} & a_{32} & a_{33} - \lambda \end{vmatrix} = 0 , \tag{8.32}$$

and, in general, given the general first-order system in 'normal' form

$$y_1' = a_{11}y_1 + a_{12}y_2 + \ldots + a_{1n}y_n \, ,$$

$$y_2' = a_{21}y_1 + a_{22}y_2 + \ldots + a_{2n}y_n \, ,$$

$$\cdots\cdots\cdots\cdots\cdots\cdots\cdots\cdots$$ (8.33)

$$y_n' = a_{n1}y_1 + a_{n2}y_2 + \ldots + a_{nn}y_n \, ,$$

its characteristic equation is

$$D(\lambda) = \begin{vmatrix} a_{11} - \lambda & a_{12} & \cdots & a_{1n} \\ a_{21} & a_{22} - \lambda & \cdots & a_{2n} \\ \cdots\cdots\cdots\cdots\cdots\cdots\cdots\cdots\cdots \\ a_{n1} & a_{n2} & \cdots & a_{nn} - \lambda \end{vmatrix} = 0 \, . \tag{8.34}$$

Expanding the determinant we have an n-th degree algebraic equation in the unknown λ, whose solution will give n roots, real or complex, distinct or multiple, exactly as in the case of an n-th order differential equation. Actually system (8.33) could be reduced, by a procedure similar to that used above in the case of a 2×2 system, to a single n-th order differential equation in one unknown function ★.

The stability of the solution of system (8.33) depends on the roots of the characteristic equation, so that to analyse the stability of the system we can concentrate on these roots, without any need to compute the coefficients $\alpha_i^{(j)}$. Of course, we can apply to the expanded form of the characteristic equation the conditions expounded in Part II, ch. 6, to check whether all the roots of the polynomial have negative real parts. However, to find the polynomial form of the characteristic equation (8.34) is quite a job when n is large, so that it would be highly desirable to have stability conditions which can be applied directly to the coefficients a_{ij} of the system, *without having to expand the determinantal equation* (8.34). Such conditions exist, and the most im-

---

★ The converse is also true, i.e. an n-th order differential equation can be transformed into a first-order system in normal form having n equations. The procedure consists in defining new variables $y_1, y_2, \ldots, y_{n-1}$ such that $y' = y_1$, $y_1' = y_2$, ..., $y_{n-2}' = y_{n-1}$. Substituting in the given n-th order equation in y, a first-order equation in $y_{n-1}', y_{n-1}, \ldots, y_1$, y is obtained, which, together with the equations defining the new variables, forms a first-order system in normal form.

portant are listed below *. In what follows by 'stability conditions' we mean,

* Here is a sketch of proofs of the various conditions.

It is a classic result in the theory of quadratic forms that a quadratic form $Q(x) =$ $x'Ax$ (primes denote transposes) is negative definite if, and only if, the principal minors of the matrix A alternate in sign, beginning with minus (this can be proved by an extension of the elementary method of 'completing the square'). Another classic result is that the roots of a symmetric matrix are all real, and this can be proved quite easily: given (a) $Ax = \lambda x$, take complex conjugates: (b) $A\bar{x} = \bar{\lambda}\bar{x}$. Premultiply (b) by x' and take transposes, obtaining (c) $\bar{x}'Ax = \bar{x}'\bar{\lambda}x$. Premultiply (a) by $\bar{x}'$ and subtract the result from (c), obtaining $0 = (\lambda - \bar{\lambda})\bar{x}'x$, which gives $\lambda = \bar{\lambda}$, a contradiction if λ is complex. Now, diagonalizing the matrix A, the quadratic form can be transformed into a sum of squares of the type $\Sigma_i \lambda_i p_i^2$ (where the λ's are the characteristic roots of A), so that the quadratic form will be negative definite if, and only if, all the λ's are negative. Since both sets of conditions are necessary and sufficient for the negative definiteness, they must be equivalent, and this proves conditions 1.

Conditions 2 can be proved by an application of Liapunov's second method (see Appendix II). Given the linear differential system $\dot{x} = Ax$ (a dot denotes differentiation with respect to time and a prime transposition), consider the Liapunov function $x'x$. Then $dx'x/dt < 0$ implies stability. Now,

$$\frac{dx'x}{dt} = \dot{x}'x + x'\dot{x} = x'A'x + x'Ax = x'\tfrac{1}{2}(A'+A)x < 0 .$$

Since $\tfrac{1}{2}(A'+A)$ is a symmetric matrix, we can apply to it conditions 1.

Conditions 3 can be proved by an application of a theorem on non-negative matrices. Given a matrix $B \geqslant 0$, let λ_M be its dominant root: the theorem states that a set of necessary and sufficient conditions that the real number λ be greater than λ_M is that all the leading principal minors of the matrix $\lambda I - B$ be positive. Now consider a matrix A with non-negative non-diagonal elements. Obviously for a certain $\lambda > 0$ the matrix $B = A + \lambda I$ is non-negative. Let λ_n be the characteristic root of A having the greatest real part and λ_M be the dominant root of B. Since the roots of B are the sums $\lambda_i + \lambda$ (λ_i are the roots of A), it follows that $\lambda_M = \lambda_n + \lambda$. Now $\lambda_M < \lambda$ if, and only if, $\lambda_n < 0$, i.e. when all the characteristic roots of A have negative real parts. Applying the theorem stated above to the matrix $-A = \lambda I - B$, we obtain conditions 3. (Gantmacher, 1959, pp. 88−9.)

To prove conditions 4, the classic result can be used that a quasi-dominant diagonal implies that the matrix is non-singular (this can be proved by showing that the contrary involves a contradiction: see McKenzie, 1960, p. 49). Now consider $A - \lambda I$. Since $a_{ii} < 0$, if λ has a non-negative real part, $|a_{ii} - \lambda| \geqslant |a_{ii}|$, all i. These inequalities imply that $A - \lambda I$ has a quasi-dominant diagonal and is non-singular: therefore, λ cannot be a characteristic root of A (McKenzie, 1960, p. 49).

To prove conditions 5 and 6 it must be recalled that in the expansion of (8.34), the coefficient of λ^{n-1} is equal to $-\Sigma_i a_{ii}$ and the constant term is equal to $(-1)^n (\det A)$. Now, from elementary algebra, the coefficient of λ^{n-1} is equal to (-1) times the sum of the roots, and the constant term is equal to $(-1)^n$ times the product of the roots. Now a necessary (but not sufficient) condition that all the roots have negative real parts is that the sum of the roots is negative, and another necessary but not sufficient condition is that the product of the roots has the sign of $(-1)^n$, where n is the number of roots.

as usual, 'conditions that the roots of the characteristic equation (8.34), be they real and/or complex, have negative real parts', or, which is the same thing, that these roots are all strictly lying in the left half of the complex plane.

Consider the matrix of the coefficients of the differential system (8.33),

$$
A \equiv \begin{bmatrix} a_{11} & a_{12} & \cdots & a_{1n} \\ a_{21} & a_{22} & \cdots & a_{2n} \\ \cdot & \cdot & \cdot & \cdot \\ a_{n1} & a_{n2} & \cdots & a_{nn} \end{bmatrix}.
$$

Then we have the following conditions:

1. *Negative definiteness.* If the matrix is symmetric ($a_{ij} = a_{ji}$), then a set of necessary and sufficient stability conditions is given by the following n inequalities

$$
a_{11} < 0, \quad \begin{vmatrix} a_{11} & a_{12} \\ a_{21} & a_{22} \end{vmatrix} > 0, \quad \begin{vmatrix} a_{11} & a_{12} & a_{13} \\ a_{21} & a_{22} & a_{23} \\ a_{31} & a_{32} & a_{33} \end{vmatrix} < 0, \quad \mathrm{sgn} \begin{vmatrix} a_{11} & a_{12} & \cdots & a_{1n} \\ a_{21} & a_{22} & \cdots & a_{2n} \\ \cdots & & & \\ a_{n1} & a_{n2} & \cdots & a_{nn} \end{vmatrix} = \mathrm{sgn}(-1)^n, \quad (8.35)
$$

i.e. the leading principal minors of A must alternate in sign, starting with minus.

2. *Quasi-negative definiteness.* Form the matrix $B \equiv \frac{1}{2}(A + A')$, i.e.

$$
B \equiv \begin{bmatrix} a_{11} & \frac{1}{2}(a_{12} + a_{21}) & \cdots & \frac{1}{2}(a_{1n} + a_{n1}) \\ \frac{1}{2}(a_{21} + a_{12}) & a_{22} & \cdots & \frac{1}{2}(a_{2n} + a_{n2}) \\ \cdots & & & \\ \frac{1}{2}(a_{n1} + a_{1n}) & \frac{1}{2}(a_{n2} + a_{2n}) & \cdots & a_{nn} \end{bmatrix}
$$

then a set of sufficient stability conditions (the stability under consideration is always that of system (8.33)) is that the leading principal minors of B alternate in sign, starting with minus.

3. If all the off-diagonal coefficients of A (i.e. the coefficients a_{ij}, $i \neq j$) are non-negative, then a set of necessary and sufficient stability conditions is the same as in case 1.

4. *Dominant negative diagonal*. A set of sufficient stability conditions is that all the coefficients on the main diagonal are negative and each is in absolute value greater than the sum of the absolute values of all the other coefficients belonging to the same row (or column). In formal terms,

$$a_{ii} < 0$$

$$|a_{ii}| > \sum_{\substack{j=1 \\ j \neq i}}^{n} |a_{ij}|, \tag{8.36}$$

or

$$a_{ii} < 0$$

$$|a_{ii}| > \sum_{\substack{j=1 \\ j \neq i}}^{n} |a_{ji}|. \tag{8.37}$$

Note that conditions (8.36) and (8.37) are alternative, in the sense that each set is by itself sufficient for stability.

Conditions (8.36) and (8.37) can be extended to the case of a quasi-dominant negative diagonal, i.e.

$$a_{ii} < 0,$$

$$h_i |a_{ii}| \geqslant \sum_{\substack{j=1 \\ j \neq i}}^{n} h_j |a_{ij}| \quad \text{(at least one strict inequality)}, \tag{8.36'}$$

or

$$a_{ii} < 0,$$

$$h_i |a_{ii}| \geqslant \sum_{\substack{j=1 \\ j \neq i}}^{n} h_j |a_{ji}| \quad \text{(at least one strict inequality)}, \tag{8.37'}$$

where the h's are all positive numbers.

5. A necessary (but not sufficient) stability condition is that the sum of the coefficients on the main diagonal is negative, i.e.

$$\sum_{i=1}^{n} a_{ii} < 0 .$$

6. A necessary (but not sufficient) stability condition is that the determinant of A has the sign of $(-1)^n$.

This completes the discussion of homogeneous first-order systems. We can now turn to the problem of finding a particular solution of system (8.1). The general method of undetermined coefficients (see Part II, ch. 1) can be applied here too, and we shall examine, as an example, the case in which $g_1(t)$, $g_2(t)$ are two given constants, say b_1, b_2. Thus we have

$$y' = a_{11}y + a_{12}z + b_1 ,$$
$$z' = a_{21}y + a_{22}z + b_2 . \qquad (8.1')$$

As a particular solution, let us try $\bar{y}(t) = B_1, \bar{z}(t) = B_2$, where B_1, B_2 are undetermined constants. Substituting in (8.1') and rearranging terms we have

$$a_{11}B_1 + a_{12}B_2 = -b_1 ,$$
$$a_{21}B_1 + a_{22}B_2 = -b_2 , \qquad (8.38)$$

which gives *

$$B_1 = \frac{-b_1 a_{22} + b_2 a_{12}}{a_{11}a_{22} - a_{12}a_{21}} , \qquad B_2 = \frac{-b_2 a_{11} + b_1 a_{21}}{a_{11}a_{22} - a_{12}a_{21}} .$$

* The method is successful only if the determinant of system (8.38) is different from zero, i.e.

$$\begin{vmatrix} a_{11} & a_{12} \\ a_{21} & a_{22} \end{vmatrix} \neq 0 .$$

Note that this condition implies that zero is *not* a root of the characteristic equation. When this occurs, a way out is to reduce the non-homogeneous system to a single equation (the procedure is the same as for the homogeneous system) and then apply to the latter the methods that we have illustrated for single equations (see e.g. Part II, ch. 4).

Finally, the determination of the arbitrary constants can be made by means of a number of additional conditions equal to the number of arbitrary constants. These conditions usually take the form that the initial values of the functions (i.e., $y_i(0)$, $i = 1, 2, ..., n$) are known. Substituting in the general solution of the system under consideration we obtain a system of linear equations which can be solved for the unknowns $A_1, A_2, ..., A_n$ [*].

The systems that we have so far examined are not the only ones. In general, the first derivatives of two or more functions and/or higher-order derivatives of one or more functions might appear in each equation. In other words, it might happen that in every equation of the system the derivatives of any order of each unknown function appear. As an illustration, consider the non-homogeneous system

$$a_3 y''' + a_2 y'' + b_1 z' + b_0 z = g_1(t) ,$$
$$c_1 y' + c_0 y + d_2 z'' = g_2(t) ,$$

(8.39)

and its homogeneous counterpart

$$a_3 y''' + a_2 y'' + b_1 z' + b_0 z = 0 ,$$
$$c_1 y' + c_0 y + d_2 z'' = 0 .$$

(8.40)

To solve system (8.40) we can follow the same direct method expounded

---

[*] Consider, for example, the case in which all the roots of the characteristic equation are distinct. Then the general solution is

$$y_i(t) = \sum_{j=1}^{n} A_j \alpha_i^{(j)} \exp(\lambda_j t) + \bar{y}_i(t) , \qquad i = 1, 2, ..., n ,$$

where $\bar{y}_i(t) \equiv 0$ if the system is homogeneous. Now, for $t = 0$, we have

$$y_i(0) - \bar{y}_i(0) = \sum_j A_j \alpha_i^{(j)}$$

(∗)

where $y_i(0)$ are the given initial conditions. A necessary and sufficient condition that (∗) be solvable is that the matrix $C \equiv [\alpha_i^{(j)}]$ is non-singular. Now, it is a well-known theorem in matrix algebra that the characteristic vectors associated with distinct characteristic roots of a matrix are linearly independent. It follows that the matrix C is formed by linearly independent vectors and so is non-singular. Some complications may arise when there are repeated roots, but we need not treat them here.

above in relation to first-order systems *. So let us try as a solution

* Alternatively, we could reduce the system to a single differential equation (but the manipulations would be more complicated than for 'normal' first-order systems) or transform the system into an equivalent first-order system by means of an appropriate introduction of new variables. In relation to system (8.40), define $y' = y_1$, $y'_1 = y_2$, $z' = z_1$ (whence $y''' = y'_2$ and $z'' = z'_1$), substitute suitably in (8.40) and rearrange terms. The result, together with the equations which define the new variables, is the following first-order system (which already is in 'normal' form):

$$y' = y_1 \,,$$

$$y'_1 = y_2 \,,$$

$$z' = z_1 \,,$$

$$y'_2 = -\frac{b_0}{a_3} z - \frac{a_2}{a_3} y_2 - \frac{b_1}{a_3} z_1 \,,$$

$$z'_1 = -\frac{c_0}{d_2} y - \frac{c_1}{d_2} y_1 \,,$$

whose characteristic equation is

$$\begin{vmatrix} -\lambda & 1 & 0 & 0 & 0 \\ 0 & -\lambda & 0 & 1 & 0 \\ 0 & 0 & -\lambda & 0 & 1 \\ 0 & 0 & -b_0/a_3 & -a_2/a_3 - \lambda & -b_1/a_3 \\ -c_0/d_2 & -c_1/d_2 & 0 & 0 & -\lambda \end{vmatrix} = 0 \,.$$

The student may check as an exercise that the expanded form of the above characteristic equation is the same as that of (8.43) in the text. It may also be noted that it is much easier to expand (8.43) than to follow the procedure indicated in this footnote. There may be, however, a reason to transform a general system into a 'normal' first-order system: see the next footnote. Let us also note that when a system is first-order (either because it is so given or because it has been so transformed from a higher-order system), but not in 'normal' form, the latter can always be obtained by means of appropriate manipulations. Two cases must be distinguished. (1) the determinant of the coefficients of the y'_i $(i = 1, 2, ..., n)$ is different from zero. Then the system can be put in normal form by 'solving' for the y'_i in terms of the y_i (in matrix terms, a first-order homogeneous system can be written as $Ay + By' = 0$, so that, if B is non-singular, $y' = -B^{-1}Ay$, which is the normal form). (2) the determinant of the coefficients of the y'_i is zero. Then by means of appropriate substitutions we can eliminate some unknown functions and some equations from the system until a first-order system is obtained such that the determinant of the remaining y'_i $(i = 1, 2, ..., r; r < n)$ is non-zero, and we can proceed as in (1) (in matrix terms, if B is singular, the number of equations and of unknowns of the system is reduced to the rank of B: see Frazer, Duncan and Collar (1938), p. 163). Of course, if we do not want to convert a first-order system into the normal form we can always derive directly the characteristic equation as expounded in the text in relation to the more general system (8.40); we can also note that when B is singular, the degree of the characteristic equation, however the latter is obtained, is not n, but r, the rank of B.

$y(t) = \alpha_1 e^{\lambda t}, z(t) = \alpha_2 e^{\lambda t}$, where α_1, α_2 are not both zero. Substituting in (8.40) and rearranging terms we have

$$e^{\lambda t}[(a_3\lambda^3 + a_2\lambda^2)\alpha_1 + (b_1\lambda + b_0)\alpha_2] = 0 ,$$

$$e^{\lambda t}[(c_1\lambda + c_0)\alpha_1 + d_2\lambda^2\alpha_2] = 0 . \tag{8.41}$$

If $\alpha_1 e^{\lambda t}, \alpha_2 e^{\lambda t}$ are a solution, system (8.41) must be identically satisfied, and this is possible if, and only if,

$$(a_3\lambda^3 + a_2\lambda^2)\alpha_1 + (b_1\lambda + b_0)\alpha_2 = 0 ,$$

$$(c_1\lambda + c_0)\alpha_1 + d_2\lambda^2\alpha_2 = 0 . \tag{8.42}$$

System (8.42) will have non-trivial solutions for α_1, α_2 if, and only if, its determinant is zero, i.e.

$$\begin{vmatrix} a_3\lambda^3 + a_2\lambda^2 & b_1\lambda + b_0 \\ \\ c_1\lambda + c_0 & d_2\lambda^2 \end{vmatrix} = 0 . \tag{8.43}$$

The determinantal equation (8.43) and its expanded form are called the characteristic equation of system (8.40). Expanding the determinant we obtain a fifth-degree equation in the unknown λ. From this point on, the procedure is the same as that expounded above for first-order systems. To each λ_i a pair of values $(\alpha_1^{(i)}, \alpha_2^{(i)})$ is associated substituting λ_i in (8.42). If, for example, the characteristic equation has five real and distinct roots, then the general solution will be

$$y(t) = \sum_{i=1}^{5} A_i \alpha_1^{(i)} \exp(\lambda_i t) ,$$

$$z(t) = \sum_{i=1}^{5} A_i \alpha_2^{(i)} \exp(\lambda_i t) , \tag{8.44}$$

where the A_i are five arbitrary constants. The stability of the system can be examined applying the stability conditions (see Part II, ch. 6) to the explicit form of the characteristic equation. Let us note that for system (8.40) — as, in general, for systems that are not of type (8.33) — there are no stability conditions directly applicable to the coefficients of the system, so that we must obtain the explicit polynomial form of the characteristic equation and then apply to it the conditions expounded in Part II, ch. 6 [*].

In the case of a non-homogeneous system, a particular solution can usually be found by means of the method of undetermined coefficients. The arbitrary constants, finally, can be determined given a sufficient number of additional conditions. In the case of system (8.39) or (8.40) such additional conditions could be, for example, that $y(0)$, $y'(0)$, $y''(0)$ and $z(0)$, $z'(0)$ are all known values.

References

Baumol, W.J., 1970, *Economic Dynamics*, chs. 15, 16.

Bellman, R., 1953, *Stability Theory of Differential Equations*, ch. 1, §§ 1, 7, 12.

Frazer, R.A., Duncan, W.J. and Collar, A.R., 1938, *Elementary Matrices and Some Applications to Dynamics and Differential Equations,* chs. V, VI.

Gantmacher, F.R., 1959, *Applications of the Theory of Matrices*, pp. 88–9.

Ince, E.L., 1956, *Ordinary Differential Equations*, pp. 144–8.

Lancaster, K., 1968, *Mathematical Economics*, Review 6, § R6.2.

McKenzie, L., 1960, Matrices with Dominant Diagonals and Economic Theory, pp. 47–9.

Samuelson, P.A., 1947, *Foundations of Economic Analysis*, Appendix A, § IV; Appendix B, §§ 30–35.

Yamane, T., 1968, *Mathematics for Economists: An Elementary Survey*, ch. 12, §§ 12.11, 12.12.

---

[*] Of course, if we prefer, we can transform the system into a 'normal' first-order system as illustrated in the previous footnote and then use, if applicable, the stability conditions expounded in this chapter.

9

Some Economic Applications
of Simultaneous Systems

A few moments of reflection will convince us that all economic models, even the simplest ones, are simultaneous systems. The fact that many of them are usually examined as giving rise to a single functional equation is due to the fact that reduction of the system to a single equation involves only direct substitutions and is actually easier than simultaneous methods. As an example, consider the homogeneous part of the Walrasian demand and supply adjustment model (see Part II, ch. 3, § 1):

$$D = a + bp \, ,$$

$$S = a_1 + b_1 p \, ,$$

$$p' = c(D - S) \, ,$$

which has the characteristic equation

$$\begin{vmatrix} 1 & 0 & -b \\ 0 & 1 & -b_1 \\ c & -c & -\lambda \end{vmatrix} = -\lambda - b_1 c + bc = 0 \, ,$$

so that $\lambda = c(b - b_1)$, etc. However, direct substitution from the first two equations into the third suggests itself quite naturally and is actually simpler. On the other hand, there are some economic models in which, after all direct substitutions have been made, two or more simultaneous equations still remain, to which simultaneous methods can be profitably applied [*].

§1. Stability of Walrasian general equilibrium of exchange

The problem of the stability of demand and supply equilibrium was examined in Part II, ch. 3, §1, in the context of a partial equilibrium analysis. In the case of a general equilibrium analysis the demand and supply functions relative to each good are in principle functions of the prices of all goods, and not only of the price of the good to which they refer. Thus we can write

$$E_j = E_j(p_1, p_2, ..., p_m) , \qquad j = 1, 2, ..., m , \tag{9.1}$$

where E_j is excess demand for the j-th good. The equilibrium point $(p_1^e, p_2^e, ..., p_m^e)$ is determined by the conditions that all excess demands are simultaneously zero. We assume that this point exists (and is economically meaningful) and propose to study its stability. Here too, as in Part II, ch. 3, §1, we can distinguish between static stability and dynamic stability. Although the relevant concept is the dynamic one, we shall examine static stability too, in order to show that as soon as we pass from one to two or more markets the static stability conditions do *not* coincide any more (except for some particular cases) with the 'true' dynamic stability conditions.

The behaviour assumption that we make is that the price of a good varies in relation to its excess demand, i.e. the price increases (decreases) if excess demand is positive (negative) [**]. This corresponds to the mechanism conceived by Walras, the famous 'tâtonnement', of which a brief account is the

---

[*] We have violated this principle in the exposition of Phillips' stabilization model. As the reader perhaps recalls, it was reduced to a single equation at the cost of some manipulations *in addition* to direct substitutions. While pleading guilty, we offer two excuses: (1) Phillips himself has used a reduction method, and (2) the exposition of this model here would have added bulk to an already crowded chapter.

[**] We shall not examine other possible behaviour assumptions, also because almost all the literature on the subject uses the Walrasian assumption (this perhaps is due to the fact that Marshall was essentially a partial equilibrium theorist, whereas Walras was the general equilibrium theorist 'par excellence').

following ‡. Assume that the market starts with arbitrary initial prices (*'prix criés au hasard'*). An 'auctioneer' collects supply offers and demand requests for each good, and if a good is in excess demand (excess supply) he raises (lowers) the price of the good, and communicates to the market the new set of prices. The process goes on until, according to Walras, equilibrium is reached. It must be noted that in this idealized process no exchanges take place until equilibrium is reached (i.e. contracts are provisional, and binding only if prices turn out to be the equilibrium prices) *.

Now, Walras did not give a rigorous proof that the *'tâtonnement'* process was indeed convergent **, nor did his successors, who only repeated what he had written. The first to tackle the problem rigorously, as far as the present writer knows, was J.R. Hicks (1939), who extended to general equilibrium – making the necessary modifications – the (static) stability condition of partial equilibrium. This condition is that a change in price provokes a change in the opposite direction in the 'own' excess demand, i.e.

$$dE_j/dp_j < 0 . \tag{9.2}$$

Of course, account must be taken of the fact that the change in a price influences not only its own excess demand, but also, in principle, all the other excess demands. Thus conditions (9.2) must be qualified, as we said above. Hicks' qualifications consist in the distinction between *imperfect* and *perfect* stability. Stability is imperfect when (9.2) holds only when, given a change in the j-th price, all the other prices have adjusted in such a way that all the other markets are again in equilibrium. Stability is instead perfect when (9.2) holds in any case, that is when (1) all the other prices have ad-

‡ The student is advised to read at least the sections of Walras' (1954) book quoted in the references and Jaffé's (1967) article.

* The reason for this assumption is that, if exchanges out of equilibrium take place then the initial endowments of the various goods owned by the single traders would change; such changes would modify the form of the excess demand functions, and so the position of the equilibrium point itself would change.

** Walras assumed that the influence of the 'own' price is equilibrating. He was well aware, of course, of the indirect influences of the changes in the other prices, but he assumed that such influences were some equilibrating and some disequilibrating, so that up to a certain point they cancelled each other out. Hence, he says, "the new system of price is closer to equilibrium than the old system of prices; and it is only necessary to continue this process along the same lines for the system to move closer and closer to equilibrium" (Walras, 1954, p. 172). This, of course, is not a proof that would satisfy a modern theorist (but Walras was breaking new ground, was writing in 1874, and Liapunov's second method had not yet been invented...).

justed as in the previous case; (2) all the other prices have remained constant; (3) any subset of k other prices have varied so that equilibrium in the respective markets has been restored, whereas the remaining $m - k$ prices have remained constant (if we let k vary from zero to $m - 1$, cases (2) and (1) are also included here).

In order to find the conditions for the two kinds of stability, let us consider the total differentials of the excess demand functions [*]:

$$dE_i = a_{i1} \, dp_1 + a_{i2} \, dp_2 + ... + a_{im} \, dp_m , \quad i = 1, 2, ..., m , \quad (9.3)$$

where $a_{ik} \equiv \partial E_i / \partial p_k$ evaluated in the equilibrium point ($k = 1, 2, ..., m$).

Now, assume that the price of the j-th good has changed and that all the other prices have varied as required by the definition of imperfect stability. Thus we have

$$dE_j = a_{j1} \, dp_1 + a_{j2} \, dp_2 + ... + a_{jm} \, dp_m , \quad (9.4)$$

whereas the remaining total differentials are all zero since equilibrium has been restored:

$$dE_k = 0 = a_{k1} \, dp_1 + a_{k2} \, dp_2 + ... + a_{km} \, dp_m \quad \left\{ \begin{array}{l} k = 1, 2, ..., m , \\ \\ k \neq j . \end{array} \right. \quad (9.4')$$

Relations (9.4) and (9.4') are a set of m equations in the m unknowns dp_i. Solving with respect to dp_j we have

$$dp_j = dE_j \, \frac{D_{jj}}{D} , \quad (9.5)$$

where

$$D \equiv \begin{vmatrix} a_{11} & a_{12} & \cdots & a_{1m} \\ a_{21} & a_{22} & \cdots & a_{2m} \\ \cdots\cdots\cdots\cdots\cdots \\ a_{m1} & a_{m2} & \cdots & a_{mm} \end{vmatrix} ,$$

[*] Since, as is well known, the total differential can approximate the variation in the function only in a sufficiently small neighbourhood of the starting point, the conditions that we shall obtain are *local* stability conditions.

and D_{jj} is the cofactor of a_{jj} in D *. Note that, since the sum of the subscripts of a_{jj} is even, the cofactor is the same as the minor; moreover, this minor, by its very definition, is a principal minor of order $m-1$. From (9.5) we immediately have

$$\frac{\mathrm{d}E_j}{\mathrm{d}p_j} = \frac{D}{D_{jj}} , \tag{9.6}$$

so that inequality (9.2) will be satisfied if, and only if, D and D_{jj} are of opposite sign. This condition must hold for any j from 1 to m, since any market may be involved. It follows that the necessary and sufficient conditions for *imperfect stability* are that all the principal minors of order $m-1$ of D have a sign opposite to the sign of D.

To obtain the perfect stability conditions let us consider first the case in which, the price of good j having varied, all the other prices have remained constant. We have

$$\mathrm{d}E_j = a_{jj}\, \mathrm{d}p_j ,$$

$$\mathrm{d}E_k = a_{kj}\, \mathrm{d}p_j \qquad \left\{ \begin{array}{l} k = 1, 2, ..., m , \\[2mm] k \neq j . \end{array} \right. \tag{9.7}$$

From the first equation in (9.7) we have

$$\mathrm{d}E_j/\mathrm{d}p_j = a_{jj} , \tag{9.8}$$

and so $a_{jj} < 0$ for all j is the first condition for perfect stability. That is, the partial derivative of the j-th excess demand with respect to the 'own' price (i.e. p_j) must be negative. Thus (9.8) implies that all markets must be stable when considered in isolation ($a_{jj} < 0$ is, in fact, equivalent to the static stability condition in the case of a partial equilibrium analysis).

Consider now the case in which, p_j having varied, another price, say p_h, adjusts in such a way that equilibrium is restored in the h-th market, while

---

* Note that D is the *Jacobian* of the m excess demand functions. Let us recall that, given m functions in the same m independent variables, their Jacobian is the determinant (or the matrix) formed in the following way: the elements in the first row are, in order, the first partial derivatives of the first function with respect to the first, second, ..., m-th variable, and so on.

all the remaining prices are constant. The relevant equations are

$$dE_j = a_{jj} \, dp_j + a_{jh} \, dp_h$$

$$dE_h = 0 = a_{hj} \, dp_j + a_{hh} \, dp_h \, ,$$

(9.9)

so that, solving for dp_j, we have

$$dp_j = dE_j \; \frac{a_{hh}}{\begin{vmatrix} a_{jj} & a_{jh} \\ a_{hj} & a_{hh} \end{vmatrix}} \, ,$$

(9.10)

and so

$$\frac{dE_j}{dp_j} = \frac{\begin{vmatrix} a_{jj} & a_{jh} \\ a_{hj} & a_{hh} \end{vmatrix}}{a_{hh}} \, ,$$

(9.11)

whence $dE_j/dp_j < 0$ if, and only if,

$$\begin{vmatrix} a_{jj} & a_{jh} \\ a_{hj} & a_{hh} \end{vmatrix} > 0 \, ,$$

(9.12)

since a_{hh} must be negative as found above. Condition (9.12) must hold for any combination of subscripts h and j ($h \neq j$), since any two markets may be involved. From its definition, the determinant which appears in (9.12) is a second-order principal minor of D. Thus condition (9.12) is that all the principal minors of the second order of D must be positive.

Proceeding thus, considering adjustments in two, three, etc., markets, we obtain the complete necessary and sufficient conditions for *perfect stability*, which are that all the principal minors of order r of D have the sign of $(-1)^r$ ★. This is the same as saying that such principal minors taken in ascending order must alternate in sign beginning with minus:

★ Where $1 \leqslant r \leqslant m$, i.e. including, as usual, also the elements on the main diagonal of D, and D itself, in the expression 'principal minors'.

$$a_{jj} < 0, \qquad \begin{vmatrix} a_{jj} & a_{jh} \\ a_{hj} & a_{hh} \end{vmatrix} > 0, \qquad \begin{vmatrix} a_{jj} & a_{jh} & a_{js} \\ a_{hj} & a_{hh} & a_{hs} \\ a_{sj} & a_{sh} & a_{ss} \end{vmatrix} < 0, \text{ etc.,} \qquad (9.13)$$

for any $j, h, s, \ldots$ (not equal).

This completes the examination of the *static stability* conditions, so that we can now study the *dynamic stability* of the model. The dynamic formalization of the behaviour assumption made by Walras is the following simultaneous system of differential equations

$$p'_j = F_j[E_j(p_1, p_2, \ldots, p_m)], \qquad j = 1, 2, \ldots, m , \qquad (9.14)$$

where F_j are sign-preserving functions with the usual properties (see Part II, ch. 3, §1) i.e.

$$\operatorname{sgn} F_j[\ldots] = \operatorname{sgn} [\ldots], \qquad F_j[0] = 0 , \qquad \mathrm{d}F_j[0]/\mathrm{d}E_j > 0 .$$

Performing the two linearizations (of the F's and of the E's: see Part II, ch. 3, §1) * we obtain

$$(p_j - p_j^e)' = k_j a_{j1}(p_1 - p_1^e) + k_j a_{j2}(p_2 - p_2^e) + \ldots + k_j a_{jm}(p_m - p_m^e) ,$$

$$j = 1, 2, \ldots, m , \qquad (9.15)$$

where $k_j \equiv F'[0]$, $a_{jk} \equiv \partial E_j/\partial p_k$ and p_j^e indicates the equilibrium value of the j-th price.

In order to simplify the exposition we shall assume that $k_j = 1$, all j **, so that the system can be written — in extended form — as

---

* This implies that we are examining *local* stability. This is no limitation here, since we are interested in a comparison of static and dynamic stability conditions, and the former have also a local nature: see above, footnote * to p. 276.

** This is not a great restriction, since it has been shown that the main dynamic stability conditions are independent of the magnitude of the k's (see the survey by Newman, 1959, p. 8).

$$\bar{p}_1' = a_{11}\bar{p}_1 + a_{12}\bar{p}_2 + \ldots + a_{1m}\bar{p}_m \; ,$$

$$\bar{p}_2' = a_{21}\bar{p}_1 + a_{22}\bar{p}_2 + \ldots + a_{2m}\bar{p}_m \; , \tag{9.15'}$$

$$\ldots\ldots\ldots\ldots\ldots\ldots\ldots\ldots\ldots\ldots$$

$$\bar{p}_m' = a_{m1}\bar{p}_1 + a_{m2}\bar{p}_2 + \ldots + a_{mm}\bar{p}_m \; ,$$

where $\bar{p}_i = (p_i - p_i^e)$. The solution of system (9.15′) will give the time path of the deviations from equilibrium, $\bar{p}_i(t)$. The conditions for the dynamic stability of equilibrium are obviously that

$$\lim_{t \to +\infty} \bar{p}_i(t) = 0 \; , \tag{9.16}$$

and this is equivalent to the condition that the roots of the characteristic equation of system (9.15′) are negative if real, and have negative real parts if complex. Now, the characteristic equation of system (9.15′) is

$$\begin{vmatrix} a_{11}-\lambda & a_{12} & \cdots & a_{1m} \\ a_{21} & a_{22}-\lambda & \cdots & a_{2m} \\ \ldots\ldots\ldots\ldots\ldots\ldots\ldots \\ a_{m1} & a_{m2} & \cdots & a_{mm}-\lambda \end{vmatrix} = 0 \; . \tag{9.17}$$

The first thing to note is that the coefficients a_{ij} are the same as those appearing in the static stability conditions. However, the static stability conditions are *not*, in general, either necessary or sufficient for the roots of (9.17) to be stable (this was first pointed out by Samuelson in his critique of the Hicksian method). In the exercises at the end of this section we shall examine the counterexamples, by means of which Samuelson proved that both imperfect and perfect static stability conditions are neither necessary nor sufficient for dynamic stability, which of course is the relevant concept of stability. However, there are some particular cases in which the Hicksian *perfect* stability conditions are related to dynamic stability. This can be shown quite easily using the dynamic stability conditions expounded in the previous chapter (see pp. 266–68).

The first case, pointed out by Samuelson himself [*], is the case of symmetry,

---

[*] He also pointed out that quasi-negative definiteness implies the Hicksian perfect stability conditions (but the converse is not true). But this case does not seem to have an economic interpretation.

i.e. $a_{ij} = a_{ji}$. In this case, the conditions

$$a_{11} < 0, \quad \begin{vmatrix} a_{11} & a_{12} \\ a_{21} & a_{22} \end{vmatrix} > 0, \quad \begin{vmatrix} a_{11} & a_{12} & a_{13} \\ a_{21} & a_{22} & a_{23} \\ a_{31} & a_{32} & a_{33} \end{vmatrix} < 0, \quad \text{etc.,} \quad (9.18)$$

are necessary and sufficient for the roots of (9.17) to be stable. Symmetry means that the effect of the i-th price on the excess demand for the j-th good is exactly the same as the effect of the j-th price on the excess demand for the i-th good, and this for all i's and j's. This is a rather strong requirement and we cannot expect it to be generally satisfied [*].

Another case, pointed out by Metzler (1945) [**], exists when all goods are gross substitutes, i.e. when each excess demand responds negatively to an increase in its 'own' price and positively to an increase in the price of any other good, i.e. $a_{ii} < 0, a_{ij} > 0$. Also in this case conditions (9.18) are necessary and sufficient for dynamic stability [‡]. It must be noted that the requirements imposed by Metzler were too strong, since — see conditions 3 in Part II, ch. 8 — there is no need for the off-diagonal elements to be all positive: they must only be non-negative. However, the gross substitutability property seems, even in its weakened form, a rather strong requirement.

An interesting case of dynamic stability is the dominant negative diagonal — see Part II, ch. 8, conditions (8.36). Its economic interpretation is the following: in each excess demand, the 'own' price effect is equilibrating, and it is in absolute value greater than the sum of the absolute values of the effects of the other prices. This sounds quite sensible and perhaps corresponds to what Walras had in mind when he stated that the '*tâtonnement*' process is stable [‡‡]. It must be noted, finally, that in the dominant negative diagonal

---

[*] It would be satisfied, for example, if all 'income effects' were absent or negligible, since the 'substitution effects' are symmetrical.

[**] He also proved that Hicks' perfect stability conditions are necessary (but not sufficient) if equilibrium is to be stable for *any* choice of (positive) speeds of adjustment (the k's in eq. (9.15) above).

[‡] See footnote [*] to p. 282

[‡‡] See footnote [**] to p. 275. The similarity between Walras' treatment and the dominant negative diagonal was pointed out by Arrow, Block and Hurwicz (1959) p. 106 (see the general list of references at the end of the volume). We can add that Walras might have thought that, since the 'own' price effect is direct, whereas the effects of the other prices are indirect, the former must prevail over the latter, and this is rather close to the

case the Hicksian conditions of perfect stability are satisfied, although the converse is not true [*].

Exercises

1. Consider the excess demand functions $E_1 = E_1(p_1, p_2), E_2 = E_2(p_1, p_2)$ and assume that their partial derivatives, computed in the equilibrium point, are

$$\frac{\partial E_1}{\partial p_1} = -2, \quad \frac{\partial E_1}{\partial p_2} = 4, \quad \frac{\partial E_2}{\partial p_1} = -1, \quad \frac{\partial E_2}{\partial p_2} = 1.$$

Show that equilibrium is dynamically stable, although both imperfect and perfect static stability conditions are not satisfied.

Calculation. The determinant which appears in the static stability conditions is

$$D = \begin{vmatrix} -2 & 4 \\ -1 & 1 \end{vmatrix} = 2.$$

One of the elements on the diagonal is positive, so that perfect stability is excluded. The ratios D/D_{jj} are $2/-2, 2/1$ and the second is positive. This excludes imperfect stability. Consider now the linearized dynamic system

$$\bar{p}'_1 = -2\bar{p}_1 + 4\bar{p}_2, \qquad \bar{p}'_2 = -\bar{p}_1 + \bar{p}_2.$$

negative dominant diagonal case. We must also add, however, that according to Jaffé (1967, pp. 14–5), the 'modern' case closest to Walras' thought is the gross substitutes case.

[*] See Newman (1959, theorem 9, p. 6). Of course, the negative dominant diagonal is by itself a sufficient stability condition, and the fact that the Hicks conditions are also satisfied does not add anything (whereas in the case of symmetry they are necessary and sufficient). We can also note that it has been proved that gross substitutability is by itself a sufficient stability condition (see Appendix II, §4.1). In other words, if all goods are gross substitutes, then this is enough to guarantee stability, without any need to check that conditions (9.18) are satisfied (it must be stressed that this is true only in general equilibrium analysis, thanks to some properties of general equilibrium; otherwise conditions $a_{ii} < 0, a_{ij} \geq 0$ are *not* sufficient for stability and so conditions (9.18) must be checked). Putting all this together with what we remarked in footnote [*] to p. 280, we conclude that in the study of the stability of general equilibrium the only case in which the Hicks conditions are useful is the case of symmetry.

Its characteristic equation is

$$\begin{vmatrix} -2-\lambda & 4 \\ -1 & 1-\lambda \end{vmatrix} = 0 ,$$

i.e.

$$\lambda^2 + \lambda + 2 = 0 ,$$

which gives $\lambda_1, \lambda_2 = -\frac{1}{2} \pm i\frac{1}{2}\sqrt{7}$. The roots are complex with negative real part, so that the equilibrium point is dynamically stable.

This counterexample shows that both imperfect and perfect stability conditions are not necessary for the dynamic stability of equilibrium.

2. The partial derivatives of the excess demand functions $E_1(p_1,p_2)$ and $E_2(p_1,p_2)$ are, in the equilibrium point,

$$\frac{\partial E_1}{\partial p_1} = 1 , \quad \frac{\partial E_1}{\partial p_2} = 1 ; \quad \frac{\partial E_2}{\partial p_1} = 2 , \quad \frac{\partial E_2}{\partial p_2} = 1 .$$

Show that equilibrium is dynamically unstable, although static imperfect stability conditions are satisfied. (This counterexample shows that imperfect stability conditions are not sufficient for dynamic stability.)

3. Exercises 1 and 2 show that both imperfect and perfect stability conditions are not necessary, and that imperfect stability conditions are not sufficient, for the dynamic stability of equilibrium. We have still to show that perfect stability conditions are not sufficient for dynamic stability. Assume that the partial derivatives of the excess demand functions are, in the equilibrium point, as laid out in the following determinant:

$$D \equiv \begin{vmatrix} -\epsilon & -1 & 0 & 0 \\ 0 & -\epsilon & -1 & 0 \\ 0 & 0 & -\epsilon & -1 \\ 1 & -1 & 1 & -1-\epsilon \end{vmatrix} ,$$

where ϵ is an arbitrary positive number. Check that perfect stability conditions are satisfied and that equilibrium is dynamically unstable.

Calculation. The student may check as an exercise that the principal minors of D alternate in sign for any positive ϵ. Consider now the characteristic equation of the corresponding dynamic system. This equation is

$$\begin{vmatrix} -\epsilon-\lambda & -1 & 0 & 0 \\ 0 & -\epsilon-\lambda & -1 & 0 \\ 0 & 0 & -\epsilon-\lambda & -1 \\ 1 & -1 & 1 & -1-\epsilon-\lambda \end{vmatrix} = 0 .$$

Expanding the determinant and rearranging terms we have

$$(\epsilon+\lambda)^4 + (\epsilon+\lambda)^3 + (\epsilon+\lambda)^2 + (\epsilon+\lambda) + 1 = 0 .$$

Now we could express this equation as a polynomial in λ and apply the stability conditions expounded in Part II, ch. 7. However, following Samuelson, we shall solve the equation as given above. Putting $y = \epsilon + \lambda$, it becomes

$$y^4 + y^3 + y^2 + y + 1 = 0 . \tag{9.19}$$

Let us now observe that

$$(y-1)(y^4+y^3+y^2+y+1) = y^5 - 1 ,$$

so that the roots of the equation $y^5 - 1 = 0$ coincide with the roots of the equations

$$y - 1 = 0 \quad (\text{whence } y = 1) ,$$

$$y^4 + y^3 + y^2 + y + 1 = 0 .$$

From this it follows that, of the five roots of $y^5 - 1 = 0$, one will be $y = 1$ and the remaining four will be the roots of (9.19). The reader may ask the reason for these apparently senseless passages (we have *increased* the degree of the equation to be solved). The reason is that the equation $y^5 - 1 = 0$ is much easier to solve than equation (9.19) [*]. Now, the roots of

---

[*] Eq. (9.19) is a reciprocal equation and can be solved by standard procedures (see, e.g., Turnbull, 1957, pp. 114–5). Since $y = 0$ is not a root, divide through by y^2 and rearrange terms, obtaining

are
$$y^5 - 1 = 0$$

$$y = \sqrt[5]{1} .$$

From elementary complex numbers theory (see, e.g., Courant (1936) p. 75) we know that the roots of unity are given by the formula

$$\cos \frac{2k\pi}{n} + i \sin \frac{2k\pi}{n} ,$$

where k is given the values 0, 1, 2, ..., $n - 1$ (n being the order of the root). In our case $n = 5$, and so we obtain

$$y_1 = 1 ,$$

$$y_2 = \cos 72° + i \sin 72° ,$$

$$y_3 = \cos 144° + i \sin 144° ,$$

$$y_4 = \cos 216° + i \sin 216° ,$$

$$y_5 = \cos 288° + i \sin 288° .$$

Discarding the spurious root $y_1 = 1$, we can rewrite the remaining four roots as

$$y_2, y_5 = \cos 72° \pm i \sin 72° , \qquad y_3, y_4 = -\cos 36° \pm i \sin 36° .$$

Since $y = \epsilon + \lambda$, then $\lambda = y - \epsilon$ and so the roots of the characteristic equation are

$$(\cos 72° - \epsilon) \pm i \sin 72° , \qquad (-\cos 36° - \epsilon) \pm i \sin 36° .$$

$$y^2 + \frac{1}{y^2} + y + \frac{1}{y} + 1 = 0 . \tag{9.19'}$$

Now let $y + 1/y = z$, from which $y^2 + 1/y^2 = z^2 - 2$. Substituting in (9.19') we have $z^2 + z - 1 = 0$, which gives $z_1, z_2 = -\frac{1}{2} \pm \frac{1}{2}\sqrt{5}$. Now, the relation $y + 1/y = z$ can be written as $y^2 - zy + 1 = 0$. Substituting in this relation first z_1 and then z_2, we solve for y, obtaining the four roots of (9.19). This procedure is more complicated, but may be preferred by the student not familiar with the roots of unity.

Now, since ϵ is an arbitrary positive number, we may freely fix it. Let us then assume that $0 < \epsilon < \cos 72°$. It follows that the first pair of roots has a positive real part, and this proves that equilibrium is unstable.

A final word. The reader may have wondered why Samuelson had to build such a complicated counterexample to disprove the sufficiency of the perfect stability conditions [*], whereas the counterexamples to disprove the necessity, etc. (exercises 1 and 2) were rather simple. The fact is that *in any 2×2 system*, perfect stability is indeed sufficient for dynamic stability. This can be proved easily as follows. Consider the 2×2 system whose coefficients are

$$\begin{bmatrix} a_{11} & a_{12} \\ a_{21} & a_{22} \end{bmatrix} .$$

The perfect stability conditions are

$$a_{11} < 0, \quad a_{22} < 0,$$

$$a_{11}a_{22} - a_{12}a_{21} > 0.$$

The characteristic equation of the system is

$$\begin{vmatrix} a_{11} - \lambda & a_{12} \\ a_{21} & a_{22} - \lambda \end{vmatrix} = 0, \quad \text{i.e.} \quad \lambda^2 - (a_{11} + a_{22})\lambda + (a_{11}a_{22} - a_{12}a_{21}) = 0.$$

Given the perfect stability conditions, the succession of the signs of the coefficients of the characteristic equation is $+ + +$, so that the roots are necessarily stable (see Part II, ch. 4, conditions (4.15)). It follows that to find counterexamples, higher systems than 2×2 systems must be used.

§2. Leontief's dynamic model

A prerequisite for understanding Leontief's dynamic model is, of course, the knowledge of his static model, which we cannot treat here. We shall only

---

[*] Actually Samuelson (1944) worked in terms of excess supply functions. We have modified his counterexample to put it on comparable terms with the others (only a change in signs is needed).

recall that in the static model the interdependency among the various sectors
of the economy is represented by a certain set of constant technical coefficients $a_{ik} \geqslant 0$; each of them is the quantity of the i-th good currently absorbed in the production of one unit of the k-th good. Thus such coefficients
refer to flows of goods currently used up by the various industries and say
nothing about capital formation. Now, in addition to the flows just mentioned,
there are other flows of goods which are not embodied in current output, but
go to increase the stock of capital, both fixed and circulating. In the static
model such flows − that is, investment − are included in the final demands
but are not 'explained', i.e. they are exogenous. However, they can be made
endogenous (and so be 'explained' by the model) by connecting the capital
requirements of each sector to the output of that sector by means of certain
other constant technical coefficients $b_{ik} \geqslant 0$; each of them represents the
stock of the i-th good (in its quality of capital good) that the k-th industry
must have at hand for each unit of its output. In other words, the assumption
is made − as in macroeconomic 'accelerator' models − of a constant capital/
output ratio; since here we are in a multisector model, we have many such
ratios, the b's. Of course, not each good can be simultaneously an intermediate
good and a capital good, so that some of the b's as well as some of the a's
will be zero.

Let S_{ik} be the stock of the i-th good owned by the k-th industry and X_k
the total output of the k-th good (industry). What we have just said is equivalent to the relations

$$S_{ik} = b_{ik}X_k \qquad \left\{ \begin{array}{l} i = 1, 2, ..., m \;, \\[2mm] k = 1, 2, ..., m \;, \end{array} \right. \qquad (9.20)$$

so that, differentiating both members with respect to time, we have

$$S'_{ik} = b_{ik}X'_k \;. \qquad (9.21)$$

Eq. (9.21) − apart from its disaggregated nature − is a continuous version of
the acceleration principle, since it links the variation in the stock of capital
(i.e. investment) to the variation in output by means of the appropriate
capital coefficients.

When we take account of (9.21), the balance equations of the static model
must be so modified:

$$X_i = \sum_{k=1}^{m} a_{ik} X_k + \sum_{k=1}^{m} b_{ik} X'_k + Y_i , \qquad i = 1, 2, ..., m . \tag{9.22}$$

The left-hand side of (9.22) is total current output of the i-th good, which in equilibrium must be equal to the quantity of that good currently demanded, the latter being made up of three components:

(1) the quantity of the i-th good currently used as an input by all industries, which is

$$\sum_{k=1}^{m} a_{ik} X_k ;$$

(2) the quantity of the i-th good currently demanded for investment purposes by all industries, which is

$$\sum_{k=1}^{m} b_{ik} X'_k ;$$

(3) the quantity of the i-th good currently used to satisfy the final demand, Y_i.

The new component with respect to the static model is of course (2). Here too we can distinguish an *open* model (in which final demands are given exogenously) and a *closed* model, in which final demands are made endogenous by means of the introduction of an n-th sector ($n = m + 1$), the sector of households. The 'output' of this sector is labour and its 'inputs' are the various consumption goods, durable and non-durable. In this case eqs. (9.22) would become

$$X_i = \sum_{k=1}^{n} a_{ik} X_k + \sum_{k=1}^{n} b_{ik} X'_k , \qquad i = 1, 2, ..., m, n , \tag{9.22'}$$

where

$$a_{in} X_n + b_{in} X'_n = Y_i .$$

Let us note that the closure of the model implies that also in the n-th sector there are fixed coefficients a_{in}, b_{in}, and this in turn means that there is strict proportionality between the quantity of goods (the number of 'baskets', which contain the various goods in fixed proportions) that households receive and the quantity of labour that they 'produce'. This, of course, sounds rather unrealistic.

Returning to eqs. (9.22), we add that the Y's must be taken as known: they can be constants or some other known functions of time. The properties of the model can be illustrated by a two-industries example:

$$X_1 = a_{11}X_1 + a_{12}X_2 + b_{11}X_1' + b_{12}X_2' + Y_1 \,,$$

$$X_2 = a_{21}X_1 + a_{22}X_2 + b_{21}X_1' + b_{22}X_2' + Y_2 \,.$$

(9.23)

Of course, to solve the model we need to know the form of the Y's. In any case, however, the solution involves the solution of the homogeneous part of the model, for which the form of the Y's is irrelevant. So let us begin with the solution of the homogeneous system; we shall next consider the various particular solutions of the non-homogeneous model according to the different assumptions made about the Y's.

The homogeneous system

$$-b_{11}X_1' + (1-a_{11})X_1 - b_{12}X_2' - a_{12}X_2 = 0$$

$$-b_{21}X_1' - a_{21}X_1 - b_{22}X_2' + (1-a_{22})X_2 = 0$$

(9.24)

is a first-order system, but is not in 'normal' form, since in each equation the derivatives of both functions appear. Thus we can proceed as expounded in the later part of Part II, ch. 8 (pp. 269 *et seq.*). We obtain the characteristic equation

$$\begin{vmatrix} -b_{11}\lambda + (1-a_{11}) & -b_{12}\lambda - a_{12} \\ -b_{21}\lambda - a_{21} & -b_{22}\lambda + (1-a_{22}) \end{vmatrix} = 0 \,,$$

i.e.

$$(b_{22}b_{11} - b_{12}b_{21})\lambda^2 - [(1-a_{11})b_{22} + (1-a_{22})b_{11} + a_{12}b_{21} + a_{21}b_{12}]\lambda$$

$$+ [(1-a_{11})(1-a_{22}) - a_{21}a_{12}] = 0 \,.$$

(9.25)

We can check that the roots are real and distinct [*]. The discriminant of (9.25) is

---

[*] This property is no longer true with more than two industries. When there are three or more industries, complex roots may also occur (see Leontief, *et al.*, 1953, p. 79).

$$\Delta = [(1-a_{11})b_{22} + (1-a_{22})b_{11} + a_{12}b_{21} + a_{21}b_{12}]^2$$

$$- 4(b_{22}b_{11} - b_{12}b_{21})[(1-a_{11})(1-a_{22}) - a_{21}a_{12}] ,$$

which can be written as

$$[(1-a_{11})b_{22} - (1-a_{22})b_{11} + a_{12}b_{21} - a_{21}b_{12}]^2 + 4[(1-a_{11})b_{22}a_{21}b_{12}$$

$$+ (1-a_{22})b_{11}a_{12}b_{21} + b_{22}b_{11}a_{21}a_{12} + b_{12}b_{21}(1-a_{11})(1-a_{22})] . \qquad (9.26)$$

Now, let us recall from the static model that for the system to be 'viable', the expressions $1 - a_{11}$ and $1 - a_{22}$ (as well as the expression $(1-a_{11})(1-a_{22}) - a_{12}a_{21}$) must be all positive *. It is sufficient that $1 - a_{11}$ and $1 - a_{22}$ be positive for (9.26) to be positive. We can also show that at least one of the roots is positive. Examination of the signs of the coefficients of (9.25) yields the following information: the coefficient of λ^2 may have any sign; the coefficient of λ is negative given the 'viability' conditions mentioned above, and for the same reason the constant term is positive. So, regardless of the sign of the coefficient of λ^2, there is certainly a variation in the succession of the signs of the coefficients, and this means − given that $\Delta > 0$ − a positive root. More precisely, three cases are possible:

Case (1)

$$b_{22}b_{11} - b_{12}b_{21} < 0 .$$

The succession of signs is − − +, and so there is one negative and one positive root.

Case (2)

$$b_{22}b_{11} - b_{12}b_{21} = 0 .$$

In this particular case the characteristic equation is a first-degree equation, whose only root is necessarily positive.

---

* These are the well-known Hawkins−Simon conditions (see any text on input−output analysis). A simple proof can be sketched here. In matrix terms the solution of the static model is $X = [I-A]^{-1}Y$. Now A is a non-negative matrix, and let us assume that it is indecomposable. Then $[I-A]^{-1} > 0$ if, and only if, $1 > \lambda_M$, where λ_M is the dominant root of A (Gantmacher, 1959, p. 83). Now, necessary and sufficient conditions that $1 > \lambda_M$ are that the leading principal minors of $I-A$ are all positive (Gantmacher, 1959, p. 88), which are the Hawkins−Simon conditions.

Case (3)

$$b_{22}b_{11} - b_{12}b_{21} > 0.$$

The succession of the signs is $+ - +$, and so there are two positive roots.

In general, the movement given by the homogeneous part of the system is divergent; for t sufficiently large, the term containing the larger positive root will dominate, so that all the variables will tend to grow at the same proportionate rate given by the dominant root.

The solution of (9.24) is then

$$X_1(t) = A_1 \exp(\lambda_1 t) + A_2 \exp(\lambda_2 t),$$

$$X_2(t) = A_1 \alpha_1 \exp(\lambda_1 t) + A_2 \alpha_2 \exp(\lambda_2 t),$$

(9.27)

where λ_1, λ_2 are the roots of (9.25) and the coefficients α_1, α_2 are

$$\alpha_1 = \frac{1 - a_{11} - b_{11}\lambda_1}{a_{12} + b_{12}\lambda_1}, \qquad \alpha_2 = \frac{1 - a_{11} - b_{11}\lambda_2}{a_{12} + b_{12}\lambda_2}.$$

We may now inquire whether the homogeneous system is capable of *balanced growth* *, that is, a state of growth in which the proportions that the variables bear to each other are constant. This, of course, is equivalent to the requirement that all the variables grow at the same (proportionate) rate. It must be noted that we are requiring an *actual* balanced growth, not an *asymptotic* balanced growth (i.e. the variables must actually grow at the same rate and not only *tend* to grow at the same rate for $t \to \infty$; this second question will be examined later). Thus balanced growth will obtain if, and only if, in the right-hand side of both eqs. (9.27) only one term (containing a positive root) remains. Let λ_1 be the positive root (or one of the positive roots). Then we must have

$$X_1(t) = A_1 \exp(\lambda_1 t),$$

$$X_2(t) = A_2 \alpha_1 \exp(\lambda_1 t).$$

(9.27′)

---

* Of course, the question has not much sense if we are considering an open system, since the behaviour of the model depends also on the particular solution of the non-homogeneous system. It has sense if we are considering a closed system. From the mathematical point of view, the homogeneous part of an open system and a closed system give rise to the same type of differential system.

Can (9.27′) occur? The answer is yes, and there are two ways.

(a) When $b_{11}b_{22} - b_{12}b_{21} = 0$. Then, as we have seen, there is only one root and the solution will be of type (9.27′), where

$$\lambda_1 = \frac{(1-a_{11})(1-a_{22}) - a_{21}a_{12}}{(1-a_{11})b_{22} + (1-a_{22})b_{11} + a_{12}b_{21} + a_{21}b_{12}}.$$

Note that $b_{11}b_{22} - b_{12}b_{21} = 0$ means that the determinant formed with the capital coefficients

$$\begin{vmatrix} b_{11} & b_{12} \\ b_{21} & b_{22} \end{vmatrix}$$

is zero, i.e. that the capital coefficients are equiproportional in the two sectors:

$$\frac{b_{11}}{b_{12}} = \frac{b_{21}}{b_{22}}, \qquad \frac{b_{11}}{b_{21}} = \frac{b_{12}}{b_{22}}.$$

(b) Choosing the initial conditions in such a way that A_2 turns out to be zero. This can always be done. Let $X_1(0), X_2(0)$ be the initial values. We want to know which relations they must satisfy in order that $A_2 = 0$. To this purpose, consider the equations for the determination of A_1, A_2:

$$X_1(0) = A_1 + A_2 ,$$

$$X_2(0) = A_1\alpha_1 + A_2\alpha_2 ,$$

from which

$$A_1 = \frac{\alpha_2 X_1(0) - X_2(0)}{\alpha_2 - \alpha_1} , \qquad A_2 = \frac{X_2(0) - \alpha_1 X_1(0)}{\alpha_2 - \alpha_1}.$$

Then a necessary and sufficient condition that $A_2 = 0$ is that $X_2(0) - \alpha_1 X_1(0) = 0$, i.e. that $X_2(0)/X_1(0) = \alpha_1$. Thus balanced growth will occur if the initial values bear a precise ratio to each other.

Case (a) cannot be extended to the general m-sector model. The fact that the determinant of the capital coefficients is zero,

$$\begin{vmatrix} b_{11} & b_{12} & \cdots & b_{1m} \\ b_{21} & b_{22} & \cdots & b_{2m} \\ \cdots\cdots\cdots\cdots\cdots \\ b_{m1} & b_{m2} & \cdots & b_{mm} \end{vmatrix} = 0,$$

implies that in the characteristic equation the coefficient of λ^m is zero, so that the equation is at most of degree $m-1$ and has at most $m-1$ roots. In the particular case in which $m = 2$, only one root remains, but this is no longer true when $m > 2$. On the contrary, case (b) can be extended to the general model. The equations for the determination of the A's are easily found [*] and are

$$X_j(0) = \sum_{i=0}^{m} A_i \alpha_j^{(i)}, \qquad j = 1, 2, ..., m. \tag{9.28}$$

Then, by Cramer's rule,

$$A_i = \frac{D_i}{D}, \qquad \text{where } D \equiv \begin{vmatrix} \alpha_1^{(1)} & \alpha_1^{(2)} & \cdots & \alpha_1^{(m)} \\ \alpha_2^{(1)} & \alpha_2^{(2)} & \cdots & \alpha_2^{(m)} \\ \cdots\cdots\cdots\cdots\cdots\cdots \\ \alpha_m^{(1)} & \alpha_m^{(2)} & \cdots & \alpha_m^{(m)} \end{vmatrix}, \tag{9.29}$$

and D_i is obtained substituting the column of the $X_j(0)$ in the place of the i-th column of D. Now let λ_1 be a positive root [**]. If we choose

[*] The solution for an m-sector model will have the form
$$X_j(t) = \sum_{i=0}^{m} A_i \alpha_j^{(i)} \exp(\lambda_i t),$$
whence, putting $t = 0$, we obtain equations (9.28). Some complications may arise when there are repeated roots, but we need not treat them here.

[**] This presumes that a positive root exists (and that the α vector associated with it is positive). It can be proved that this presumption is true. In matrix terms, the general differential system is $X = AX + B\dot{X}$ and its characteristic equation is $|I - (A + \lambda B)| = 0$, where A is the matrix of the current input coefficients and B is the matrix of the capital coefficients. Now let A be indecomposable and its dominant root λ_M be smaller than unity (see footnote [**], p. 290). B is non-negative. Let us recall that the dominant root

$X_1(0), X_2(0), ..., X_m(0)$ proportional to $\alpha_1^{(1)}, \alpha_2^{(1)}, ..., \alpha_m^{(1)}$, it follows that each D_i (except D_1) will have two proportional columns, and so $A_j = 0, i \neq 1$. The value of A_1 will be c, the proportionality factor ($c = X_j(0)/\alpha_j^{(1)}$, all j).

Let us now turn to the particular solution of the non-homogeneous system (9.23). We shall examine two cases: constant final demands and exponentially increasing final demands.

1. *Constant final demands*

Let $Y_1 = C_1$, $Y_2 = C_2$, where C_1, C_2 are given positive constants. As a particular solution, try $\bar{X}_1 = B_1$, $\bar{X}_2 = B_2$, where B_1, B_2 are undetermined constants. Substitution in (9.23) yields

$$(1-a_{11})B_1 - a_{12}B_2 = C_1 ,$$

$$-a_{21}B_1 + (1-a_{22})B_2 = C_2 ,$$

which give

$$B_1 = \frac{(1-a_{22})C_1 + a_{12}C_2}{(1-a_{11})(1-a_{22}) - a_{12}a_{21}} ,$$

$$B_2 = \frac{(1-a_{11})C_2 + a_{21}C_1}{(1-a_{11})(1-a_{22}) - a_{12}a_{21}} . \tag{9.30}$$

It can be observed that the 'viability' conditions already used are sufficient for (9.30) to be positive. Indeed, relations (9.30) coincide with the solution of the static system. The general solution of (9.23) is then

$$X_1(t) = A_1 \exp(\lambda_1 t) + A_2 \exp(\lambda_2 t) + B_1 ,$$

$$X_2(t) = A_1\alpha_1 \exp(\lambda_1 t) + A_2\alpha_2 \exp(\lambda_2 t) + B_2 , \tag{9.31}$$

of a non-negative indecomposable matrix is a continuous and strictly increasing function of the elements of the matrix (Schwartz, 1961, p. 24). Then there is a positive λ such that the dominant root of the matrix $A + \lambda B$ is unity, and such a λ obviously satisfies the equation $|I - (A+\lambda B)| = 0$ (this equation can be considered as $|\rho I - (A+\lambda B)| = 0$, the characteristic equation of the matrix $A + \lambda B$, for a latent root $\rho = 1$). This proves that $|I - (A+\lambda B)| = 0$ has a positive root, given by the above value of λ, say λ_1. The $\alpha_j^{(1)}$ will be given by the system of equations $\alpha^{(1)} = (A+\lambda_1 B)\alpha^{(1)}$, i:e. $\alpha^{(1)}$ is the latent vector of the matrix $A + \lambda_1 B$ associated with the unit latent root of such a matrix. But, as we have seen above, the dominant root of such a matrix equals 1 and so, from the Frobenius theorem (Gantmacher 1959, p. 65), α is a positive vector.

where B_1, B_2 are given by (9.30).

Given the initial values $X_1(0), X_2(0)$, we can determine A_1, A_2. Substituting in (9.31) we have

$$A_1 + A_2 = X_1(0) - B_1 ,$$

$$\alpha_1 A_1 + \alpha_2 A_2 = X_2(0) - B_2 ,$$

(9.31')

from which

$$A_1 = \frac{[X_1(0) - B_1]\alpha_2 - [X_2(0) - B_2]}{\alpha_2 - \alpha_1} ,$$

$$A_2 = \frac{[X_2(0) - B_2] - [X_1(0) - B_1]\alpha_1}{\alpha_2 - \alpha_1} .$$

2. *Exponentially increasing final demands*

Let $Y_1 = d_1 e^{\mu t}$, $Y_2 = d_2 e^{\mu t}$, where d_1, d_2, μ are given positive constants. As a particular solution try $\bar{X}_1(t) = B_1 e^{\mu t}$, $\bar{X}_2(t) = B_2 e^{\mu t}$, where B_1, B_2 are undetermined constants. Substituting in (9.23) we have

$$B_1 e^{\mu t} = a_{11} B_1 e^{\mu t} + a_{12} B_2 e^{\mu t} + b_{11} \mu B_1 e^{\mu t} + b_{12} \mu B_2 e^{\mu t} + d_1 e^{\mu t} ,$$

$$B_2 e^{\mu t} = a_{21} B_1 e^{\mu t} + a_{22} B_2 e^{\mu t} + b_{21} \mu B_1 e^{\mu t} + b_{22} \mu B_2 e^{\mu t} + d_2 e^{\mu t} ,$$

so that

$$e^{\mu t}[(1 - a_{11} - \mu b_{11})B_1 - (a_{12} + b_{12}\mu)B_2 - d_1] = 0 ,$$

$$e^{\mu t}[-(a_{21} + b_{21}\mu)B_1 + (1 - a_{22} - \mu b_{22})B_2 - d_2] = 0 .$$

(9.32)

Eqs. (9.32) must be satisfied for any t, and this is possible if, and only if, both expressions in square brackets are zero, i.e.

$$(1 - a_{11} - \mu b_{11})B_1 - (a_{12} + b_{12}\mu)B_2 = d_1 ,$$

$$-(a_{21} + b_{21}\mu)B_1 + (1 - a_{22} - \mu b_{22})B_2 = d_2 ,$$

(9.33)

which give

$$B_1 = \frac{(1 - a_{22} - \mu b_{22})d_1 + (a_{12} + b_{12}\mu)d_2}{(1 - a_{11} - \mu b_{11})(1 - a_{22} - \mu b_{22}) - (a_{12} + b_{12}\mu)(a_{21} + b_{21}\mu)} ,$$

(9.34)

$$B_2 = \frac{(1 - a_{11} - \mu b_{11}) d_2 + (a_{21} + b_{21}\mu) d_1}{(1 - a_{11} - \mu b_{11})(1 - a_{22} - \mu b_{22}) - (a_{12} + b_{12}\mu)(a_{21} + b_{21}\mu)}. \tag{9.34}$$

Therefore, the general solution of system (9.23) is now

$$X_1(t) = A_1 \exp(\lambda_1 t) + A_2 \exp(\lambda_2 t) + B_1 \exp(\mu t),$$

$$X_2(t) = A_1 \alpha_1 \exp(\lambda_1 t) + A_2 \alpha_2 \exp(\lambda_2 t) + B_2 \exp(\mu t), \tag{9.35}$$

where B_1, B_2 are given by (9.34).

Given the initial values $X_1(0), X_2(0)$, we can determine A_1, A_2. Substituting in (9.35) we have

$$A_1 + A_2 = X_1(0) - B_1,$$

$$\alpha_1 A_1 + \alpha_2 A_2 = X_2(0) - B_2, \tag{9.35'}$$

which give

$$A_1 = \frac{[X_1(0) - B_1]\alpha_2 - [X_2(0) - B_2]}{\alpha_2 - \alpha_1},$$

$$A_2 = \frac{[X_2(0) - B_2] - [X_1(0) - B_1]\alpha_1}{\alpha_2 - \alpha_1}.$$

The model with exponential final demands can be generalized to the case in which the two final demands grow at different rates, i.e. $Y_1 = d_1 \exp(\mu_1 t)$, $Y_2 = d_2 \exp(\mu_2 t)$. Correspondingly, the particular solution will be of the type

$$\overline{X}_1(t) = B_{11} \exp(\mu_1 t) + B_{12} \exp(\mu_2 t),$$

$$\overline{X}_2(t) = B_{21} \exp(\mu_1 t) + B_{22} \exp(\mu_2 t);$$

the four undetermined constants $B_{11}, B_{12}, B_{21}, B_{22}$ can be determined by the usual method.

Up to this point we have considered only the quantity side of the model. Let us now turn to the determination of prices; for simplicity we shall consider only the closed model. It has been shown by Solow that, in formulating the price equations, account must be taken of the capital losses (or gains), i.e. of the variations in the value of the stocks of capital goods brought about by price changes. Thus, in equilibrium, the price level of each sector equals the costs of the current inputs plus interest charges plus capital losses (or minus capital gains). The price equations are then ★

$$p_1 = (a_{11}p_1 + a_{21}p_2) + r(b_{11}p_1 + b_{21}p_2) - (b_{11}p_1' + b_{21}p_2'),$$
$$(9.36)$$
$$p_2 = (a_{12}p_1 + a_{22}p_2) + r(b_{12}p_1 + b_{22}p_2) - (b_{12}p_1' + b_{22}p_2'),$$

where r is the (given) rate of interest. System (9.36) can be rewritten as

$$b_{11}p_1' + (1 - a_{11} - rb_{11})p_1 + b_{21}p_2' - (a_{21} + rb_{21})p_2 = 0,$$
$$(9.36')$$
$$b_{12}p_1' - (a_{12} + rb_{12})p_1 + b_{22}p_2' + (1 - a_{22} - rb_{22})p_2 = 0,$$

and its characteristic equation is

$$\begin{vmatrix} b_{11}\rho + 1 - a_{11} - rb_{11} & b_{21}\rho - a_{21} - rb_{21} \\ b_{12}\rho - a_{12} - rb_{12} & b_{22}\rho + 1 - a_{22} - rb_{22} \end{vmatrix} = 0, \qquad (9.37)$$

where the ρ's are the characteristic roots. Eq. (9.37) can be rewritten as

$$\begin{vmatrix} -b_{11}\lambda + (1 - a_{11}) & -b_{21}\lambda - a_{21} \\ -b_{12}\lambda - a_{12} & -b_{22}\lambda + (1 - a_{22}) \end{vmatrix} = 0, \qquad (9.37')$$

where $\lambda \equiv r - \rho$. It is apparent that (9.37') is the same as the characteristic equation of the physical system (9.24) ★★. Thus, since $\rho \equiv r - \lambda$, it follows that the characteristic roots of the price system are obtained subtracting from r the characteristic roots of the physical system. This allows us to draw some interesting conclusions. First of all, the prices corresponding to the balanced growth path ‡ are *constant* if, and only if, $r = \lambda_1$, where λ_1 is the positive

---

★ If we put $p_1' = p_2' \equiv 0$ in (9.36), we obtain the static price equations. By such an expression we do not mean the price equations of the static model, but the price equations of the dynamic model in which no account is taken of capital losses (or gains).

★★ Remember that when the rows and columns of a determinant are interchanged the value of the latter does not vary.

‡ Let $\rho_1 = r - \lambda_1$. Then the prices corresponding to the balanced growth path are those obtained when $p_2(0)/p_1(0) = \alpha_1$ (the procedure is the same as for the physical system: see above in the text). It can be checked that when $r = \lambda_1$ these prices are the same as the 'static' prices obtained as indicated in footnote ★ above. (*Hint*: the system for the

root giving rise to this path (see above). This proves that the dynamic price equations (9.36) do not necessarily give rise to a changing price level on the balanced growth path. But, if $r \neq \lambda_1$ (and this surely is the most probable case), then the prices corresponding to the balanced growth path will be changing over time, converging or diverging if $r \lessgtr \lambda_1$. Secondly, consider the solution for the time paths of outputs as given in (9.27) and let λ_1 be a positive root to which $\alpha_1 > 0$ corresponds. The system is called *relatively stable* if, as $t \to +\infty$, all outputs tend to grow at the same proportionate rate λ_1 (in other words, the actual path converges relative to the balanced growth path) i.e., in formal terms, if

$$\lim_{t \to +\infty} \frac{X_i'(t)}{X_i(t)} = \lambda_1 , \qquad \text{all } i .$$

It can easily be seen that, in our 2×2 system, the necessary and sufficient condition for relative stability is that $\lambda_1 > \lambda_2$. In fact,

$$\lim_{t \to +\infty} \frac{X_1'(t)}{X_1(t)} = \lim_{t \to +\infty} \frac{\lambda_1 A_1 \exp(\lambda_1 t) + \lambda_2 A_2 \exp(\lambda_2 t)}{A_1 \exp(\lambda_1 t) + A_2 \exp(\lambda_2 t)}$$

$$= \lambda_1 \lim_{t \to +\infty} \frac{1}{1 + (A_2/A_1) \exp[(\lambda_2 - \lambda_1)t]}$$

$$+ \lambda_2 \lim_{t \to +\infty} \frac{1}{1 + (A_1/A_2) \exp[(\lambda_1 - \lambda_2)t]}$$

$$= \lambda_1 ,$$

if, and only if, $\lambda_1 > \lambda_2$. The same is true for $X_2(t)$. Consider now the solution for the time paths of prices, given by

$$p_1(t) = B_1 \exp(\rho_1 t) + B_2 \exp(\rho_2 t) ,$$

$$p_2(t) = B_2 \alpha_1 \exp(\rho_1 t) + B_2 \alpha_2 \exp(\rho_2 t) ,$$

(9.38)

static prices is homogeneous, so that its determinant must be zero for it to give nontrivial solutions. Note that this determinant is the same as the determinant appearing in the characteristic equation of the output system, with r instead of λ; thus if $r = \lambda_1$, then $p_2/p_1 = \alpha_1$.)

where B_1, B_2 are arbitrary constants and α_1, α_2 are the same as for the output system (with $\lambda_i \equiv r - \rho_i$). Let us consider the term containing α_1, since $\alpha_1 > 0$. By the same procedure as for the output system, we obtain that $\rho_1 > \rho_2$ is the necessary and sufficient condition for the relative stability of the price system. But $\rho_i \equiv r - \lambda_i$, and so $\rho_1 > \rho_2$ is the same as $\lambda_2 > \lambda_1$, which is exactly the opposite of the condition for the relative stability of the output system. This illustrates the *dual stability theorem*: if the output system is relatively stable, the price system is relatively unstable, and vice versa (Jorgenson, 1960) *.

Exercises

1. The following data are given: $a_{11} = 0.1, a_{12} = 0.9, a_{21} = 0.4, a_{22} = 0.2$; $b_{11} = b_{22} = 0, b_{12} = 2, b_{21} = 3; Y_1 = 90, Y_2 = 80; X_1(0) = 500, X_2(0) = 400$. Determine the general solution of the output system.

Calculation. Let us begin with the homogeneous part, which is

$$0.9\, X_1 - 2\, X_2' - 0.9\, X_2 = 0\ ,$$

$$-3\, X_1' - 0.4\, X_1 + 0.8\, X_2 = 0\ .$$

Its characteristic equation is

$$\begin{vmatrix} 0.9 & -2\lambda - 0.9 \\ -3\lambda - 0.4 & 0.8 \end{vmatrix} = -6\lambda^2 - 3.5\,\lambda + 0.36 = 0\ ,$$

with roots

$$\lambda_1, \lambda_2 = \frac{3.5 \pm \sqrt{20.89}}{12} \simeq \frac{3.5 \pm 4.57}{12} = -0.6725,\, 0.0891\overline{6}\ .$$

The coefficients α_1, α_2 are given by the relations

---

* The reader is referred to Jorgenson's (1960) paper for the general case. Here we shall only note that the theorem is no longer generally true in the open system (Jorgenson, 1960). Another aspect of the dual stability theorem is the following: "If output levels can be guaranteed to remain non-negative for any — meaningful — initial levels (that is, output levels which are themselves non-negative), then prices must become negative for some meaningful initial price levels, and conversely" (Jorgenson, 1961, *Rev. Econ. Stud.*, pp. 105–6; see also Jorgenson, 1961, *Int. Economic Review*, §3).

$$\alpha_1 = \frac{0.9}{0.9 - 2 \times 0.6725} \simeq -2.0225 , \quad \alpha_2 = \frac{0.9}{0.9 + 2 \times 0.08916} \simeq 0.8346 ,$$

and so the general solution of the homogeneous system is

$$X_1(t) = A_1 \exp(-0.6725t) + A_2 \exp(0.08916t)$$

$$X_2(t) = -2.0225 A_1 \exp(-0.6725t) + 0.8346 A_2 \exp(0.08916t) .$$

As a particular solution of the non-homogeneous system

$$0.9 X_1 - 2 X_2' - 0.9 X_2 = 90 ,$$

$$-3 X_1' - 0.4 X_1 + 0.8 X_2 = 80 ,$$

try $\overline{X}_1 = B_1, \overline{X}_2 = B_2$, where B_1, B_2 are undetermined constants. Substituting in the non-homogeneous system we have

$$0.9 B_1 - 0.9 B_2 = 90 ,$$

$$-0.4 B_1 + 0.8 B_2 = 80 ,$$

which give $B_1 = 400, B_2 = 300$. Thus the general solution of the non-homogeneous system is

$$X_1(t) = A_1 \exp(-0.6725t) + A_2 \exp(0.08916t) + 400 ,$$

$$X_2(t) = -2.0225 A_1 \exp(-0.6725t) + 0.8346 A_2 \exp(0.08916t) + 300 .$$

For $t = 0$ and given the initial conditions, we have

$$500 = A_1 + A_2 + 400$$

$$400 = -2.0225 A_1 + 0.8346 A_2 + 300 ,$$

which give $A_1 \simeq -5.789, A_2 \simeq 105.789$. The final form of the solution is then

$$X_1(t) = -5.789 \exp(-0.6725t) + 105.789 \exp(0.08916t) + 400 ,$$

$$X_2(t) = 11.708 \exp(-0.6725t) + 88.292 \exp(0.08916t) + 300 .$$

2. Same data as in the previous exercise, but for $Y_1 = 500\,e^{0.10t}$, $Y_2 = 400\,e^{0.10t}$.

§3. The stability of a barter international equilibrium (Marshall–Kemp)

Let us consider a trading world composed of two countries — the 'home country' and the 'rest of the world' — both being barter economies. Each country produces two goods, say good 1 and good 2, which are the same in both countries. International trade is possible if, and only if, in the two countries the structures of production and of demand are such that, for some range of the relative price, when within one country a situation obtains in which there is a positive (negative) excess demand for good 1 (good 2), then in the other country the opposite situation obtains. Assuming that the conditions for the existence of international trade are satisfied, let us recall from elementary international economics that the equilibrium point in international exchange is determined by the intersection of the *offer curve* (also called the *reciprocal demand* or *demand and supply* curve) of one country with the offer curve of the other country ★. The offer curve of a country can be defined as the locus of all points which represent the various terms of trade at which the country is willing to trade. Each point of such curve, in other words, indicates the (maximum) quantity of the exported good that the country is willing to give in exchange for a given amount of the imported good (or, if you prefer, the (minimum) quantity of the imported good that the country is willing to accept in exchange for a given amount of the exported good). In what follows we shall use the following symbols:

p = terms of trade, expressed as number of units of good 1 exchanged for one unit of good 2. On the assumption of no transport costs, free trade etc., p coincides with the internal price (in each country) of good 2 in terms of good 1 taken as the standard of measurement ('*numéraire*').

$E_1(p), E_2(p)$ = excess demands for good 1 and for good 2 within the home country.

$E_1^*(p), E_2^*(p)$ = excess demands for good 1 and for good 2 within the rest of the world.

★ It may also be recalled that the 'law of reciprocal demand' was introduced (in verbal terms) by J.S. Mill in order to determine the terms of trade, which were left undetermined between two extremes by the theory of comparative costs. The graphical apparatus of the offer curves was introduced by A. Marshall, who also studied the problem of the stability of the equilibrium point(s) by means of a graphical analysis; this justifies the name of Marshall in the title of this section. A modern (and rather concise) treatment in mathematical terms of the same stability problem under various behaviour assumptions has been given by Kemp, and this explains his name in the title. See also Amano (1968).

We assume that, within the range of values of the terms of trade at which international trade is possible, the production and demand conditions in the two countries are such that the home country wishes to import good 2 and to export good 1, whereas the opposite is true for the rest of the world. Therefore, in the home country there is a positive excess demand for good 2 (this excess demand is the demand for imports) and a negative excess demand for good 1 (the supply of exports). The opposite situation obtains in the rest of the world. Thus we can write

$$E_1(p)<0, \quad E_2(p)>0; \quad E_1^*(p)>0, \quad E_2^*(p)<0.$$

Let

$$-E_1 = G_1(E_2),$$

$$-E_2^* = G_2(E_1^*)$$

be the offer curves of the home country and of the rest of the world. The minus signs are due to the fact that E_1 and E_2^* are negative magnitudes, and we want to work with all positive magnitudes for graphical convenience. In fig. 9.1 two 'normal' offer curves are drawn. The equilibrium point is Q and the corresponding quantities traded are $\overline{OA}$ of good 1 (exported by the home country and imported by the rest of the world) and $\overline{OB}$ of good 2 (imported

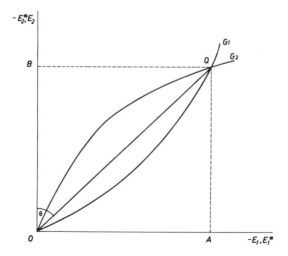

Fig. 9.1.

by the home country and exported by the rest of the world). The equilibrium terms of trade are measured by $\tan\theta$.

In order to study the stability of the equilibrium point, as we know, behaviour assumptions are needed. We shall examine two different behaviour assumptions, both based on quantity adjustments *. In our treatment we shall follow Kemp in using barred symbols for *actual* quantities and unbarred symbols for the corresponding 'ideal' quantities (i.e. quantities lying on the offer curves).

Behaviour assumption I

Consider any non-equilibrium point P. Each country, owing to the competition between its traders, adjusts the quantity of its exports towards that quantity which it would offer at the terms of trade actually prevailing, if such terms remained fixed for all the time needed to complete the adjustment. With reference to fig. 9.2, assume that the initial non-equilibrium point is P. Now, $-\bar{E}_1(0)$ is the initial quantity of exports of the home country and $-\bar{E}_2^*(0)$ is the initial quantity of exports of the rest of the world; the terms of trade are measured by the slope (referred to the vertical axis) of the straight line passing through P and O. Given such terms of trade, the quantity of exports that the home country desires to export is determined, by the very definition of an offer curve, by the abscissa of point A. Therefore the home country is inclined to decrease its exports, adjusting them from $-\bar{E}_1(0)$ towards $-E_1(0)$. By similar reasoning it can be seen that the rest of the world tends to expand its exports, adjusting them from $-\bar{E}_2^*(0)$ towards $-E_2^*(0)$. Thus point P tends to move in a direction included between the two arrows. From this fact, however, no definite conclusion about the stability of point Q can be drawn. We should like to stress that the pointed arrows do *not*, by themselves, allow us to determine the actual 'trajectory' of point P and even less to say whether this point will converge, and how, to the equilibrium point. It is true that the arrows point towards equilibrium, but this is not enough: nothing excludes, for example, that point P overtakes point Q and is then pushed back, giving rise to oscillations that in principle might be of increasing amplitude. In other words, recalling what we said in Part II, ch. 3, §1,

---

* See Kemp (1964, ch. 4), where a third assumption is also examined, based on price adjustment. Let us note that Kemp attributes assumption II to Marshall, while leaving unnamed assumption I. We believe that, owing to the ambiguity of Marshall's statements on this topic, both assumptions are consistent with what he wrote in *The Pure Theory of Foreign Trade* and in Appendix J of *Money, Credit and Commerce*. However, we do not think that this attribution problem is important enough to justify an exegesis of the cited works of Marshall in order to support our impression.

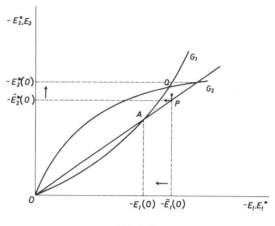

Fig. 9.2.

the arrows demonstrate only the existence of equilibrating forces (*static stability*) but cannot as such tell us anything on the actual dynamic convergence to equilibrium (*dynamic stability*). Some general comments on arrow diagrams will be made in the next section.

To study rigorously the dynamic stability of equilibrium under the stated behaviour assumption we must base the analysis on a system of functional equations. Such a system is

$$\frac{d(-\bar{E}_1)}{dt} = f_1 [-E_1(\bar{p}) - (-\bar{E}_1)], \quad \mathrm{sgn} f_1 [...] = \mathrm{sgn}[...], \quad f_1[0] = 0, \quad f_1'[0] > 0,$$

$$\frac{d(-\bar{E}_2^*)}{dt} = f_2 [-E_2^*(\bar{p}) - (-\bar{E}_2^*)], \quad \mathrm{sgn} f_2 [...] = \mathrm{sgn}[...], \quad f_2[0] = 0, \quad f_2'[0] > 0. \tag{9.39}$$

The first differential equation expresses formally the fact that, if $-E_1(\bar{p})$, the quantity of exports that the home country desires to supply at the current terms of trade $\bar{p}$, is greater (smaller) than the quantity actually supplied, $-\bar{E}_1$, then the latter is increased (decreased). The second differential equation expresses a similar fact for the rest of the world.

The system can be rewritten as

$$-\frac{d\bar{E}_1}{dt} = f_1 [\bar{E}_1 - E_1(\bar{p})], \tag{9.39'}$$

$$-\frac{d\bar{E}_2^*}{dt} = f_2[\bar{E}_2^* - E_2^*(\bar{p})] \ . \tag{9.39'}$$

Let us now linearize the system at the equilibrium point. The linearization of f_1 and f_2 is straightforward; choosing the units of quantity in both countries we can put $f_1'[0] = f_2'[0] = 1$. The linearization of the arguments of f_1 and of f_2 requires some manipulations $\star$, after which we obtain

$$-\frac{d\bar{E}_1}{dt} = (1+\epsilon)[\bar{E}_1 - E_1(p^e)] - p^e\epsilon[\bar{E}_2^* - E_2^*(p^e)] \ ,$$

$$-\frac{d\bar{E}_2^*}{dt} = -\frac{\epsilon^*}{p^e}[\bar{E}_1 - E_1(p^e)] + (1+\epsilon^*)[\bar{E}_2^* - E_2^*(p^e)] \ , \tag{9.40}$$

$\star$ Linearizing $\bar{E}_1 - E_1(\bar{p})$ we have

$$\bar{E}_1 - E_1(\bar{p}) = \bar{E}_1 - \frac{dE_1}{dp}(\bar{p} - p^e) - E_1(p^e) \ . \tag{1}$$

Now we must recall from the static system the budget restraint $\bar{E}_1 + \bar{p}\bar{E}_2 = 0$ (the sum of the values of the excess demands must be zero) and, since $\bar{E}_2 = -\bar{E}_2^*$ (the imports of the home country are the exports of the rest of the world), we have $\bar{E}_1 = \bar{p}\bar{E}_2^*$. Linearizing this relation we obtain

$$\bar{E}_1 - E_1(p^e) = p^e[\bar{E}_2^* - E_2^*(p^e)] + E_2^*(p^e)(\bar{p} - p^e) \ ,$$

so that

$$\bar{p} - p^e = \frac{\bar{E}_1 - E_1(p^e)}{E_2^*(p^e)} - \frac{p^e[\bar{E}_2^* - E_2^*(p^e)]}{E_2^*(p^e)} \ . \tag{2}$$

Substituting in (1) and since $E_1(p^e) = p^eE_2^*(p^e)$ (whence $E_2^*(p^e) = E_1(p^e)/p^e$), we obtain

$$\bar{E}_1 - E_1(p^e) = \left(1 - \frac{dE_1}{dp}\frac{p^e}{E_1(p^e)}\right)[\bar{E}_1 - E_1(p^e)] + \frac{dE_1}{dp}\frac{p^e}{E_1(p^e)}p^e[\bar{E}_2^* - E_2^*(p^e)] \ . \tag{3}$$

Defining $\epsilon \equiv -(dE_1/dp)[p^e/E_1(p^e)]$ we have the first equation of system (9.40). For the second equation, linearizing $\bar{E}_2^* - E_2^*(\bar{p})$ we have

$$\bar{E}_2^* - E_2^*(\bar{p}) = \bar{E}_2^* - \frac{dE_2^*}{dp}(\bar{p} - p^e) - E_2^*(p^e) \ . \tag{4}$$

Substituting (2) in (4) and rearranging terms we have

$$\bar{E}_2^* - E_2^*(\bar{p}) = -\frac{dE_2^*}{dp}\frac{p^e}{E_2^*(p^e)}\frac{1}{p^e}[\bar{E}_1 - E_1(p^e)] + \left(1 + \frac{dE_2^*}{dp}\frac{p^e}{E_2^*(p^e)}\right)[\bar{E}_2^* - E_2^*(p^e)] \ . \tag{5}$$

Defining $\epsilon^* \equiv (dE_2/dp)[p^e/E_2^*(p^e)]$ we have the second equation of system (9.40).

where

$$\epsilon \equiv -\frac{dE_1}{dp}\frac{p}{E_1}\,, \qquad \epsilon^* \equiv \frac{dE_2^*}{dp}\frac{p}{E_2^*}$$

are the elasticity of the supply of exports with respect to the terms of trade, respectively, of the home country and of the rest of the world (of course both are computed at the equilibrium point).

The characteristic equation of system (9.40) is

$$\begin{vmatrix} 1+\epsilon+\lambda & -p^e\epsilon \\ -\epsilon^*/p^e & 1+\epsilon^*+\lambda \end{vmatrix} = \lambda^2 + (2+\epsilon+\epsilon^*)\lambda + 1 + \epsilon + \epsilon^* = 0\,, \qquad (9.41)$$

whose roots are

$$\lambda_1 = -1\,, \qquad \lambda_2 = -(1+\epsilon+\epsilon^*)\,.$$

Thus the movement is monotonic, and it will converge if, and only if,

$$1+\epsilon+\epsilon^* > 0\,. \qquad (9.42)$$

We can now use the relations holding between the ϵ, ϵ^* elasticities and the elasticities of the offer curves *. These relations are

$$\epsilon = \frac{e}{1-e}\,, \qquad \epsilon^* = \frac{e^*}{1-e^*}\,, \qquad (9.43)$$

where

$$e \equiv \frac{dG_1}{dE_2}\frac{E_2}{G_1}\,, \qquad e^* \equiv \frac{dG_2}{dE_1^*}\frac{E_1^*}{G_2}\,.$$

Using (9.43), inequality (9.42) can be rewritten as

$$\frac{1-ee^*}{(1-e)(1-e^*)} > 0\,. \qquad (9.42')$$

Now, from fig. 9.2 it can be seen that e and e^* are both positive, and — using

* See Kemp (1964, p. 303).

the well-known graphical measure of the elasticity of a curve at a point – that both are smaller than unity. It follows that, if the offer curves have the shape represented in fig. 9.2, the equilibrium point is dynamically stable according to the behaviour assumption under consideration. Of course, if the curves have other shapes, condition (9.42′) need not be satisfied any more, so that equilibrium may be unstable.

Behaviour assumption II

Consider any point P different from the equilibrium point. Each country adjusts its supply of exports towards that quantity of exports which it would offer if the actual quantity of imports (corresponding to point P) remained fixed for all the time needed to complete the adjustment. In other words, each country moves towards the point on the respective offer curve corresponding to the prevailing quantity of the country's imports. With reference to fig. 9.3, assume that the initial non-equilibrium point is P. Now, $-\bar{E}_2^*(0)$ is the initial quantity of imports of the home country and $-\bar{E}_1(0)$ is the initial quantity of imports of the rest of the world. The quantity of exports that the home country desires to offer in exchange for the actual quantity of imports is $-E_1(0)$; consequently, the home country adjusts its exports from the actual quantity $-\bar{E}_1(0)$ towards the desired quantity $-E_1(0)$. Similarly, it can be seen that the rest of the world adjusts its exports from the actual quantity $-\bar{E}_2^*(0)$ towards the desired quantity $-E_2^*(0)$. Thus point P tends to move in a direction included between the two arrows. To reach definite conclusions about the stability of the equilibrium point, however, we need as before an

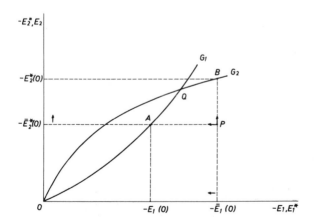

Fig. 9.3.

explicit formal system of dynamic equations. This system is

$$\frac{d(-\bar{E}_1)}{dt} = g_1[G_1(\bar{E}_2) - (-\bar{E}_1)], \qquad \mathrm{sgn}\,g_1[...] = \mathrm{sgn}\,[...],$$

$$g_1[0] = 0, \qquad g_1'[0] > 0, \qquad\qquad (9.44)$$

$$\frac{d(-\bar{E}_2^*)}{dt} = g_2[G_2(\bar{E}_1^*) - (-\bar{E}_2^*)], \qquad \mathrm{sgn}\,g_2[...] = \mathrm{sgn}\,[...],$$

$$g_2[0] = 0, \qquad g_2'[0] > 0.$$

The first equation expresses formally the fact that, if $G_1(\bar{E}_2)$ — that is, the quantity of exports that the home country is willing to supply, given its offer curve, in exchange for the quantity $-\bar{E}_2^* = \bar{E}_2$ of imports — is greater (smaller) than $-\bar{E}_1$, the actual quantity of exports, then the latter is increased (decreased). The second equation expresses a similar fact for the rest of the world. Thus system (9.44) reflects formally the behaviour assumption under consideration.

Choosing the units of quantity so that $g_1'[0] = g_2'[0] = 1$, the linearized form of system (9.44) turns out to be, after some manipulations ★,

$$-\frac{d\bar{E}_1}{dt} = [\bar{E}_1 - E_1(p^e)] + p^e e[\bar{E}_2^* - E_2^*(p^e)],$$

$$\qquad\qquad (9.44')$$

$$-\frac{d\bar{E}_2^*}{dt} = \frac{e^*}{p^e}[\bar{E}_1 - E_1(p^e)] + [\bar{E}_2^* - E_2^*(p^e)].$$

★ Linearizing $G_1(\bar{E}_2) + \bar{E}_1$ we have

$$G_1(\bar{E}_2) + \bar{E}_1 = \frac{dG_1}{dE_2}[\bar{E}_2 - E_2(p^e)] + G_1^e + \bar{E}_1. \qquad (1)$$

Since $E_1(p^e) + p^e E_2(p^e) = 0$ owing to the budget restraint, and $G_1^e = -E_1(p^e)$ by definition, we have

$$G_1(\bar{E}_2) + \bar{E}_1 = \bar{E}_1 - E_1(p^e) + \frac{dG_1}{dE_2}\frac{E_2(p^e)}{-E_1(p^e)}p^e[\bar{E}_2 - E_2(p^e)]. \qquad (2)$$

Now, $\bar{E}_2 = -\bar{E}_2^*$ (the imports of the home country are the exports of the rest of the world) and $E_2(p^e) = -E_2^*(p^e)$ by definition of the equilibrium point, so that $\bar{E}_2 - E_2(p^e) = -[\bar{E}_2^* - E_2^*(p^e)]$. Substituting in (2) and defining $e \equiv (dG_1/dE_2)$ $\times [E_2(p^e)/E_1(p^e)]$ we obtain the first equation of system (9.44'). For the second equation, linearizing $G_2(\bar{E}_1^*) + \bar{E}_2^*$ we have

The characteristic equation is

$$\begin{vmatrix} 1+\lambda & p^e e \\ e^*/p^e & 1+\lambda \end{vmatrix} = \lambda^2 + 2\lambda + 1 - ee^* = 0 , \tag{9.45}$$

whose roots are

$$\lambda_1, \lambda_2 = -1 \pm (ee^*)^{\frac{1}{2}} .$$

Thus we have two cases: (1) if one of the quantities e, e^* is negative while the other is positive, the roots are complex, and their real part is negative, so that equilibrium is stable; (2) if e, e^* have the same sign, then the roots are real, and in order that both are negative, we must have $ee^* < 1$. Thus the necessary and sufficient stability condition is now

$$ee^* < 1 . \tag{9.46}$$

In the case of fig. 9.3 both elasticities are positive and smaller than unity, so that the equilibrium point is stable and the approach to it is monotonic.

Thus we have seen that the equilibrium point Q is stable according to both behaviour assumptions. But this has occurred because we have assumed that the offer curves have the so called 'normal' form, i.e. that they are both monotonically increasing and each one concave with respect to its import axis. As a general remark, when the functions are 'well-behaved', different behaviour assumptions usually give the same results, as we have seen in other contexts (e.g., Part II, ch. 3, §1). But other shapes of the offer curves are admissible, so that cases may arise in which equilibrium is unstable according to both behaviour assumptions as well as cases in which equilibrium is stable accord-

$$G_2(\bar{E}_1^*) + \bar{E}_2^* = \frac{dG_2}{dE_1^*} [\bar{E}_1^* - E_1^*(p^e)] + G_2^e + \bar{E}_2^* . \tag{3}$$

Since $E_1^*(p^e) + p^e E_2^*(p^e) = 0$ because of the budget restraint, and $G_2^e = -E_2^*(p^e)$ by definition, we have

$$G_2(\bar{E}_1^*) + \bar{E}_2^* = \frac{dG_2}{dE_1^*} \frac{E_1^*(p^e)}{-E_2^*(p^e)} \frac{1}{p^e} [\bar{E}_1^* - E_1^*(p^e)] + \bar{E}_2^* - E_2^*(p^e) . \tag{4}$$

Now $\bar{E}_1^* - E_1^*(p^e) = -[\bar{E}_1 - E_1(p^e)]$; substituting in (4) and defining $e^* \equiv (dG_2/dE_1^*)$ $\times [E_1^*(p^e)/E_2^*(p^e)]$, we obtain the second equation of system (9.44').

ing to one assumption and unstable according to the other (for some examples, see Kemp, 1964, pp. 68–9).

Exercises

1. At the equilibrium point, the quantities exchanged are 100 of good 1 and 100 of good 2, and the linearized form of the offer curves is $-E_1 = 76 + 0.24 E_2$; $-E_2^* = -50 + 1.5 E_1^*$. Examine the stability of the equilibrium point according to behaviour assumption II.

Calculation. Computing the elasticities, we have $e = 0.24 E_2/-E_1 = 0.24$ (since in the equilibrium point $-E_1 = E_2 = 100$) and $e^* = 1.5 E_1^*/-E_2^* = 1.5$. The relative price (terms of trade) is 1. With the given numerical values the characteristic equation of the dynamic system corresponding to behaviour assumption II becomes

$$\lambda^2 + 2\lambda + 0.64 = 0 ,$$

which gives $\lambda_1, \lambda_2 = -1.6, -0.4$. The equilibrium point is stable.

2. Same data as in the previous exercise, but use the first behaviour assumption.

§4. A digression on 'arrow diagrams'

We have inserted here this digression because the first economist to use 'arrow diagrams' (we call them so for lack of a better name) to study stability problems was, as far as we know, A. Marshall in his work on the offer curves examined (in modern terms) in the previous section. We stated there that such arrows, *by themselves alone*, cannot be used to study the *dynamic stability* of the equilibrium point, since they cannot tell us whether the initial point actually converges, and with which path, to the equilibrium point. Here we call generically y_1, y_2 the two variables that appear on the axes.

Now, the precise 'trajectory' of the initial non-equilibrium point can be drawn only *after* having formalized the problem by means of a system of functional equations, whose solution yields the time path of each variable. Knowing these time paths, we can draw the 'trajectory' of the system as a whole; this trajectory is actually a curve expressed in parametric form *. The

---

* That is, a 'phase path'. See Appendix III, §5.2. The trajectory can also be obtained

parametric equations of such a curve are

$$y_1 = y_1(t), \qquad y_2 = y_2(t),$$

where the functions $y_1(t), y_2(t)$ are given by the solution of the system of functional equations. In fig. 9.4 we have drawn schematically the equilibrium point E and the initial point P (from the economic point of view, the system under examination can be any model involving only two variables to be expressed as functions of time). In the second and fourth quadrants we have

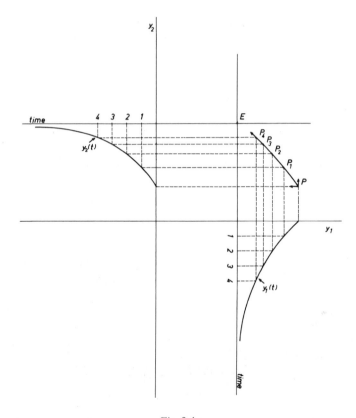

Fig. 9.4.

without knowing the functions $y_1(t), y_2(t)$, but finding the 'integral curves' of the system (Appendix III, §5.2). In any case, however, the differential equations governing the motion of the system must be explicitly written and formally analysed.

drawn the functions $y_1(t)$, $y_2(t)$ (obtained as the solution of a functional system), which as an example we have assumed both monotonic and convergent. Given the unit of time, we can find, by means of the self-explaining graphical procedure depicted in the diagram, the successive points $P_1, P_2, P_3, ...$, and so build, with the desired degree of approximation, the trajectory of point P, which, of course, will be monotonic and convergent. Using the arrows alone we could not draw this trajectory. Even if the arrows both 'point' towards equilibrium, we cannot be sure that the equilibrium point is stable.

The main purpose of this digression is to warn the student against using arrow diagrams *alone* to analyse a stability problem. Such diagrams can at most be used to obtain a first idea of the situation, but to obtain rigorous results the problem must always be analysed by means of functional equations: if not, wrong conclusions are highly likely to be drawn, especially in non-'normal' cases ★. Of course, it is perfectly legitimate to use such diagrams *after* the problem has been formally solved: then they are a useful expository device and very helpful in expounding the results in an intuitive manner for the benefit of the non-mathematical reader ★★.

§5. Flexible exchange rates and the level of national income (Laursen and Metzler)

Before 1950, the interactions between the two basic mechanisms on which

---

★ Even Marshall, who believed that arrow diagrams were not only a perfect substitute for differential equations, but actually a better tool – see *The Pure Theory of Foreign Trade*, p. 19, note 1, and p. 25, note 1, and *Money, Credit and Commerce*, p. 341, note 1 – was led by them to make some wrong statements. Thus from his Proposition XII (*The Pure Theory*, ..., p. 21) it follows that an intersection of the offer curves, such that in it one curve is negatively sloped while the other is positively sloped, determines a stable equilibrium point. Now, this is true according to behaviour assumption II (see the previous section) but is not always true according to behaviour assumption I. It can easily be seen from (9.42') of the previous section that, if one elasticitity is negative (negatively sloped offer curve), the equilibrium point will be unstable if the other elasticity, although positive, is greater than 1 (e.g., the offer curve is increasing, but convex and not concave – with respect to its import axis – in the neighbourhood of the equilibrium point).

★★ The first modern writer to have used arrow diagrams again seems to be Metzler (1951) (in Wealth, Saving and the Rate of Interest). They have been popularized in international monetary economics by Mundell (1960) (see The Monetary Dynamics ... , and the other papers reprinted in Mundell (1968), *International Economics*). Both authors of course rely on mathematical appendixes to prove the results concerning stability rigorously.

the balance of payments * adjustment is based, i.e. the 'classical' mechanism working through variations in relative prices and the 'Keynesian' mechanism working through variations in income (the foreign trade multiplier), had not been formally explored. In that year, different authors had the idea of combining the two hitherto distinct mechanisms in a more general model. Among the various papers which then appeared on the subject, we have selected for exposition here that by Laursen and Metzler (1950) **, which, we think, is a 'classic' on this topic.

The two authors wanted to insert the flexibility of the exchange rate into a macroeconomic model of the Keynesian type, not to analyse the adjustment of the balance of payments *per se*, but rather to prove the falsity of the (then) widely held belief that a system of flexible exchange rates would be capable of 'insulating' a country from changes in other countries' national incomes. The analysis in which we are interested here is an 'intermediate product' of their work, since it is a necessary step for what they wanted to prove. While referring to Appendix I, §7.2, for the exposition of that aspect of Laursen's and Metzler's work, we shall expound here the basic model and the dynamics of the adjustment.

Let Y be national money income; assuming that the prices of domestic goods and services are constant (we can then, without loss of generality, put the price level equal to 1), variations in Y measure variations in the physical output of goods and services ‡. The subscripts 1 and 2 refer to country 1 (e.g., the home country) and to country 2 (e.g., the rest of the world), in a two-country world.

Imports M are measured in local currency (i.e. the currency of the importing country), and are assumed to depend on national income and on the relative price of imports with respect to home goods; given the assumption that in each country the price level of home goods is constant, this relative price is measured by the exchange rate. The exchange rate π is defined as the number of units of the currency of country 2 for one unit of the currency of country 1; of course, from the point of view of the other country the exchange rate is $1/\pi$. Now, an increase in national income has a positive effect on imports, whereas the effect of a variation in the exchange rate is uncertain,

---

* It must be noted that the balance of payments considered here is only the balance concerning the exports and imports of goods and services.

** Two other papers published in the same year on the same subject, are Harberger's (1950) and Stolper's (1950). However, the first has no dynamics, and the second (based on difference equations) contains a less sophisticated analysis than Laursen's and Metzler's.

‡ From now on, by 'goods' we shall mean both goods and services.

since it depends on the elasticity of the demand for imports (remember that we are dealing not with physical quantities, but with expenditure on imported goods).

For brevity, aggregate national expenditure (consumption plus investment) is indicated as ω. The marginal propensity to spend (the marginal propensity to consume plus the marginal propensity to invest) is, of course, positive. *Another variable which influences ω is the relative price π of imports.* This is an important point and must be discussed further.

Total expenditure ω includes both expenditure on domestic and on foreign goods. Now, if we did not take account of π as an argument on which ω depends, we would implicitly assume that when the price of imports changes, the consequent change in the expenditure on imports [*] is exactly offset by a change of equal absolute amount, and in the opposite direction, in the expenditure on domestic goods, so that the total expenditure ω remains the same. This sounds rather unrealistic, so that an effect of π on ω must be introduced. It remains to determine the nature of this effect. Let us consider a fall in the relative price of imports. Since the prices of domestic goods have been assumed constant, this fall means a fall in the absolute price of imports. This, of course, increases the real income corresponding to any given level of money income. Now, the short-run consumption function is non-proportional, so that the average propensity to consume decreases as real income increases, and vice versa. From this it follows that "as import prices fall and the real income corresponding to a given money income increases, the amount spent on goods and services out of a given money income will fall. The argument is applicable in reverse, of course, to a rise of import prices. In short, our basic premise is that, other things being the same, the expenditure schedule of any given country rises when import prices rise and falls when import prices fall" (Laursen and Metzler, 1950, p. 286) [**].

We can express formally all this as follows:

$$\omega_1 = \omega_1(Y_1,\pi), \qquad 0 < \frac{\partial \omega_1}{\partial Y_1} < 1, \qquad \frac{\partial \omega_1}{\partial \pi} > 0,$$

$$\omega_2 = \omega_2\left(Y_2,\frac{1}{\pi}\right), \qquad 0 < \frac{\partial \omega_2}{\partial Y_2} < 1, \qquad \frac{\partial \omega_2}{\partial (1/\pi)} > 0,$$

[*] We neglect the exceptional case in which the demand for imports has a unit elasticity.
[**] This conclusion has been disputed by White (1954). See also the authors' Reply.

$$M_1 = M_1(Y_1, \pi), \qquad 0 < \frac{\partial M_1}{\partial Y_1} < 1, \qquad \frac{\partial M_1}{\partial \pi} \; ?$$

$$M_2 = M_2 \left(Y_2, \frac{1}{\pi} \right), \qquad 0 < \frac{\partial M_2}{\partial Y_2} < 1, \qquad \frac{\partial M_2}{\partial (1/\pi)} \; ?$$

The (static) model is:

$$Y_1 = \omega_1(Y_1, \pi) + \pi M_2 \left(Y_2, \frac{1}{\pi} \right) - M_1(Y_1, \pi), \qquad (9.47)$$

$$Y_2 = \omega_2 \left(Y_2, \frac{1}{\pi} \right) + \frac{1}{\pi} M_1(Y_1, \pi) - M_2 \left(Y_2, \frac{1}{\pi} \right), \qquad (9.48)$$

$$B_2 = \frac{1}{\pi} M_1(Y_1, \pi) - M_2 \left(Y_2, \frac{1}{\pi} \right). \qquad (9.49)$$

The first and second equations express the national income determination in the two countries (recall that exports of country 1 are the imports of country 2 and vice versa; exports must be multiplied by the exchange rate to convert them into local currency). The third equation defines the balance of payments of country 2, expressed in country 2's currency; there is no need of a separate equation for the balance of payments of country 1, since in our two-country world the balance of payments of country 1 equals minus the balance of payments of country 2 multiplied by π.

The above model is indeterminate, since there are three equations and four unknowns (Y_1, Y_2, π, B_2). Thus we can use the degree of freedom to impose the condition that the balance of payments is in equilibrium, i.e. $B_2 = 0$, so that we have

$$Y_1 = \omega_1(Y_1, \pi), \qquad (9.47')$$

$$Y_2 = \omega_2 \left(Y_2, \frac{1}{\pi} \right), \qquad (9.48')$$

$$\frac{1}{\pi} M_1(Y_1, \pi) - M_2 \left(Y_2, \frac{1}{\pi} \right) = 0, \qquad (9.49')$$

which determine the equilibrium point Y_1^e, Y_2^e, π^e.

Let us now consider the adjustment process. The behaviour assumptions are the following:

(1) The level of national income (output) varies in relation to excess demand, and, more precisely, it tends to increase if aggregate demand exceeds aggregate supply (i.e. the level of current output), and to decrease in the opposite case. This behaviour assumption is commonly considered valid in the context of a model with rigid prices and less than full employment. It must be noted that, since we are examining disequilibrium situations, the excess demands must be computed using (9.47) and (9.48), and not (9.47'), (9.48'), which refer only to the equilibrium situation. Thus excess demand in country 1 is

$$[\omega_1(Y_1, \pi) + \pi M_2 \left(Y_2, \frac{1}{\pi} \right) - M_1(Y_1, \pi)] - Y_1$$

and similarly for country 2.

(2) The rate of exchange, which is the price of the foreign currency, tends to increase (decrease) if in the foreign exchange market there is a positive (negative) excess demand for the foreign currency. This is an extension to the foreign exchange market (where the 'good' exchanged is the foreign currency) of the Walrasian behaviour assumption that we have examined in Part II, ch. 3, §1. We assume that the 'dominant' currency, which is used in international transactions, is the currency of country 2. Thus the relevant price is π; the demand for such currency emanates from the import demand of country 1 and so is $(1/\pi)M_1$, the supply emanates from exports revenue and so is M_2.

Such assumptions can be formally expressed by the following system of differential equations:

$$\frac{dY_1}{dt} = k_1 \left[\omega_1(Y_1, \pi) + \pi M_2 \left(Y_2, \frac{1}{\pi} \right) - M_1(Y_1, \pi) - Y_1 \right],$$

$$\frac{dY_2}{dt} = k_2 \left[\omega_2 \left(Y_2, \frac{1}{\pi} \right) + \frac{1}{\pi} M_1(Y_1, \pi) - M_2 \left(Y_2, \frac{1}{\pi} \right) - Y_2 \right], \quad (9.50)$$

$$\frac{d\pi}{dt} = k_3 \left[\frac{1}{\pi} M_1(Y_1, \pi) - M_2 \left(Y_2, \frac{1}{\pi} \right) \right],$$

where k_1, k_2, k_3 are positive constants. We shall now perform a linear approximation at the equilibrium point; for simplicity of notation we put

$$w_1 \equiv \frac{\partial \omega_1}{\partial Y_1}, \qquad w_2 \equiv \frac{\partial \omega_2}{\partial Y_2}, \qquad m_1 \equiv \frac{\partial M_1}{\partial Y_1}, \qquad m_2 \equiv \frac{\partial M_2}{\partial Y_2},$$

$$s_1 \equiv \frac{\partial \omega_1}{\partial \pi}, \qquad s_2 \equiv \frac{\partial \omega_2}{\partial (1/\pi)}.$$

We also note that at the equilibrium point the following relation holds:

$$M_1 - \frac{\partial M_1}{\partial \pi} - \frac{\partial M_2}{\partial (1/\pi)} = M_1(\eta_1 + \eta_2 - 1), \tag{9.51}$$

where η_1, η_2 are the price elasticities of the import demands of the two countries. In fact, let x_1 and x_2 denote the physical quantities of imports; we then have $M_1 = \pi x_1$ and

$$\frac{\partial M_1}{\partial \pi} = x_1 + \pi \frac{\partial x_1}{\partial \pi} = x_1 \left(1 + \frac{\pi}{x_1} \frac{\partial x_1}{\partial \pi}\right) = x_1(1 - \eta_1)$$

where by definition

$$\eta_1 \equiv -\frac{\pi}{x_1} \frac{\partial x_1}{\partial \pi}$$

(remember that the price level in each country is 1 by assumption). Similarly we obtain

$$\frac{\partial M_2}{\partial (1/\pi)} = x_2(1 - \eta_2).$$

Now, choosing the units of measurement in such a way that *at the equilibrium point* the exchange rate is equal to 1, we have $M_1 = x_1, M_2 = x_2$ and, given (9.49'), $M_1 = M_2$. From all this eq. (9.51) follows.

When we take account of (9.51) and of the notation stated above, the linearized form of system (9.50) turns out to be

$$\frac{d\bar{Y}_1}{dt} = k_1(w_1 - m_1 - 1)\bar{Y}_1 + k_1 m_2 \bar{Y}_2 + k_1[s_1 + M_1(\eta_1 + \eta_2 - 1)]\bar{\pi},$$

$$\tag{9.52}$$

$$\frac{d\bar{Y}_2}{dt} = k_2 m_1 \bar{Y}_1 + k_2(w_2 - m_2 - 1)\bar{Y}_2 - k_2[s_2 + M_1(\eta_1 + \eta_2 - 1)]\bar{\pi},$$

$$\frac{d\bar{\pi}}{dt} = k_3 m_1 \bar{Y}_1 - k_3 m_2 \bar{Y}_2 - k_3 M_1 (\eta_1 + \eta_2 - 1)\bar{\pi} , \qquad (9.52)$$

where barred symbols denote deviations from equilibrium ($\bar{Y}_1 = Y_1 - Y_1^e$, etc.). The characteristic equation of system (9.52) is

$$\begin{vmatrix} k_1(w_1 - m_1 - 1) - \lambda & k_1 m_2 & k_1[s_1 + M_1(\eta_1 + \eta_2 - 1)] \\ k_2 m_1 & k_2(w_2 - m_2 - 1) - \lambda & -k_2[s_2 + M_1(\eta_1 + \eta_2 - 1)] \\ k_3 m_1 & -k_3 m_2 & -k_3 M_1(\eta_1 + \eta_2 - 1) - \lambda \end{vmatrix} = 0 ,$$

that is, expanding the determinant,

$$\lambda^3 + c_1 \lambda^2 + c_2 \lambda + c_3 = 0 , \qquad (9.53)$$

where

$$c_1 \equiv k_1(1 + m_1 - w_1) + k_2(1 + m_2 - w_2) + k_3 M_1(\eta_1 + \eta_2 - 1) ,$$

$$c_2 \equiv M_1(\eta_1 + \eta_2 - 1)[k_2 k_3(1 - w_2) + k_1 k_3(1 - w_1)]$$

$$+ k_1 k_2[m_1(1 - w_2) + (1 - w_1)(1 + m_2 - w_2)] - k_1 k_3 m_1 s_1 - k_2 k_3 m_2 s_2 ,$$

$$c_3 \equiv k_1 k_2 k_3 [(1 - w_1)(1 - w_2)M_1(\eta_1 + \eta_2 - 1) - s_1 m_1(1 - w_2) - s_2 m_2(1 - w_1)] .$$

We can now apply the stability conditions expounded in Part II, ch. 6 (see inequalities (6.11′) there), that are

$$c_1 > 0 , \qquad (9.54a)$$

$$c_3 > 0 , \qquad (9.54b)$$

$$c_1 c_2 - c_3 > 0 , \qquad (9.54c)$$

that is

$$k_1(1 + m_1 - w_1) + k_2(1 + m_2 - w_2) + k_3 M_1(\eta_1 + \eta_2 - 1) > 0 , \qquad (9.55a)$$

$$k_1 k_2 k_3 [(1 - w_1)(1 - w_2)M_1(\eta_1 + \eta_2 - 1) - s_1 m_1(1 - w_2)$$

$$- s_2 m_2(1 - w_1)] > 0 , \qquad (9.55b)$$

$k_1k_3[k_1(1+m_1-w_1)+k_2m_2+k_3M_1(\eta_1+\eta_2-1)]$

$\times[M_1(\eta_1+\eta_2-1)(1-w_1)-m_1s_1]+k_2k_3[k_1m_1+k_2(1+m_2-w_2)$

$+k_3M_1(\eta_1+\eta_2-1)][M_1(\eta_1+\eta_2-1)(1-w_2)-m_2s_2]$

$+k_1k_2[m_1(1-w_2)+(1-w_1)(1+m_2-w_2)][k_1(1+m_1-w_1)$

$+k_2(1+m_2-w_2)+k_3M_1(\eta_1+\eta_2-1)]$

$+k_1k_2k_3[M_1(\eta_1+\eta_2-1)(1-w_1)(1-w_2)]>0.$ (9.55c)

Notwithstanding the formidable aspect of the above inequalities, it is possible to show — taking account of the assumptions made about the various derivatives — that the relevant one is the second one, i.e. if we remember that k_1, k_2, k_3 are positive constants, the inequality

$$(1-w_1)(1-w_2)M_1(\eta_1+\eta_2-1)-s_1m_1(1-w_2)-s_2m_2(1-w_1)>0$$
(9.56)

implies that also (9.55a) and (9.55c) are satisfied. Let us note first of all that, since $1-w_1, 1-w_2, s_1, s_2, m_1, m_2$ are positive, inequality (9.56) implies that $M_1(\eta_1+\eta_2-1)>0$. Therefore, since $k_1, k_2, k_3, 1+m_1-w_1$, $1+m_2-w_2$ are positive, it follows that if (9.56) is satisfied, then (9.55a) is satisfied too.

Moreover, if (9.56) is satisfied, the following inequalities are *a fortiori* satisfied:

$$M_1(\eta_1+\eta_2-1)(1-w_1)-m_1s_1>0,$$
$$M_1(\eta_1+\eta_2-1)(1-w_2)-m_2s_2>0.$$
(9.57)

In fact, write (9.57) as

$$M_1(\eta_1+\eta_2-1)>\frac{m_1s_1}{1-w_1},$$

$$M_1(\eta_1+\eta_2-1)>\frac{m_2s_2}{1-w_2},$$
(9.57′)

and (9.56) as

$$M_1(\eta_1 + \eta_2 - 1) > \frac{m_1 s_1}{1 - w_1} + \frac{m_2 s_2}{1 - w_2}, \tag{9.56'}$$

so that it is apparent that (9.56') implies both inequalities in (9.57'). Taking account of (9.57), of $M_1(\eta_1 + \eta_2 - 1) > 0$ and of the assumptions on the various derivatives, it can easily be checked that all the expressions in square brackets in (9.55c) are positive, so that (9.55b) implies (9.55c) too. This completes the proof that the crucial inequality is (9.55b). In order to have a better idea of its economic implications, let us rewrite it as

$$\eta_1 + \eta_2 > 1 + \frac{1}{M_1} \left(\frac{m_1 s_1}{1 - w_1} + \frac{m_2 s_2}{1 - w_2} \right), \tag{9.56''}$$

and let us compare it with the traditional condition of stability of the balance of payments adjustment mechanism based on exchange rate variations alone, which is the so-called 'Marshall–Lerner' condition [*]:

$$\eta_1 + \eta_2 > 1 . \tag{9.58}$$

We can immediately note that the difference between (9.58) and (9.56'') is due to the coefficients s_1 and s_2. If there were no effect of the exchange rate on aggregate demand, then $s_1 = s_2 = 0$ and the two conditions would be the same. If, on the contrary, we agree with Laursen and Metzler that $s_1 > 0$, $s_2 > 0$, then the stability condition becomes more restrictive, as can easily be seen from the fact that the right-hand side of (9.56'') is greater than 1. The

---

[*] Assuming that M_1 and M_2 are functions only of π and that Y_1, Y_2 are constants (that is, making a partial equilibrium analysis), behaviour assumption (2) of the text gives rise to the differential equation:

$$\frac{d\pi}{dt} = a \left[\frac{1}{\pi} M_1(\pi) - M_2 \left(\frac{1}{\pi} \right) \right], \qquad a > 0 .$$

Linearizing and considering deviations from equilibrium we have, taking account of (9.51) – where now simple and not partial derivatives are involved – and of the fact that π^e has been put equal to 1,

$$\frac{d\bar{\pi}}{dt} = - a M_1(\eta_1 + \eta_2 - 1)\bar{\pi} ,$$

whose solution is $\bar{\pi}(t) = \bar{\pi}(0) \exp\left[-a M_1(\eta_1 + \eta_2 - 1)t \right]$, so that the stability condition is $\eta_1 + \eta_2 - 1 > 0$, which gives (9.58). We could arrive at the same condition by examining

economic reason for this result can be understood intuitively as follows. Suppose that the balance of payments shows a deficit. The exchange rate undergoes a devaluation, and, if there were no other effects than the direct ones on imports and exports, then the stability condition would be (9.58). Let us assume that (9.58) holds, so that these direct effects are favourable. Now, the devaluation increases aggregate demand, which in turn causes an increase in income and so also *imports increase*. This, of course, tends to counteract the favourable effects of the devaluation on the balance of payments, so that for stability the sum of the elasticities has to be greater than it would have to be if there were no such counteracting effects.

We can also observe that the stability condition is, *ceteris paribus*, the more restrictive the greater are s_1 and s_2, that is the greater is the effect, in each country, of the exchange rate on aggregate demand.

It must be noted, finally, that the results expounded here concern only the balance of goods and services, since capital movements are not considered in Laursen's and Metzler's model.

Exercises

1. The following data are given

Country 1	Country 2
$m_1 = 0.30$	$m_2 = 0.20$
$w_1 = 0.90$	$w_2 = 0.95$
$s_1 = 10$	$s_2 = 5$
$\eta_1 = 0.5$	$\eta_2 = 0.6$
$M_1 = 100$	

where the various coefficients are evaluated at the equilibrium point. Assume

the conditions under which a devaluation improves the balance of payments. Let $b_1 = \pi M_2(1/\pi) - M_1(\pi)$ be the balance of payments of country 1, for whom a devaluation means an increase in π. Differentiating we have

$$\frac{db_1}{d\pi} = M_2 - \frac{1}{\pi} \frac{dM_2}{d(1/\pi)} - \frac{dM_1}{d\pi} .$$

Now, assuming that in the initial situation the balance of payments is in equilibrium, putting $\pi^e = 1$ and taking account of (9.51), we have

$$\frac{db_1}{d\pi} = M_1(\eta_1 + \eta_2 - 1) ,$$

so that $db_1/d\pi > 0$ if, and only if, $\eta_1 + \eta_2 - 1 > 0$, which is (9.58) again.

that $k_1 = k_2 = k_3 = 1$ and study the stability of the model.

Calculation. With the given numerical data, the characteristic equation turns out to be

$$\lambda^3 + 10.65 \lambda^2 - 2.46 \lambda - 0.20 = 0.$$

The constant term is negative and this is sufficient to exclude stability. In economic terms, the reason for this instability is due to the fact that the sum of the elasticities, although greater than 1 is not sufficiently high to satisfy the more stringent condition (9.56″), according to which the critical value of the sum of the elasticities is 1.5.

2. Same data as in exercise 1, but for $s_1 = 1, s_2 = 0.5$. Compare the results with those of exercise 1 and comment.

§6. **Full employment and balance of payments equilibrium under fixed exchange rates: the 'assignment problem'.**

One of the most troublesome problems facing an open economy working under a system of fixed exchange rates is to reconcile the full employment target with the balance of payments equilibrium. If, for example, there is an external deficit and expansionary policies are required to reach full employment income, the increase in income causes an increase in imports so that the balance of payments deteriorates still further. On the other hand, if restrictive policies are undertaken for the sake of the balance of payments, they move income still further away from the full employment target. Thus the two targets (full employment and balance of payments equilibrium) seem to be in contrast except in two cases: (1) less than full employment and external surplus (expansionary policies are beneficial for both targets); (2) 'overfull' employment (inflationary pressure) and external deficit (restrictive policies are beneficial for both targets). In the other two main cases ★ (less than full employment and external deficit; overfull employment and external surplus) seemingly contradictory policies are required. A solution to this dilemma was suggested by Mundell (1962) ★★: since fiscal policy and monetary policy have

---

★ We neglect the particular cases in which there is full employment, but not external equilibrium or vice versa. They can be treated similarly to the main cases.

★★ After Mundell's article there has been a proliferation of papers on the subject (with

different impacts on the balance of payments (owing to the fact that the latter influences also the capital movements through the rate of interest), it is in principle possible to find a mix of the two policies such that the two targets are simultaneously reached. Moreover — he suggested — the convergence of the process towards the two objectives requires that monetary policy is manoeuvered in relation to the external situation and fiscal policy in relation to the internal situation. This is what Cooper later called the 'assignment problem' (Mundell called it the 'principle of effective market classification'). A few words of explanation are needed here. If the structural parameters of the economy (propensities, etc., see below) and the consequences of the policy actions were exactly known to the policy maker, he could compute exactly the values of the instruments needed to reach the objectives and have those values obtaining, so that no assignment problem would arise. But, if (1) the policy maker does not know exactly the values of the parameters nor the (quantitative) effects of his actions, so that he has to make for the targets by a more or less trial-and-error process, and/or (2) the different instruments are manoeuvered more or less independently by different agencies (decentralized economic policy), then it is necessary to know according to which 'indexes' or 'guidelines' each instrument should be adjusted in order to lead to the solution, and this is the assignment problem. Conditions (1) and/or (2) seem to prevail in the real world, and this justifies the importance of the assignment problem.

Now, the reason for the suggestion made above is that, for the model to converge, each instrument should be assigned to the target on which it has the greatest relative influence. This can be explained intuitively. It is easy to see that monetary policy has a greater impact than fiscal policy on the balance of payments, since it influences this balance, not only because it causes variations in income and so in imports (this influence is the same as that of fiscal policy), but also because it causes variations in capital movements, as said above. Now consider, for example, the case of less than full employment and external deficit. A restrictive monetary policy can be offset, as to the effect on income, by an expansionary fiscal policy in such a way that there is a net increase in income. And, at least in principle, the magnitude of the said increase can be made such that the consequent increase in imports is *smaller*

extensions to a system of flexible exchange rates). We indicate, in addition to the papers of Cooper (1969), Ott and Ott (1968), Grubel (1968), Willet and Forte (1969), Johnson (1965) cited below, the (partial) survey by Helliwell (1969) and the essays contained in Mundell and Swoboda (1969) (especially Part 4). Further references will be found in such works.

than the improvement in the capital movements balance caused by the restrictive monetary policy. Thus we can obtain an increase in income *and* a reduction in the external deficit [*]. The student may check as an exercise that, reversing the policies (expansionary monetary policy and restrictive fiscal policy), an increase in income can be obtained only at the expense of a worsening in the external balance (and vice versa), so that the process diverges from the point where both objectives are fulfilled.

Let us now put all this in formal terms. The exchange rate and the level of prices, both at home and abroad, are assumed to be rigid, and without loss of generality we can take them both as unity. Foreign repercussions are ignored, i.e. the country under consideration is 'small' with respect to the rest of the world. The equations of the model are the following:

$$C = C(Y,R) , \qquad 0 < \frac{\partial C}{\partial Y} < 1 , \qquad \frac{\partial C}{\partial R} \leqslant 0 , \qquad (9.59)$$

i.e. consumption demand depends positively on income and negatively (or not at all) on the rate of interest;

$$I = I(Y,R) , \qquad 0 < \frac{\partial I}{\partial Y} < 1 , \qquad \frac{\partial I}{\partial R} < 0 , \qquad (9.60)$$

i.e. investment demand depends positively on income and negatively on the rate of interest;

---

[*] It is only fair to say that many objections have been raised to this solution of the policy dilemma. We can group them under three headings: (1) the values that the instruments have to take on might be practically unattainable (Ott and Ott, 1968, pp. 323–5); this critique, as well as (2) below, is directed more to the possibility itself of solving the conflict between the two objectives than to the solution of the assignment problem, whereas objections (3) refer more specifically to the latter; (2) the capital flows induced by a *given* interest rates differential are limited in amount, so that ever-increasing differentials might be required to reach the objectives (Grubel, 1968, pp. 1312–13); (3) increasing interest rates cause an increasing burden for interest payments abroad, and the latter might at a certain point more than offset the gain from increased capital flows. In other words, the capital movement balance, including interest payments, might respond *negatively* to an increase in interest rates at home. In this case, of course, the assignment is *a priori* uncertain (Willet and Forte, 1969, p. 260). Another objection is based on the possible income sensitiveness of capital flows, in the presence of which the 'comparative advantage' of monetary over fiscal policy as to the balance of payments is no longer certain (Johnson, 1965, pp. 552–3).

$$M = M(Y,R) , \qquad 0 < \frac{\partial M}{\partial Y} < 1 , \qquad \frac{\partial M}{\partial R} < 0 , \qquad (9.61)$$

i.e. import demand depends positively on income and negatively on the rate of interest. The reason for assuming a direct influence of the rate of interest on imports is that, if the rate of interest influences aggregate demand as assumed in (9.59) and (9.60), it influences the demand for both home and foreign goods, the latter being included in imports.

$$X = X_0 , \qquad (9.62)$$

i.e. exports are exogeneously given.

$$K = K_0 + K(R) , \qquad \frac{dK}{dR} > 0 , \qquad (9.63)$$

i.e. the balance of short term 'autonomous' (as distinct from 'compensating') capital movements responds positively to the interest rate differential (home minus foreign level of interest rates). Since the foreign interest rate level is assumed exogenously given, we can write K as a function of the home level only.

$$Y = C + I + X - M + G , \qquad (9.64)$$

where G is government expenditure. To simplify the following analysis we assume that (9.64) holds instantaneously as an equilibrium relation, i.e. that the current level of income is always an equilibrium income (which, of course, does not necessarily occur at the full employment level) in the sense that excess demand is never present.

$$B = X - M + K + E_0 , \qquad (9.65)$$

where B is the balance of payments surplus or deficit and E_0 are exogenous elements (as e.g. unilateral transfers).

The variables G and R are the policy variables *. Substituting from the

* To keep the model as simple as possible, we have identified fiscal policy with a variation in government expenditure (taxes have not been considered explicitly) and monetary policy with a variation in 'the' interest rate (actually monetary policy acts primarily on the money supply and this reacts on the interest rate, but we have neglected this mechanism and considered R as if it were a direct policy variable).

first five equations in the remaining two we have

$$C(Y,R) + I(Y,R) + X_0 - M(Y,R) + G - Y = 0 , \qquad (9.66)$$

$$X_0 - M(Y,R) + K_0 + E_0 + K(R) - B = 0 . \qquad (9.67)$$

Eqs. (9.66) and (9.67) — that 'sum up' the model — contain four variables (Y, B, G, R) so that we can use the two degrees of freedom to fix two variables at the desired levels and determine the other two, that is

$$C(Y_F,R) + I(Y_F,R) + X_0 - M(Y_F,R) + G - Y_F = 0 , \qquad (9.66')$$

$$X_0 - M(Y_F,R) + K(R) + K_0 + E_0 = 0 , \qquad (9.67')$$

where Y_F is full employment income and B has been put equal to zero. This is the 'static' policy model of the well-known Tinbergen type; its solution determines the required values of G and R. Let us now examine the dynamic policy problem, that is the assignment problem.

Assignment I
    Government expenditure increases (decreases) of national income falls short of (exceeds) the full employment level. The interest rate increases (decreases) if there is an external deficit (surplus). In formal terms,

$$\frac{dG}{dt} = f_1(Y_F - Y) \qquad \operatorname{sgn} f_1(...) = \operatorname{sgn}(...) , \qquad f_1(0) = 0 , \qquad f_1'(0) > 0 ,$$
$$(9.68)$$
$$\frac{dR}{dt} = f_2(-B) \qquad \operatorname{sgn} f_2(...) = \operatorname{sgn}(...) , \qquad f_2(0) = 0 , \qquad f_2'(0) > 0 .$$

We shall study only local stability, so that we linearize the f's and also their arguments, of course at the equilibrium point. On the first linearization we have

$$\frac{dG}{dt} = v_1(Y_F - Y) ,$$
$$(9.68')$$
$$\frac{dR}{dt} = -v_2 B ,$$

where $v_i \equiv f_i'(0)$. On the second linearization we have $\star$

$$\frac{d\bar{G}}{dt} = -v_1 \frac{1}{1-\delta}\,\bar{G} - v_1 \frac{1}{1-\delta}\,\bar{R}\,,$$

$$\frac{d\bar{R}}{dt} = v_2 \frac{\partial M/\partial Y}{1-\delta}\,\bar{G} + v_2 \frac{(\partial M/\partial Y)\epsilon + (\partial M/\partial R - dK/dR)(1-\delta)}{1-\delta}\,\bar{R}\,,$$

$$(9.68'')$$

where barred symbols denote deviations from equilibrium and

$$\delta \equiv \frac{\partial C}{\partial Y} + \frac{\partial I}{\partial Y} - \frac{\partial M}{\partial Y}\,,$$

$$\epsilon \equiv \frac{\partial C}{\partial R} + \frac{\partial I}{\partial R} - \frac{\partial M}{\partial R}\,.$$

$$(9.69)$$

Before continuing, a few remarks on (9.69) are necessary. With regard to ϵ, it is certainly negative since the effect of the rate of interest on total national expenditure $(\partial C/\partial R + \partial I/\partial R)$ is greater in absolute value than the effect of the rate of interest on that part of total expenditure that falls on foreign goods $(\partial M/\partial R)$. With regard to δ, it is surely positive for the same reason (it can be interpreted as the marginal propensity to spend on home goods by the residents of the home country). It is less certain that it is smaller than unity: it will the more likely be so the more 'open' is the economy, *ceteris paribus* (i.e. the greater $\partial M/\partial Y$ is in relation to $\partial C/\partial Y + \partial I/\partial Y$). Anyway, it can be noted that δ can be smaller than 1 even if $\partial C/\partial Y + \partial I/\partial Y > 1$, whereas if the system is stable in isolation $(\partial C/\partial Y + \partial I/\partial Y < 1)$, then $\delta < 1$ certainly.

The characteristic equation of system (9.68'') is

$$\begin{vmatrix} -v_1\dfrac{1}{1-\delta} - \lambda & -v_1\dfrac{\epsilon}{1-\delta} \\[3mm] v_2\dfrac{\partial M/\partial Y}{1-\delta} & v_2\dfrac{(\partial M/\partial Y)\epsilon + (\partial M/\partial R - dK/dR)(1-\delta)}{1-\delta} - \lambda \end{vmatrix} = 0\,,$$

i.e.

---

* To perform correctly this linearization it must be recalled that (9.64) is assumed to hold instantaneously, whence

$$\bar{Y} = Y - Y_F = \frac{\bar{G} + (\partial C/\partial R + \partial I/\partial R - \partial M/\partial R)\,\bar{R}}{1 - (\partial C/\partial Y + \partial I/\partial Y - \partial M/\partial Y)}\,.$$

$$\lambda^2 + \frac{v_1 - v_2\left[(\partial M/\partial Y)\epsilon + (\partial M/\partial R - dK/dR)(1-\delta)\right]}{1-\delta} \lambda + v_1 v_2 \frac{dK/dR - \partial M/\partial R}{1-\delta}.$$

$$(9.70)$$

In order that the system be stable, the following inequalities must be satisfied

$$\frac{v_1 - v_2\left[(\partial M/\partial Y)\epsilon + (\partial M/\partial R - dK/dR)(1-\delta)\right]}{1-\delta} > 0,$$

$$(9.71)$$

$$v_1 v_2 \frac{dK/dR - \partial M/\partial R}{1-\delta} > 0.$$

Given the signs of the various derivatives, it follows that the system will be stable if, and only if,

$$1 - \delta > 0.$$

$$(9.72)$$

Thus we can conclude that in 'normal' cases, that is when the marginal propensity of residents to spend on home goods is smaller than unity, the assignment under consideration gives rise to a convergent path towards equilibrium.

Assignment II

Government expenditure increases (decreases) if there is an external surplus (deficit), and the rate of interest increases (decreases) if national income exceeds (falls short of) the full employment level. In formal terms,

$$\frac{dG}{dt} = g_1(B), \qquad \text{sgn } g_1(\ldots) = \text{sgn } (\ldots), \qquad g_1(0) = 0, \qquad g_1'(0) > 0,$$

$$(9.73)$$

$$\frac{dR}{dt} = g_2(Y - Y_F), \qquad \text{sgn } g_2(\ldots) = \text{sgn } (\ldots), \qquad g_2(0) = 0, \qquad g_2'(0) > 0,$$

so that, linearizing g_1, g_2 and their arguments at the equilibrium point, we have

$$\frac{d\overline{G}}{dt} = -c_1 \frac{\partial M/\partial Y}{1-\delta} \overline{G} + c_1 \frac{(dK/dR - \partial M/\partial R)(1-\delta) - (\partial M/\partial Y)\epsilon}{1-\delta},$$

$$(9.74)$$

$$\frac{d\overline{R}}{dt} = c_2 \frac{1}{1-\delta} \overline{G} + c_2 \frac{\epsilon}{1-\delta} \overline{R},$$

where $c_i \equiv g_i'(0)$. The characteristic equation of system (9.74) is

$$\begin{vmatrix} -c_1 \dfrac{\partial M/\partial Y}{1-\delta} - \lambda & c_1 \dfrac{(\mathrm{d}K/\mathrm{d}R - \partial M/\partial R)(1-\delta) - (\partial M/\partial Y)\epsilon}{1-\delta} \\[3mm] c_2 \dfrac{1}{1-\delta} & c_2 \dfrac{\epsilon}{1-\delta} - \lambda \end{vmatrix} = 0 ,$$

i.e.

$$\lambda^2 + \frac{c_1 \partial M/\partial Y - c_2 \epsilon}{1-\delta} \lambda + c_1 c_2 \frac{\partial M/\partial R - \mathrm{d}K/\mathrm{d}R}{1-\delta} = 0 . \tag{9.75}$$

The stability conditions are

$$\frac{c_1 \partial M/\partial Y - c_2 \epsilon}{1-\delta} > 0 ,$$

$$c_1 c_2 \frac{\partial M/\partial R - \mathrm{d}K/\mathrm{d}R}{1-\delta} > 0 . \tag{9.76}$$

Now, given the signs of the various derivatives, the first inequality requires that $1 - \delta > 0$, whereas the second inequality requires that $1 - \delta < 0$. Thus the two inequalities *cannot* be satisfied simultaneously and so equilibrium is necessarily unstable *. The conclusion is that the assignment under consideration is wrong and that the correct assignment is the one previously examined.

It would be tempting to draw some conclusions as to real world problems from our simplified model, e.g. that Germany, when it experiences inflationary pressures and balance of payments surplus, should *not* use a tight monetary policy as it has done in the past (such policy causes an increase in capital inflows, which add to the surplus and to internal liquidity, and this runs contrary to the anti-inflationary intentions), but should, instead, use a tight fiscal policy and let interest rates go down (capital inflows decrease, etc.). But the student — as anybody else — *must be warned emphatically* that it is dangerous to derive concrete policy prescriptions from oversimplified models.

---

* It is interesting to note that such instability exists regardless of the magnitude of δ (provided of course that $\delta \neq 1$, which is necessary for the model to make economic sense). Note also that if $1 - \delta < 0$, equilibrium can be made stable putting $c_1 < 0$, $c_2 < 0$. But in the 'normal' case $1 - \delta > 0$, it is not possible to choose the signs of c_1, c_2 in such a way to be sure *a priori* that (9.76) are both satisfied.

Exercises

1. The following data are given:
$\partial C/\partial Y = 0.75$, $\partial I/\partial Y = 0.25$, $\partial M/\partial Y = 0.10$, $dK/dR = 0.675$, $\partial C/\partial R = -0.5$, $\partial I/\partial R = -4.825$, $\partial M/\partial R = -1.5$, $v_1 = v_2 = 1$, $\bar{B}(0) = -0.01$, $\bar{Y}(0) = -0.1$.
Check that equilibrium is stable according to the pairing fiscal policy–internal equilibrium, monetary policy–external equilibrium, and determine the time path of the balance of payments and of national income (both as deviations).

Calculation. Since $\delta = 0.90$, the stability condition is satisfied. With the given numerical data, the characteristic equation becomes

$$\lambda^2 + 16\lambda + 21.75 = 0 \,,$$

which gives

$$\lambda_1, \lambda_2 = \tfrac{1}{2}[-16 \pm (256-87)^{\frac{1}{2}}] = -14.5, \, -1.5 \,.$$

Thus the solution for the time path of the policy variables is

$$\bar{G}(t) = A_1 e^{-14.5t} + A_2 e^{-1.5t} \,,$$

$$\bar{R}(t) = A_1 \frac{4.5}{38.25} e^{-14.5t} - A_2 \frac{8.5}{38.25} e^{-1.5t} \,.$$

We are asked, however, to determine the time path of $\bar{Y}(t)$ and of $\bar{B}(t)$. Since we are considering small deviations from the equilibrium point, $\bar{Y}$ and $\bar{B}$ can be approximated by the total differentials of (9.64) and of (9.65), computed for $Y = Y_F$ and $B = 0$, so that

$$\bar{Y}(t) = \frac{1}{1-\delta} \bar{G}(t) + \frac{\epsilon}{1-\delta} \bar{R}(t) \,,$$

$$\bar{B}(t) = \left(\frac{dK}{dR} - \frac{\partial M}{\partial R} \right) \bar{R}(t) - \frac{\partial M}{\partial Y} \bar{Y}(t)$$

$$= \frac{-\partial M/\partial Y}{1-\delta} \bar{G}(t) + \frac{(1-\delta)(dK/dR - \partial M/\partial R) - (\partial M/\partial Y)\epsilon}{1-\delta} \bar{R}(t) \,,$$

and so

$$\bar{Y}(t) = 10 A_1 e^{-14.5t} + 10 A_2 e^{-1.5t} - 38.25 A_1 \frac{4.5}{38.25} e^{-14.5t}$$

$$+ 38.25 A_2 \frac{8.5}{38.25} e^{-1.5t}$$

$$= 5.5 A_1 e^{-14.5t} + 18.5 A_2 e^{-1.5t} ,$$

$$\bar{B}(t) = - A_1 e^{-14.5t} - A_2 e^{-1.5t} + 6 A_1 \frac{4.5}{38.25} e^{-14.5t} - 6 A_2 \frac{8.5}{38.25} e^{-1.5t}$$

$$\simeq - 0.29412 A_1 e^{-14.5t} - 2.33333 A_2 e^{-1.5t} .$$

Given the initial deviations, we can compute the values of A_1, A_2 by means of the system

$$-0.1 = 5.5 A_1 + 18.5 A_2 ,$$

$$-0.01 = -0.29412 A_1 - 2.33333 A_2 ,$$

which give $A_1 \simeq - 0.05665, A_2 \simeq 0.01142$.

2. Same data as in exercise 1, but for $v_1 = v_2 = 10$.

3. Same data as in exercise 1, but for $dK/dR = 6$.

§7. A two-sector growth model (Shinkai)

After the aggregate growth models of the Harrod, Domar and Solow varieties, economic growth theory has progressed to two-sector growth models [*], that is, models in which two productive sectors are distinguished. One produces capital goods using as inputs capital goods and labour; the other produces consumption goods using capital goods and labour. Consumption goods are produced and consumed in fixed proportions and also capital goods are produced and used in fixed proportions. This means that in effect we can talk of a single homogeneous consumption good and of a single homogeneous capital good; however, the capital good is not homogeneous with the con-

[*] Of course the idea of a two-sector model can be traced back to Marx. See also Robinson (1956).

sumption good because it it were so we would be back in an aggregate model.

The main problem analysed in the context of two-sector models is, as in aggregate models, the existence and stability of a balanced growth path (that is, a path where all magnitudes grow at the same proportionate rate), with capital and labour always fully employed. The answer can be condensed in the 'capital intensity theorem', according to which the balanced growth path is stable if the capital intensity (that is, the capital/labour ratio) is greater in the consumption good sector than in the capital good sector. It must be pointed out that the first published work in which this condition was stated is Shinkai's (1960) paper. We have chosen this model also because it allows us to derive the above-stated theorem in a rather simple manner.

The technological assumptions are the simplest possible ones: in each sector there is only one technique, with fixed and constant technical coefficients. Capital and labour are freely transferable from one sector to the other. Labour is homogeneous and all workers obtain the same real wage rate; they consume all their income, while capitalists save and invest all their income. The labour force grows at a constant proportionate rate. The output of the capital good sector is defined net of the depreciation of the whole capital stock of the economy, so that such output coincides with net investment.

The following symbols will be used:

subscript 1 = capital good sector,
subscript 2 = consumption good sector,

      X_i = output of sector i,
      N_i = labour employed in sector i,
      a_i = capital/labour ratio in sector i,
      b_i = labour input coefficient in sector i,
      W = real wage rate,
      N = total labour force,
      K = total stock of capital,
      n = growth rate of N.

The equilibrium conditions are the following:

$$K = a_1 N_1 + a_2 N_2 , \tag{9.77}$$

$$X_2 = W(N_1 + N_2) , \tag{9.78}$$

$$N = N_1 + N_2 , \tag{9.79}$$

Eq. (9.77) is the condition of full utilization of the capital stock. In fact, since the technical coefficients are constant and given the definition of a_i,

$a_i N_i$ is the quantity of capital utilized in sector i.

Eq. (9.78) is the condition of no excess demand for consumption goods. In fact, given the assumption that workers only consume and that capitalists only save, total consumption demand is $WN_1 + WN_2$.

Finally, eq. (9.79) is the condition of full employment of labour. Given K and N, the system can be solved for N_1, N_2, W (we can reduce X_2 to N_2, since $X_2 = b_2 N_2$). Having determined N_i, we also determine X_i. The dynamics of the model can be analysed taking account of the fact that the output of sector 1 is equal to net investment, so that

$$K' = X_1 . \tag{9.80}$$

Differentiating, with respect to time, eq. (9.77), we have

$$K' = a_1 N_1' + a_2 N_2' , \tag{9.81}$$

and, since, by definition, $b_1 X_1 = N_1$, we have from (9.80) that $K' = mN_1$, where $m \equiv 1/b_1$, so that (9.81) can be rewritten as

$$a_1 N_1' + a_2 N_2' = mN_1 . \tag{9.82}$$

Differentiating, with respect to time, eq. (9.79), we have

$$N' = N_1' + N_2' . \tag{9.83}$$

But $N' = nN$ by assumption, and $nN = n(N_1 + N_2)$ because of (9.79), so that we can rewrite (9.83) as

$$N_1' + N_2' = nN_1 + nN_2 . \tag{9.84}$$

Eqs. (9.82) and (9.84) form a system of two differential equations in the two unknown functions $N_1(t), N_2(t)$ [*]. Substituting $N_1(t) = \alpha_1 e^{\lambda t}$, $N_2(t) = \alpha_2 e^{\lambda t}$

---

[*] Shinkai (1960, p. 109) states that "In order for these equations [his equations (5), which are the same as (9.82) and (9.84) here] to have solutions, the determinant $\begin{vmatrix} a_1 & a_2 \\ 1 & 1 \end{vmatrix}$ must not vanish, that is $a \equiv a_1 - a_2 \neq 0$". This statement is not correct. From the mathematical point of view, the system can also be solved if this determinant is zero; the only consequence is that the characteristic equation reduces to a first-degree equation whose only root is n, so that the solution of the system is $N_1(t) = A_1 e^{nt}$, $N_2(t) = [(m - a_1 n)/a_2 n] A_1 e^{nt}$. It is, however, true that if $a_1 - a_2 = 0$, the *static* system (9.77)–

and eliminating $e^{\lambda t}$, we obtain

$$(m - a_1 \lambda)\alpha_1 - a_2 \lambda \alpha_2 = 0 \,,$$

$$(n - \lambda)\alpha_1 + (n - \lambda)\alpha_2 = 0 \,, \tag{9.85}$$

from which we derive the characteristic equation

$$\begin{vmatrix} m - a_1 \lambda & -a_2 \lambda \\ n - \lambda & n - \lambda \end{vmatrix} = a\lambda^2 - (an + m)\lambda + mn = 0 \,, \tag{9.86}$$

where $a \equiv a_1 - a_2$. The roots are $\lambda_1 = n$, $\lambda_2 = 1/ab_1$, and so the solution will be

$$N_1(t) = A_1 \alpha_1^{(1)} e^{nt} + A_2 \alpha_1^{(2)} \exp\left(\frac{1}{ab_1} t\right) \,,$$

$$N_2(t) = A_1 \alpha_2^{(1)} e^{nt} + A_2 \alpha_2^{(2)} \exp\left(\frac{1}{ab_1} t\right) \,, \tag{9.87}$$

or, using Shinkai's notation,

$$N_1(t) = A e^{nt} + B \exp\left(\frac{1}{ab_1} t\right) \,,$$

$$N_2(t) = C e^{nt} + D \exp\left(\frac{1}{ab_1} t\right) \,, \tag{9.87'}$$

where, of course, $C/A = \alpha_2^{(1)}/\alpha_1^{(1)}$, $D/B = \alpha_2^{(2)}/\alpha_1^{(2)}$. Putting $\alpha_1^{(1)} = \alpha_1^{(2)} = 1$, from the first equation of (9.85) we obtain

$$\alpha_2^{(1)} = \frac{m - a_1 n}{a_2 n} = \frac{1 - a_1 b_1 n}{a_2 b_1 n} \,, \qquad \alpha_2^{(2)} = \frac{m - a_1/ab_1}{a_2/ab_1} = -1 \,. \tag{9.88}$$

(9.79) cannot be solved, as Shinkai notes. He also correctly points out that, if $a_1 = a_2$, the model loses most of the characteristics of a two-sector model. In fact, if the capital/labour ratio is the same in both sectors, the capital good and the consumption good can be considered from the production point of view as the same good but for a scale factor. Thus, if we want a true two-sector model, we must assume that $a_1 \neq a_2$.

To determine the values of the arbitrary constants we need to know the initial conditions N_1^0, N_2^0. Instead of assuming known N_1^0, N_2^0, Shinkai gives as known K^0, N^0. From eqs. (9.77) and (9.79) we have

$$a_1 N_1^0 + a_2 N_2^0 = K^0 ,$$

$$N_1^0 + N_2^0 = N^0 ,$$

(9.89)

so that

$$N_1^0 = \frac{K^0 - a_2 N^0}{a} , \qquad N_2^0 = \frac{a_1 N^0 - K^0}{a} .$$

Thus, to determine the arbitrary constants, we have the equations

$$A + B = N_1^0 = \frac{K^0 - a_2 N^0}{a} ,$$

$$\frac{1 - a_1 b_1 n}{a_2 b_1 n} A - B = N_2^0 = \frac{a_1 N^0 - K^0}{a} ,$$

(9.90)

whose solution yields

$$A = \frac{a_2 b_1 n}{1 - a b_1 n} \; N^0 = c N^0 ,$$

$$B = \frac{K^0}{a} - \frac{a_2}{(1 - a b_1 n) a} N^0 = \left(\frac{K^0}{c} - \frac{N^0}{b_1 n} \right) d ,$$

(9.91)

where

$$c \equiv \frac{a_2 b_1 n}{1 - a b_1 n} , \qquad d \equiv \frac{c}{a} .$$

Given the relations between C and A, D and B, we have

$$C = \frac{1 - a_1 b_1 n}{a_2 b_1 n} A = (1 - c) N^0 ,$$

$$D = -B .$$

(9.92)

We can now observe that normally the capital coefficient $(a_1 b_1)$ of sector

1 does not exceed 10 and that the growth rate of labour is not greater than 0.02, so that we may safely assume that

$$1 - a_1 b_1 n > 0 .$$ (9.93)

It follows that c is positive and less than 1, so that both A and C are positive.

Let us consider first the possibility of balanced growth. From (9.91) and (9.92) it follows that, if K^0 is equal to $cN^0/b_1 n$, B and D turn out to be zero. Thus in the solution only the exponential term containing n remains, and this means that N_1, N_2 (as well as X_1, X_2, K_1, K_2, given the assumption of fixed technical coefficients) grow at the same proportionate rate n (the growth rate of the labour force). Next, let us consider the stability of the balanced growth path. It is apparent that, if $a < 0$, then the second exponential in the solution tends to zero as t increases, so that the solution approaches the balanced growth path. On the other hand, if $a > 0$, then the opposite conclusion holds. Since $a \lessgtr 0$ means $a_1 \lessgtr a_2$, it follows that the balanced growth path is stable (unstable) if the consumption good sector is more (less) capital intensive than the capital good sector[*].

It must be noted that the above treatment concerns stability in the absolute sense (i.e. whether the absolute distance of the actual time path from the balanced growth path decreases) and not *relative* stability (i.e. whether the relative distance of the actual time path from the balanced growth path decreases, that is whether the actual proportionate rate of growth approaches the balanced growth rate n: see what we said in the treatment of Leontief's dynamic model). For relative stability it is enough that

$$1/ab_1 < n ,$$ (9.94)

and this does not require that $a < 0$. However, given assumption (9.93), it is easy to see that, if $a > 0$, then inequality (9.94) cannot hold, since it can be rewritten as $1 - ab_1 n < 0$, that is, $1 - a_1 b_1 n < - a_2 b_1 n$, which cannot be

---

[*] It must be noted that the capital intensity theorem remains valid also in more general two-sector models, which allow continuous substitutability between capital and labour and use less extreme assumptions about the saving behaviour of the two classes. In such models, however, the capital intensity condition is only a *sufficient* condition, whereas in Shinkai's (1960) model it is also necessary. Another sufficient condition in some of those more general models is that the sum of the elasticities of substitution in the two sectors is greater than 1. The most important results on two-sector models are summarized in Hahn and Matthews (1964, §I.8) and in Stiglitz and Uzawa (1969, pp. 406–7). See also Morishima (1969, ch. III) and Appendix III here, §7.5.

true if (9.93) is true. Thus we can conclude that the model under consideration does not admit of relative stability, as distinct from stability in the absolute sense: if it is unstable in the absolute sense it cannot be relatively stable
either.

Exercises

1. The following data are given: $n = 0.01, a_1 = 5, a_2 = 7, b_1 = 2, b_2 = 3$.
Determine the time path of the system.

Calculation. The basic differential equations are

$$5 N_1' + 7 N_2' = 0.5 N_1 \ ,$$

$$N_1' + N_2' = 0.01 N_1 + 0.01 N_2 \ ,$$

with the characteristic equation

$$\begin{vmatrix} 5\lambda - 0.5 & 7\lambda \\ \lambda - 0.01 & \lambda - 0.01 \end{vmatrix} = -2\lambda^2 - 0.48\lambda + 0.005 = 0 \ ,$$

which gives $\lambda_1 = 0.01, \lambda_2 = -0.25$. The balanced growth path is stable.

2. With the same data of the previous exercise and given $N^0 = 100, K^0 = 600$,
determine the coefficients A, B, C, D. Determine also the time paths of
X_1, X_2, K_1, K_2.

References

Allen, R.G.D., 1959, *Mathematical Economics*, ch. 11, §§ 11.8, 11.9.
Amano, A., 1968, Stability Conditions in the Pure Theory of International Trade: A
    Rehabilitation of the Marshallian Approach.
Cooper, R.N., 1969, Comment: "The Assignment Problem".
Courant, R., 1937, *Differential and Integral Calculus*, Vol. I, p. 75.
Dernburg, T.F. and Dernburg, J.D., 1969, *Macroeconomic Analysis: An Introduction to
    Comparative Statics and Dynamics*, ch. 15.
Gantmacher, F.R., 1959, *Applications of the Theory of Matrices*, pp. 83, 88.
Grubel, H.G., 1968, International Diversified Portfolios: Welfare Gains and Capital Flows.
Hahn, F.H. and Matthews, R.C.O., 1964, The Theory of Economic Growth: A Survey,
    §I.8.
Harberger, A.C., 1950, Currency Depreciation, Income and the Balance of Trade.

Helliwell, J.F., 1969, Monetary and Fiscal Policies for an Open Economy.

Henderson, J.M. and Quandt, R.E., 1958, *Microeconomic Theory: A Mathematical Approach*, ch. 5, §5.4.

Hicks, J.R., 1946, *Value and Capital*, chs. IV, V and relative Mathematical Appendixes; Additional Note C.

Jaffé, W., 1967, Walras' Theory of *Tâtonnement*: A Critique of Recent Interpretations.

Johnson, H.G., 1965, Some Aspects of the Theory of Economic Policy in a World of Capital Mobility.

Jorgenson, D.W., 1960, A Dual Stability Theorem.

Jorgenson, D.W., 1961, Stability of a Dynamic Input–Output System.

Jorgenson, D.W., 1961, The Structure of Multi-Sector Dynamic Models.

Kemp, M.C., 1964, *The Pure Theory of International Trade*, ch. 5.

Kuenne, R.E., 1963, *The Theory of General Economic Equilibrium*, ch. 8, §4.

Lange, O., 1952, *Price Flexibility and Employment*, Appendix, pp. 91–99.

Laursen, S. and Metzler, L.A., 1950, Flexible Exchange Rates and the Theory of Employment.

Leontief, W., *et al.*, 1953, *Studies in the Structure of the American Economy*, ch. 3.

Marshall, A., 1923, *Money, Credit and Commerce*, Appendix J.

Marshall, A., 1937, *The Pure Theory of Foreign Trade*.

Metzler, L.A., 1945, Stability of Multiple Markets: The Hicks Conditions.

Morishima, M., 1969, *Theory of Economic Growth*, ch. III.

Mundell, R.A., 1962, The Appropriate Use of Monetary and Fiscal Policy for Internal and External Stability.

Mundell, R.A. and Swoboda, A.K., eds., 1969, *Monetary Problems of the International Economy*, Part 4.

Negishi, T., 1962, The Stability of a Competitive Economy: A Survey Article, §§1, 2, 3.

Newman, P.K., 1959, Some Notes on Stability Conditions.

Ott, D.J. and Ott, A.F., 1968, Monetary and Fiscal Policy: Goals and the Choice of Instruments.

Patinkin, D., 1965, *Money, Interest and Prices*, Supplementary Note B.

Quirk, J. and Saposnick, R., 1968, *Introduction to General Equilibrium Theory and Welfare Economics*, ch. 5, §§5.1, 5.2, 5.3, 5.5.

Robinson, J., 1956, *The Accumulation of Capital*.

Samuelson, P.A., 1944, The Relation between Hicksian Stability and True Dynamic Stability.

Samuelson, P.A., 1947, *Foundations of Economic Analysis*, ch. IX, pp. 269–74.

Schwartz, J.T., 1961, *Lectures on the Mathematical Method in Analytical Economics*, p. 24.

Shinkai, Y., 1960, On Equilibrium Growth of Capital and Labor.

Solow, R.M., 1959, Competitive Valuation in a Dynamic Input–Output System.

Stiglitz, J.E. and Uzawa, H., eds., 1969, *Readings in the Modern Theory of Economic Growth*, pp. 406–7.

Stolper, W.F., 1950, The Multiplier, Flexible Exchanges and International Equilibrium.

Turnbull, H.W., 1957, *Theory of Equations*, pp. 114–15.

Walras, L., 1954, *Elements of Pure Economics*, Lesson 12, §§124–30.

White, 1954, The Employment-Insulating Advantages of Flexible Exchange Rates: A Comment on Professors Laursen and Metzler.

Willet, T. and Forte, F., 1969, Interest Rate Policy and External Balance.

APPENDICES

APPENDIX I

Comparative Statics
and the Correspondence Principle

§1. Introduction

Let there be given a situation of static equilibrium, formally described by the solution of a system of static equations in which, in addition to the variables (whose equilibrium values are given by the solution of the system), various parameters also appear, considered as exogenously given.

Comparative statics purposes to examine how the equilibrium values of the variables respond to a change in one or more parameters, that is in which direction they change and establish a new equilibrium to match the new configuration of the parameters.

The traditional example of the demand and supply equilibrium may be useful to clarify such concepts. Let us suppose that in the demand function there is a parameter representing, for example, consumers' tastes: call it α. An increase in α means that consumer tastes have changed in favour of the good in question, i.e. that the demand curve shifts upwards (more is demanded at any given price). The intersection of the demand curve in the new position with the supply curve (which we assume to have remained in the same position) determines the new equilibrium point. We now want to know whether in the new equilibrium the quantity exchanged and the price are greater or smaller than before. That is, how the variable q^e and the variable p^e have reacted to a change in the parameter α? The task of comparative statics is to answer questions of this type.

It must be stressed that comparative statics does not say anything about the time path of the variables from the initial to the final equilibrium point; *nor can it say whether the new equilibrium point will actually be approached.* The answer to these other questions does not pertain to comparative statics but to dynamics, and precisely to that branch of dynamics which deals with the stability of equilibrium. However, as we shall see, there exists a strict connection between comparative statics and dynamics. This connection is expressed by the principle which Samuelson has called the '*correspondence principle*'.

§2. The method of comparative statics

The mathematics of comparative statics consists of two well-known theorems: the implicit function theorem and the chain rule for the differentiation of composite functions.

Let there be given n equations in implicit form, whose solution determines the equilibrium point which we were discussing in the previous section. Of course, such equations will be obtained from economic considerations, which for the moment need not interest us. In the said equations n variables and m ($m \gtreqless n$) parameters appear. In symbols,

$$f^i(x_1, x_2, ..., x_n; \alpha_1, \alpha_2, ..., \alpha_m) = 0 , \quad i = 1, 2, ..., n . \tag{I.1}$$

Given a certain configuration of the parameters, say $(\alpha_1^0, \alpha_2^0, ..., \alpha_m^0)$, the solution of system (I.1) determines the corresponding equilibrium values $(x_1^0, x_2^0, ..., x_n^0)$ of the variables x_i. Since the comparative statics method takes the equilibrium point as given, we assume that this solution exists and is economically meaningful. Now, if the conditions required by the implicit function theorem * are satisfied, we can express the x_i as differentiable functions of the α's in a neighbourhood of the point $(x_1^0, x_2^0, ..., x_n^0; \alpha_1^0, \alpha_2^0, ..., \alpha_m^0)$, i.e.

$$x_i = x_i(\alpha_1, \alpha_2, ..., \alpha_m) , \quad i = 1, 2, ..., n . \tag{I.2}$$

---

* This theorem can be formulated in various ways with different degrees of generality. The version which interest us here is the following. The functions

$$f^i(x_1, x_2, ..., x_n; \alpha_1, \alpha_2, ..., \alpha_m) , \quad i = 1, 2, ..., n ,$$

The problem of comparative statics would seem therefore solved: substituting the new values of the parameters $(\alpha'_1, \alpha'_2, ..., \alpha'_m)$ in (I.2) we can obtain immediately the new equilibrium point $(x'_1, x'_2, ..., x'_n)$ ★. Unfortunately, the fact is that usually we must be content with the knowledge that eqs. (I.2) exist, without being able to express them in terms of known functions. This impossibility may be purely mathematic, in the sense that, given the f^i, it is not always possible to solve for the x_i; but it usually derives from the fact that in economic theory the desire to reach general results, not depending on a particular form of the f^i, leads us *to leave this form unspecified and to make only 'qualitative' assumptions, consisting of the assumptions on the signs of the partial derivatives of the f^i at most.*

These difficulties, however, can be overcome if we are satisfied with qualitative results. In fact, if we succeed in determining the *signs* of the partial derivatives ★★

together with their first-order partial derivatives, are continuous with respect to the $n+m$ variables $(x_1, x_2, ..., x_n; \alpha_1, \alpha_2, ..., \alpha_m)$ in a neighbourhood N of the point $(x^0_1, x^0_2, ..., x^0_n; \alpha^0_1, \alpha^0_2, ..., \alpha^0_m)$, which point satisfies the relations

$$f^i(x^0_1, x^0_2, ..., x^0_n; \alpha^0_1, \alpha^0_2, ..., \alpha^0_m) = 0 , \qquad i = 1, 2, ..., n .$$

Moreover, the value of the Jacobian of the f^i with respect to the x_i is non-zero at the point $(x^0_1, x^0_2, ..., x^0_n; \alpha^0_1, \alpha^0_2, ..., \alpha^0_m)$. If such conditions are satisfied, there exists a set of functions

$$x_i = x_i(\alpha_1, \alpha_2, ..., \alpha_m) , \qquad i = 1, 2, ..., n ,$$

which in a neighbourhood of the point $(x^0_1, x^0_2, ..., x^0_n; \alpha^0_1, \alpha^0_2, ..., \alpha^0_m)$ are single valued, continuous, are the only functions to satisfy the relations

$$f^i(x_1(\alpha_1, \alpha_2, ..., \alpha_m), x_2(\alpha_1, \alpha_2, ..., \alpha_m), ..., x_n(\alpha_1, \alpha_2, ..., \alpha_m); \alpha_1, \alpha_2, ..., \alpha_m) = 0 ,$$

$$i = 1, 2, ..., n ,$$

and have continuous partial derivatives of as many orders as are possessed by the f^i in the neighbourhood N. For the proof of this theorem, see e.g. Hobson (1957, Vol. I, §319), or any advanced calculus textbook. It must be noted that the above is the traditional 'local' implicit function theorem. Recently Gale and Nikaidô (1965) (see also Nikaido, 1968) have proved a global version of this theorem, according to which sufficient conditions for global univalence are that the Jacobian and all its principal minors be everywhere positive.

★ Of course, we could also substitute the new set $(\alpha'_1, \alpha'_2, ..., \alpha'_m)$ directly in (I.1) and solve them again for the x_i. This, however, would not change the difficulties listed in the text.

★★ With the notation $(\ )^0$ we want to specify that the partial derivatives are evaluated at the point $(x^0_1, x^0_2, ..., x^0_n; \alpha^0_1, \alpha^0_2, ..., \alpha^0_m)$. From now on for simplicity we shall drop this notation, it being clear from the context that the various derivatives are evaluated at the said point.

$$\left(\frac{\partial x_i}{\partial \alpha_j}\right)^0 , \qquad \begin{matrix} i = 1, 2, ..., n , \\ \\ j = 1, 2, ..., m , \end{matrix} \qquad (\text{I.3})$$

we have determined the *direction* in which the (new) equilibrium value of the i-th variable lies as a result of a sufficiently small change in the j-th parameter [*], that is, *we know whether at the new equilibrium point the i-th variable has a value which is greater than, smaller than or equal to the value that it had at the initial equilibrium point*, although we cannot say by how much. Such 'ordinal' comparison is the most than we can hope for in 'qualitative' economic theory.

Now, the comparative statics method suggests how to compute the partial derivatives (I.3) [**]. Since (I.2) satisfy (I.1), that is

$$f^i(x_1(\alpha_1, \alpha_2, ..., \alpha_m), x_2(\alpha_1, \alpha_2, ..., \alpha_m),$$

$$..., x_n(\alpha_1, \alpha_2, ..., \alpha_m); \alpha_1, \alpha_2, ..., \alpha_m) = 0 ,$$

$$i = 1, 2, ..., n ,$$

we can compute, by means of the chain rule theorem, the total derivative of each f^i with respect to any parameter α_j, obtaining [‡]

---

[*] If all parameters change simultaneously, we have only to evaluate, instead of the partial differentials $(\partial x_i/\partial \alpha_j) \, d\alpha_j$ (it must be noted that the variations $d\alpha_j$ are known exogenously), the total differentials

$$\frac{\partial x_i}{\partial \alpha_1} \, d\alpha_1 + \frac{\partial x_i}{\partial \alpha_2} \, d\alpha_2 + ... + \frac{\partial x_i}{\partial \alpha_m} \, d\alpha_m ,$$

and similarly if any group of k $(k < m)$ parameters vary simultaneously.

[**] This method is the one 'codified' by Samuelson. Of course earlier applications of the method can be found in the mathematical economics literature: without going back to the last century, we can indicate Slutsky's (1953) famous article and, of course, Hicks' (1939) *Value and Capital*. However, Samuelson was the first to give a systematic account of this method and to point out its general nature. It can also be noted, from the purely mathematical point of view, that the same result − i.e. eqs. (I.5) − could be reached by linearizing the f^i in the equilibrium point, solving explicitly for the x_i in terms of the α_j and computing the partial derivatives of the resulting linear expressions.

[‡] The left-hand side of (I.4) is the total derivative of the i-th function with respect to the j-th parameter; this derivative is evaluated at the point

$$(x_1^0, x_2^0, ..., x_n^0; \alpha_1^0, \alpha_2^0, ..., \alpha_m^0) .$$

Since each f^i is identically zero in a neighbourhood N of this point and so is stationary here, the above total derivative must be zero, from which (I.4) follows.

$$\sum_{s=1}^{n} \frac{\partial f^i}{\partial x_s} \frac{\partial x_s}{\partial \alpha_j} + \frac{\partial f^i}{\partial \alpha_j} = 0 , \qquad i = 1, 2, ..., n , \tag{I.4}$$

that is, shifting $\partial f^i / \partial \alpha_j$ to the right-hand side and writing the equations in extended form:

$$\frac{\partial f^1}{\partial x_1} \frac{\partial x_1}{\partial \alpha_j} + \frac{\partial f^1}{\partial x_2} \frac{\partial x_2}{\partial \alpha_j} + \ldots + \frac{\partial f^1}{\partial x_n} \frac{\partial x_n}{\partial \alpha_j} = - \frac{\partial f^1}{\partial \alpha_j} ,$$

$$\frac{\partial f^2}{\partial x_1} \frac{\partial x_1}{\partial \alpha_j} + \frac{\partial f^2}{\partial x_2} \frac{\partial x_2}{\partial \alpha_j} + \ldots + \frac{\partial f^2}{\partial x_n} \frac{\partial x_n}{\partial \alpha_j} = - \frac{\partial f^2}{\partial \alpha_j} , \tag{I.4'}$$

$$\cdots\cdots\cdots\cdots\cdots\cdots\cdots\cdots\cdots$$

$$\frac{\partial f^n}{\partial x_1} \frac{\partial x_1}{\partial \alpha_j} + \frac{\partial f^n}{\partial x_2} \frac{\partial x_2}{\partial \alpha_j} + \ldots + \frac{\partial f^n}{\partial x_n} \frac{\partial x_n}{\partial \alpha_j} = - \frac{\partial f^n}{\partial \alpha_j} .$$

Eqs. (I.4') are a linear system of n equations in the n unknowns $\partial x_i/\partial \alpha_j$, $i = 1, 2, ..., n$. Solving such a system we have

$$\frac{\partial x_i}{\partial \alpha_j} = \frac{\Delta_i}{\Delta} \tag{I.5}$$

where

$$\Delta \equiv \begin{vmatrix} \dfrac{\partial f^1}{\partial x_1} & \dfrac{\partial f^1}{\partial x_2} & \cdots & \dfrac{\partial f^1}{\partial x_n} \\[2mm] \dfrac{\partial f^2}{\partial x_1} & \dfrac{\partial f^2}{\partial x_2} & \cdots & \dfrac{\partial f^2}{\partial x_n} \\[2mm] \cdots & \cdots & \cdots & \cdots \\[2mm] \dfrac{\partial f^n}{\partial x_1} & \dfrac{\partial f^n}{\partial x_2} & \cdots & \dfrac{\partial f^n}{\partial x_n} \end{vmatrix}$$

is the determinant of the system and Δ_i is the determinant that we obtain substituting in Δ the column of the known terms $- \partial f^k / \partial \alpha_j$ to the column of the coefficients concerning the i-th unknown, which are $\partial f^k / \partial x_i, k = 1, 2, ...$ ..., n. We can immediately note that Δ is the Jacobian of the functions f^i with respect to the x_i, which we have assumed non-vanishing in order that the functions (I.2) exist ★; therefore system (I.4') is always solvable.

★ See pp. 342–3, footnote ★.

We have at this point the problem of determining the sign of Δ and of Δ_j. We have said above that we know only the signs of the $\partial f^k/\partial \alpha_j$ and of the $\partial f^k/\partial x_i$, and it is obvious that such knowledge is not, except for particular cases [*], sufficient to determine the sign of Δ and of Δ_j. However, this difficulty can be (partially) overcome. It is well known that two powerful tools in the economic theorist's tool-kit are *the assumption of maximizing behaviour* and *the assumption that the equilibrium point is dynamically stable*. By means of such assumptions it is usually possible to determine the sign of Δ; sometimes they also help in determining the sign of Δ_j.

Although a book on dynamics, such as this is, need only present the relation between comparative statics and the stability assumption (which is the correspondence principle), the relation between comparative statics and the maximizing assumption is also given, to complete the description of the comparative statics method.

We have said above that in some cases the signs of the relevant determinants can be ascertained knowing only the signs of the partial derivatives which appear in them. Research is in progress to find those special cases where the knowledge of the signs of the elements of a determinant is sufficient to determine the sign of the determinant and an algorithm has been devised for this determination (see Lancaster (1966) [**]). We should like to stress that this algorithm is a method of obtaining in a more efficient way the *same* information (i.e. whether the sign of the determinant is determinate or not) which could be obtained more laboriously by explicit expansion of the determinant (see, however, Basset (1968) for a counterexample, in which the explicit expansion of the determinant allows the determination of its sign, whereas Lancaster's algorithm leaves it indeterminate. This is due to the fact that in economic

---

[*] For example, if a determinant has the following sign pattern

$$
\begin{array}{cccccc}
+ & + & + & + & + & + \\
- & + & + & + & + & + \\
0 & - & + & + & + & + \\
0 & 0 & - & + & + & + \\
0 & 0 & 0 & - & + & + \\
0 & 0 & 0 & 0 & - & +
\end{array} \, ,
$$

then it is clearly positive.

[**] It has been shown by Lloyd (1969) that Lancaster's algorithm is, in fact, just a transformation of Samuelson's early proposals about a purely 'qualitative' calculus (*Foundations*, pp. 23–9). Lloyd also shows that, except for large equation systems, the conventional techniques are preferable.

problems we usually know not only the sign but also the form of the element
— for example, that it is a marginal propensity to spend, etc. — so that in the
expansion some terms may cancel out). The said algorithm cannot, of course,
make sign-determinate a determinant which is not so; therefore, it cannot
substitute the additional information that we obtain from the maximizing
assumption and from the stability assumption.

§3. Comparative statics and maximizing behaviour: an example from traditional demand theory

By 'maximizing' behaviour we mean, of course, not only maximizing but
also minimizing behaviour. The reader is assumed to know the first- and
second-order conditions for a (free or constrained) maximum or minimum
(in case of need, consult Appendix A of Samuelson's (1947) *Foundations* or
a good advanced calculus textbook).

The maximizing behaviour assumption is one of the basic principles of
neoclassical economic theory, in which the principle of 'rational' behaviour
is equivalent to the assumption that the economic agents maximize or minimize something. The best-known examples are, of course, the theory of
consumer's behaviour and the theory of cost and production.

From the formal point of view, let us assume that eqs. (I.1) of the previous
section are the first-order conditions for an extremum (maximum or minimum,
free or constrained). In other words, the f^i are the n first-order partial derivatives of a function F to be maximized or minimized (in the F, and so in the
f^i also, one or more Lagrange multipliers will appear if the extremum is constrained). For the point determined by the solution of (I.1) to be a solution
of the extremum problem and so to establish an equilibrium point, the
second-order conditions ★ must, of course, be satisfied. Now the satisfaction
of the second-order conditions implies, among other things, that the *Hessian*
of the F is non-zero and has a precise sign depending on the number of variables and on the type of extremum. By definition, the Hessian of a function
coincides with the Jacobian of the first-order partial derivatives of the function, so that we can immediately draw two important conclusions. The first
is that, since the Jacobian is different from zero, the essential condition re-

---

★ In the older literature the second-order conditions for an extremum are often called
'stability conditions' (see e.g. Hicks (1939), *Value and Capital*, mathematical appendixes).
They must not be confused with dynamic stability conditions, although they are not
completely unrelated, as we shall see in Appendix I, §5.

quired by the implicit function theorem is satisfied, so that the functions
(I.2) of the previous section exist. The second is that, when the sign of the
said Jacobian is determined, the sign of Δ is automatically determined, since,
as we have seen in the previous section, Δ and the Jacobian are the same. From
this follows the importance, to which Samuelson has called attention, of the
second-order conditions for an extremum, not only to establish whether the
stationary point is a maximum or minimum, but also to have useful information for comparative statics purposes.

As a simple illustration we shall examine the consumer's choice problem.
Let $U = U(x_1, x_2)$ be the (ordinal) utility function of the consumer, which
he is assumed to maximize subject to the budget constraint $R - p_1 x_1 - p_2 x_2$
$= 0$. Let us form the function

$$F = U(x_1, x_2) + \lambda(R - p_1 x_1 - p_2 x_2) ,$$

where λ is a Lagrange multiplier. The first-order conditions for a maximum are

$$\frac{\partial F}{\partial x_1} = \frac{\partial U}{\partial x_1} - \lambda p_1 = 0 ,$$

$$\frac{\partial F}{\partial x_2} = \frac{\partial U}{\partial x_2} - \lambda p_2 = 0 ,$$

$$\frac{\partial F}{\partial \lambda} = R - p_1 x_1 - p_2 x_2 = 0 ,$$

and the second-order conditions are that the following bordered ★ Hessian

$$\begin{vmatrix} \dfrac{\partial^2 U}{\partial x_1^2} & \dfrac{\partial^2 U}{\partial x_1 \partial x_2} & -p_1 \\[2ex] \dfrac{\partial^2 U}{\partial x_1 \partial x_2} & \dfrac{\partial^2 U}{\partial x_2^2} & -p_2 \\[2ex] -p_1 & -p_2 & 0 \end{vmatrix}$$

★ Note that the Hessian is bordered if we start from the Hessian of the utility function, but is a normal Hessian if we consider it as the Hessian of the F function.

be positive. The first-order conditions are a system of three equations in implicit form in the three variables x_1, x_2, λ and in the three parameters $p_1, p_2,$ R, whose solution yields the point of the consumer's equilibrium, provided that the second-order conditions are satisfied. It can easily be checked that the Jacobian of the first-order equations with respect to x_1, x_2, λ is the same as the above-written Hessian. Thus the following functions exist:

$$x_1 = x_1(p_1, p_2, R) ,$$

$$x_2 = x_2(p_1, p_2, R) ,$$

$$\lambda = \lambda(p_1, p_2, R) ,$$

where the first two functions are the consumer's demand functions. We now want to examine, for example, how the quantity demanded of x_1 responds to a change in p_1. Differentiating totally the first-order conditions with respect to p_1 we have

$$\frac{\partial^2 U}{\partial x_1^2} \frac{\partial x_1}{\partial p_1} + \frac{\partial^2 U}{\partial x_1 \partial x_2} \frac{\partial x_2}{\partial p_1} - p_1 \frac{\partial \lambda}{\partial p_1} = \lambda ,$$

$$\frac{\partial^2 U}{\partial x_1 \partial x_2} \frac{\partial x_1}{\partial p_1} + \frac{\partial^2 U}{\partial x_2^2} \frac{\partial x_2}{\partial p_1} - p_2 \frac{\partial \lambda}{\partial p_1} = 0 ,$$

$$- p_1 \frac{\partial x_1}{\partial p_1} - p_2 \frac{\partial x_2}{\partial p_2} = x_1 ,$$

so that

$$\frac{\partial x_1}{\partial p_1} = x_1 \begin{vmatrix} \dfrac{\partial^2 U}{\partial x_1 \partial x_2} & -p_1 \\ \dfrac{\partial^2 U}{\partial x_2^2} & -p_2 \end{vmatrix} \Delta^{-1} + \lambda \frac{-p_2^2}{\Delta}$$

$$= - x_1 \frac{\partial x_1}{\partial R} + \lambda \frac{-p_2^2}{\Delta} , \bigstar$$

where Δ is the determinant of the system, which coincides with the above-written Hessian. Thus we know that $\Delta > 0$. Therefore, if we also take into account the fact that $\lambda > 0$, it follows that the second term in the last expression is negative (substitution effect), whereas the first term (income effect) remains with an uncertain sign.

The above succinct treatment seems sufficient to illustrate the relation between comparative statics and the maximizing behaviour assumption, so we pass on to the treatment of the correspondence principle.

§4. Comparative statics and the dynamic stability of equilibrium: the 'correspondence principle'

The importance of the study of the dynamic stability of equilibrium as such is very great. In fact, an equilibrium point which exists in principle, but which cannot be approached and which (supposing that it has been hit by chance) is such that the slightest disturbance starts a movement away from it — that is, an unstable equilibrium point — is obviously not very relevant from an economic point of view. It turns out that the study of the dynamic stability of equilibrium is often important also in obtaining determinate comparative statics results.

Let the equilibrium point be determined by relations (I.2) of Appendix I, §2. It often happens that in the study of the dynamic stability of this point plausible behaviour assumptions lead to dynamic equations or systems of the type

$$\frac{dx_i}{dt} = k_i f^i(x_1, x_2, ..., x_n),\tag{I.6}$$

where the k_i are positive constants **. It is enough to recall, as an example,

---

* In the last equality the following relation is implicit

$$\frac{\partial x_1}{\partial R} = - \begin{vmatrix} \dfrac{\partial^2 U}{\partial x_1 \partial x_2} & -p_1 \\ \dfrac{\partial^2 U}{\partial x_2^2} & -p_2 \end{vmatrix} \Delta^{-1}.$$

In fact, differentiating with respect to R the first order conditions and solving for $\partial x_1/\partial R$ we obtain the above relation.

** The substance of the following treatment would not be significantly changed if we considered difference equations instead of differential equations. It can also be noted that the right-hand side of eqs. (I.6) can be considered as originating from the linearization at the equilibrium point of the functions $h_i[f^i(...)]$, where the h_i are sign-preserving functions and $h_i'[0] \equiv k_i$.

the study of the stability of Walrasian general equilibrium of exchange (see Part II, ch. 9, §1, of the text), where the equilibrium point is determined by the set of equations $E_i(p_1, p_2, ..., p_m) = 0$ and the *tâtonnement* process can be formalized as $dp_i/dt = k_i E_i$.

Not knowing the form of the functions f^i, we can make a linear approximation at the equilibrium point ★. Considering the deviations from equilibrium, $\bar{x}_i = x_i - x_i^0$, we obtain

$$\frac{d\bar{x}_i}{dt} = k_i \sum_{j=1}^{n} \frac{\partial f^i}{\partial x_j} \bar{x}_j , \qquad i = 1, 2, ..., n , \tag{I.7}$$

where the $\partial f^i/\partial x_j$ are evaluated at the equilibrium point. The characteristic equation of system (I.7) is

$$\begin{vmatrix} k_1 \dfrac{\partial f^1}{\partial x_1} - \lambda & k_1 \dfrac{\partial f^1}{\partial x_2} & \cdots & k_1 \dfrac{\partial f^1}{\partial x_n} \\[2ex] k_2 \dfrac{\partial f^2}{\partial x_1} & k_2 \dfrac{\partial f^2}{\partial x_2} - \lambda & \cdots & k_2 \dfrac{\partial f^2}{\partial x_n} \\[2ex] \cdots & \cdots & \cdots & \cdots \\[2ex] k_n \dfrac{\partial f^n}{\partial x_1} & k_n \dfrac{\partial f^n}{\partial x_2} & \cdots & k_n \dfrac{\partial f^n}{\partial x_n} - \lambda \end{vmatrix} = 0 .$$

Expanding the determinant we obtain an equation of the type

$$(-1)^n \lambda^n + (-1)^{n-1} c_1 \lambda^{n-1} + ... + (-1)^{n-r} c_r \lambda^{n-r} + ... + c_n = 0 , \tag{I.8}$$

where the coefficients c_i are expressed in terms of the elements of the matrix

---

★ This implies that we are studying local stability. What if we study global stability? No linearization is required applying Liapunov's second method (see Appendix II), so that it would seem that we cannot obtain any information from global stability considerations. Of course, this is not true, since if global stability obtains, local stability obtains *a fortiori*.

$$\begin{bmatrix} k_1 \dfrac{\partial f^1}{\partial x_1} & k_1 \dfrac{\partial f^1}{\partial x_2} & \cdots & k_1 \dfrac{\partial f^1}{\partial x_n} \\ k_2 \dfrac{\partial f^2}{\partial x_1} & k_2 \dfrac{\partial f^2}{\partial x_2} & \cdots & k_2 \dfrac{\partial f^2}{\partial x_n} \\ \cdots & & & \\ k_n \dfrac{\partial f^n}{\partial x_1} & k_n \dfrac{\partial f^n}{\partial x_2} & \cdots & k_n \dfrac{\partial f^n}{\partial x_n} \end{bmatrix}$$

and are defined as follows:

c_1 = sum of all principal minors of the first order
c_2 = sum of all principal minors of the second order
. . . .
c_r = sum of all $n!/r!(n-r)!$ principal minors of the r-th order
. . . .
c_n = determinant of the matrix.

Let us note that, from the properties of determinants,

$$c_n = k_1 k_2 \ldots k_n \begin{vmatrix} \dfrac{\partial f^1}{\partial x_1} & \dfrac{\partial f^1}{\partial x_2} & \cdots & \dfrac{\partial f^1}{\partial x_n} \\ \dfrac{\partial f^2}{\partial x_1} & \dfrac{\partial f^2}{\partial x_2} & \cdots & \dfrac{\partial f^2}{\partial x_n} \\ \cdots & & & \\ \dfrac{\partial f^n}{\partial x_1} & \dfrac{\partial f^n}{\partial x_2} & \cdots & \dfrac{\partial f^n}{\partial x_n} \end{vmatrix},$$

that is

$$c_n = k_1 k_2 \ldots k_n \Delta,$$

where Δ is the same determinant which appears in the comparative statics results (see Appendix I, §2).

Let us now examine the stability conditions. We know that a necessary, although not sufficient stability condition, is that $c_n \neq 0$ (this excludes any zero real root) and that all the coefficients $(-1)^n$, $(-1)^{n-1}c_1$, ..., c_n have the same sign (this excludes, by Descartes' theorem, any positive root). Therefore c_n, and consequently Δ (since the k_i are positive constants), must have the sign of $(-1)^n$. Thus, by means of stability considerations, we are able to determine the sign of the determinant which appears in the denominators of the comparative statics results. Moreover, the fact that also the signs of the other coefficients $(c_1, c_2, ..., c_{n-1})$ are determined, may be useful to determine the signs of the Δ_i.

The determination of the sign of Δ (and where possible also of Δ_i) by means of dynamic stability considerations is the essence of the *correspondence principle*.

Of course, this principle is not without limitations, which were pointed out by Patinkin (1952). Cases may occur in which the perfect 'correspondence' between the comparative statics and the dynamic system — perfect in the sense that the comparative statics Δ is the same, apart from the positive multiplicative constants, as the constant term in the characteristic equation of the dynamic system — is not possible. Such cases are all those in which the behaviour assumptions made in the study of dynamic stability do *not* lead to equations of type (I.6) *. However, it often turns out that equations of type (I.6) are indeed appropriate for the study of the dynamic stability of the equilibrium point. Moreover, even when this is not the case, it may be possible to obtain some information about comparative statics from dynamic considerations **. In conclusion, it seems fair to say that the correspondence principle, while not being a panacea, can be a useful tool in many instances.

Let us note that by applying the correspondence principle we kill two birds with one stone, since in addition to obtaining information about comparative statics, we check at the same time that the system will actually approach the new equilibrium point, a result that cannot be derived from comparative statics alone.

As we have shown, the sign of Δ has been determined *assuming* that equilibrium is stable. To this approach the objection could be raised that to *impose* on the model from the outside that the equilibrium point should be stable is not legitimate, or at least not logically satisfactory. We think that this objection is not valid; the answer to it is that, since — as we have said at the beginning of this section — unstable equilibria are not meaningful from

---

* Patinkin illustrates the case in which the dynamic equations for the study of the stability of equilibrium are of the type

$$\frac{dx_i}{dt} = \sum_{j=1}^{n} k_{ij} f^j(x_1, x_2, ..., x_n; \alpha_1, \alpha_2, ..., \alpha_m) , \qquad i = 1, 2, ..., n .$$

However, in this case too it is possible to obtain some information about comparative statics (note (2), p. 42, in Patinkin's (1952) article).

** See the previous footnote.

the economic point of view, we are interested in analysing the comparative statics properties of stable equilibria only. It would be completely useless to know where the new equilibrium point lies if this point cannot be approached. However, if somebody is not satisfied with this, the way out is to drop the stability *assumption*, and to make conditional (or taxonomic) statements of the type "*if* equilibrium is stable (unstable) then the comparative statics results are so and so".

It must be noted, finally, that when different behaviour assumptions are possible *, different stability conditions (and so different comparative statics results) may be obtained.

§5. Extrema and dynamic stability: an application to the theory of the firm

The 'static' considerations concerning the second-order conditions for an extremum and the dynamic considerations concerning stability can sometimes be put together. This is another aspect of the relations between statics and dynamics, which can be considered as a special case of a generalized correspondence principle.

Formally, if the equations

$$f^i(x_1, x_2, ..., x_n; \alpha_1, \alpha_2, ..., \alpha_m) = 0 , \quad i = 1, 2, ..., n ,$$

determine a stationary point (maximum, minimum or a point not an extremum) of a function F, of which the f^i are the first-order partial derivatives, and if the behaviour assumptions concerning the dynamic stability of the same point give rise to a dynamic system of the type

$$\frac{dx_i}{dt} = k_i f^i(x_1, x_2, ..., x_n; \alpha_1, \alpha_2, ..., \alpha_m) , \quad \begin{matrix} i = 1, 2, ..., n \\ k_i > 0 \end{matrix}$$

then:

(I) if the stationary point is a maximum, it is locally stable;

(II) if the stationary point is a minimum, it is unstable;

(III) if the stationary point is not an extremum, it is stable or unstable according to the initial position of the system (one-sided stability–instability).

The above theorem can easily be proved if we consider the simple case in

---

* For some general considerations on the 'relativity' of stability conditions, see Part II, ch. 3, §1.

which there is only one function in one independent variable. Let $y = F(x)$ be such a function, and let x^0 be the stationary point determined by the equation

$$f(x) = F'(x) = 0 \ .$$

From the theory of maxima and minima, we know that, if $F'(x^0) = F''(x^0) = \ldots = F^{(n-1)}(x^0) = 0$, while $F^{(n)}(x^0) \neq 0$, then:

(1) if n is even, the stationary point is an extremum, and precisely a maximum (minimum) if $F^{(n)}(x^0) \lessgtr 0$;

(2) if n is odd, the stationary point is not an extremum but a horizontal inflection point, in the neighbourhood of which the function is increasing (decreasing) if $F^{(n)}(x^0) \gtrless 0$.

Let us begin with the special cases in which $n = 2$ or 3. Let us consider the differential equation

$$dx/dt = kf(x) \ , \qquad k > 0 \ ,$$

and expand the right-hand side in Taylor's series at the point x^0. Omitting all non-linear terms we have

$$d\bar{x}/dt = kf'(x^0)\bar{x} \ ,$$

where $\bar{x} = x - x^0$ denotes deviations from equilibrium. The solution of the last differential equation is

$$\bar{x}(t) = \bar{x}(0) \exp [kf'(x^0)t] \ ,$$

where $\bar{x}(0)$ indicates the initial deviation $x(0) - x^0$ for $t = 0$. Since $f'(x^0) \equiv F''(x^0)$, we have

$$\bar{x}(t) = \bar{x}(0) \exp [kF''(x^0)t] \ ,$$

from which it can be immediately seen that the point x^0 is stable or unstable if $F''(x^0) \lessgtr 0$, that is if x^0 affords a maximum (minimum) to the function $F(x)$.

Let us now suppose that $f'(x^0) = 0$, but that $f''(x^0) \equiv F'''(x^0) \neq 0$; in Taylor's expansion of $f(x)$ the first-order term is zero, so that we must consider the second-order term (higher-order terms are neglected). Thus we have

$$d\bar{x}/dt = kf''(x^0)\tfrac{1}{2}\bar{x}^2 .$$

This can be considered as a Bernoulli equation *, whose solution is

$$\bar{x}(t) = \frac{1}{-\tfrac{1}{2}kf''(x^0)t + 1/\bar{x}(0)} = \frac{1}{-\tfrac{1}{2}kF'''(x^0)t + 1/\bar{x}(0)} .$$

It can easily be checked that, if $\bar{x}(0)$ has the opposite sign of $-F'''(x^0)$, there will be a positive value of t for which the denominator will vanish, that is $\bar{x}$ becomes infinite and the equilibrium is not stable. On the other hand, if $\bar{x}(0)$ has the same sign as $-F'''(x^0)$, then the denominator always has the same sign for $t \geqslant 0$ and tends in absolute value to infinity as $t \to +\infty$, so that $\bar{x}(t) \to 0$ and the equilibrium is stable. Therefore, we have stability or instability according to the position of the initial point $x(0)$ which determines the initial deviation $\bar{x}(0)$.

What we have shown for $n = 2, 3$ can be generalized. In what follows we put $m \equiv n - 1$ and we assume that $m > 2$ (and so that $n > 3$) since the cases up to $n = 3$ have just been examined. Let us then suppose that the first m derivatives of F, that is the first $m - 1$ derivatives of f are zero at $x = x^0$, whereas $F^{(n)}(x^0) \equiv f^{(m)}(x^0) \neq 0$. The differential equation is

$$\frac{d\bar{x}}{dt} = \frac{k}{m!} f^{(m)}(x^0)\bar{x}^m ,$$

which still is a Bernoulli equation and has the solution

$$\bar{x}(t) = 1 \Big/ \left\{ \frac{k}{m!}(1-m)f^{(m)}(x^0)t + \frac{1}{[\bar{x}(0)]^{m-1}} \right\}^{1/(m-1)}$$

$$= 1 \Big/ \left\{ \frac{k}{m!}(1-m)F^{(n)}(x^0)t + \frac{1}{[\bar{x}(0)]^{n-2}} \right\}^{1/(n-2)} .$$

We must now distinguish two cases:
(1) n is even, so that also $n-2$ is even and so $1/[\bar{x}(0)]^{n-2} > 0$. Since $1 - m < 0$, we have the following results:

(a) if $F^{(n)}(x^0) < 0$, that is if the stationary point is a maximum, the denominator is positive for any $t \geqslant 0$ and tends to infinity as $t \to +\infty$, so that $\bar{x}(t) \to 0$ and the equilibrium is stable;

---

* See Appendix III, §4.

(b) if $F^{(n)}(x^0) > 0$, that is, if the stationary point is a minimum, the denominator becomes zero for a positive value of t, that is, $\bar{x}$ becomes infinite and the equilibrium is not stable.

(2) n is odd, so that also $n-2$ is odd and $1/[\bar{x}(0)]^{n-2} \gtreqless 0$ if $\bar{x}(0) \gtreqless 0$. It can easily be checked that the denominator always maintains the same sign (for any $t \geqslant 0$) and tends in absolute value to infinity as $t \to +\infty$, or vanishes for a certain (positive) value of t, according to whether $\bar{x}(0)$ has the same or the opposite sign of $(1-m)F^{(n)}(x^0)$. Thus we have stability or instability according to the position of the initial point.

Thus we have proved propositions (I), (II) and (III) for the case in which only one independent variable is involved. We can also say that, even when the relation $f(x) = 0$ has been derived from considerations other than the maximizing behaviour assumption, if the point x^0 is stable, unstable, stable—unstable, then it must necessarily correspond respectively to a maximum, minimum, horizontal inflection point, of a function $F(x) \equiv \int f(x) \, dx$. However, this is a purely formal result, since the construction *a posteriori* of the $F(x)$ has no economic meaning.

Propositions (I), (II) and (III) can be extended to the general case of a function in n independent variables. As an illustration, we shall treat the case in which the stationary point is a maximum. If $y = F(x_1, x_2, ..., x_n)$ is the function to maximize, the first-order conditions are

$$\frac{\partial F}{\partial x_i} = f^i(x_1, x_2, ..., x_n) = 0 , \qquad i = 1, 2, ..., n ,$$

and the second-order conditions are that the principal minors of the following Hessian matrix

$$\begin{bmatrix} \dfrac{\partial^2 F}{\partial x_1^2} & \dfrac{\partial^2 F}{\partial x_1 \partial x_2} & \cdots & \dfrac{\partial^2 F}{\partial x_1 \partial x_n} \\[2ex] \dfrac{\partial^2 F}{\partial x_2 \partial x_1} & \dfrac{\partial^2 F}{\partial x_2^2} & \cdots & \dfrac{\partial^2 F}{\partial x_2 \partial x_n} \\[2ex] \dfrac{\partial^2 F}{\partial x_n \partial x_1} & \dfrac{\partial^2 F}{\partial x_n \partial x_2} & \cdots & \dfrac{\partial^2 F}{\partial x_n^2} \end{bmatrix} \equiv \begin{bmatrix} \dfrac{\partial f^1}{\partial x_1} & \dfrac{\partial f^1}{\partial x_2} & \cdots & \dfrac{\partial f^1}{\partial x_n} \\[2ex] \dfrac{\partial f^2}{\partial x_1} & \dfrac{\partial f^2}{\partial x_2} & \cdots & \dfrac{\partial f^2}{\partial x_n} \\[2ex] \dfrac{\partial f^n}{\partial x_1} & \dfrac{\partial f^n}{\partial x_2} & \cdots & \dfrac{\partial f^n}{\partial x_n} \end{bmatrix}$$

alternate in sign, beginning with minus.

Let us now examine the dynamic system

$$\frac{dx_i}{dt} = f^i(x_1, x_2, ..., x_n), \qquad i = 1, 2, ..., n, \qquad (I.9)$$

where for simplicity's sake we have put $k_i = 1$ *. Performing a linear approximation at the equilibrium point and considering the deviations $\bar{x}_i = x_i - x_i^0$, we have

$$\frac{d\bar{x}_i}{dt} = \frac{\partial f^i}{\partial x_1}\bar{x}_1 + \frac{\partial f^i}{\partial x_2}\bar{x}_2 + ... + \frac{\partial f^i}{\partial x_n}\bar{x}_n, \qquad i = 1, 2, ..., n.$$

The matrix of the coefficients of such a system coincides with the above-written Hessian and is symmetrical, given the commutative property of partial differentiation ($\partial^2 F/\partial x_i \partial x_j = \partial^2 F/\partial x_j \partial x_i$). Now, when the matrix of the coefficients of a differential system is symmetric, the alternation (starting with minus) of the signs of the principal minors is a necessary and sufficient stability condition (see Part II, ch. 8, conditions 1). It follows that the maximum point is stable, of course if the dynamic behaviour assumptions give rise to the differential system (I.9).

We want to conclude this section with a simple economic application to the elementary theory of the monopolistic firm. The 'traditional' monopolist wants to maximize profit, so that, calling q the quantity produced and sold, $R(q)$ total revenue, and $C(q)$ total cost, the first- and second-order conditions for maximum profit are

$$R'(q) - C'(q) = 0,$$

$$R''(q) - C''(q) < 0.$$

Let us now make the following behaviour assumption: the monopolist increases (decreases) the quantity produced and sold if marginal revenue is greater (smaller) than marginal cost. This looks like a very plausible assumption, since if marginal revenue is greater (smaller) than marginal cost, the monopolist's profit increases (decreases) as the quantity produced and sold increases (decreases). Thus the assumption reflects the presumed behaviour of

---

* It can be shown that if a symmetric matrix A is stable, also the matrix DA — where D is the diagonal matrix $[k_1, k_2, ..., k_n]$; $k_i > 0$ — is stable (Arrow and McManus, 1958). Thus the argument in the text is also valid if the k_i are not unity.

a monopolist in his search for the maximum profit. The formal counterpart of this assumption is

$$dq/dt = \varphi[R'(q) - C'(q)], \quad \text{sgn}\,\varphi[...] = \text{sgn}\,[...], \quad \varphi[0] = 0, \quad \varphi'[0] > 0.$$

Performing a linear approximation of the function φ at the equilibrium point and putting $\varphi'[0] \equiv k$, we have

$$\frac{dq}{dt} = k[R'(q) - C'(q)].$$

We must now linearize the function $R'(q) - C'(q)$ at the equilibrium point, after which we obtain

$$\frac{d\bar{q}}{dt} = k[R''(q^0) - C''(q^0)]\bar{q},$$

where $\bar{q} = q - q^0$. The solution is

$$\bar{q}(t) = \bar{q}(0) \exp\{k[R''(q^0) - C''(q^0)]t\},$$

from which, given the second-order conditions for a maximum, $\lim_{t \to +\infty} \bar{q}(t) = 0$, and so the equilibrium point is stable.

§6. Elements of comparative dynamics

The concept of comparative dynamics is closely related to that of comparative statics. The main difference lies in the fact that comparative dynamics is concerned with the effects of changes in parameters, etc., on the whole *motion over time* of a dynamic economic model. According to Samuelson, the changes which are the concern of comparative dynamics can be any one of the following:

(1) changes in initial conditions;

(2) changes in exogenous forces (as, e.g., in autonomous investment);

(3) changes in internal parameters (as, e.g., in the propensity to save).

The basic method of comparative dynamics can be summarized as follows: we have a set of functional equations, whose solution gives the time path of the economic system. In this solution initial conditions, exogenous elements and internal parameters also appear. Differentiating totally the solution functions (or the functional equations themselves) with respect to the argument representing the element whose shift we are interested in, we try to determine the effect of this shift.

The comparative dynamics method has been so far almost exclusively employed in growth models to analyse the effects of shifts in some exogenous elements or internal parameters on the steady-state equilibrium growth path of the model. Consider, for example, the neoclassical growth model (Part II, ch. 3, §4) and ask: what is the effect of an increase in the propensity to save on the steady-state equilibrium growth path? The answer is: none, since in this path all variables grow at the rate n, which is independent of s. Another comparative dynamics exercise has been explicitly carried out in relation to the neoclassical growth model in a monetary economy (Part II, ch. 3, §5, especially eqs. (3.63) and (3.64)).

The conditions of stability of the equilibrium path may be useful in obtaining information on comparative dynamics (see the above-mentioned neoclassical monetary growth model), and this can be regarded as the analogue of the correspondence principle, where 'dynamic equilibrium path' has been substituted for 'static equilibrium point'.

It must be noted, finally, that comparative dynamics, as such, does not say anything about the transition from one equilibrium growth path to another; the study of this transition belongs to stability analysis.

§7. Some economic applications of the correspondence principle

§7.1. The 'complete' Keynesian model

By 'complete' Keynesian model (Ackley's terminology) we mean the following well-known macroeconomic model:

$$S = S(Y,R), \qquad 0 < \frac{\partial S}{\partial Y} < 1, \qquad \frac{\partial S}{\partial R} > 0, \tag{I.10}$$

$$I = I(Y,R), \qquad 0 < \frac{\partial I}{\partial Y} < 1, \qquad \frac{\partial I}{\partial R} < 0, \tag{I.11}$$

$$I = S, \tag{I.12}$$

$$L = L(Y,R) \qquad \frac{\partial L}{\partial Y} > 0, \qquad \frac{\partial L}{\partial R} < 0, \tag{I.13}$$

$$L = L_s^*. \tag{I.14}$$

The price level is assumed to be rigid. The symbols are the usual ones and the equations are self-explanatory: in order, they are the saving function, the investment function, the *ex ante* equality between investment and saving, the demand for money function, the equality between the demand for and the (exogenously given) supply of money. The *a priori* assumptions on the various functions are condensed in the assumed signs of the various partial derivatives. Substituting from the first two equations in the third and from the fourth in the fifth, we obtain

$$I(Y,R) - S(Y,R) = 0 , \tag{I.12'}$$

$$L(Y,R) - L_s^* = 0 . \tag{I.14'}$$

Eqs. (I.12') and (I.14') determine, in the (R, Y) plane, two curves which are the well-known *IS* and *LM* (or *LL*) curves, following the terminology suggested by Hicks (1937). The intersection of these curves determines the equilibrium point, say R_e, Y_e, in which real and monetary equilibrium obtain simultaneously.

In the system composed of eqs. (I.12') and (I.14') a parameter L_s^* is already present. We can introduce at least three other parameters, one for each of the functions S, I, L, that is

$$I(Y,R,\alpha_1) - S(Y,R,\alpha_2) = 0 , \tag{I.15}$$

$$L(Y,R,\alpha_3) - L_s^* = 0 , \tag{I.16}$$

where we conventionally establish that $\partial I/\partial\alpha_1 > 0$, $\partial S/\partial\alpha_2 > 0$, $\partial L/\partial\alpha_3 > 0$. In other words, α_1 is defined in such a way that I varies in the same direction as α_1 (α_1 is, for example, autonomous investment), and similarly for α_2, α_3.

Provided that the Jacobian

$$\begin{vmatrix} \dfrac{\partial I}{\partial Y} - \dfrac{\partial S}{\partial Y} & \dfrac{\partial I}{\partial R} - \dfrac{\partial S}{\partial R} \\[2ex] \dfrac{\partial L}{\partial Y} & \dfrac{\partial L}{\partial R} \end{vmatrix}$$

is non-zero at the point R_e, Y_e, there exist the functions

$$Y = Y(\alpha_1, \alpha_2, \alpha_3, L_s^*) , \tag{I.17}$$

$$R = R(\alpha_1, x_2, \alpha_3, L_s^*), \tag{I.18}$$

of which we want to know the partial derivatives $\partial Y/\partial\alpha_1$, $\partial R/\partial\alpha_1$, etc., which give us the reaction of the equilibrium values of income and of the rate of interest to a shift in the parameters. Let us note that not all the parameters appear in each of the relations (I.15) and (I.16), and this is an element which, in general, makes it easier to obtain the desired comparative statics results. We shall examine only the effects of a shift in the money supply; the student can complete the analysis as an exercise.

Differentiating totally (I.15) and (I.16) with respect to L_s^* — account being taken of (I.17) and (I.18) — we have

$$\left(\frac{\partial I}{\partial Y} - \frac{\partial S}{\partial Y}\right)\frac{\partial Y}{\partial L_s^*} + \left(\frac{\partial I}{\partial R} - \frac{\partial S}{\partial R}\right)\frac{\partial R}{\partial L_s^*} = 0 ,$$

$$\tag{I.19}$$

$$\frac{\partial L}{\partial Y}\frac{\partial Y}{\partial L_s^*} + \frac{\partial L}{\partial R}\frac{\partial R}{\partial L_s^*} = 1 ,$$

whose solution is

$$\frac{\partial Y}{\partial L_s^*} = \frac{\partial S/\partial R - \partial I/\partial R}{\Delta} ,$$

$$\tag{I.20}$$

$$\frac{\partial R}{\partial L_s^*} = \frac{\partial I/\partial Y - \partial S/\partial Y}{\Delta} ,$$

where

$$\Delta \equiv \left(\frac{\partial I}{\partial Y} - \frac{\partial S}{\partial Y}\right)\frac{\partial L}{\partial R} - \left(\frac{\partial I}{\partial R} - \frac{\partial S}{\partial R}\right)\frac{\partial L}{\partial Y} . \tag{I.21}$$

The assumptions made at the beginning on the various partial derivatives allow us to determine the sign of the numerator of $\partial Y/\partial L_s^*$ only, which turns out to be positive, but do not allow us to determine the sign of Δ and of the numerator of $\partial R/\partial L_s^*$.

Let us then examine the problem of the stability of the equilibrium point in the model under consideration ★. Plausible behaviour assumptions, which are commonly used in studying the dynamics of the Keynesian model are the

---

★ The order of the exposition could also have been inverted. That is, one could examine first the stability problem and then the comparative statics problem.

following:

(1) In a context of rigid prices and less than full employment, an *ex ante* difference between investment and saving reacts on income, which increases (decreases) if investment exceeds (falls short of) saving. Let us note, incidentally, that this assumption is the same as the following: income increases (decreases) if aggregate demand exceeds (falls short of) current output (which is the same as income) [*]. In the latter form we have already seen this assumption (Part II, ch. 5, §2, and Part II, ch. 9, §5 of the text).

(2) The rate of interest tends to increase (decrease) if the demand for money exceeds (falls short of) the supply. The rationale of this assumption is the following. Consider, for example, a positive excess demand for money. The scarcity of liquidity drives the owners of bonds to try to sell them; this brings about a fall in bond prices, that is, an increase in the interest rate, the latter being inversely proportional to the price of bonds.

The formal counterpart of these assumptions is

$$dY/dt = \varphi_1[I(Y,R) - S(Y,R)], \quad \text{sgn}\,\varphi_1[...] = \text{sgn}\,[...],$$

$$\varphi_1[0] = 0, \quad \varphi_1'[0] > 0,$$

$$dR/dt = \varphi_2[L(Y,R) - L_s^*], \quad \text{sgn}\,\varphi_2[...] = \text{sgn}\,[...],$$

$$\varphi_2[0] = 0, \quad \varphi_2'[0] > 0.$$

Performing a linear approximation at the equilibrium point and denoting with a bar the deviations from equilibrium, we have

$$\frac{d\bar{Y}}{dt} = c_1\left(\frac{\partial I}{\partial Y} - \frac{\partial S}{\partial Y}\right)\bar{Y} + c_1\left(\frac{\partial I}{\partial R} - \frac{\partial S}{\partial R}\right)\bar{R},$$

$$\frac{d\bar{R}}{dt} = c_2\frac{\partial L}{\partial Y}\bar{Y} + c_2\frac{\partial L}{\partial R}\bar{R},$$

(I.22)

where $c_1 \equiv \varphi_1'[0]$, $c_2 \equiv \varphi_2'[0]$. The characteristic equation of system (I.22) is

---

[*] Since consumption is income minus saving, the inequality $I \gtrless S$ is the same as $I \gtrless Y - C$, that is, as $C + I \gtrless Y$.

$$\begin{vmatrix} c_1 \left(\dfrac{\partial I}{\partial Y} - \dfrac{\partial S}{\partial Y} \right) - \lambda & c_1 \left(\dfrac{\partial I}{\partial R} - \dfrac{\partial S}{\partial R} \right) \\ \\ c_2 \dfrac{\partial L}{\partial Y} & c_2 \dfrac{\partial L}{\partial R} - \lambda \end{vmatrix} = 0 \,,$$

that is

$$\lambda^2 - \left[c_1 \left(\frac{\partial I}{\partial Y} - \frac{\partial S}{\partial Y} \right) + c_2 \frac{\partial L}{\partial R} \right] \lambda + c_1 c_2 \Delta \,, \tag{I.23}$$

where Δ is the same expression defined in (I.21). The necessary and sufficient stability conditions are

$$c_1 \left(\frac{\partial I}{\partial Y} - \frac{\partial S}{\partial Y} \right) + c_2 \frac{\partial L}{\partial R} < 0 \,,$$

$$\Delta > 0 \,.$$

Using these results we can establish that $\partial Y / \partial L_s^* > 0$, whereas the sign of $\partial R / \partial L_s^*$ remains indeterminate.

Let us note, finally, that in the 'pure' Keynesian case, that is $\partial I / \partial Y \simeq 0$, $\partial S / \partial R \simeq 0$, complete comparative statics results can be obtained without any dynamic considerations.

§7.2. The foreign trade multiplier under flexible exchange rates

First of all, let us note that any static analysis of the multiplier type is actually a comparative statics analysis, since it proposes to study how the equilibrium value of income changes in response to a shift in any one of the autonomous components of expenditure.

In the text we have met the foreign trade multiplier several times – Part I, ch. 3, §2, and Part I, ch. 9, §1 – but always in a regime of fixed exchange rates. Here we shall examine it under flexible exchange rates, following the analysis contained in the classic paper by Laursen and Metzler (1950). The dynamic part of this paper has been examined in the text – Part II, ch. 9, §5 – and we shall not repeat it here. For the comparative statics analysis, let us introduce a parameter which represents an exogenous increase in aggregate demand in country 1. Thus we have

$$Y_1 = \omega_1(Y_1, \pi) + \alpha_1 \,,$$

$$Y_2 = \omega_2 \left(Y_2, \frac{1}{\pi} \right), \qquad (I.24)$$

$$\frac{1}{\pi} M_1(Y_1, \pi) = M_2 \left(Y_2, \frac{1}{\pi} \right).$$

On the assumption that the required conditions are satisfied, there exist the functions

$$Y_1 = Y_1(\alpha_1) \,,$$

$$Y_2 = Y_2(\alpha_1) \,, \qquad (I.25)$$

$$\pi = \pi(\alpha_1) \,.$$

The multiplier we are interested in is given by the derivative $dY_1/d\alpha_1$; as a by-product we shall obtain also the derivatives $dY_2/d\alpha_1$ and $d\pi/d\alpha_1$. Differentiating totally eqs. (I.24) with respect to α_1 (account being taken of eqs. (I.25), setting $\pi^0 = 1$ in the initial equilibrium situation (this involves only a change in units of measurement) and rearranging terms, we obtain

$$(1 - w_1) \frac{dY_1}{d\alpha_1} - s_1 \frac{d\pi}{d\alpha_1} = 1 \,,$$

$$(1 - w_2) \frac{dY_2}{d\alpha_1} + s_2 \frac{d\pi}{d\alpha_1} = 0 \,, \qquad (I.26)$$

$$-m_1 \frac{dY_1}{d\alpha_1} + m_2 \frac{dY_2}{d\alpha_1} + M_1(\eta_1 + \eta_2 - 1) \frac{d\pi}{d\alpha_1} = 0 \,,$$

where the symbols are as defined in Part II, ch. 9, §5. The solution of system (I.26) is

$$\frac{dY_1}{d\alpha_1} = \frac{(1 - w_2)M_1(\eta_1 + \eta_2 - 1) - m_2 s_2}{\Delta} \,,$$

$$\frac{dY_2}{d\alpha_1} = \frac{-m_1 s_2}{\Delta} \,, \qquad (I.27)$$

$$\frac{d\pi}{d\alpha_1} = \frac{m_1(1-w_2)}{\Delta},$$ (I.27)

where

$$\Delta \equiv \begin{vmatrix} 1-w_1 & 0 & -s_1 \\ 0 & 1-w_2 & s_2 \\ -m_1 & m_2 & M_1(\eta_1+\eta_2-1) \end{vmatrix},$$

that is

$$\Delta \equiv (1-w_1)(1-w_2)M_1(\eta_1+\eta_2-1) - s_1m_1(1-w_2) - s_2m_2(1-w_1).$$ (I.28)

The sign of Δ is indeterminate, since expression (I.28) contains both positive and negative terms and also a term whose sign is not known *a priori* $(\eta_1+\eta_2-1)$. However, from the dynamic analysis we know that a necessary (and in this case also sufficient) stability condition is that $\Delta > 0$: see relation (9.56) in Part II, ch. 9, §5. Moreover, $\Delta > 0$ implies that

$$(1-w_2)M_1(\eta_1+\eta_2-1) - m_2s_2 > 0,$$ (I.29)

as can easily be seen from the fact that $\Delta > 0$ can be rewritten as

$$(1-w_2)M_1(\eta_1+\eta_2-1) - m_2s_2 > s_1m_1\frac{1-w_2}{1-w_1},$$ (I.30)

where the right-hand side is a positive quantity. Thus we may conclude that $dY_1/d\alpha_1 > 0$, $d\pi/d\alpha_1 > 0$, $dY_2/d\alpha_1 < 0$. Let us note, incidentally, that this is a case in which the correspondence principle makes it possible to eliminate *completely* the indeterminacy of the comparative statics results.

The fact that, notwithstanding the full flexibility of the exchange rate, a change in income in country 1 brings about a change in income in country 2, is sufficient to show the falseness of the opinion which attributes an 'insulating' property to flexible exchange rates. The fact is that, although the exchange rate adjusts so as to eliminate any effect of the trade balance, keeping it at a zero level, the variations in the exchange rate, however, have a direct effect on aggregate expenditure $C + I$. It follows that $Y = C + I + X - M$ cannot remain constant, although $X - M = 0$. This is the essence of Laursen's and Metzler's argument. The conclusions reached above on the signs of $dY_1/d\alpha_1$ and of $d\pi/d\alpha_1$ are not a surprise: an increase in autonomous expenditure in country 1 brings about, account being taken of all the repercussions, an increase in national income and thus an increase in imports; the consequent deficit in country 1's balance of payments is corrected by a devaluation, that is by an increase in π. But the result on the sign of $dY_2/d\alpha_1$ may be somewhat surprising: a boom in one country causes a recession in the other country. However, this result will become intuitively clear if we remember that an increase in π — that is, an *appreciation* in country 2's currency — brings about a *fall* in the aggregate expenditure schedule of country 2, whose national income must therefore decrease, being the balance of trade in equilibrium.

References

Ackley, G., 1961, *Macroeconomic Theory*, ch. XIV.

Arrow, K.J. and McManus, M., 1958, A Note on Dynamic Stability.

Basset, L., 1968, The Solution of Qualitative Comparative Static Problems: Comment.

Basset, L., Maybee, J. and Quirk, J., 1968, Qualitative Economics and the Scope of the Correspondence Principle.

Gale, D. and Nikaidô, H., 1965, The Jacobian Matrix and Global Univalence of Mappings.

Hicks, J.R., 1937, Mr. Keynes and the "Classics": A Suggested Interpretation.

Hicks, J.R., 1939, *Value and Capital*, Parts I and II, and Mathematical Appendixes.

Hobson, E.W., 1957, *The Theory of Functions of a Real Variable & the Theory of Fourier's Series*, Vol. I, § 319.

Lancaster, K., 1966, The Solution of Qualitative Comparative Statics Problems.

Laursen, S. and Metzler, L.A., 1950, Flexible Exchange Rates and the Theory of Employment.

Lloyd, P.J., 1969, Qualitative Calculus and Comparative Static Analysis.

Nikaido, H., 1968, *Convex Structures and Economic Theory*, ch. VII.

Patinkin, D., 1952, The Limitations of Samuelson's "Correspondence Principle".

Quirk, J. and Saposnick, R., 1968, *Introduction to General Equilibrium Theory and Welfare Economics*, ch. 6.

Samuelson, P.A., 1941, The Stability of Equilibrium: Comparative Statics and Dynamics.

Samuelson, P.A., 1947, *Foundations of Economic Analysis*, chs. II, III, IX, X (pp. 294–6 and 301–2), XII.

Slutsky, E., 1953, On the Theory of the Budget of the Consumer.

APPENDIX II

The Stability of Equilibrium
and Liapunov's Second Method

§1. The concept of stability

Some brief remarks will be made on the concept of stability before tackling Liapunov's 'second' method. Stability analysis is concerned with the following general problem: to ascertain whether, and under what conditions, the variables present in a given economic model converge over time to their respective equilibrium value ⋆, i.e. towards the equilibrium point of the model. It is immaterial, for this purpose, whether we imagine that the model has never been in equilibrium before or that the model was previously in equilibrium and has been brought out of it by an occasional disturbance (these are obviously two aspects of the same problem). What matters is that in the period that we take as initial the system is not in equilibrium.

In formal terms, the problem is to ascertain whether

$$\lim_{t \to +\infty} y_i(t) = y_i^e , \qquad i = 1, 2, ..., n ,$$ (II.1)

⋆ This value may be a stationary equilibrium or a moving equilibrium. The latter is sometimes represented by a situation in which all the relevant variables grow together at the same constant rate of growth.

or, which is the same thing, whether

$$\lim_{t \to +\infty} [y_i(t) - y_i^e] = 0 , \qquad i = 1, 2, ..., n , \qquad (II.2)$$

where y_i^e indicates the equilibrium value of the variable y_i. The time path of the i-th variable $y_i(t)$ is determined by the solution of a system of functional equations (or of a single functional equation, if $i = 1$) [*]. The first relation above means that every variable converges towards its equilibrium value as t increases; the second relation means that the deviations of each variable from its equilibrium value converge to zero as t increases. The two ways of defining stability are obviously equivalent.

The general concept of stability must now be qualified. We use the expression '*local stability*' when (II.1) (and so (II.2)) hold only if the initial point — i.e. the vector of the initial values $y_i(0)$ — is sufficiently near to the equilibrium point. The expression '*global stability*' is used instead when (II.1) (and so (II.2)) hold for any initial point, however far from the equilibrium point. 'Local stability' and 'global stability' correspond to "stability of the first kind in the small" and to "perfect stability of the first kind" in Samuelson's terminology (*Foundations*, pp. 261–2). However, the terminology 'local stability' and 'global stability' is now more usual. As a matter of terminology, 'local stability' and 'global stability' correspond to what mathemathicians call 'uniform asymptotic stability' and 'uniform asymptotic stability in the large', respectively. Other concepts of stability are also defined in mathematics [**], but we need not bother about them since the relevant concepts used in economics are those stated above.

§2. Liapunov's 'second method': general concepts

This method, also called the 'direct' method, serves to answer questions of stability of differential or difference systems (Liapunov, 1907) [‡] *without*

---

[*] In this appendix we shall use 'systems' in the sense of both systems proper and a single equation. Let us note, incidentally, that in this appendix by 'stability' we mean *dynamic* stability, as is implicit in the fact that we use functional equations. See Part II, ch. 3, §1, of the text.

[**] See, e.g., Kalman and Bertram (1960, pp. 375–7) for a list of definitions of 'stability'.

[‡] Liapunov's original memoir was published in Russian in 1893; a French translation (Problème général de la stabilité du mouvement) appeared in 1907 in *Annales de la Faculté de Sciences de Toulouse*, and has been reprinted in facsimile in *Annals of Mathe-*

solving the system. On the other hand, the 'first method' (also called the 'indirect' method) consists of finding the solution of the system and utilizing it to check whether (II.1) or (II.2) are satisfied.

The advantage of the direct method over the indirect one lies in the fact that we do not need to know the solution of the system. Indeed, only in some special cases — among which the linear and constant coefficients case is the easiest to handle — are we able to find the solution of a differential or difference system. When the system is non-linear it may be — and it usually is — impossible to find its solution, and to know that the solution exists because the existence theorem tells us so is a meagre solace. It is true, of course, that we may always try a numerical integration of the system (electronic computers will do the job), but this possibility is not of great help to the economic theorist. He seeks general answers, independent of numerical analyses which hold only for the single case, and so he works with functions which are specified only *qualitatively* (e.g., he assumes that $y = f(x)$, where $f'(x)$ (and perhaps $f''(x)$ too) has a certain sign, and that is all). Moreover, sometimes the problems are such that even if the analyst were ready to use numerically specified functions, it would be impossible to find them empirically (think of the problem of the stability of general equilibrium).

When we are confronted with a non-solvable non-linear system, then, if we want to examine its stability by the 'first' method we must make a linear approximation at the equilibrium point, and so the stability results that we obtain will hold only in a sufficiently small neighbourhood of that point, i.e. they will be only local stability results. If we want global stability results we cannot use the linear approximation, and it is here that the 'second' method proves particularly useful. It is, however, advisable to inform the reader now that, as far as the second method is concerned, only some general theorems exist. There are no hard and fast rules according to which we are sure to find, if it exists, the 'Liapunov function' on which the method is based. It is perhaps safe to say that much depends on the ingenuity of the user.

Let us note, incidentally, that in the text we have always used the first method, either because the models treated there were such as to give rise to systems of linear difference or differential equations with constant coefficients or because, when the models were non-linear, we used the linear approximation method.

---

matics Studies No. 17, Princeton University Press, 1949; see especially pp. 255–67. It must be noted that in Liapunov's original memoir only systems of differential equations are treated. The extension of the 'second method' to systems of difference equations has been made successively.

§3. The fundamental theorems

We shall examine only the so-called *autonomous* systems, i.e. systems of differential or of difference equations of the type

$$\frac{dy_i}{dt} = f_i(y_1, y_2, ..., y_n), \qquad i = 1, 2, ..., n,$$ (II.3)

$$y_{i_{t+1}} = f_i(y_{1_t}, y_{2_t}, ..., y_{n_t}), \qquad i = 1, 2, ..., n,$$ (II.3′)

and not the more general systems ($u_i(t)$ = known functions)

$$\frac{dy_i}{dt} = f_i(y_1, y_2, ..., y_n, t, u_i(t)), \qquad i = 1, 2, ..., n,$$ (II.4)

$$y_{i_{t+1}} = f_i(y_{1_t}, y_{2_t}, ..., y_{n_t}, t, u_i(t)), \qquad i = 1, 2, ..., n.$$ (II.4′)

At the moment, only autonomous systems are used in the economic applications of the second method.

The functions f_i have the following properties *, respectively in the case of system (II.3) and of system (II.3′):

$$f_i(y_1, y_2, ..., y_n) = 0 \quad \text{for} \quad y_i = y_i^e, \quad i = 1, 2, ..., n.$$ (II.5)

$$f_i(y_{1_t}, y_{2_t}, ..., y_{n_t}) = y_i^e \quad \text{for} \quad y_{i_t} = y_i^e, \quad i = 1, 2, ..., n.$$ (II.5′)

Sometimes the system is built in such a way that the variables y_i represent the *deviations* of other variables from an equilibrium point, i.e. $y_i = x_i - x_i^e$, all i. In this case it is obvious that $y_i^e = 0$ (the so-called '*null solution*').

Before going any further, a review of the meaning of '*distance*' in mathematics is necessary.

The *distance* from the origin of a point in an n-dimensional metric space (or, if we prefer, the *norm* of the vector $\mathbf{y} = (y_1, y_2, ..., y_n)$, i.e. of the vector whose elements are the coordinates of the point) is defined as any scalar function of the variables $y_1, y_2, ..., y_n$ which has some specific properties. Such properties are (in what follows the distance will be indicated as $D(\mathbf{y})$. Equivalent notation is $\|\mathbf{y}\|$).

(1) $D(\mathbf{y}) > 0$ if $\mathbf{y} \neq \mathbf{0}$, i.e. if at least one of the numbers $y_1, y_2, ..., y_n$ is not zero;

---

* We assume also that the f_i have all the properties needed for the solution of system (II.3) or (II.3′) to exist and be unique.

(2) $D(\mathbf{y}) = 0$ if, and only if, $\mathbf{y} = \mathbf{0}$, i.e. if, and only if, $y_i = 0$ for all i;

(3) $D(\mu\mathbf{y}) = |\mu| D(\mathbf{y})$ for any constant μ;

(4) $D(\mathbf{y}' + \mathbf{y}'') \leqslant D(\mathbf{y}') + D(\mathbf{y}'')$, where $\mathbf{y}' = (y'_1, y'_2, ..., y'_n)$ and $\mathbf{y}'' = (y''_1, y''_2, ..., y''_n)$ are any two points (vectors).

The concept of distance, and its properties, does not change if instead of the origin we refer to any other point, say P^e; in such a case, for the elements $(y_1, y_2, ..., y_n)$ we can substitute the differences $(y_1 - y_1^e, y_2 - y_2^e, ..., y_n - y_n^e)$ and reinterpret properties (1) to (4) in terms of such differences.

The functions which satisfy the stated properties are theoretically infinite; a list of the more usual ones is given below:

(a) the Euclidean distance, $D(\mathbf{y}) = + (y_1^2 + y_2^2 + ... + y_n^2)^{1/2}$ − this is perhaps the first function which everyone immediately thinks of, since it measures the length of the straight line segment joining the point with the origin (the 'length' or 'modulus' of the vector $\mathbf{y}$);

(b) the modified Euclidean distance, $D(\mathbf{y}) = + (a_1 y_1^2 + a_2 y_2^2 + ... + a_n y_n^2)^{1/2}$, where the a_i are given positive constants;

(c) the absolute value distance, $D(\mathbf{y}) = \sum_{i=1}^{n} h_i |y_i|$, where the h_i are given positive constants;

(d) the 'maximum' distance, $D(\mathbf{y}) = \max_i c_i |y_i|$, where the c_i are given positive constants.

The reader may check as a simple exercise that all the stated functions satisfy properties (1) to (4) above.

We may now state the fundamental theorems.

Theorem I. Consider the autonomous system

$$\frac{dy_i}{dt} = f_i(y_1, y_2, ..., y_n), \qquad i = 1, 2, ..., n,$$

where

$$f_i = 0 \quad \text{for} \quad y_i = y_i^e, \qquad i = 1, 2, ..., n.$$

Suppose there exists a scalar function

$$V(y_1 - y_1^e, y_2 - y_2^e, ..., y_n - y_n^e)$$

with continuous first partial derivatives with respect to $y_i - y_i^e$, all i, and such that

(i) V is positive definite, i.e. $V > 0$ if at least one of the quantities $y_1 - y_1^e$, $y_2 - y_2^e$, ..., $y_n - y_n^e$ is different from zero; and $V = 0$ if, and only if,

$y_i - y_i^e = 0$ for all i;

(ii) $V \to +\infty$ as $\| \mathbf{y} - \mathbf{y}^e \| \to +\infty$;

(iii) $\quad \dfrac{\mathrm{d}V}{\mathrm{d}t} = \displaystyle\sum_{i=1}^{n} \dfrac{\partial V}{\partial(y_i - y_i^e)} \dfrac{\mathrm{d}(y_i - y_i^e)}{\mathrm{d}t}$

is negative if at least one of the quantities $y_1 - y_1^e, y_2 - y_2^e, ..., y_n - y_n^e$ is different from zero; and $\mathrm{d}V/\mathrm{d}t = 0$ if, and only if, $y_i - y_i^e = 0$ for all i.

Then the equilibrium state $(y_1^e, y_2^e, ..., y_n^e)$, is globally stable (uniformly asymptotically stable in the large).

A heuristic proof of the theorem is straightforward [*]. The existence of the '*Liapunov function*' V implies that the point whose coordinates are $y_1(t)$, $y_2(t), ..., y_n(t)$, where the $y_i(t)$ are determined by the solution of system (II.3), approaches more and more, as t increases, the point $(y_1^e, y_2^e, ..., y_n^e)$. The latter is therefore globally stable. The interesting thing is that, as we have already noted, properties (i) to (iii) can be checked without solving the system, since the explicit knowledge of the functions $y_i(t)$ is not required.

It must be noted that the converse of Theorem I is also true, i.e. *if* the equilibrium state is globally stable, *then* there exists a 'Liapunov function' which satisfies all the conditions of Theorem I. Thus the existence of a Liapunov function as required by Theorem I is a necessary and sufficient condition for global stability.

The second method may serve also to prove the *instability*, since the theorem is true that, *if* there exists a function V having the same properties (i) and (ii) of Theorem I and $\mathrm{d}V/\mathrm{d}t$ is always *positive* (being zero if, and only if, $y_i - y_i^e = 0$ for all i), *then* the equilibrium state is globally unstable. This theorem, too, is intuitive, since $\mathrm{d}V/\mathrm{d}t > 0$ implies that the point whose co-ordinates are $y_1(t), y_2(t), ..., y_n(t)$ moves farther and farther away from the equilibrium point.

In the intuitive proofs of the theorems above we have used the expressions 'to approach' and 'to move away from' the equilibrium point, which imply that the 'distance' between the point whose position is given by the solution of system (II.3) and the equilibrium point decreases or increases with time. These considerations give us a hint: *the simplest way to apply Liapunov's second method* — and this is the only practical suggestion that we can give — *is to try, in the search for a Liapunov function, the functions which define the*

---

[*] For rigorous formal proofs, see any of the following: Kalman and Bertram (1960), Krasovskiĭ (1963), LaSalle and Lefschetz (1961), Sansone and Conti (1964).

'*distance*'. Such functions, by their very definition, satisfy conditions (i) and (ii) of Theorem I, and so it only remains to check (but this is the difficulty) that $dV/dt < 0$ (or $dV/dt > 0$, if we are interested in proving instability) [*]. If the 'distance' fails to give the desired results, then we shall have to look for more general functions satisfying the requirements of the theorem. Actually, all the economic results so far obtained applying Liapunov's second method have been reached using the 'distance' functions.

We have so far treated systems of differential equations; let us now state a theorem for systems of difference equations.

Theorem II. Consider the autonomous system

$$y_{i_{t+1}} = f_i(y_{1_t}, y_{2_t}, ..., y_{n_t}), \qquad i = 1, 2, ..., n,$$

where $f_i = y_i^e$ for $y_{i_t} = y_i^e$, all i.
Suppose there exists a continuous scalar function

$$V(y_1 - y_1^e, y_2 - y_2^e, ..., y_n - y_n^e),$$

such that
   (i) V is positive definite, i.e. $V > 0$ if at least one of the quantities $y_1 - y_1^e, y_2 - y_2^e, ..., y_n - y_n^e$ is different from zero; and $V = 0$ if, and only if, $y_i - y_i^e = 0$ for all i;
   (ii) $V \to +\infty$ as $\| \mathbf{y} - \mathbf{y}^e \| \to +\infty$;
   (iii) ΔV is negative if at least one of the quantities $y_1 - y_1^e, y_2 - y_2^e, ...$ $..., y_n - y_n^e$ is different from zero; and $\Delta V = 0$ if, and only if, $y_i - y_i^e = 0$, all i.
Then the equilibrium state $(y_1^e, y_2^e, ..., y_n^e)$ is globally stable (uniformly asymptotically stable in the large).

A heuristic proof of this theorem can be given as for Theorem I, and we need not repeat it here.
   Let us note that, when the functions f_i are such that

$$\| \mathbf{f} \| < \| \mathbf{y} \| \qquad (\mathbf{f}(0) = 0)$$

___

[*] A word of caution: some 'distance' may not be everywhere differentiable (the maximum norm is one of them). In such cases, provided that the distance is a continuous function, requirement (iii) may be replaced, at those points where the function is not differentiable, by the proof that the function is strictly decreasing at those points.

for *some* norm, they are called a *contraction*. In this case equilibrium is stable, since choosing $V = \|\mathbf{y}_t\|$ we have

$$\Delta V = \|\mathbf{y}_{t+1}\| - \|\mathbf{y}_t\| = \|\mathbf{f}\| - \|\mathbf{y}\| < 0 .$$

A final remark: Theorems I and II are applicable only to first-order systems in 'normal' form, i.e. to systems having the form (II.3) or (II.3'). If the system that we have to analyse is not in this form, it must be transformed into a 'normal' first-order system before we can apply the 'second method'. The transformation into a first-order system is in principle always possible by introducing new variables appropriately defined. Suppose that $d^2 y_i/dt^2$ appears in a differential system; then define a new variable z_i such that $dy_i/dt = z_i$ and substitute dz_i/dt for $d^2 y_i/dt^2$. If $y_{i_{t+2}}$ appears in a difference system, define z_{i_t} such that $y_{i_{t+1}} = z_{i_t}$ and substitute $z_{i_{t+1}}$ for $y_{i_{t+2}}$. Derivatives (or lags) higher than the second can be eliminated in a similar way (e.g., if $d^3 y_i/dt^3$ also appears, define a new variable w_i such that $dz_i/dt = w_i$ and substitute dw_i/dt for $d^3 y_i/dt^3$). After having transformed the system into a first-order system, however, we must still put it in the 'normal' form (II.3) or (II.3'). Suppose that we have the first-order systems

$$\varphi_i(y_1, y_2, ..., y_n; y'_1, y'_2, ..., y'_n) = 0 ,$$

or

$$\varphi_i(y_{1_t}, y_{2_t}, ..., y_{n_t}; y_{1_{t+1}}, y_{2_{t+1}}, ..., y_{n_{t+1}}) = 0 ,$$

where the functions φ_i have continuous first partial derivatives. A sufficient condition that such systems may be put, at least in principle, in the 'normal' forms (II.3) or (II.3') is that the Jacobian of the φ_i with respect to the y'_i or to the $y_{i_{t+1}}$ be different from zero *. Otherwise, the normal form cannot be obtained with certainty.

§4. Some economic applications **

§4.1. *Global stability of Walrasian general equilibrium (Arrow et al.)*
Let us recall from Part II, ch. 9, §1, of the text that Walras' '*tâtonnement*'

---

* This is the implicit function theorem in its 'local' form. If we want a 'global' univalence, then the condition is that all the principal minors of the said Jacobian be everywhere positive. See the article by Gale and Nikaido (1965) and Nikaido (1968).

can be formalized in the following system of differential equations:

$$\frac{dp_i}{dt} = k_i E_i(p_1, p_2, ..., p_n), \qquad i = 1, 2, ..., n,$$

where the p's are the prices, the E's the aggregate excess demand functions and the k's are positive constants.

Now, choose as the Liapunov function the square of the modified Euclidean distance, i.e.

$$V(p_1 - p_1^e, p_2 - p_2^e, ..., p_n - p_n^e) = \sum_{i=1}^{n} \frac{1}{k_i}(p_i - p_i^e)^2 .$$

We have (remember that the p_i^e's are constants)

$$\frac{dV}{dt} = 2 \sum_{i=1}^{n} \frac{1}{k_i}(p_i - p_i^e)\frac{dp_i}{dt},$$

so that, since

$$\frac{dp_i}{dt} = k_i E_i(p_1, p_2, ..., p_n),$$

we have

$$\frac{dV}{dt} = 2 \sum_{i=1}^{n} (p_i - p_i^e)E_i(p_1, p_2, ..., p_n)$$

$$= 2 \sum_{i=1}^{n} p_i E_i(p_1, p_2, ..., p_n) - 2 \sum_{i=1}^{n} p_i^e E_i(p_1, p_2, ..., p_n).$$

From static general equilibrium theory we know that

$$\sum_{i=1}^{n} p_i E_i = 0 \quad \text{(Walras' law)},$$

** As far as we know, the first to mention Liapunov's second method in the economic literature have been Clower and Bushaw, 1954, pp. 335–6 and 339). However, the first extensive application of this method to economics was made some years later, in the paper by Arrow, Block and Hurwicz (1959).

and so

$$\frac{dV}{dt} = -2\sum_{i=1}^{n} p_i^e E_i(p_1, p_2, ..., p_n) .$$

Now, let us state without proof the following [*]:

Lemma. If the equilibrium prices are all positive and gross substitutability prevails, and Walras' law, together with positive homogeneity, holds, then

$$\sum_{i=1}^{n} p_i^e E_i(p_1, p_2, ..., p_n)$$

is always positive for any non-equilibrium positive price vector $(p_1, p_2, ..., p_n)$.

Positive homogeneity (of degree zero) means that, if all prices are multiplied by the same positive constant, the excess demands do not vary, and this is a well-known consequence of the utility maximization postulate. Gross substitutability means, as we saw in Part II, ch. 9, §1 of the text, that $\partial E_j / \partial p_i > 0$ for all $i, j; i \neq j$.

Using the lemma, it follows immediately that dV/dt is always negative out of equilibrium, becoming zero only at the equilibrium point (by definition, $E_i = 0$ for $p_i = p_i^e$, all i).

Gross substitutability, then, implies global stability of general equilibrium.

Another interesting case of global stability is when

$$\frac{\partial E_j}{\partial p_j} < 0 , \qquad \left| \frac{\partial E_j}{\partial p_j} \right| > \sum_{\substack{s=1 \\ s \neq j}}^{n} \left| \frac{\partial E_j}{\partial p_s} \right| \qquad \text{for all } j ,$$

i.e. the case of the *dominant negative diagonal*. For the Liapunov function choose

$$V = \max_{j} |k_j E_j| , \qquad k_j \text{ positive constants.}$$

Let $|k_w E_w| \geqslant |k_j E_j|$ for all j, where w is a subscript belonging to some excess demand function. Then

---

[*] See Arrow, Block and Hurwicz (1959, p. 90). Note that the positivity of the expression $\sum_{i=1}^{n} p_i^e E_i(p_1, p_2, ..., p_n)$ means that the aggregate excess demand functions satisfy the weak axiom of revealed preference.

$$V = |k_w E_w|,$$

and so, wherever dV/dt exists [*], we have [**]

$$\frac{dV}{dt} = k_w (\operatorname{sgn} E_w) \sum_j \frac{\partial E_w}{\partial p_j} \frac{dp_j}{dt} = k_w (\operatorname{sgn} E_w) \sum_j \frac{\partial E_w}{\partial p_j} k_j E_j . \tag{II.6}$$

It can immediately be checked that $dV/dt = 0$ in equilibrium, where $E_j = 0$ for all j. If we are out of equilibrium, then $E_j \neq 0$ for at least one j, and so $|E_w| > 0$. Given the assumption made at the beginning, we have, for $j = w$,

$$\left| \frac{\partial E_w}{\partial p_w} \right| > \sum_{s \neq w} \left| \frac{\partial E_w}{\partial p_s} \right| ,$$

and, multiplying both members by $|E_w|$, we have

$$\left| \frac{\partial E_w}{\partial p_w} \right| |E_w| > \sum_{s \neq w} \left| \frac{\partial E_w}{\partial p_s} \right| |E_w| . \tag{II.7}$$

Now, since $|k_w E_w| \geq |k_j E_j|$, we have $|E_w| \geq (k_j/k_w)|E_j|$ and so, using s instead of j,

$$\sum_{s \neq w} \left| \frac{\partial E_w}{\partial p_s} \right| |E_w| \geq \sum_{s \neq w} \left| \frac{\partial E_w}{\partial p_s} \right| \frac{k_s}{k_w} |E_s| = \frac{1}{k_w} \sum_{s \neq w} \left| \frac{\partial E_w}{\partial p_s} \right| k_s |E_s| . \tag{II.8}$$

From (II.7) and (II.8) we have

$$\left| \frac{\partial E_w}{\partial p_w} \right| |E_w| > \frac{1}{k_w} \sum_{s \neq w} \left| \frac{\partial E_w}{\partial p_s} \right| |E_s| k_s ;$$

therefore

$$\left| \frac{\partial E_w}{\partial p_w} \right| |E_w| k_w > \sum_{s \neq w} \left| \frac{\partial E_w}{\partial p_s} \right| |E_s| k_s .$$

---

[*] In the following proof we assume that dV/dt exists everywhere. For the case where it does not exist, see Arrow, Block and Hurwicz (1959, p. 106).

[**] The notation $(\operatorname{sgn} E_w)$ means 'the sign of E_w', i.e. $(\operatorname{sgn} E_w) = +1$ if $E_w > 0$, $(\operatorname{sgn} E_w) = -1$ if $E_w < 0$, $(\operatorname{sgn} E_w) = 0$ if $E_w = 0$. Note that $|k_w E_w| = k_w |E_w|$ since $k_w > 0$. Now, $k_w |E_w| = k_w (\operatorname{sgn} E_w) E_w$, from which, differentiating with respect to t, we have relation (II.6).

Since $\partial E_w/\partial p_w < 0$ by assumption, the last inequality may be written as

$$-\frac{\partial E_w}{\partial p_w}(\operatorname{sgn} E_w)E_w k_w > \sum_{s \neq w}\left|\frac{\partial E_w}{\partial p_s}\right||E_s|k_s . \qquad (\text{II.9})$$

Now, the quantity

$$\sum_{s \neq w}\left|\frac{\partial E_w}{\partial p_s}\right||E_s|k_s$$

is certainly not smaller than the quantity

$$\sum_{s \neq w}(\operatorname{sgn} E_w)\frac{\partial E_w}{\partial p_s}E_s k_s .$$

Indeed, three cases are possible ★:

(1) For one or more subscripts s, it happens that $\partial E_w/\partial p_s$ and E_s have the same sign, and so

$$\frac{\partial E_w}{\partial p_s}E_s = \left|\frac{\partial E_w}{\partial p_s}\right||E_s| .$$

Now, if $(\operatorname{sgn} E_w) = +1$, the corresponding elements in the two sums are equal, whereas, if $(\operatorname{sgn} E_w) = -1$, the elements in the first sum are greater than the corresponding elements in the second sum.

(2) For one or more subscripts s, it happens that $\partial E_w/\partial p_s$ and/or E_s are equal to zero: in this case the corresponding elements in the two sums are equal.

(3) For one or more subscripts s, it happens that $\partial E_w/\partial p_s$ and E_s are of opposite sign. Now, if $(\operatorname{sgn} E_w) = -1$, then

$$(\operatorname{sgn} E_w)\frac{\partial E_w}{\partial p_s}E_s = \left|\frac{\partial E_w}{\partial p_s}\right||E_s|$$

and the corresponding elements in the two sums are equal; if $(\operatorname{sgn} E_w) = +1$, then $(\operatorname{sgn} E_w)(\partial E_w/\partial p_s)E_s$ is a negative quantity and the elements in the first sum are greater than the corresponding elements in the second sum.

★ Apart from the trivial case $(\operatorname{sgn} E_w) = 0$, which anyway is excluded since we are out of equilibrium. Of course, the possible cases are not mutually exclusive.

This proves that the elements in the first sum are not smaller than the corresponding elements in the second sum, and so [*]

$$\sum_{s \neq w} \left| \frac{\partial E_w}{\partial p_s} \right| |E_s| k_s \geq (\operatorname{sgn} E_w) \sum_{s \neq w} \frac{\partial E_w}{\partial p_s} E_s k_s .$$ (II.10)

Now, from (II.9) and (II.10) it follows that

$$-\frac{\partial E_w}{\partial p_w} (\operatorname{sgn} E_w) E_w k_w > (\operatorname{sgn} E_w) \sum_{s \neq w} \frac{\partial E_w}{\partial p_s} E_s k_s ;$$ (II.11)

therefore

$$0 > (\operatorname{sgn} E_w) \frac{\partial E_w}{\partial p_w} E_w k_w + (\operatorname{sgn} E_w) \sum_{s \neq w} \frac{\partial E_w}{\partial p_s} E_s k_s ,$$

so that, putting under the Σ sign the term $(\operatorname{sgn} E_w)(\partial E_w / \partial p_w) E_w k_w$, we have

$$0 > (\operatorname{sgn} E_w) \sum_s \frac{\partial E_w}{\partial p_s} E_s k_s .$$ (II.12)

Since the subscript s runs over the same set of indices as the subscript j, we have

$$0 > (\operatorname{sgn} E_w) \sum_j \frac{\partial E_w}{\partial p_j} E_j k_j .$$ (II.12′)

Thus we have proved that in any non-equilibrium point inequality (II.12′) holds. From (II.12′) and (II.6) it follows that $dV/dt < 0$ out of equilibrium, and this proves the global stability of equilibrium in the case under consideration. The proof can be easily extended to the case of a *quasi-dominant* negative diagonal, in which

[*] Since $(\operatorname{sgn} E_w)$ does not depend on s, we may write

$$\sum_{s \neq w} (\operatorname{sgn} E_w) \frac{\partial E_w}{\partial p_s} E_s k_s$$

in the form

$$(\operatorname{sgn} E_w) \sum_{s \neq w} \frac{\partial E_w}{\partial p_s} E_s k_s .$$

$$\frac{\partial E_j}{\partial p_j} < 0 \, , \qquad c_j \left| \frac{\partial E_j}{\partial p_j} \right| > \sum_{s \neq j} c_s \left| \frac{\partial E_j}{\partial p_s} \right| \, , \qquad j = 1, 2, ..., n \, ,$$

where the c's are positive constants. In this case, take

$$V = \frac{k_w}{c_w} |E_w| \, ,$$

and then proceed as in the previous case.

The two cases of global stability examined — gross substitutability and negative dominance — generalize the results already obtained 'locally' (see Part II, ch. 9, §1, of the text for the economic meaning of gross substitutability and of negative dominance).

In their first paper on the stability of the competitive equilibrium, Arrow and Hurwicz (1958) said that "in none of the cases studied have we found the system to be unstable under the (perfectly competitive) adjustment process" (p. 529), and suggested tentatively the proposition that under perfect competition the system is always stable, admitting, however, that "it is conceivable... that...an example of unstable unique competitive equilibrium may be found" (p. 530). Some such examples were found by Scarf. Here we shall examine the first of Scarf's counterexamples to the stability of general equilibrium.

Consider an economy involving only three consumers and three goods. The utility functions are such that each consumer desires only two commodities in a fixed ratio (i.e. the two commodities are perfectly complementary), which is taken to be one to one, and has no desire for the remaining commodity. It is assumed that the first consumer desires only goods 1 and 2, the second consumer desires only goods 2 and 3 and the third consumer desires only goods 3 and 1. Formally, the utility functions can be written as

$$U_1(x_{11}, x_{12}, x_{13}) = \min (x_{11}, x_{12}) \, ,$$

$$U_2(x_{21}, x_{22}, x_{23}) = \min (x_{22}, x_{23}) \, ,$$

$$U_3(x_{31}, x_{32}, x_{33}) = \min (x_{33}, x_{31}) \, ,$$

where x_{ij} is the quantity of good j consumed by the i-th individual. For example, the typical indifference curve of the first consumer is shown in fig. A.1. Finally, it is assumed that the initial endowments are

$$\bar{x}_{ij} = \begin{cases} 1 & \text{for } i = j, \\ 0 & \text{for } i \neq j, \end{cases}$$

that is, the first consumer possesses initially one unit of the first good and zero units of goods 2 and 3, and so on.

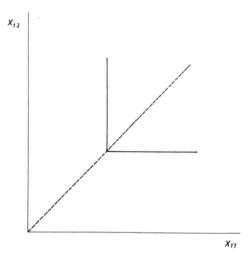

Fig. A.1.

Let us consider the first consumer. For any income M_1 he will demand the same quantity of goods 1 and 2 and, therefore, putting $x_{11} = x_{12}$ and $x_{13} = 0$ in his budget constraint $p_1 x_{11} + p_2 x_{12} + p_3 x_{13} = M_1$, we obtain his demand functions

$$x_{11}(p_1, p_2, p_3, M_1) = \frac{M_1}{p_1 + p_2},$$

$$x_{12}(p_1, p_2, p_3, M_1) = \frac{M_1}{p_1 + p_2},$$

$$x_{13}(p_1, p_2, p_3, M_1) = 0.$$

Now the 'income' of the first consumer is derived from his initial holding of the first good, so that $M_1 = p_1$. Thus the excess demand functions of the first consumer are

$$E_{11}(p_1,p_2,p_3) = x_{11}(p_1,p_2,p_3,M_1) - 1 = \frac{-p_2}{p_1 + p_2},$$

$$E_{12}(p_1,p_2,p_3) = x_{12}(p_1,p_2,p_3,M_1) - 0 = \frac{p_1}{p_1 + p_2},$$

$$E_{13}(p_1,p_2,p_3) = 0.$$

In a similar way we can derive the excess demand functions of the second and third consumers, and adding the three excess demand functions for each good we obtain the following aggregate excess demand functions:

$$E_1(p_1,p_2,p_3) = \frac{-p_2}{p_1 + p_2} + \frac{p_3}{p_3 + p_1},$$

$$E_2(p_1,p_2,p_3) = \frac{-p_3}{p_2 + p_3} + \frac{p_1}{p_1 + p_2}, \tag{II.13}$$

$$E_3(p_1,p_2,p_3) = \frac{-p_1}{p_3 + p_1} + \frac{p_2}{p_2 + p_3}.$$

It can easily be verified that the only equilibrium situation is $p_1 = p_2 = p_3$. To determine 'absolute' prices we need a normalization condition, e.g. $p_1^2 + p_2^2 + p_3^2 = 3$ (alternatively we could choose one good as 'numéraire' and put its price equal to 1); the equilibrium point is then $(1, 1, 1)$.

Consider now the dynamic adjustment process

$$\frac{dp_i}{dt} = E_i(p_1,p_2,p_3). \tag{II.14}$$

We shall show that

$$p_1 p_2 p_3 = \text{constant} \tag{II.15}$$

for any solution of (II.14). Differentiation of (II.15) with respect to time yields

$$\frac{dp_1}{dt} p_2 p_3 + \frac{dp_2}{dt} p_1 p_3 + \frac{dp_3}{dt} p_1 p_2 = 0, \tag{II.16}$$

and using (II.14) and (II.13) we have

$$\frac{p_3(p_1^2 - p_2^2)}{p_1 + p_2} + \frac{p_2(p_3^2 - p_1^2)}{p_3 + p_1} + \frac{p_1(p_2^2 - p_3^2)}{p_2 + p_3}$$

$$= p_3(p_1 - p_2) + p_2(p_3 - p_1) + p_1(p_2 - p_3) = 0 , \qquad (II.16')$$

which proves (II.15). It follows that equilibrium is unstable. In fact, the value of $p_1 p_2 p_3$ at equilibrium is 1, and, if $p_1(0)p_2(0)p_3(0) \neq 1$, equilibrium will never be reached, since by (II.15) we have $p_1(t)p_2(t)p_3(t) = p_1(0)p_2(0)p_3(0)$.

This completes our treatment of the global stability of general equilibrium. The student who wishes to pursue the matter further may consult, as a first step, Negishi's (1962) survey article.

§4.2. *Rules of thumb in business management (Baumol and Quandt)*

The complete information required to compute exactly the optimum point of a firm as indicated by economic theory, is not freely available in real life; it is conceivable that it might be obtained, but only at a cost which would exceed the benefits. Business management, then, uses rules of thumb in its decision making.

Baumol and Quandt (1964) have investigated how 'good' rules of thumb can be constructed and tested. A 'learning' rule of thumb is the following: a price change is made, and the resulting change in profits is observed; if the latter is positive, price is changed again in the same direction; if, instead, it is negative, price is changed in the opposite direction to that of the previous change; if, finally, the level of profits is stationary, price is not changed again. This rule of thumb can be proved to converge globally to the optimum point, provided that the latter exists and that no shifts occur in the profit function.

The rule under examination can be formalized as follows (a dot denotes d/dt):

$$\dot{p} = g\left(\frac{\dot{\pi}}{\dot{p}}\right) \quad \text{if } \dot{p} \neq 0 ,$$

$$\dot{p} = 0 \quad \text{otherwise} ,$$

where p is price, π is profit and g is a sign-preserving function, i.e. $g \gtreqless 0$ if $\dot{\pi}/\dot{p} \gtreqless 0$ *. Let us now assume that the (unknown) profit function is a concave,

---

* This is a generalization of Baumol's and Quandt's analysis (they use the relation $\dot{p} = k\dot{\pi}/\dot{p}$, k a positive constant).

differentiable function of p and that an optimum exists, i.e.

$$\pi = f(p) , \quad f'' < 0 \text{ everywhere} ,$$

$$f'(p) = 0 \quad \text{for } p = p_e .$$

Now, $\dot{\pi} = f'(p)\dot{p}$, and so the basic dynamical equation can be written as

$$\dot{p} = g(f'(p)) .$$

As a Liapunov function, choose [*] the square of the Euclidean distance:

$$V = (p - p_e)^2 .$$

We have

$$\frac{dV}{dt} = 2(p - p_e)\dot{p} = 2(p - p_e)g(f'(p)) .$$

Given the assumptions on the profit function, it must be $f'(p) \gtrless 0$ for $p \lessgtr p_e$, and so dV/dt is always negative out of equilibrium, which proves global stability.

References

Arrow, K.J., Block, H.D. and Hurwicz, L., 1959, On the Stability of the Competitive Equilibrium, II.

Arrow, K.J. and Hurwicz, L., 1958, On the Stability of the Competitive Equilibrium, I.

Baumol, W.J. and Quandt, R.E., 1964, Rules of Thumb and Optimally Imperfect Decisions, Appendix A.

Clower, R.W. and Bushaw, D.W., 1954, Price Determination in a Stock-Flow Economy.

Gale, D. and Nikaidô, H., 1965, The Jacobian Matrix and Global Univalence of Mappings.

Kalman, R.E. and Bertram, J.E., 1960, Control System Analysis and Design Via the "Second Method" of Liapunov, I and II.

Karlin, S., 1959, *Mathematical Method and Theory in Games, Programming and Economics*, Vol. I, ch. 9, §§9.4, 9.5.

Krasovskiĭ, N.N., 1963, *Stability of Motion, Applications of Liapunov's Second Method to Differential Systems and Equations with Delay*.

Lancaster, K., 1968, *Mathematical Economics*, ch. 12, § 12.2.

[*] Baumol and Quandt use $V = \frac{1}{2}(\dot{p} - 0)^2$, but this does not seem quite correct, since such a V does not necessarily satisfy requirement (ii) of Theorem I.

LaSalle, J.P. and Lefschetz, S., 1961, *Stability by Liapunov's Direct Method with Applications.*
Liapunov, A., 1907, *Problème général de la stabilité du mouvement*, pp. 255–67.
Morishima, M., 1964, *Equilibrium Stability and Growth*, ch. II.
Negishi, T., 1962, The Stability of a Competitive Economy: A Survey Article.
Newman, P.K., 1961, Approaches to Stability Analysis.
Nikaido, H., 1968, *Convex Structures and Economic Theory*, ch. VII.
Sansone, G. and Conti, R., 1964, *Non-linear Differential Equations*, ch. I, § 3.3; ch. IX, § 1.
Scarf, H., 1960, Some Examples of Global Instability of the Competitive Equilibrium.

APPENDIX III

Other Topics in Differential
and Difference Equations

§1. Introduction

Economic phenomena are not necessarily linear, so that linear and constant-coefficient differential and difference equations (l.c. equations for brevity) cannot be considered as a generally adequate tool to analyse dynamic problems. The widespread use of l.c. equations is of course mainly due to the fact that such equations are always solvable, whereas as soon as we venture into the field of non-l.c. equations we are not sure of finding the explicit solution. Such use can be justified as a first approximation (think, e.g., of the study of local stability) or as a simplifying assumption (think, e.g., of linear business cycle models). It would be highly desirable, however, to be able, when the need arises, to go further than 'first approximations' and 'simplifying assumptions'. This appendix is devoted to various topics in non-l.c. equations analysis.

It is a well-known fact that when an equation is non-l.c., more often than not it turns out that, although we know the solution exists (by the existence and uniqueness theorem ★), we are not able to 'find' it, since it cannot be

---

★ Consider the differential equation $dy/dt = f(y, t)$ and let $f(y, t)$ be a single-valued and continuous function of y and t in a rectangular domain D surrounding a point

expressed in terms of (a finite number of) known functions. There are, however, several types of non-l.c. equations which are explicitly integrable. It
would be impossible — and useless — to expound them all here [*], so we shall
examine only a few types, which have had some, although limited, applications in economic dynamics. We shall examine only differential equations,
both because in the field of non-l.c. equations only differential equations are
normally met in economic applications, and because a difference equation
can, if necessary, easily be analysed numerically, the precise time path corresponding to the given numerical values of the parameters and of the initial
conditions being obtained [**]. However, in expounding the elements of the
qualitative theory of non-linear equations we shall examine difference equations too.

§2. Exact equations of the first order and of the first degree

The general equation of the first order and of the first degree can be
written as

$$P(t,y) + Q(t,y)\frac{dy}{dt} = 0 , \tag{III.1}$$

(y_0, t_0) and defined by the inequalities $|y - y_0| \leq b$, $|t - t_0| \leq a$. Let M be the upper
bound of $|f(y, t)|$ in D, and let h be the smaller of a and of b/M. If $h < a$, the more
stringent restriction $|t - t_0| \leq h$ is imposed upon t. Moreover, $f(y, t)$ is Lipschitzian, that
is, if (y, t) and (Y, t) are two points in D with the same abscissa, then $|f(Y, t) - f(y, t)| < K|Y - y|$, where K is a constant. All these conditions being satisfied, there exists a unique
continuous function of t, say $y(t)$, defined for all values of t such that $|t - t_0| < h$, which
satisfies the differential equation and reduces to y_0 when $t = t_0$. This theorem can be extended to systems of first-order equations. For proofs see, for example, Ince (1956),
ch. III. For existence and uniqueness theorems concerning difference equations see, for
example, Milne-Thomson (1933).

[*] The interested student may consult, for example, Ince's two books (1956, 1959)
for differential equations and the books by Boole (1960) and by Milne-Thomson (1933)
for difference equations.

[**] Of course, differential equations can also be analysed numerically, but the method
is not easy and in any case yields only approximate results. On the other hand, the
precise numerical solution of a difference equation can always and easily be obtained by
applying the recurrent method. If, for example, the equation is of the type $y_{t+1} = f(y_t, t)$,
then, given y_0, we compute $y_1 = f(y_0, 0)$; from y_1 we compute $y_2 = f(y_1, 1)$, and so on.

and it is called of the first degree because the power to which the derivative dy/dt is raised is 1. Eq. (III.1) can also be written in the form of a total differential equation:

$$P(t,y)\,dt + Q(t,y)\,dy = 0 \,.\tag{III.2}$$

When the left-hand side of (III.2) is *immediately* (that is, without previous multiplication by any factor) recognizable as the total differential dz of a function $z(t,y)$, equation (III.2) is said to be *exact* and its solution is

$$z(t,y) = A \,,\tag{III.3}$$

where A is an arbitrary constant. For this to be true it must, of course, be the case that

$$P(t,y) = \frac{\partial z}{\partial t}\,,$$
$$\tag{III.4}$$
$$Q(t,y) = \frac{\partial z}{\partial y}\,.$$

Now, for (III.4) to hold, P and Q being differentiable functions, it must be true that

$$\frac{\partial P}{\partial y} = \frac{\partial Q}{\partial t}\,,\tag{III.5}$$

since by the *commutative theorem* on partial differentiation the following relation:

$$\frac{\partial^2 z}{\partial y \partial t} = \frac{\partial^2 z}{\partial t \partial y}$$

must hold, so that (III.5) is a consequence of (III.4).

  Condition (III.5) – called the *integrability condition* – is not only necessary but also sufficient in order that (III.2) be an exact equation. After having checked that the integrability condition is satisfied, we can find the solution (III.3) by integrating P with respect to t and Q with respect to y, that is

$$\int\limits_{t_0}^{t} P(t,y)\,dt + \int\limits_{y_0}^{y} Q(t_0,y)\,dy = A \;, \tag{III.6}$$

where A is an arbitrary constant and t_0, y_0 may be chosen as convenient. Let us note that this does not mean that there are three arbitrary constants. The arbitrary constant is actually only one, since a change in t_0 or in y_0 is the same as adding an arbitrary constant to the left-hand side of (III.6), which can then be shifted to the right-hand side and absorbed in A. For this reason the limits of integration can also be left indeterminate and omitted, the solution being written as

$$\int P(t,y)\,dt + \int Q(t,y)\,dy = A \;. \tag{III.6$'$}$$

When condition (III.5) does not hold, the solution cannot be given by (III.6), and it is necessary to find an *integrating factor*, that is, a function $\mu(t,y)$ such that the expression

$$\mu(t,y)(P\,dt + Q\,dy)$$

is a total differential. In other words, the integrating factor must be such that the integrability condition is satisfied with respect to $\mu(t,y)P(t,y)$ and to $\mu(t,y)Q(t,y)$, i.e.

$$\frac{\partial[\mu(t,y)P(t,y)]}{\partial y} = \frac{\partial[\mu(t,y)Q(t,y)]}{\partial t}.$$

When the integrating factor has been found, the solution can be given as

$$\int \mu(t,y)P(t,y)\,dt + \int \mu(t,y)Q(t,y)\,dy = A \;.$$

Although it can be proved ★ that there exists an infinite number of integrating factors (so that eq. (III.1) is always integrable, at least in principle), it turns out that the direct evaluation of μ requires the solution of a partial differen-

---

★ See, e.g., Ince (1956, pp. 27–9). The only condition is that eq. (III.2) has a unique solution, that is, the conditions of the existence and uniqueness theorem are assumed to hold.

tial equation, that is, an equation of a more advanced type than the equation whose solution we are looking for. Fortunately, in many cases the partial differential equation has an obvious solution which gives the required integrating factor. We shall not pursue this matter further, turning instead to the study of two special cases of exact equations.

The first occurs when P depends on t alone and Q on y alone, that is

$$P(t)\,dt + Q(y)\,dy = 0 . \tag{III.7}$$

The equation is then said to have *separated variables*, and the integrability condition is necessarily satisfied, since

$$\frac{\partial P}{\partial y} = \frac{\partial Q}{\partial t} = 0 . \tag{III.8}$$

Therefore, the solution is

$$\int P(t)\,dt + \int Q(y)\,dy = A . \tag{III.9}$$

The second case occurs when P and Q are both functions of t and y, but such that they can be factorized into the product of a function of t alone and of a function of y alone, that is, say

$$P(t,y) = T(t) \times Y_1(y) ,$$
$$\tag{III.10}$$
$$Q(t,y) = T_1(t) \times Y(y) .$$

The equation is then said to have *separable variables*, since it may be written – if we divide by $T_1(t) \times Y_1(y)$ – in the form

$$\frac{T(t)}{T_1(t)}\,dt + \frac{Y(y)}{Y_1(y)}\,dy = 0 , \tag{III.11}$$

which has separated variables.

§3. Linear equations of the first order with variable coefficients

The general first-order linear equation is

$$a_1(t)\frac{dy}{dt} + a_0(t)y = g(t) \ , \tag{III.12}$$

where $a_1(t), a_0(t), g(t)$ are known functions. As in constant-coefficient linear equations, eq. (III.12) is said to be non-homogeneous; the corresponding homogeneous form is, of course,

$$a_1(t)\frac{dy}{dt} + a_0(t)y = 0 \ . \tag{III.13}$$

Setting

$$h(t) \equiv \frac{a_0(t)}{a_1(t)}$$

$$\varphi(t) \equiv \frac{g(t)}{a_1(t)} \ ,$$

we can rewrite (III.12) and (III.13) as

$$\frac{dy}{dt} + h(t)y = \varphi(t) \ , \tag{III.12'}$$

$$\frac{dy}{dt} + h(t)y = 0 \ . \tag{III.13'}$$

Let us consider first eq. (III.13'). It can be written as

$$dy + h(t)y \, dt = 0 \ , \tag{III.14}$$

which has separable variables: in fact, dividing through by y we have

$$\frac{1}{y}dy + h(t) \, dt = 0 \ , \tag{III.15}$$

whose solution – see eq. (III.9) in the previous section – is

$$\int \frac{1}{y}dy + \int h(t) \, dt = A \ , \tag{III.16}$$

that is,

$$\log_e y = A - \int h(t)\,dt ,$$

so that

$$y(t) = \exp\left[A - \int h(t)\,dt\right] . \tag{III.17}$$

Setting $e^A \equiv C$, we have

$$y(t) = C \exp\left[- \int h(t)\,dt\right] . \tag{III.18}$$

Let us now tackle eq. (III.13'). To solve it we shall apply Lagrange's method of *variation of parameters* ★. This is a general method of solving an equation by considering as variables as a function of t the arbitrary constants which appear in the solution of a simpler equation, trying then to determine them in such a way that the equation to solve is identically satisfied. In our case we put

$$y(t) = C(t) \exp\left[- \int h(t)\,dt\right] , \tag{III.19}$$

where $C(t)$ is an undetermined function. Differentiating we have

$$\frac{dy}{dt} = \frac{dC}{dt} \exp\left[- \int h(t)\,dt\right] - h(t)C(t)\exp\left[- \int h(t)\,dt\right] . \tag{III.20}$$

Substituting (III.19) and (III.20) in (III.12') we obtain

$$\frac{dC}{dt} \exp\left[- \int h(t)\,dt\right] = \varphi(t) , \tag{III.21}$$

that is,

$$\frac{dC}{dt} = \varphi(t) \exp\left[\int h(t)\,dt\right] , \tag{III.21'}$$

★ This method was devised by John Bernoulli in relation to the first-order linear equation, but its generalization is due to Lagrange, and this explains why the method is usually referred to as Lagrange's.

which gives

$$C(t) = \int \{\varphi(t) \exp [\int h(t) \, dt]\} \, dt + B \ , \tag{III.22}$$

where B is an arbitrary constant. From (III.19) and (III.22) we have

$$y(t) = B \exp [-\int h(t) \, dt] + \exp [-\int h(t) \, dt] \int \{\varphi(t) \exp [\int h(t) \, dt]\} \, dt \ . \tag{III.23}$$

which is the required solution of (III.12$'$).

Let us note, finally, that the methods expounded in this section can be applied also when the coefficients are constant. In particular, the method of variation of parameters can be applied when the method of undetermined coefficients to find a particular solution of the non-homogeneous equation (see Part II, ch. 2) fails.

§4. The Bernoulli equation

The non-linear first-order equation

$$\frac{dy}{dt} + h(t)y = \varphi(t)y^n \ , \tag{III.24}$$

where n is any real number (different from 0 and from $+1$), is known in the mathematical literature as the Bernoulli equation[*]. It can be put in linear form by a change of dependent variable. If we put

$$z = y^{1-n} \ , \tag{III.25}$$

then

$$\frac{dz}{dt} = (1-n)y^{-n}\frac{dy}{dt} \ . \tag{III.26}$$

Multiplying both members of (III.24) by $(1-n)y^{-n}$, we have

---

[*] The name derives from the fact that it was proposed for solution by James Bernoulli (in 1695); the method of solution expounded here was discovered by Leibniz in the following year.

$$(1-n)y^{-n}\frac{dy}{dt} + (1-n)h(t)y^{1-n} = \varphi(t) , \tag{III.27}$$

and so, taking account of (III.25) and (III.26), we have

$$\frac{dz}{dt} + (1-n)h(t)z = \varphi(t) , \tag{III.28}$$

which is linear in z and can be solved by the methods expounded in the previous section. Having found the function $z(t)$, from (III.25) we obtain

$$y(t) = [z(t)]^{1/(1-n)} , \tag{III.29}$$

which is the required solution of eq. (III.24).

§5. Elements of the qualitative theory of non-linear differential equations

By 'qualitative' or 'topological' theory of differential equations we mean the analysis of the properties of the solution of a differential equation (or of a system) without actually knowing the solution itself nor trying to approximate it by means of power series or other 'quantitative' methods [*]. The same definition applies of course to difference equations.

We shall examine single first-order equations and systems of two simultaneous first-order equations (the latter can also be considered as the transformation of a second-order equation). In any case the equations considered will be *autonomous,* that is, not involving time explicitly nor involving given function(s) of time. The techniques used will be mainly geometric.

§5.1. *Single equations*
A graphical technique widely used to analyse first-order autonomous equations, that is, equations of the type

$$\varphi\left(y, \frac{dy}{dt}\right) = 0 , \tag{III.30}$$

---

[*] Given this definition, Liapunov's second method for the study of stability problems also belongs to the qualitative analysis. However, the importance of the said method is such that we have treated it in an appendix of its own (Appendix II).

is the so-called *phase diagram*. Before expounding this technique a few considerations are necessary. Let us assume that (III.30) is explicit or can be made so, that is having (or such that it can be put in) the form

$$\frac{dy}{dt} = f(y) .$$
(III.30′)

Eq. (III.30′) has separable variables, since we can write it as $dy - f(y)\,dt = 0$, that is,

$$\frac{1}{f(y)}\,dy - dt = 0 ,$$
(III.31)

which gives

$$\int \frac{1}{f(y)}\,dy - t = A .$$
(III.32)

A legitimate question is now the following: since the equation is integrable, why the need to use other methods? The reasons are formal and economic. Formally we can note the following:

(1) the function $f(y)$ may be such that the integral $\int [1/f(y)]\,dy$ cannot be expressed in terms of known functions **★**;

(2) even if difficulty (1) does not occur, so that

$$\int \frac{1}{f(y)}\,dy = G(y) ,$$

where G is a known function, it may happen that the relation $t = H(y)$ (where $H(y) \equiv G(y) - A$) is not invertible, and so we cannot obtain the explicit form of the solution, $y = y(t) \equiv H^{-1}(t)$, which is the one we are interested in to determine the time path of y.

From the economic point of view there is the usual motive: in economic theory, more often than not the form of the function $f(y)$ is not specified, but only its qualitative properties are given, so that only a qualitative analysis is possible. If we add the (formal) fact that it may happen that eq. (III.30) cannot be put into the explicit form (III.30′), we have more than enough to justify the great usefulness of the phase diagram.

★ This, of course, may occur also in relation to eqs. (III.6), (III.9), (III.18), and (III.23). When this happens, we can try to expand the integrands in power series and to integrate term by term. This belongs to the domain of 'quantitative' approximations.

Consider two orthogonal Cartesian axes; on the abscissae we measure y and on the ordinates we measure dy/dt, that is, $f(y)$ if (III.30) can be made explicit. Then the graphical counterpart of eq. (III.30) or (III.30') is a well-defined curve, which is the *phase diagram* of the equation. In fig. A.2 some of the ways in which $\varphi(dy/dt, y) = 0$ might qualitatively behave are represented.

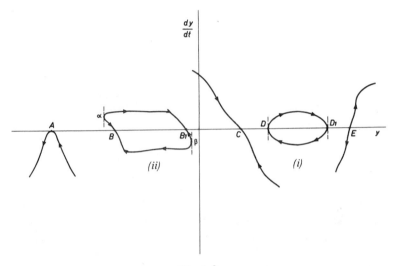

Fig. A.2.

The basic rules for interpreting these diagrams are very simple: *in all the points above the y-axis, dy/dt is positive and so y is increasing; in all the points below the y-axis, dy/dt is negative and so y is decreasing; in all the points falling on the y-axis, dy/dt is zero and so y is stationary.*
The arrows indicate the direction of the movement: if $dy/dt > 0$, we move from the left to the right on the phase curve (y increases); if $dy/dt < 0$, we move from the right to the left along the phase curve (y decreases). An equilibrium point occurs where $dy/dt = 0$, that is, where the phase curve intersects the y-axis. Of course, there may be more than one such point.
It is then quite simple to analyse the stability of an equilibrium point: for example, point A is stable from the right but unstable from the left (one-sided stability—instability), point C is stable, point E is unstable. In other words, it is true, in general, that:
(a) if the phase curve intersects the y-axis with a positive slope, the equilibrium point (that is, the intersection point) is unstable (points like E);

(b) if the phase curve intersects the y-axis with a negative slope, the equilibrium point is stable (points like C);

(c) if the phase curve is tangential to the y-axis, remaining wholly on one side of it (that is, if the point of tangency is a maximum or a minimum of the phase curve), the equilibrium point is stable from one side and unstable from the other (points like A); if, instead, the point of tangency corresponds to a horizontal inflection point of the phase curve, then the equilibrium point is stable if the phase curve lies above (below) the y-axis to the left (right) of the inflection point and unstable in the opposite case.

More generally, global stability obtains if the phase curve lies wholly above (below) the y-axis to the left (right) of the equilibrium point ★.

An interesting case occurs when the phase curve forms a *closed loop*. Of course, this is possible only if the function $f(y)$ is multivalued. When the phase diagram has the form of a closed curve, an oscillatory movement (necessarily of constant amplitude) may occur. The conditions for the occurrence of a cycle when the phase curve is closed are the following:

(1) that the curve lies partly above and partly below the y-axis, so that there can be a stage of increase and one of decrease in y;

(2) that the phase curve has an infinite slope (tangent parallel to the dy/dt axis) at the points of intersection with the y-axis. In fact, if it were not so, such intersection points would be stable or unstable according to the rules outlined above, under (a) and (b), so that the movement in the first case would converge monotonically to the equilibrium point and would not cross the y-axis, and in the second case would diverge from the equilibrium point and would not cross the y-axis either.

In fig. A.2, the phase curve of type (i) satisfies both conditions, so that it gives rise to a constant amplitude oscillatory movement. The phase curve of type (ii) does not satisfy condition (2), and the movement converges towards point B or B_1 according to whether the initial point falls in the portion $\alpha B \beta$ or $\alpha B_1 \beta$ of the phase curve.

It must be stressed that the oscillatory movements that may occur are not necessarily of constant amplitude. Oscillatory movements of the convergent or divergent kind may also occur with multivalued functions $f(y)$. Of course, the phase curve must not be a closed loop, but must have a spiral-like form, as

---

★ Apart from intuitive graphical considerations, this condition can be proved rigorously by means of Liapunov's second method (see Appendix II, §3, theorem I). Let $V = \frac{1}{2}(y - y_e)^2$ be a Liapunov function. Then $dV/dt = (y - y_e)\, dy/dt = (y - y_e)f(y)$, which is zero for $y = y_e$, and $dV/dt < 0$ if $f(y) \gtrless 0$ for $y - y_e \lessgtr 0$, which is the condition stated in the text.

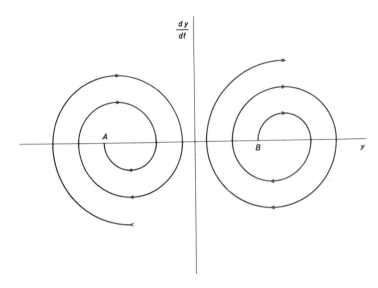

Fig. A.3.

in fig. A.3. In any case the same conditions (1) and (2) must hold. Spirals like A give rise to an oscillatory movement which converges to the equilibrium point A, whereas the opposite is true in the case of spirals like B.

What we have said in this section, of course, does not exhaust all the possible cases. But a complete taxonomy would not be possible and anyway not of much interest, since once we have understood the rather simple principles which underlie phase diagrams, we are sufficiently equipped to understand any such diagram that we may meet.

Let us note, finally, that the phase diagram can be applied also to first-order linear equations with constant coefficients (a particular case of the general first-order autonomous equation) of the type

$$\frac{dy}{dt} = ay + b \, ,$$

which were examined in Part II, ch. 2. The phase diagram of that equation is a straight line which intersects the y-axis in the point $-b/a$ and which has a positive (negative) slope if a is positive (negative).

§5.2. *Systems of two simultaneous equations*

Here we shall examine autonomous systems of the type

$$\frac{dy_1}{dt} = \varphi_1(y_1, y_2),$$

$$\frac{dy_2}{dt} = \varphi_2(y_1, y_2).$$ (III.33)

System (III.33) can be given as such or it may arise by a second-order equation. Consider, for example, the equation

$$\frac{d^2 y_1}{dt^2} + f\left(y_1, \frac{dy_1}{dt}\right) = 0,$$ (III.34)

and define a new variable y_2 such that $dy_1/dt = y_2$. Then the system

$$\frac{dy_1}{dt} = y_2$$

$$\frac{dy_2}{dt} = -f(y_1, y_2)$$ (III.35)

is equivalent to eq. (III.34) and is of type (III.33). The reason for transforming eq. (III.34) into system (III.35) is that by so doing we can use the qualitative techniques that we are going to expound.

Let us now give some definitions. By *phase plane* (also called the *plane of the states*) we mean the plane (y_1, y_2). To each 'state' of the system, that is to each pair of coordinates y_1, y_2, there corresponds a point in the phase plane. Thus the motion of the system can be represented by a succession of points in the phase plane, that is by a *phase path* ★ or *trajectory* (also called 'characteristic curve' or simply 'characteristic'). This path, in other words, is described by the parametric equations

$$y_1 = y_1(t),$$

$$y_2 = y_2(t),$$ (III.36)

★ The *phase path* must not be confused with the *phase diagram* treated in the previous section. The analogue of the phase path for a single equation would be the y-axis itself.

where $y_1(t), y_2(t)$ is the solution of system (III.33) [*]. Eliminating t from (III.36) we have

$$\psi(y_1, y_2) = 0 , \qquad (III.37)$$

which is the implicit equation of the phase path.

The same trajectory can also be obtained in a different way. Eliminating dt from (III.33) we have the differential equation

$$\frac{dy_2}{dy_1} = \frac{\varphi_2(y_1, y_2)}{\varphi_1(y_1, y_2)} , \qquad (III.38)$$

whose solution yields the *integral curves* of system (III.33) in the phase plane, each curve corresponding to given values of the arbitrary constants. Now, such integral curves are the same [**] as the trajectory obtained by (III.36) — actually, the solution of (III.38) is the same as (III.37), apart from arbitrary constants — with the difference that from (III.36) we also obtain the direction of the movement of the representative point on the phase path, whereas from the integration of (III.38) we obtain a purely geometric curve, without any reference to what is happening in time. However, the 'direction of travel' along the integral curves can be obtained from eqs. (III.33), it being observed that $dy_i/dt \gtrless 0$ when $\varphi_i(y_1, y_2) \gtrless 0$, and this tells us whether y_i is increasing or decreasing [‡].

The practical reason for obtaining the integral curves is that it may happen that eq. (III.38) is integrable [‡‡] whereas eqs. (III.36) are not obtainable from the solution of system (III.33), either because such a solution cannot be found (and this is a very common case with non-linear systems) or because it can be given only in the form of an integral curve. Even if eq. (III.38) is not integrable [‡‡], a graphic analysis of it to obtain the approximate shape of the

[*] For the graphic construction of a phase path by means of (III.36), see Part II, ch. 9. §4.

[**] Some authors, e.g. Andronov *et al.* (1966, pp. 7, 34), prefer to distinguish between *phase paths* and *integral curves*, since an integral curve may consist of several phase paths. Consider, for example, fig. A.4(a) below. Each integral curve consists of three phase paths, two of which are the two branches of the typical integral curve, and the third is the equilibrium point itself; it is, however, true that the integral curves are the loci of all the phase paths.

[‡] Here, as well as in the remaining treatment (unless otherwise explicitly stated), the direction of the movement is to be understood for $t \to +\infty$.

[‡‡] By 'integrable' we mean that the integral can be explicitly expressed in terms of (a finite number of) known functions. Thus by 'not integrable' we do not mean that the integral does not exist, but that it cannot be expressed, etc.

integral curves may be simpler than the analysis of system (III.33).

Any point in which the two functions $\varphi_1(y_1, y_2)$ and $\varphi_2(y_1, y_2)$ do not vanish simultaneously is called an *ordinary point* (or regular point), whereas any point in which the two functions are simultaneously zero is called a *singular point*. It is clear that singular points represent states of rest, that is, of equilibrium of the system, since in a singular point $dy_1/dt = dy_2/dt = 0$ by definition. Thus the analysis of the integral curves usually starts by trying to determine the singular points, if any, around which the integral curves are then constructed. In what follows, for graphical simplicity we shall take the origin as the singular point. This does not involve any loss of generality, since if the singular point is elsewhere, we can always imagine making a transformation of coordinates so that the origin and the singular point coincide; if there are several singular points, one of them is taken as the origin.

The 'elementary' singular points are the *node*, the *saddle point* (or *col*), the *focus* (or *vortex*) and the *centre*, the classification being made according to the shape of the integral curves.

A *node* is a singular point such that all integral curves pass through it. Some examples are given in fig. A.4. In the particular case in which the integral curves are straight lines passing through the singular point the node is called a stellar node or *star*.

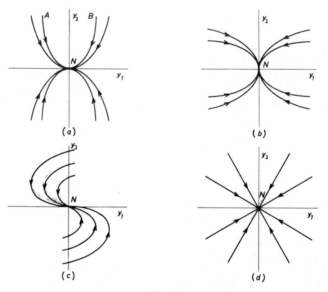

Fig. A.4.

If the direction of the movement (indicated by the arrows) is towards (away from) the singular point, the latter is, of course, stable (unstable).

A *saddle point* is a singular point through which only two integral curves pass, which are asymptotes to all the remaining curves. The asymptotes can be the axes themselves, as in fig. A.5(a), or not, as in fig. A.5(b). It can be seen that, whatever the direction of the movement along an integral curve, the motion is always away from the equilibrium point (except for the one along one of the two asymptotes).

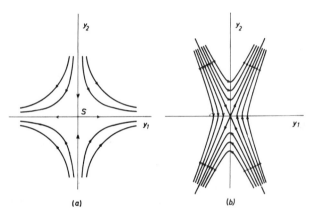

Fig. A.5.

A *focus* is a singular point which is the limit point of all integral curves, which have the form of spirals enclosed in each other (fig. A.6). The direction of the movement can be towards or away from the equilibrium point.

Finally, a *centre* is a singular point through which no integral curve passes (that is, an isolated singular point) surrounded by closed integral curves (fig. A.7). In this case, no matter what the direction of the movement is, the variables y_1, y_2 have a periodic motion whose amplitude is neither decreasing nor increasing, whereas in the case of a focus they have an oscillatory movement whose amplitude is either decreasing or increasing.

In general, a system may have several singular points of different types. Thus, if we 'map' the whole phase plane, we obtain certain domains possessing different properties. The boundaries of these domains are certain asymptotic trajectories called *separatrices* (see e.g. fig. A.8).

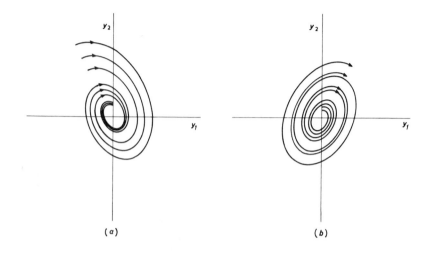

Fig. A.6.

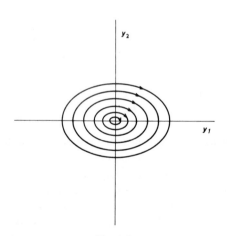

Fig. A.7.

Incidentally, we may note that the graphical technique of the integral curves can be applied also to linear systems with constant coefficients. But this application, though interesting in itself, does not add anything to our knowledge of the solution of such systems, since the latter can always be obtained explicitly ★. Thus the technique of the integral curves is most useful in

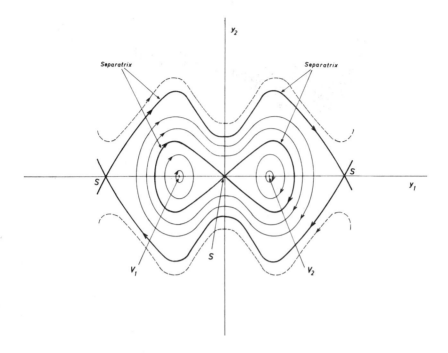

Fig. A.8.

the analysis of non-linear systems which cannot be integrated or whose solution cannot be put in explicit form, as we said above. An illustration will be given in the next section.

The notion of centre defined above leads us to investigate the problem of

---

★ Moreover, it may happen that the difficulty of the problem is increased. For example, consider the system

$$dy_1/dt = y_2 \,,$$

$$dy_2/dt = -\omega^2 y_1 - 2by_2 \,,$$

which is easily integrable by the standard procedure expounded in Part II, ch. 8 (the characteristic equation is $\lambda^2 + 2b\lambda + \omega^2 = 0$, etc.). Eliminating dt we obtain the differential equation of the integral curves

$$\frac{dy_2}{dy_1} = -\frac{2by_2 + \omega^2 y_1}{y_2} \,,$$

which is rather more difficult to integrate than the original system.

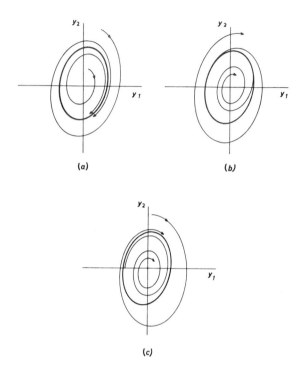

Fig. A.9.

the existence and stability of *limit cycles* (fig. A.9). A limit cycle is an isolated closed integral curve to which all nearby paths approach from both sides in a spiral fashion. If the direction of movement along the nearby paths is towards (away from) the limit cycle, the latter is called *orbitally stable (unstable)*. Intermediate cases may also occur in which all paths on one side of the limit cycle approach it, while on the other side they move away from it; in such cases the limit cycle can be called *semi-stable*. The (local) stability of a limit cycle can be investigated by means of the following theorem:

Theorem I. Let $y_1 = y_1(t), y_2 = y_2(t)$ be a periodic motion (limit cycle) of system (III.33). This limit cycle is locally stable (unstable) if its *characteristic exponent*

$$h = \frac{1}{T} \int_0^T \left\{ \frac{\partial \varphi_1[y_1(t), y_2(t)]}{\partial y_1} + \frac{\partial \varphi_2[y_1(t), y_2(t)]}{\partial y_2} \right\} dt$$

is respectively negative (positive). For a proof the reader is referred, for example, to Andronov *et al.*, 1966, pp. 289–90 and 296–300.

In the above theorem we started with an existing limit cycle. But to determine whether a given system has limit cycles is not an easy matter. A sufficient condition for the *absence* of closed integral curves (that is, the non-satisfaction of this condition is a necessary condition for the presence of limit cycles) is given by the following:

Theorem II (negative criterion of Bendixon). Given system (III.33), if the expression $\partial\varphi_1/\partial y_1 + \partial\varphi_2/\partial y_2$ does not change its sign (or vanish identically) within a region D of the phase plane, no closed path can exist in D [*].

Another negative criterion is the following:

Theorem III. If a system has no singular points, then it cannot have limit cycles [**].

We shall now state a set of *sufficient* conditions for the existence of limit cycles [‡]:

Theorem IV (Poincaré–Bendixon). Let D indicate the finite domain in the phase plane, contained between two closed curves C_1 and C_2. Then, if (1) in D and on C_1 and C_2 no singular points exist, and (2) the integral curves passing through the points of C_1 and C_2 penetrate in D all for t increasing or all for t decreasing, then D contains at least one limit cycle. It can also be shown that the limit cycle contained in D must be alternately stable and unstable (the outermost and innermost being stable), so that if there is only one limit cycle it is necessarily stable.

Another useful theorem, which allows us to establish simultaneously the existence *and* the stability (or instability) of a limit cycle, is the following [‡‡]:

Theorem V (Nemitzky). If it is possible to determine two positive constants ρ_1 and ρ_2 ($\rho_2 > \rho_1$) such that for ρ_1 the expression $y_1\varphi_1 + y_2\varphi_2 \geqslant 0$, and, for $\rho_2, y_1\varphi_1 + y_2\varphi_2 \leqslant 0$, and, if, moreover, the circular ring between the circles of radii ρ_2 and ρ_1 has no singular points, then there exists a stable

[*] Andronov *et al.*, 1966, p. 305; Minorsky, 1962, pp. 82–4.
[**] Andronov *et al.*, 1966, p. 306.
[‡] Minorsky, 1962, p. 84; Sansone and Conti, 1964, ch. IV, §IV.2.9.
[‡‡] Minorsky, 1962, p. 90.

limit cycle in D. If the signs of $y_1\varphi_1 + y_2\varphi_2$ are reversed, other conditions being the same, the limit cycle is unstable.

Finally, let us state two theorems [*], one relative to periodic motions of the second-order equation

$$\frac{d^2y}{dt^2} + f(y)\frac{dy}{dt} + g(y) = 0 , \tag{III.39}$$

which is an equation of the Liénard type (a generalization of the van der Pol equation for relaxation oscillations [**]), and the other relative to periodic motions of the second-order equation

$$\frac{d^2y}{dt^2} + f\left(y, \frac{dy}{dt}\right)\frac{dy}{dt} + g(y) = 0 , \tag{III.40}$$

which, in turn, is a generalization of the previous one.

Theorem VI. The differential eq. (III.39) has a unique periodic solution if the following conditions are satisfied:
  (1) $f(y)$ and $g(y)$ are differentiable;
  (2) there exist two positive numbers y_1, y_2 such that $f(y) < 0$ for $-y_1 < y < y_2$ and $f(y) \geqslant 0$ otherwise;
  (3) $yg(y) > 0$ for $y \neq 0$;
  (4) $\lim\limits_{y \to \pm\infty} F(y) = \lim\limits_{y \to \pm\infty} G(y) = \infty$,
where

$$F(y) = \int_0^y f(y)\,dy , \qquad G(y) = \int_0^y g(y)\,dy ;$$

  (5) $G(-y_1) = G(y_2)$.

---

[*] Minorsky, 1962, ch. 4, § 2; Sansone and Conti, 1964, ch. VI, §§ VI.3 and VI.4. The theorems stated here are due to Levinson and Smith and have been successively sharpened by Dragilev, de Castro, Sansone and Conti and others. See Sansone and Conti, *loc. cit.*
[**] This equation has the form

$$\frac{d^2y}{dt^2} + \mu(y^2 - 1)\frac{dy}{dt} + y = 0 ,$$

where μ is a positive parameter.

Theorem VII. The differential eq. (III.40) has at least one limit cycle if the following conditions are satisfied:

(1) $yg(y) > 0$ for $y \neq 0$;

(2) $\lim_{y \to \pm\infty} G(y) = \infty$, where

$$G(y) = \int_0^y g(y)\,dy\;;$$

(3) $f(0,0) < 0$;

(4) there exists a positive number y_0 such that $f(y, dy/dt) \geqslant 0$ for $|y| \geqslant y_0$;

(5) there exists a constant M such that, for $|y| \leqslant y_0$, $f(y,v) \geqslant -M$ for any v;

(6) there exists a $y_1 > y_0$ such that

$$\int_{y_0}^{y_1} f(y, v(y))\,dy \geqslant 10My_0\;,$$

where $v(y)$ is an arbitrary positive decreasing function of y.

The limit cycle is unique if:

(7) there exist two positive numbers y_0, y_1 such that $f(y, dy/dt) < 0$ for $-y_1 < y < y_2$ and $f(y, dy/dt) \geqslant 0$ otherwise;

(8) $\dfrac{dy}{dt}\,\dfrac{\partial f}{\partial(dy/dt)} = 0$;

(9) $G(-y_1) = G(y_0)$.

§5.3. *The Lotka–Volterra equations*

The treatment which follows is actually an illustration of the technique of the integral curves explained in the previous section. However, both to avoid interrupting the main line of the argument there and because such equations are of interest in themselves, we have decided to treat them in a separate section.

In the mathematical literature [*] such equations are usually attributed to Volterra. However, this particular aspect of Volterra's work on mathematical

---

[*] See, for example, Andronov *et al.* (1966, pp. 142–5), and Minorsky (1962, pp. 65–70). The following mathematical treatment is based on those works, as well as on Volterra's.

biology was anticipated by Lotka, who developed and studied the same equations earlier than Volterra [*]. This is why we think that the denomination 'Lotka–Volterra equations' is more appropriate. Here we shall, of course, leave aside the biological problems [**] which gave rise to such equations, and examine them from the purely mathematical point of view [‡].

The equations under consideration have the form

$$\frac{dy_1}{dt} = (a_1 - b_1 y_2) y_1 ,$$

$$\frac{dy_2}{dt} = -(a_2 - b_2 y_1) y_2 ,$$

(III.41)

where a_1, b_1, a_2, b_2 are positive constants and only non-negative values of y_1, y_2 are considered. The integral curves of (III.41) can be obtained as follows. Multiply the first equation by a_2/y_1, the second by a_1/y_2 and add, obtaining

$$\frac{a_2}{y_1} \frac{dy_1}{dt} + \frac{a_1}{y_2} \frac{dy_2}{dt} = -a_2 b_1 y_2 + a_1 b_2 y_1 ,$$

(III.42)

that is,

$$a_2 \frac{d \log y_1}{dt} + a_1 \frac{d \log y_2}{dt} = -a_2 b_1 y_2 + a_1 b_2 y_1 ,$$

(III.42′)

where, of course, the logarithms are to the base e.

Now, multiply the first equation of (III.41) by b_2, the second by b_1 and add, obtaining,

$$b_2 \frac{dy_1}{dt} + b_1 \frac{dy_2}{dt} = a_1 b_2 y_1 - a_2 b_1 y_2 .$$

(III.43)

Since the right-hand members of (III.42′) and of (III.43) are equal, the left-hand members must also be equal, so that

[*] See Lotka (1956, pp. 88–92); see also E.T. Whittaker's *Biography of Vito Volterra*, reprinted in Volterra's *Theory of Functionals*, etc., pp. 20–1 of the reprint.

[**] The interested reader can consult Volterra (1931) and Lotka, *loc. cit.*

[‡] Of course, the ultimate reason for our having treated such equations at length is that they have had an interesting economic application. See §7.4 of this appendix.

$$-a_2 \frac{\mathrm{d}\log y_1}{\mathrm{d}t} - a_1 \frac{\mathrm{d}\log y_2}{\mathrm{d}t} + b_2 \frac{\mathrm{d}y_1}{\mathrm{d}t} + b_1 \frac{\mathrm{d}y_2}{\mathrm{d}t} = 0 . \qquad \text{(III.44)}$$

This differential equation is directly integrable and yields the single-valued integral

$$b_2 y_1 + b_1 y_2 - a_2 \log y_1 - a_1 \log y_2 = A , \qquad \text{(III.45)}$$

where A is an arbitrary constant. Another way of arriving at the same result is to follow the standard procedure for obtaining the integral curves explained in the previous section, that is, to eliminate $\mathrm{d}t$ from the original system and to integrate the resulting differential equation. Eliminating $\mathrm{d}t$ from system (III.41) we have

$$\frac{\mathrm{d}y_2}{\mathrm{d}y_1} = -\frac{(a_2 - b_2 y_1) y_2}{(a_1 - b_1 y_2) y_1} ,$$

that is,

$$- (a_1 - b_1 y_2) y_1 \, \mathrm{d}y_2 - (a_2 - b_2 y_1) y_2 \, \mathrm{d}y_1 = 0 .$$

The variables are separable (see Appendix III, §2) through the division by $y_1 y_2$, so that

$$- (a_1 y_2^{-1} - b_1) \, \mathrm{d}y_2 - (a_2 y_1^{-1} - b_2) \, \mathrm{d}y_1 = 0 .$$

Integrating we have

$$- \int (a_1 y_2^{-1} - b_1) \, \mathrm{d}y_2 - \int (a_2 y_1^{-1} - b_2) \, \mathrm{d}y_1 = A ,$$

that is,

$$- a_1 \log y_2 + b_1 y_2 - a_2 \log y_1 + b_2 y_1 = A ,$$

which is the same as eq. (III.45).

Setting $B \equiv e^A$, eq. (III.45) can be rewritten as

$$\exp (b_2 y_1) \exp (b_1 y_2) y_1^{-a_2} y_2^{-a_1} = B , \qquad \text{(III.45')}$$

which gives

$$y_1^{-a_2} \exp (b_2 y_1) = B y_2^{a_1} \exp (-b_1 y_2) . \qquad \text{(III.46)}$$

Now, consider the functions

$$X_1 = X_1(y_1) = y_1^{-a_2} \exp(b_2 y_1),$$

$$X_2 = X_2(y_2) = y_2^{a_1} \exp(-b_1 y_2). \tag{III.47}$$

The required integral curves are determined by the relation

$$X_1 = B X_2, \tag{III.48}$$

that is, are obtained equating the function X_1 to the function X_2 multiplied by an arbitrary constant. Of course, to each value of the arbitrary constant B there corresponds one integral curve.

In order to construct the integral curves, let us first investigate the form of the functions $X_1(y_1)$ and $X_2(y_2)$. We have

$$\frac{dX_1}{dy_1} = -a_2 y_1^{-a_2-1} \exp(b_2 y_1) + b_2 y_1^{-a_2} \exp(b_2 y_1) = X_1\left(b_2 - \frac{a_2}{y_1}\right), \tag{III.49}$$

from which we see that $dX_1/dy_1 = 0$ for $y_1 = a_2/b_2$ and that dX_1/dy_1 is always negative for $0 \leqslant y_1 < a_2/b_2$ and always positive for $y_1 > a_2/b_2$. Thus the shape of X_1 is as shown in fig. A.10. The curve has been drawn everywhere

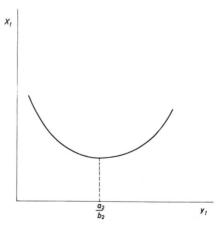

Fig. A.10.

convex to the y_1-axis since the second derivative $d^2 X_1/dy_1^2$ is always positive for $y_1 \geqslant 0$ [*].

With regard to X_2, we have

$$\frac{dX_2}{dy_2} = a_1 y_2^{a_1 - 1} \exp(-b_1 y_2) - b_1 y_2^{a_1} \exp(-b_1 y_2) = X_2 \left(\frac{a_1}{y_2} - b_1 \right), \quad \text{(III.50)}$$

from which we see that $dX_2/dy_2 = 0$ for $y_2 = a_1/b_1$ and that dX_2/dy_2 is always positive for $0 \leqslant y_1 < a_1/b_1$ and always negative for $y_2 > a_1/b_1$. Therefore the shape of X_2 is as shown in fig. A.11. Actually the curve has inflection points [**], but we have neglected them for graphical simplicity [‡].

[*] It turns out that

$$\frac{d^2 X_1}{dy_1^2} = X_1 [(a_2 + 1) a_2 y_1^{-2} - 2 a_2 b_2 y_1^{-1} + b_2^2].$$

Consider the inequality $d^2 X_1/dy_1^2 \gtreqless 0$. Since $X_1 > 0$ for $y_1 \geqslant 0$, we can consider only the inequality

$$(a_2 + 1) a_2 y_1^{-2} - 2 a_2 b_2 y_1^{-1} + b_2^2 \gtreqless 0.$$

For $y_1 = 0$, it certainly holds with the $>$ sign; so let us multiply through by y_1^2, $(y_1 > 0)$ and consider the inequality

$$f(y_1) = b_2^2 y_1^2 - 2 a_2 b_2 y_1 + (a_2 + 1) a_2 \gtreqless 0.$$

It can be checked that the equation $f(y_1) = 0$ has no real roots, so that the inequality is always satisfied with the $>$ sign for $y_1 > 0$.

[**] It turns out that

$$\frac{d^2 X_2}{dy_2^2} = X_2 [a_1 (a_1 - 1) y_2^{-2} - 2 a_1 b_1 y_2^{-1} + b_1^2].$$

Consider the inequality $d^2 X_2/dy_2^2 \gtreqless 0$. For $y_2 = 0$ it is not possible to know what happens without knowing the magnitude of a_1. Let us then consider the range $y_2 > 0$, where $X_2 > 0$, so that we may examine only the inequality $a_1 (a_1 - 1) y_2^{-2} - 2 a_1 b_1 y_2^{-1} + b_1^2 \gtreqless 0$, that is

$$h(y_2) = b_1^2 y_2^2 - 2 a_1 b_1 y_2 + (a_1 - 1) a_1 \gtreqless 0.$$

The equation $h(y_2) = 0$ has two real roots, $a_1/b_1 \pm \sqrt{a_1/b_1}$, which determine the inflection points, that are symmetrical with respect to the maximum point of the curve X_2. The one to the right is certainly relevant; regarding the one to the left, since — as we said at the beginning of this section — only the range $y_2 \geqslant 0$ is considered, its relevance or not depends on the magnitude of a_1.

[‡] In Andronov et al. (1966, pp. 144–5) the inflection points are not even mentioned, and the curve is drawn as in fig. A.11 after consideration of dX_2/dy_2 only.

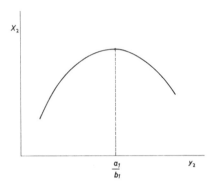

Fig. A.11.

We can now construct the integral curves by means of the diagram below ★ (fig. A.12). In the second and fourth quadrant the curves X_2 and X_1 found above are drawn; in the third quadrant the straight line represents eq. (III.48). Let us take an arbitrary point P_0 on the line OK. Draw from it two straight lines, one perpendicular to the OX_1 axis and the other perpendicular to the OX_2 axis. Call D, E, F, G the points of intersection of those lines with the X_1 and X_2 curves. From points D and E draw two straight lines parallel to the OX_1 axis and from F and G draw two straight lines parallel to the OX_2 axis. The four points of intersection of these four straight lines (points 1, 2, 3, 4) belong to the integral curve $X_1(y_1) = BX_2(y_2)$. In fact, each one of these points by construction is such as to equate $X_1(y_1)$ to $BX_2(y_2)$. The locus of these points when the point P slides along the OK line in the interval P'P'' is the required integral curve for the value $\tan \alpha$ of the arbitrary constant B. To each value of B an integral curve corresponds and can be constructed in the same way. All such curves are closed (except one corresponding to the coordinate axes), so that the state of equilibrium (i.e. the singular point whose coordinates are $y_1 = a_2/b_2, y_2 = a_1/b_1$) ★★ is a *centre*.

By inspection of the diagram and using eqs. (III.41) it can be seen that the direction of the movement along the integral curve is that shown by the arrows (anticlockwise). Take, for example, point 2. There y_2 is greater than a_1/b_1, so that $a_1 - b_1 y_2 < 0$ and $dy_1/dt < 0$ (y_1 decreases); y_1 is smaller

---

★ Andronov *et al.*, 1966, p. 144; Volterra, 1931, p. 16. We have changed the positions of the various curves so as to obtain the integral curves in the north-east quadrant.

★★ The origin too is a state of equilibrium, since $dy_1/dt = dy_2/dt = 0$ also for $y_1 = y_2$ = 0. Note that the singular point in the origin is of the *saddle-point* type.

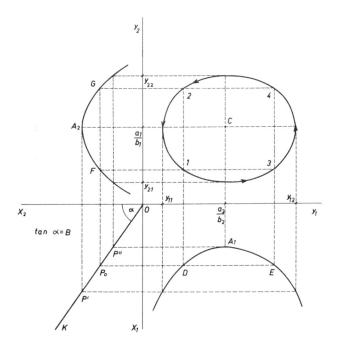

Fig. A.12.

than a_2/b_2 so that $a_2 - b_2y_1 > 0$ and $dy_2/dt < 0$ (y_2 decreases). Therefore the point travels in an anticlockwise direction ★. As the representative point travels around the integral curve, y_1 oscillates between points y_{11} and y_{12}, and y_2 oscillates between points y_{21} and y_{22}. Given the initial conditions, the slope of OK (and so the corresponding integral curve) is determined, as well as the point on the integral curve from which the movement starts. It is also interesting to note that any external shock simply brings about a shift from one to another integral curve, where the system returns to its endless periodic motion.

Let us note, finally, that the system that we have examined in this section is a non-linear 'conservative' system. This name is drawn from physical systems, which are called conservative when their total energy (potential plus kinetic) remains constant during the motion over time. For non-physical sys-

---

★ This depends on how we draw the diagram. If we had put y_2 on the horizontal, and y_1 on the vertical, axis, the resulting integral curves would have been traversed in a clockwise direction.

tems (such as the one considered here) the 'conservative' character is attributed on purely formal grounds and need not interest us here ★.

§6. Elements of the qualitative theory of non-linear difference equations

The concept of 'qualitative' or 'topological' theory of difference equations is the same as for differential equations. We shall only add that the qualitative theory of difference equations is underdeveloped compared with the qualitative theory of differential equations, to which mathematicians have devoted most of their efforts. A reason for this relative neglect is perhaps that in the case of difference equations *exact* 'quantitative' results can always and easily be obtained once the numerical data are given; also historical and practical reasons may have played a role. In this section we shall examine only the first-order non-linear autonomous difference equation, that is the equation of the type

$$\varphi(y_{t+1}, y_t) = 0 . \tag{III.51}$$

The graphical analysis of eq. (III.51) can be made by means of a diagram in which y_t is measured on the abscissae and y_{t+1} is measured on the ordinates. We shall call it the *phase diagram* by analogy with the similar diagram used for differential equations (Appendix III, §5.1) ★★. It may happen that eq. (III.51) can be made explicit as

$$y_{t+1} = f(y_t) , \tag{III.51'}$$

★ From the formal point of view, a system $dy_i/dt = \varphi_i(y_1, y_2)$, $i = 1, 2$, is 'conservative' in domain D if it has a first integral in D, and D has the property that every trajectory having one point in D lies entirely in D for $t \to +\infty$ or for $t \to -\infty$. A 'first integral' is a single-valued differentiable function $F(y_1, y_2)$ defined on D and not identically constant, such that $F(y_1, y_2) =$ constant when $y_1 = y_1(t)$, $y_2 = y_2(t)$, $y_i(t)$ being a solution of the differential system. It can easily be checked that these properties are satisfied by the Lotka–Volterra equations (a first integral is, for example, the function on the left-hand side of (III.45′)). For a treatment of non-linear conservative systems from both the physical and the purely formal point of view, see Andronov *et al.* (1966, ch. II) and Minorsky (1962, ch. 2).

★★ The analogy, however, must be taken with caution. For example, the analogue of dy/dt is Δy_t and not y_{t+1}. If Δy_t instead of y_{t+1} were used, the horizontal axis would become what is now the 45° line. In other words, the 45° line plays the role of the horizontal axis used in differential equations (points above the 45° line represent points of increasing y, etc.).

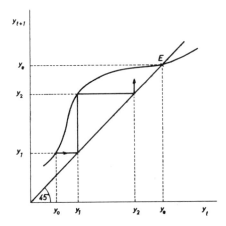

Fig. A.13.

but, if this is not possible, the graphical analysis can be made equally well, using (III.51). In fig. A.13 we have a possible form of the phase line. The 45° line is useful given its property of being the locus of all points such that the abscissa and the ordinate are equal. We consider only the first quadrant, since the variables which appear in economic applications must be non-negative.

Suppose that the arbitrary initial point is y_0. The successive value y_1 is obtained finding the point on the phase line having the abscissa y_0. By means of the 45° line we transfer graphically y_1 onto the horizontal axis and then we obtain y_2 as the ordinate of the point on the phase line corresponding to the abscissa y_1; we transfer y_2 onto the horizontal axis by means of the 45° line, and so on. The time path of y is given by the succession of the values $y_0, y_1, y_2, \ldots$ so obtained. Let us note, incidentally, that the path is monotonic and convergent towards the equilibrium point E (the same result would be obtained if the initial point were to the right of E). An equilibrium point is by definition a point such that y is stationary over time, that is, a point such that $y_{t+1} = y_t$. Therefore *the equilibrium points are the points of contact of the phase line with the 45° line* ★.

We shall now expound some general properties of the phase diagrams under consideration.

★ In other words, given (III.51'), equilibrium points are the 'fixed points' of the mapping $y \to f(y)$.

Case (1): monotonic movements

Monotonic movements arise when the phase line is a monotonically increasing function; if it is everywhere or in some stretches decreasing, oscillating movements occur (see the next case (2)). The movement may be convergent (as in fig. A.13) or divergent (as in fig. A.14). It can be noted that in the first case the phase line is such that it lies *above* the 45° line to the *left* of, and *below* the 45° line to the *right* of, the equilibrium point, whereas in the second case exactly the opposite is true. Thus it is the *position* of the phase line with respect to the 45° line that determines the stability of the equilibrium point ★.

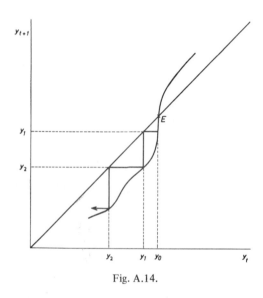

Fig. A.14.

The reader can check as an exercise that: (a) when the phase line is tangent to the 45° line and lies wholly on one side of it, the point of tangency is semi-stable, that is, stable or unstable according to whether the initial point is situated on one side or on the other of the equilibrium point; (b) when there

---

★ Baumol (1970, pp. 259–61) states that the time path will converge to the equilibrium point if $0 < df/dy_t < 1$ and diverge if $df/dy_t > 1$. These conditions, however, are necessary and sufficient only for *local* stability (or instability), whereas in general they are unduly restrictive, being only sufficient but not necessary. In fact, it can easily be checked that $df/dy_t > 1$ in some stretches of the phase line in fig. A.13 and that $0 < df/dy_t < 1$ in some stretches of the phase line in fig. A.14; and this is enough to show the lack of necessity. Given that $f(y_t)$ is an increasing function, the general necessary and

are multiple equilibria they are alternatively stable (or semistable) and unstable (or semistable); (c) when there are no equilibrium points the movement is in any case divergent to $+\infty$ or to $-\infty$.

Case (2): oscillations

Oscillatory movements occur when the phase line has a negative slope at least in some stretches. For simplicity, we shall examine only the case in which it has a negative slope everywhere. The oscillations may be damped, explosive or of constant amplitude, as in figs. A.15(a), A.15(b) and A.15(c), respectively *. Also *limit cycles* may occur, that is, a cycle of constant amplitude surrounded by other cycles whose amplitude is either decreasing or increasing. The limit cycle is stable if all the nearby cycles tend to it from both sides, as in fig. A.15(d), and unstable in the opposite case. It can also be semistable, that is, when the nearby cycles approach it from one side and move away from it on the other side. Of course, multiple limit cycles may also occur.

---

sufficient conditions are those given in the text in terms of the position of the phase line with respect to the 45° line. Apart from intuitive graphical considerations, they can be proved rigorously. The sufficiency can be proved using Liapunov's second method (see Appendix II, §3, Theorem II). Consider the equation $y_{t+1} = f(y_t)$. As a Liapunov function, take $V_t = |y_t - y_e|$. Then

$$\Delta V_t = |y_{t+1} - y_e| - |y_t - y_e| = |f(y_t) - y_e| - |y_t - y_e|.$$

Suppose now that $y_t < y_e$ and that $f(y_t) > y_t$ (that is, $f(y_t)$ lies above the 45° line to the left of the equilibrium point). Since f is an increasing function, it will also be $f(y_t) < y_e$. Thus we have

$$y_t < f(y_t) < y_e \quad \text{for} \quad y_t < y_e. \tag{1}$$

From inequality (1) we obtain $y_t - y_e < f(y_t) - y_e < 0$, so that, taking absolute values,

$$|y_t - y_e| > |f(y_t) - y_e|,$$

and so $\Delta V_t < 0$. Similar reasoning shows that $\Delta V_t < 0$ also for $y_t > y_e$ if $f(y_t) < y_t$ (that is, if $f(y_t)$ lies below the 45° line to the right of the equilibrium point). Therefore $\Delta V_t < 0$ everywhere except for $y_t = y_e$, and the equilibrium point is (globally) stable. The necessity can be proved by showing a case in which the condition is not satisfied and the equilibrium is unstable, and this case is, for example, the one in fig. A.14. This completes the proof.

* It is interesting to note that the presence of oscillations does not require that the phase line forms a closed loop. Closed-loop phase lines, however, allow constant amplitude oscillations which are not alternations (an alternation is an oscillation such that y reverses the direction of movement each period, as in diagrams A.15(a), A.15(b) and A.15(c)), that is, periodic movements such that the direction of movement is reversed every n periods, n being greater than 1. For a closed-loop phase diagram, see Baumol, 1970, p. 264.

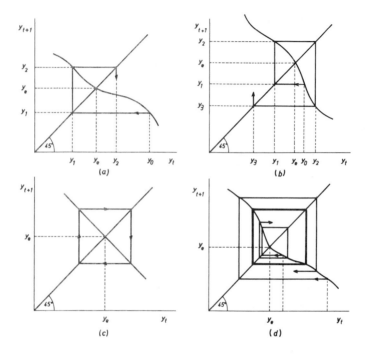

Fig. A.15.

We do not think that further exemplification is necessary. Once the reader has grasped the simple rules underlying the phase diagram method, he can continue by himself, if he likes, to draw and analyse a great variety of such diagrams. Let us note, finally, that the phase diagram can also be applied to the first-order linear equation with constant coefficients

$$y_{t+1} = ay_t + b ,$$

which gives rise to a straight line in the phase diagram; an economic application *ante litteram* has been made in Part I, ch. 3, §2, of the text, to which we refer the reader ★.

★ The phase plane diagram for the second-order linear equation with constant coefficients is expounded in Baumol's (1958) article, where an economic application is made to Hicks' trade cycle model.

§7. Some economic applications

The economic applications of the topics expounded in the previous sections are relatively few with respect to the applications of linear and constant-coefficient equations, which are still dominant ★. It should, however, be noted that non-linear methods are now used more frequently than they were, especially in growth theory. For other applications, in addition to those expounded here, the reader is referred (the list is by no means exhaustive, but only gives examples) to Ichimura's (1955) paper on non-linear cyclical models (limit cycles in generalized van der Pol equations), to Goodwin's (1951, 1955) various cyclical models (phase diagrams), to Jorgenson's (1961) model of a dual economy (Bernouilli's equation), to Rose's non-linear employment cycle model (Poincaré—Bendixon theorem), to Beckmann and Ryder's (1969) model of simultaneous price and quantity adjustment (phase paths, limit cycles), and to much of the recent literature on two-sector neoclassical growth models (phase diagrams, limit cycles).

§7.1. *The neoclassical aggregate growth model again (Solow)*
This model was examined in Part II, ch. 3, §4, of the text. Here we shall see what happens if we assume that the production function is

$$Y = (aK^p + L^p)^{1/p}, \quad 0 < p < 1, \quad a > 0, \tag{III.52}$$

a case examined by Solow (1956). As an example, let us take $p = \frac{1}{2}$, so that

$$Y = a^2 K + L + 2a(KL)^{\frac{1}{2}}. \tag{III.52'}$$

Given (III.52′), the basic differential equation of the model becomes

$$r' = s(a\sqrt{r} + 1)^2 - nr. \tag{III.53}$$

that is,

$$r' = s[(a^2 - n/s)r + 2a\sqrt{r} + 1]. \tag{III.54}$$

The equilibrium situation is obtained setting $r' = 0$, which gives

---

★ This, of course, is the reason why we have devoted all the text to them and only two appendixes – the present one and Appendix II – to non-l.c. equations. We think, however, that the material contained in them is sufficient for understanding all the relevant economic literature.

$$(a^2 - n/s)r + 2a\sqrt{r} + 1 = 0 . \tag{III.55}$$

It can immediately be seen that if $a^2 - n/s \geqslant 0$, eq. (III.55) has no real roots, that is, it is not possible to find any capital/labour ratio such that it brings about a capital/output ratio which equals the rate of growth to the natural rate. If, on the other hand, $a^2 - n/s < 0$, then (III.55) has one, and only one, economically meaningful solution, which turns out to be ★

$$r_e = \frac{1}{[(n/s)^{1/2} - a]^2} . \tag{III.56}$$

Let us now solve the differential eq. (III.54). If we let

$$A \equiv a - (n/s)^{1/2} ,$$

$$B \equiv a + (n/s)^{1/2} ,$$

it can be rewritten as

$$\frac{dr}{dt} = s(A\sqrt{r} + 1)(B\sqrt{r} + 1) , \tag{III.57}$$

that is,

$$\frac{1}{s(A\sqrt{r} + 1)(B\sqrt{r} + 1)} dr - dt = 0 , \tag{III.58}$$

which has separated variables. To simplify the integration, let us multiply through by $(ns)^{1/2}$, obtaining

---

★ Consider the equation

$$(a^2 - n/s)x^2 + 2ax + 1 = 0 , \tag{III.55'}$$

where $x \equiv \sqrt{r}$. We are interested in real roots of (III.55), that is, in non-negative roots of (III.55'). Solving the latter equation we obtain

$$x_1, x_2 = \frac{1}{(n/s)^{1/2} - a} , \frac{-1}{(n/s)^{1/2} + a} .$$

The second root gives rise to complex r's, whereas a real r corresponds to the first root if, and only if, $(n/s)^{1/2} - a > 0$, that is, $a - (n/s)^{1/2} < 0$, which is the same as $a^2 - n/s < 0$ (since $a^2 - n/s = [a - (n/s)^{1/2}][a + (n/s)^{1/2}]$).

$$\frac{(n/s)^{\frac{1}{2}}}{(A\sqrt{r}+1)(B\sqrt{r}+1)}\, dr - (ns)^{\frac{1}{2}}\, dt = 0\ , \tag{III.59}$$

whose solution is

$$-\int (ns)^{\frac{1}{2}}\, dt + \int \frac{(n/s)^{\frac{1}{2}}}{(A\sqrt{r}+1)(B\sqrt{r}+1)}\, dr = C\ . \tag{III.60}$$

Also the second integral can be explicitly solved, so that we obtain

$$-(ns)^{\frac{1}{2}}t + \left[\frac{1}{A}\log_e (A\sqrt{r}+1) - \frac{1}{B}\log_e (B\sqrt{r}+1)\right] = C\ , \tag{III.61}$$

from which

$$(A\sqrt{r}+1)^{1/A}(B\sqrt{r}+1)^{-1/B} = D \exp\left[(ns)^{\frac{1}{2}}t\right]\ , \tag{III.62}$$

where $D \equiv e^{-C}$ is the new arbitrary constant. Assuming $r = r_0$ known for $t = 0$, from (III.62) we have

$$D = (A\sqrt{r_0}+1)^{1/A}(B\sqrt{r_0}+1)^{-1/B}\ ,$$

and so

$$\left(\frac{A\sqrt{r}+1}{A\sqrt{r_0}+1}\right)^{1/A}\left(\frac{B\sqrt{r}+1}{B\sqrt{r_0}+1}\right)^{-1/B} = \exp\left[(ns)^{\frac{1}{2}}t\right]\ , \tag{III.63}$$

which is the final form of the solution of (III.54). From eq. (III.63) it is not possible to make r explicit as a function of t, so that the solution is not very useful for obtaining in a simple way a clear picture of the behaviour of r over time. This, however, can be obtained easily by means of the phase diagram. Consider the function

$$f(r) = s[(a^2 - n/s)r + 2a\sqrt{r} + 1]\ .$$

We have

$$f(0) = s > 0\ ,$$

$$\frac{df}{dr} = s\left[\left(a^2 - \frac{n}{s}\right) + \frac{a}{\sqrt{r}}\right]\ ,$$

$$\frac{d^2 f}{dr^2} = -\frac{as}{2\sqrt{r^3}}.$$

The second derivative is always negative for $r \geqslant 0$. With regard to the first derivative, it is always positive for $r \geqslant 0$ if $a^2 - n/s > 0$ (fig. A.16(a)), whereas, if $a^2 - n/s < 0$, it is positive, zero, negative, respectively, for $r \lesseqgtr a^2/(n/s - a^2)^2$, $r \geqslant 0$. The critical value $a^2/(n/s - a^2)^2$ is smaller than r_e [*], so that we have fig. A.16(b). From the phase diagrams of fig. A.16 it can easily be seen that in case (a), r increases beyond all bounds, whereas in case (b) it tends monotonically from both sides to the equilibrium point r_e, which is therefore globally stable.

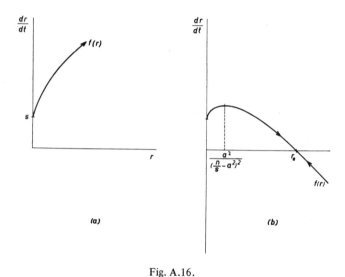

Fig. A.16.

Let us note that this section provides an example of those cases in which, although the differential equation is explicitly integrable, qualitative methods yield better results. This is due to the fact that from the integral the explicit function $r = r(t)$ cannot be obtained, as we remarked above (see also Appendix III, §5.1, remark (2)).

---

[*] Consider the inequality $a^2/(a^2 - n/s)^2 < 1/[(n/s)^{1/2} - a]^2$, which gives $a^2[(n/s)^{1/2} - a]^2 < (a^2 - n/s)^2$. This can be written as $a^2[(n/s)^{1/2} - a]^2 < \{[(n/s)^{1/2} - a][(n/s)^{1/2} + a]\}^2$, that is, $a^2 < [(n/s)^{1/2} + a]^2$, which is certainly satisfied.

§7.2. *Embodied technical progress and 'vintage' models (Solow–Bergstrom)*
The older formulations of technical progress postulated a production function of the type

$$Y(t) = f(K(t), L(t); t) , \qquad \partial f/\partial t > 0 ,$$

or of the type

$$Y(t) = A(t)f(K(t), L(t)) , \qquad dA/dt > 0 ,$$

which imply a technical progress of the 'disembodied' kind, that is, something like 'manna' which falls from heaven on *all* capital goods, old and new, and which therefore explicates its influence on output even if the capital stock (and the labour force) remain the same both quantitatively and qualitatively. It is as if technical progress were simply "a way of improving the organization and operation of inputs without reference to the nature of inputs themselves" (Solow, 1960, §2). This, of course, is in striking contrast with reality, where most of technical progress is *embodied* in the *new* capital goods which are being installed both to replace old capital goods and to make additions to the existing capital stock. It is therefore necessary to take account of the fact that the capital goods have a different productivity according to their dates of construction * or *vintages* **; of course, because of technical progress such productivity is the greater the more recent is the vintage.
A related problem is that of the substitutability between labour and capital. In a situation in which several productive techniques are known, there is obviously an *ex ante substitutability*, which means simply the possibility of choice among the various techniques *before* the installation of the capital goods. But once the choice has been made and the capital goods relative to the technique chosen have been installed, does substitutability still exist, that is, is there also an *ex post substitutability*? At first sight the answer is *no*, since any given type of capital good normally requires for its operation a well-defined number of workers. But, if we look more closely at the matter, we discover that some *ex post* substitutability exists, and is obtainable by varying the number of hours of operation of the capital goods per unit of time (say, the

* The date of construction need not coincide with the date of installation, so that, in principle, it is possible that in time t capital goods constructed in different times $t - \theta_i$ are installed. In what follows we shall neglect this problem.
** The analogy with wines, although suggestive, is perhaps misleading. For most of great wines, apart from exceptional vintages and within certain limits, the dictum "the older the better" is true. This is exactly contrary to what happens for capital goods.

day); this substitutability, however, is presumably more limited than the *ex ante* substitutability.

Therefore we think that the most realistic assumption is an intermediate one between no *ex post* substitutability and complete (that is, equal to the *ex ante*) *ex post* substitutability. In any case we think that an *ex ante* substitutability exists, so that the case of no substitutability both *ex ante* and *ex post* is the less realistic one ★.

In this section we shall examine Solow's (1960) vintage model, following, however, not the original presentation but Bergstrom's (1967) presentation.

The following symbols will be used:

v	= vintage; this symbol is used to avoid confusion with t, which indicates the generic time; both v and t are measured from a common origin (e.g., in calendar time);
$K_v(t)$	= quantity of capital of vintage v still existing in time t;
$Q_v(t)$	= quantity of output produced in time t using capital goods of vintage v;
$L_v(t)$	= quantity of labour working, at time t, with capital of vintage v;
$I(t)$	= real gross investment at time t;
$C(t)$	= real consumption at time t;
$Q(t)$	= total gross output at time t;
$p(t)$	= price level at time t;
$w(t)$	= real wage rate at time t;
$L(t)$	= total amount of labour employed at time t;
$L_s(t)$	= supply of labour at time t;
$A, B, \alpha, b,$ $s, \rho, \delta, \lambda, l$	$\}$ = positive constants ($\alpha < 1$, $b > 1$, $s < 1$).

The model postulates a continuous substitutability both *ex ante* and *ex post* according to a Cobb-Douglas production function. We shall now write the basic equations of the model, giving then their interpretation:

$$Q_v(t) = A\,e^{\lambda v}K_v(t)^{\alpha}L_v(t)^{1-\alpha} \quad \Big\} \qquad \qquad \text{(III.64)}$$
$$v \leqslant t,$$
$$L_v(t) = B\,e^{-\rho v}Q_v(t)^{b}K_v(t)^{1-b} \qquad \qquad \text{(III.64')}$$

★ The following terminology is now common:
'clay–clay'   = no substitutability, both *ex ante* and *ex post*;
'putty–putty' = continuous substitutability, both *ex ante* and *ex post*;
'putty–clay'   = continuous substitutability *ex ante*, no substitutability *ex post*.

$$K_v(t) = I(v) \exp\left[-\delta(t-v)\right],$$ (III.65)

$$C(t) = (1-s)Q(t),$$ (III.66)

$$w(t)\frac{\partial L_v(t)}{\partial Q_v(t)} = p(t),$$ (III.67)

$$Q(t) = \int_{-\infty}^{t} Q_v(t)\,dv,$$ (III.68)

$$L(t) = \int_{-\infty}^{t} L_v(t)\,dv,$$ (III.69)

$$L_s(t) = L_0\,e^{lt},$$ (III.70)

$$Q(t) = C(t) + I(t),$$ (III.71)

$$L(t) = L_s(t).$$ (III.72)

Eq. (III.64) is the production function; since it holds both for $v < t$ and for $v = t$, we have both *ex ante* and *ex post* substitutability. The multiplicative exponential function represents the influence of technical progress: this influence is the greater, the greater is v, that is, the nearer is the date of construction of capital goods.

Eq. (III.64′) is obtained from eq. (III.64), expressing $L_v(t)$ in terms of the other variables. We have $B = A^{-1/(1-\alpha)}$, $\rho = \lambda/(1-\alpha)$, $b = 1/(1-\alpha)$. Let us note that $b > 1$, since $0 < \alpha < 1$.

Eq. (III.65) expresses the assumption of 'radioactive' depreciation (or depreciation 'by evaporation'); that is, the physical depreciation of capital goods occurs at a constant proportionate rate δ, so that at time t the quantity of the capital goods of vintage v (which initially was $I(v)$) still surviving is given by (III.65).

Eq. (III.66) is the usual proportional consumption function.

Eq. (III.67) expresses the condition for profit maximization under perfect competition. As we know from microeconomics, profit maximization requires that each factor be employed up to the point in which its price equals the value of its marginal product, that is $w(t) = p(t)(\partial Q_v/\partial L_v)$. Let us note that this relationship must hold for any v, that is, *workers must be allocated to the capital goods of the various vintages in such a way that the marginal products of the labour employed with capital goods of different vintages be equal.* Dividing both members of the above relationship by $\partial Q_v/\partial L_v$ and noting that $(\partial Q_v/\partial L_v)^{-1} = \partial L_v/\partial Q_v$, we have (III.67).

Eqs. (III.68) and (III.69) follow directly from the definitions of the variables.

Eq. (III.70) expresses the assumption that the supply of labour grows at an exogenous constant proportionate rate l.

Eq. (III.71) expresses the equilibrium condition, that total output equals total demand.

Eq. (III.72) expresses the assumption of a continuous full employment of the labour force.

If we make the assumption that the wage rate $w(t)$ is exogenously given, the time path of the remaining variables is determined by the model.

From eqs. (III.64′), (III.65) and (III.67) we obtain ★

$$L_v(t) = B^{1/(1-b)} \left[\frac{p(t)}{bw(t)} \right]^{b/(b-1)} \exp\,(\sigma v - \delta t)\,I(v)\,, \qquad \text{(III.73)}$$

$$Q_v(t) = B^{1/(1-b)} \left[\frac{p(t)}{bw(t)} \right]^{1/(b-1)} \exp\,(\sigma v - \delta t)\,I(v)\,, \qquad \text{(III.74)}$$

where $\sigma = \delta + \rho/(b-1)$.

From (III.73) and (III.74), together with (III.68) and (III.69), we have ★★

$$L(t) = B^{1/(1-b)} \left[\frac{p(t)}{bw(t)} \right]^{b/(b-1)} e^{-\delta t} \int_{-\infty}^{t} e^{\sigma v} I(v)\,dv\,, \qquad \text{(III.75)}$$

$$Q(t) = B^{1/(1-b)} \left[\frac{p(t)}{bw(t)} \right]^{1/(b-1)} e^{-\delta t} \int_{-\infty}^{t} e^{\sigma v} I(v)\,dv\,, \qquad \text{(III.76)}$$

★ Substitute (III.65) in (III.64′) and differentiate to obtain $\partial L_v(t)/\partial Q_v(t)$. Insert the result in (III.67) and express $Q_v(t)$ in terms of the other variables. This is (III.74). Then insert (III.65) and (III.74) in (III.64′) and obtain (III.73).

★★ Substitute (III.73) and (III.74) in (III.68) and (III.69). Noting that the integration variable is v, take out of the integral sign the multiplicative factors not containing v which yields (III.75) and (III.76).

which yield ★

$$L(t) = Be^{-\rho t}[Q(t)]^b \{ \int_{-\infty}^{t} \exp[-\sigma(t-v)]I(v)\,dv \}^{1-b} . \qquad \text{(III.77)}$$

From (III.70), (III.72) and (III.77) we obtain ★★

$$\frac{dQ}{dt} = \frac{b-1}{b}\left(\frac{L_0}{B}\right)^{1/(b-1)} \exp\left(\frac{\rho+l}{b-1}t\right) Q(t)^{1/(1-b)}I(t) + \frac{1}{b}[l-\delta(b-1)]Q(t),$$

$$\text{(III.78)}$$

which, together with (III.66) and (III.71), yields ‡

$$\frac{dQ}{dt} = \frac{s(b-1)}{b}\left(\frac{L_0}{B}\right)^{1/(b-1)} \exp\left(\frac{\rho+l}{b-1}t\right) Q^{(b-2)/(b-1)} + \frac{1}{b}[l-\delta(b-1)]Q .$$

$$\text{(III.79)}$$

Eq. (III.79) is the basic differential equation of the model. It is an equation of the Bernoulli type (see Appendix III, §4). Let us make the substitution

$$z = Q^{1-(b-2)/(b-1)} = Q^{1/(b-1)} ,$$

so that

$$\frac{dz}{dt} = \frac{1}{b-1} Q^{-(b-2)/(b-1)} \frac{dQ}{dt} .$$

Multiplying both members of (III.79) by $[1/(b-1)]Q^{-(b-2)/(b-1)}$, we have

---

★ From (III.76) express $p(t)/bw(t)$ in terms of the other variables and then substitute in (III.75). In the resulting expression a term $\exp[(\delta b-\delta)t]$ appears. Noting that $\delta b - \delta = -\rho - \sigma(1-b)$, this term can be written as $\exp(-\rho t)\exp[-\sigma(1-b)t]$ and the second exponential can be brought under the integral sign. This yields (III.77).

★★ Substitute (III.70) into (III.72) and then the result in (III.77). Call this (III.77'). Differentiate both members of (III.77') with respect to time (the following rules must be used: (1) differentiation of a product; (2) differentiation of a composite function; (3) differentiation of an integral with respect to a parameter). From the resulting relation express dQ/dt in terms of remaining variables. Use (III.77') to express the integral in terms of the other variables. The result is (III.78).

‡ From (III.66) and (III.71) we obtain $sQ(t) = I(t)$, which, of course, is the saving–investment equality. Substituting in (III.78) we have (III.79).

$$\frac{1}{b-1} Q^{-(b-2)/(b-1)} \frac{dQ}{dt}$$

$$= \frac{s}{b} \left(\frac{L_0}{B}\right)^{1/(b-1)} \exp\left(\frac{\rho+l}{b-1} t\right) + \frac{1}{b(b-1)} [l-\delta(b-1)]Q^{1/(b-1)} ,$$

that is, in terms of z,

$$\frac{dz}{dt} - \frac{1}{b(b-1)} [l-\delta(b-1)]z = \frac{s}{b} \left(\frac{L_0}{B}\right)^{1/(b-1)} \exp\left(\frac{\rho+l}{b-1} t\right) . \tag{III.80}$$

Eq. (III.80) is a first-order linear equation with constant coefficients, non-homogeneous. Applying the method expounded in Part II, ch. 2, we find that the general solution of the corresponding homogeneous equation is

$$z = M \exp\left[\frac{l-\delta(b-1)}{b(b-1)} t\right] .$$

As a particular solution try $H \exp\{[(\rho+l)/(b-1)]t\}$. Substituting in (III.80) we obtain

$$H = \frac{s(b-1)(L_0/B)^{1/(b-1)}}{(l+\delta)(b-1)+\rho b} ,$$

and so the general solution of (III.80) is

$$z = M \exp\left[\frac{l-\delta(b-1)}{b(b-1)} t\right] + H \exp\left(\frac{\rho+l}{b-1} t\right) , \tag{III.81}$$

where M is an arbitrary constant. Another way of obtaining the same result is to apply formula (III.23) of Appendix III, §3.

We can then return to Q by means of the inverse transformation $Q = z^{b-1}$, so that

$$Q = \left\{M \exp\left[\frac{l-\delta(b-1)}{b(b-1)} t\right] + H \exp\left(\frac{\rho+l}{b-1} t\right)\right\}^{b-1} , \tag{III.82}$$

where, on the assumption of known $Q(t) = Q(0)$ for $t = 0$, the arbitrary constant M is determined as

$$M = Q(0)^{1/(b-1)} - H.$$

From (III.82) we obtain the result that $Q(t)$ tends asymptotically to grow at the rate $\rho + l$. In other words, the equilibrium growth path $H \exp[(\rho + l)t]$ is *relatively stable*. To show this, we have to prove that

$$\lim_{t \to +\infty} \frac{dQ/dt}{Q} = \rho + l.$$

From (III.82) we have

$$\frac{dQ/dt}{Q}$$

$$= \frac{(b-1)\{M\exp[\frac{l-\delta(b-1)}{b(b-1)}t] + H\exp(\frac{\rho+l}{b-1}t)\}^{b-2}\{\frac{l-\delta(b-1)}{b(b-1)}M\exp[\frac{l-\delta(b-1)}{b(b-1)}t] + \frac{\rho+l}{b-1}H\exp(\frac{\rho+l}{b-1}t)\}}{\{M\exp[\frac{l-\delta(b-1)}{b(b-1)}t] + H\exp(\frac{\rho+l}{b-1}t)\}^{b-1}}$$

$$= \frac{\frac{l-\delta(b-1)}{b}M\exp[\frac{l-\delta(b-1)}{b(b-1)}t] + (\rho+l)H\exp(\frac{\rho+l}{b-1}t)}{M\exp[\frac{l-\delta(b-1)}{b(b-1)}t] + H\exp(\frac{\rho+l}{b-1}t)}$$

$$= \frac{\frac{l-\delta(b-1)}{b}M\exp[\frac{l-\delta(b-1)}{b(b-1)}t]}{M\exp[\frac{l-\delta(b-1)}{b(b-1)}t] + H\exp(\frac{\rho+l}{b-1}t)} + \frac{(\rho+l)H\exp(\frac{\rho+l}{b-1}t)}{M\exp[\frac{l-\delta(b-1)}{b(b-1)}t] + H\exp(\frac{\rho+l}{b-1}t)}$$

$$= \frac{\frac{l-\delta(b-1)}{b}}{1 + \frac{H}{M}\exp[\frac{b\rho+(b-1)(l+\delta)}{b(b-1)}t]} + \frac{\rho+l}{\frac{M}{H}\exp[\frac{(l+\delta)(1-b)-b\rho}{b(b-1)}t]+1}.$$

Therefore

$$\lim_{t \to +\infty} \frac{dQ/dt}{Q} = \frac{l-\delta(b-1)}{b}\lim_{t \to +\infty}\left\{1 + \frac{H}{M}\exp\left[\frac{b\rho+(b-1)(l+\delta)}{b(b-1)}t\right]\right\}^{-1}$$

$$+ (\rho+l)\lim_{t \to +\infty}\left\{\frac{M}{H}\exp\left[\frac{(l+\delta)(1-b)-b\rho}{b(b-1)}t\right]+1\right\}^{-1}. \qquad \text{(III.83)}$$

Since $b > 1$, it follows that

$$\frac{b\rho + (b-1)(l+\delta)}{b(b-1)} > 0$$

and that

$$\frac{(l+\delta)(1-b) - b\rho}{b(b-1)} < 0 .$$

Therefore the first limit on the right-hand side of (III.83) is zero and the second is 1. This completes the proof that

$$\lim_{t \to +\infty} \frac{dQ/dt}{Q} = \rho + l . \tag{III.84}$$

Let us note that this result coincides with that obtaining in the neoclassical aggregate growth model with disembodied technical progress. In fact, if in the model expounded in Part II, ch. 3, §4, of the text we insert in the production function a multiplicative $e^{\lambda t}$, where λ is a constant, we obtain the result that the rate of growth to which the system tends is $\lambda/(1-\alpha) + n$ [*]. This result, remembering that here we have used the symbol l for n and the symbol ρ for $\lambda/(1-\alpha)$, is the same as (III.84).

In fact, the main difference between 'vintage' and traditional neoclassical aggregate growth models is the fact that, in the former the 'manna' of technical progress falls only on the new machines, whereas in the latter it falls on all the capital stock, that is both on new and on old machines. This, after all, is not so great a difference, and consequently it is no wonder that the long-run result is the same (with both *ex ante* and *ex post* substitutability) [**].

§7.3. *A cyclical model by Goodwin*

Goodwin is one of the first and more strenuous supporters of the need for non-linear cyclical and growth–cyclical models, and he has built several such models. Here we shall examine his first non-linear cyclical model. In the next section we shall expound his latest growth–cyclical model.

The model is based on the capital stock adjustment principle (that Goodwin

---

[*] The easiest way to prove this is the following. Consider the production function $Y = e^{\lambda t} K^{\alpha} L^{1-\alpha}$. Since there is full employment and $L = L_0 e^{nt}$, we can write $Y = K^{\alpha} L^{*1-\alpha}$, where $L^* = L_0 \exp(n^*t)$, $n^* \equiv n + \lambda/(1-\alpha)$. Then the analysis can proceed as before.

[**] However, the conclusion that vintage models represent no progress would be unwarranted. In fact, such models are more appropriate, for example, for the treatment of the 'learning' theory of technical progress. See Hahn and Matthews (1964, § II.4).

calls the *flexible* or *non-linear accelerator*). The basic equations of the model are the following

$$K^* = kY \, , \tag{III.85}$$

$$C = bY + a \, , \tag{III.86}$$

$$Y = C + K' \, , \tag{III.87}$$

where K^* is the desired capital stock and the other symbols have the usual meanings. Eq. (III.85) expresses the desired capital stock as proportional, given a constant desired capital/output ratio, to current output. Eq. (III.86) is the consumption function. Eq. (III.87) is the determination of income, where K' is (net) investment (we neglect depreciation). We must now 'close' the model by means of an investment function. Investment expresses the reaction of entrepreneurs to a discrepancy between desired and actual capital stock. A possible assumption is the following: when $K^* \neq K$, entrepreneurs try to fill the gap as rapidly as possible. Therefore when $K^* > K$ investment is kept at the maximum rate allowed by the existing productive capacity, and when $K^* < K$ disinvestment occurs at the maximum rate allowed by not replacing capital goods which are being scrapped for normal depreciation. Thus we may write

$$K' = \begin{cases} K_1 & \text{if} \quad K^* - K > 0 \, , \\ 0 & \text{if} \quad K^* - K = 0 \, , \\ K_2 & \text{if} \quad K^* - K < 0 \, , \end{cases} \tag{III.88}$$

where K_1 is a positive, and K_2 a negative, constant.
From eqs. (III.85), (III.86) and (III.87) we obtain

$$Y = \frac{1}{1-b} K' + \frac{a}{1-b} \, , \tag{III.89}$$

$$K^* = \frac{k}{1-b} K' + \frac{ka}{1-b} \, , \tag{III.90}$$

where K' is given by (III.88).
We can immediately note that the model has an equilibrium point for $K' = 0$, so that $Y_e = a/(1-b)$ and $K_e = kY_e$. Such equilibrium, however, is

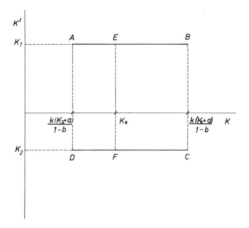

Fig. A.17.

not stable, although it cannot be considered unstable either. In other words, any deviation from equilibrium gives rise to a constant-amplitude oscillation. The phase diagram of the model is drawn in fig. A.17. Suppose that the initial point is A. The capital stock in existence is smaller than the desired capital stock, so that investment takes place at the rate K_1; from (III.89) we have that the income is

$$Y = \frac{1}{1-b} K_1 + \frac{a}{1-b}$$

and consequently the desired capital stock is

$$K^* = \frac{k}{1-b} K_1 + \frac{ka}{1-b}.$$

The actual capital stock increases and passes through K_e, but it cannot stop there because we still have $K' = K_1 > 0$ (point E). Thus the capital stock goes on increasing up to the point in which it reaches its desired level (corresponding to point B), where K' falls sharply to zero given (III.88). But then income falls to $a/(1-b)$ and the desired capital stock to $ka/(1-b)$, which is now smaller than the existing capital stock. Therefore, K' falls to K_2 (point C); consequently, income falls to $(a+K_2)/(1-b)$ and the desired capital stock to $k(a+K_2)/(1-b)$. The stock of capital goes on decreasing: it passes through

K_e, but it cannot remain there since K' is still negative ($K' = K_2 < 0$: point F), so that it decreases more and more until it reaches its desired value $k(a + K_2)/(1-b)$, corresponding to point D. Here K' falls to zero, Y increases to $a/(1-b)$ and the desired capital stock is $ka/(1-b)$, so that K' rises immediately to K_1, and we are again at point A. In other words, in the phase diagram we have a continuous movement in the segments $\overline{AB}$ and $\overline{CD}$, with a discontinuous jump from C to D and from B to A.

The time path of Y and K is described in fig. A.18. Let us note that the descending phase is longer than the upward swing, given that the time required to reduce the capital stock is presumably greater than the time needed to increase it (i.e. $|K_2| < K_1$).

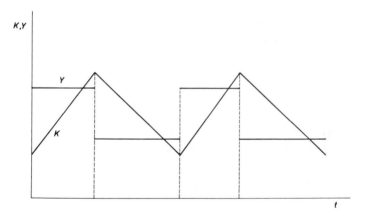

Fig. A.18.

This rather simple and admittedly crude model is sufficient to illustrate the features of non-linear cyclical models:

(1) The final result is independent of initial conditions (this is not true in linear models).

(2) The oscillation is self-sustaining, without any need of exogenous factors nor of implausible assumptions about the coefficients (the latter, as we know, are necessary in linear models to obtain a constant-amplitude oscillation).

(3) The equilibrium point is unstable, and therefore the slightest disturbance sets the mechanism into motion. However, notwithstanding such instability, the theory works, because the mechanism does not explode but is maintained within the limits of a constant-amplitude oscillation (this cannot occur in explosive linear models ★) thanks to its intrinsic non-linearities.

§7.4. *Goodwin's growth cycle*

This is a model of cycles in growth rates and, as such, it is a step towards more realistic interpretations of cycles and growth. In fact, after the Second World War in most Western countries there has been a continual growth in real national income, which has, however, occurred at different rates over time. Thus the cycle is actually a cycle in growth rates, not in absolute levels of national income, the latter being always on the increase or, at least not on the decrease.

The assumptions of the model are the following:

(1) Steady technical progress, of the disembodied type. If we call a the labour productivity, that is, output per unit of labour, we can then write

$$Y/L = a = a_0\, e^{\alpha t}\,, \tag{III.91}$$

where α is a positive constant.

(2) Steady growth in the labour force N:

$$N = N_0\, e^{\beta t}\,, \tag{III.92}$$

where β is a positive constant. Note that the labour force, that is, the labour supply N, and employment L in this model do *not* coincide, i.e. there is no full employment assumption.

(3) There are only two factors of production, labour and 'capital', both homogeneous and non-specific.

(4) All quantities are real and net.

(5) All wages are consumed; all profits are saved and automatically invested.

(6) The capital/output ratio $k = K/Y$ is constant.

(7) The real wage rate w rises in the neighbourhood of full employment.

The first five assumptions, as Goodwin says, are made for convenience, whereas the last two are of a more empirical, and disputable, sort.

Given the definition of a, we can write the workers' share of the product (call u such a share) as

$$u = w/a\,. \tag{III.93}$$

★ This statement is not in contrast with the features of Hicks' trade cycle model – see Part I, ch. 5, § 2, in the text – which, in effect, is not a linear model but is actually a non-linear model, which can be treated by linear methods since it consists of several connected linear segments.

Consequently, the capitalists' share is *

$$1 - w/a .$$ (III.94)

It follows that the rate of profit is

$$\frac{(1 - w/a)Y}{K} ,$$ (III.95)

that is, given assumptions (4), (5) and (6),

$$\frac{(1 - w/a)Y}{K} = \frac{1 - w/a}{k} = \frac{\dot{K}}{K} = \frac{\dot{Y}}{Y}$$ (III.95′)

where a dot denotes the time derivative d/dt.
    Consider now eq. (III.91), take logarithms to the base e and differentiate with respect to time: the result is

$$\frac{\dot{Y}}{Y} - \frac{\dot{L}}{L} = \alpha ,$$ (III.96)

so that

$$\frac{\dot{L}}{L} = \frac{\dot{Y}}{Y} - \alpha ,$$ (III.97)

that is, given (III.95′),

$$\frac{\dot{L}}{L} = \frac{1 - w/a}{k} - \alpha .$$ (III.98)

Define now the employment ratio v as

$$v = \frac{L}{N} .$$ (III.99)

Logarithmic differentiation yields

* There is a misprint in Goodwin's (1967) paper, where the capitalists' share is indicated as $l - w/a$, whereas, of course, it is $1 - w/a$. The misprint has, however, no effect on the final equations, which are correct.

$$\frac{\dot{v}}{v} = \frac{\dot{L}}{L} - \frac{\dot{N}}{N} \tag{III.100}$$

that is, given (III.98) and since $\dot{N}/N = \beta$,

$$\frac{\dot{v}}{v} = \frac{1 - w/a}{k} - (\alpha + \beta) = \frac{1 - u}{k} - (\alpha + \beta) . \tag{III.101}$$

Let us now consider assumption (7). It can be written as $\dot{w}/w = f(v)$, where f is an increasing function of the kind drawn in fig. A.19. Taking a linear approximation, we can write

$$\dot{w}/w = -\gamma + \rho v , \tag{III.102}$$

where γ and ρ are positive constants. Logarithmic differentiation of (III.93) yields

$$\dot{u}/u = \dot{w}/w - \alpha , \tag{III.103}$$

whence, given (III.102),

$$\dot{u}/u = -(\alpha + \gamma) + \rho v . \tag{III.104}$$

From eqs. (III.101) and (III.104) we obtain the fundamental dynamic equations of the model:

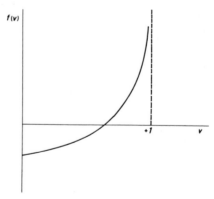

Fig. A.19.

$$\dot{v} = \left\{ \left[\frac{1}{k} - (\alpha + \beta) \right] - \frac{1}{k} u \right\} v ,$$ (III.105)

$$\dot{u} = [-(\alpha + \gamma) + \rho v] u .$$ (III.106)

Letting

$$1/k - (\alpha + \beta) = a_1 , \quad 1/k = b_1 , \quad (\alpha + \gamma) = a_2 , \quad \rho = b_2 ,$$

we have the Lotka–Volterra equations *

$$\dot{v} = (a_1 - b_1 u)v ,$$
$$\dot{u} = -(a_2 - b_2 v)u .$$ (III.107)

Applying the procedure expounded in Appendix III, §5.3, we can draw the integral curves using the relation

$$\phi(v) = B\psi(u) ,$$

where $\phi(v) = v^{-a_2} \exp(b_2 v)$, $\psi(u) = u^{a_1} \exp(-b_1 u)$; the shapes of these two functions have already been discussed in Part III, §5.3. The final result is shown in the diagram (fig. A.20), which is constructed as explained in Appendix III, §5.3 (the only difference is that the variable appearing in the first equation is now measured on the vertical axis instead of on the horizontal axis, so that the direction of the movement along the integral curve is clockwise). The variables by their definition are restricted in the interval from zero to $+1$ **.

A point on the u-axis will give us the distribution of income: workers' share is the segment from the origin to the point; capitalists' is the segment from the point to $+1$. The latter share multiplied by the constant $1/k$ gives the profit rate and the rate of growth in output and in the capital stock (see eqs. (III.95) and (III.95′) above). From v we obtain the rate of growth of the wage rate (see eq. (III.102) above).

As the representative point travels around the closed curve, u vibrates

---

* The parameters b_1, a_2, b_2 are by definition positive. It seems realistic to assume that $1/k > \alpha + \beta$ (e.g., 0.2 can be taken as a safe lower limit for $1/k$, and 0.12 as a safe upper limit for $\alpha + \beta$), so that also $a_1 > 0$.

** It must be noted that u may exceptionally be greater than 1, since wages (= consumption) may exceed total product if there is disinvestment.

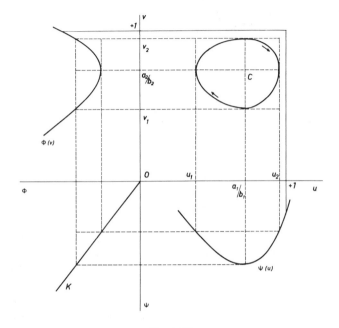

Fig. A.20.

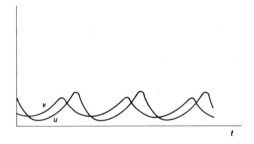

Fig. A.21.

between u_1 and u_2, and v between v_1 and v_2. A rough approximation to the typical time paths of u and v is illustrated in fig. A.21. Thus we have a cycle in the employment ratio and in the growth rate of income. Whether the descending phase of the cycle implies also a fall in absolute values or means only that the latter increase less rapidly depends on the severity of the cycle. The same is true for real wages.

The economic mechanism underlying the motion of the representative point is, in Goodwin's (1967) words, the following: "When profit is greatest, $u = u_1$, employment is average, $v = a_2/b_2$, and the high growth rate pushes employment to its maximum v_2, which squeezes the profit rate to its average value a_1/b_1. The deceleration in growth lowers employment (relative) to its average value again, where profit and growth are again at their nadir u_2. This low growth rate leads to a fall in output and employment to well below full employment, thus restoring profitability to its average value because productivity is now rising faster than wage rates ... . The improved profitability carries the seed of its own destruction by engendering a too vigorous expansion of output and employment, thus destroying the reserve army of labour and strengthening labour's bargaining power" (pp. 57–8; symbols have been changed in accordance with the notation used here). According to Goodwin, this is essentially Marx's idea of the 'contradictions' of capitalism; there is, however, a difference, since in the model the wage rate need not fall in absolute value. As we said above, in the descending phase the rate of growth of the wage rate falls, and whether or not this implies a fall in absolute value depends on the severity of the cycle.

As we know, external shocks will not alter the features of the (u,v) cycle, since they merely shift the representative point onto another integral curve, having the same shape and enclosing (or enclosed in) the previous one. In any case, that is both for undisturbed and for disturbed systems, the very long-run average values of u and v, which can be taken as the coordinates of the singular point C (a centre) are independent of initial conditions and external shocks. This interesting property, just stated by Goodwin, can be proved as follows. Rewrite eqs. (III.107) as

$$\frac{d \log v}{dt} = a_1 - b_1 u \, ,$$

$$\text{(III.107')}$$

$$\frac{d \log u}{dt} = -a_2 + b_2 v \, ,$$

and integrate between two arbitrary values of t, say t' and t'', corresponding to which v and u take on, respectively, the values v', v'' and u', u''. The result is

$$\log \frac{v''}{v'} = a_1 (t'' - t') - b_1 \int_{t'}^{t''} u \, dt \, , \qquad \text{(III.108)}$$

$$\log\frac{u''}{u'} = -a_2(t'' - t') + b_2 \int_{t'}^{t''} v \, dt \, . \tag{III.108}$$

Now call T the period of the oscillation, and let the limits of integration differ by T. It follows that $v' = v''$, $u' = u''$, $t'' - t' = T$, and so

$$0 = a_1 T - b_1 \int_0^T u \, dt \, ,$$

$$0 = -a_2 T + b_2 \int_0^T v \, dt \, ,$$

so that

$$\frac{1}{T} \int_0^T u \, dt = \frac{a_1}{b_1} \, ,$$

$$\tag{III.109}$$

$$\frac{1}{T} \int_0^T v \, dt = \frac{a_2}{b_2} \, .$$

Therefore the average values of u and v over a whole cycle are constant and respectively equal to a_1/b_1 and a_2/b_2, the coordinates of the centre of the fluctuation.

§7.5. *Uzawa's two-sector model of economic growth*

A two-sector model of economic growth is a model in which two sectors are distinguished, one producing a homogeneous consumption good (the consumption sector) and the other producing a homogeneous capital good (the investment sector); both goods are produced by two homogeneous factors of production: labour and capital, which are freely transferable from one sector to the other. One such model — based on fixed-coefficient production functions — has been treated in the text (Part II, ch. 9, §7); here we shall examine a more general model, in which the production functions allow for continuous substitutability between capital and labour. The treatment is based essentially on Uzawa's (1963) work; at the end of this section, however, we shall summarize the rather lengthy discussion of this class of models which has taken place during the 1960's.

The basic equations of the model are the following (a dot over a symbol denotes the operator d/dt, and the subscripts I and C denote, respectively, the investment sector and the consumption sector):

$$L(t) = L_0 e^{nt},$$

$$\hfill \text{(III.110)}$$

$$\dot{K}(t) = Y_I(t) - \gamma K(t),$$

$$\hfill \text{(III.111)}$$

$$Y_C(t) = F_C(K_C(t), L_C(t)),$$

$$\hfill \text{(III.112)}$$

$$Y_I(t) = F_I(K_I(t), L_I(t)),$$

$$\hfill \text{(III.113)}$$

$$Y(t) = Y_C(t) + p(t)Y_I(t),$$

$$\hfill \text{(III.114)}$$

$$K_I(t) + K_C(t) = K(t),$$

$$\hfill \text{(III.115)}$$

$$L_I(t) + L_C(t) = L(t),$$

$$\hfill \text{(III.116)}$$

$$w(t) = \frac{\partial F_C}{\partial L_C} = p(t)\frac{\partial F_I}{\partial L_I},$$

$$\hfill \text{(III.117)}$$

$$r(t) = \frac{\partial F_C}{\partial K_C} = p(t)\frac{\partial F_I}{\partial K_I},$$

$$\hfill \text{(III.118)}$$

$$p(t)Y_I(t) = sY(t).$$

$$\hfill \text{(III.119)}$$

Eq. (III.110) expresses the usual assumption of a constant proportionate rate of growth in the labour force.

Eq. (III.111) defines the net increase in the total capital stock, given by the output of the investment sector, $Y_I(t)$, minus depreciation, which is assumed to be proportional to the existing capital stock ('radioactive' depreciation or depreciation 'by evaporation').

Eqs. (III.112) and (III.113) express the production functions of the consumption sector and of the investment sector; the output of a sector, of course, depends on the quantities of capital and labour employed in that sector. Such production functions are assumed to be of the 'well-behaved' kind, i.e. they show constant returns to scale and the marginal productivities are positive and decreasing; properties (III.122) and (III.123) below complete this well-behaved nature.

Eq. (III.114) defines gross national product measured in terms of the consumption good; $p(t)$ is the price of the capital good in terms of the consumption good.

Eqs. (III.115) and (III.116) express the full employment condition for both factors of production.

Eqs. (III.117) and (III.118) determine the wage rate and the rentals of the capital good under the assumption of perfect competition: the wage rate $w(t)$ is equal to the value of the marginal product of labour in both sectors, and the rentals rate $r(t)$ is equal to the value of the marginal product of capital in both sectors.

Finally, eq. (III.119) is the investment–saving *ex ante* equality, given the assumption that a constant fraction is saved out of current gross national product and is automatically invested.

At any moment of time, the labour force and the capital stock are given (the former exogenously and the latter as a result of past accumulation), so that eqs. (III.112)–(III.119) determine the equilibrium quantities and prices (momentary or *short-run equilibrium*), whereas eqs. (III.110) and (III.111) determine the path of growth equilibrium (*long-run equilibrium*).

Let us now define the following derived variables (for brevity, the indication of t is dropped):

$$k = \frac{K}{L}, \quad y = \frac{Y}{L}, \quad \omega = \frac{w}{r},$$

$$k_i = \frac{K_i}{L_i}, \quad y_i = \frac{Y_i}{L}, \quad l_i = \frac{L_i}{L},$$

where $i = I, C$.

Using the properties of homogeneous functions of the first degree, eqs. (III.112) and (III.113) can be written as

$$Y_i = L_i F_i \left(\frac{K_i}{L_i}, 1 \right) = L_i f_i \left(\frac{K_i}{L_i} \right),$$

so that

$$\frac{Y_i}{L} = \frac{L_i}{L} f_i \left(\frac{K_i}{L_i} \right),$$

that is, using the notation defined above,

$$y_i = f_i(k_i) l_i. \tag{III.120}$$

Since $\partial F_i / \partial K_i = f_i'(k_i)$, from the assumptions made on F_i we have

$$f_i(k_i) > 0, \quad f'(k_i) > 0, \quad f''(k_i) < 0, \quad \text{for all } k_i > 0 . \tag{III.121}$$

Moreover, to complete the 'well-behaved' nature of the production functions the following assumptions are made:

$$f_i(0) = 0 , \quad f_i(\infty) = \infty , \tag{III.122}$$

$$f_i'(0) = \infty , \quad f_i'(\infty) = 0 . \tag{III.123}$$

We can now turn to the determination of the short-run equilibrium. Eqs. (III.112)–(III.119) can be reduced to the following:

$$\omega = \frac{f_i(k_i)}{f_i'(k_i)} - k_i , \tag{III.124}$$

$$p = \frac{f_C'(k_C)}{f_I'(k_I)} , \tag{III.125}$$

$$y = y_C + p y_I , \tag{III.126}$$

$$y_I = f_I(k_I) \frac{k_C - k}{k_C - k_I} , \qquad y_C = f_C(k_C) \frac{k - k_I}{k_C - k_I} , \tag{III.127}$$

$$p y_I = s y . \tag{III.128}$$

A derivation of eqs. (III.124)–(III.128) from eqs. (III.112)–(III.119) is the following.

From (III.117) and (III.118) we have

$$\omega = \frac{w}{r} = \frac{\partial F_i / \partial L_i}{\partial F_i / \partial K_i} .$$

Using Euler's theorem,

$$L_i \frac{\partial F_i}{\partial L_i} = Y_i - K_i \frac{\partial F_i}{\partial K_i} ,$$

so that

$$\frac{\partial F_i}{\partial L_i} = \frac{Y_i}{L_i} - \frac{K_i}{L_i}\frac{\partial F_i}{\partial K_i},$$

and so

$$\omega = \frac{Y_i/L_i}{\partial F_i/\partial K_i} - \frac{K_i}{L_i} = \frac{f_i(k_i)}{f_i'(k_i)} - k_i,$$

given the definitions of the variables.

Using the second equality in (III.118) we have

$$p = \frac{\partial F_C/\partial K_C}{\partial F_I/\partial K_I}$$

from which (III.125) follows.

Dividing both members of (III.114) by L and using the definitions of the symbols, we have (III.126).

To obtain eq. (III.127), consider eqs. (III.115) and (III.116). They can be rewritten as

$$\frac{L_I}{L}\frac{K_I}{L_I} + \frac{L_C}{L}\frac{K_C}{L_C} = \frac{K}{L},$$

$$\frac{L_I}{L} + \frac{L_C}{L} = 1,$$

that is,

$$l_I k_I + l_C k_C = k,$$

$$l_I + l_C = 1,$$

so that, solving for l_I and l_C, we obtain

$$l_I = \frac{k_C - k}{k_C - k_I}, \qquad l_C = \frac{k - k_I}{k_C - k_I}.$$

Substituting these last relations in (III.120) we have (III.127).

Finally, eq. (III.128) is obtained dividing both members of (III.119) by L.

Consider now eq. (III.124). Given an arbitrary positive ω it can be solved uniquely for the capital–labour ratio $k_i = k_i(\omega)$ in each sector. To prove this, consider the function

$$h(k_i) = \frac{f_i(k_i)}{f_i'(k_i)} - k_i = \frac{f_i(k_i) - k_i f_i'(k_i)}{f_i'(k_i)} . \tag{III.129}$$

We have $\lim_{k_i \to 0} h(k_i) = 0$ using (III.122) and (III.123), and $\lim_{k_i \to +\infty} h(k_i) = +\infty$ using (III.122), (III.123) and the fact that

$$\lim_{k_i \to +\infty} k_i f_i'(k_i) = \lim_{k_i \to +\infty} \frac{k_i}{1/f_i'(k_i)}$$

$$= \text{(by l'Hôpital's theorem)} \lim_{k_i \to +\infty} -\frac{[f_i'(k_i)]^2}{f_i''(k_i)} = 0 .$$

Therefore the function $z = h(k_i)$ crosses the function $z = \omega$ at least once in the positive quadrant; the abscissa of any such intersection is a value of k_i which satisfies (III.124). To show that there is only one such intersection, it is sufficient to prove that $h(k_i)$ is a monotonically increasing function for any $k_i > 0$. The first derivative of $h(k_i)$ is

$$h'(k_i) = \frac{[f_i'(k_i)]^2 - f_i''(k_i)f_i(k_i)}{[f_i'(k_i)]^2} - 1 = -\frac{f_i''(k_i)f_i(k_i)}{[f_i'(k_i)]^2} > 0 , \tag{III.130}$$

since $f''(k_i) < 0$ by assumption. From this it also follows that the equilibrium value of k_i increases as ω increases.

We shall now show that given the aggregate capital–labour ratio $k = K/L$, the wage–rentals ratio ω is uniquely determined. The solution of the model then runs as follows: at any moment of time, K and L and therefore k are given, so we can determine ω and then k_I, k_C. Given k_I and $k_C, f_i(k_i)$ and $f_i'(k_i)$ are also determined, so that we can determine the remaining variables $(p, y_C, y_I, \text{etc.})$.

From (III.126) and (III.128) we have $(1-s)py_I = sy_C$, and substituting p, y_I, y_C from (III.125) and (III.127) we obtain

$$(1-s)\frac{f_C'}{f_I'} f_I \frac{k_C - k}{k_C - k_I} = sf_C \frac{k - k_I}{k_C - k_I} ;$$

therefore

$$\frac{(1-s)f_C'f_Ik_C}{f_I'(k_C - k_I)} - \frac{(1-s)f_C'f_I}{f_I'(k_C - k_I)} k = \frac{sf_Cf_I'}{f_I'(k_C - k_I)} k - \frac{sf_Cf_I'k_I}{f_I'(k_C - k_I)} ,$$

which gives

$$[sf_Cf_I' + (1-s)f_C'f_I]k = sf_Cf_I'k_I + (1-s)f_C'f_Ik_C ,$$

and so

$$k = \frac{sf_Cf_I'k_I + (1-s)f_C'f_Ik_C}{sf_Cf_I' + (1-s)f_C'f_I} .$$

Dividing both numerator and denominator by $f_C'f_I'$ we have

$$k = \frac{s(f_C/f_C')k_I + (1-s)(f_I/f_I')k_C}{s(f_C/f_C') + (1-s)(f_I/f_I')} ,$$

that is,

$$k = \frac{s[k_C(\omega)+\omega]k_I(\omega) + (1-s)[k_I(\omega)+\omega]k_C(\omega)}{s[k_C(\omega)+\omega] + (1-s)[k_I(\omega)+\omega]} , \qquad \text{(III.131)}$$

since $k_i + \omega = f_i/f_i'$ from (III.124) and $k_i = k_i(\omega)$, as we have seen above.

Let us note for future reference that, if we add ω to both sides, eq. (III.131) can be transformed into

$$k + \omega = \frac{[k_C(\omega)+\omega][k_I(\omega)+\omega]}{s[k_C(\omega)+\omega] + (1-s)[k_I(\omega)+\omega]} . \qquad \text{(III.132)}$$

Consider the function (which takes on positive values for $\omega > 0$):

$$g(\omega) = \frac{s[k_C(\omega)+\omega]k_I(\omega) + (1-s)[k_I(\omega)+\omega]k_C(\omega)}{s[k_C(\omega)+\omega] + (1-s)[k_I(\omega)+\omega]}$$

$$= \frac{[k_C(\omega)+\omega][k_I(\omega)+\omega]}{s[k_C(\omega)+\omega] + (1-s)[k_I(\omega)+\omega]} - \omega . \qquad \text{(III.133)}$$

If we show that

$$\lim_{\omega\to 0} g(\omega) = 0 , \qquad \lim_{\omega\to+\infty} g(\omega) = +\infty ,$$

then the function $z = g(\omega)$ will cross the function $z = k$ at least once, k being a given positive number, and therefore eq. (III.131) will have at least one solution *. Now

* Uzawa's proof is different and, we believe, not correct. He uses (III.132) and shows that the function on the right-hand side takes on positive values and has a derivative

$$g(\omega) = \frac{1}{s/[k_I(\omega) + \omega] + (1-s)/[k_C(\omega) + \omega]} - \omega \,,$$

from which

$$g(\omega) = \frac{1 - s\omega/[k_I(\omega) + \omega] - (1-s)\omega/[k_C(\omega) + \omega]}{s/[k_I(\omega) + \omega] + (1-s)/[k_C(\omega) + \omega]} \,. \tag{III.134}$$

Since, from (III.124), $k_i(\omega) \to 0$ as $\omega \to 0$, we have that the denominator of $g(\omega)$ tends to infinity as ω tends to zero. To evaluate the limit of the numerator, we use l'Hôpital's theorem, so that

$$- \lim_{\omega \to 0} \frac{s\omega}{k_I(\omega) + \omega} = - \lim_{\omega \to 0} \frac{s}{dk_I/d\omega + 1} \,.$$

This limit is zero since, from (III.124),

$$\frac{dk_I}{d\omega} = - \frac{[f_I'(k_I)]^2}{f(k_I)f_I''(k_I)} \,, \tag{III.135}$$

which, using (III.122) and (III.123), tends to infinity as $\omega \to 0$. We also have

$$- \lim_{\omega \to 0} \frac{(1-s)\omega}{k_C(\omega) + \omega} = - \lim_{\omega \to 0} \frac{1-s}{dk_C/d\omega + 1} = 0 \,.$$

From all the above it follows that $g(\omega) \to 0$ as $\omega \to 0$. In a similar way it can be proved that $g(\omega) \to +\infty$ as $\omega \to +\infty$ (as $\omega \to +\infty$, $k_i(\omega) \to +\infty$ and $dk_i/d\omega \to 0$, etc.).

To prove uniqueness, it is sufficient to prove that $g'(\omega) > 0$. Rewrite $g(\omega)$ as

$$g(\omega) = \frac{Z_C Z_I}{s Z_C + (1-s)Z_I} - \omega \,,$$

where

$$Z_i \equiv k_i(\omega) + \omega \,.$$

greater than 1 for $\omega > 0$. This is clearly not sufficient, since it proves only that the solution, if it exists, is unique, but does not prove its existence. Similar remarks could be made with reference to other proofs in Uzawa's paper, which we have suitably modified.

We have

$$g'(\omega) = \frac{sZ_C^2 Z_I' + (1-s)Z_I^2 Z_C'}{[sZ_C + (1-s)Z_I]^2} - 1 \,. \tag{III.136}$$

Since $Z_i' = 1 + dk_i/d\omega > 1$ (k_i being an increasing function of ω as we saw above), it follows that

$$g'(\omega) > \frac{sZ_C^2 + (1-s)Z_I^2}{[sZ_C + (1-s)Z_I]^2} - 1 \,. \tag{III.137}$$

The fraction on the right-hand side of (III.137) is not smaller than 1, since

$$sZ_C^2 + (1-s)Z_I^2 \geqslant s^2 Z_C^2 + (1-s)^2 Z_I^2 + 2s(1-s)Z_C Z_I \,,$$

which gives

$$s(1-s)Z_C^2 + (1-s)sZ_I^2 \geqslant 2s(1-s)Z_C Z_I \,,$$

from which

$$Z_C^2 + Z_I^2 - 2Z_C Z_I = (Z_C - Z_I)^2 \geqslant 0 \,.$$

This proves that $g'(\omega)$ is positive, which completes our demonstration. From the above it also follows that the equilibrium value $\omega = \omega(k)$ is an increasing function of k (and vice versa, if ω is considered as the independent variable).

We can now turn to the determination of the *long-run equilibrium*.

From (III.111) we have, dividing through by kL,

$$\frac{\dot{K}}{K} = \frac{y_1}{k} - \gamma \,,$$

from which, subtracting $n = \dot{L}/L$ from both sides, we have

$$\frac{\dot{K}}{K} - \frac{\dot{L}}{L} = \frac{y_1}{k} - n - \gamma \,.$$

The left-hand side is $\dot{k}/k$ and so

$$\frac{\dot{k}}{k} = \frac{y_1}{k} - n - \gamma \,. \tag{III.138}$$

Consider now the distributional identity $Y = rK + wL$ and divide both sides by L, obtaining

$$y = rk + w = r(k + \omega)$$

that is, using (III.118)

$$y = pf_I'(k_I)(k + \omega) .$$ (III.139)

From (III.128) we have

$$y_I = s\frac{y}{p}$$

that is, using (III.139),

$$y_I = sf_I'(k_I)(k + \omega) .$$ (III.140)

Substituting (III.140) into (III.138) we have

$$\frac{\dot{k}}{k} = sf_I'(k_I)\frac{k + \omega}{k} - n - \gamma ,$$ (III.141)

which is the fundamental dynamic equation of the model. Note that the right-hand side is a continuous function of ω. Since k is also a continuous and differentiable function of ω (the derivative $dk/d\omega$ can be computed from (III.131)), we can transform (III.141) into a differential equation in ω. In fact,

$$\frac{\dot{k}}{k} = \frac{(dk/d\omega)\,\dot{\omega}}{k(\omega)} ,$$

and so

$$\dot{\omega} = \frac{k(\omega)}{dk/d\omega}[\phi(\omega) - (n + \gamma)] ,$$ (III.142)

where

$$\phi(\omega) = sf_I'(k_I(\omega))\frac{k(\omega) + \omega}{k} .$$ (III.143)

Of course, $k(\omega) + \omega$ is given by (III.132). The equilibrium value of ω (and therefore the corresponding equilibrium value of k, which we may call a *balanced capital–labour ratio*) is determined by solving the equation

$$\phi(\omega) = n + \gamma, \qquad (\text{III}.144)$$

since when (III.144) holds, $\dot{\omega} = 0$.

We now show that eq. (III.144) always has at least one solution. The solution is unique under the *capital intensity condition*, that is if $k_C > k_I$ (the consumption sector is more capital intensive than the investment sector). It is important to note that this is a sufficient, but not a necessary, condition.

To prove its existence, we have to show that

$$\lim_{\omega \to 0} \phi(\omega) = +\infty, \qquad \lim_{\omega \to +\infty} \phi(\omega) = 0. \qquad (\text{III}.145)$$

The first limit is easily proved, since $k_I \to 0$ as $\omega \to 0$ and $f_I'(0) = \infty$ by (III.123); moreover, $(k + \omega)/k \to 1$ as $\omega \to 0$.

To prove the second limit we proceed as follows. From (III.131) and (III.132) we have

$$\frac{k + \omega}{k} = \frac{(k_I + \omega)(k_C + \omega)}{s(k_C + \omega)k_I + (1 - s)(k_I + \omega)k_C}, \qquad (\text{III}.146)$$

From (III.124) we obtain

$$f_I' = \frac{f_I}{k_I + \omega} \qquad (\text{III}.147)$$

and so, substituting (III.146) and (III.147) into the expression for $\phi(\omega)$, we have

$$\frac{1}{s} \phi(\omega) = \frac{f_I(k_C + \omega)}{s(k_C + \omega)k_I + (1 - s)(k_I + \omega)k_C}$$

$$= \frac{f_I}{sk_I + (1 - s)(k_I + \omega)k_C/(k_C + \omega)} < \frac{f_I}{sk_I}.$$

Now, using l'Hôpital's theorem,

$$\lim_{\omega \to +\infty} \frac{f_I(k_I(\omega))}{sk_I(\omega)} = \lim_{\omega \to +\infty} \frac{f_I' \, dk_I/d\omega}{s \, dk_I/d\omega} = \lim_{\omega \to +\infty} \frac{f_I'}{s} = 0,$$

since $k_I \to +\infty$ as $\omega \to +\infty$ and $f_I'(\infty) = 0$ by (III.123). It follows that also $\phi(\omega) \to 0$ as $\omega \to 0$. To prove uniqueness, it is sufficient to show that $\phi(\omega)$ is a monotonically decreasing function. Consider eq. (III.143), take logarithms of both sides and differentiate with respect to ω, obtaining

$$\frac{1}{\phi(\omega)} \frac{d\phi}{d\omega} = \frac{f_I'' \, dk_I/d\omega}{f_I'} + \frac{dk_I/d\omega + 1}{\omega + k(\omega)} - \frac{dk/d\omega}{k(\omega)}$$

$$= \frac{f_I'' \, dk_I/d\omega}{f_I'} + \frac{1}{\omega + k(\omega)} + \left[\frac{1}{\omega + k(\omega)} - \frac{1}{k(\omega)}\right] \frac{dk}{d\omega}.$$

Using (III.135) and (III.124) we have

$$\frac{f_I'' \, dk_I/d\omega}{f_I'} = -\frac{f_I'}{f_I} = -\frac{1}{\omega + k_I(\omega)},$$

and so

$$\frac{1}{\phi(\omega)} \frac{d\phi}{d\omega} = -\frac{1}{\omega + k_I(\omega)} + \frac{1}{\omega + k(\omega)} + \left[\frac{1}{\omega + k(\omega)} - \frac{1}{k(\omega)}\right] \frac{dk}{d\omega}. \quad \text{(III.148)}$$

Now, if $k_C > k_I$, then $k > k_I$ since $l_C = (k - k_I)/(k_C - k_I)$ is a positive magnitude. And $k > k_I$ is a *sufficient* condition that the right-hand side of (III.148) be negative (remember that $dk/d\omega > 0$). Therefore, since $\phi(\omega) > 0$, $d\phi/d\omega < 0$ if $k_C > k_I$.

Let us finally examine the problem of *stability*. Consider eq. (III.142), which can be written as

$$\dot{\omega} = \theta(\omega), \quad \text{(III.142')}$$

where $\theta(\omega)$ is the right-hand side of (III.142). Since $k(\omega)/(dk/d\omega)$ is a positive magnitude, the sign of $\theta(\omega)$ depends on the sign of $\phi(\omega) - (n + \gamma)$. Now, if the capital intensity condition holds, it follows from what we have shown above that $\phi(\omega) - (n + \gamma)$ is positive (negative) to the left (right) of the equilibrium point ω^*, which is therefore monotonically stable.

Thus we have reached the important theorem that *the capital intensity condition is a sufficient condition both for uniqueness and for stability of the balanced growth equilibrium.*

If this condition does not hold, there may be multiple equilibria. In this case, as we know from phase diagram considerations, they will be alternatively stable and unstable. From (III.145) we can also say that they will be odd in number and that — ranking them in order of increasing magnitude of ω^* — the first will be stable, the second unstable, etc. Therefore we can conclude that, even when the capital intensity condition is *not* satisfied, at worst the system converges to *some* balanced growth equilibrium ★.

After Uzawa's work, there has been a proliferation of papers on two-sector models. Another sufficient condition has been found to replace the rather inadequate capital intensity condition (inadequate because — as Solow (1961) noted — it is unsatisfactory that an important property such as stability should depend on a casual property of technology). We summarize below the most important results obtained in the 1960's. The list is taken from Stiglitz and Uzawa, eds., 1969, pp. 406–7; we have supplemented it with some more recent findings (Morishima, 1969).

(1) All of wages consumed, constant fraction of profits saved.
    (a) Sufficient conditions for uniqueness of momentary equilibrium:
        (i) capital intensity in consumption good sector $\geqslant$ capital intensity in capital good sector;
        or
        (ii) sum of elasticities of substitution greater than 1.
    (b) Balanced growth always uniquely determined.
    (c) System stable if (sufficient conditions):
        (i) capital intensity in consumption good sector $\geqslant$ capital intensity in capital good sector;
        or
        (ii) sum of elasticities of substitution greater than 1.

(2) Some of wages saved, but a smaller proportion than out of profits.
    (a) Same sufficient conditions for uniqueness of momentary equilibrium as (1a).
    (b) Sufficient conditions for uniqueness and stability of balanced growth:
        (i) capital intensity in consumption good sector $\geqslant$ capital intensity in capital good sector;
        or
        (ii) elasticity of substitution in each sector not smaller than 1.

★ Uzawa and other authors call this property 'global stability'. However, to avoid confusion with the other meaning given to this expression (i.e. the system converges to its (unique) equilibrium state from any initial position: see Appendix II) we prefer not to use it in this context.

(3) Same proportion of profits as wages saved.
   (a) Momentary equilibrium always uniquely determined.
   (b) Sufficient conditions for uniqueness and stability of balanced growth:
      (i) elasticity of substitution in each sector not smaller than one;
      or
      (ii) capital intensity in capital good sector ≤ capital intensity in con-
         sumption good sector.

(4) Proportion of savings of capitalists greater than that of workers (Pasinetti
   savings assumption)
   (a) Same sufficient conditions for uniqueness of momentary equilibrium
      as (1a).
   (b) If it exists, two-class balanced growth path is always unique.
   (c) Necessary and sufficient conditions for the existence of two-class
      balanced growth path:
      (i) ratio of workers' savings propensity to capitalists' less than share of
         profit;
      or
      (ii) ratio of investment to income greater than savings rate of workers.
   (d) Sufficient condition for local stability of two-class balanced growth
      path: capital intensity in capital good sector ≤ capital intensity in con-
      sumption good sector.

A (not exhaustive) list of references to the literature where proofs may be
found of the above-stated results would include the following (in alphabetical
order): Amano, 1964; Burmeister, 1967, 1968; Drandakis, 1963; Hahn, 1965;
Inada, 1963, 1964; Ramaswami, 1969; Stiglitz, 1967; Takayama, 1963;
Uzawa, 1961, 1963.

In all the models used to obtain the above-listed results the assumption is
made of an exogenously given steady population growth. In a more general
model of flexible population growth (where the rate of growth of the labour
force is assumed to depend on the real wage rate) the capital intensity condition is no longer a sufficient condition of stability, since the balanced growth
equilibrium may be unstable even though this condition is satisfied. In such
a model, stability is seen to depend not only on the relative capital intensities
of the two industries but also on the workers' and capitalists' consumption-
saving decisions and on the flexibility of the population growth (Morishima,
1969, ch. III).

§7.6. *A multi-sector extension of the neoclassical growth model and the
'Hahn problem' (Burmeister et al.)*

Hahn (1966) was the first to investigate, as an extension of the two-sector
model, a neoclassical growth model in which there is one homogeneous consumption good and m different kinds of capital goods. He reached the following conclusions:

(1) momentary equilibrium may not be unique;

(2) not all equilibrium paths, where they exist, converge to a balanced
growth path. The latter will be unstable unless asset prices take on certain
initial values.

Shell and Stiglitz (1967) investigated the conditions under which a competitive system may be presumed to lead asset prices to the unique 'correct'
values for balanced growth.

It was subsequently shown by Burmeister, Dobell and Kuga (1968) that
the 'Hahn phenomenon' is not inevitable. In other words, the introduction of
many capital goods does not necessarily lead to result (2) — which was
accepted also by Shell and Stiglitz — but this result depends in an essential
way on the fact that there is a market for old capital goods whose price is
influenced by anticipated capital gains (or losses). If one assumes that old
capital goods are not traded in practice, then the opposite of Hahn's result
is true: the model is stable.

Here we shall examine the Burmeister–Dobell–Kuga model, simplifying
it by assuming only two different capital goods, which, however, is sufficient
to illustrate the features of the model.

The basic equations are the following:

$$Y_j = L_j^{\alpha_{0j}} K_{1j}^{\alpha_{1j}} K_{2j}^{\alpha_{2j}} , \qquad j = 0, 1, 2 , \qquad\qquad \text{(III.149)}$$

$$\alpha_{0j} > 0 , \quad a_{1j} \geqslant 0 , \quad \alpha_{2j} \geqslant 0 , \quad \sum_{i=0}^{2} \alpha_{ij} = 1 .$$

$$\sum_{j=0}^{2} L_j = L$$

$$\sum_{j=0}^{2} K_{ij} = K_i , \qquad\qquad i = 1, 2 , \qquad\qquad \text{(III.150)}$$

$$w = P_j \frac{\partial Y_j}{\partial L_j} , \qquad\qquad j = 0, 1, 2 , \qquad\qquad \text{(III.151)}$$

$$r_i = P_j \frac{\partial Y_j}{\partial K_{ij}}, \qquad \begin{array}{l} i = 1, 2 , \\[4pt] j = 0, 1, 2 , \end{array} \qquad \text{(III.152)}$$

$$P_i Y_i = s_i r_i K_i , \qquad i = 1, 2 ; \quad 0 < s_i < 1 ,$$

$$\text{(III.153)}$$

$$P_0 Y_0 = wL + \sum_{i=1}^{2} (1 - s_i) r_i K_i .$$

The first equation defines the production functions in the various sectors. The subscript zero refers to the consumption good and the subscripts 1, 2 refer to the two capital goods; thus Y_0 is the output of the consumption good, L_0 is the labour input in the consumption sector, etc. The production functions are assumed to be of the Cobb–Douglas type (which has the required 'well-behaved' nature) and labour is assumed to be required directly to produce a positive quantity of any good.

Eqs. (III.150) express the full employment condition for all factors, which are assumed to be freely transferable from one sector to another.

Eqs. (III.151) and (III.152) determine the wage rate and the rentals of the capital goods under the assumption of perfect competition: the wage rate w is equal to the value of the marginal product of labour in all sectors and the rentals rate of the i-th capital good, r_i, is equal to the value of the marginal product of that capital good in all sectors.

The first equation in (III.153) is the investment–saving *ex ante* equality and the second equation is the equality between supply and demand of the consumption good. Underlying (III.153) there are the following assumptions:

(1) the services of capital goods are rented; each capital good is owned by a firm which saves a part of current rentals * and invests it in further equipment of the same type, distributing the remaining part to households;

(2) households consume all their income, whichever its source (wages and/or dividends).

We shall now reduce the system to an intensive form, as a function of the ratios K_i/L alone (aggregate capital–labour ratios). This will occupy us for most of the remaining part of this section **.

The second set of equations in (III.150) can be written as

---

* Since the opportunity of trading in old capital goods is assumed non-existent, the earnings of firms consist entirely of current rentals.

** The reader who is not interested in the reduction process may go on directly to equations (III.172) below.

$$\frac{K_{10}}{L_0}\frac{L_0}{L}+\frac{K_{11}}{L_1}\frac{L_1}{L}+\frac{K_{12}}{L_2}\frac{L_2}{L}=\frac{K_1}{L},$$

$$\frac{K_{20}}{L_0}\frac{L_0}{L}+\frac{K_{21}}{L_1}\frac{L_1}{L}+\frac{K_{22}}{L_2}\frac{L_2}{L}=\frac{K_2}{L}.$$

$$(III.154)$$

From (III.151) and (III.152) we have

$$\frac{w}{r_1}=\frac{\partial Y_j/\partial L_j}{\partial Y_j/\partial K_{1j}},\qquad \frac{w}{r_2}=\frac{\partial Y_j/\partial L_j}{\partial Y_j/\partial K_{2j}}.$$

$$(III.155)$$

Computing the partial derivatives from (III.149), we have

$$\frac{w}{r_1}=\frac{\alpha_{0j}}{\alpha_{1j}}\frac{K_{1j}}{L_j},$$

$$\frac{w}{r_2}=\frac{\alpha_{2j}}{\alpha_{0j}}\frac{K_{2j}}{L_j},$$

$$(III.155')$$

so that

$$\frac{K_{1j}}{L_j}=\frac{\alpha_{1j}}{\alpha_{0j}}\frac{w}{r_1},$$

$$\frac{K_{2j}}{L_j}=\frac{\alpha_{2j}}{\alpha_{0j}}\frac{w}{r_2}.$$

$$(III.156)$$

Substituting (III.156) into (III.154) and using the notation $k_i = K_i/L$, $l_j = L_j/L$, we have

$$l_0\frac{\alpha_{10}}{\alpha_{00}}\frac{w}{r_1}+l_1\frac{\alpha_{11}}{\alpha_{01}}\frac{w}{r_1}+l_2\frac{\alpha_{12}}{\alpha_{02}}\frac{w}{r_1}=k_1,$$

$$l_0\frac{\alpha_{20}}{\alpha_{00}}\frac{w}{r_2}+l_1\frac{\alpha_{21}}{\alpha_{01}}\frac{w}{r_2}+l_2\frac{\alpha_{22}}{\alpha_{02}}\frac{w}{r_2}=k_2,$$

$$(III.157)$$

that is

$$l_0\frac{\alpha_{10}}{\alpha_{00}}+l_1\frac{\alpha_{11}}{\alpha_{01}}+l_2\frac{\alpha_{12}}{\alpha_{02}}=k_1\frac{r_1}{w},$$

$$l_0\frac{\alpha_{20}}{\alpha_{00}}+l_1\frac{\alpha_{21}}{\alpha_{01}}+l_2\frac{\alpha_{22}}{\alpha_{02}}=k_2\frac{r_2}{w}.$$

$$(III.157')$$

From (III.151) we have

$$P_j = \frac{w}{\partial Y_j / \partial L_j} ,$$

whence, computing $\partial Y_j / \partial L_j$ from (III.149),

$$P_j = \frac{w}{\alpha_{0j} Y_j / L_j} , \qquad (III.158)$$

and so, using (III.158), we have

$$P_1 Y_1 = w \frac{L_1}{\alpha_{01}} ,$$
$$\qquad\qquad\qquad\qquad (III.159)$$
$$P_2 Y_2 = w \frac{L_2}{\alpha_{02}} .$$

Substituting (III.159) into the first equations of (III.153) and dividing through by L we obtain

$$w \frac{l_1}{\alpha_{01}} = s_1 r_1 k_1 ,$$

$$w \frac{l_2}{\alpha_{02}} = s_2 r_2 k_2 ,$$

from which

$$l_1 = s_1 \alpha_{01} k_1 \frac{r_1}{w}$$
$$\qquad\qquad\qquad\qquad (III.160)$$
$$l_2 = s_2 \alpha_{02} k_2 \frac{r_2}{w} .$$

Consider now the second equation in (III.153). Dividing through by wL we have

$$\frac{P_0 Y_0}{wL} = 1 + (1 - s_1) \frac{r_1}{w} k_1 + (1 - s_2) \frac{r_2}{w} k_2 . \qquad (III.161)$$

Now, from (III.151) we have, for $j = 0$,

$$w = P_0 \frac{\alpha_{00}}{L_0} Y_0 ,$$

(III.162)

and so, substituting (III.162) into the denominator of the fraction in the left-hand side of (III.161), we have

$$\frac{l_0}{\alpha_{00}} = 1 + (1 - s_1) \frac{r_1}{w} k_1 + (1 - s_2) \frac{r_2}{w} k_2 ,$$

which gives

$$l_0 = \alpha_{00} [1 + (1 - s_1) \frac{r_1}{w} k_1 + (1 - s_2) \frac{r_2}{w} k_2] .$$

(III.163)

Substituting (III.160) and (III.163) in (III.157') and rearranging terms, we have

$$\{1 - [(1 - s_1)\alpha_{10} + \alpha_{11}s_1]\} k_1 \frac{r_1}{w} - [(1 - s_2)\alpha_{10} + \alpha_{12}s_2] k_2 \frac{r_2}{w} = \alpha_{10} ,$$

(III.164)

$$- [(1 - s_1)\alpha_{20} + \alpha_{21}s_1] k_1 \frac{r_1}{w} + \{1 - [(1 - s_2)\alpha_{20} + \alpha_{22}s_2]\} k_2 \frac{r_2}{w} = \alpha_{20} .$$

System (III.164) can be solved for $k_1 r_1/w$, $k_2 r_2/w$. It is left as an exercise to show that this solution is positive *. Thus we have, say,

$$k_1 \frac{r_1}{w} = b_1 ,$$

$$k_2 \frac{r_2}{w} = b_2 ,$$

(III.165)

(where b_1, b_2 are positive constants), so that

$$\frac{k_1}{b_1} = \frac{w}{r_1} , \qquad \frac{k_2}{b_2} = \frac{w}{r_2} .$$

(III.165')

---

* *Hint*: write the system in matrix terms as $(I - A)x = \alpha$, and note that A is a positive matrix whose column sums are smaller than unity. Use then the theorems on positive matrices to show that $(I - A)^{-1} > 0$.

The production functions (III.149) can also be written, being homogeneous of the first degree, as

$$Y_j = L_j \left(\frac{K_{1j}}{L_j}\right)^{\alpha_{1j}} \left(\frac{K_{2j}}{L_j}\right)^{\alpha_{2j}}, \tag{III.149'}$$

from which

$$Y_1 = \frac{L_1}{K_{11}} K_{11} \left(\frac{K_{11}}{L_1}\right)^{\alpha_{11}} \left(\frac{K_{21}}{L_1}\right)^{\alpha_{21}} = K_{11} \left(\frac{K_{11}}{L_1}\right)^{\alpha_{11}-1} \left(\frac{K_{21}}{L_1}\right)^{\alpha_{21}},$$

$$\tag{III.166}$$

$$Y_2 = \frac{L_2}{K_{22}} K_{22} \left(\frac{K_{12}}{L_2}\right)^{\alpha_{12}} \left(\frac{K_{22}}{L_2}\right)^{\alpha_{22}} = K_{22} \left(\frac{K_{12}}{L_2}\right)^{\alpha_{12}} \left(\frac{K_{22}}{L_2}\right)^{\alpha_{22}-1},$$

that is, using (III.156),

$$Y_1 = K_{11} \left(\frac{w}{r_1}\right)^{\alpha_{11}-1} \left(\frac{w}{r_2}\right)^{\alpha_{21}} \left(\frac{\alpha_{11}}{\alpha_{01}}\right)^{\alpha_{11}-1} \left(\frac{\alpha_{21}}{\alpha_{01}}\right)^{\alpha_{21}},$$

$$\tag{III.167}$$

$$Y_2 = K_{22} \left(\frac{w}{r_1}\right)^{\alpha_{12}} \left(\frac{w}{r_2}\right)^{\alpha_{22}-1} \left(\frac{\alpha_{12}}{\alpha_{02}}\right)^{\alpha_{12}} \left(\frac{\alpha_{22}}{\alpha_{02}}\right)^{\alpha_{22}-1}.$$

From (III.152) we have

$$\frac{r_1}{P_1} = \frac{\partial Y_1}{\partial K_{11}} = \alpha_{11} \frac{Y_1}{K_{11}},$$

$$\tag{III.168}$$

$$\frac{r_2}{P_2} = \frac{\partial Y_2}{\partial K_{22}} = \alpha_{22} \frac{Y_2}{K_{22}}.$$

Substituting (III.167) in (III.168) we have

$$\frac{r_1}{P_1} = d_1 \left(\frac{w}{r_1}\right)^{\alpha_{11}-1} \left(\frac{w}{r_2}\right)^{\alpha_{21}},$$

$$\tag{III.169}$$

$$\frac{r_2}{P_2} = d_2 \left(\frac{w}{r_1}\right)^{\alpha_{12}} \left(\frac{w}{r_2}\right)^{\alpha_{22}-1},$$

where

$$d_1 = \alpha_{01}^{\alpha_{01}} \alpha_{11}^{\alpha_{11}} \alpha_{21}^{\alpha_{21}}, \qquad d_2 = \alpha_{02}^{\alpha_{02}} \alpha_{12}^{\alpha_{12}} \alpha_{22}^{\alpha_{22}}. \tag{III.170}$$

Using (III.165') we can rewrite (III.169) as

$$\frac{r_1}{P_1} = d_1 b_1^{1-\alpha_{11}} b_2^{-\alpha_{21}} k_1^{\alpha_{11}-1} k_2^{\alpha_{21}} \, ,$$

$$\frac{r_2}{P_2} = d_2 b_1^{-\alpha_{12}} b_2^{1-\alpha_{22}} k_1^{\alpha_{12}} k_2^{\alpha_{22}-1} \, .$$

(III.169')

From the first equations in (III.153) we have

$$\frac{r_1}{P_1} = \frac{Y_1}{s_1 K_1} \, ,$$

$$\frac{r_2}{P_2} = \frac{Y_2}{s_2 K_2} \, .$$

(III.171)

Equating the right-hand members of (III.169') and (III.171) and multiplying through the first equation by $s_1 K_1 / L = s_1 k_1$ and the second equation by $s_2 K_2 / L = s_2 k_2$, we have finally

$$y_1 = m_1 k_1^{\alpha_{11}} k_2^{\alpha_{21}} \, ,$$

$$y_2 = m_2 k_1^{\alpha_{12}} k_2^{\alpha_{22}} \, ,$$

(III.172)

where

$$m_1 = s_1 d_1 b_1^{1-\alpha_{11}} b_2^{-\alpha_{21}} \, , \qquad m_2 = s_2 d_2 b_1^{-\alpha_{12}} b_2^{1-\alpha_{22}} \, ,$$

$$y_1 = Y_1 / L \, , \qquad y_2 = Y_2 / L \, .$$

(III.173)

Eqs. (III.172) are the required intensive form of the model.

We now introduce the usual dynamic equations:

$$\dot{L}/L = n \, ,$$

(III.174)

$$\dot{K}_1 = Y_1 - \gamma_1 K_1 \, ,$$

$$\dot{K}_2 = Y_2 - \gamma_2 K_2 \, ,$$

(III.175)

where n is the constant growth rate of population and γ_i is the constant rate of depreciation of the i-th capital good. We can rewrite (III.175) as

$$\frac{\dot{K}_1}{K_1} = \frac{Y_1}{L}\frac{L}{K_1} - \gamma_1 = \frac{y_1}{k_1} - \gamma_1 \ ,$$

$$\frac{\dot{K}_2}{K_2} = \frac{Y_2}{L}\frac{L}{K_2} - \gamma_2 = \frac{y_2}{k_2} - \gamma_2 \ ,$$

and, using (III.174),

$$\frac{\dot{K}_1}{K_1} - \frac{\dot{L}}{L} = \frac{y_1}{k_1} - (\gamma_1 + n) \ ,$$

$$\frac{\dot{K}_2}{K_2} - \frac{\dot{L}}{L} = \frac{y_2}{k_2} - (\gamma_2 + n) \ .$$

(III.176)

The left-hand side of (III.176) is $\dot{k}_i/k_i$ and so

$$\dot{k}_1 = y_1 - (\gamma_1 + n)k_1 \ ,$$

$$\dot{k}_2 = y_2 - (\gamma_2 + n)k_2 \ ,$$

(III.177)

whence, using (III.172), we obtain

$$\dot{k}_1 = m_1 k_1^{\alpha_{11}} k_2^{\alpha_{21}} - (n + \gamma_1)k_1 \ ,$$

$$\dot{k}_2 = m_2 k_1^{\alpha_{12}} k_2^{\alpha_{22}} - (n + \gamma_2)k_2 \ ,$$

(III.178)

which is the fundamental dynamic system of the model. The equilibrium point is obtained by putting $\dot{k}_1 = 0$, $\dot{k}_2 = 0$, that is by solving the system

$$m_1 k_1^{\alpha_{11}} k_2^{\alpha_{21}} = (n + \gamma_1)k_1 \ ,$$

$$m_2 k_1^{\alpha_{12}} k_2^{\alpha_{22}} = (n + \gamma_2)k_2 \ .$$

(III.179)

It can easily be proved that, apart from the trivial solution $k_1 = k_2 = 0$, system (III.179) has a unique positive solution, say (k_1^*, k_2^*) ★. For convenience

---

★ A simple proof is sketched here. Express, for example, k_1 in terms of k_2 from both equations in (III.179), obtaining, say, $k_1 = f_1(k_2)$, $k_1 = f_2(k_2)$. Equate, and the equilibrium value k_2^* is obtained as a solution of $f_1(k_2) = f_2(k_2)$. The study of the two functions reveals that — excluding the origin — they intersect only once in the positive quadrant.

we introduce the variables

$$z_i = k_i/k_i^*$$ (III.180)

and, since from (III.179) we have

$$k_i^* = \frac{m_i}{n + \gamma_i} k_1^{*\alpha_{1i}} k_2^{*\alpha_{2i}},$$ (III.181)

we can rewrite (III.178) as

$$\dot{z}_1 = c_1(z_1^{\alpha_{11}} z_2^{\alpha_{21}} - z_1),$$
$$\dot{z}_2 = c_2(z_1^{\alpha_{12}} z_2^{\alpha_{22}} - z_2),$$ (III.182)

where $c_i = n + \gamma_i$.

We shall now study system (III.182) and show that it is locally stable [*]. In terms of z_i, the equilibrium point is $(1, 1)$. Let us then make a linear approximation of the functions on the right-hand sides of eqs. (III.182) in $(1, 1)$ [**]. Expanding in Taylor's series and neglecting the terms of order higher than the first, we have

$$\dot{\bar{z}}_1 = c_1(\alpha_{11} - 1)\bar{z}_1 + c_1\alpha_{21}\bar{z}_2,$$
$$\dot{\bar{z}}_2 = c_2\alpha_{12}\bar{z}_1 + c_2(\alpha_{22} - 1)\bar{z}_2,$$ (III.183)

where $\bar{z}_i$ denotes the deviations from equilibrium.

The matrix

$$\begin{bmatrix} c_1(\alpha_{11} - 1) & c_1\alpha_{21} \\ c_2\alpha_{12} & c_2(\alpha_{22} - 1) \end{bmatrix}$$

[*] For a proof of its global stability, see Burmeister, Dobell and Kuga (1968).

[**] Following rigorously the correspondence between mathematical tools and economic models, the model under consideration should have been treated in Part II, ch.9, since we are examining the stability of the equilibrium point by means of an approximating linear differential system. However, we believe that here an exception is called for, because, as we said at the beginning, this multi-sector model appears as a natural extension of the two-sector neoclassical model treated in the previous section.

has a negative dominant diagonal, since $\alpha_{ii} < 1$ and $1 - \alpha_{11} = \alpha_{01} + \alpha_{21} > \alpha_{21}$, $1 - \alpha_{22} = \alpha_{02} + \alpha_{12} > \alpha_{12}$. Therefore its latent roots have negative real parts, and consequently the equilibrium point is stable.

References

Amano, A., 1964, A Further Note on Professor Uzawa's Two-Sector Model of Economic Growth.

Andronov, A.A., Vitt, A.A. and Khaikin, S.E., 1966, *Theory of Oscillators*, chs. I–V.

Baumol, W.J., 1958, Topology of Second order Linear Difference Equations with Constant Coefficients.

Baumol, W.J., 1970, *Economic Dynamics*, ch. 13; ch. 14, § 10.

Beckmann, M.J. and Ryder, H.E., 1969, Simultaneous Price and Quantity Adjustment in a Single Market.

Bergstrom, A.R., 1967, *The Construction and Use of Economic Models*, ch. 7.

Boole, G., 1960, *A Treatise on the Calculus of Finite Differences*, chs. IX, X, XII, XIII.

Burmeister, E., 1967, The Existence of Golden Ages and Stability in the Two-Sector Model.

Burmeister, E., 1968, The Role of the Jacobian Determinant in the Two-Sector Model.

Burmeister, E., Dobell, R. and Kuga, K., 1968, A Note on the Global Stability of a Simple Growth Model with Many Capital Goods.

Drandakis, E.M., 1963, Factor Substitution in the Two-Sector Growth Model.

Goodwin, R.M., 1951, The Nonlinear Accelerator and the Persistence of Business Cycles.

Goodwin, R.M., 1955, A Model of Cyclical Growth.

Goodwin, R.M., 1967, A Growth Cycle.

Hahn, F.H., 1965, On Two-Sector Growth Models.

Hahn, F.H., 1966, Equilibrium Dynamics with Heterogeneous Capital Goods.

Hahn, F.H. and Matthews, R.C.O., 1964, The Theory of Economic Growth: A Survey, § II.3.

Ichimura, S., 1955, Toward a General Nonlinear Macrodynamic Theory of Economic Fluctuations.

Inada, K.-I., 1963, On a Two-Sector Model of Economic Growth: Comments and a Generalization.

Inada, K.-I., 1964, On the Stability of Growth Equilibria in Two-Sector Models.

Ince, E.L., 1956, *Ordinary Differential Equations*, ch. II.

Ince, E.L., 1959, *Integration of Ordinary Differential Equations*, ch. I.

Jorgenson, D.W., 1961, The Development of a Dual Economy.

Lotka, A.J., 1956, *Elements of Mathematical Biology*, pp. 88–92.

Milne-Thomson, L.M., 1933, *The Calculus of Finite Differences*, ch. XI.

Minorsky, N., 1962, *Nonlinear Oscillations*, chs. 1–4.

Morishima, M., 1969, *Theory of Economic Growth*, ch. III.

Ramaswami, V.K., 1969, On Two-Sector Neo-Classical Growth.

Rose, H., 1967, On the Non-Linear Theory of the Employment Cycle.

Sansone, G. and Conti, R., 1964, *Non-Linear Differential Equations*, chs. I, II, IV, VI..

Shell, K. and Stiglitz, J.E., 1967, The Allocation of Investment in a Dynamic Economy.
Solow, R.M., 1956, A Contribution to the Theory of Economic Growth.
Solow, R.M., 1960, Investment and Technical Progress.
Solow, R.M., 1961, Note on Uzawa's Two-Sector Model of Economic Growth.
Stiglitz, J.E., 1967, A Two-Sector Two Class Model of Economic Growth.
Stiglitz, J.E. and Uzawa, H., eds, 1969, *Readings in the Modern Theory of Economic Growth*, pp. 405–7.
Takayama, A., 1963, On a Two-Sector Model of Economic Growth: A Comparative Statics Analysis.
Thalberg, B., 1966, *A Trade Cycle Analysis.*
Uzawa, H., 1961, On a Two-Sector Model of Economic Growth.
Uzawa, H., 1963, On a Two-Sector Model of Economic Growth, II.
Volterra, V., 1931, *Leçons sur la théorie mathématique de la lutte pour la vie,* ch. I, §II.

APPENDIX IV

Linear Mixed Differential and Difference Equations

§1. General concepts

A mixed differential–difference equation is a functional equation in an unknown function of time and certain of its derivatives, evaluated at different values of t *. If we recall the definitions of order of a differential equation and of order of a difference equation, it is clear that a mixed differential–difference equation has both a differential order and a difference order. The general form of an equation of differential order n and of difference order m is the following:

$$F[t, y(t), y(t - \omega_1), ..., y(t - \omega_m), y'(t), y'(t - \omega_1), ..., y'(t - \omega_m), ...$$

$$..., y^{(n)}(t), y^{(n)}(t - \omega_1), ..., y^{(n)}(t - \omega_m)] = 0 , \qquad (IV.1)$$

where F is a given function, and the positive numbers ω_i, $\omega_1 < \omega_2 < ... < \omega_m$,

---

* We shall consider only functions having one independent variable, so that the derivatives and the differences which appear in the equation are ordinary, and not partial, derivatives and differences. It must be noted that both the function and its derivatives may be evaluated at different points of time.

(the 'retardations' or lags) are also given. In the particular case in which the ω_i are equispaced, we can put $\omega_1 = 1, \omega_2 = 2, ..., \omega_m = m$.

The treatment here will be limited to linear equations with constant coefficients and of the first order both in derivatives and in differences, which have the form

$$a_0 y'(t) + a_1 y'(t - \omega) + b_0 y(t) + b_1 y(t - \omega) = g(t) , \qquad \text{(IV.2)}$$

where $a_0, a_1, b_0, b_1, \omega$ are given constants and $g(t)$ is a known function. Eq. (IV.2) is non-homogeneous; the corresponding homogeneous equation is the same but for $g(t) \equiv 0$.

We shall now give a few more definitions. An equation having form (IV.2) is called 'of retarded type' if $a_0 \neq 0, a_1 = 0$; 'of neutral type' if $a_0 \neq 0$, $a_1 \neq 0$; 'of advanced type' if $a_0 = 0, a_1 \neq 0$. We shall further limit our treatment to equations of retarded type ★, both because their study is sufficient to illustrate the general method of solution based on the characteristic equation and because it is this type which has been more frequently used in economic applications.

We shall then consider equations of the type

$$a_0 y'(t) + b_0 y(t) + b_1 y(t - \omega) = g(t) , \qquad \text{(IV.3)}$$

and of the type

$$a_0 y'(t) + b_0 y(t) + b_1 y(t - \omega) = 0 . \qquad \text{(IV.4)}$$

For such equations the same general principles hold as for difference equations (see Part I, ch. 1) and differential equations (see Part II, ch. 1), that is:

(1) if $y_1(t)$ is a solution of (IV.4), $A y_1(t)$ also is a solution, where A is an arbitrary constant;

(2) if $y_1(t)$ and $y_2(t)$ are two linearly independent solutions of (IV.4), $A_1 y_1(t) + A_2 y_2(t)$ is also a solution, where A_1 and A_2 are arbitrary constants; this property (the principle of superposition) can be extended to any number of linearly independent solutions;

(3) if $w(t)$ is a solution of (IV.4) and $\bar{y}(t)$ is a solution of (IV.3), then $w(t) + \bar{y}(t)$ is a solution of (IV.3).

The reader can check these principles by direct substitution in (IV.4) and

---

★ Mixed differential–difference equations of retarded type are also called *differential equations with time delay* and *hystero-differential equations*.

in (IV.3). Given (3), the main problem is to find the solution of (IV.4), then adding to this solution, if the equation is non-homogeneous, a particular solution of (IV.3).

§2. The method of solution and the stability conditions

Property (2) of the previous section suggests the possibility of finding the general solution of (IV.4) as a linear combination of elementary solutions, according to the procedure already applied with success to differential and to difference equations. Moreover, analogy suggests that such elementary solutions might be of exponential type $e^{\lambda t}$, where λ is a constant to be determined *. Substituting in (IV.4) and collecting terms, we have

$$e^{\lambda t}(a_0\lambda + b_0 + b_1 e^{-\omega\lambda}) = 0 . \tag{IV.5}$$

Therefore $e^{\lambda t}$ is a solution of (IV.4) if, and only if, eq. (IV.5) is identically satisfied, which in turn is true if, and only if,

$$a_0\lambda + b_0 + b_1 e^{-\omega\lambda} = 0 . \tag{IV.6}$$

Eq. (IV.6) is called the *characteristic equation* of (IV.4) and its roots are called the *characteristic roots*.

Eq. (IV.6) is a *transcendental* equation, which has an infinite number of roots; the general solution of (IV.4) has then the form

$$y(t) = \sum_{r=1}^{\infty} c_r \exp(\lambda_r t) , \tag{IV.7}$$

if all the characteristic roots λ_r are distinct (the coefficients c_r are arbitrary constants), and the form

$$y(t) = \sum_{r=1}^{\infty} p_r(t) \exp(\lambda_r t) , \tag{IV.7'}$$

---

* The reader may wonder why $e^{\lambda t}$ and not μ^t (the former is suggested by differential, and the latter by difference, equations). An intuitive reason is that, if the unknown function is differentiable, the 'differential' nature is stronger than the 'difference' nature. Another (practical) reason is that, when differentiability obtains, the function $e^{\lambda t}$ is easier to treat than the function μ^t.

if there are multiple roots, where $p_r(t)$ is a polynomial in t (of degree less than the multiplicity of the corresponding root). As far as multiple roots are concerned, it can be proved that eq. (IV.6) has at most one multiple root, and that, if

$$a_0 \neq b_1 \omega \exp \left(1 + \frac{b_0 \omega}{a_0}\right),$$ (IV.8)

then all the roots are simple *.

If we define a new variable $s \equiv \omega\lambda$, eq. (IV.6) can be rewritten as

$$\frac{a_0}{\omega} s + b_0 + b_1 e^{-s} = 0 .$$ (IV.9)

Let us now multiply through by $(-\omega/a_0)e^s$. Defining $a \equiv -b_0\omega/a_0$, $b \equiv -b_1\omega/a_0$ and rearranging terms we have

$$a e^s + b - s e^s = 0 .$$ (IV.9′)

If, instead, we multiply by $-\omega/a_0$ only, we obtain (a and b are defined as before)

$$s = a + b e^{-s} .$$ (IV.9″)

Of course, the reason for these transformations is that the alternative forms (IV.9′) and (IV.9″) will be useful in the following treatment.

We can now tackle the problem of locating the characteristic roots. For this purpose we shall use (IV.9″), which is in a more convenient form. Consider the function

$$z = f(s) = s - b e^{-s}$$ (IV.10)

so that the real roots of (IV.9″) are given by the intersection of $f(s)$ with the function $z = a$, a straight line parallel to the s axis. We have

$$\frac{df}{ds} = 1 + b e^{-s} , \qquad \frac{d^2f}{ds^2} = -b e^{-s} .$$ (IV.11)

---

* See Bellman and Cooke (1963, p. 109). See also below, footnotes * and ** to p. 471.

Two cases must be distinguished:

(1) $b > 0$. Then df/ds is always positive, and from (IV.10), $\lim_{s \to \pm \infty} f(s) = \pm \infty$. Therefore the function $f(s)$ will intersect once, and only once, the function $z = a$; furthermore, the intersection point cannot be an inflection point, so that the real root will be a simple root $\star$.

(2) $b < 0$. Then df/ds is zero for

$$-be^{-s} = 1 , \tag{IV.12}$$

that is

$$s = \log(-b) . \tag{IV.12'}$$

Furthermore, d^2f/ds^2 is always positive, so that (IV.12') yields a unique global minimum to $f(s)$. Substituting (IV.12') in (IV.10) we have

$$\min f(s) = \log(-b) + 1 . \tag{IV.13}$$

Now, from obvious geometric considerations, if $\min f(s) \gtreqless a$, the function $f(s)$ will lie entirely above, be tangent to, intersect twice, the straight line $z = a$. Therefore, eq. (IV.9'') will have no real roots, two equal real roots, two distinct real roots according to whether $\star\star$

$$\log(-b) + 1 \gtreqless a , \tag{IV.14}$$

that is, rearranged,

$$a - \log(-b) \lesseqgtr 1 .. \tag{IV.15}$$

Thus we are able to conclude that the characteristic equation under examination has at most two real roots. Therefore all the other roots (which are infinite in number) are complex.

Regarding complex roots, let

$$s = \alpha \pm i\theta \tag{IV.16}$$

$\star$ Given the definition of b, if $b > 0$ then $b_1\omega$ and a_0 have opposite signs, so that (IV.8) is satisfied, and conversely.

$\star\star$ Therefore, if $\log(-b) + 1 \neq a$ no multiple real roots may occur. The condition can be written as $\log(-b) \neq -1 + a$, that is $-b \neq e^{-1+a}$, i.e., given the definitions of a and b, $b_1\omega/a_0 \neq \exp[-1 - (b_0\omega/a_0)]$, from which, taking reciprocals and multiplying through by $b_1\omega$, we obtain (IV.8).

be the representative pair of complex roots [*]. Substituting in (IV.9″) we have

$$\alpha \pm i\theta = a + be^{-\alpha} \exp\left(\mp i\theta\right),$$

and, using the well-known transformation

$$\exp\left(\mp i\theta\right) = \cos\theta \mp i\sin\theta,$$

we obtain

$$\alpha \pm i\theta = (a + be^{-\alpha}\cos\theta) \mp ibe^{-\alpha}\sin\theta,$$

so that, equating the corresponding real and imaginary parts,

$$\alpha = a + be^{-\alpha}\cos\theta,$$
$$\theta = -be^{-\alpha}\sin\theta.$$

(IV.17)

We are not in a much better position than before, since eqs. (IV.17) are transcendental equations too. However, some conclusions concerning the intervals in which θ lies can be reached. Since, in (IV.16), θ can be taken as a positive number, from the second equation of (IV.17) we obtain the information that $\sin\theta$ and b must have opposite sign. This restricts the values of θ within the following intervals:

$$2k\pi < \theta < (2k+1)\pi \qquad \text{if } b < 0,$$
$$k = 0, 1, 2, ..., n, ... ,$$
$$(2k+1)\pi < \theta < (2k+2)\pi \qquad \text{if } b > 0.$$

(IV.18)

Further information can be obtained by means of a graphical analysis, an illustration of which will be given in the next section (fig. A.22).

The general conclusion of the foregoing analysis is that the solution of eq. (IV.6) shows in any case an oscillatory path, to which a monotonic path may or may not be superimposed.

It would be desirable, at this point, to have at hand *stability conditions* to check whether the real parts of the roots of the characteristic equation – be

---

[*] We have implicitly assumed that complex roots always occur in conjugate pairs. It can be proved that it is indeed so. See Bellman and Cooke (1963, p. 108). Another way to prove this is to observe that if $\alpha + i\theta$ satisfies (IV.17) below, also $\alpha - i\theta$ satisfies them.

they real or complex — are all negative without having to solve the characteristic equation itself. Fortunately, such conditions exist, and can be given in two forms. Before proceeding further, note that, since ω is a positive magnitude, the negativity of the real part of s is necessary and sufficient for the negativity of the real part of λ. We can now state [*]:

Hayes' Theorem. All the roots of (IV.9′) have negative real parts if, and only if,

(1) $a < 1$,

and

(2) $a < -b < (a_1^2 + a^2)^{1/2}$,

where a_1 is the root of the equation $x = a \tan x$ such that $0 < x < \pi$. If $a = 0$, we take $a_1 = \frac{1}{2}\pi$.

The stability conditions given in this theorem are not easy to apply, since we must first solve the transcendental equation $x = a \tan x$. Therefore we think that the conditions given by Burger are preferable, since their application requires only the solution of the simpler equation $\cos x = \alpha$ (where α is a given constant). Therefore we state [**]:

Burger's Theorem. For all roots of (IV.9″) to possess negative real parts it is necessary and sufficient

(1) in the case $b \geqslant -1$ that $a < -b$;

(2) in the case $b < -1$ that $a < b$ or that $b \leqslant a < -b$ and arc $\cos(-a/b) >$ $(b^2 - a^2)^{1/2}$, where the value of the function arc $\cos$ is restricted by $0 <$ arc $\cos(-a/b) \leqslant \pi$.

As we said above, Burger's conditions are, in general, simpler to apply than Hayes' since to solve the equation $\cos x = -a/b$ is simpler than to solve the equation $a \tan x = x$. The only case in which Hayes' theorem is easier to apply is when $a = 0$. In that case, in fact, the stability condition is $0 < -b < \frac{1}{2}\pi$, which we can obtain immediately using Hayes' theorem, whereas applying Burger's theorem is a slightly longer business.

Because of property (3) of the previous section, to complete our analysis it is sufficient to show how a particular solution $\bar{y}(t)$ of (IV.3) can be found.

---

[*] See Bellman and Cooke (1963, pp. 444–6).

[**] For the proof of this theorem and of its equivalence with Hayes' theorem, see Burger. Given its superiority over Hayes' theorem, it is surprising that this theorem has generally passed unnoticed both in the mathematical and in the mathematical economics literature (e.g., in Bellman's and Cooke's treatise on differential–difference equations Burger's theorem is not even mentioned; and in the mathematical economics literature, as far as we know, only Hayes' theorem has been used).

The simplest case occurs when $g(t)$ is a constant, let us call it B. As a particular solution, we can try $\bar{y}(t) = D$, where D is an undetermined constant. Substituting in (IV.3) we have

$$b_0 D + b_1 D = B ,$$

which gives ★

$$D = \frac{B}{b_0 + b_1} .$$

The above is nothing else but an application of the general principle of *undetermined coefficients*, which has already served us well in difference and in differential equations. We recall that this method consists in trying as a particular solution a function having the same form of the given function $g(t)$ but with undetermined coefficients; substituting in (IV.3) one tries to determine such coefficients so that the equation is identically satisfied. If the first attempt does not succeed, one tries next the same type of function but multiplied by a polynomial in t (starting with the first degree) and proceeds in like manner ★★.

★ If $b_0 + b_1 = 0$, try $\bar{y}(t) = Dt$. Substitution in (IV.3) yields, after manipulation, $D = B/(a_0 - b_1\omega)$. If also $a_0 - b_1\omega = 0$, try $\bar{y}(t) = Dt^2$; substitution in (IV.3) and manipulation yields $D = B/b_1\omega^2$, where it must be true that $b_1\omega^2 \neq 0$, since in the contrary case eq. (IV.3) would no more be a mixed differential–difference equation, but would reduce to a simple differential equation.

★★ We give as an example $g(t) = Be^{\gamma t}$, where B and γ are given constants. As a particular solution let us try $\bar{y}(t) = De^{\gamma t}$, where D is an undetermined constant. Substituting in (IV.3) and collecting terms, we have

$$e^{\gamma t}[D(a_0\gamma + b_0 + b_1 e^{-\gamma\omega}) - B] = 0 ,$$

which will be identically satisfied if, and only if, the expression in square brackets is zero, so that

$$D = \frac{B}{a_0\gamma + b_0 + b_1 e^{-\gamma\omega}} .$$

In the case in which γ happens to coincide with one of the real roots of (IV.6) the denominator of the fraction is zero. In such a case we try $\bar{y}(t) = Dte^{\gamma t}$. Substituting in (IV.3) and proceeding as above we obtain

$$D = \frac{B}{a_0 - b_1\omega e^{-\gamma\omega}} .$$

The reader may examine as an exercise the case in which $a_0 - b_1\omega e^{-\gamma\omega} = 0$.

§3. Some economic applications

Whereas differential equations and difference equations both have a lot of economic applications, the economic applications of mixed differential–difference equations are so far very few [*].

If this is so, the reader might wonder why we have felt the need to devote an appendix to these equations. One reason is that among the applications there is Kalecki's (1935) model which, successively elaborated upon by the same author [**], is by now a 'classic' in macrodynamics and cannot be ignored by any 'dynamicist'. But this would not be a sufficient reason, mainly because in this book we have ignored many other important dynamic models. The fundamental reason is that we think that *mixed differential–difference equations are much more suitable than differential equations alone, or difference equations alone, for an adequate treatment of dynamic economic phenomena.* We think so because we believe that real life dynamic economic phenomena are approximately continuous phenomena, in which, however, are present in an essential way discontinuous lags, influences on the current value of a variable of previous values of the same variable (placed at a finite, and not infinitesimal, distance), etc. The reason why we believe that economic phenomena are mainly continuous (although approximately so) is the following. Though many individual economic decisions are taken at discrete intervals of time (e.g. daily, or weekly, or monthly, etc.), the variables which are considered (and observed) by the economist are usually the result of a great number of decisions taken by different agents at different points of time, so that it seems natural to treat economic phenomena as approximately continuous [‡]. But this must not lead us to neglect the other aspect (discon-

---

[*] In addition to the applications expounded in this section, we recall – no claim to exhaustiveness being made – Tinbergen's (1959) shipbuilding cycle model, Frisch's (1933) essay, an application by Leontief (1953) to their own dynamic model, some applications cited by Burger (1956), and an application by Furuno (1965) to two-sector growth models.

[**] See Kalecki (1954). Here we shall examine only the 1935 model.

[‡] These considerations have led some authors (see, e.g., Bergstrom, 1967, pp. 1–2) to suggest that economic dynamic models should be formulated as systems of differential equations. We think that such a conclusion is unwarranted. In fact, the other aspect (discontinuous lags, etc.) is not less important, so that, if we do not use the most appropriate mathematical tool (mixed differential–difference equations or other types of functional equations, as integral equations, integro–differential equations, etc.), we must ascertain which is the more relevant aspect in any given case, using then either differential or difference equations (see, in relation to this, what we have written at the end of ch. II.1 (p. 166), and of §2 of ch. II.3 (p. 185), in the text).

tinuous lags, etc.). Using differential equations we neglect the latter aspect in favour of the former (continuity); using difference equations we neglect the former aspect in favour of the latter. Both aspects can be taken into account using mixed differential–difference equations instead.

Perhaps it is the greater formal difficulty of mixed equations with respect to 'pure' differential or difference equations that has prevented a larger use of mixed equations in economic dynamics. But the formal difficulty should be no hindrance if the superiority of mixed equations with respect to pure equations were definitely proved.

Let us now pass to the applications. The first is Kalecki's model; the second is a formalization of ours concerning the classical price-specie-flow mechanism of balance of payments adjustment.

§3.1. Kalecki's (1935) model

The model concerns a closed economic system without trend (we are then in the short run). Indicating with B total real income of capitalists, we have the relation

$$B = C + A , \qquad\qquad (IV.19)$$

where C is capitalists' consumption, while A — if we neglect workers' saving and capital incomes — coincides with gross capital accumulation ★. Capitalists' consumption can be related to gross real profits (capitalists' income) by means of the linear function

$$C = C_1 + \lambda B , \qquad\qquad (IV.20)$$

where C_1 is a positive constant and λ is a positive constant too, but smaller than 1. From (IV.19) and (IV.20) we obtain

$$B = \frac{C_1 + A}{1 - \lambda} . \qquad\qquad (IV.21)$$

Although Kalecki's model is pre-Keynesian, we have here the ingredients made famous by Keynes: the consumption function and the multiplier.

Regarding investment, Kalecki assumes that there is an average *gestation*

★ This amounts to the assumption that all wages are consumed, an extreme case — made to simplify the analysis — of the plausible assumption that workers' propensity to consume is greater than capitalists' propensity to consume.

lag of investment equal to a positive constant θ. The gestation period of investment is the time interval between the decision to invest and the delivery of the finished capital goods. More precisely, in each investment three stages can be distinguished:

(1) investment orders, i.e. all the orders for capital goods, both for replacement purposes and for net additions to the capital stock; they are called I;

(2) production of capital goods, that is gross capital accumulation;

(3) deliveries of finished capital goods, call them L.

Given the assumption made above, we can write

$$L(t) = I(t - \theta) . \tag{IV.22}$$

To find the relation between A and I we proceed as follows. Let $W(t)$ be the total amount in time t of unfilled investment orders. Since each order requires a period of time θ to be filled, and assuming that the construction of the ordered capital goods proceeds at an even pace (that is, $1/\theta$ of each order is executed per unit of time) *, it follows that the production of capital goods is equal to $(1/\theta)W$; therefore

$$A = \frac{W}{\theta} . \tag{IV.23}$$

As regards $W(t)$, it equals the sum of all orders made in the interval $(t - \theta, t)$; in fact, since θ is the gestation period of investment, all orders placed during the said interval are still unfilled, whereas all orders placed previously are already filled. Therefore

$$W(t) = \int_{t-\theta}^{t} I(\tau)\, d\tau \tag{IV.24}$$

and so, given (IV.23),

$$A(t) = \frac{1}{\theta} \int_{t-\theta}^{t} I(\tau)\, d\tau . \tag{IV.25}$$

---

* Kalecki (1935, p. 328) seems to consider this fact as a consequence of the existence of a gestation lag. We think that it is more correct to regard it as a separate assumption.

The meaning of eq. (IV.25) is that the output of capital goods at time t is equal to an average — expressed in continuous terms — of the orders placed in the interval $(t - \theta, t)$.

If we call K the capital stock, its first derivative with respect to time is its net increment, so that

$$K'(t) = L(t) - U , \tag{IV.26}$$

where U indicates physical depreciation. Kalecki assumes that in the period under consideration U is a constant.

To 'close' the model we need an investment function. According to Kalecki, there are two main determinants of investment: the gross profit rate B/K and the money rate of interest which he calls p. However, such variables, in Kalecki's opinion, do not influence the absolute level of investment but rather its level relative to the capital stock, that is the ratio I/K; in fact, when B and K increase in the same proportion, so that the ratio B/K remains unchanged, I probably rises. Thus we have the equation

$$\frac{I}{K} = f\left(\frac{B}{K}, p\right) . \tag{IV.27}$$

In the absence of external actions and except for situations of 'financial panic', the money rate of interest usually varies according to the general business conditions, which are represented by B/K. Thus the money rate p can be assumed to be an increasing function of B/K, and consequently f is a function of B/K only. Since B is proportional to $C_1 + A$ by eq. (IV.21), we can write

$$\frac{I}{K} = \phi\left(\frac{C_1 + A}{K}\right) , \tag{IV.28}$$

where ϕ is an increasing function. Taking a linear approximation we have

$$\frac{I}{K} = m\frac{C_1 + A}{K} - n ,$$

where m and n are positive constants ★; from the above equation we have

---

★ The positivity of m is obvious, given the assumption that ϕ is an increasing function. The assumption $n > 0$ is not made by Kalecki, but we think that it is rather plausible. In

$$I = m(C_1 + A) - nK \, . \tag{IV.29}$$

Let us list here for the sake of convenience the basic equations of the model:

$$L(t) = I(t - \theta) \, , \tag{IV.22}$$

$$A(t) = \frac{1}{\theta} \int_{t-\theta}^{t} I(\tau) \, d\tau \, , \tag{IV.25}$$

$$K'(t) = L(t) - U \, , \tag{IV.26}$$

$$I = m(C_1 + A) - nK \, . \tag{IV.29}$$

Differentiating (IV.29) we have

$$I'(t) = mA'(t) - nK'(t) \, , \tag{IV.30}$$

and differentiating (IV.25) we obtain

$$A'(t) = \frac{I(t) - I(t - \theta)}{\theta} \, . \tag{IV.31}$$

From (IV.22) and (IV.26) we obtain

$$K'(t) = I(t - \theta) - U \, . \tag{IV.32}$$

Substituting in (IV.30) from (IV.31) and from (IV.32) we have

$$I'(t) = \frac{m}{\theta} \left[I(t) - I(t-\theta) \right] - n \left[I(t-\theta) - U \right] \, . \tag{IV.33}$$

Denoting by $J(t)$ the difference $I(t) - U$, that is net investment, we have, taking account of the fact that U is a constant, so that $J'(t) = I'(t)$, the equation

fact, we can plausibly assume that investment becomes zero if the rate of profit falls below a certain minimum, and this implies the positivity of n.

$$J'(t) = \frac{m}{\theta} \left[J(t) - J(t - \theta) \right] - n J(t - \theta) ,$$

that is

$$\theta J'(t) - m J(t) + (m + \theta n) J(t - \theta) = 0 . \tag{IV.34}$$

Eq. (IV.34) is a mixed differential–difference equation of the type analysed in the previous section. Its characteristic equation is

$$\theta \lambda - m + (m + \theta n) e^{-\theta \lambda} = 0 , \tag{IV.35}$$

that is, letting $\theta \lambda \equiv s$ and rearranging terms, we have

$$s = m - (m + \theta n) e^{-s} , \tag{IV.36}$$

which has the form of (IV.9″) in Appendix IV, §2. For the real roots, applying eq. (IV.15) of the previous section we obtain the result that eq. (IV.36) will have no real roots, two equal real roots, two distinct real roots according to whether

$$m - \log (m + \theta n) \gtreqless 1 . \tag{IV.37}$$

On *a priori* grounds it is not possible to determine which is the sign which obtains in inequality (IV.37) ★.

For the complex roots, applying eqs. (IV.17) of Appendix IV, §2, we have

---

★ The reader who feels inclined to try with numerical values of the parameters may find the following transformations useful. Consider eq. (IV.29) and write it as

$$I = n \left[\frac{m}{n} (C_1 + A) - K \right] .$$

Now, from (IV.21), $C_1 + A = (1 - \lambda) B$. Let $\rho = B/Y$ be the capitalists' share in national income. Then

$$I = n \left\{ \left[\frac{m}{n} (1 - \lambda) \rho \right] Y - K \right\} . \tag{IV.29'}$$

Eq. (IV.29') is the usual capital stock adjustment equation, where n = reaction coefficient, and $[(m/n)(1 - \lambda) \rho]$ can be interpreted as the (desired) capital/output ratio. Thus given the values of the capital/output ratio and of n, λ, ρ, the value of m can be determined.

$$\alpha = m - (m + \theta n)e^{-\alpha}\cos\beta ,$$

$$\beta = (m + \theta n)e^{-\alpha}\sin\beta ,$$ \hfill (IV.38)

where $\alpha \pm i\beta$ is the typical pair of complex conjugate roots. From the second equation in (IV.38) we have **

$$e^{\alpha} = (m + \theta n)\frac{\sin\beta}{\beta} ,$$

which gives

$$\alpha = \log(m + \theta n) + \log\frac{\sin\beta}{\beta} .$$

Substituting in the first equation of (IV.38) we have

$$\log(m + \theta n) + \log\frac{\sin\beta}{\beta} = m - (m + \theta n)\left(\frac{i}{m + \theta n}\frac{\beta}{\sin\beta}\right)\cos\beta ,$$

so that

$$\log\frac{\sin\beta}{\beta} + \frac{\beta}{\tan\beta} = m - \log(m + \theta n) .$$ \hfill (IV.39)

Letting

$$f(\beta) = \log\frac{\sin\beta}{\beta} + \frac{\beta}{\tan\beta} ,$$

$$C = m - \log(m + \theta n) ,$$

we obtain the values of β as the intersections of $f(\beta)$ with C. The function $f(\beta)$ does not depend on the 'structural' parameters of the model and so can be plotted once and for all. The diagram below (fig. A.22) is due to Frisch and Holme.

Imagine a straight line parallel to the β-axis. It will, in any case, have one intersection with $f(\beta)$ in each of the intervals

$$2k\pi < \beta < (2k + 1)\pi , \qquad k = 1, 2, ..., n , ... ,$$ \hfill (IV.40)

** The following treatment is due to Frisch and Holme (1935).

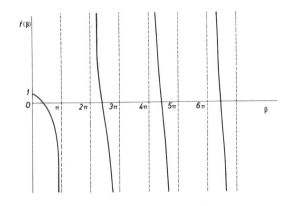

Fig. A.22.

and, if $C < 1$, it will also have one intersection in the interval

$$0 < \beta < \pi . \tag{IV.41}$$

If $C > 1$, the latter intersection does not exist, and, if $C = 1$, it exists for $\beta = 0$, which is irrelevant.

The cycle corresponding to the intersection in interval (IV.41) is called by Frisch and Holme and by Kalecki a *major* cycle, since its period is greater than 2θ (twice the gestation lag) [*], whereas the other cycles, given by intersections in intervals (IV.40), all have periods smaller than θ (*minor* cycles).

Thus, taking account of the definition of C and of (IV.37), we can conclude that the necessary and sufficient condition for the existence of a major cycle is that the characteristic equation has no real roots.

Let us now examine the stability of the model. Applying Burger's theorem we obtain the following necessary and sufficient stability conditions:

(1) if $-(m + \theta n) \geqslant -1$, that is if $m + \theta n \leqslant 1$, the condition is

$$m < m + \theta n ,$$

which is obviously satisfied;

(2) if $-(m + \theta n) < -1$, that is, if $m + \theta n > 1$, the conditions are

---

[*] Remember that $s \equiv \theta \lambda$ and so $\lambda = \alpha/\theta \pm i\beta/\theta$, so that the period of the oscillation is $2\pi/(\beta/\theta)$. If β falls in range (IV.41), then clearly $2\pi\theta/\beta > 2\theta$.

(a) $-(m + \theta n) < m < m + \theta n$,

(b) $\arccos \left(\dfrac{m}{m + \theta n} \right) > (\theta^2 n^2 + 2m\theta n)^{1/2}$.

Condition (b) is the crucial one, since condition (a) is obviously satisfied. Now, since $m/(m + \theta n) < 1$, $\arccos(\ldots) < \frac{1}{2}\pi \simeq 1.57$. Thus, if the expression under square root is not smaller than $(1.57)^2 = 2.4649$, inequality (b) is certainly not satisfied (of course, the converse is not true).

§3.2. *A formalization of the classical price-specie-flow mechanism of balance of payments adjustment.*

The classical price-specie-flow mechanism can thus be described: a balance of payments ★ surplus causes an inflow of gold in the surplus country, that is an increase in the supply of money and consequently, according to the quantity theory, an increase in the price level. This increase, on the one hand, tends to curb exports, since the goods of the surplus country are now relatively dearer on the international market, and to stimulate imports, since foreign goods are now relatively cheaper. Therefore, a gradual disappearance of the surplus takes place ★★. Similar reasoning explains the elimination of a deficit: gold flows out, that is, the supply of money decreases, the price level decreases and this stimulates exports and curbs imports, thus leading to a gradual disappearance of the deficit ★★.

We shall now formalize this theory. First of all, let us state some assumptions which we believe are present, explicitly or implicitly, in the classical theory:

(1) There is free trade, with no interference by government or by monopolistic agents.

(2) The level of national output is given, normally at the full employment level.

(3) During the adjustment period changes in the supply of money are occurring only because of the surpluses (or deficits) in the balance of payments ‡. We could introduce other causes of variation, but this would complicate the analysis without any great advantage.

The following are simplifying assumptions:

★ 'Balance of payments' here is used in the sense of 'balance of trade' only.

★★ As we shall see, this requires that certain stability conditions are satisfied.

‡ Let us note that, in the case in which the circulating medium is paper money, it must be of the type with 100% gold reserve or with a fixed fractional gold reserve.

(4) Since the rate of exchange is fixed, we assume that it is equal to unity (this does not involve any loss of generality, since it is only a matter of choice of units). Moreover, we assume that international payments take place in gold.

(5) Transport costs, insurance, etc., are neglected both for goods and for gold.

(6) Interactions with the 'rest of the world' are neglected, that is, we are considering a 'small' country.

In what follows we shall use the following symbols:

Q = supply of money,
V = velocity of circulation of money (assumed constant),
Y = level of national output (assumed given),
P = level of home prices,
P_M = level of international prices (assumed given),
M = quantity of imports,
X = quantity of exports.

The model can be expressed by the following equations:

$$QV = PY , \qquad\qquad\qquad (IV.42)$$

which expresses the quantity theory;

$$X = X(P) , \qquad dX/dP < 0 , \qquad\qquad (IV.43)$$

i.e. exports are a decreasing function of the home price level, given the foreign price level;

$$M = M(P) , \qquad dM/dP > 0 , \qquad\qquad (IV.44)$$

i.e. imports are an increasing function of the home price level;

$$PX(P) - P_M M(P) = 0 , \qquad\qquad (IV.45)$$

the above being the balance of payments equilibrium equation.

We have four equations to determine the four unknowns Q, X, M, P. Note that Q is also an unknown. In fact, there can be no equilibrium if the supply of money is not such as to give rise to a price level which is the one appropriate for the balance of payments equilibrium (this is an aspect of the 'optimum distribution of specie'). We shall assume that the equilibrium point exists and is economically meaningful.

If the system is not in equilibrium, flows of gold will take place. Assuming that the supply of money and the quantity of gold coincide ★, we have that the variation in the supply of money is in each instant equal to the surplus or deficit in the balance of payments, so that

$$dQ/dt = PX(P) - P_M M(P) .$$ (IV.46)

In turn, the variation in the supply of money causes a change in the price level, given (IV.42). It seems plausible to believe that this change does not occur immediately, but after some lag, say ω. In other words, the change in the price level occurring at time t depends, through (IV.42), on the change in the money supply which occurred at time $t - \omega$, where ω is fixed. Thus we have the equation

$$\frac{dP}{dt} = \frac{V}{Y} \frac{dQ}{d(t - \omega)} .$$ (IV.47)

From (IV.46) and (IV.47) we have

$$\frac{dP}{dt} = \frac{V}{Y} \{ P(t-\omega) X[P(t-\omega)] - P_M M[P(t-\omega)] \} .$$ (IV.48)

We shall study local stability, so that we can use the linear approximation

$$\frac{d\bar{P}}{dt} = \frac{V}{Y} \alpha \bar{P}(t - \omega) ,$$ (IV.48')

where $\bar{P} = P - P^e$ indicates deviations from equilibrium, and

$$\alpha \equiv X^e + P^e \left(\frac{dX}{dP} \right)^e - P_M \left(\frac{dM}{dP} \right)^e .$$

The characteristic equation of (IV.48') is

$$\lambda - \frac{V}{Y} \alpha e^{-\lambda \omega} = 0 .$$ (IV.49)

★ If it were not so, the only difference would be a multiplicative constant in the right-hand side of (IV.46).

Setting $s \equiv \lambda \omega$ and multiplying both members of (IV.49) by $- \omega e^s$, we obtain

$$\frac{V\omega}{Y} \alpha - s e^s = 0 \, , \tag{IV.49'}$$

which has the form (IV.9') of Appendix IV, §2. Applying Hayes' theorem we obtain the following necessary and sufficient stability conditions

$$0 < - \frac{V\omega}{Y} \alpha < \tfrac{1}{2} \pi \, . \tag{IV.50}$$

The left-hand part of the double inequality (IV.50) implies that $\alpha < 0$, the right-hand part that α be in absolute value smaller than $\tfrac{1}{2} \pi Y / V\omega$. It is interesting to note that such conditions are *more restrictive* than those holding in the case in which no lag is assumed. In fact, in the latter case we would obtain the differential equation

$$\frac{\mathrm{d}\bar{P}}{\mathrm{d}t} = \frac{V}{Y} \alpha \bar{P}(t) \, ,$$

whose characteristic equation is $\lambda - (V/Y)\alpha = 0$, so that the stability condition would be $\alpha < 0$. ★

We want now to give an economic interpretation to the stability conditions. For this purpose some manipulations on α are required. We have

---

★ The same condition would hold also if, instead of a lag, we postulated a continuous adjustment process in the price level of the type

$$\frac{\mathrm{d}P}{\mathrm{d}t} = c(QV - PY) \, , \qquad c > 0 \, .$$

Differentiating and using (IV.46) we would obtain, after linearization, the second-order differential equation

$$\frac{\mathrm{d}^2\bar{P}}{\mathrm{d}t^2} + cY \frac{\mathrm{d}\bar{P}}{\mathrm{d}t} - cV\alpha\bar{P} = 0 \, ,$$

whose characteristic equation is

$$\lambda^2 + cY\lambda - cV\alpha = 0 \, ,$$

and the stability condition turns out to be $\alpha < 0$ again.

$$X^e + P^e \left(\frac{dX}{dP}\right)^e - P_M \left(\frac{dM}{dP}\right)^e = X^e \left[1 + \frac{P^e}{X^e}\left(\frac{dX}{dP}\right)^e - \frac{P_M}{X^e}\left(\frac{dM}{dP}\right)^e\right].$$

Now, in the equilibrium point we have $P^e X^e = P_M M^e$, which gives $P_M/X^e = P^e/M^e$, and so

$$X^e \left[1 + \frac{P^e}{X^e}\left(\frac{dX}{dP}\right)^e - \frac{P_M}{X^e}\left(\frac{dM}{dP}\right)^e\right] = X^e \left[1 + \frac{P^e}{X^e}\left(\frac{dX}{dP}\right)^e - \frac{P^e}{M^e}\left(\frac{dM}{dP}\right)^e\right],$$

from which

$$\alpha \equiv X^e \left[1 - \eta_X^e - \eta_M^e\right],$$

where

$$\eta_X^e \equiv -\frac{P^e}{X^e}\left(\frac{dX}{dP}\right)^e, \qquad \eta_M^e \equiv \frac{P^e}{M^e}\left(\frac{dM}{dP}\right)^e$$

are, respectively, the elasticity of exports and of imports with respect to P. Since $X^e > 0$, the condition $\alpha < 0$ is equivalent to

$$1 - \eta_X^e - \eta_M^e < 0,$$

that is,

$$\eta_X^e + \eta_M^e > 1,$$

which coincides with the so-called 'Marshall–Lerner' condition.

The condition $-\alpha < \frac{1}{2}\pi Y/V\omega$ can be written, after simple manipulation, as

$$\eta_X^e + \eta_M^e < 1 + \frac{Y}{X^e V\omega}\frac{\pi}{2}.$$

Thus, finally, we can rewrite (IV.50) as

$$1 < \eta_X^e + \eta_M^e < 1 + \frac{Y\pi}{2X^e V\omega}. \tag{IV.50$'$}$$

The economic interpretation is straightforward: the sum of the elasticities must not only be greater than 1 (and this is the usual condition, well-known in monetary international economics), but also *smaller* than another critical value (of course, the latter is greater than 1), as given by (IV.50′). Therefore, instability might occur not only because the sum of the elasticities is too small, but also because such a sum is *too great*.

References

Allen, R.G.D., 1959, *Mathematical Economics*, ch. 8, §§8.4, 8.5.
Allen, R.G.D., 1967, *Macro-Economic Theory: A Mathematical Treatment*, ch. 19, §§19.3, 19.4.
Bellman, R. and Cooke, K.L., 1963, *Differential–Difference Equations*, chs. 3, 4, 13.
Bergstrom, A.R., 1967, *The Construction and Use of Economic Models*, pp. 1–2.
Boole, G., 1960, *A Treatise on the Calculus of Finite Differences*, pp. 277–88.
Burger, E., 1956, On the Stability of Certain Economic Systems.
Frisch, R., 1933, Propagation Problems and Impulse Problems in Dynamic Economics.
Frisch, R. and Holme, H., 1935, The Characteristic Solutions of a Mixed Difference and Differential Equation Occurring in Economic Dynamics.
Furuno, Y., 1965, The Period of Production in Two-Sector Models of Economic Growth.
Kalecki, M., 1935, A Macrodynamic Theory of Business Cycles.
Kalecki, M., 1954, *Theory of Economic Dynamics*.
Leontief, W., *et al.*, 1953, *Studies in the Structure of the American Economy*, ch. 3, Mathematical Note 2.
Tinbergen, J., 1959, *Selected Papers*, pp. 1–14.

Bibliography

This is not a comprehensive bibliography but only a general list of the works that have been cited in this book.

Ackley, G., 1961, *Macroeconomic Theory* (Macmillan, New York).

Allen, R.G.D., 1938, *Mathematical Analysis for Economists* (Macmillan, London).

Allen, R.G.D., 1959, *Mathematical Economics*, 2nd edn. (Macmillan, London).

Allen, R.G.D., 1967, *Macro-Economic Theory: A Mathematical Treatment* (Macmillan, London).

Amano, A., 1964, A Further Note on Professor Uzawa's Two-Sector Model of Economic Growth, *Rev. Econ. Stud.* 31, 97–102.

Amano, A., 1968, Stability Conditions in the Pure Theory of International Trade: A Rehabilitation of the Marshallian Approach, *Q. J. Econ.* 82, 326–39.

American Economic Association and Royal Economic Society, 1966, *Surveys of Economic Theory*, Vols. I, II, III (Macmillan, London).

Andronov, A.A., Vitt, A.A. and Khaikin, S.E., 1966, *Theory of Oscillators* (Pergamon Press, London).

Archibald, G.C. and Lipsey, R.G., 1967, *An Introduction to a Mathematical Treatment of Economics* (Weidenfeld and Nicolson, London).

Arrow, K.J., Block, H.D. and Hurwicz, L., 1959, On the Stability of the Competitive Equilibrium, II, *Econometrica* 27, 82–109.

Arrow, K.J. and Hurwicz, L., 1958, On the Stability of the Competitive Equilibrium, I, *Econometrica* 26, 522–52.

Arrow, K.J., Karlin, S. and Suppes, P., eds., 1960, *Mathematical Methods in the Social Sciences, 1959* (Stanford University Press).

Arrow, K.J. and McManus, M., 1958, A Note on Dynamic Stability, *Econometrica* **26**, 448–54.

Basset, L., 1968, The Solution of Qualitative Comparative Static Problems: Comment, *Q. J. Econ.* **82**, 519–23.

Basset, L., Maybee, J. and Quirk, J., 1968, Qualitative Economics and the Scope of the Correspondence Principle, *Econometrica* **36**, 544–63.

Baumol, W.J., 1957, Speculation, Profitability and Stability, *Rev. Econ. Statist.* **39**, 263–71.

Baumol, W.J., 1958, Topology of Second Order Linear Difference Equations with Constant Coefficients, *Econometrica* **26**, 258–85.

Baumol, W.J., 1970, *Economic Dynamics*, 3rd edn. (Macmillan, New York).

Baumol, W.J. and Quandt, R.E., 1964, Rules of Thumb and Optimally Imperfect Decisions, *Am. Econ. Rev.* **54**, 23–46.

Beach, E.F., 1957, *Economic Models* (John Wiley, New York).

Beckmann, M.J. and Ryder, H.E., 1969, Simultaneous Price and Quantity Adjustment in a Single Market, *Econometrica* **37**, 470–84.

Beckmann, M.J. and Wallace, J.P., 1967, Marshallian versus Walrasian Stability, *Kyklos* **20**, 935–48.

Bellman, R., 1953, *Stability Theory of Differential Equations* (McGraw-Hill, New York).

Bellman, R. and Cooke, K.L., 1963, *Differential–Difference Equations* (Academic Press, New York).

Bergstrom, A.R., 1967, *The Construction and Use of Economic Models* (The English Universities Press, London).

Boole, G., 1960, *A Treatise on the Calculus of Finite Differences* (Dover Publications reprint, New York).

Boulding, K.E. and Stigler, G.J., eds., 1953, *Readings in Price Theory* (Allen & Unwin, London).

Bronfenbrenner, M. and Holzman, F.D., 1963, Survey of Inflation Theory, *Am. Econ. Rev.* **53**, 593–661. Reprinted in: American Economic Association and Royal Economic Society, 1966, *Surveys of Economic Theory*, Vol. I, pp. 46–107.

Buchanan, N.S., 1939, A Reconsideration of the Cobweb Theorem, *J. Polit. Econ.* **47**, 67–81.

Burger, E., 1956, On the Stability of Certain Economic Systems, *Econometrica* **24**, 488–93.

Burmeister, E., 1967, The Existence of Golden Ages and Stability in the Two-Sector Model, *Q. J. Econ.* **81**, 146–54.

Burmeister, E., 1968, The Role of the Jacobian Determinant in the Two-Sector Model, *Int. Econ. Rev.* **9**, 195–203.

Burmeister, E., Dobell, R. and Kuga, K., 1968, A Note on the Global Stability of a Simple Growth Model with Many Capital Goods, *Q. J. Econ.* **82**, 657–65.

Bushaw, D.W. and Clower, R.W., 1957, *Introduction to Mathematical Economics* (Irwin, Homewood, Ill.).

Caves, R.E. and Johnson, H.G., eds., 1968, *Readings in International Economics* (Allen & Unwin, London).

Chiang, A.C., 1967, *Fundamental Methods of Mathematical Economics* (McGraw-Hill, New York).

Chipman, J.S., 1950, The Multi-Sector Multiplier, *Econometrica* **18**, 355–74.

Clower, R.W. and Bushaw, D.W., 1954, Price Determination in a Stock-Flow Economy, *Econometrica* **22**, 328–43.

Cooper, R.N., 1969, Comment: "The Assignment Problem". In: Mundell, R.A. and Swoboda, A.K., eds., 1969, *Monetary Problems of the International Economy*, pp. 235–41.

Coppock, D.J., 1965, The Post-War Short Cycle in the U.S.A., *The Manchester School of Economic and Social Studies* 33, 17–44.

Courant, R., 1937, *Differential and Integral Calculus*, Vol. I, 2nd edn. (Blackie & Son, London).

Cutilli, B., 1963, The Role of Commercial Banks in Foreign Exchange Speculation, with Mathematical Appendix by G. Gandolfo, *Banca Nazionale del Lavoro Q. Rev*, No. 65, 216–31.

Deardoff, A.V., 1970, Growth Paths in the Solow Neoclassical Growth Model, *Q. J. Econ.* 84, 134–9.

Dernburg, T.F. and Dernburg, J.D., 1969, *Macroeconomic Analysis: An Introduction to Comparative Statics and Dynamics* (Addison-Wesley, Reading, Mass.).

Domar, E.D., 1946, Capital Expansion, Rate of Growth and Employment, *Econometrica* 14, 137–47. Reprinted in: Domar, E.D., 1957, *Essays in the Theory of Economic Growth*, pp. 70–82; Stiglitz, J.E. and Uzawa, H., eds., 1969, *Readings in the Modern Theory of Economic Growth*, pp. 34–44.

Domar, E.D., 1957, *Essays in the Theory of Economic Growth* (Oxford University Press, New York).

Drandakis, E.M., 1963, Factor Substitution in the Two-Sector Growth Model, *Rev. Econ. Stud.* 30, 217–28.

Duesenberry, J.S., 1949, *Income, Saving and the Theory of Consumer Behavior* (Harvard University Press).

Duesenberry, J.S., 1958, *Business Cycles and Economic Growth* (McGraw-Hill, New York).

Ezekiel, M., 1938, The Cobweb Theorem, *Q. J. Econ.* 52, 255–80. Reprinted in: Haberler, G., ed., 1950, *Readings in Business Cycle Theory*, pp. 422–42.

Fellner, W. and Haley, B.F., eds., 1950, *Readings in the Theory of Income Distribution* (Allen & Unwin, London).

Fisher, F.M., 1962, An Alternate Proof and Extension of Solow's Theorem on Nonnegative Square Matrices, *Econometrica* 30, 349–50.

Fisher, F.M., 1965, Choice of Units, Column Sums, and Stability in Linear Dynamic Systems with Nonnegative Square Matrices, *Econometrica* 33, 445–50.

Frazer, R.A., Duncan, W.J. and Collar, A.R., 1938, *Elementary Matrices and Some Applications to Dynamics and Differential Equations* (Cambridge University Press, London).

Friedman, M., 1953, The Case for Flexible Exchange Rates. In: Friedman, M., *Essays in Positive Economics* (Chicago University Press) pp. 157–203. Reprinted in abridged form in: Caves, R.E. and Johnson, H.G., eds., 1968, *Readings in International Economics*, pp. 413–37 (pages refer to the original).

Frisch, R., 1933, Propagation Problems and Impulse Problems in Dynamic Economics. In: *Economic Essays in Honor of Gustav Cassel* (Allen & Unwin, London). Reprinted in: Gordon, R.A. and Klein, L.R., eds., 1966, *Readings in Business Cycles,* pp. 155–85.

Frisch, R., 1936, On the Notion of Equilibrium and Disequilibrium, *Rev. Econ. Stud.* 3, 100–5.

Frisch, R., 1963, Parametric Solution and Programming of the Hicksian Model. In: Rao, C.R., *et al.*, eds., *Essays on Econometrics and Planning* (in Honor of P.C. Mahalanobis) (Pergamon Press, London) pp. 45–82.

Frisch, R. and Holme, H., 1935, The Characteristic Solutions of a Mixed Difference and Differential Equation Occurring in Economic Dynamics, *Econometrica* 3, 225–39.

Furuno, Y., 1965, The Period of Production in Two-Sector Models of Economic Growth, *Int. Econ. Rev.* 6, 240–4.

Gale, D. and Nikaidô, H., 1965, The Jacobian Matrix and Global Univalence of Mappings, *Mathematische Annln.* 159, 81–93. Reprinted in: Newman, P.K., ed., 1968, *Readings in Mathematical Economics*, Vol. I, pp. 68–80.

Gantmacher, F.R., 1959, *Applications of the Theory of Matrices* (Interscience, New York).

Glahe, F.R., Professional and Nonprofessional Speculation, Profitability, and Stability, *Southern Econ. J.* 23, 43–8.

Goldberg, S., 1958, *Introduction to Difference Equations* (John Wiley, New York).

Goodwin, R.M., 1947, Dynamical Coupling with Especial Reference to Markets having Production Lags, *Econometrica* 15, 181–204.

Goodwin, R.M., 1951, The Nonlinear Accelerator and the Persistence of Business Cycles, *Econometrica* 19, 1–17.

Goodwin, R.M., 1955, A Model of Cyclical Growth. In: Lundberg, E., ed., *The Business Cycle in the Post-War World* (Macmillan, London) pp. 203–21. Reprinted in: Gordon, R.A. and Klein, L.R., eds., 1966, *Readings in Business Cycles*, pp. 6–22.

Goodwin, R.M., 1967, A Growth Cycle. In: Feinstein, C.H., ed., *Socialism, Capitalism and Economic Growth* (Essays presented to Maurice Dobb) (Cambridge University Press, London) pp. 54–8.

Gordon, R.A. and Klein, L.R., eds., 1966, *Readings in Business Cycles* (Allen & Unwin, London).

Grubel, H.G., 1968, International Diversified Portfolios: Welfare Gains and Capital Flows, *Am. Econ. Rev.* 58, 1299–314.

Haberler, G., ed., 1950, *Readings in Business Cycles Theory* (Allen & Unwin, London).

Hadar, J., 1965, A Note on Dominant Diagonals in Stability Analysis, *Econometrica* 33, 442–4.

Hahn, F.H., 1965, On Two-Sector Growth Models, *Rev. Econ. Stud.* 32, 339–46.

Hahn, F.H., 1966, Equilibrium Dynamics with Heterogeneous Capital Goods, *Q. J. Econ.* 80, 633–46.

Hahn, F.H. and Matthews, R.C.O., 1964, The Theory of Economic Growth: A Survey, *Econ. J.* 74, 779–902. Reprinted in: American Economic Association and Royal Economic Society, 1966, *Surveys of Economic Theory*, Vol. II, pp. 1–124.

Hansen, A.H. and Clemence, R.V., 1953, *Readings in Business Cycles and National Income* (Norton, New York).

Harberger, A.C., 1950, Currency Depreciation, Income and the Balance of Trade, *J. Polit. Econ.* 58, 47–60. Reprinted in: Caves, R.E. and Johnson, H.G., eds., 1968, *Readings in International Economics*, pp. 341–58.

Harrod, R.F., 1939, An Essay in Dynamic Theory, *Econ. J.* 49, 14–33. Reprinted in: Hansen, A.H. and Clemence, R.V., eds., 1953, *Readings in Business Cycles and National Income*, pp. 200–19; Stiglitz, J.E. and Uzawa, H., eds., 1969, *Readings in the Modern Theory of Economic Growth*, pp. 14–33.

Harrod, R.F., 1948, *Towards a Dynamic Economics* (Macmillan, London).

Helliwell, J.F., 1969, Monetary and Fiscal Policies for an Open Economy, *Oxford Econ. Pap.* 21, 35–55.

Henderson, J.M. and Quandt, R.E., 1958, *Microeconomic Theory: A Mathematical Approach* (McGraw-Hill, New York).

Hicks, J.R., 1937, Mr. Keynes and the "Classics": A Suggested Interpretation, *Economet-rica* 5, 147–59. Reprinted in: Fellner, W. and Haley, B.F., eds., 1950, *Readings in the Theory of Income Distribution*, pp. 461–76; Hicks, J.R., 1967, *Critical Essays in Monetary Theory* (Oxford University Press, London) pp. 126–42.

Hicks, J.R., 1939, *Value and Capital*, 1st edn. (Oxford University Press, London).

Hicks, J.R., 1946, *Value and Capital*, 2nd edn. (Oxford University Press, London).

Hicks, J.R., 1949, Mr. Harrod's Dynamic Theory, *Economica* (n.s.) 16, 106–21. Re-printed in: Gordon, R.A. and Klein, L.R., eds., 1966, *Readings in Business Cycles*, pp. 23–38.

Hicks, J.R., 1950, *A Contribution to the Theory of the Trade Cycle* (Oxford University Press, London).

Hicks, J.R., 1965, *Capital and Growth* (Oxford University Press, London).

Hobson, E.W., 1957, *The Theory of Functions of a Real Variable & The Theory of Fourier's Series*, Vols. I, II (Dover Publications reprint, New York).

Huang, D.S., 1964, *Introduction to the Use of Mathematics in Economic Analysis* (John Wiley, New York).

Ichimura, S., 1955, Toward a General Nonlinear Macrodynamic Theory of Economic Fluctuations. In: Kurihara, K.K., ed., *Post-Keynesian Economics* (Allen & Unwin, London) pp. 192–226.

Inada, K.-I., 1963, On a Two-Sector Model of Economic Growth: Comments and a Generalization, *Rev. Econ. Stud.* 30, 105–18.

Inada, K.-I., 1964, On the Stability of Growth Equilibria in Two-Sector Models, *Rev. Econ. Stud.* 31, 127–42.

Ince, E.L., 1956, *Ordinary Differential Equations* (Dover Publications reprint, New York).

Ince, E L., 1959, *Integration of Ordinary Differential Equations* (Oliver and Boyd, London).

Jaffé, W., 1967, Walras' Theory of *Tâtonnement*: A Critique of Recent Interpretations, *J. Polit. Econ.* 75, 1–19.

Johnson, H.G., 1965, Some Aspects of the Theory of Economic Policy in a World of Capital Mobility, *Rivista Internazionale di Scienze Economiche e Commercialia* 12, 545–59. Reprinted in: Bagiotti, T., ed., 1966, *Essays in Honour of Marco Fanno* (Cedam, Padova) 345–59.

Jorgenson, D.W., 1960, A Dual Stability Theorem, *Econometrica* 28, 892–9.

Jorgenson, D.W., 1961, Stability of a Dynamic Input–Output System, *Rev. Econ. Stud.* 28, 105–16.

Jorgenson, D.W., 1961, The Development of a Dual Economy, *Econ. J.* 71, 309–34.

Jorgenson, D.W., 1961, The Structure of Multi-Sector Dynamic Models, *Int. Econ. Rev.* 2, 276–93.

Kaldor, N., 1934, A Classificatory Note on the Determinateness of Equilibrium, *Rev. Econ. Stud.* 1, 122–36. Reprinted as: Kaldor, N., 1960, Determinateness of Static Equilibrium, *Essays on Value and Distribution*.

Kaldor, N., 1960, Determinateness of Static Equilibrium, *Essays on Value and Distribu-tion* (G. Duckworth, London) pp. 13–33.

Kalecki, M., 1935, A Macrodynamic Theory of Business Cycles, *Econometrica* 3, 327–44.

Kalecki, M., 1954, *Theory of Economic Dynamics* (Allen & Unwin, London).

Kalman, R.E. and Bertram, J.E., 1960, Control System Analysis and Design Via the "Second Method" of Lyapunov, I (Continuous-Time Systems) and II (Discrete-Time Systems), *J. of Basic Eng.* (Trans. ASME) pp. 371–400.

Karlin, S., 1959, *Mathematical Methods and Theory in Games, Programming and Economics*, Vols. I, II (Addison-Wesley, Reading, Mass.).

Kemp, M.C., 1963, Speculation, Profitability, and Price Stability, *Rev. Econ. Statist.* **45**, 185–9.

Kemp, M.C., 1964, *The Pure Theory of International Trade* (Prentice-Hall, Englewood Cliffs, N.J.).

Kindleberger, C.P., 1968, *International Economics*, 4th edn. (Irwin, Homewood, Ill.).

Kogiku, K.C., 1968, *An Introduction to Macroeconomic Models* (McGraw Hill, New York).

Kooros, A., 1965, *Elements of Mathematical Economics* (Houghton Mifflin, Boston).

Krasovskiĭ, N.N., 1963, *Stability of Motion, Applications of Lyapunov's Second Method to Differential Systems and Equations with Delay* (Stanford University Press).

Kuenne, R.E., 1963, *The Theory of General Economic Equilibrium* (Princeton University Press).

Kuh, E., 1963, *Capital Stock Growth: A Micro-Econometric Approach* (North-Holland, Amsterdam).

Lancaster, K., 1966, The Solution of Qualitative Comparative Static Problems, *Q. J. Econ.* **80**, 278–95.

Lancaster, K., 1968, *Mathematical Economics* (Macmillan, New York).

Lange, O., 1952, *Price Flexibility and Employment* (Principia Press, Bloomington, Indiana).

LaSalle, J.P. and Lefschetz, S., 1961, *Stability by Liapunov's Direct Method with Applications* (Academic Press, New York).

Laursen, S. and Metzler, L.A., 1950, Flexible Exchange Rates and the Theory of Employment, *Rev. Econ. Statist.* **32**, 281–99.

Leontief, W., *et al.*, 1953, *Studies in the Structure of the American Economy* (Oxford University Press, New York).

Levhari, D. and Patinkin, D., 1968, The Role of Money in a Simple Growth Model, *Am. Econ. Rev.* **58**, 713–53.

Liapounoff, A., 1907, Problème général de la stabilité du mouvement, *Annales de la Faculté des Sciences de Toulouse* (2), 9. Reprinted in: 1949, *Ann. Math. Stud.*, No. 17 (Princeton University Press).

Lloyd, P.J., 1969, Qualitative Calculus and Comparative Static Analysis, *Econ. Rec.* **45**, 343–53.

Lotka, A.J., 1956, *Elements of Mathematical Biology* (formerly published under the title *Elements of Physical Biology*) (Dover Publications reprint, New York).

Machlup, F., 1943, *International Trade and the National Income Multiplier* (Blakiston, Philadelphia).

Machlup, F., 1959, Statics and Dynamics: Kaleidoscopic Words, *Southern Econ. J.* **26**, 91–110. Reprinted in: Machlup, F., 1963, *Essays in Economic Semantics* (Prentice-Hall, Englewood Cliffs, N.J.) pp. 4–42.

Marshall, A., 1920, *Principles of Economics*, 8th edn. (Macmillan, London).

Marshall, A., 1923, *Money, Credit and Commerce* (Macmillan, London).

Marshall, A., 1937, *The Pure Theory of Foreign Trade*, privately circulated in 1877. Reprinted by: London School of Economics, 1937, *Reprints of Scarce Tracts on Political Economy* (Lund Humpries, London).

McKenzie, L., 1960, Matrices with Dominant Diagonals and Economic Theory. In: Arrow, K.J., Karlin, S. and Suppes, P., eds., 1960, *Mathematical Methods in the Social Sciences* pp. 47–62.

Metzler, L.A., 1941, The Nature and Stability of Inventory Cycles, *Rev. Econ. Statist.* 23, 113–29. Reprinted in: Gordon, R.A. and Klein, L.R., eds., 1966, *Readings in Business Cycles*, pp. 100–29 (pages refer to the reprint).

Metzler, L.A., 1942, Underemployment Equilibrium in International Trade, *Econometrica* 10, 97–112.

Metzler, L.A., 1945, Stability of Multiple Markets: The Hicks Conditions, *Econometrica* 13, 277–92. Reprinted in Newman, P.K., ed., 1968, *Readings in Mathematical Economics*, Vol. I, pp. 197–212.

Metzler, L.A., 1950, A Multiple Region Theory of Income and Trade, *Econometrica* 18, 329–54.

Metzler, L.A., 1951, Wealth, Saving and the Rate of Interest, *J. Polit. Econ.* 59, 93–116.

Miconi, B., 1967, On Harrod's Model and Instability, *L'industria*, October–December, 455–78.

Milne-Thomson, L.M., 1933, *The Calculus of Finite Differences* (Macmillan, London).

Minorsky, N., 1962, *Nonlinear Oscillations* (Van Nostrand, New York).

Minsky, H.P., 1959, A Linear Model of Cyclical Growth, *Rev. Econ. Statist.* 41, 133–45. Reprinted in: Gordon, R.A. and Klein, L.R., eds., 1966, *Readings in Business Cycles*, pp. 79–99.

Modigliani, F., 1949, Fluctuations in the Saving–Income Ratio: A Problem in Economic Forecasting. In: *National Bureau of Economic Research, Studies in Income and Wealth*, Vol. XI (N.B.E.R., New York) pp. 371–443.

Morishima, M., 1964, *Equilibrium Stability, and Growth* (Oxford University Press, London).

Morishima, M., 1969, *Theory of Economic Growth* (Oxford University Press, London).

Mundell, R.A., 1960, The Monetary Dynamics of International Adjustment under Fixed and Flexible Exchange Rates, *Q. J. Econ.* 74, 227–57. Reprinted as ch. 11 in: Mundell, R.A., 1968, *International Economics*, pp. 152–76.

Mundell, R.A., 1962, The Appropriate Use of Monetary and Fiscal Policy for Internal and External Stability, *I.M.F. Staff Pap.* 9, 70–6. Reprinted as ch. 16 in: Mundell, R.A., 1968, *International Economics*, pp. 233–9.

Mundell, R.A., 1968, *International Economics* (Macmillan, New York).

Mundell, R.A. and Swoboda, A.K., eds., 1969, *Monetary Problems of the International Economy* (University of Chicago Press).

Negishi, T., 1962, The Stability of a Competitive Economy: A Survey Article, *Econometrica* 30, 635–69.

Newman, P.K., 1959, Some Notes on Stability Conditions, *Rev. Econ. Stud.* 27, 1–9.

Newman, P.K., 1961, Approaches to Stability Analysis, *Economica* (n.s.) 28, 12–29.

Newman, P.K., ed., 1968, *Readings in Mathematical Economics*, Vols. I, II (Johns Hopkins Press, Baltimore).

Nikaido, H., 1968, *Convex Structures and Economic Theory* (Academic Press, New York).

Obst, N.P., 1967, A Connection between Speculation and Stability in the Foreign Exchange Market, *Southern Econ. J.* 34, 146–9.

Okuguchi, K., 1968, The Labour Participation Ratio and the Speed of Adjustment, *Economica* (n.s.) 35, 445–50.

Ott, D.J. and Ott, A.F., 1968, Monetary and Fiscal Policy: Goals and the Choice of Instruments, *Q. J. Econ.* 82, 313–25.

Papandreou, A.G., 1965, *Introduction to Macroeconomic Models* (Centre of Planning and Economic Research, Athens).

Pasinetti, L.L., 1960, Cyclical Fluctuations and Growth, *Oxford Econ. Pap.* **12**, 215–41.

Patinkin, D., 1952, The Limitations of Samuelson's "Correspondence Principle", *Metroeconomica* **4**, 37–43.

Patinkin, D., 1965, *Money, Interest and Prices*, 2nd edn. (Harper & Row, New York).

Phelps, E., 1966, *Golden Rules of Economic Growth* (Norton, New York).

Phillips, A.W., 1954, Stabilisation Policy in a Closed Economy, *Econ. J.* **64**, 290–323.

Phillips, A.W., 1957, Stabilisation Policy and the Time-Form of Lagged Responses, *Econ. J.* **67**, 265–77.

Quirk, J. and Saposnick, R., 1968, *Introduction to General Equilibrium Theory and Welfare Economics* (McGraw-Hill, New York).

Ramaswami, V.K., 1969, On Two-Sector Neo-Classical Growth, *Oxford Econ. Pap.* **21**, 142–60.

Robinson, J., 1956, *The Accumulation of Capital* (Macmillan, London).

Rose, H., 1967, On the Non-Linear Theory of the Employment Cycle, *Rev. Econ. Stud.* **34**, 153–73.

Samuelson, P.A., 1939, Interactions between the Multiplier Analysis and the Principle of Acceleration, *Rev. of Econ. Statist.* **21**, 75–8. Reprinted in: Stiglitz, J.E., ed., 1966, *Collected Scientific Papers of Paul A. Samuelson*, Vol. II, pp. 1107–10.

Samuelson, P.A., 1941, Conditions that the Roots of a Polynomial be less than Unity in Absolute Value, *Ann. Math. Statist.* **12**, 360–4. Reprinted in: *Collected Scientific Papers of Paul A. Samuelson*, Vol. I, pp. 689–93.

Samuelson, P.A., 1941, The Stability of Equilibrium: Comparative Statics and Dynamics, *Econometrica* **9**, 97–120. Reprinted in: *Collected Scientific Papers of Paul. A. Samuelson*, Vol. I, pp. 539–62.

Samuelson, P.A., 1944, The Relation between Hicksian Stability and True Dynamic Stability, *Econometrica* **12**, 256–7. Reprinted in: *Collected Scientific Papers of Paul A. Samuelson*, Vol. I, pp. 563–4.

Samuelson, P.A., 1947, *Foundations of Economic Analysis* (Harvard University Press).

Samuelson, P.A., 1949, Dynamic Process Analysis. In: Ellis, H.S., ed., *A Survey of Contemporary Economics* (Blakiston, Philadelphia) ch. 10. Reprinted in: *Collected Scientific Papers of Paul A. Samuelson*, Vol. I, pp. 590–625.

Sansone, G. and Conti, R., 1964, *Non-Linear Differential Equations* (Pergamon Press, London).

Sato, R., 1963, Fiscal Policy in a Neo-Classical Growth Model: An Analysis of Time Required for Equilibrating Adjustment, *Rev. Econ. Stud.* **30**, 16–23.

Sato, R., 1970, A Further Note on a Difference Equation Recurring in Growth Theory, *J. Econ. Theory* **2**, 95–102.

Scarf, H., 1960, Some Examples of Global Instability of the Competitive Equilibrium, *Int. Econ. Rev.* **1**, 157–72.

Schwartz, J.T., 1961, *Lectures on the Mathematical Method in Analytical Economics* (Gordon and Breach, New York).

Shell, K. and Stiglitz, J.E., 1967, The Allocation of Investment in a Dynamic Economy, *Q. J. Econ.* **81**, 592–609.

Shinkai, Y., 1960, On Equilibrium Growth of Capital and Labor, *Int. Econ. Rev.* **1**, 107–11.

Slutsky, E., 1953, On the Theory of the Budget of the Consumer, transl. by O. Ragusa. In: Boulding, K.E. and Stigler, G.J., eds., 1953, *Readings in Price Theory*, pp. 27–56.

Smithies, A., 1942, The Stability of Competitive Equilibrium, *Econometrica* **10**, 258–74.

Smithies, A., 1957, Economic Fluctuations and Growth, *Econometrica* 25, 1–52. Reprinted in a condensed form in: Gordon, R.A. and Klein, L.R., eds., 1966, *Readings in Business Cycles*, pp. 39–78.

Smyth, D.J., 1963, Monetary Factors and Multiplier–Acceleration Interaction, *Economica* (n.s.) 30, 400–7.

Smyth, D.J., 1964, Empirical Evidence on the Acceleration Principle, *Rev. Econ. Stud.* 31, 185–202.

Solow, R.M., 1952, On the Structure of Linear Models, *Econometrica* 20, 29–46.

Solow, R.M., 1956, A Contribution to the Theory of Economic Growth, *Q. J. Econ.* 70, 65–94. Reprinted in: Newman, P.K., ed., 1968, *Readings in Mathematical Economics*, Vol. II, pp. 142–71; Stiglitz, J.E. and Uzawa, H., eds., 1969, *Readings in the Modern Theory of Economic Growth*, pp. 58–87.

Solow, R.M., 1959, Competitive Valuation in a Dynamic Input–Output System, *Econometrica* 27, 30–53.

Solow, R.M., 1960, Investment and Technical Progress. In: Arrow, K.J., Karlin, S. and Suppes, P., eds., 1960, *Mathematical Methods in the Social Sciences, 1959*, pp. 89–104. Reprinted in: Stiglitz, J.E. and Uzawa, H., eds., 1969, *Readings in the Modern Theory of Economic Growth*, pp. 156–71.

Solow, R.M., 1961, Note on Uzawa's Two-Sector Model of Economic Growth, *Rev. Econ. Stud.* 29, 48–50.

Stein, J.L., 1969, "Neo-classical" and "Keynes-Wicksell" Monetary Growth Models, *J. Money, Credit and Banking,* 1, 153–71.

Stein, J.L., 1970, Monetary Growth Theory in Perspective, *Am. Econ. Rev.* 60, 85–106.

Stiglitz, J.E., ed., 1966, *Collected Scientific Papers of Paul A. Samuelson*, Vols. I, II (M.I.T. Press).

Stiglitz, J.E., 1967, A Two-Sector Two Class Model of Economic Growth, *Rev. Econ. Stud.* 34, 227–38.

Stiglitz, J.E. and Uzawa, H., eds., 1969, *Readings in the Modern Theory of Economic Growth* (M.I.T. Press).

Stolper, W.F., 1950, The Multiplier, Flexible Exchanges and International Equilibrium, *Q. J. Econ.* 64, 559–82.

Swan, T., 1956, Economic Growth and Capital Accumulation, *Econ. Rec.* 32, 334–61. Reprinted in: Newman, P.K., ed., 1968, *Readings in Mathematical Economics,* Vol. II, pp. 172–99; Stiglitz, J.E. and Uzawa, H., eds., 1969, *Readings in the Modern Theory of Economic Growth*, pp. 88–115.

Takayama, A., 1963, On a Two-Sector Model of Economic Growth: A Comparative Statics Analysis, *Rev. Econ. Stud.* 30, 95–104.

Telser, L.G., 1959, A Theory of Speculation Relating Profitability and Stability, *Rev. Econ. Statist.* 41, 295–301.

Thalberg, B., 1966, *A Trade Cycle Analysis* (Lund Economic Studies, Lund).

Tinbergen, J., 1959, *Selected Papers*, eds. Klaassen, L.H., Koyck, L.M. and Witteveen, H.J. (North-Holland, Amsterdam).

Tintner, G. and Millham, C.B., 1970, *Mathematics and Statistics for Economists*, 2nd edn. (Holt, Rinehart and Winston, New York).

Turnbull, H.W., 1957, *Theory of Equations* (Oliver and Boyd, London).

Uzawa, H., 1961, On a Two-Sector Model of Economic Growth, *Rev. Econ. Stud.* 29, 40–7.

Uzawa, H., 1963, On a Two-Sector Model of Economic Growth, II, *Rev. Econ. Stud.* 30, 105–18.

Vanek, J., 1962, *International Trade: Theory and Economic Policy* (Irwin, Homewood, Ill.).

Volterra, V., 1931, *Leçons sur la théorie mathématique de la lutte pour la vie* (Gauthier-Villars, Paris).

Volterra, V., 1959, *Theory of Functionals and of Integral and Integro-Differential Equations* (Dover Publications reprint, New York).

Walras, L., 1954, *Elements of Pure Economics*, transl. by W. Jaffé (Allen & Unwin, London).

White, W.H., 1954, The Employment-Insulating Advantages of Flexible Exchange Rates: A Comment on Professors Laursen and Metzler, *Rev. Econ. Statist.* 36, 225–8.

Willet, T. and Forte, F., 1969, Interest Rate Policy and External Balance, *Q. J. Econ.* 83, 242–62.

Yamane, T., 1968, *Mathematics for Economists: An Elementary Survey*, 2nd edn. (Prentice-Hall, Englewood Cliffs, N.J.).

Author Index

(see also Bibliography) *

* Numbers refer to pages; those followed by n to footnotes, and those followed by r to references at the end of each chapter or appendix.

499

Subject Index

---

* Numbers refer to pages, and those followed by n to footnotes.

−, static and dynamic, 175−6, 274, 280, 304
Stability conditions (*see* Burger's, Characteristic equation, Difference equations, Differential equations, Hayes', Liapunov's second method, Liénard−Chipart, Mixed differential−difference equations, Routh−Hurwitz, Samuelson's, Schur's)
Stability conditions and comparative statics, 343, 350−4
Stabilization policies, 98−9, 219−27, 245−9
Star or stellar node, 402
Statics
− and dynamics, 1
−, comparative (*see* Comparative statics)
Substitution effect, 350
Superposition theorem, 11, 165, 468
Supply
− and demand equilibrium, 25, 91, 175, 274
− of labour, 191, 194, 201, 428, 436, 443
Symmetry, 266, 281, 282n

Tâtonnement, 274−5, 375
Technical coefficients, 287

Technical progress, 152−3, 196−7, 425−6, 427, 432, 436
Topological theory
− of difference equations, 416−20
− of differential equations, 395−416
Trade balance (*see* Balance of payments)
Trade cycle (*see* Business cycle)
Trend, 74, 113, 151, 152, 157, 158
Two-sector models, 331−7, 442−55

Undetermined coefficients method, 12, 18−22, 58, 106, 106n, 134, 165, 170−3, 216−7, 238, 268, 474, 474n
Univalence of mappings
−, global, 342−3n, 375n
−, local, 342−3n, 375n

Variable coefficients, 391−4
Variation of parameters method, 393−4
Vintage models, 425−32
Vortex, 402

Walrasian v. Marshallian stability conditions, 176−81
Walras' law, 376
Warranted rate of growth, 42, 158
Wronksian, 238n